MW01618478

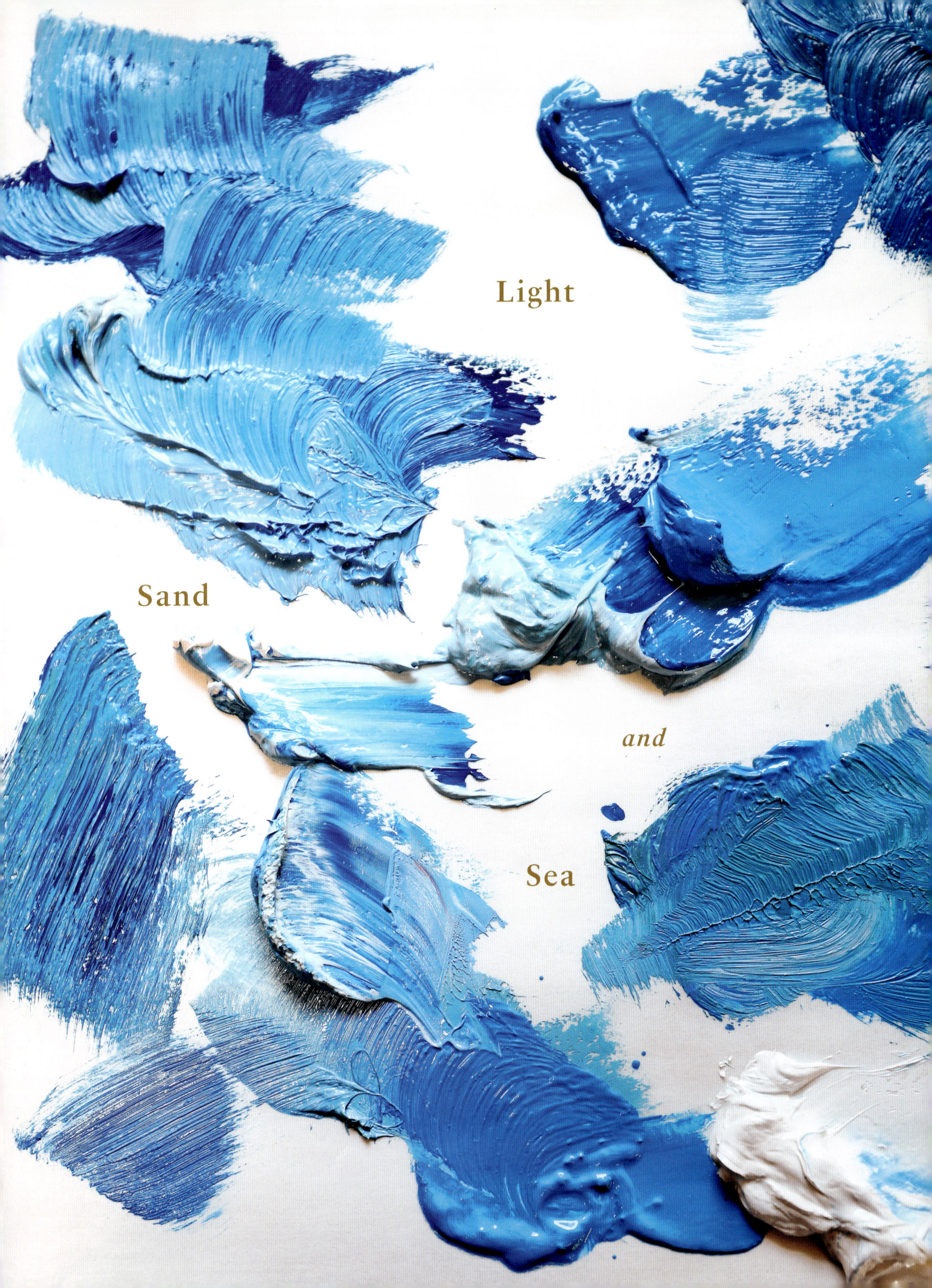
Light
Sand
and
Sea

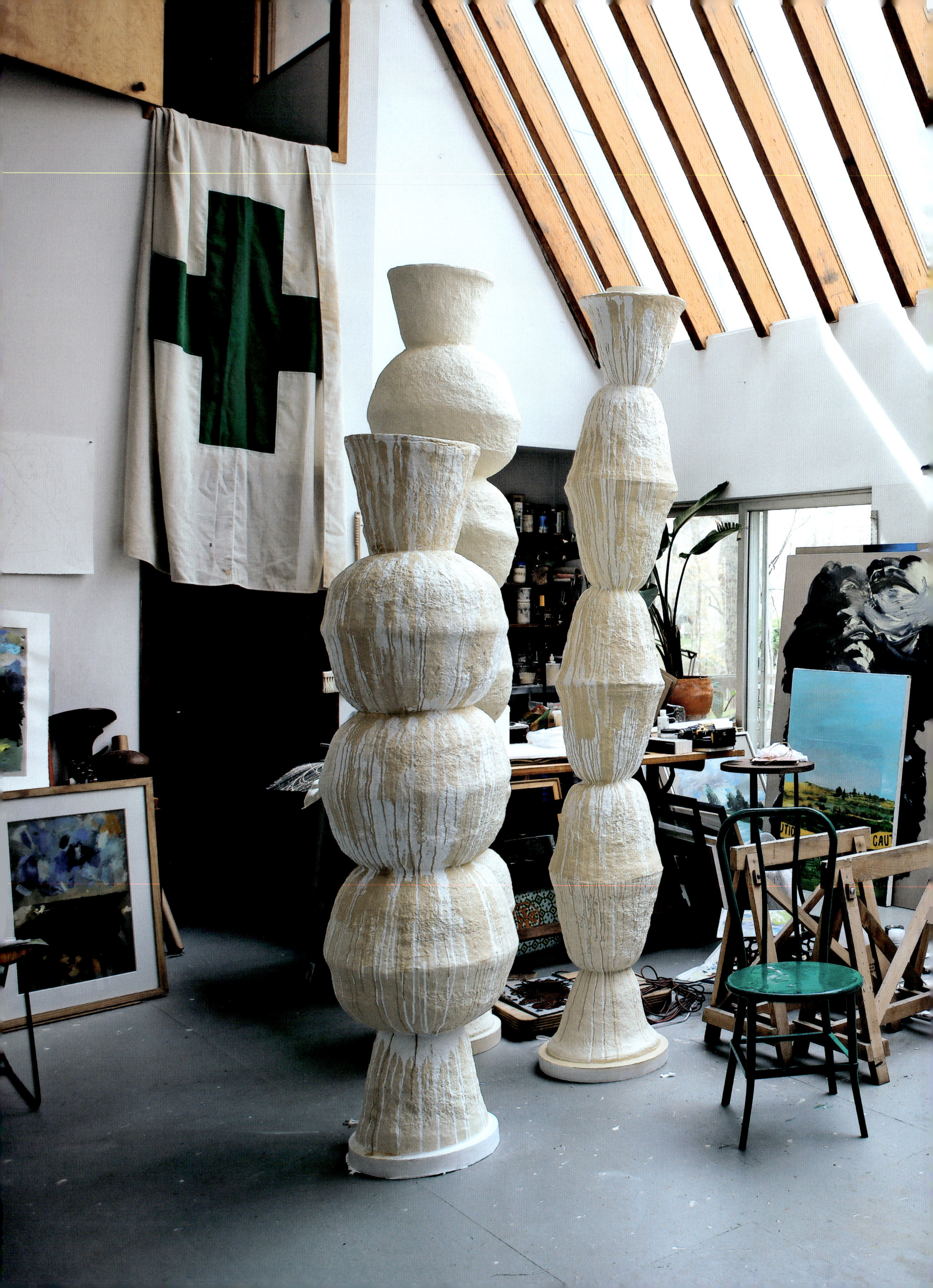

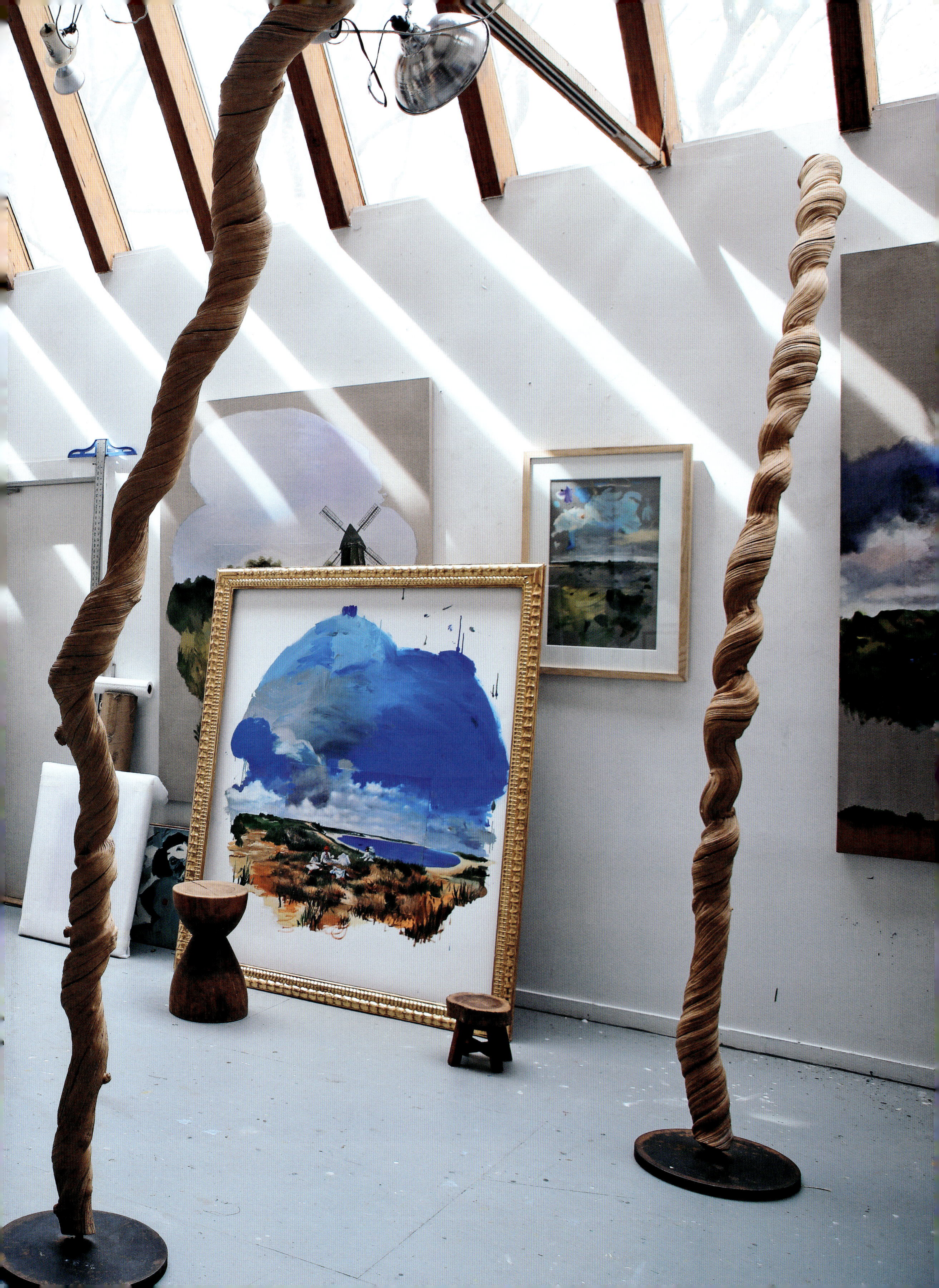

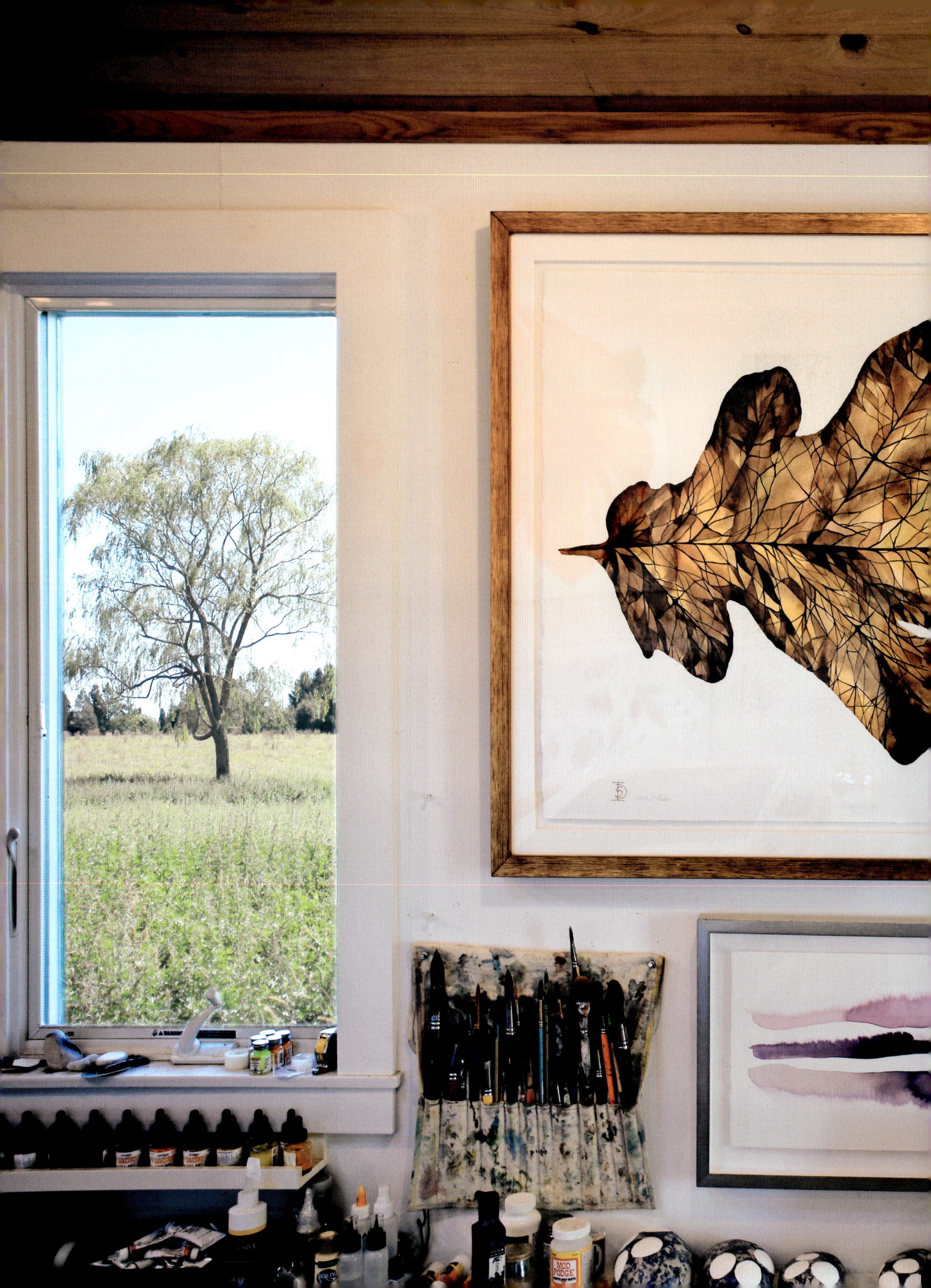
MOD PODGE

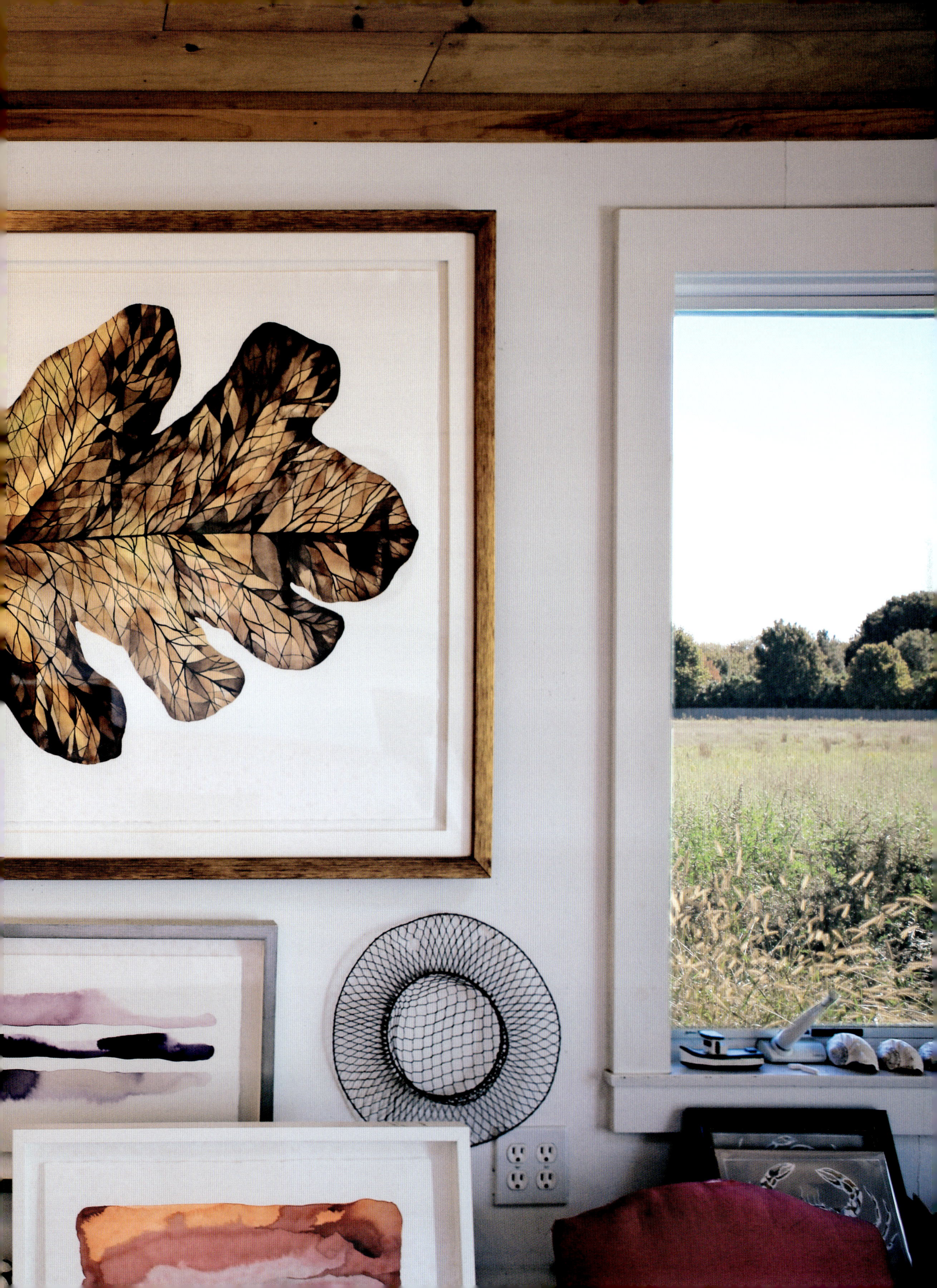

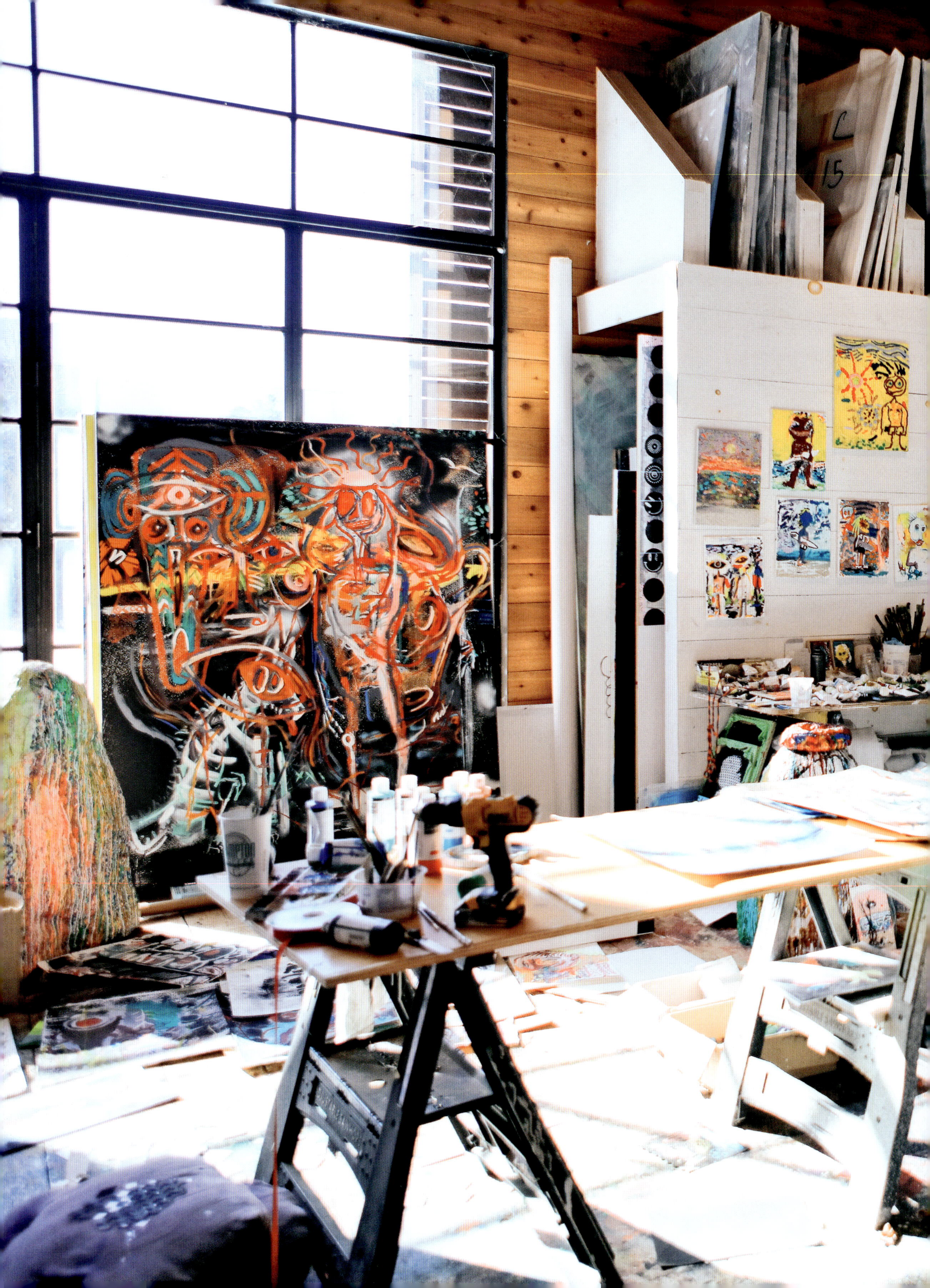

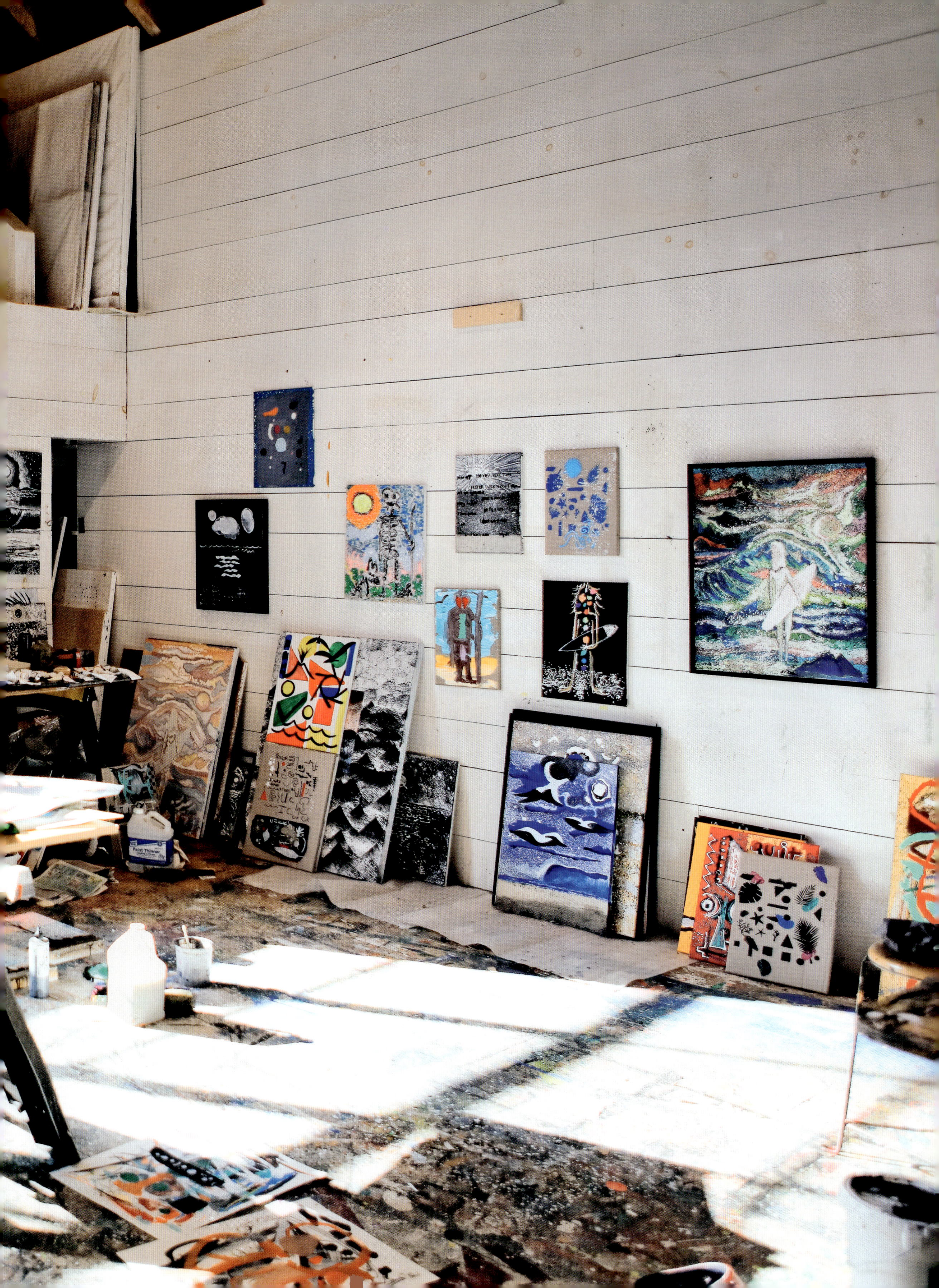

LIGHT SAND AND SEA

HAMPTONS ARTISTS — and — THEIR STUDIOS

Jaime Lopez *and* Coco Myers

Photography by Jaime Lopez

Text by Coco Myers

Foreword by Mónica Ramírez-Montagut, PhD

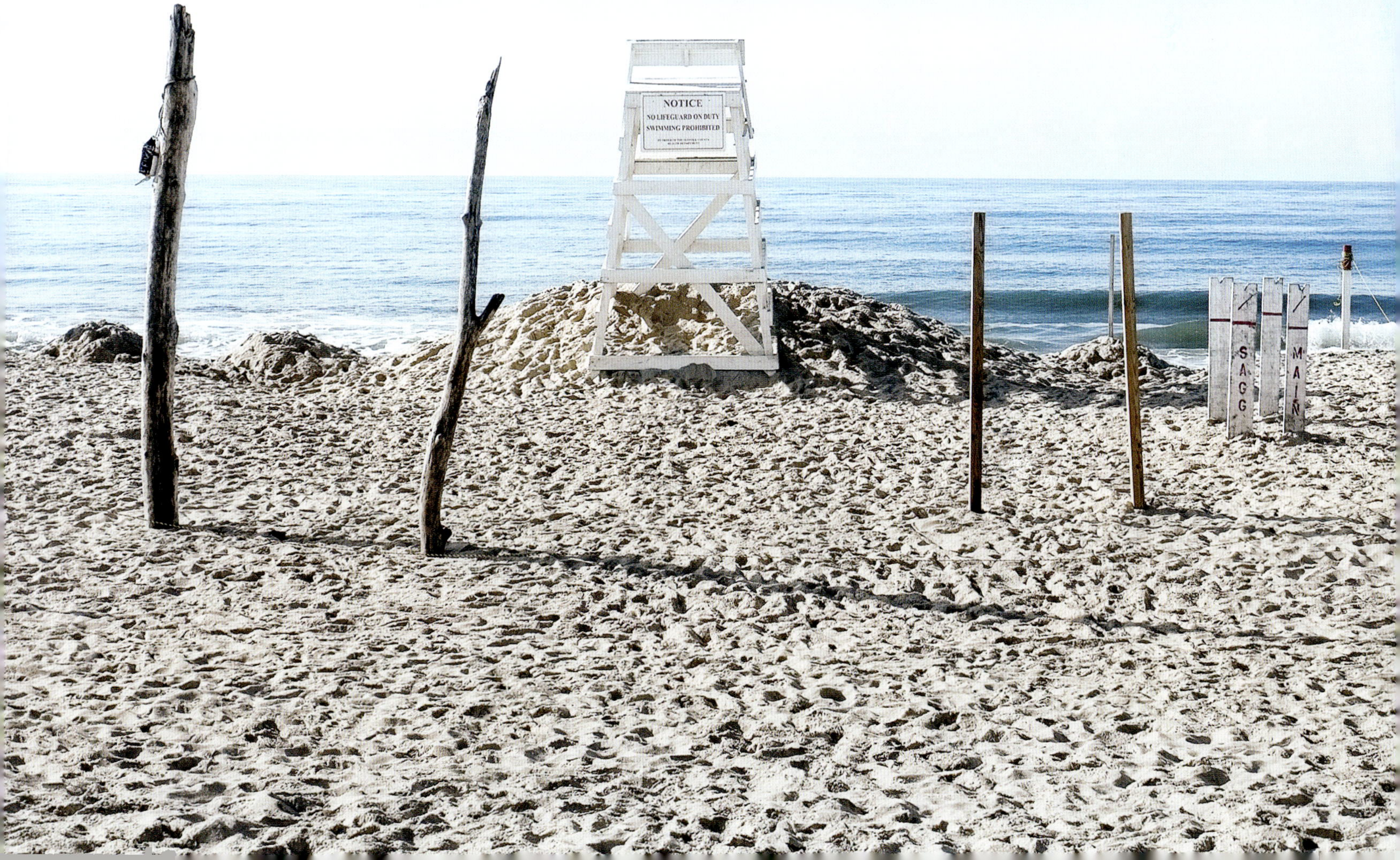

CONTENTS

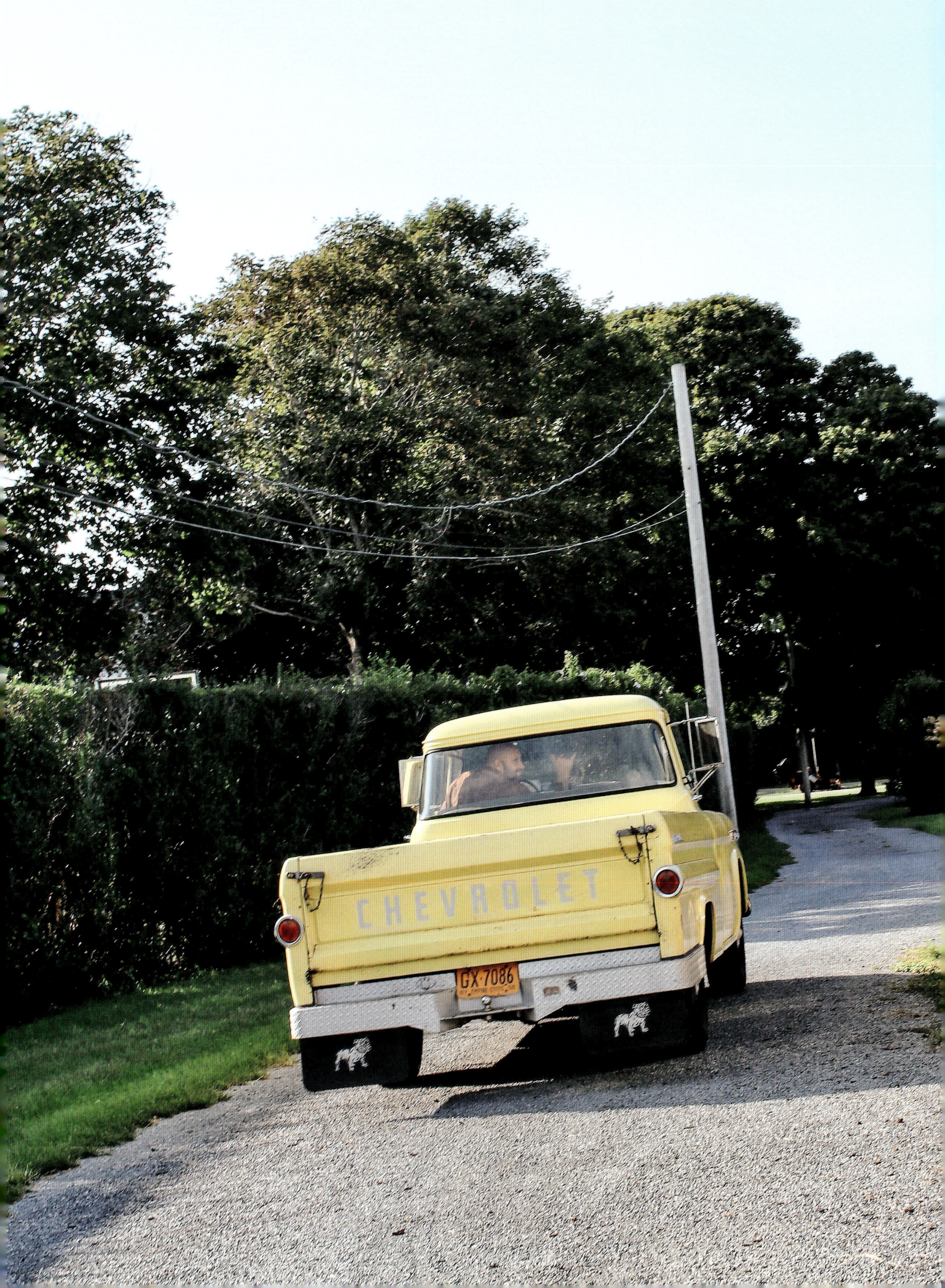
CHEVROLET
GX-7086

Mónica Ramírez-Montagut, PhD

Executive Director, Parrish Art Museum

FOREWORD

IT IS WITH IMMENSE PLEASURE and delight that I write the foreword for this wondrous publication by Jaime Lopez and Coco Myers. My deepest congratulations and gratitude to them both for this labor of love, which gives visibility to the creative petri dish that is the East End of Long Island. Documenting and recording the spaces, personalities, and works of the artists in our region was a Herculean effort that they undertook not only out of love and respect but also out of a need to showcase the current vibrant creative scene of an area that has been an incubator in which American art movements have matured and thrived for generations.

Begun in the 1830s, the railroad system that reached all the way from New York City to the eastern tip of Long Island by the end of the nineteenth century afforded artists the opportunity to discover and paint the Native American landscapes on the East End, such as Shinnecock Hills and Montauk. Enchanted by the region, some of the artists converted existing barns into studios and only reluctantly returned to New York City. Ever since, artists have been captivated by the area's natural beauty—its open fields, lush woods, expansive seascapes, pristine beaches, and unique, world-renowned light. And many have chosen to move here permanently.

In the East End, artists find peace, quiet, time, and space to contemplate and create, as well as a tight-knit community of peers that is more akin in lifestyle to a small European village than to the urban whirlwind of New York City. Life here offers a perfect balance: easy access to New York's high intensity and global reach on the one hand and on the other the bucolic, laid-back East End communities such as the historic Hamptons villages, the quiet hamlet of Springs, and the tony village of Sag Harbor on the South Fork, and Orient and Greenport on the North Fork.

The Parrish Art Museum, the preeminent museum in the region since 1898, often illustrates the history of the regional, national, and international migration of artists to the area in its exhibitions and permanent collection. It takes as a point of departure the American Impressionists such as William Merritt Chase, William Sidney Mount, Thomas Moran, and Childe Hassam in the 1880s. It then moves on to the Abstract Expressionists, including Jackson Pollock, Lee Krasner, Willem and Elaine de Kooning, James Brooks and Charlotte Park, and John Chamberlain, in the late 1940s and 1950s; the Pop Art artists, led by Roy Lichtenstein

A Herculean effort to showcase the current vibrant creative scene.

and Andy Warhol, and the Land Art artists such as Dennis Oppenheim, Michelle Stuart, and Alice Aycock in the 1960s; the remarkable community of Black artists in Sag Harbor, including Frank Wimberley, Al Loving, Reynold and Joan Ruffins, who settled in the town in the 1960s, and more recently, Nanette Carter, Claude Lawrence, Leslee Stradford, and Hank Willis Thomas; the feminist artists Audrey Flack, Lynda Benglis, and Joan Semmel, the Photorealists such as Chuck Close, and the Post-Minimalists like Jennifer Bartlett and Mary Heilmann in the 1970s; and

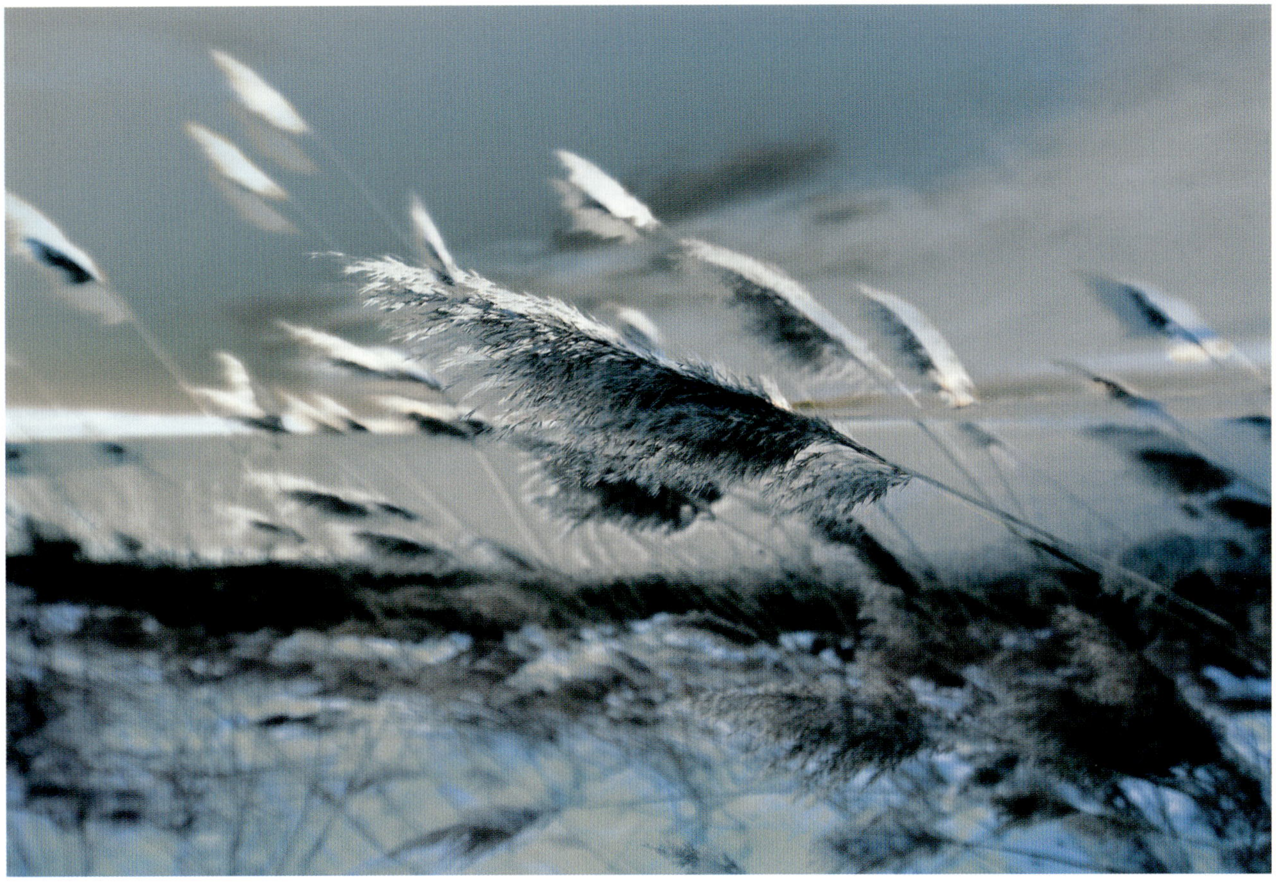

the leading Neo-Expressionists and Postmodernists, including Eric Fischl, Julian Schnabel, Cindy Sherman, David Salle, Robert Longo, Ross Bleckner, and Pat Steir, in the 1980s. Many in this extraordinary pantheon of nationally and internationally recognized artists with deep roots in the East End were celebrated in the museum's 125th-anniversary exhibition, *Artists Choose Parrish*, in 2023. In addition to those mentioned above, the exhibition featured Marina Adams, Richard Aldrich, Tony Bechara, Vija Celmins, Pamela Council, Jeremy Dennis, Rachel Feinstein, Ralph Gibson, Joanne Greenbaum, Robert Gober, Sheree Hovsepian, Virginia Jaramillo, Rashid Johnson, Mel Kendrick, Eddie Martinez, Suzanne McClelland, Sam Moyer, Alix Pearlstein, Enoc Perez, Ugo Rondinone, Amy Sillman, Ned Smyth, Donald Sultan, John Torreano, Stanley Whitney, Nina Yankowitz, and Joe Zucker.

A number of these artists are profiled in the pages of this beautiful and evocative book, which is a testament to the extraordinary artistic talent that continues to flourish in the East End.

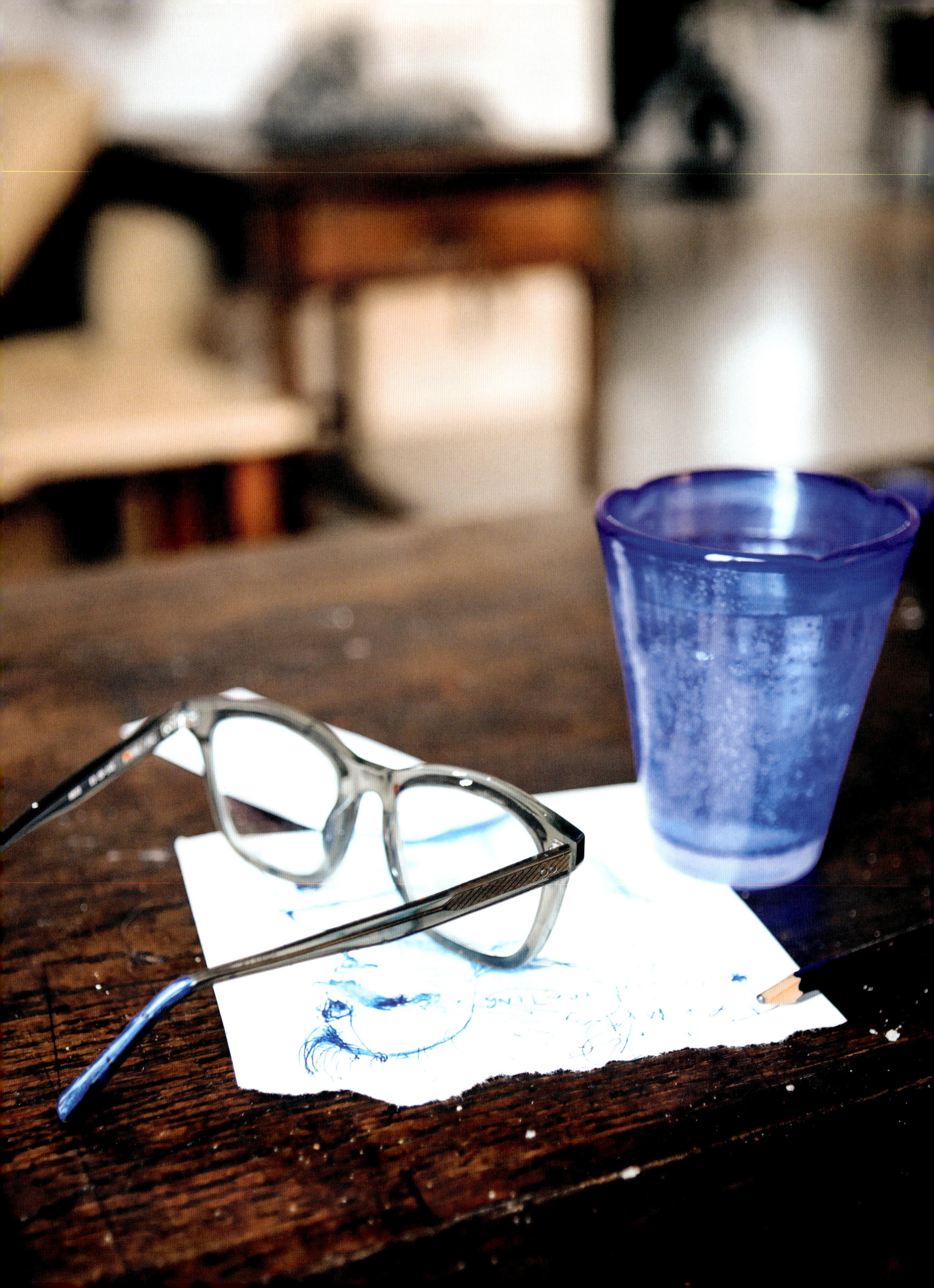

Coco Myers

INTRODUCTION

PART OF WHAT GIVES the Hamptons its illustrious reputation is the beauty of the landscape—the sea, the farms, the wide-open fields. But its character is also shaped by the artistic vein that runs through it. The East End of Long Island has long been a magnet for all manner of artists, drawn here by the bucolic lifestyle and the legendary light. It was these qualities that attracted the landscape painters Thomas Moran and William Merritt Chase in the late 1800s, the Abstract Expressionists, including Willem and Elaine de Kooning, Jackson Pollock, and Lee Krasner, in the 1950s and 1960s, and of course, the current crop of Hamptons artists—the subject of this book.

Our criteria for selecting the fifty artists who appear in the book were basic: first, we admired their work, and second, they had achieved a certain prominence in the Hamptons art world and beyond. Several summers ago, after initial visits to meet and talk to potential participants, we embarked on a series of photo shoots and interviews. We focused on painters, sculptors, photographers, and mixed-media artists who we believed represented the wide range of locally based talent and worked in a great variety of studios, from converted garages and basements to standalone structures—both the compact and the lofty.

More than merely documenting Hamptons artists and their workspaces, our goal was to showcase these artists in a fresh, authentic way—to capture them without artifice and to present them as they may not have been seen or perceived before. Most of the artists are already well known locally, but we hoped to reveal something unknown about each one—to unveil nuances of their personalities and work through the photos and through their own words.

Our goal was to capture these artists without artifice.

To that end, we got up close and personal. Each artist was first photographed in a portrait session. We chose not to provide hair, makeup, or styling, as the idea was to show the artists naturally. We asked them to come wearing whatever they felt comfortable in and to bring any trademark accessory, tool, or gear. Sculptor Joel Perlman came with his welding shield, which he donned in the studio. Painter Mary Heilmann brought a flower from her garden and held on to it for the photo. Photographer Michael O'Neill, known for his collection of colorful eyewear, wore his lime-green glasses to match his lime-green jacket. And painter Eva Faye brought her handsome dog, which had a starring role in the shoot. The photo sessions had an organic feel, resulting in expressions and postures that we couldn't have predicted.

The next phase of the shoots took us to the artists' own studios, where we could glean more of the artistic process and the person—to fill in the picture, so to speak. These visits allowed us to see the artists in their element—working, talking, explaining, demonstrating. We always came away from these sessions inspired and invigorated. There was so much to absorb besides the smell of paint or the touch of sculpted wood. Occasionally, we were treated to an impromptu musical performance (many of the artists are also musicians, we discovered): Dalton Portella on guitar, Don Christensen on drums, Caio Fonseca playing his latest original piano composition.

We were lucky. All of the featured artists welcomed us into their work worlds. They were generous with their time, forthcoming about their techniques, and enthusiastic about the book project. Given the nature of an artist's life—working in solitude—it could have been different. For many artists, their studios are sacred, private places, their realms of escape. But for this endeavor, they opened their doors. As our mission was to reveal the artists' everyday working environment, any corner could be a subject of interest: tables full of paint cans and brushes, bottles and tubes of oils, little boxes of watercolors, drill bits, wood shavings, a paint-spattered chair, photos—of people and places—tacked up on the walls, piles of books or magazines. We also wanted to document the artwork itself—recent works, older works stacked in closets, and works in progress. Because we were after authenticity, we specifically asked the artists not to tidy up or alter their studios before the shoots, as many said they wanted to. "No, no," we said. "Please don't!"

Their studios are sacred, private places, their realms of escape.

The interviews for the book evolved organically over time. Conversations that were started in the studios continued over months, allowing the artists in their own voices to illuminate their connection to the Hamptons, their inspirations, artistic goals, and work habits. They volunteered stories about their upbringing and career twists, and the narratives were by turn enlightening, amusing, even surprising. Most of the artists were reverent about the light and the sea—or some other aspect of nature—hence the title of this book. Even those who said their work is more internally generated, rather than directly inspired by the landscape, told us that they love living here and that the environment affords them the freedom to do their best work.

We feel fortunate to be able to say the same.

Jaime Lopez

PHOTOGRAPHER'S NOTE

AS HAS BEEN SAID many times, "Every portrait tells a story." I remember the first time I understood the truth of this adage. I was a young student of graphic design in New York City, and a celebrated photographer showed me a photograph of a Peruvian farmer dressed in clothing that seemed to date back to the sixteenth century. I was captivated, not only by the superb graphic quality of the print but also by the man's clothing, his hands as big and strong as tools, his calloused feet. But what made the greatest impression on me was the photographer's comment that the key to portraiture is all in the eyes. I looked at the photo again and saw what I had been missing: the portal to the man's soul was right there, seen through his eyes.

At that moment my passion for photography—for photographing people in particular—began. Little did I know that, as with anything worth doing, photographing people would have its challenges. When you place a camera between you and the subject, you are in effect creating a veil. My intention was to pull back the veil between photographer and subject so that the result would not be contrived, posed, or pretentious. To achieve this, one has to be sensitive to the subject's personality and character, as well as to his or her expectations of the shoot. And one must take the pictures in an instant!

PHOTOGRAPHER'S NOTE

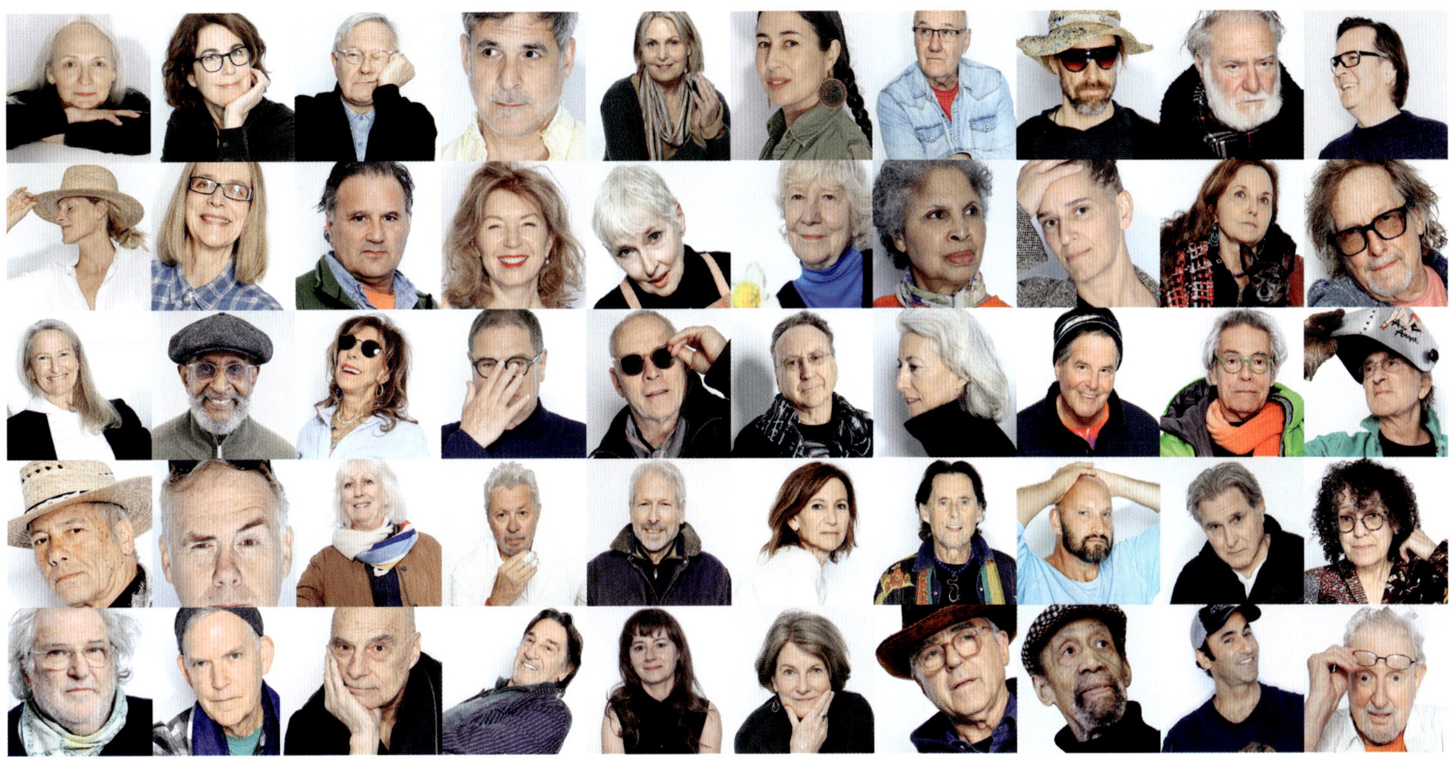

When I look back on my long career as a fashion photographer, I realize that all along I had wanted to tell stories free of the industry's expectations—portraying "perfect" beauty or selling a line of clothing. This desire led to a new project: photographing local artists—both in my studio and in theirs. I wanted to create pure and honest reflections of the artists, to capture the essence of their personalities. I tried to make them feel comfortable and at home in front of the camera. Most important, I wanted to understand what moved these artists—their ardor, intensity, warmth, and eagerness—in the hope of conveying their creative processes and what it is that they see.

The days I spent photographing these artists are among the most rewarding of my career. I felt reconnected to the basics of photography: an idea, a subject, light, a camera, and a background that complements the narrative. Every page in this book tells a story, not only about how and why these artists do what they do, but also who they are as people. I hope their personalities reveal themselves to you as they did to me—through their work, their expressions, and, of course, their eyes.

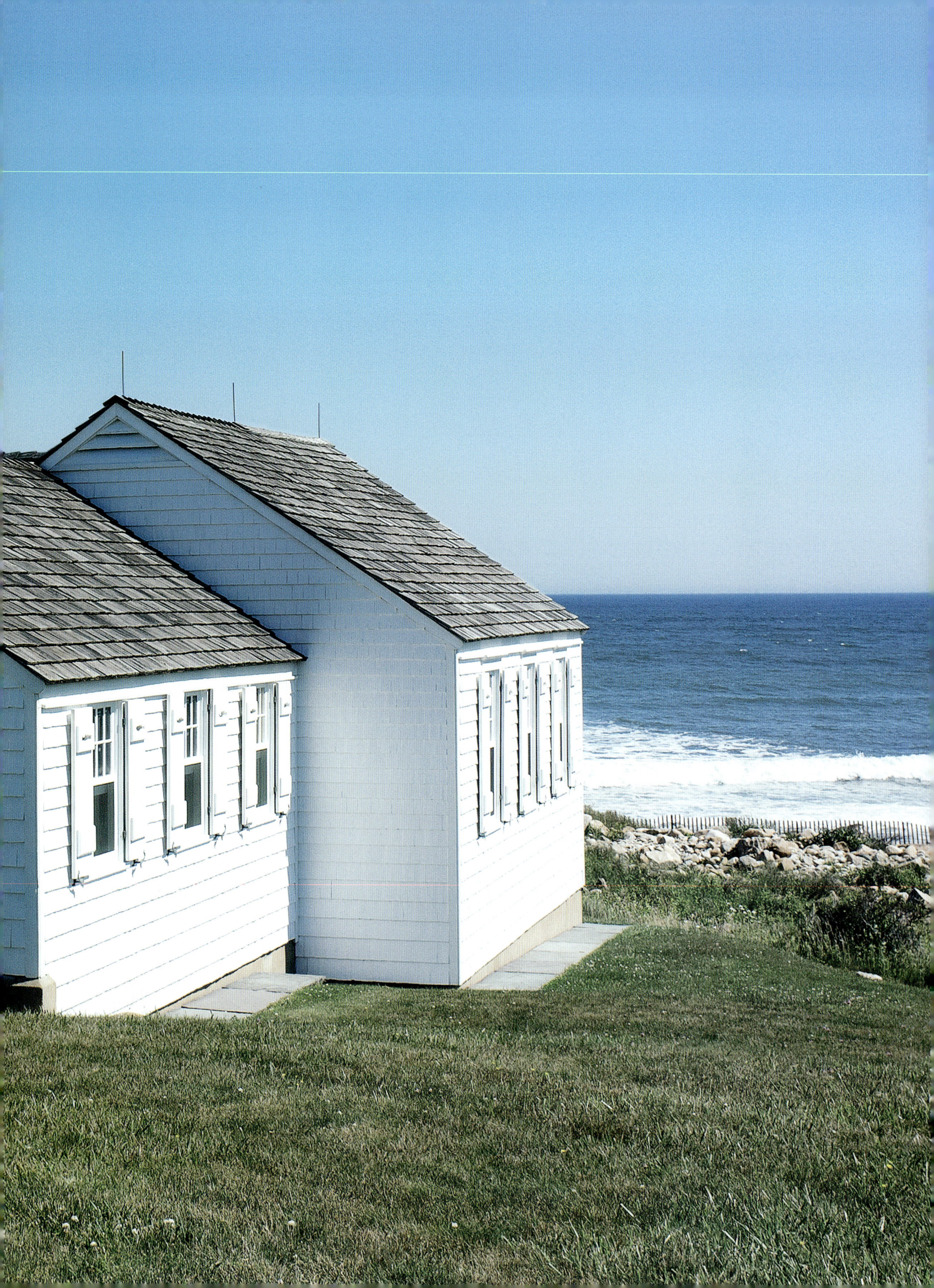

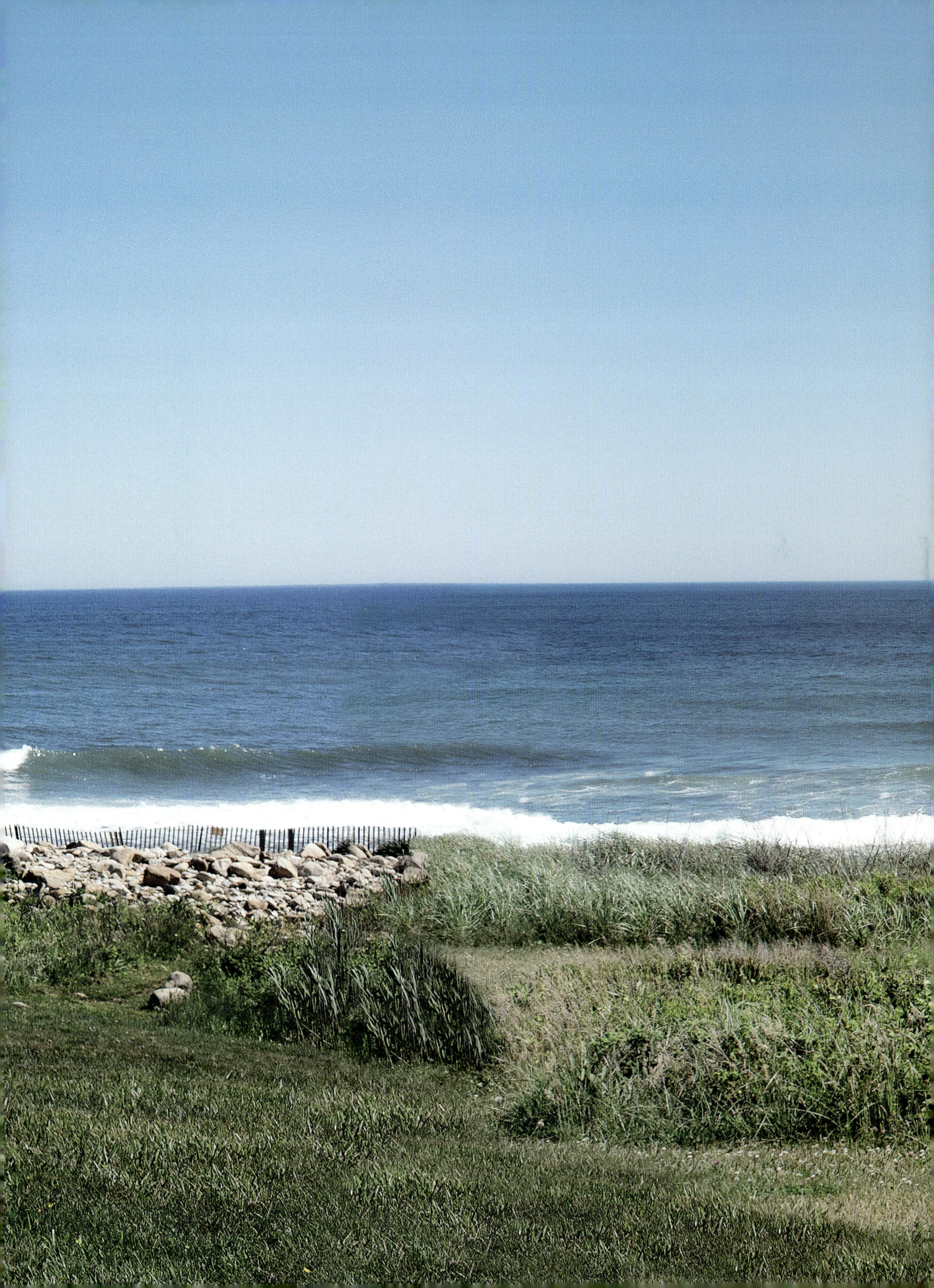

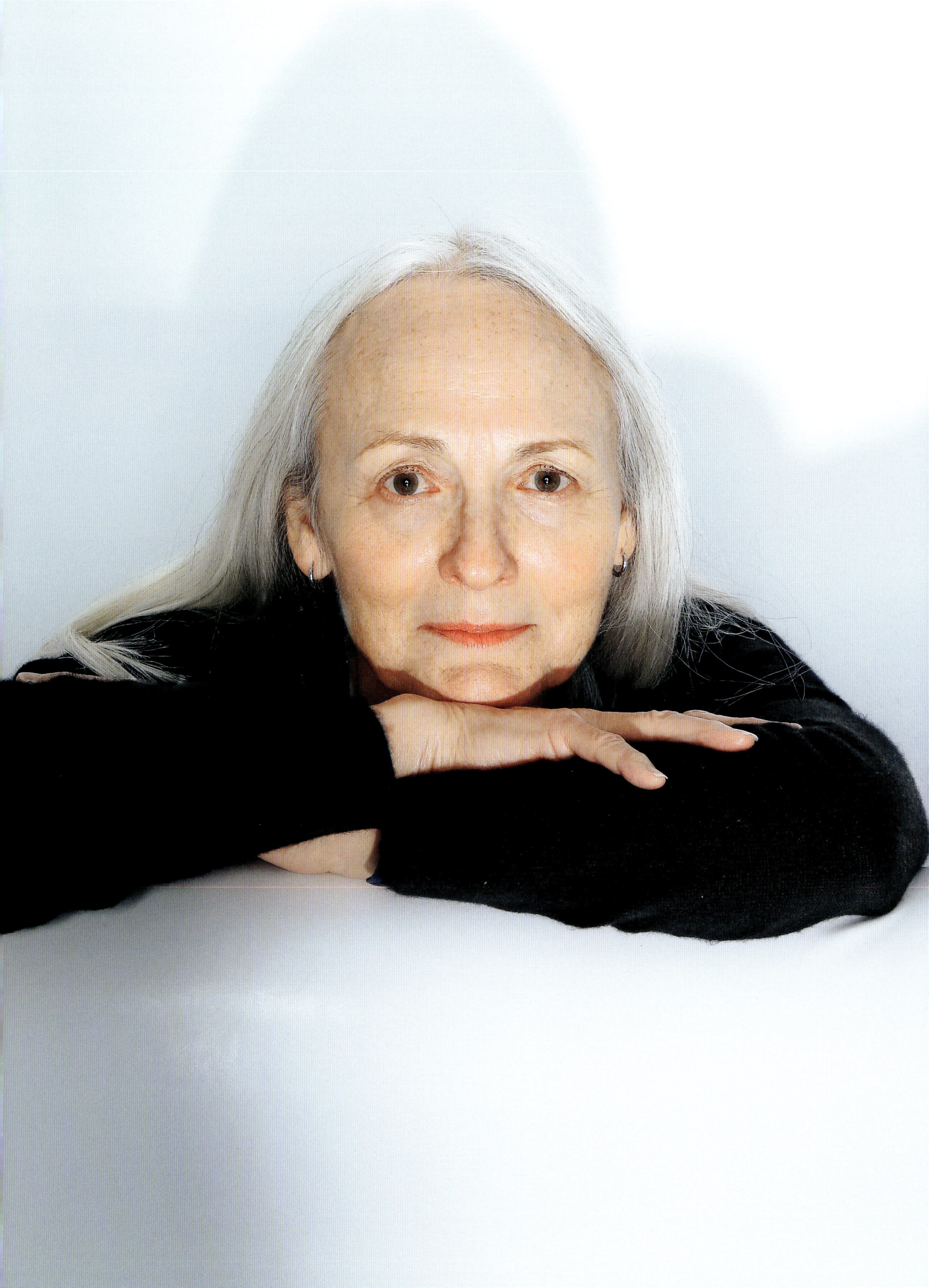

My work owes a great debt to de Kooning—his idea of "the slipping glimpse" and his practice of representing the feeling that the landscape engenders, rather than creating a literal illustration of that landscape.

ELISE ANSEL

Ansel's family bought a home in East Hampton in the mid-1970s, when she was fourteen. "Coming from New York City, it felt like a balm. Ever since, I've been spending parts of the year on the East End of Long Island. I fell in love with the spacious sense of freedom, the beach grass and dunes, the bayberry trees, the smell of wild beach roses, the landscape, the light. I remember skipping stones at Louse Point and looking at the phosphorescence in the bay at night." She and her husband live in the same family house. "A couple of years ago, I converted the old garage into a studio, the realization of a lifelong dream. I love working there, in the open air, next to the trees, the hedge, and the dahlia bed, with the smell and sound of the ocean nearby."

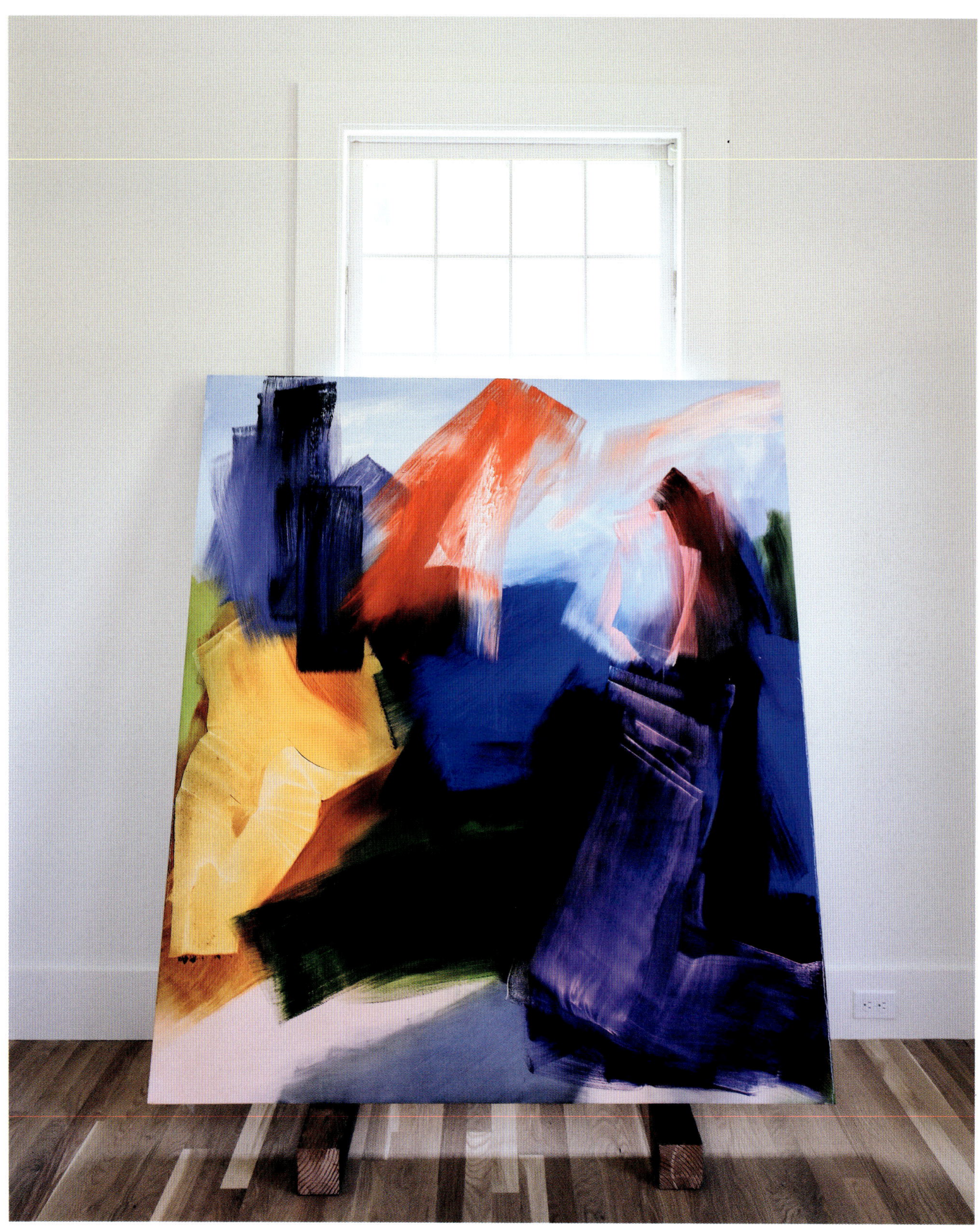

"The legacy of the Abstract Expressionists has had a profound influence on my work. For many years, I worked in a lexicon of gestural abstraction, using nature as inspiration and source. But in 2008, I experimented with interpreting historical art through the lens of gestural abstraction. I focused on bringing elements from old master figuration into a more completely abstract picture space."

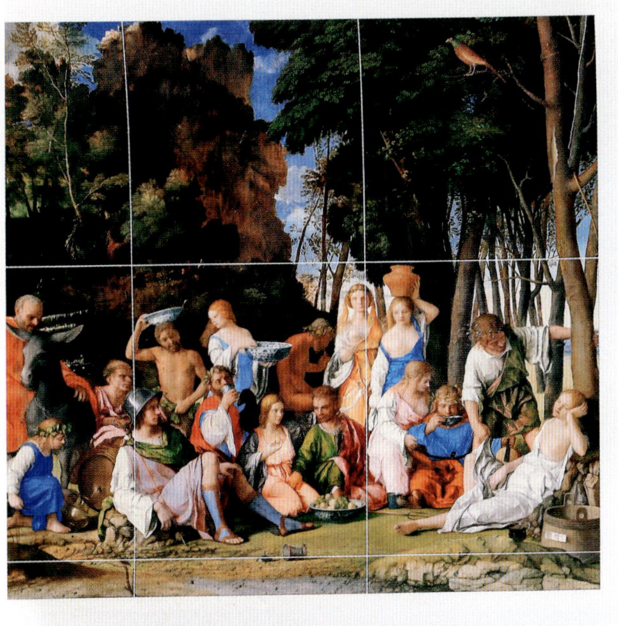
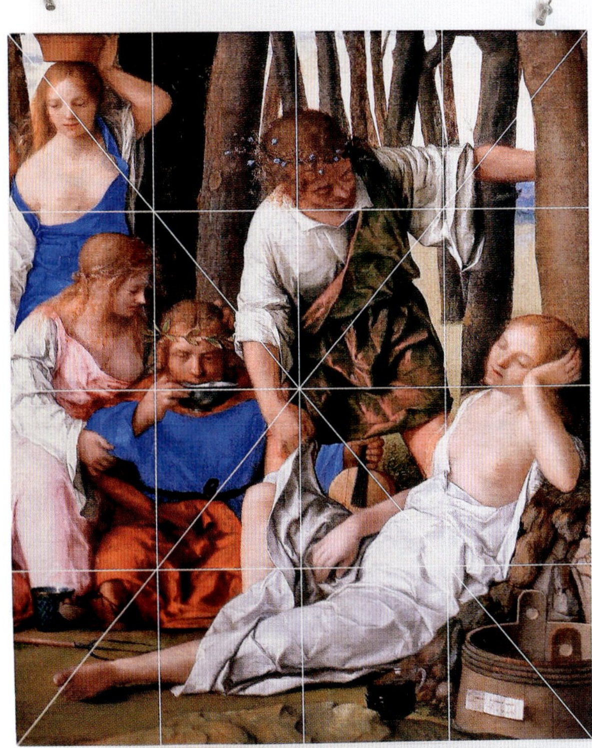
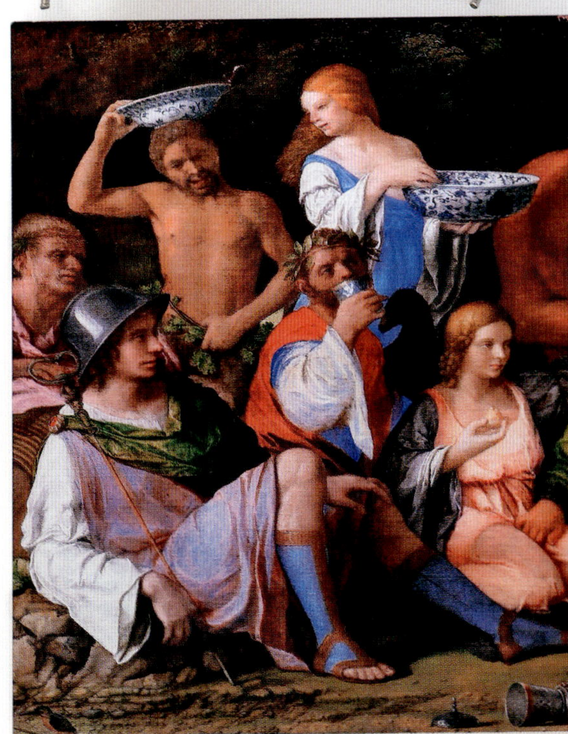
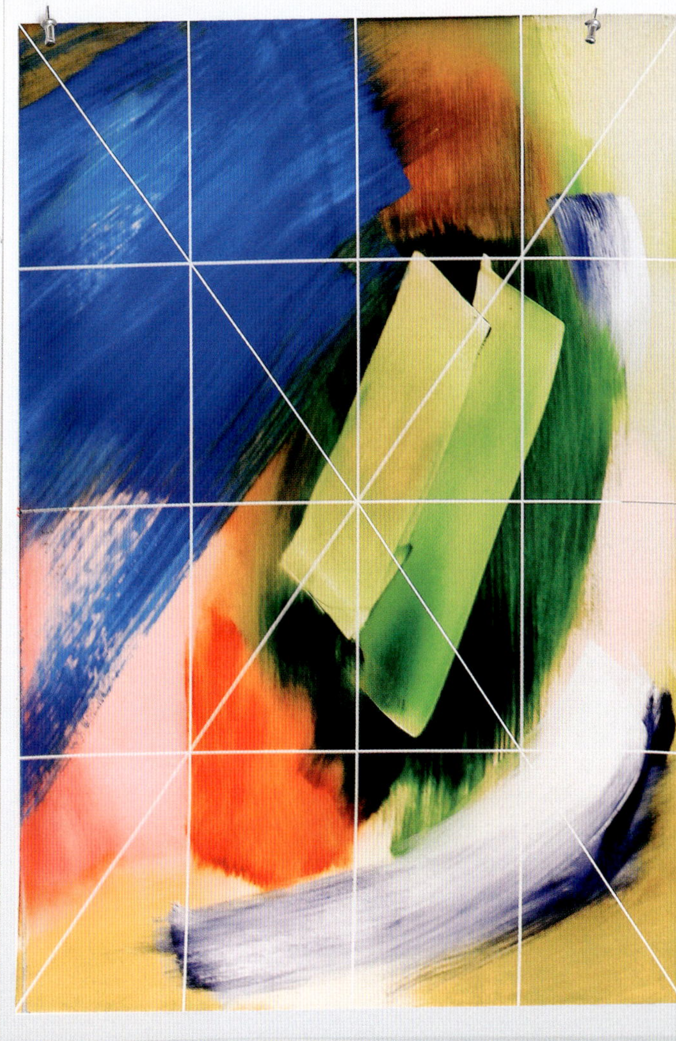

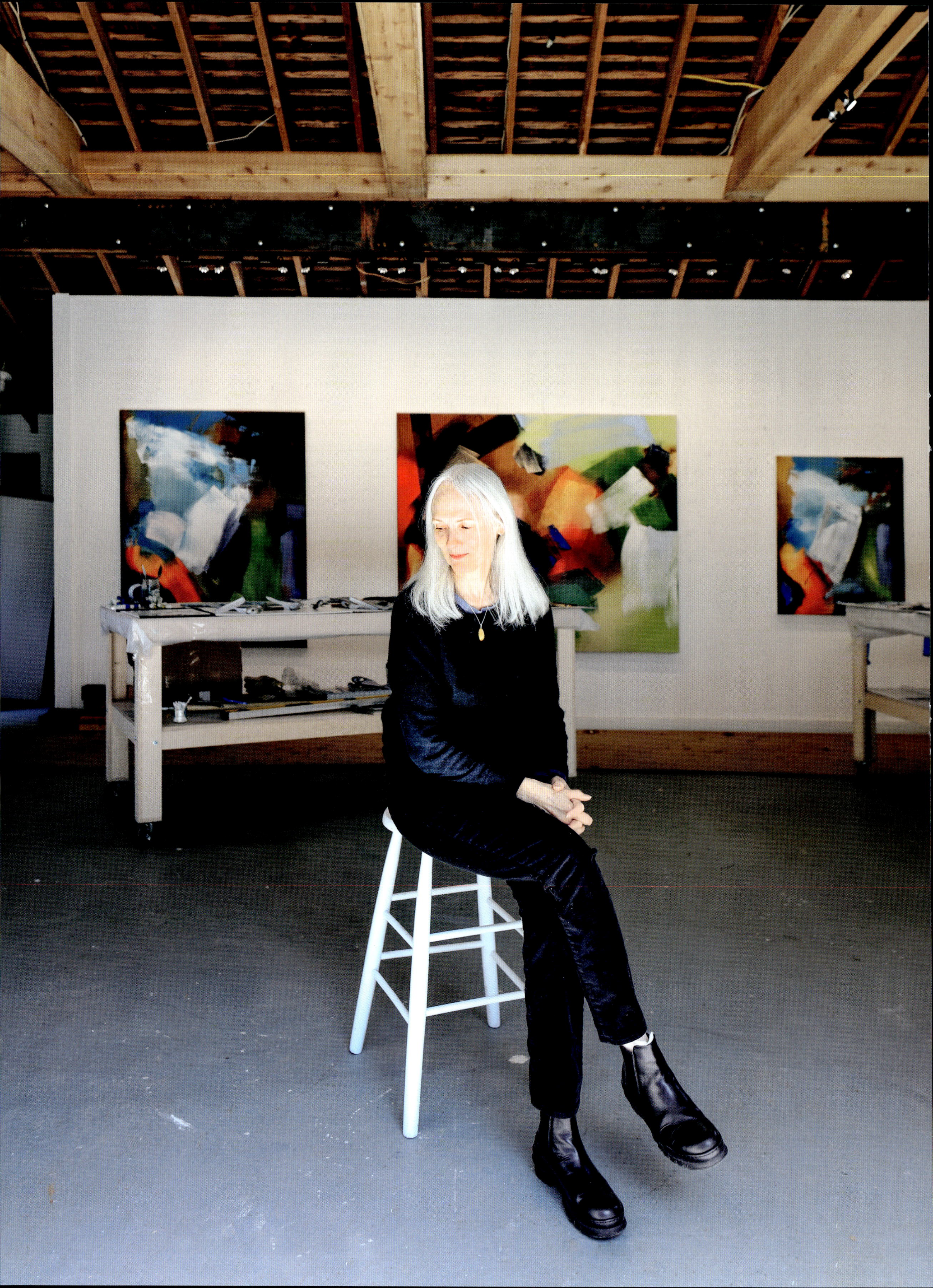

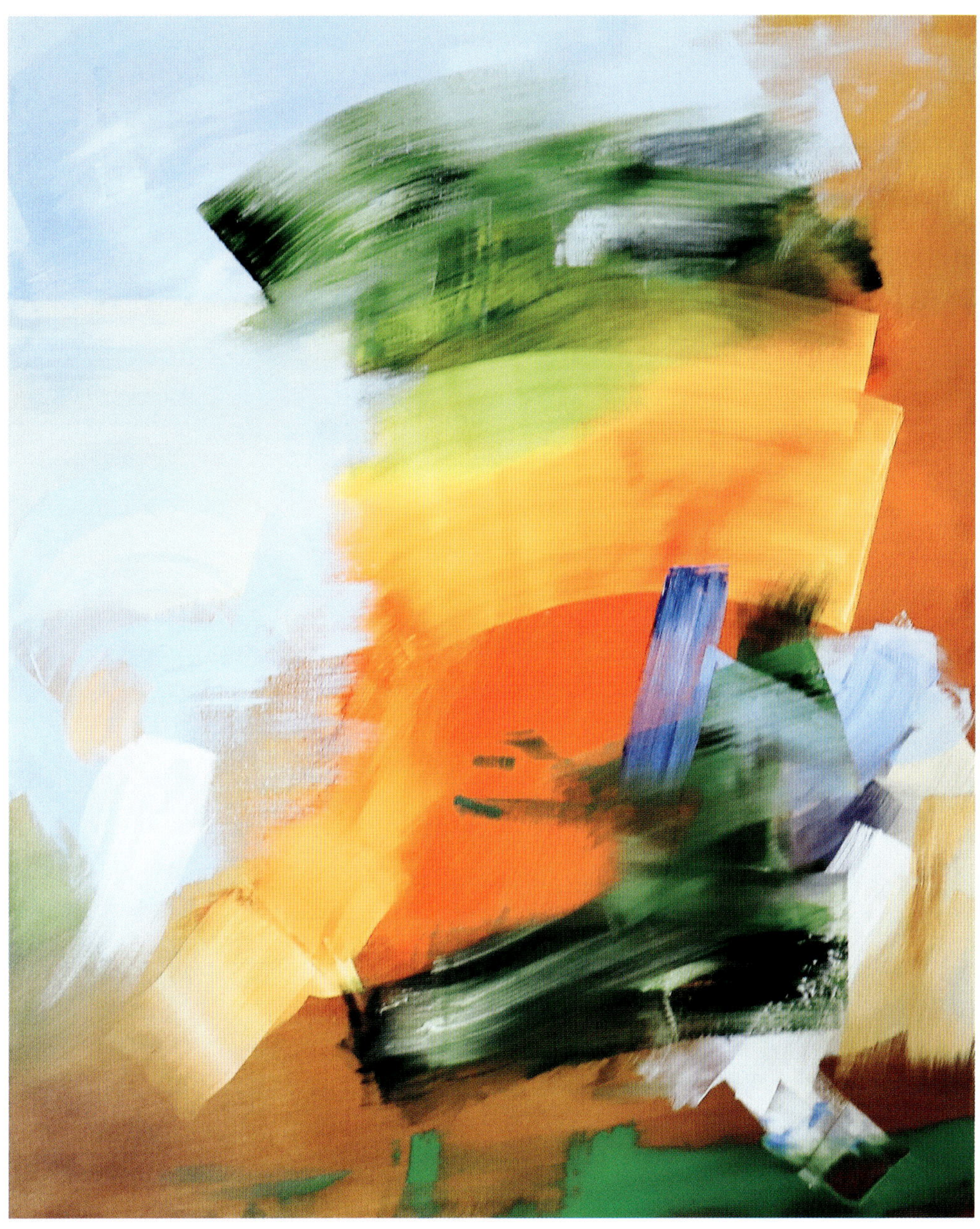

"I work in oil on linen and watercolor on Arches paper. I am particularly interested in the quality of transparency in both oil and watercolor. My main tools are large brushes and squeegees. I bought the large brushes on the recommendation of the sculptor Keith Sonnier. We were in a show together, and at the dinner after the opening he said, 'I understand what you're doing; try larger brushes.' So I did! My favorite brushes are made of hog's-hair bristles with wooden handles. Sometimes they fly like feathers in my hands; on bad days they feel like lead, but mostly they are light and quick. I use additive and subtractive methods of paint application and removal. This echoes the meaning of my work. I use brushes to put the paint on and squeegees and scrapers to take it off. On, off, on, off, and so it goes."

OPPOSITE Ansel's paintings—watercolors on paper and oil on linen—fill her airy East Hampton studio with lush color.

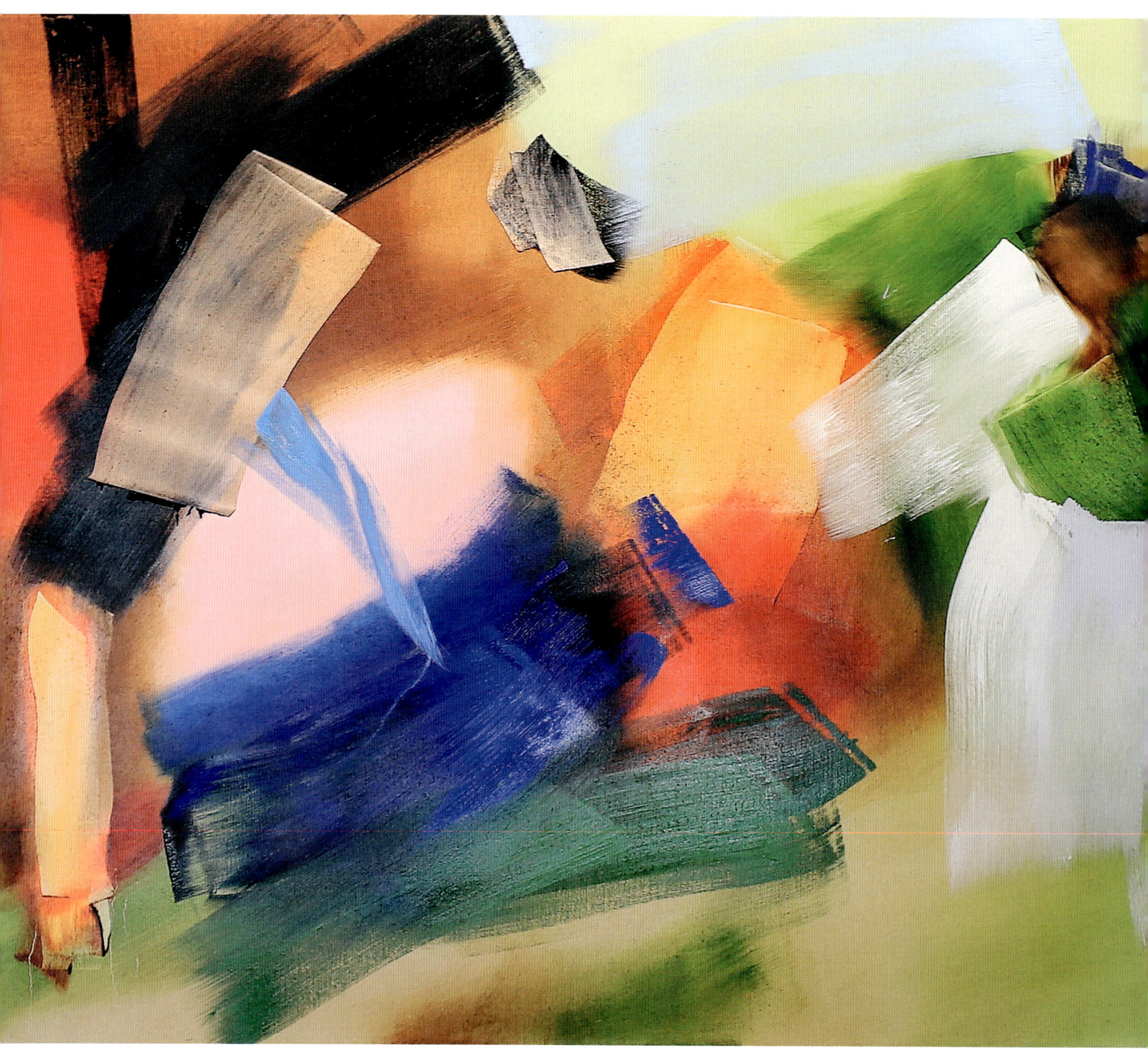

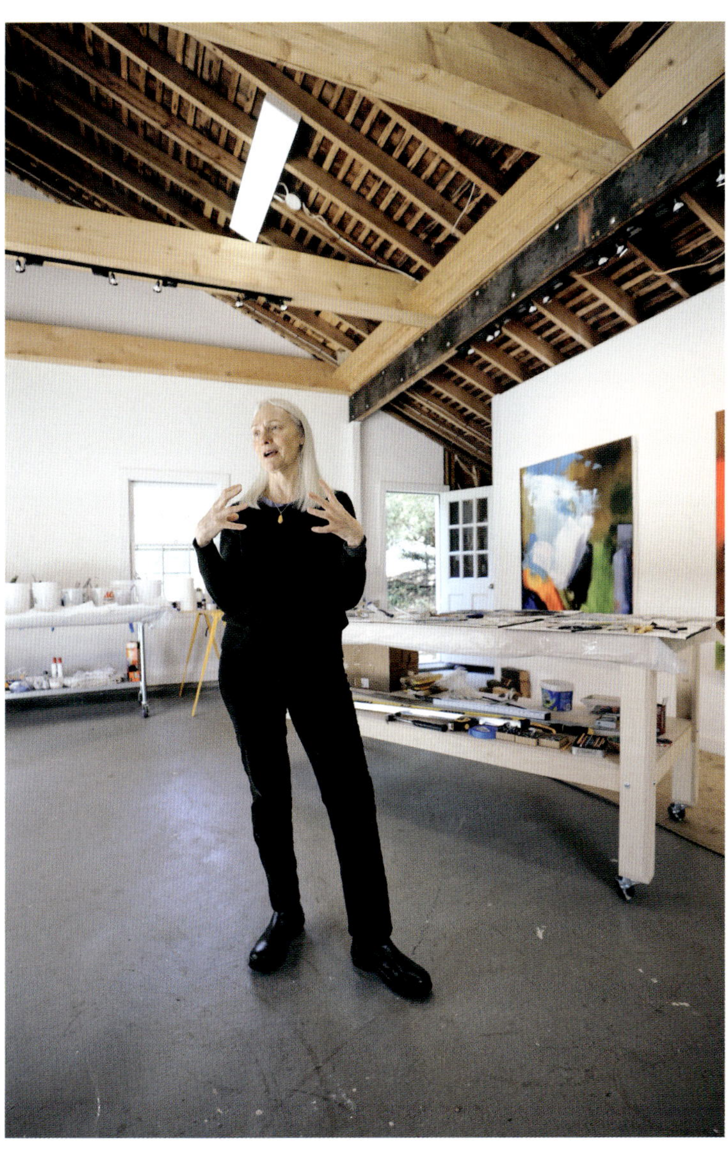

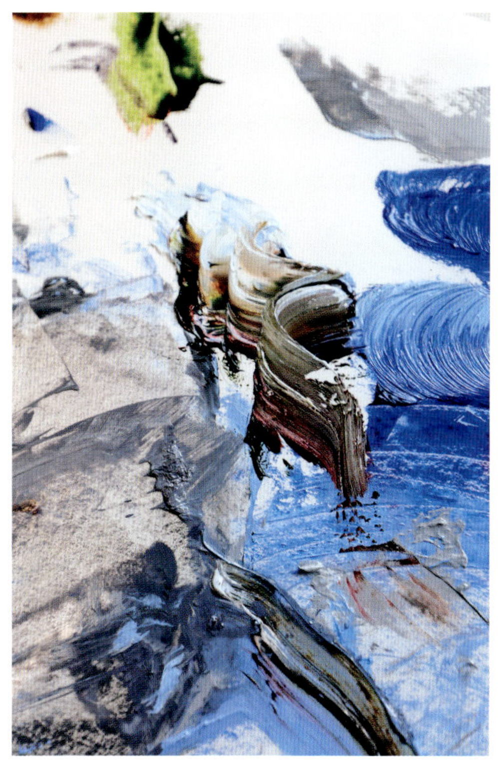

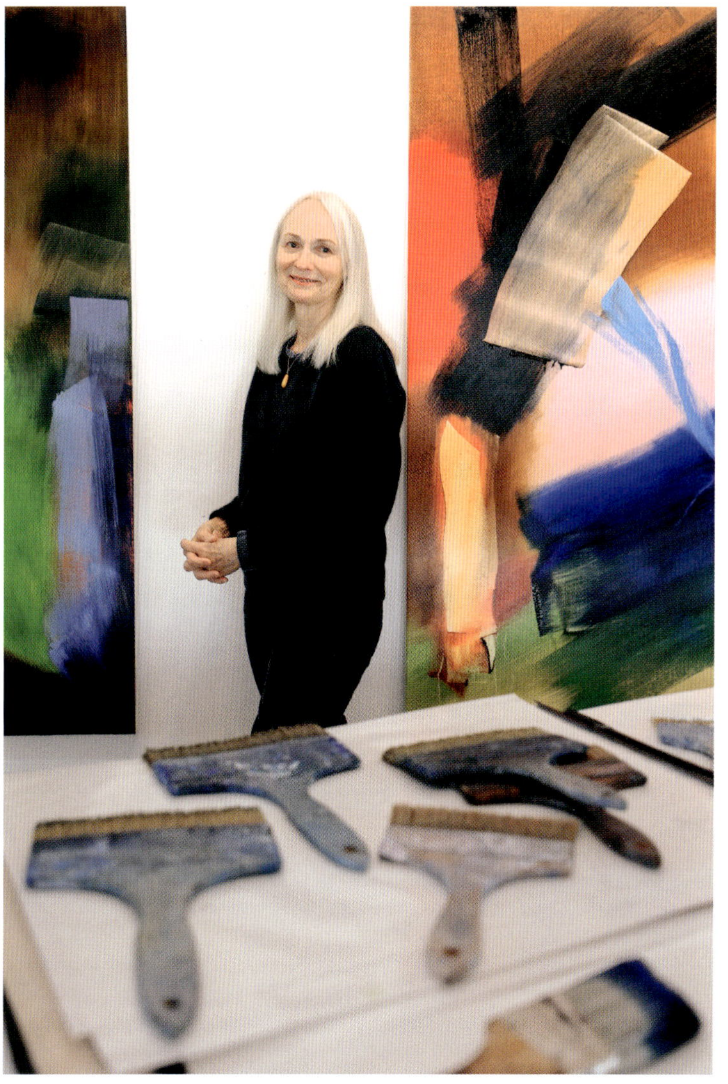

OPPOSITE AND THIS PAGE

Ansel's work involves translating old master paintings into a contemporary visual language, interpreting historical art through gestural abstraction. She uses large brushes and squeegees to lay down color in broad strokes and is particularly attuned to the quality of transparency in the paints.

I've chosen a subject that's very rich and I've stuck with it. For me, it's helpful to have parameters to work within. Expansiveness can come from limitations. I don't think I'll ever run out of new projects.

MARY ELLEN BARTLEY

Bartley first visited East Hampton more than thirty-five years ago. "I fell under the spell of this place—the water, the light, the legacy of artists, and a sense of possibilities." She and her then husband had a friend who grew up in East Hampton and whose father helped them look for a house. "He would buy funky houses and fix them up in a slapdash chic style, featuring art and overflowing bookcases. He found us a little house in Springs for $99,000—the best purchase we ever made. I still try to live in that scrappy, inspired spirit."

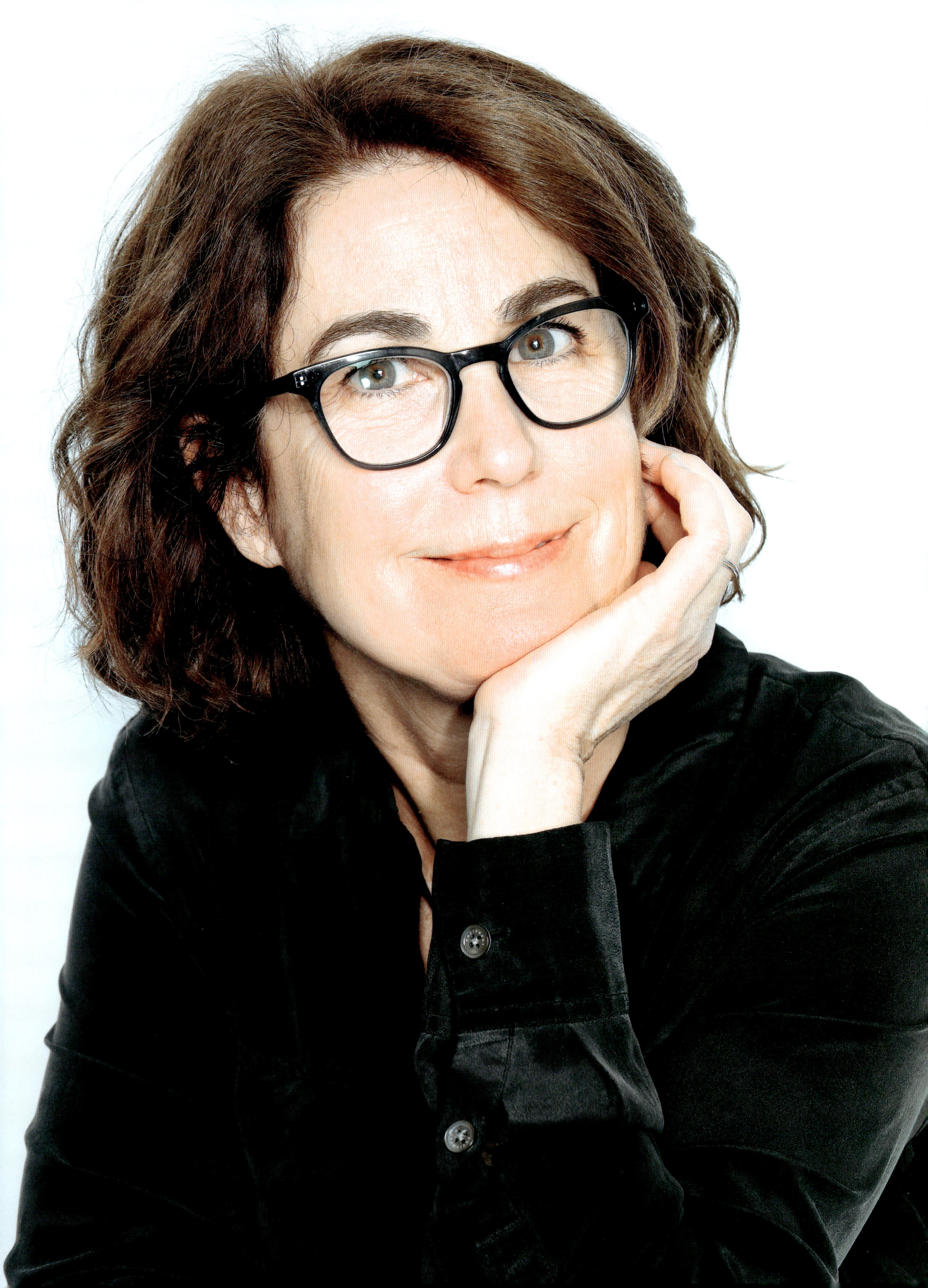

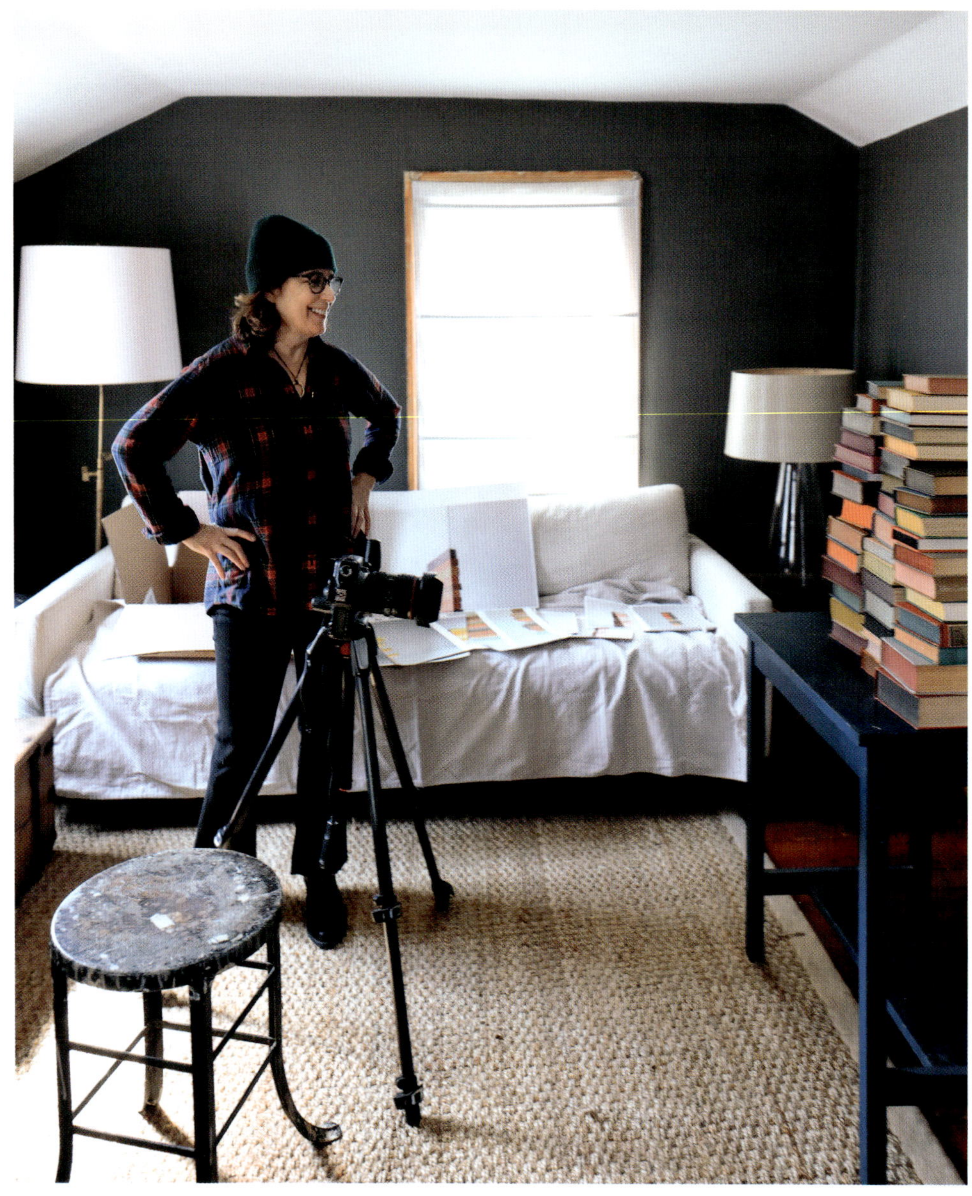

The book theme—how did that begin? "I'd had an interest in Giorgio Morandi since discovering his work in books in art school. But when I saw his retrospective at the Met in 2008, I left with a clear intention to find my own still-life objects that I could study and photograph again and again. I found stacks of paperback books and began making quiet, pale arrangements showing just the pages' edges and hiding any clues as to their content. I meant to deemphasize the narrative in photography and focus on formal and abstract qualities. I'm fascinated with artists' relationships to their books. Out here I've worked with the libraries of Jackson Pollock and Lee Krasner and Robert Wilson. I also had the lucky opportunity to photograph the Bouvier Beale books at Grey Gardens before the house was sold."

ABOVE Bartley's books can be shot in small spaces—whether in her Sag Harbor studio or in one of the many libraries she explores around the world. **OVERLEAF** For Bartley, books are both meaningful as objects to be artfully arranged and as symbols of the inner world of literature.

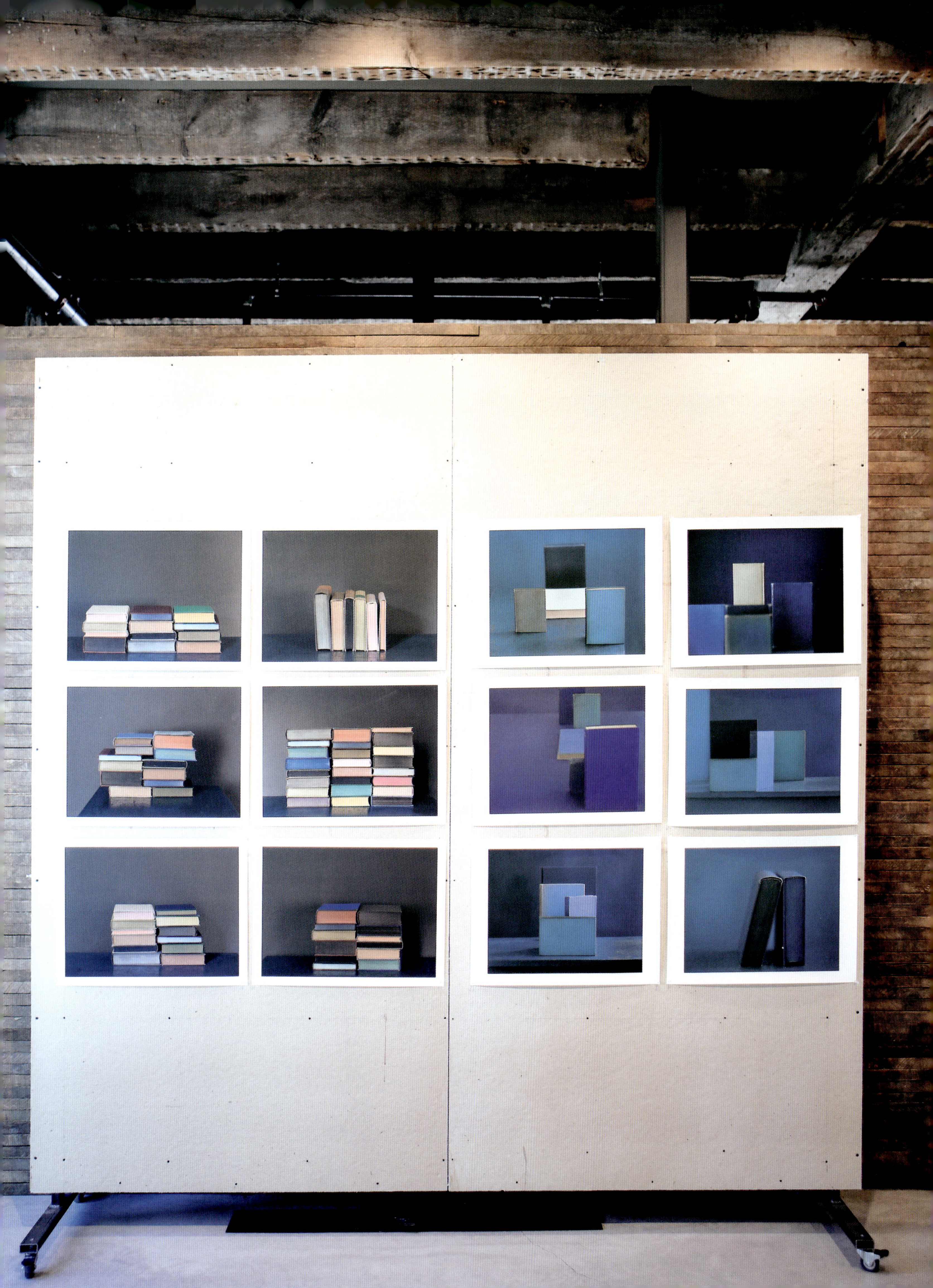

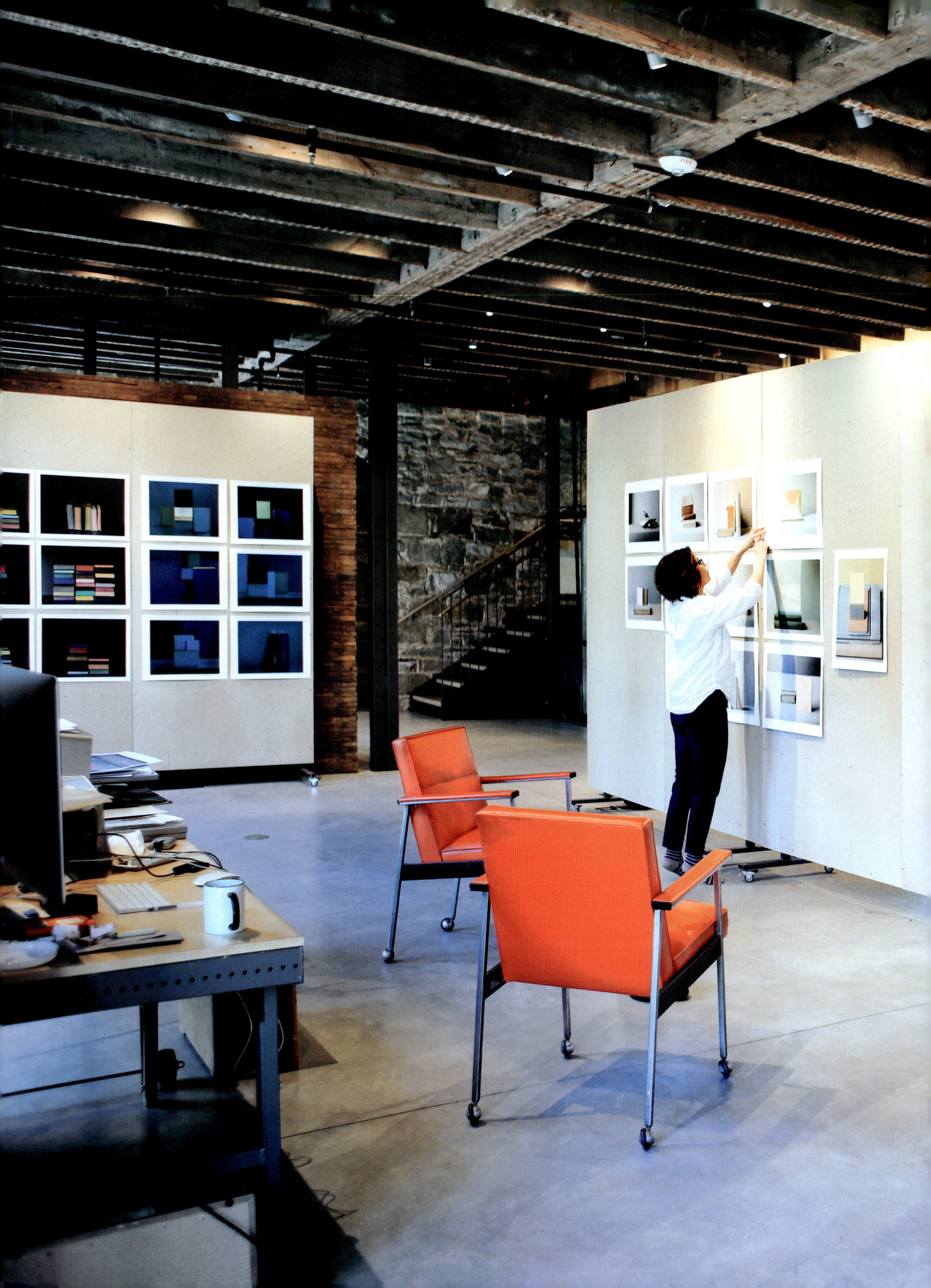

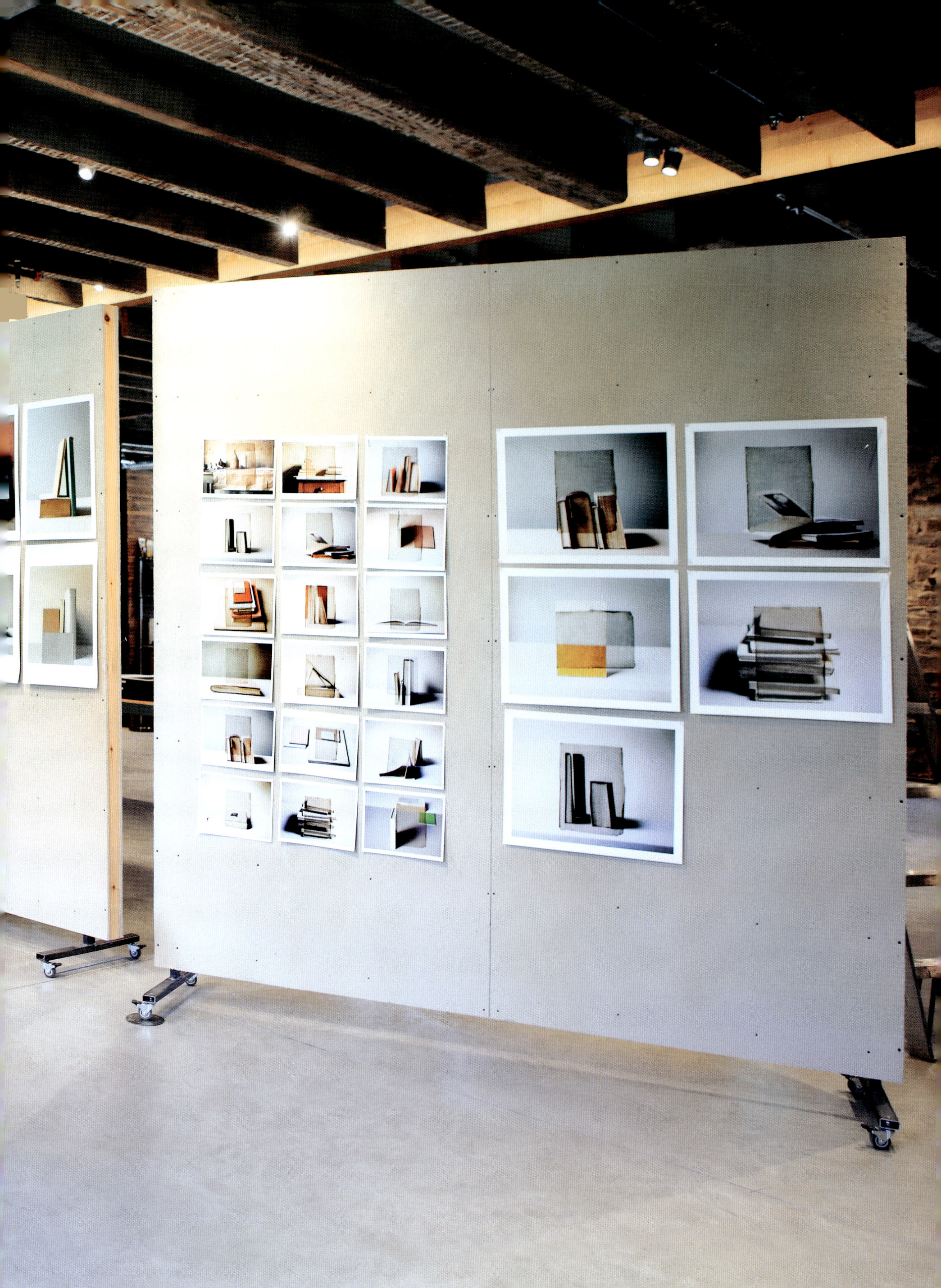

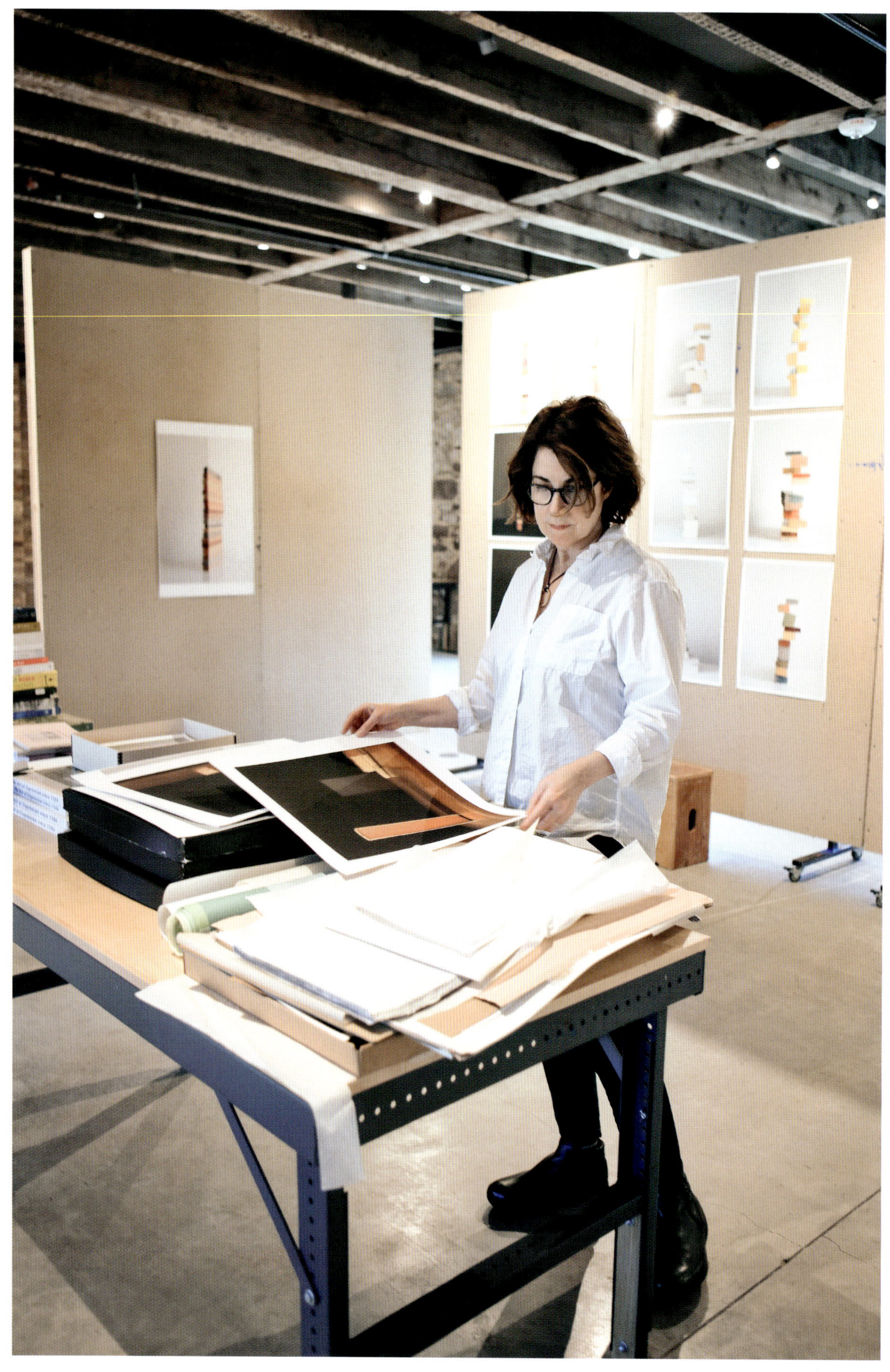

ABOVE Working as an artist in residence—here at The Church in Sag Harbor—Bartley creates endless variations on a theme, composing books in stacks or towers, or propped open to reveal the pages.

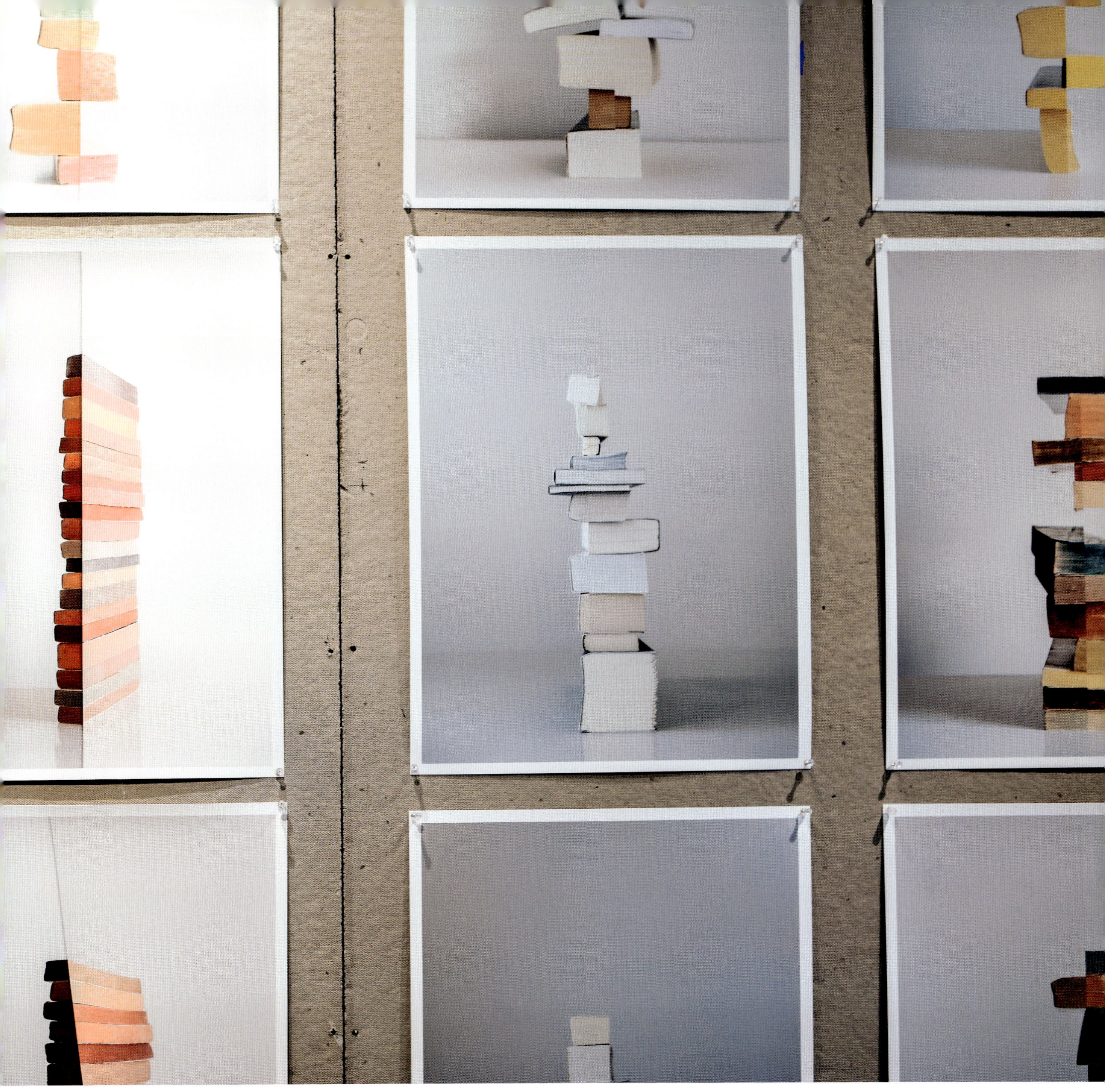

"When I travel to certain libraries as an artist in residence, I have limited time to acquaint myself with the collection, so I come up with a strategy to photograph it. This is an intense and somewhat pressurized work situation. It's usually when I'm running out of time that I have a breakthrough by overcoming some obstacle, and then the way through is clear. In the studio, which right now is wherever I can carve out a bit of space with daylight in my tiny house in Sag Harbor, I can leave things set up and come back over time. But I still seem to work in bursts, excited to see the next version of an idea."

Years ago, I acted in a play at the Actors Theatre of Louisville. A girl dressed as a young angel would intermittently walk onstage. She'd switch on a light bulb suspended over her head and say: "Be amazed!" I often imagine she walks into my studio.

WALTER BOBBIE

"I have drawn and painted since I could hold a pencil. My father carved out a studio in a corner of his garage after I won a prize for an oil painting in the New Jersey High School Art Competition." Bobbie got his masters in theater, which led to an acting career on and off Broadway. In 1992, his directing career took flight and eventually earned him a Best Director Tony award for *Chicago*. "Theater paralleled my painter's life, expanding my visual vocabulary as I collaborated with the great visual artists and designers of the stage."

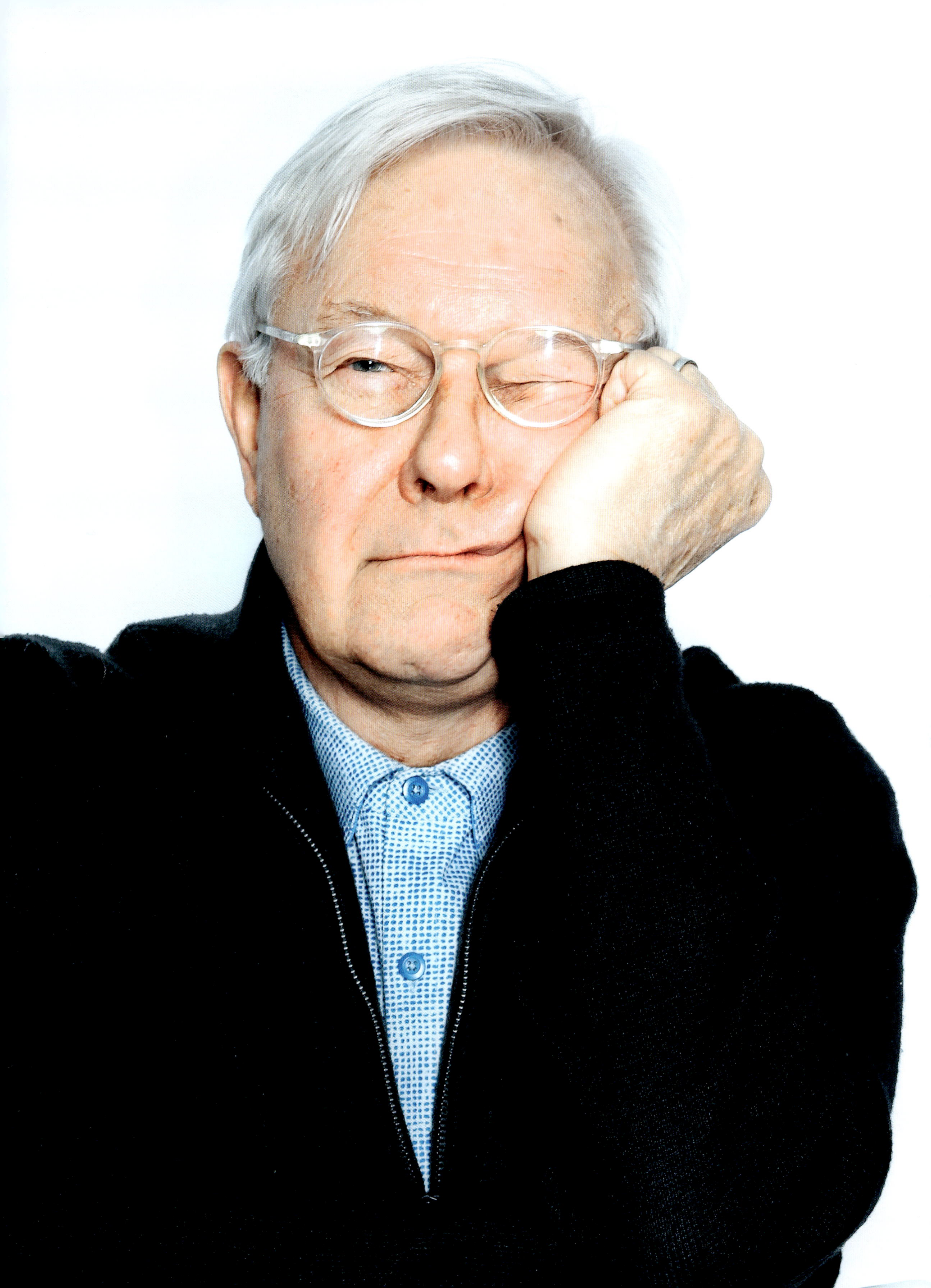

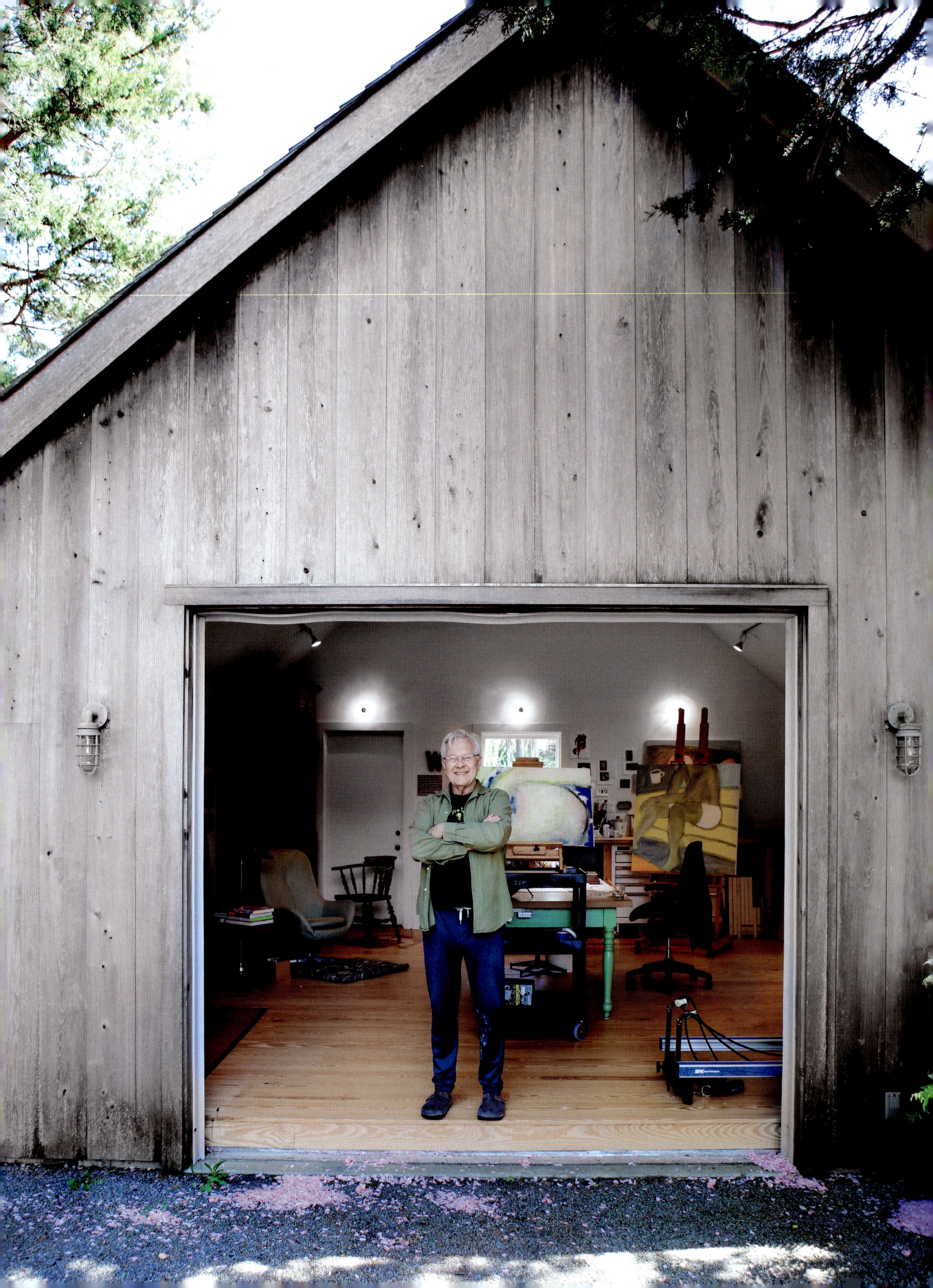

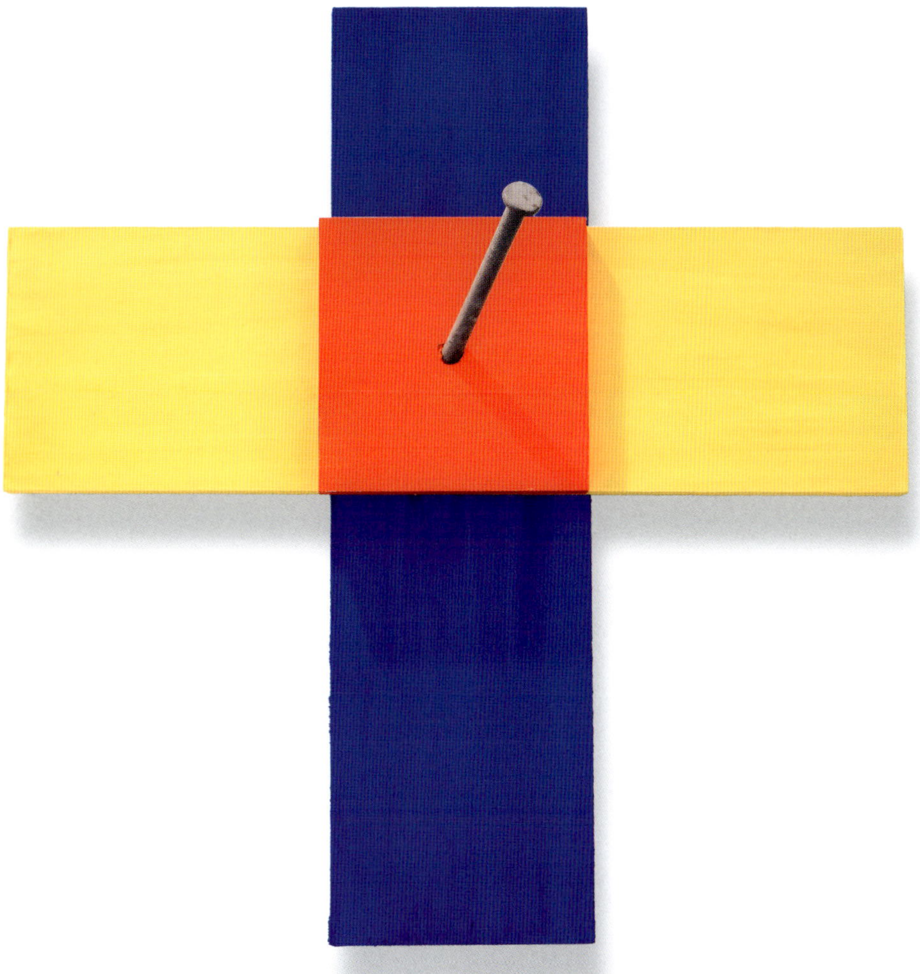

"After decades of visiting the East End, we bought a house in East Hampton in 1992 and a few years later built a house in Water Mill, where we live year-round." His spacious white studio takes up the entire former garage. "Being an artist full-time allows me to try and fail privately. In theater, my creative expression is a public event with deadlines and financial investment. As a painter, the expression is completely personal. It's you. Or I should say, me. Rise or fall, it is me."

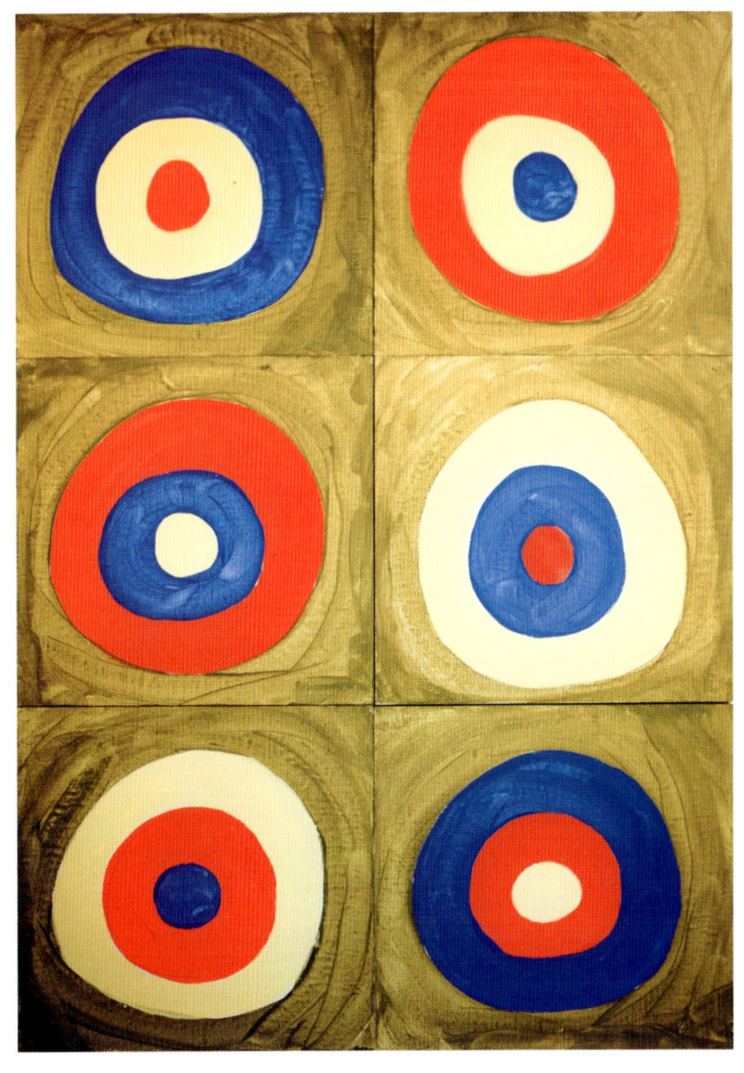

OPPOSITE

Bobbie transformed the garage into a studio once he decided to make Water Mill home and to paint full-time.

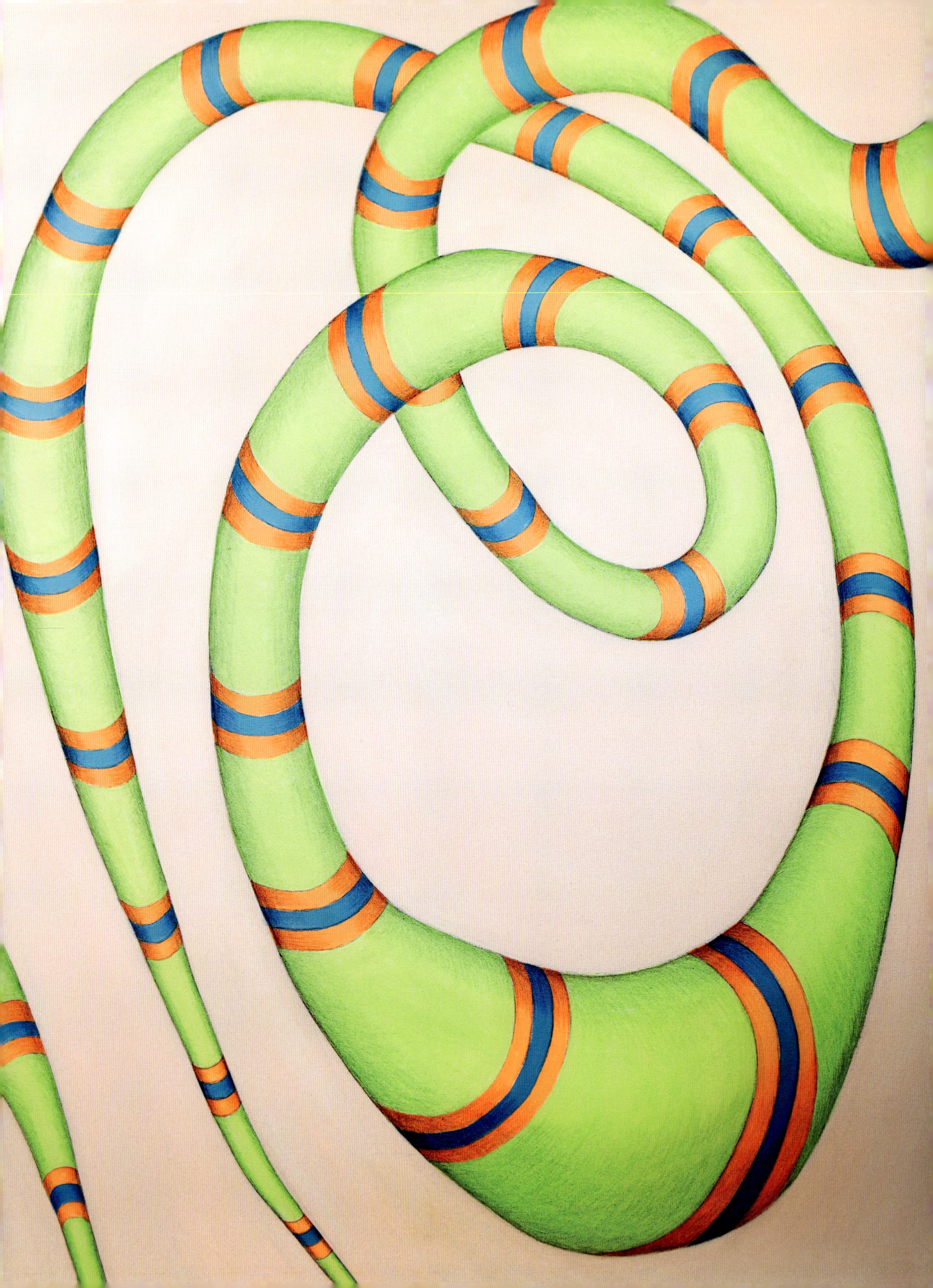

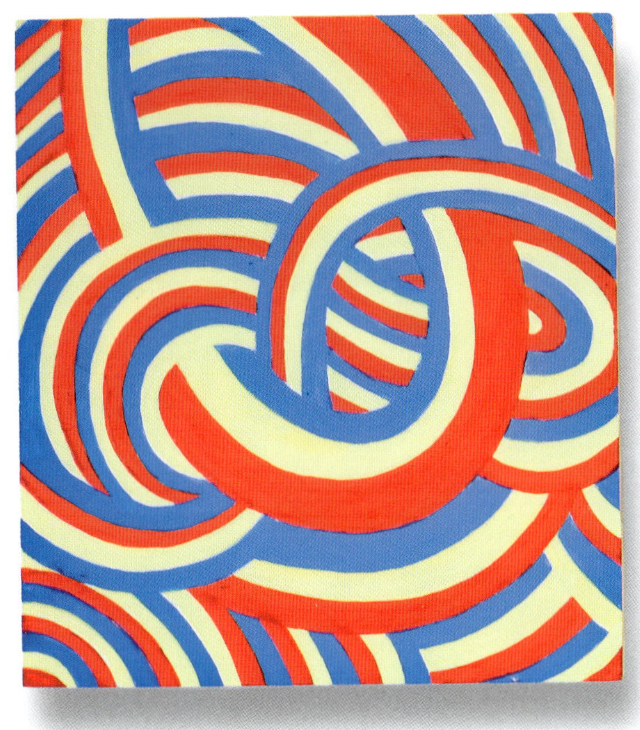

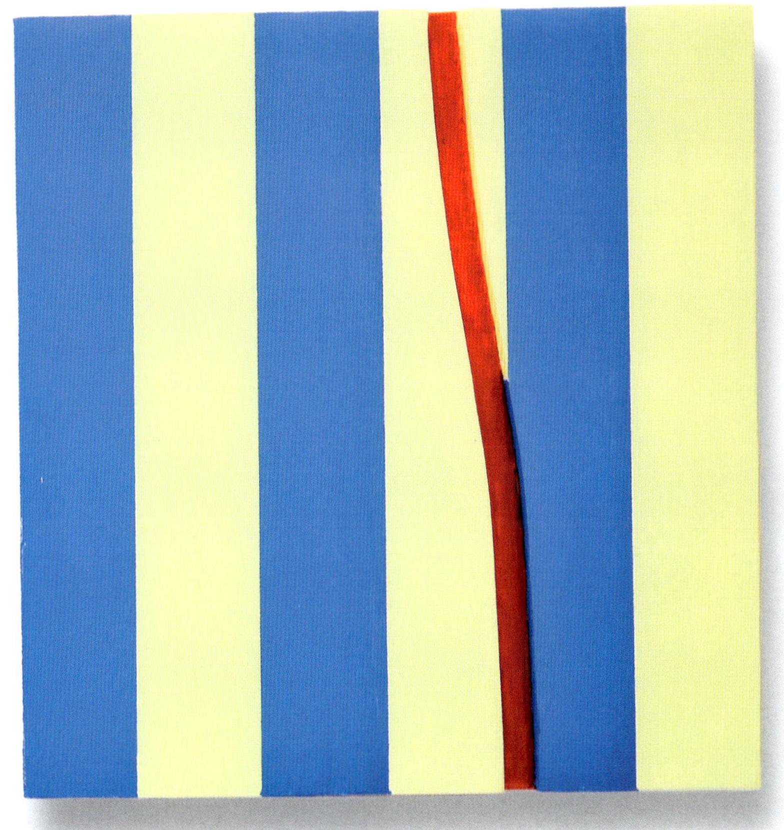

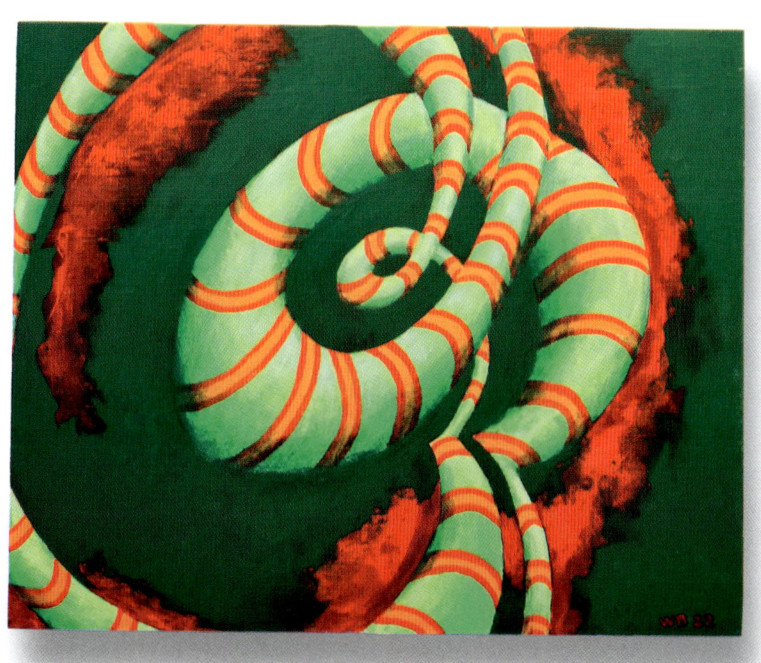

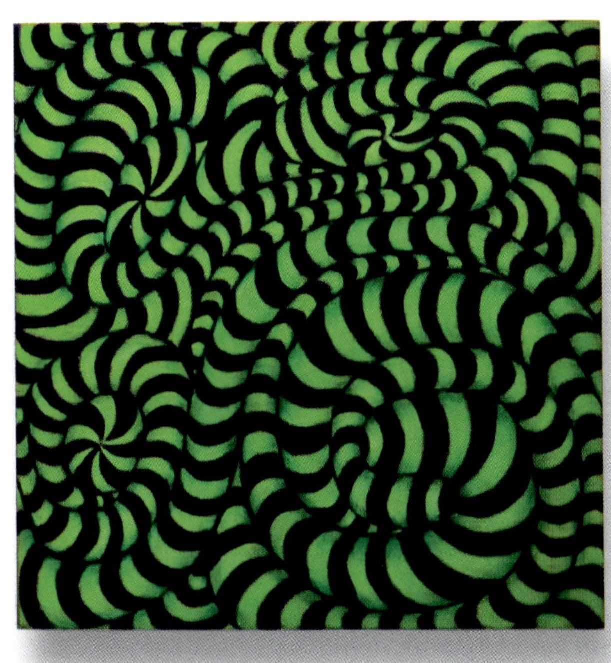

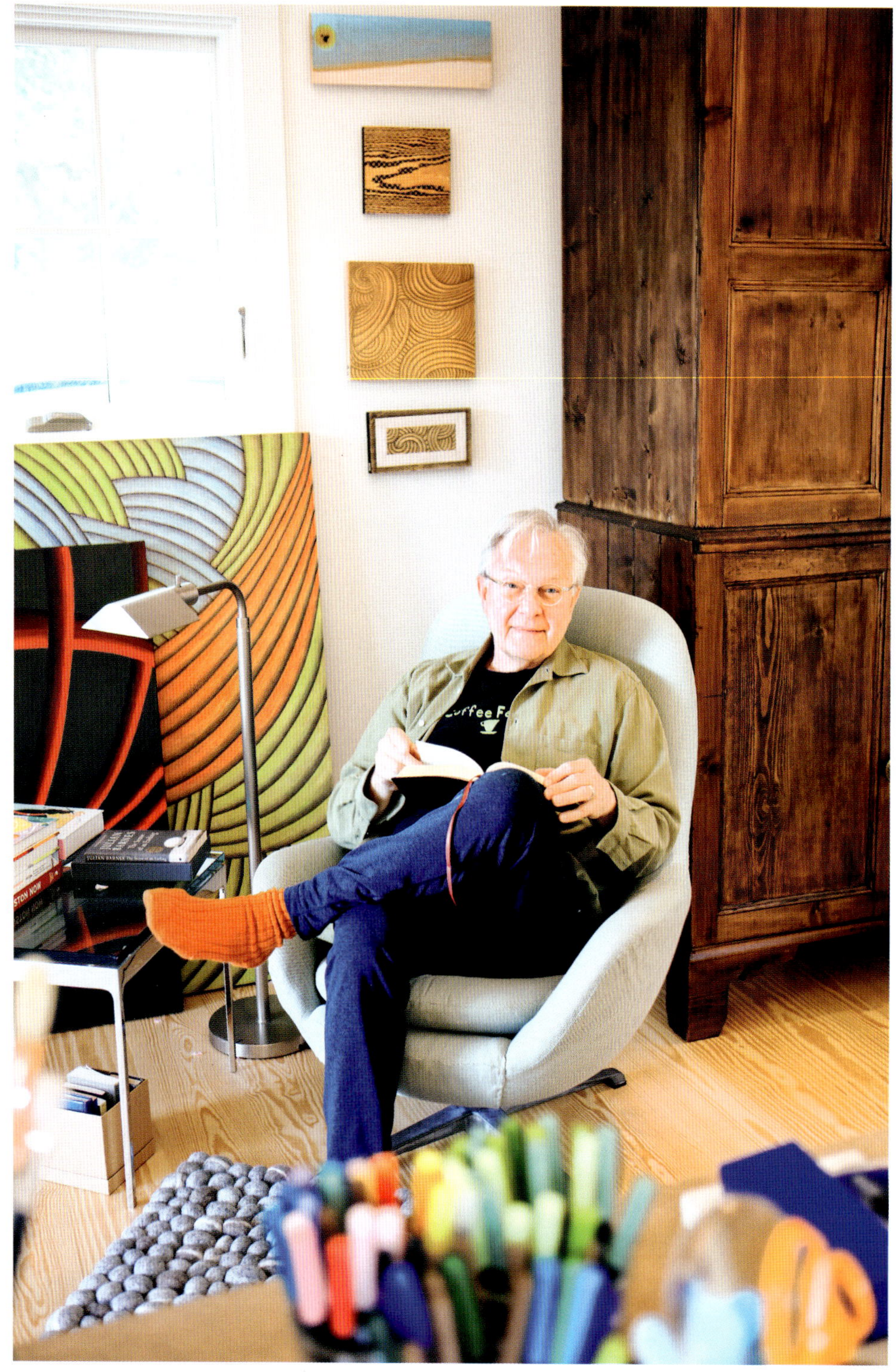

"In 2018, I shook up my art practice by drawing in a journal that had been a recent gift. The pencil liberated me from oils, solvents, and cleaning brushes, from imitation, homage, psychological narrative, and self-portraits. Ultimately, pencils and ink again gave way to brushes, acrylics, and a renewed enchantment with oils. A new expression had slowly emerged, and I went public with that renewal a few years ago."

ABOVE Bobbie begins his day drawing in a sketchbook in pencil. Many of the fanciful abstract doodles turn into vibrant, dynamic, full-scale paintings.

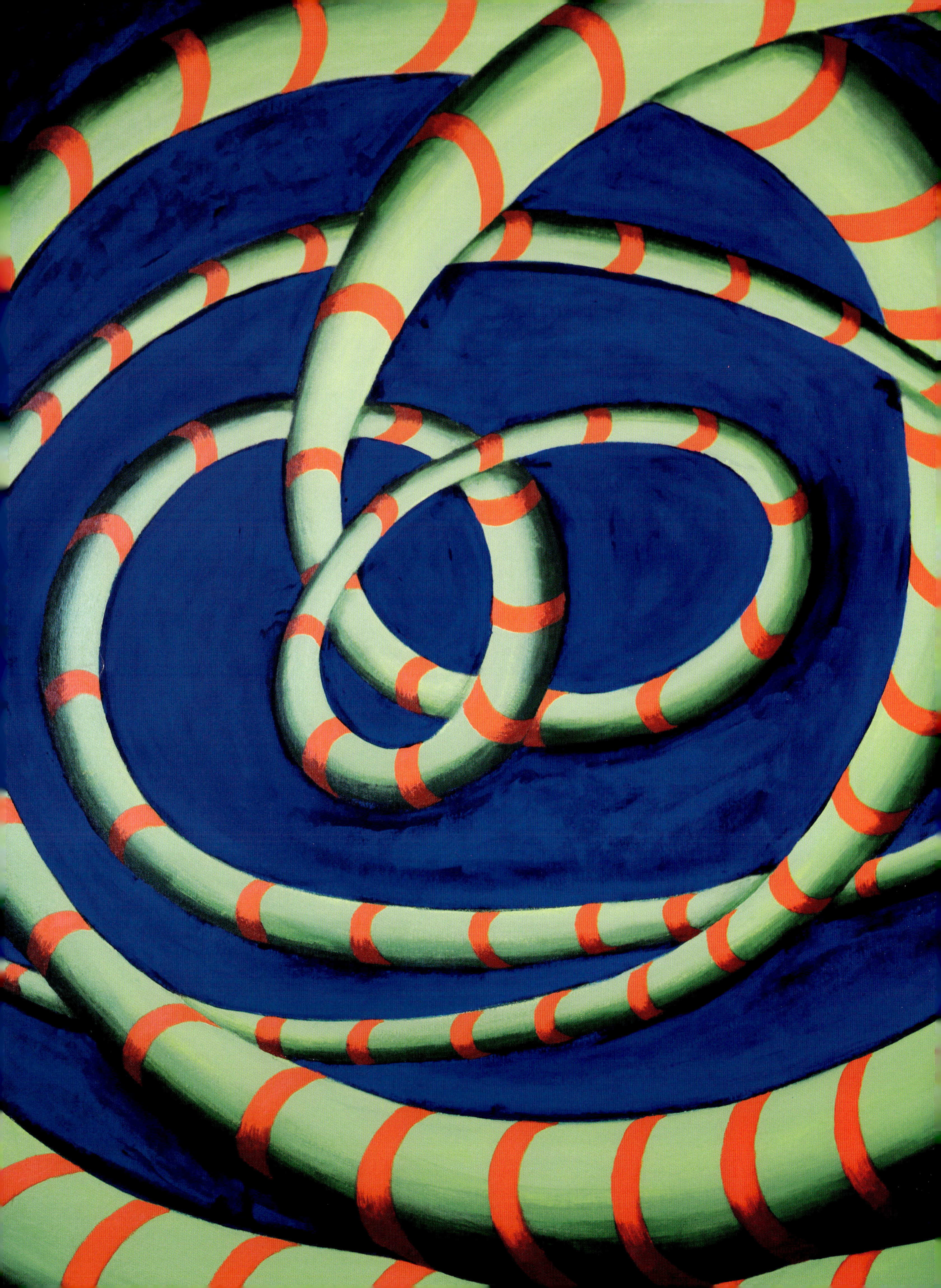

What takes me to the studio each day is habit,
the rhythm of routine, and when necessary, discipline.
Inspiration is what comes from hard work.

GUSTAVO BONEVARDI

Though his work is mostly abstract, or, as he puts it, "rarely strictly figurative," Bonevardi often includes allusions to the East End landscape and his life and experiences here. "Some paintings suggest that monumental thick fog that often rolls in off the ocean, and some sculptures capture something of my experiences of sailing at night. But these things are always unplanned—they emerge."

"There are few places I've considered home. One is the West Village in New York City, where I was born and raised. Another is East Hampton, where I now live. My earliest memories of this place are from one of the summers I spent out here with family friends. Home movies show me, at three, on the beach with my mother, as happy as I've ever been." Years later, he helped build a house for his parents' friends in East Hampton—a dream come true for a kid on his way to becoming an architect. "I belong to a long tradition of artist/architects. It has less to do with practicing architecture—I myself haven't practiced for many years—and more to do with a way of seeing and approaching things."

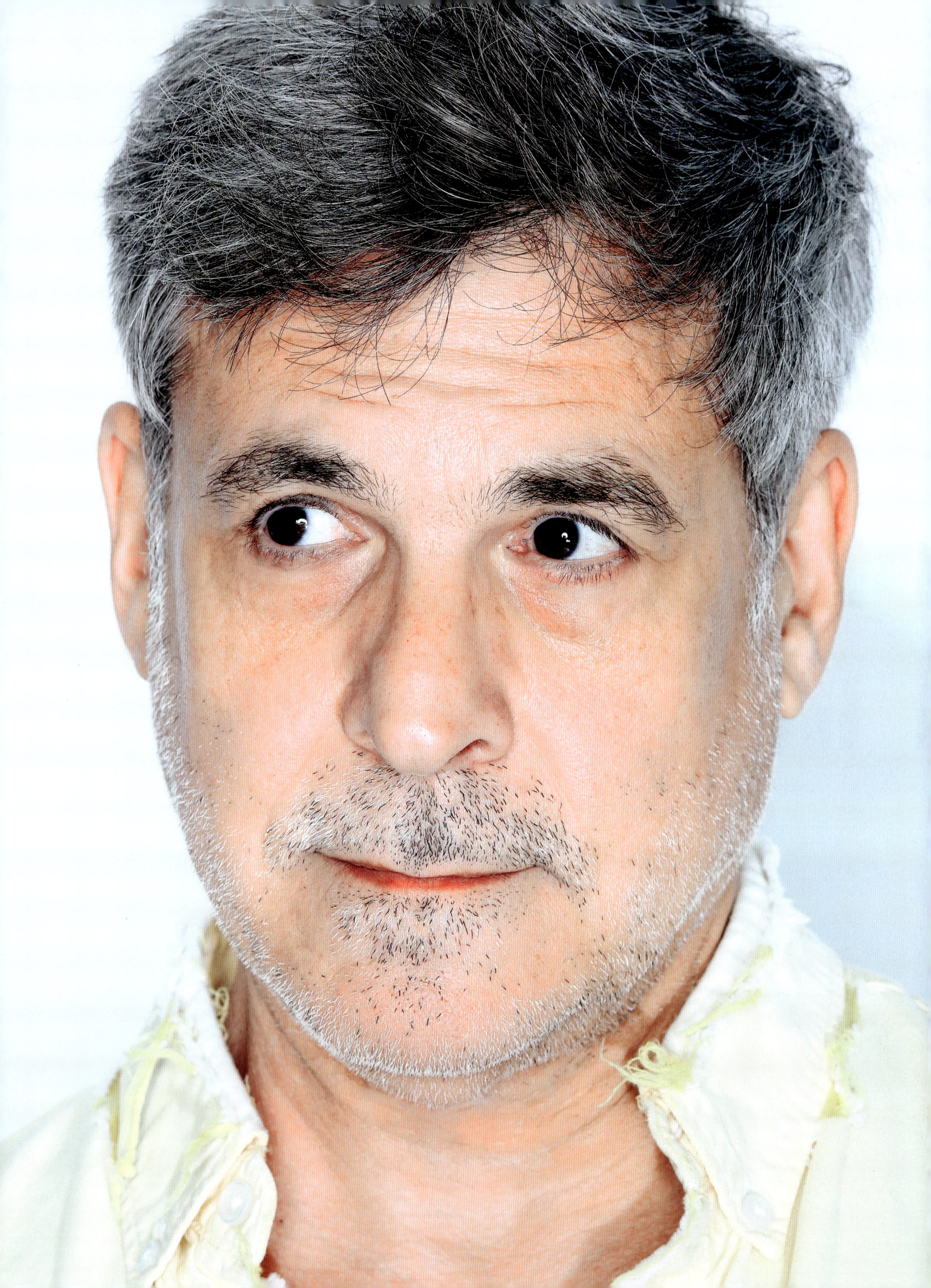

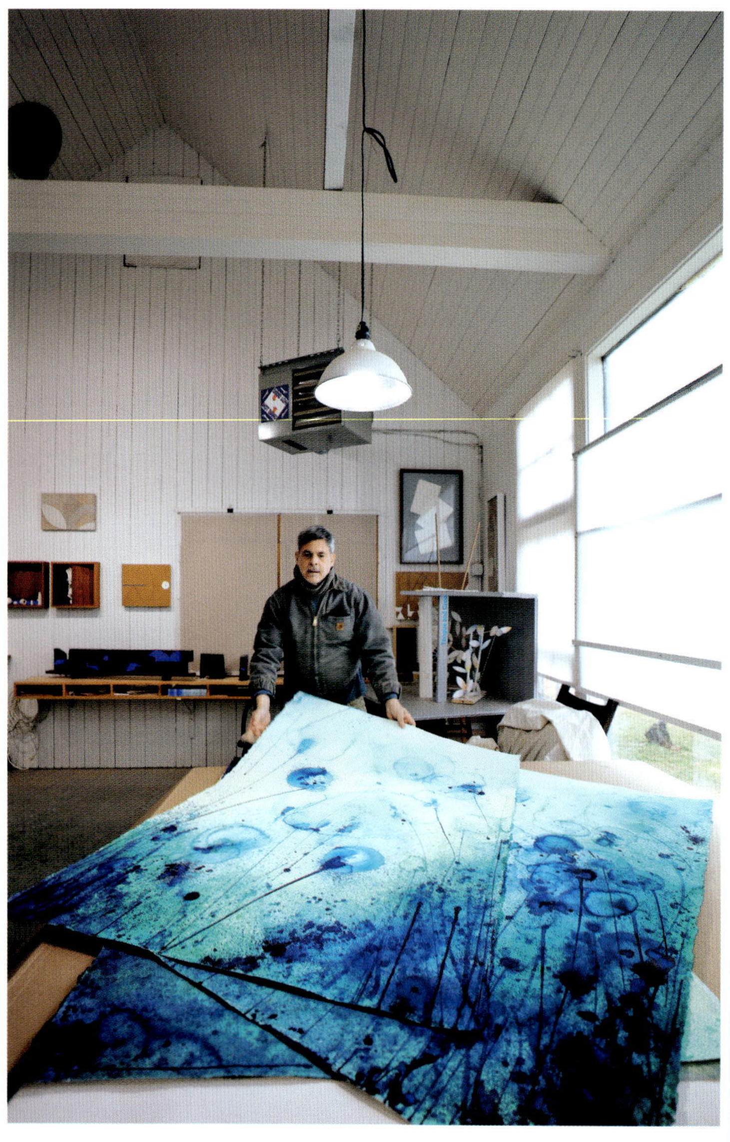

LEFT

Bonevardi has used one particular technique for years—a brushless form of watercolor painting that explores how pigment, water, and paper interact and give rise to form. What started as small, restrained works has evolved into exuberant, expansive landscapes, including triptychs measuring more than ten feet wide.

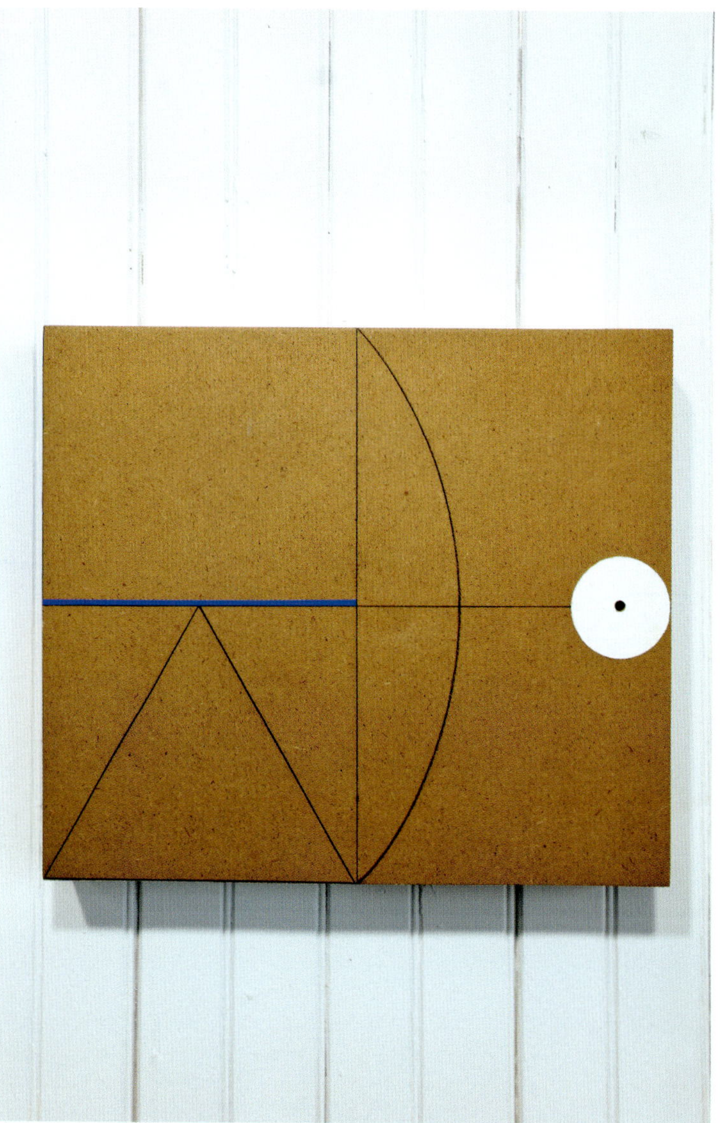

Bonevardi's studio is light-filled, open, and very neat. "It's important to me for everything to be in its place." Especially his collection of tools. Given his propensity for experimenting in many mediums, he often finds himself learning to use new tools, some of which he makes himself. "I love how each trade has its own set: hammers, saws, planes, and lathes for carpentry; T squares, erasing shields, and compasses for architecture. I greatly respect tools, but I often find myself applying them in ways other than originally intended."

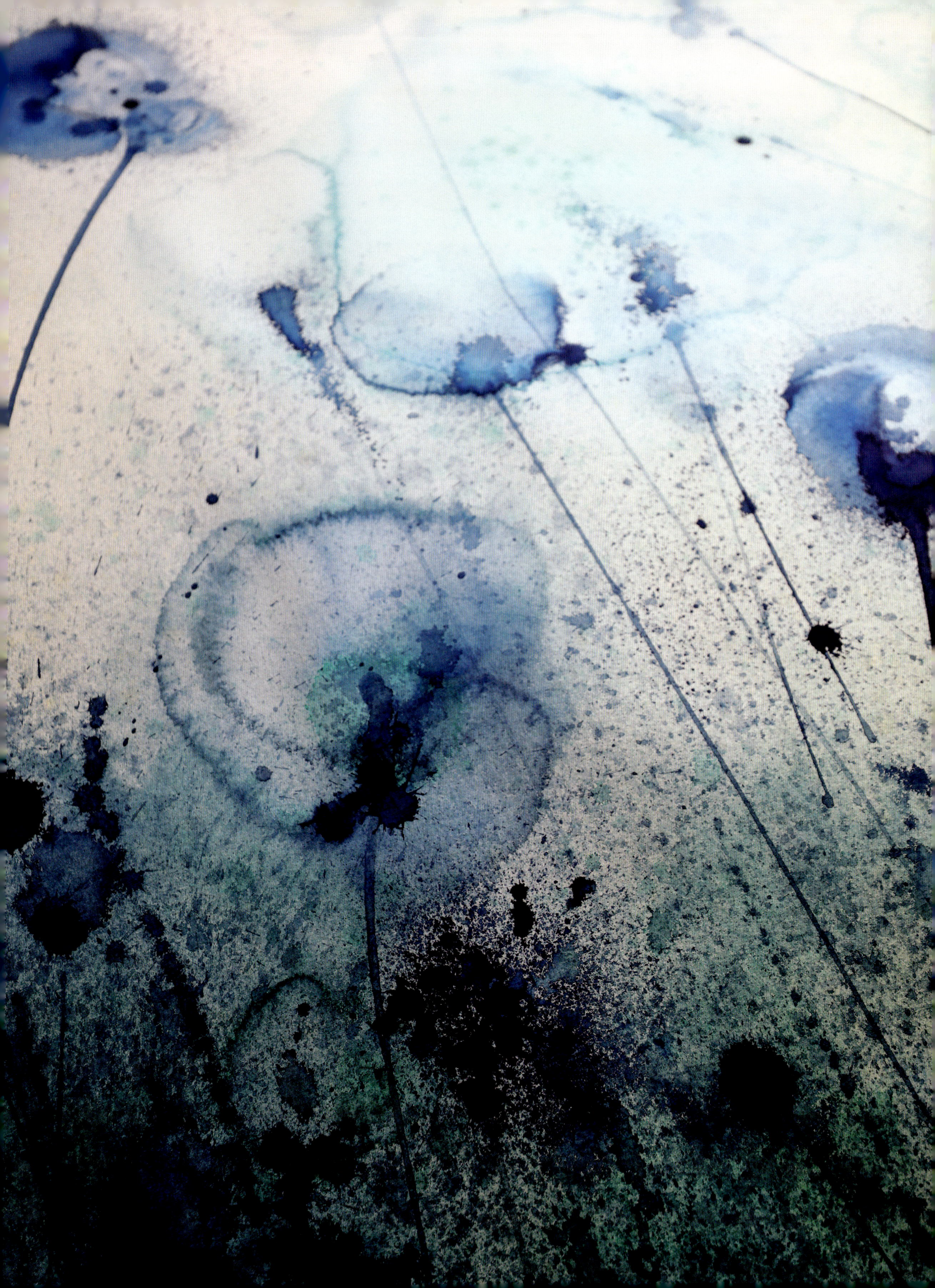

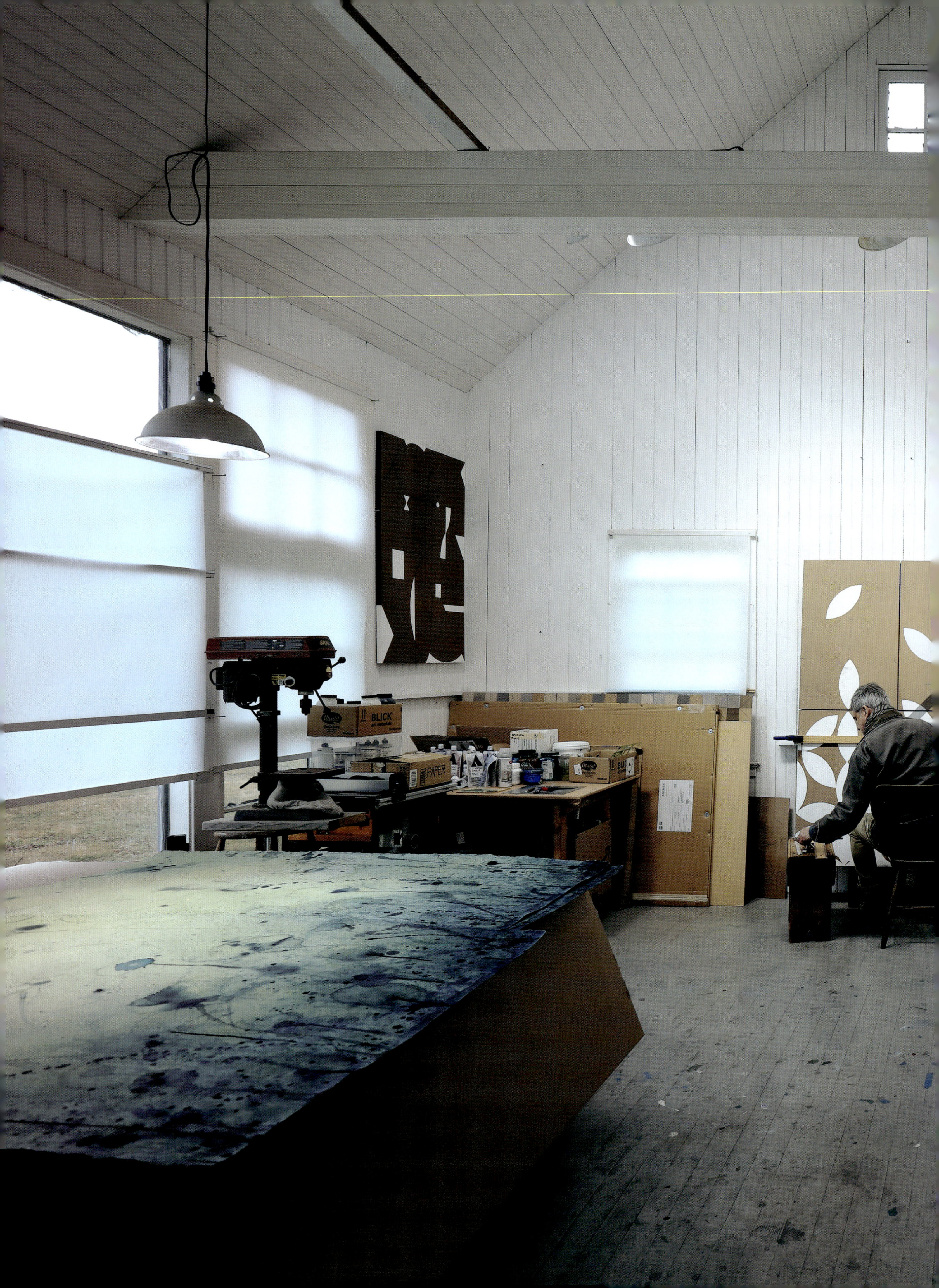
BLICK
PAPER

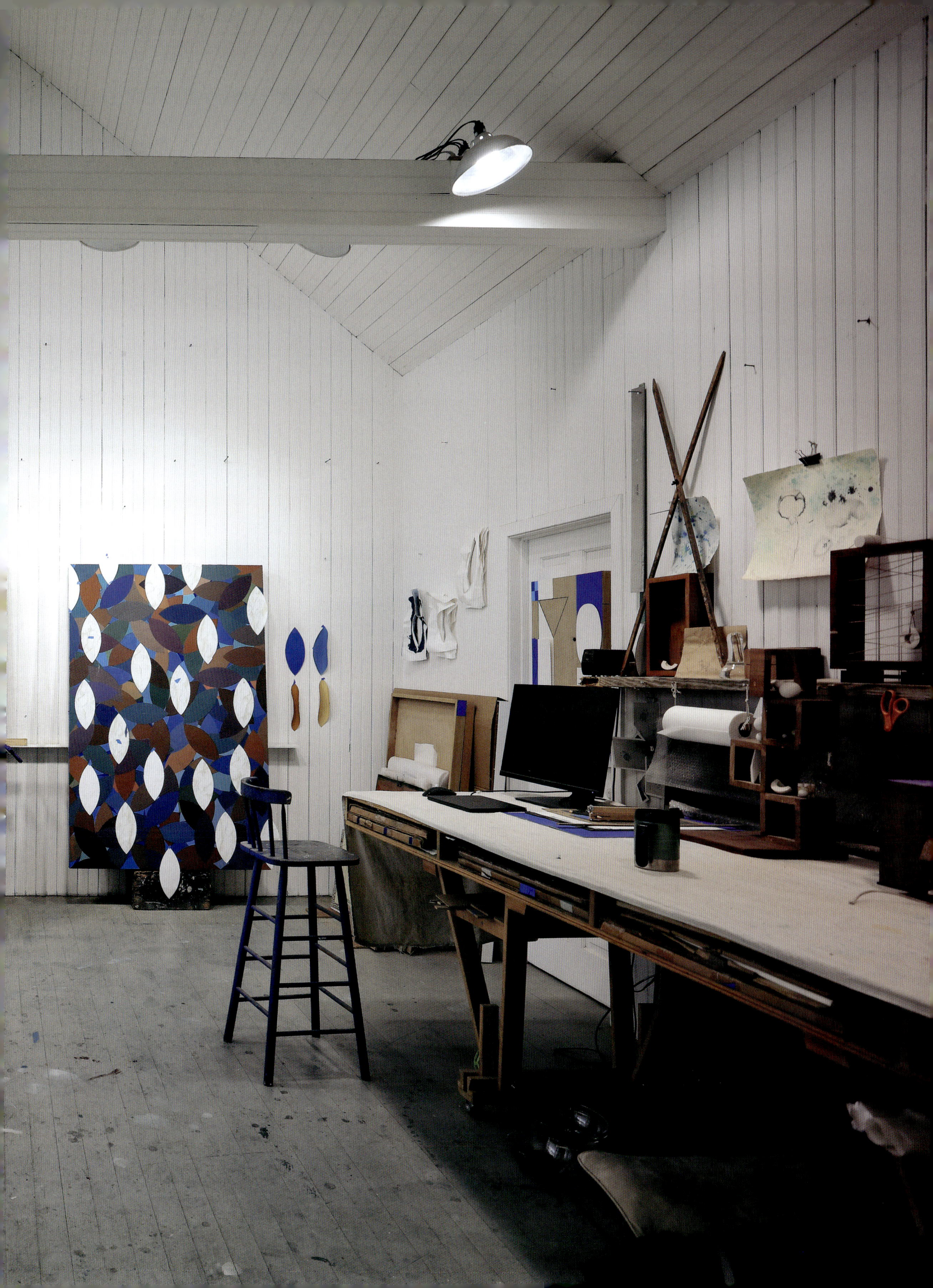

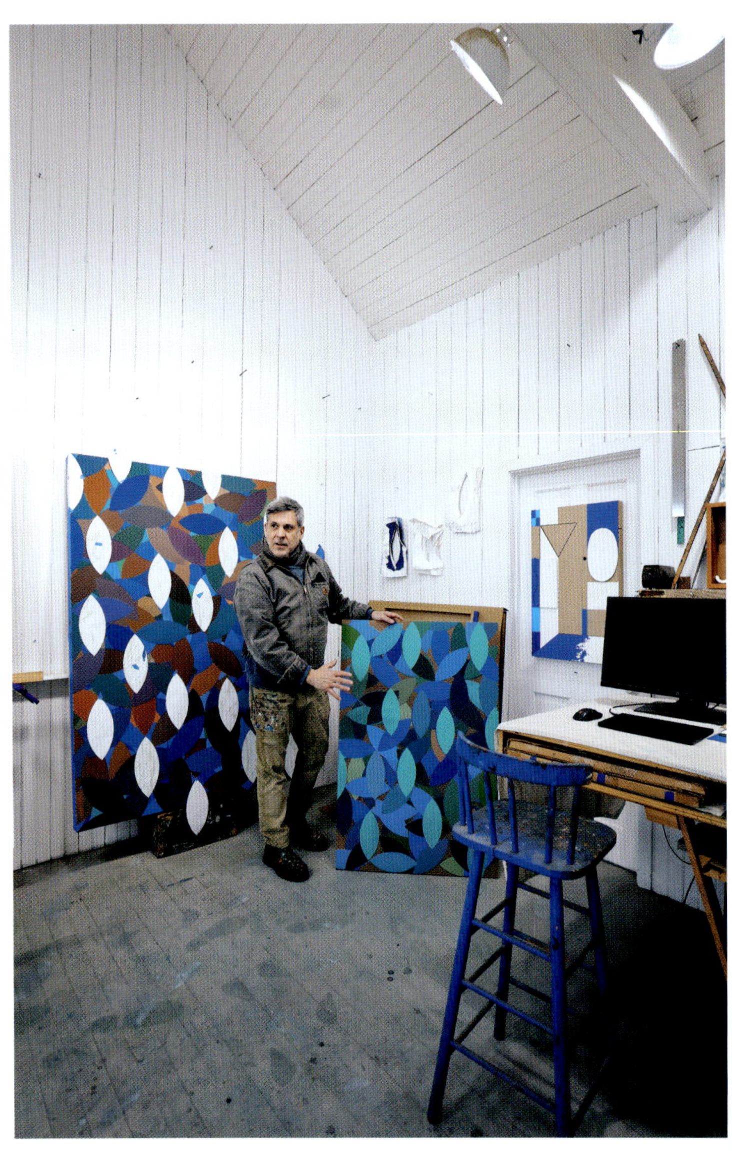

PRECEDING PAGES

Bonevardi is continually organizing and reorganizing his studio space, to the point of designing and constructing easels and tables for particular series of works; the table on the right is designed with a lower tier for drying watercolors while leaving the surface free for work.

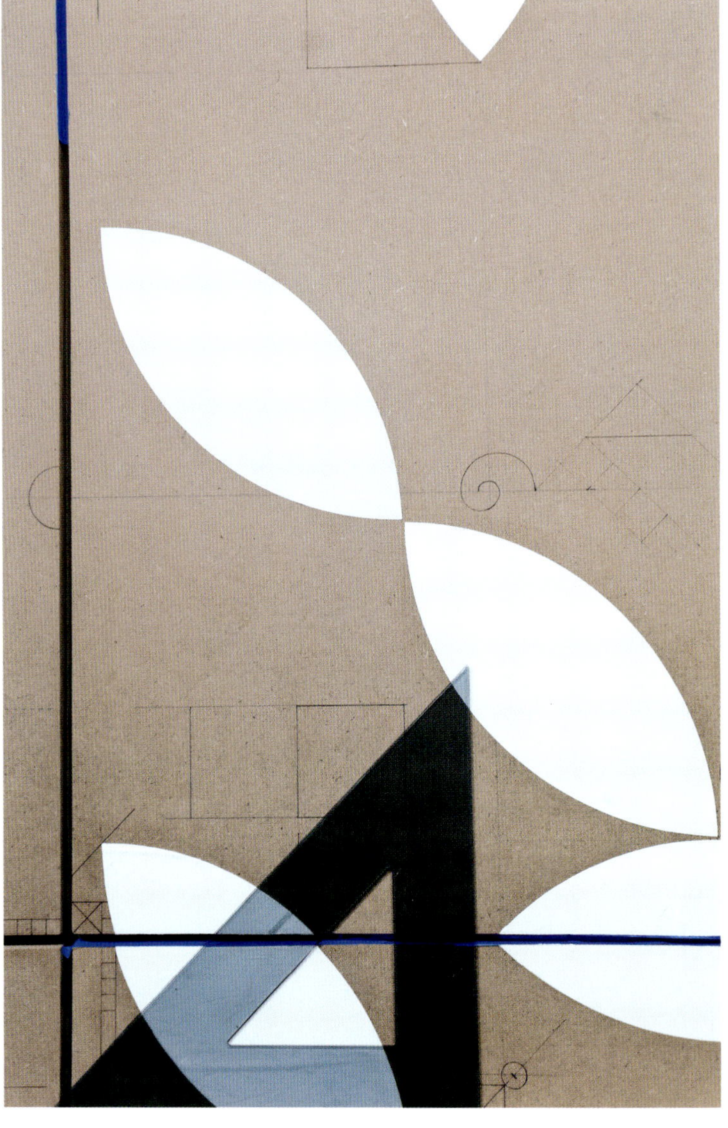

ABOVE

For this series of paintings (acrylic and charcoal on panel), Bonevardi used a set of simple geometric rules. At times, the geometry—rendered with T squares, rulers, and compasses—suggests architectural plans. At others, it gives rise to a loose sense of layered space and organic abundance.

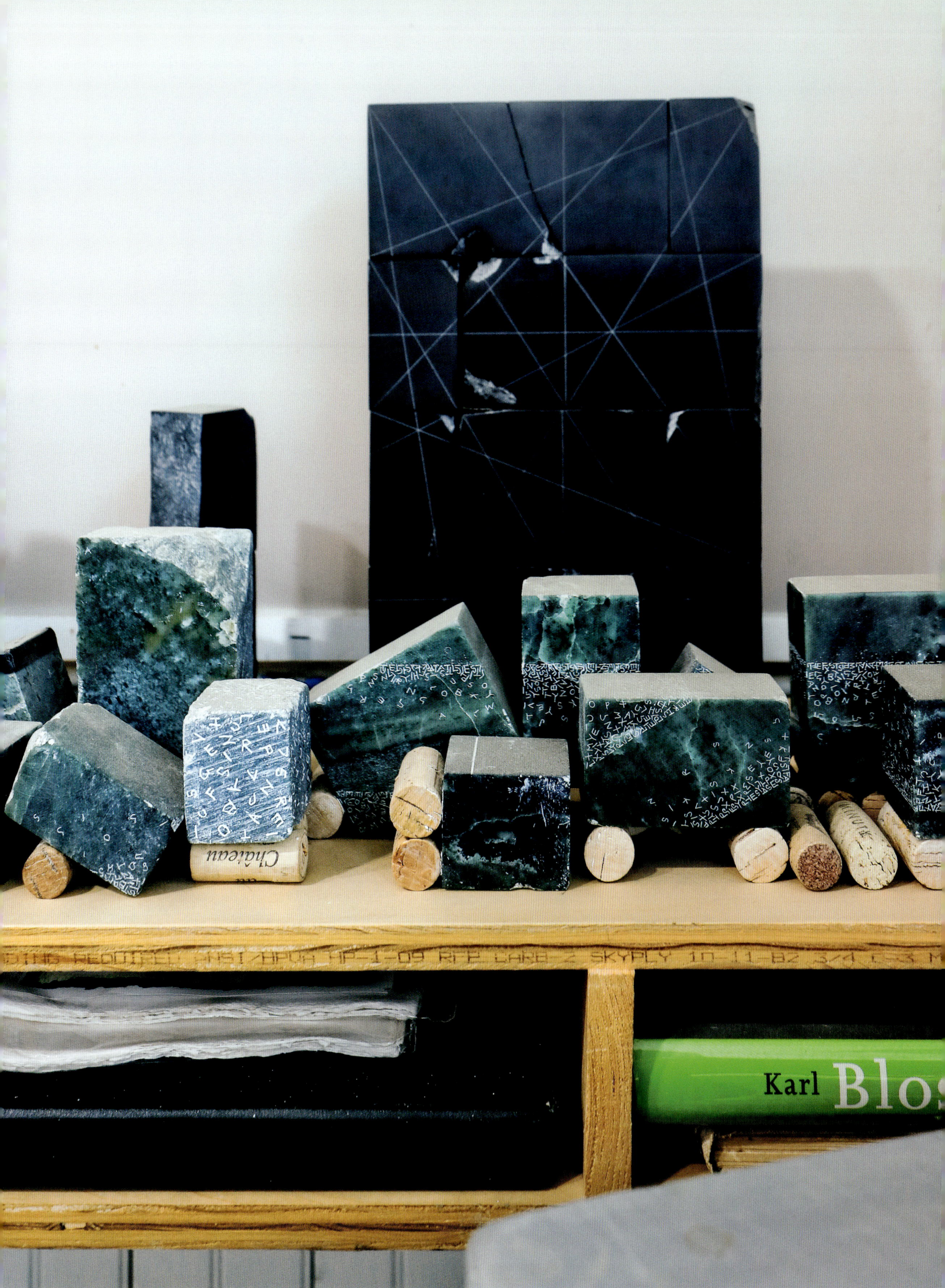
Château
SKYPLY
Karl Blos

I am drawn to the contemplative nature of abstraction. It is more akin to music and poetry.

MARY BOOCHEVER

Born in Washington, D.C., and into a foreign-service family, Boochever ended up studying at the Akademie der Bildenden Künste in Munich, Germany. She has been a painter and sculptor ever since. In 1978, she moved to New York City, where she taught at the School of Visual Arts and guest-lectured at Yale University. She and her husband, artist Kevin Teare, relocated to Sag Harbor in 1993 and built his-and-her studios. "I am a longtime practitioner of tai chi, a Taoist practice; some of the ancient Chinese philosophy has informed my work and how I live. My studio has eight sides, a form known in Chinese as the *bagua*. The octagon has a variety of meanings in many cultures and religions. In feng shui, it is considered a symbol of protection to ward off negative spiritual activity."

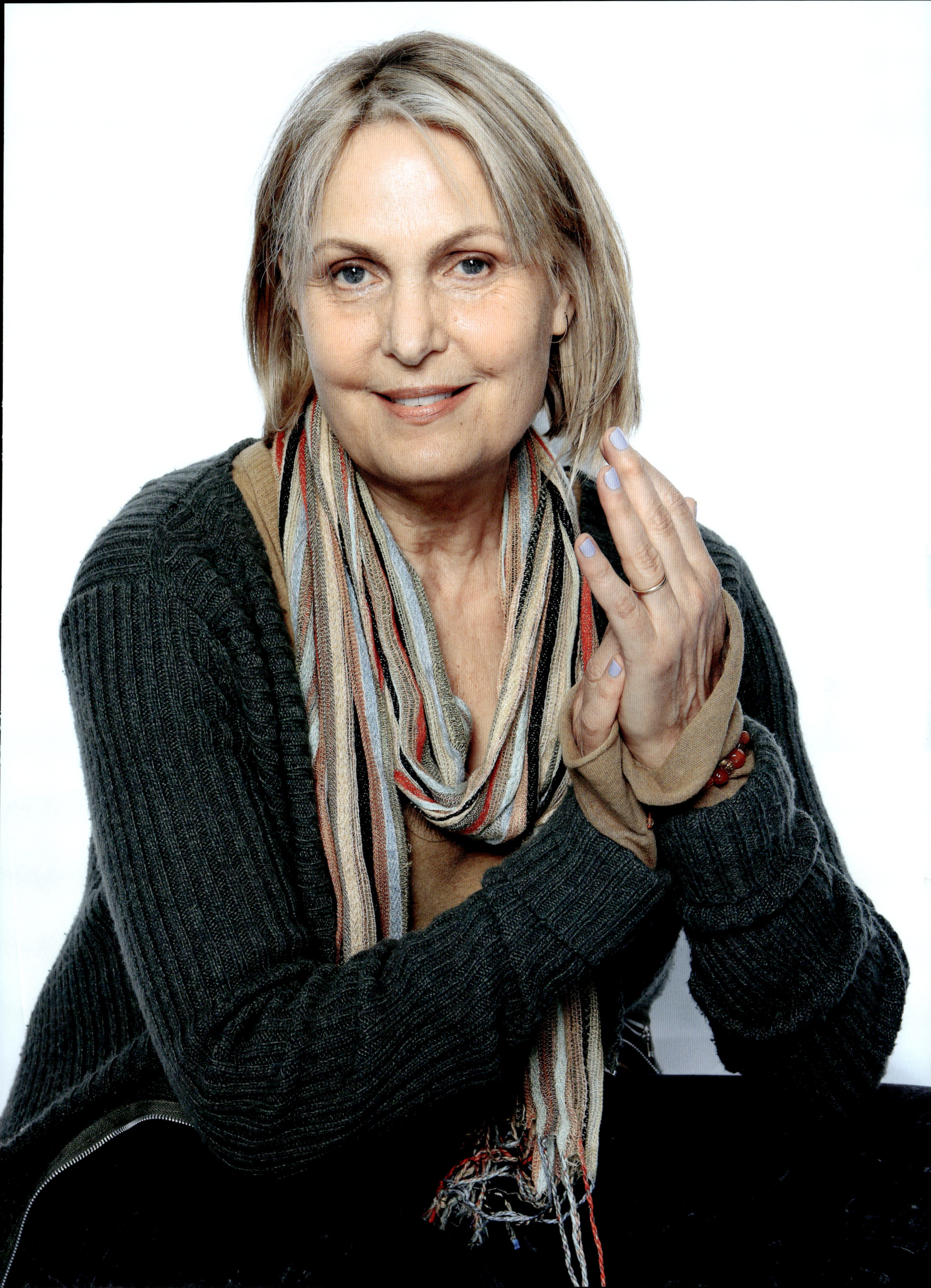

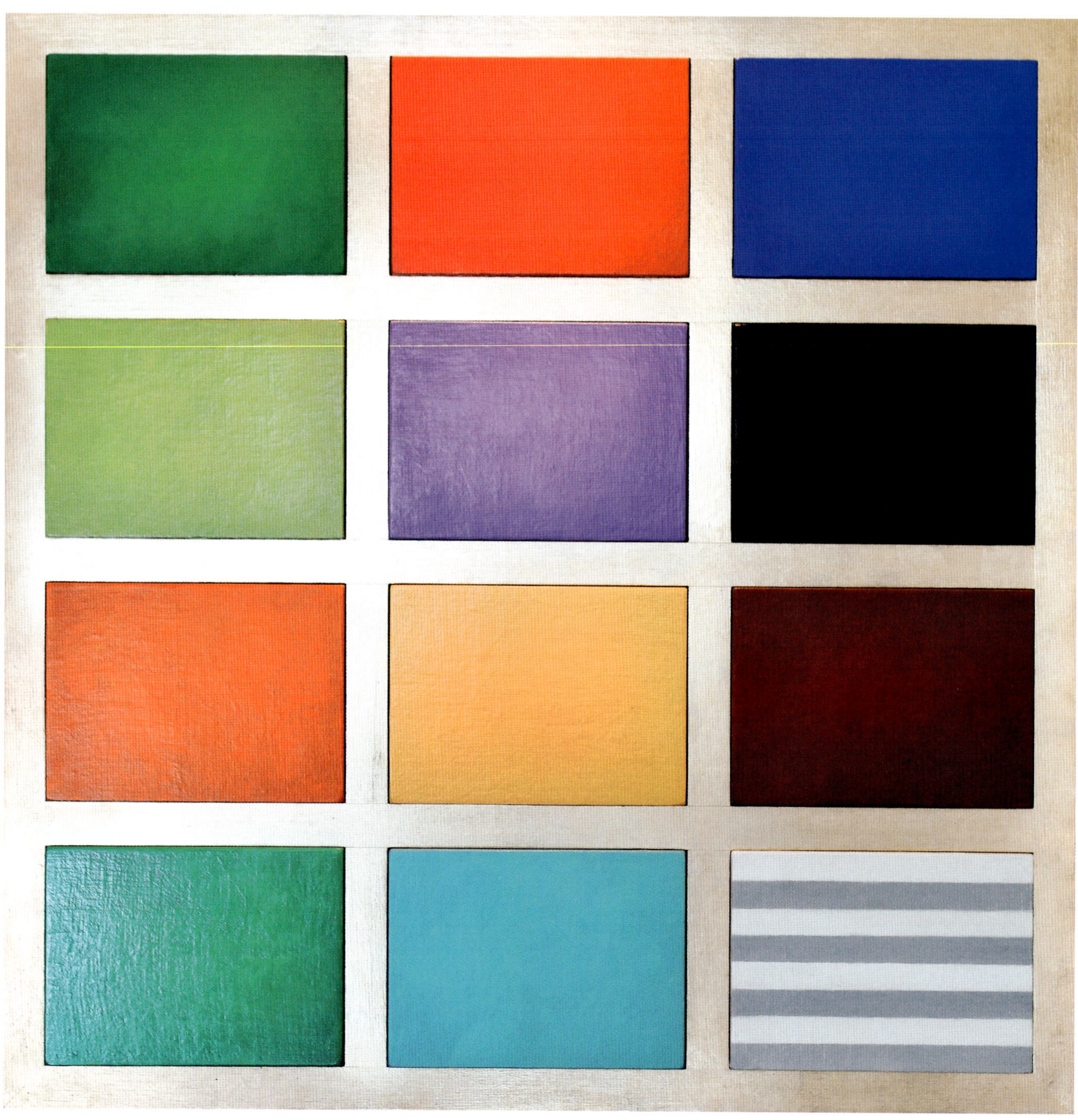

"In my work, I use color in its role as a transformative agent. I am particularly interested in color systems attached to socio-religious philosophies, and I use these as a framework for various themes. The Cabala, feng shui, theosophy, and alchemy all view color as a dynamic principle through which the life of the individual can be affected or transformed. I also use color gradations as a tool to express the gradual nature of change or the movement of energy. And I use the ladder or staircase as a tool to convey ideas about ascension and descension."

OPPOSITE A place of study and contemplation: Boochever's desk in her studio is a testament to her fascination with and exploration of color theory.

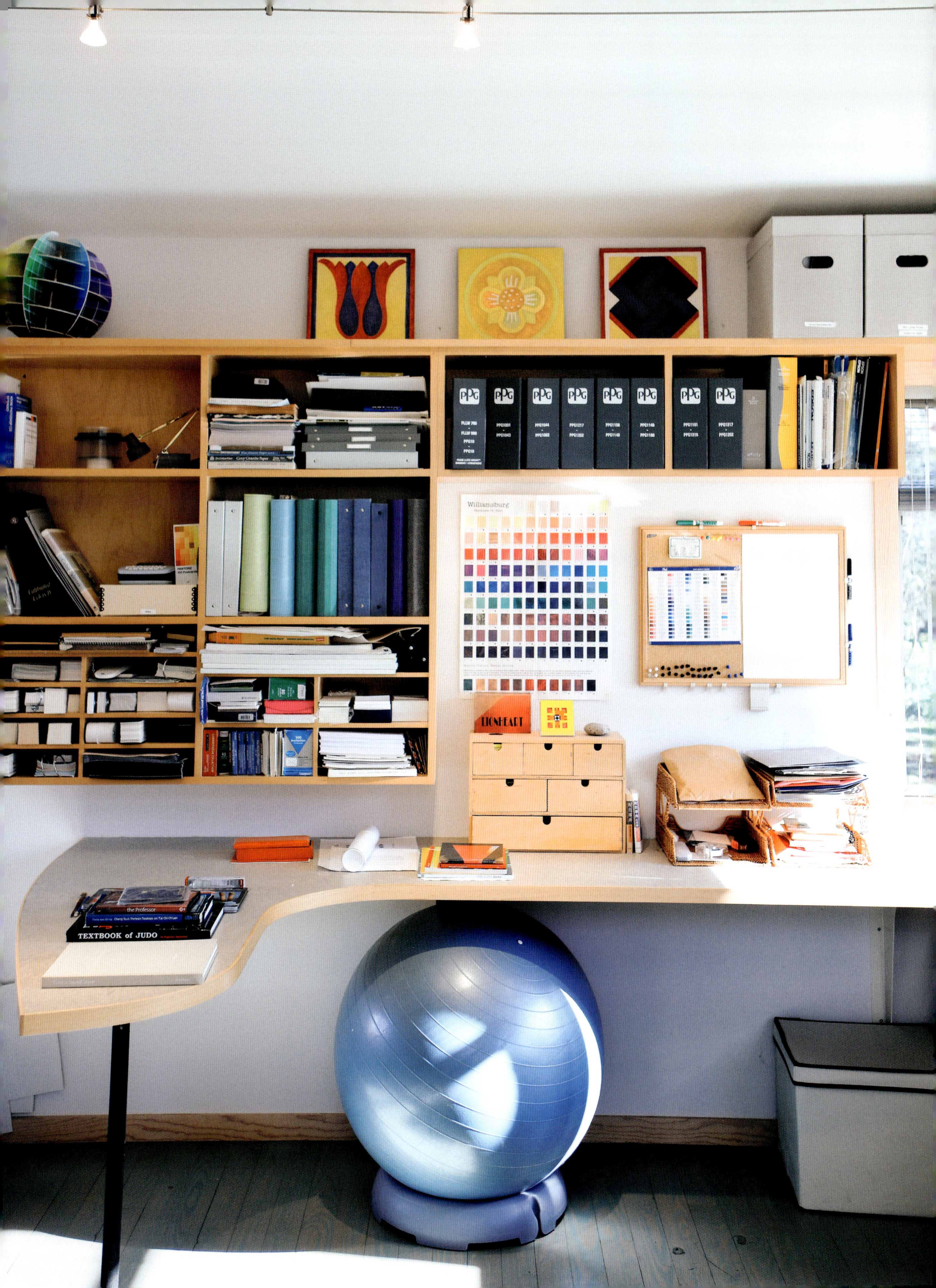
PPG
Williamsburg
LIONHEART
the Professor
TEXTBOOK of JUDO

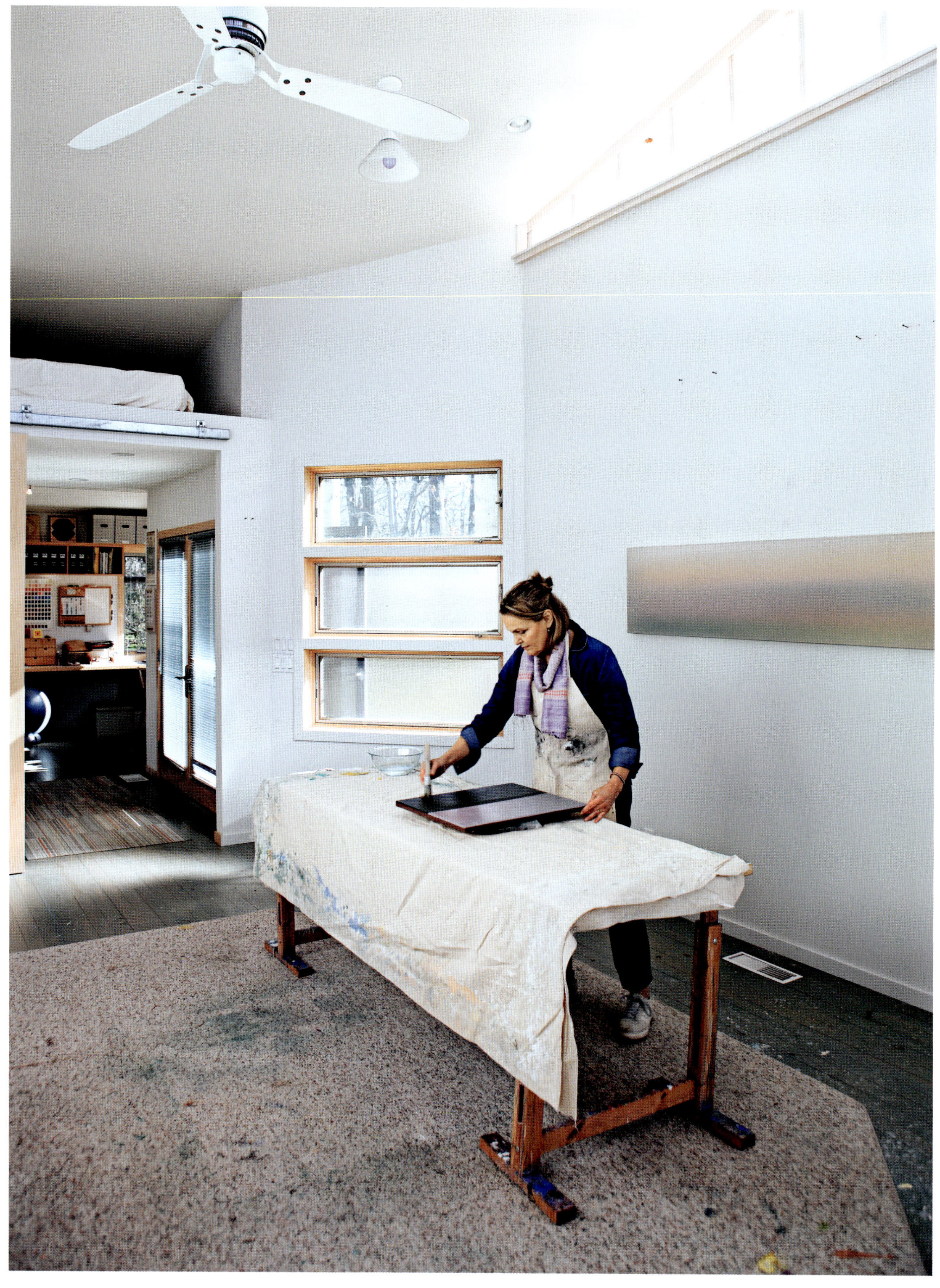

ABOVE Boochever makes some of her own paint with raw pigment in an acrylic or oil binder and has developed her own color language, inspired by sources ranging from Goethe's *Theory of Colors* to the Kabala.

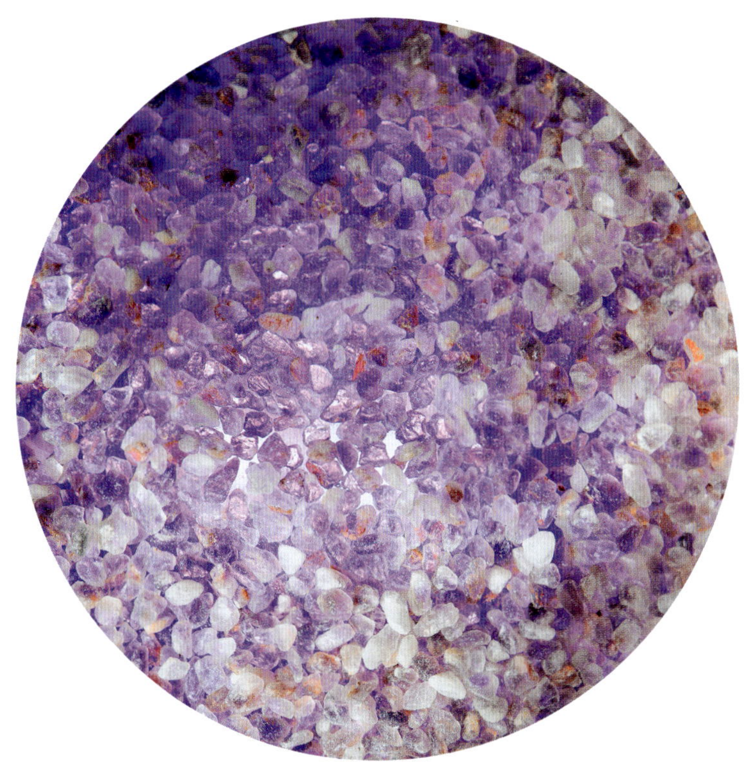

Boochever works in a variety of mediums. "I make some of my own paint with raw pigment in an acrylic or oil binder. Works on paper are usually gouache. The selection of materials in my sculptures is based on color and the philosophical implications of the medium, such as reflection, transparency, or weight. The mediums I choose are connected by my concept of color's role as a transformative agent. The desire for foreknowledge, protection, wealth, love, power, health, and healing has been with us since the dawn of humanity. The various avenues for pursuing these desired aims often include recipes and treatments replete with symbolism."

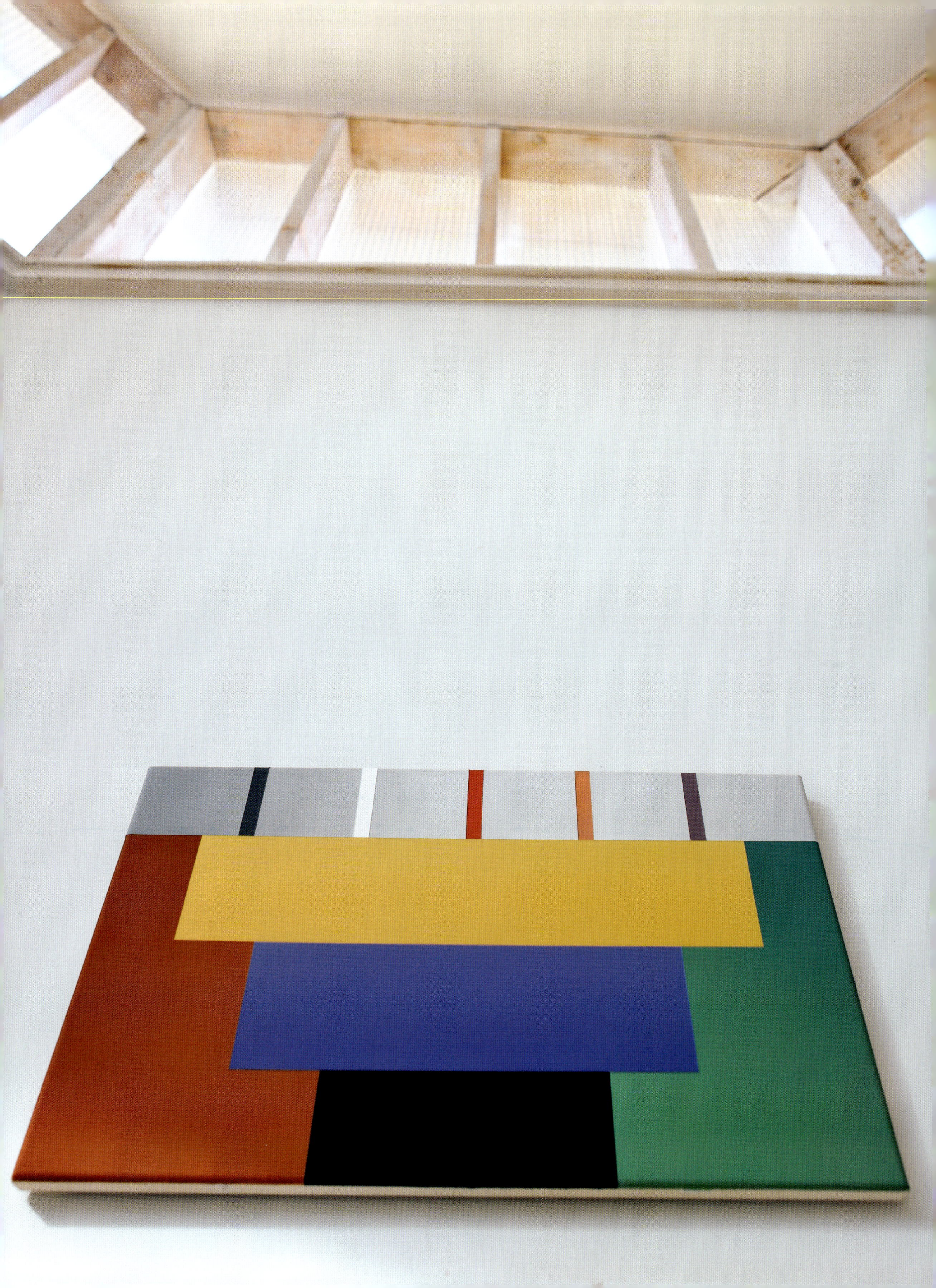

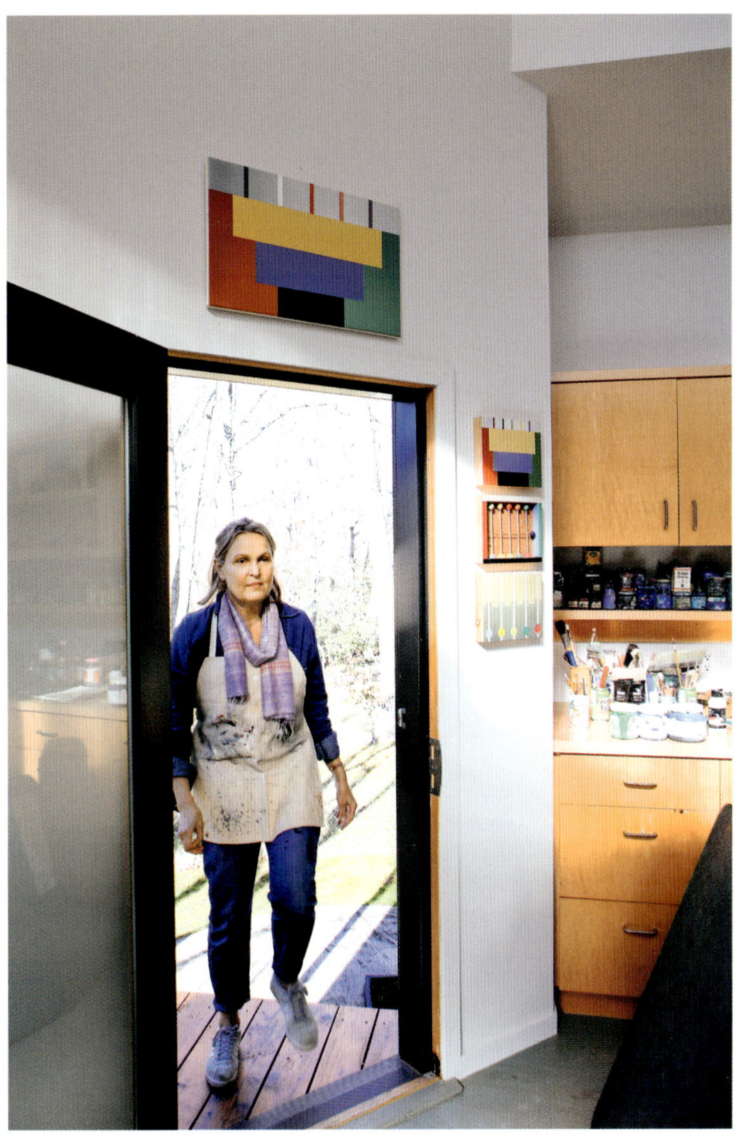

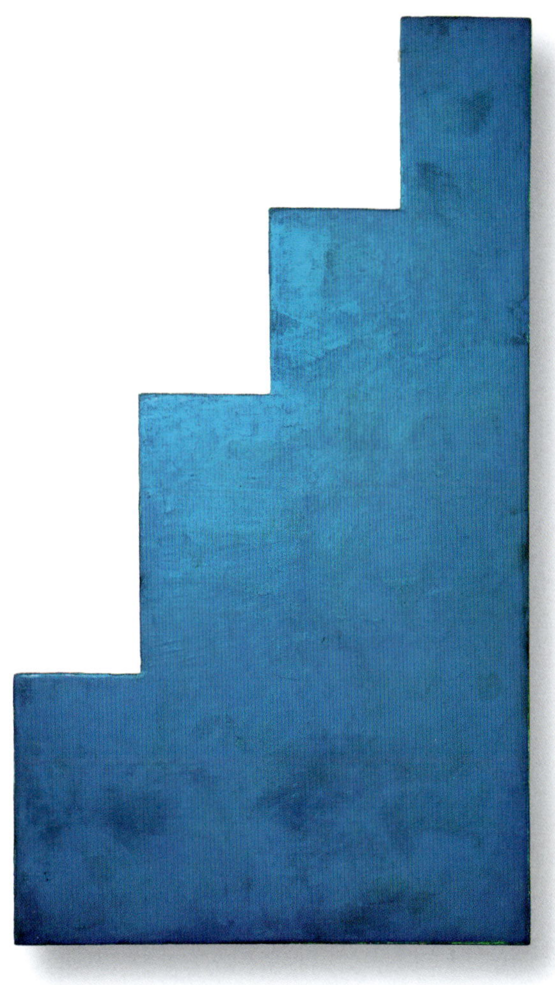

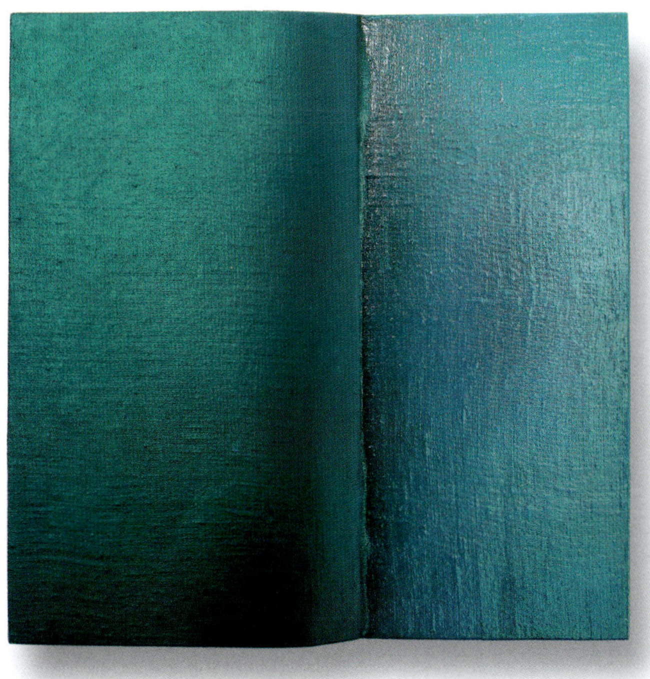

OPPOSITE AND ABOVE

Boochever, a devotee of Taoism, designed her studio to have eight sides. The octagon, a form known in Chinese as the *bagua*, is a symbol of protection. Her use of color ranges from the subtle and seemingly monochromatic to bold, striking juxtapositions of primary hues.

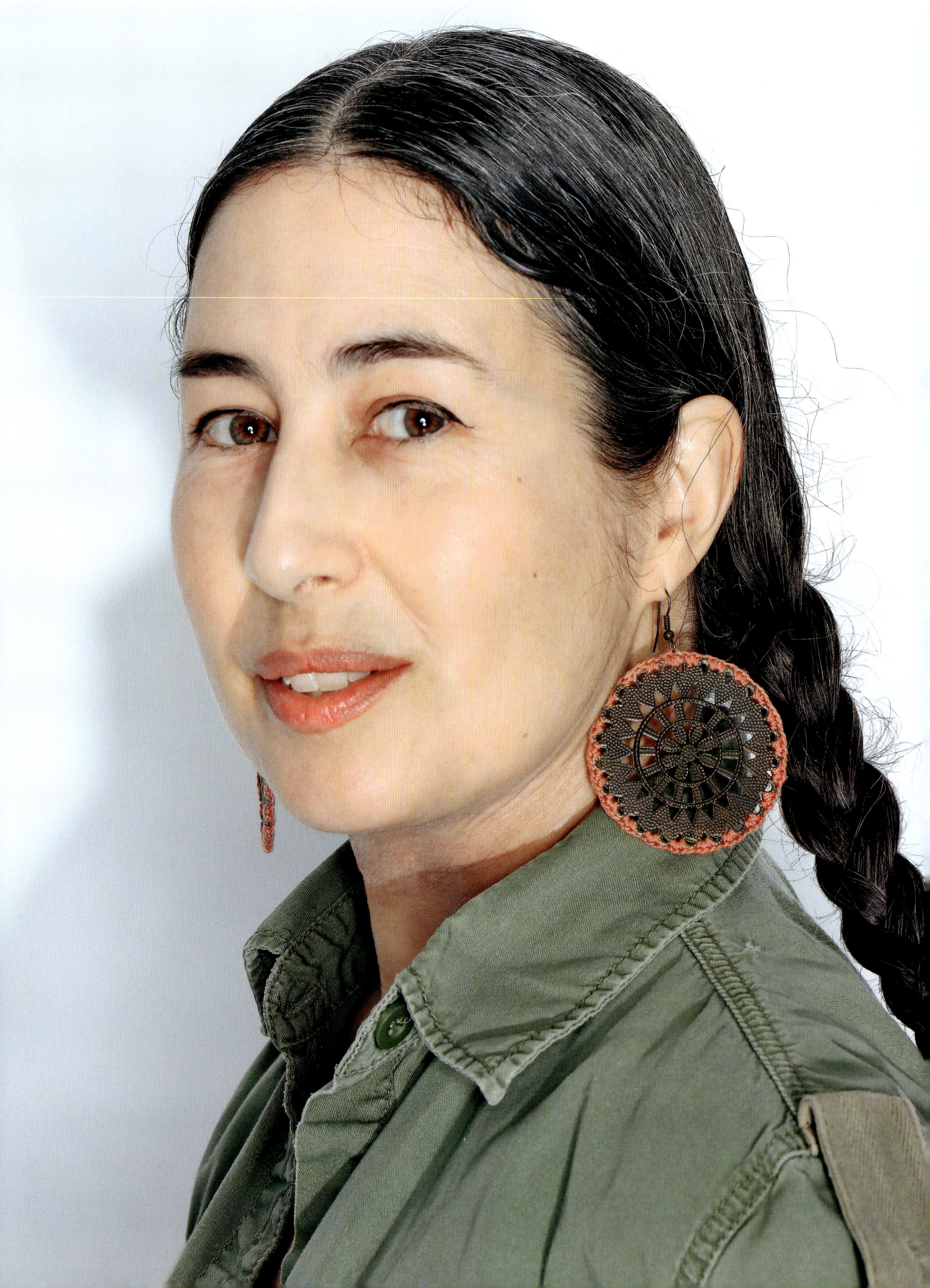

The novelty of the material—nails—
was never my aim. It's more like I found
a musical instrument through which I
can express and channel my songs.

DARLENE CHARNECO

Charneco was born to Puerto Rican parents who moved from the Bronx to Ronkonkoma, Long Island, where she was raised. "My father was a wonderful artist and nature lover. I grew up inspired by our walks and explorations of different parts of the island, including Orient Point and Montauk." In 1989, she studied art at Southampton College. "After a few sojourns in other places, I returned to the magic bays of Southampton. I missed this 'home.' It's my hope and intention to grow into an old Mother Tree here on the East End."

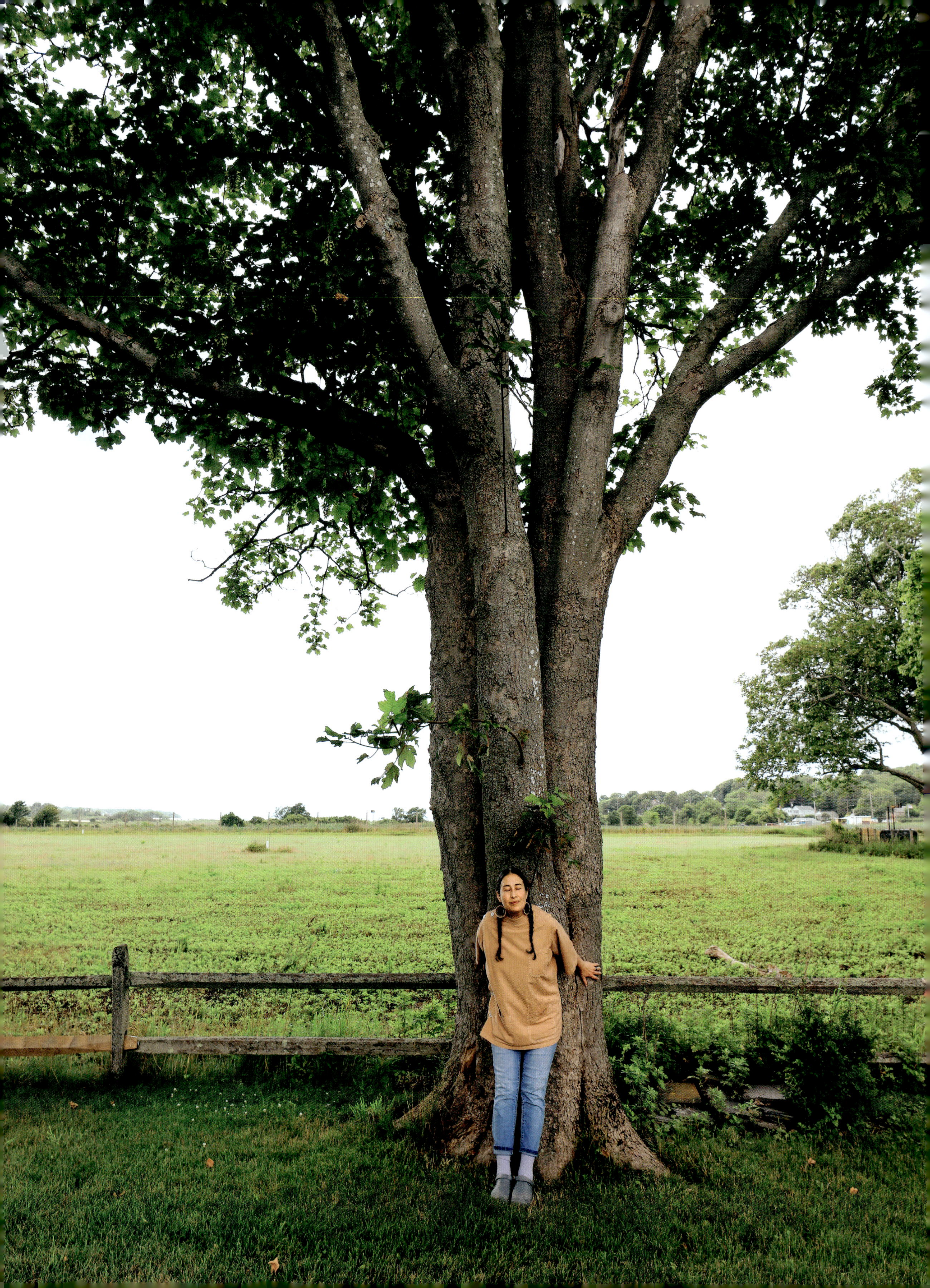

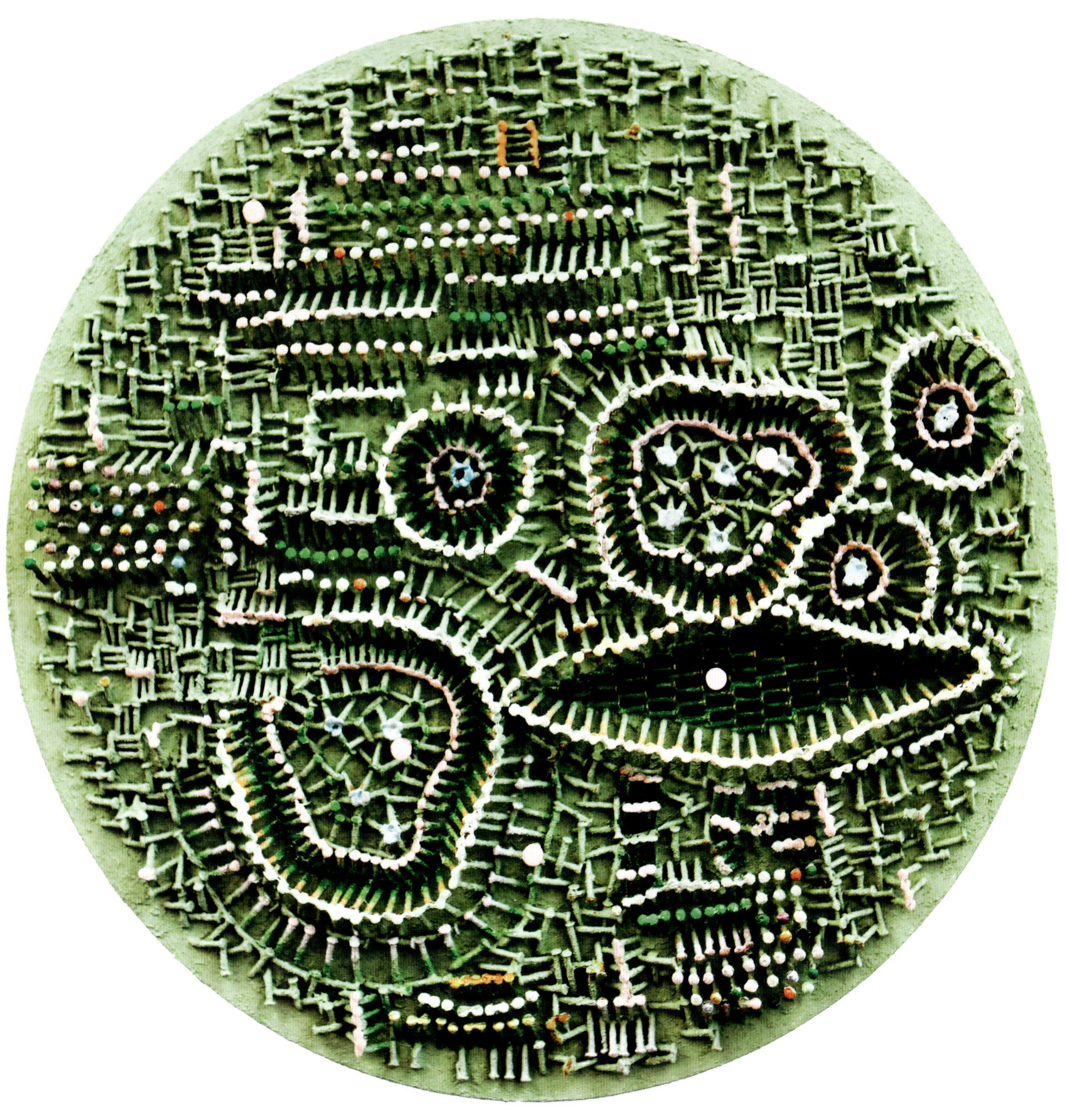

Charneco's work with nails began around 1995. "I had explored many other materials in search of a way to create a tactile, three-dimensional language that would be similar to Braille. I was focusing on creating something to 'read' with fingertips, but when I first started the hammering, I realized that this process felt like tapping out a code, which simultaneously both lifted and grounded me. The hammering process is the right combination of tactile writing and trance-inducing sound."

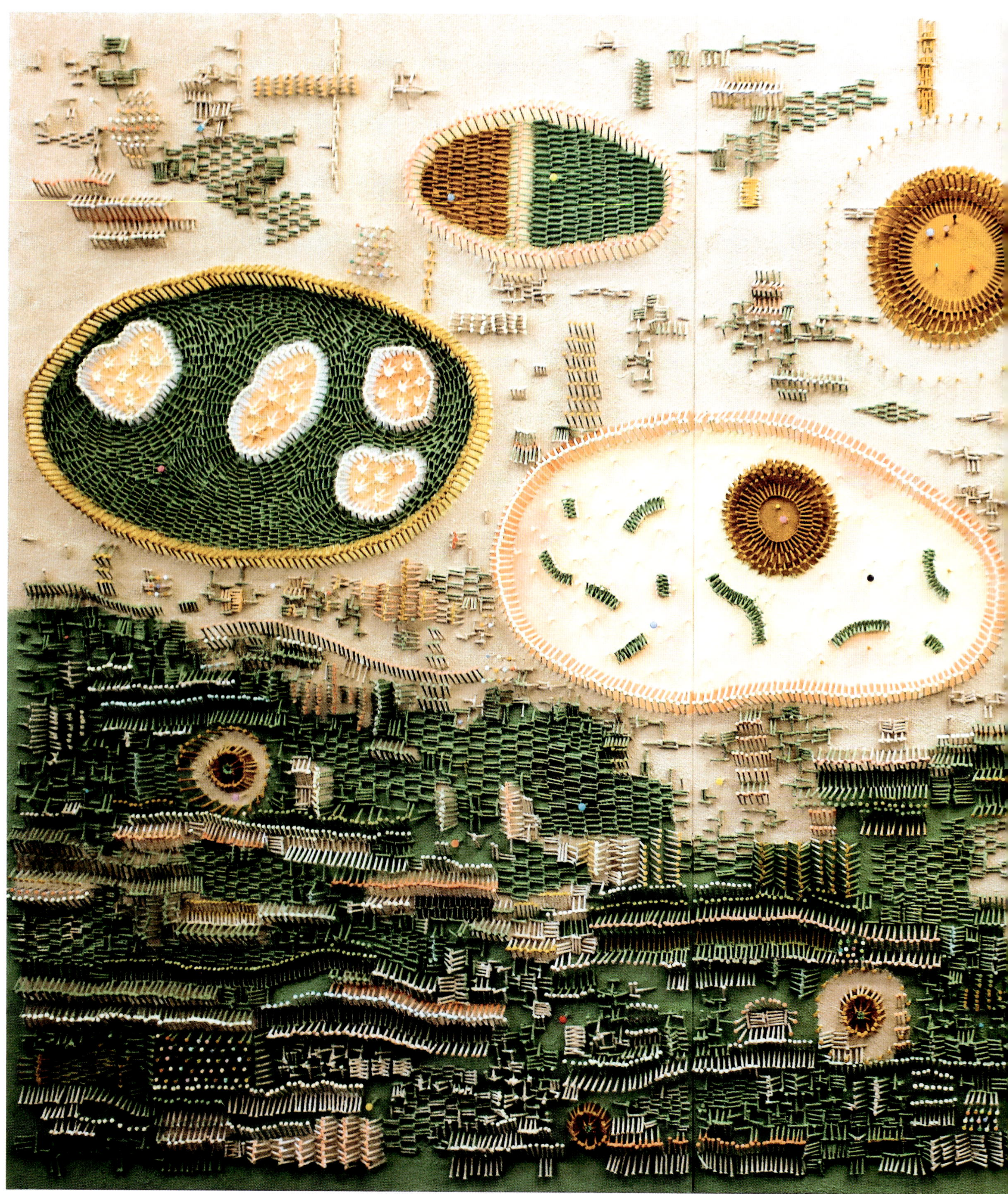

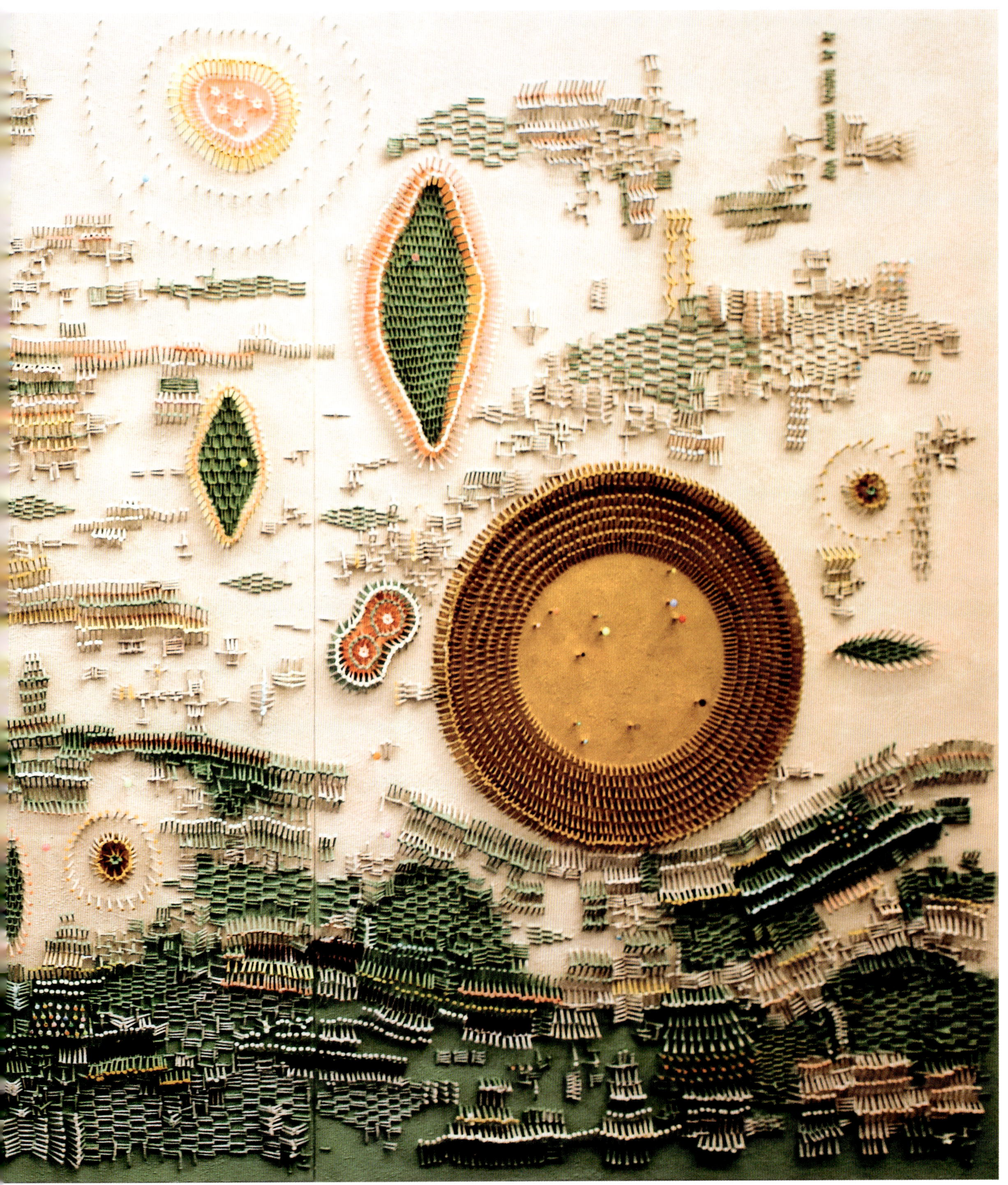

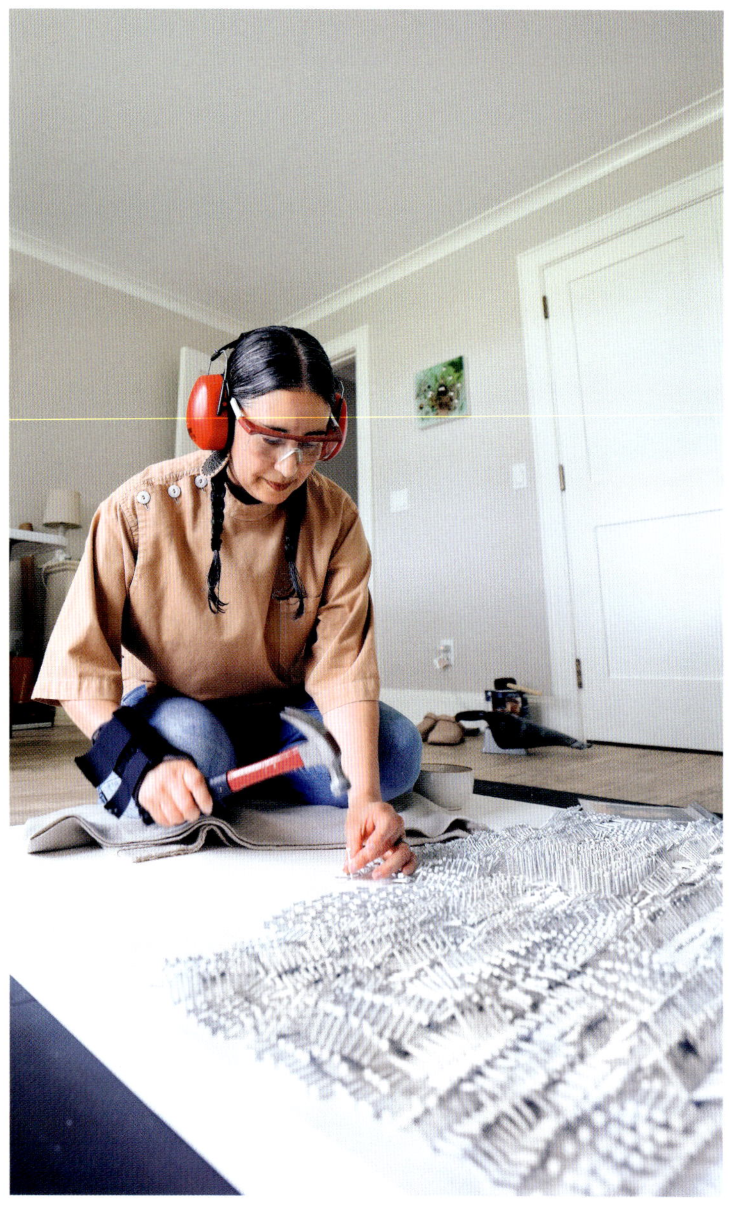

LEFT

The main surface Charneco uses is a medium-soft, thickly layered plywood that can hold the nails without splitting. After making a pattern, she builds up and melds the nail-studded surface with layers of paint and texture until it looks less like nails and more like something else.

BELOW

Charneco refers to her works as "weaves" or "touch maps." To her, they feel like a combination of woven tapestries, microscopy images, lacy textiles, and topographical maps.

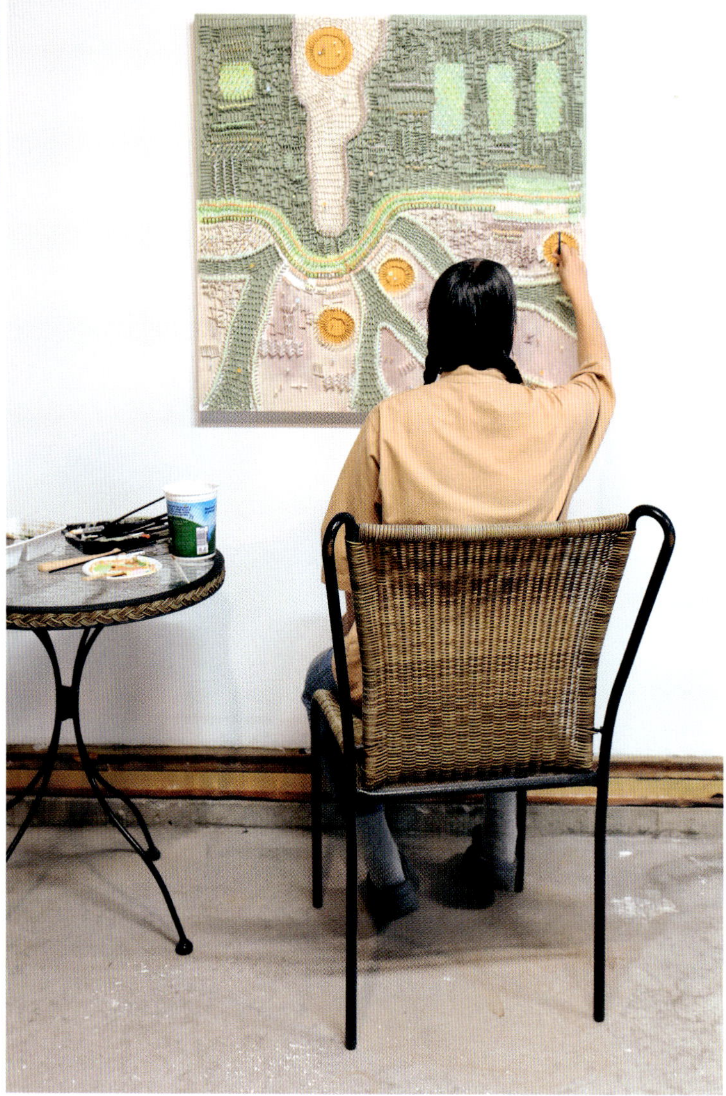

How does she go about it? "I sit, take a few deep breaths, and ask for guidance. I pour a handful of nails into one palm, cup them in both, whispering a mantra, and place them into a small bowl. Then I take one nail at a time and tap it slowly into the wood, in the direction that feels right. The colors I use are intuitive and add another layer of language. I have a resin series in which I use color as part of what I think of as a coded visual perfume, in order to re-create a complex memory."

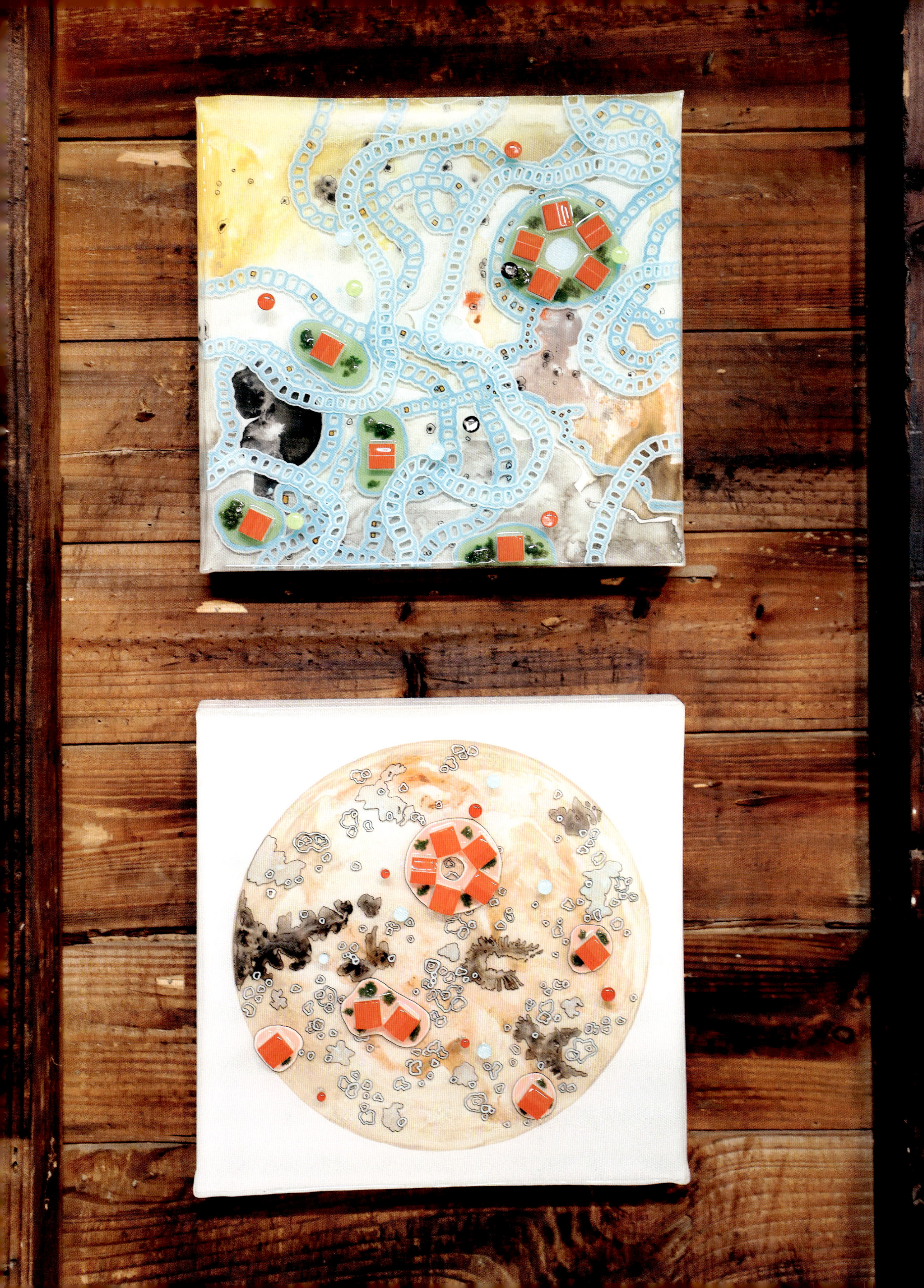

I'm a drummer, so I'm very aware of rhythm and try to use it in my work. There is a similarity between drumming and painting, and that is my hands. Both activities require touch.

DON CHRISTENSEN

"I started coming to the East End in the late sixties, while I was still in high school. I would visit my older brother, Dan, who was a painter in New York and was renting summer places in Montauk, Southampton, and Springs. He brought me to the beach in Southampton, and I was blown away. It was my first experience with the ocean—I was born and raised in Nebraska. I saw it as the 'mother of us all'! When I moved to New York, I also rented on the East End and in 2010 moved full-time to Springs with my partner, Sara DeLuca. I built a studio—basically a steel barn—on the hillside below the house and connected it to the basement. Two years later, I was working in a 1,200-square-foot space. It's fabulous that I can just walk downstairs and through the basement into my studio, my domain."

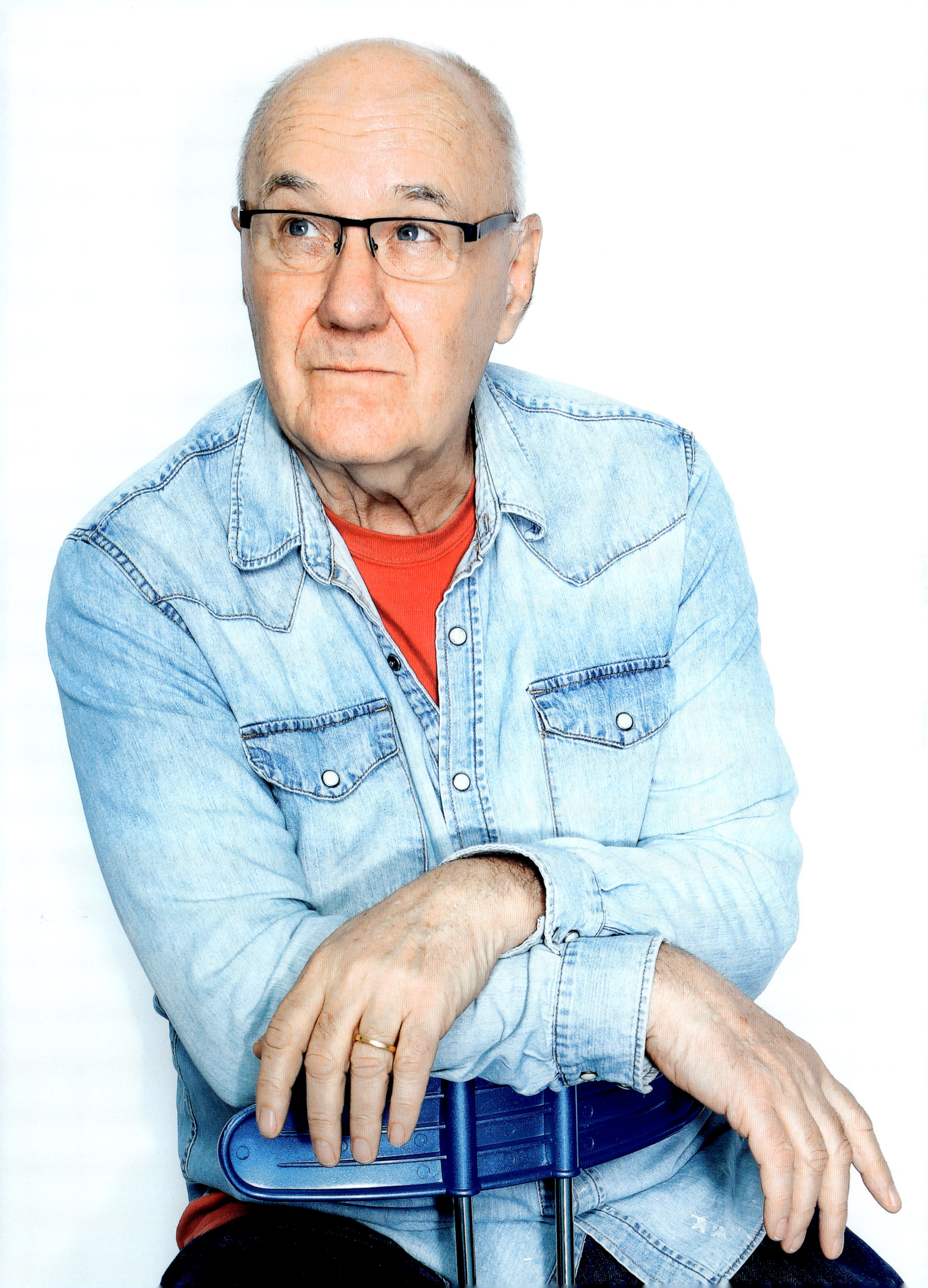

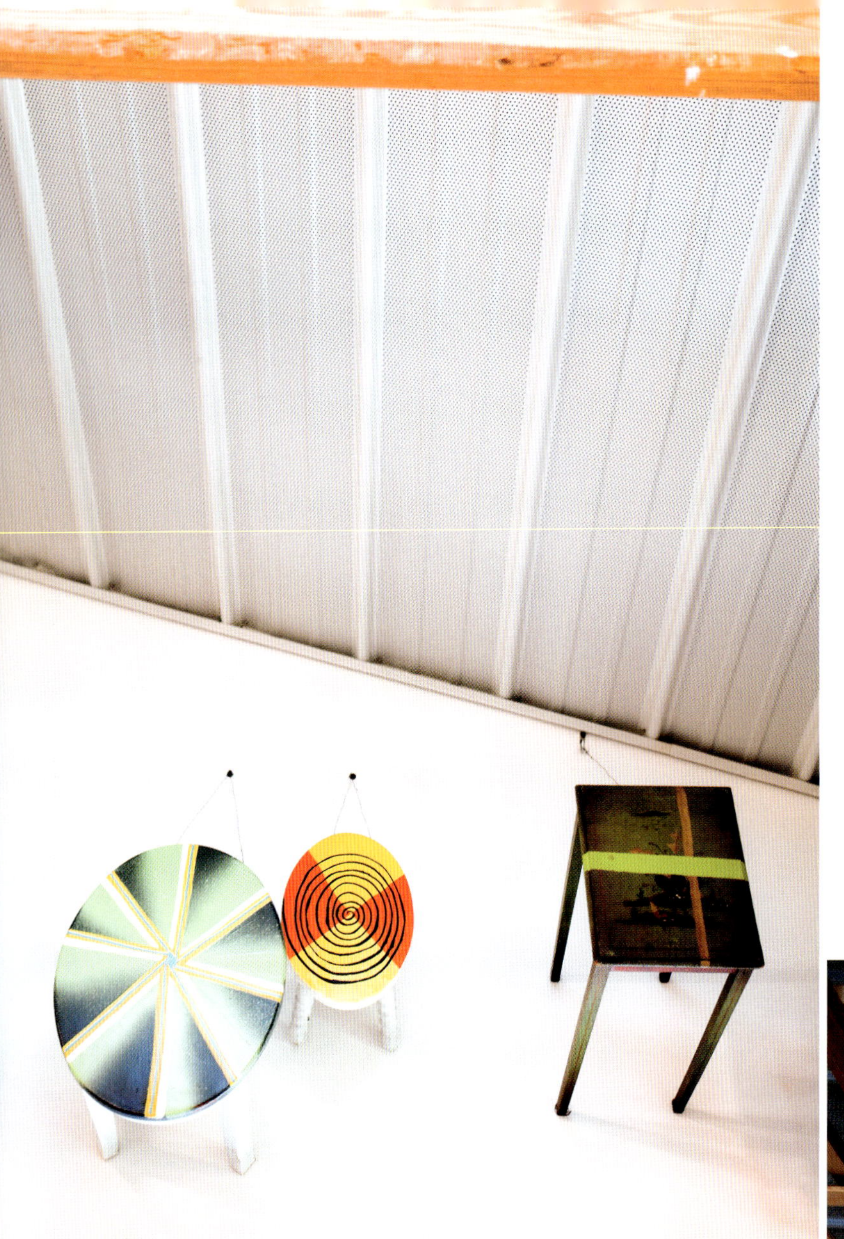

THIS PAGE AND OPPOSITE
Whether on wood, canvas, or pieces of furniture, Christensen's creativity finds expression through exuberant use of color and pattern. And though pure abstraction dominates his work, he allows himself to go toward figurative elements if they appear.

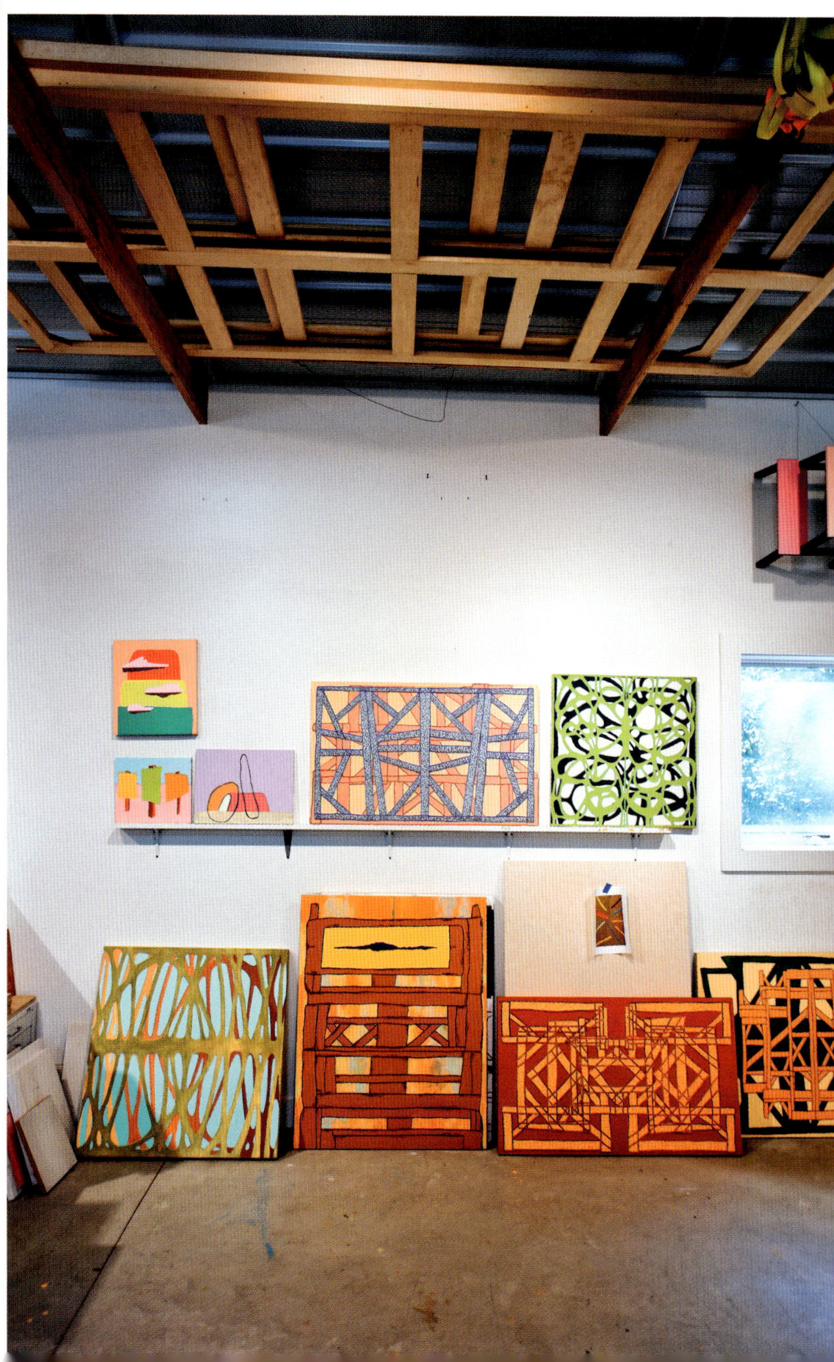

You can't envision a Christensen painting without thinking of color. "I see color everywhere, and when a particular shade or combination of colors strikes me, I try to remember it and make notes or take photos. I don't have a favorite color, and I think that idea is ridiculous. I love all color. Color only exists in context with other colors—it looks different depending on what color is next to it. My color choices are intuitive and tend to be rather impulsive. I trust my color sense. One sees colors the way one hears harmony, which is a combination of pitches, and the choices and combinations have specific emotional qualities. I don't think most of us are really aware that this process is going on in our lives all the time."

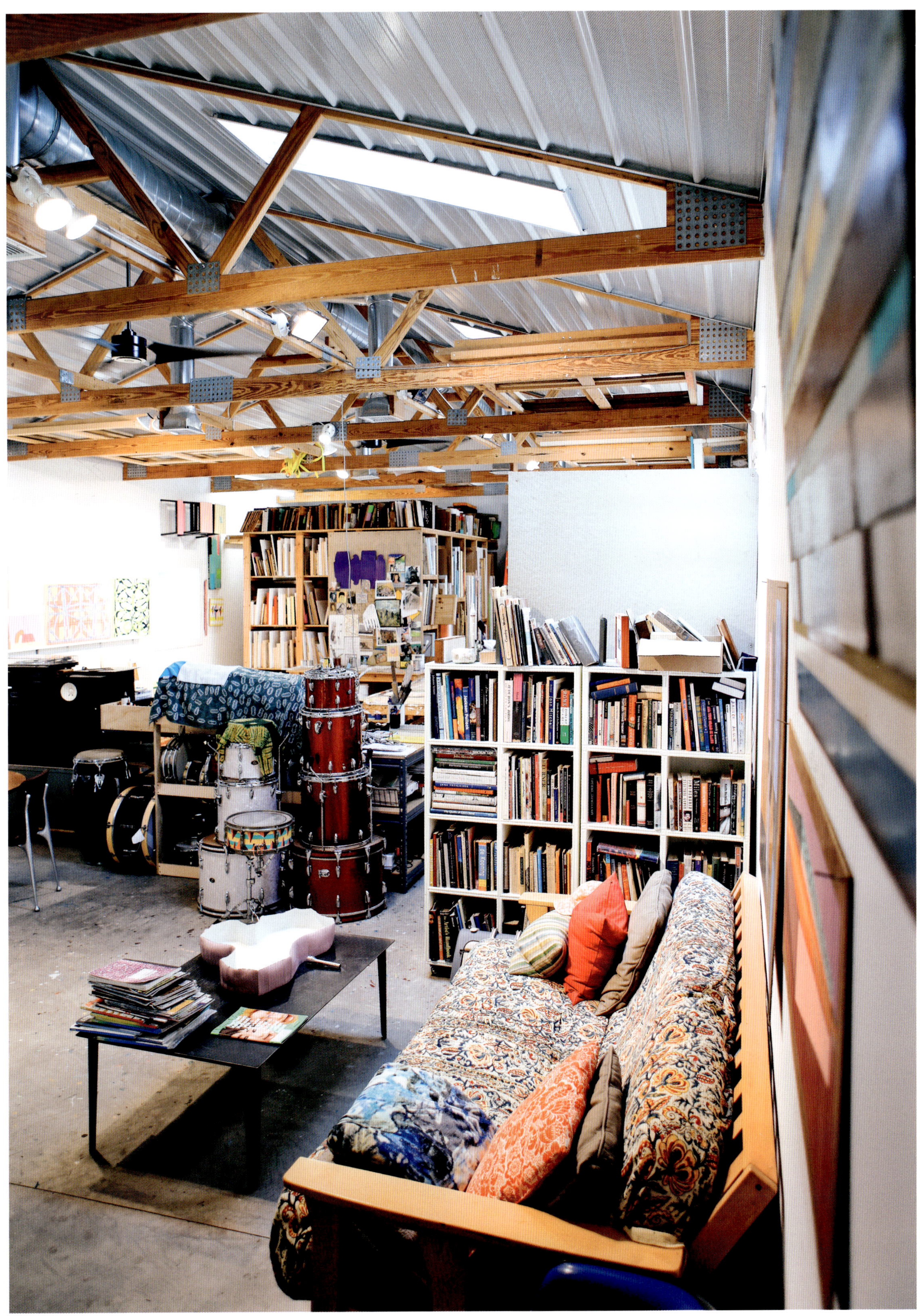

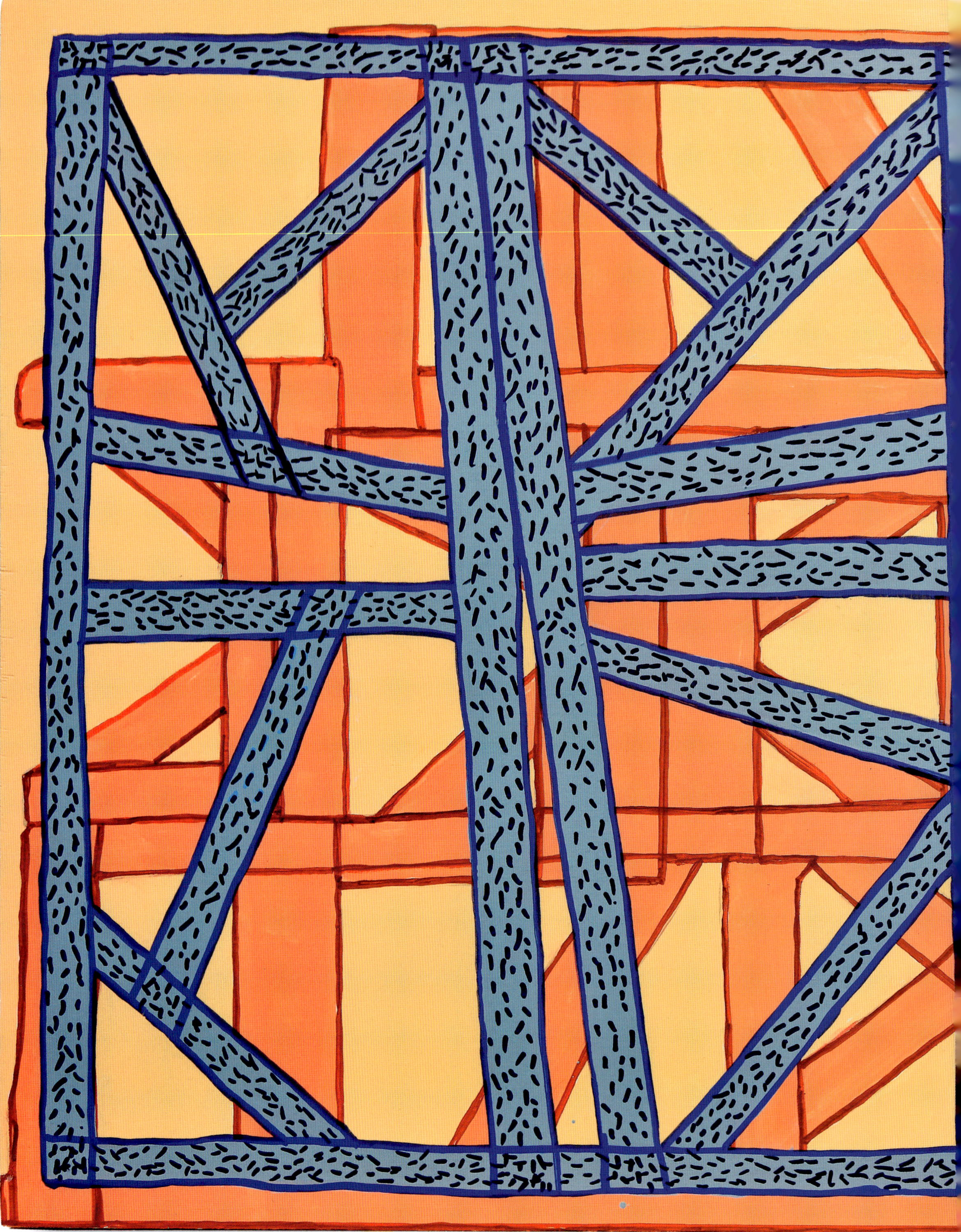

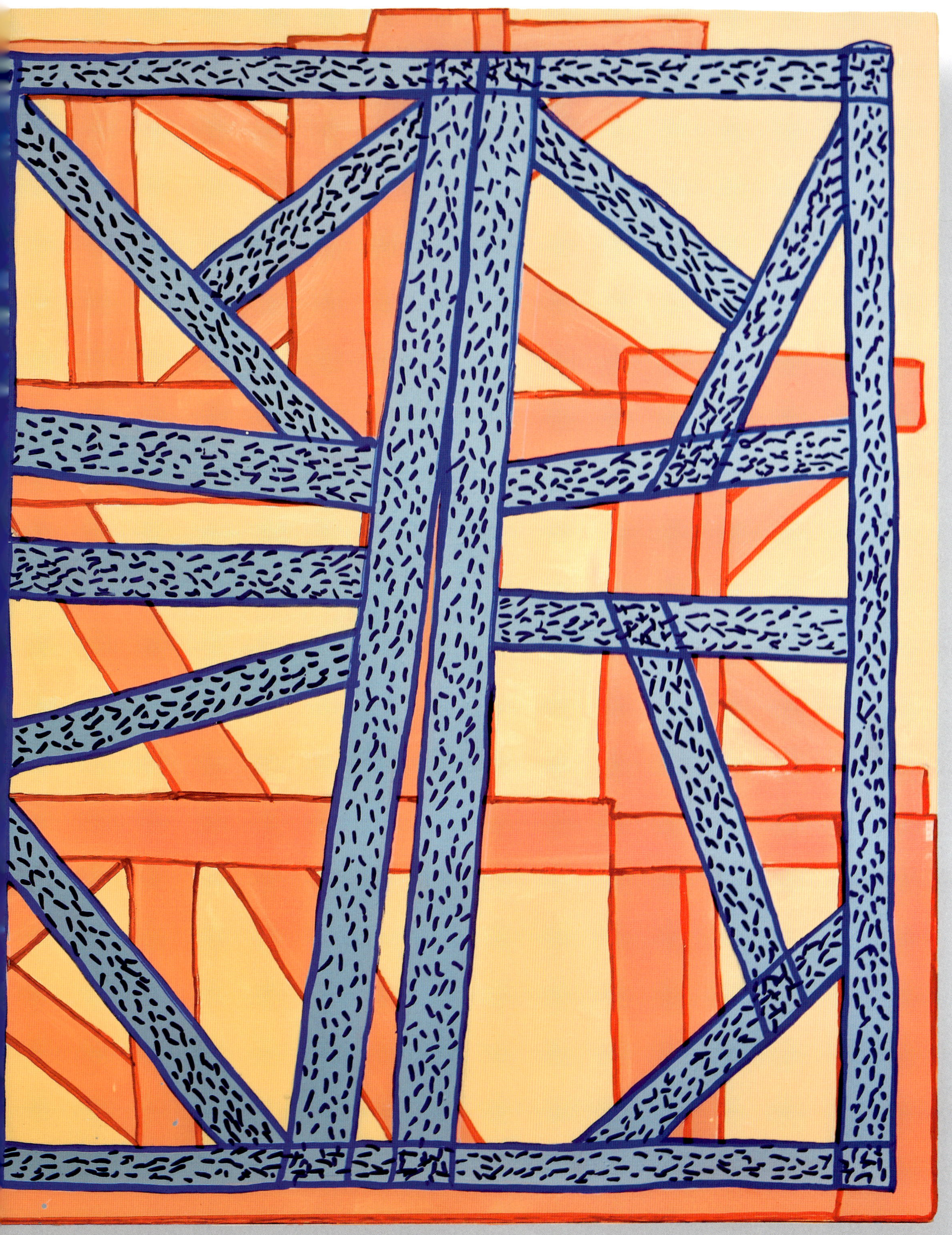

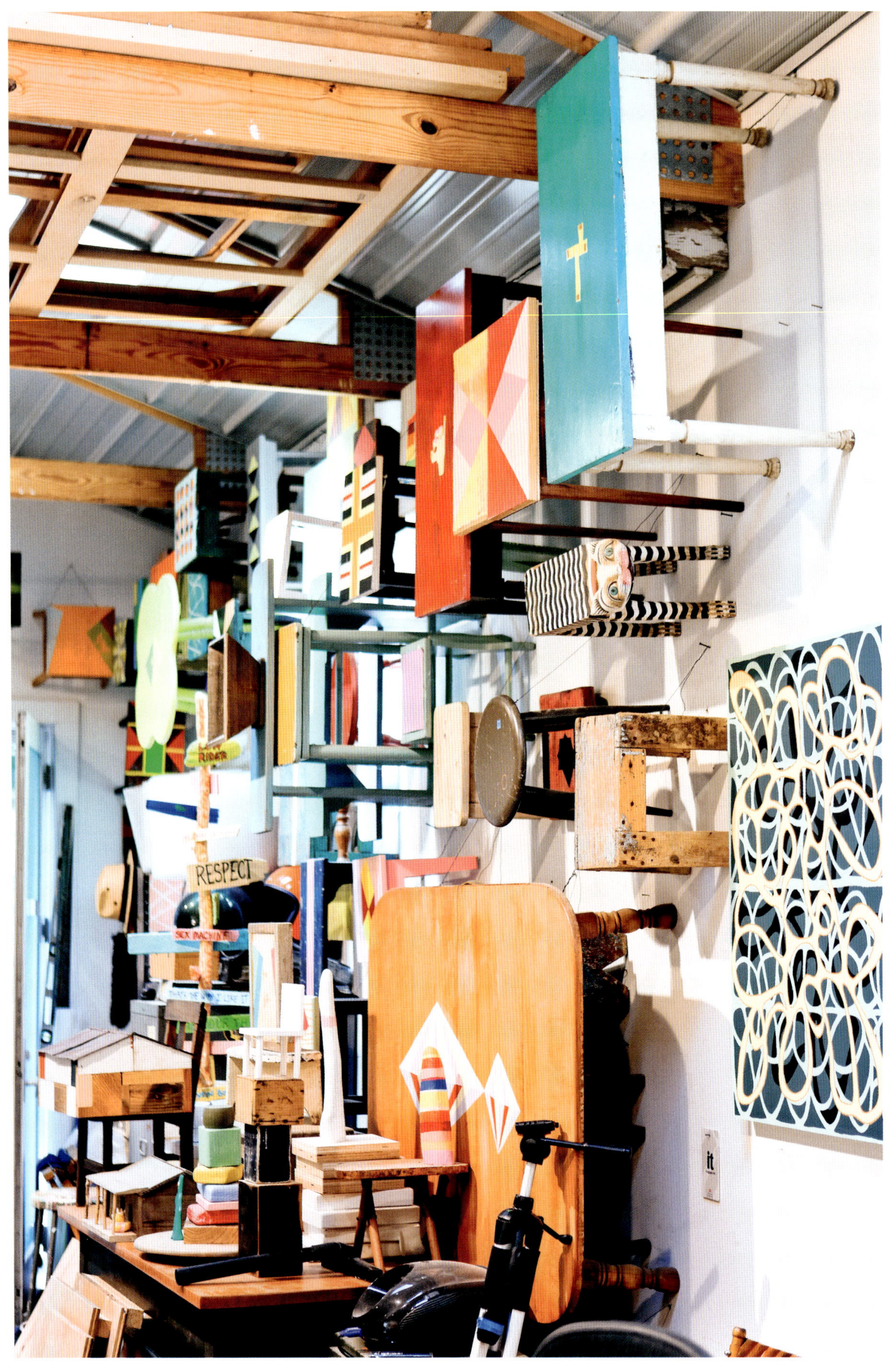

ABOVE Painted stools and tables hang on the walls of Christensen's spacious East Hampton studio.

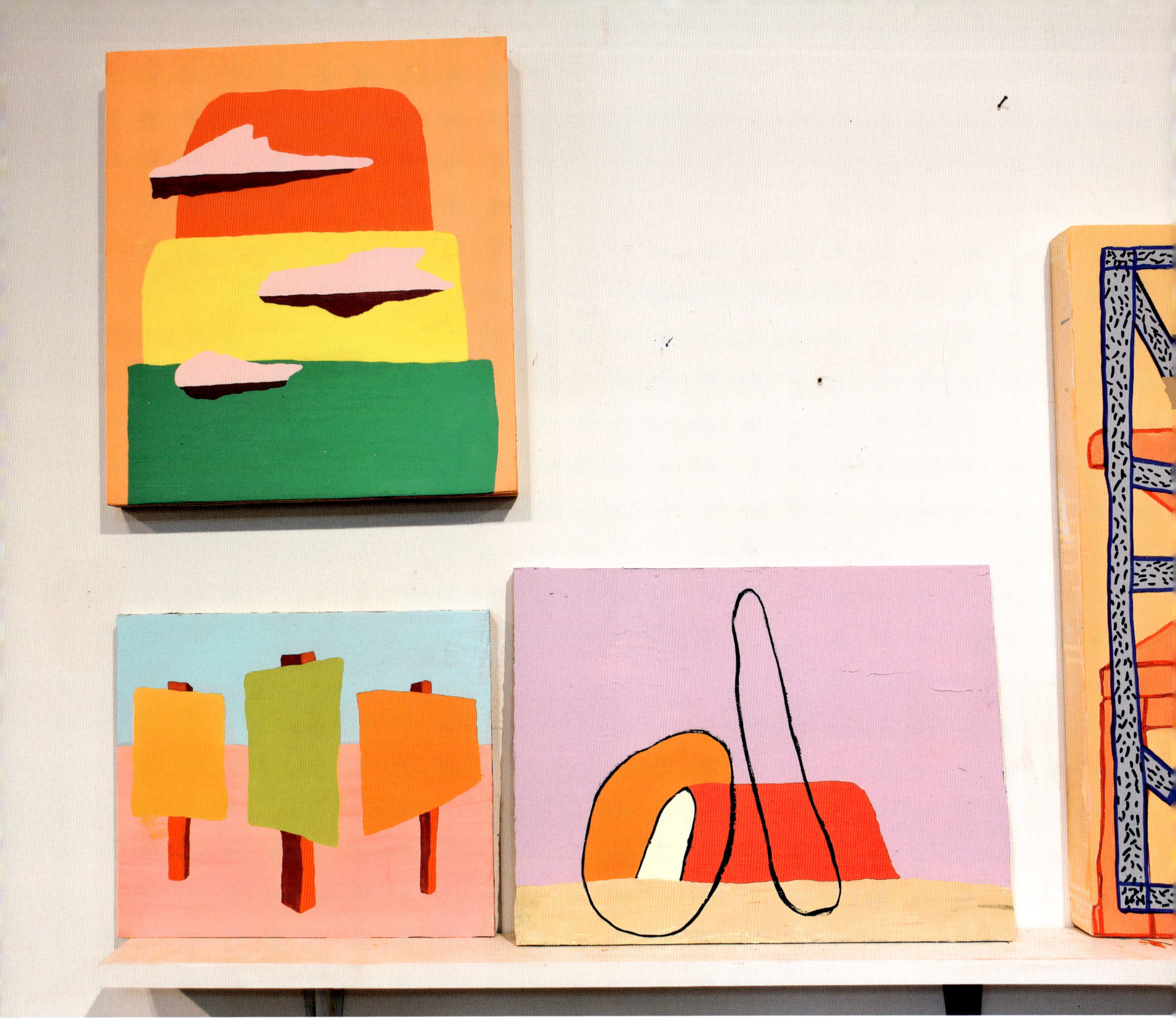

"I embraced abstraction as soon as I left art school. While I liked figure drawing and painting still lifes, to me the real joy of painting has always been the actual application of paint to a surface. By eliminating pictorial, narrative, political, or contextual concerns, one is free to just enjoy that application of paint. Maybe painters have always wanted this freedom, and it took the Cubists, Impressionists, Ab-Exers, and Minimalists to get us there. That being said, I think my work has become more subjective after years of painting pure abstraction. I've always had a tendency to look for the pictorial in abstractions, and now I allow myself to go toward the imagery if it shows up. Nearly all the ideas for my shapes are from outside or around me—commercial graphics, billboards, trucks, and the landscape. What I see influences me. What draws me to a certain composition or color or geometry is totally intuitive. I don't know what really causes this."

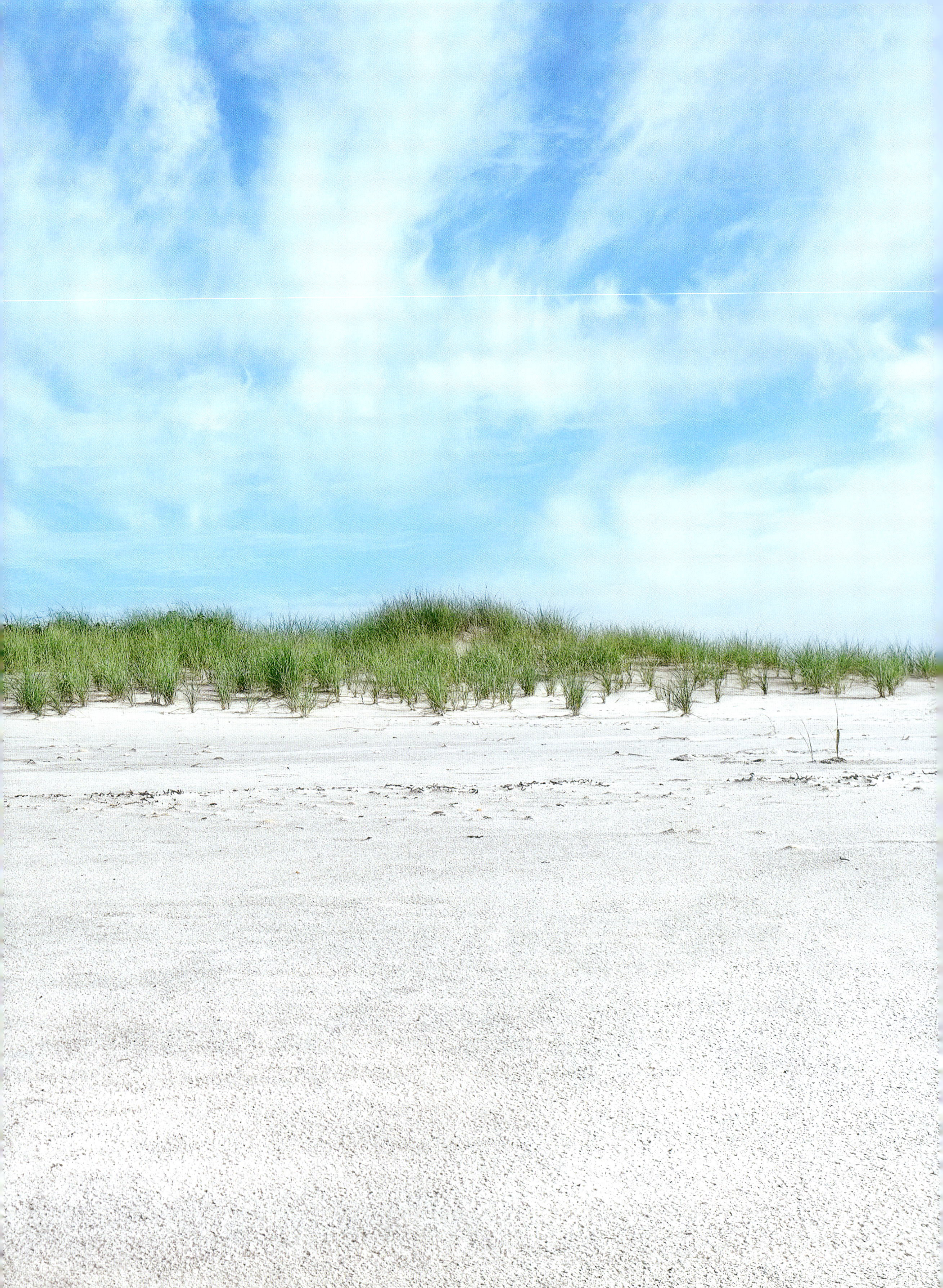

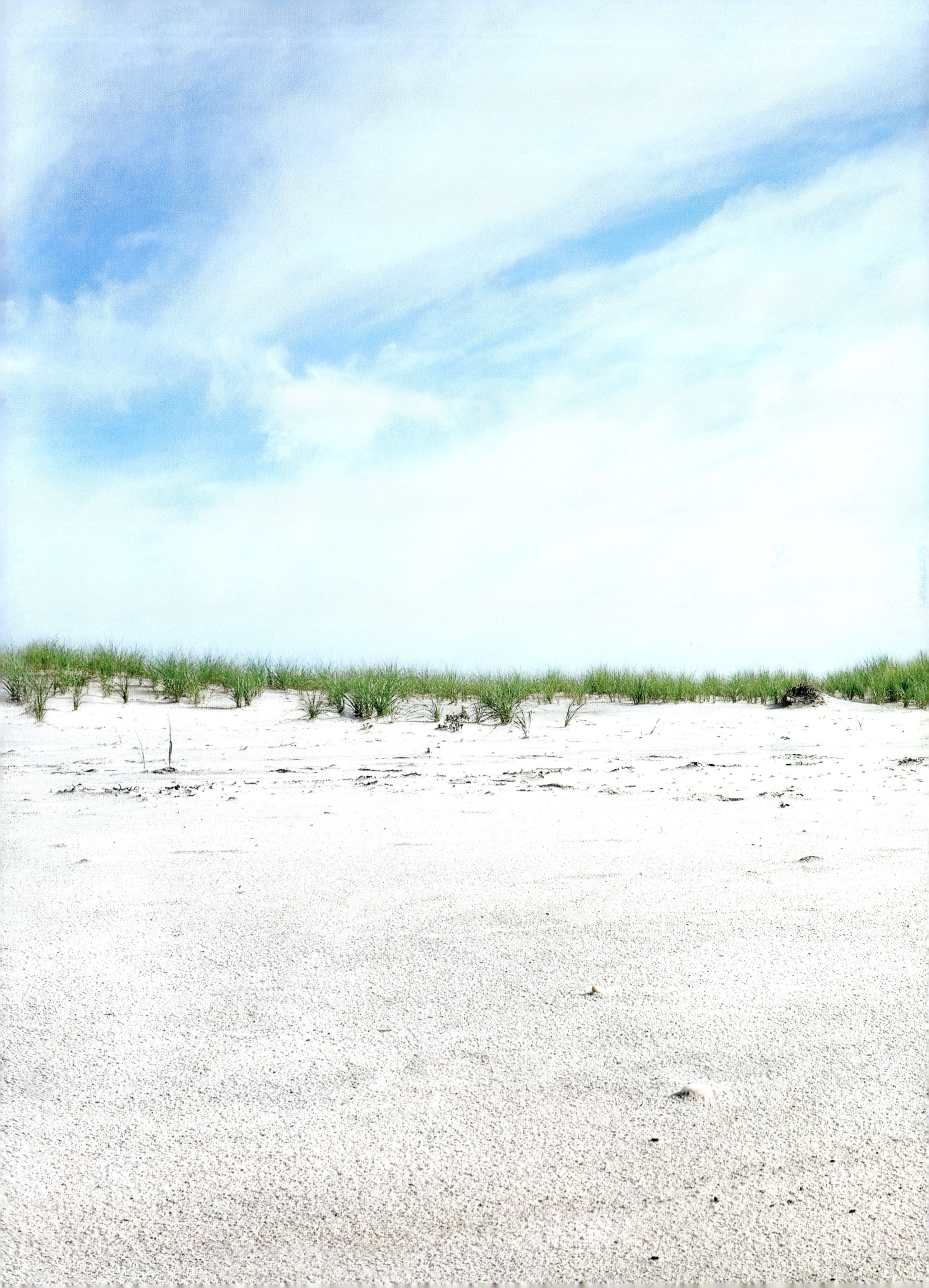

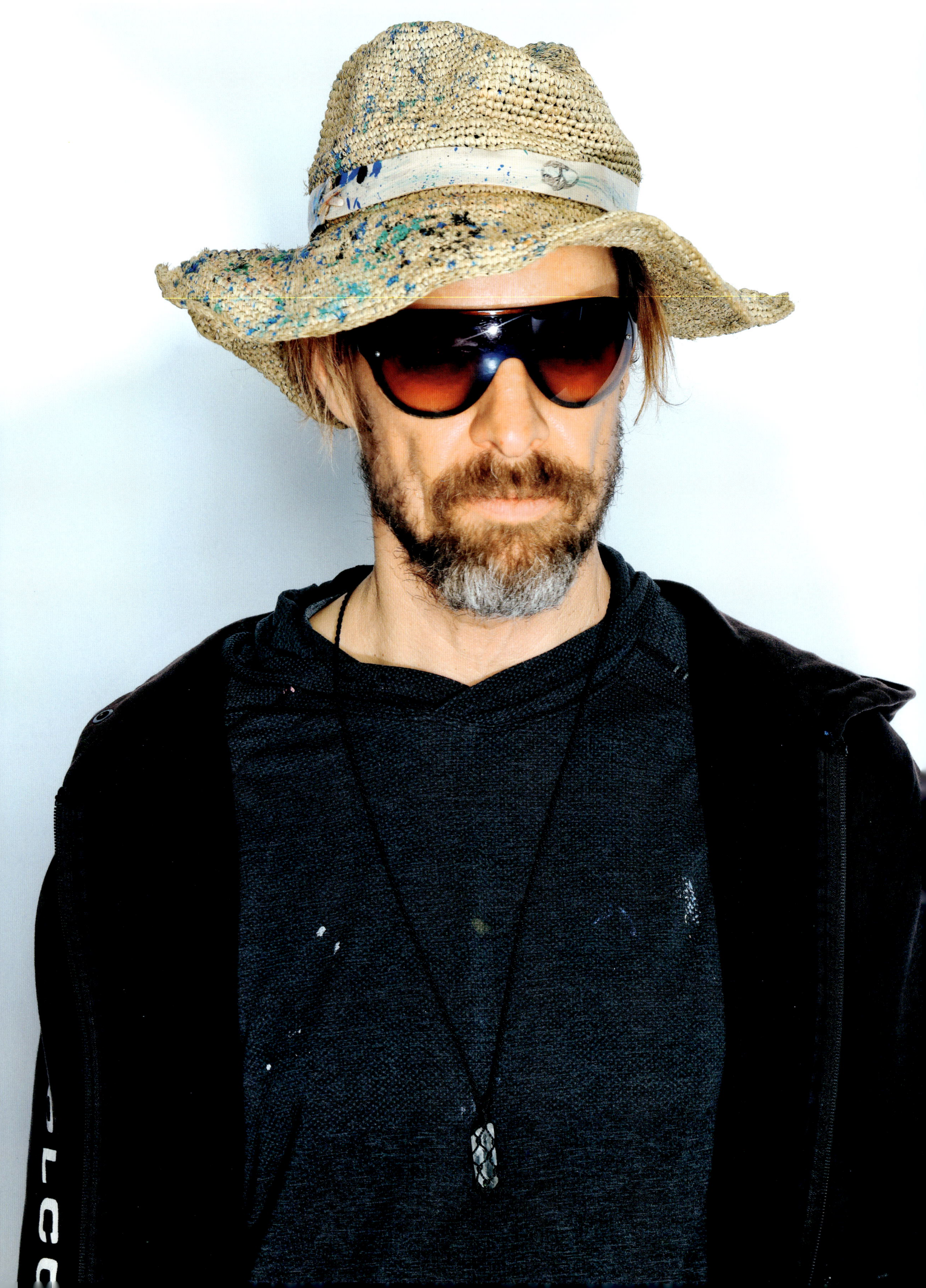

I'm a conceptualist.
Where my mind goes, my ass follows.

QUENTIN CURRY

Born in Johnstown, Pennsylvania, Curry spent his formative years in the Appalachian Mountains. "This instilled in me a love for the wild and a fascination with the counterculture movements of the eighties. After a turbulent time in school, I found solace and inspiration in skateboarding, snowboarding, and the emerging punk music scene. These experiences laid the groundwork for my future artistic endeavors, providing a backdrop of rebellion and personal expression that continues to inform my work to this day."

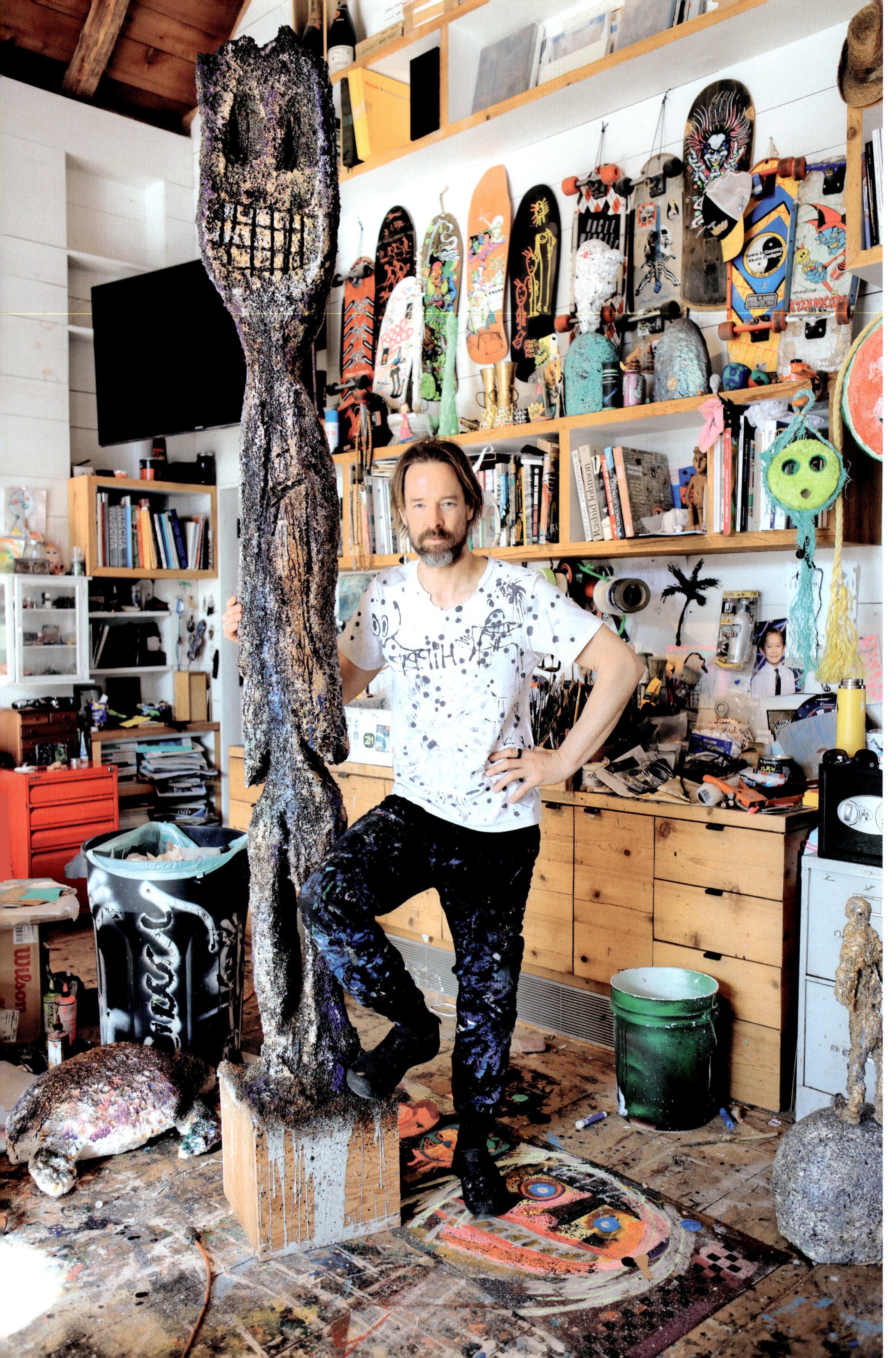

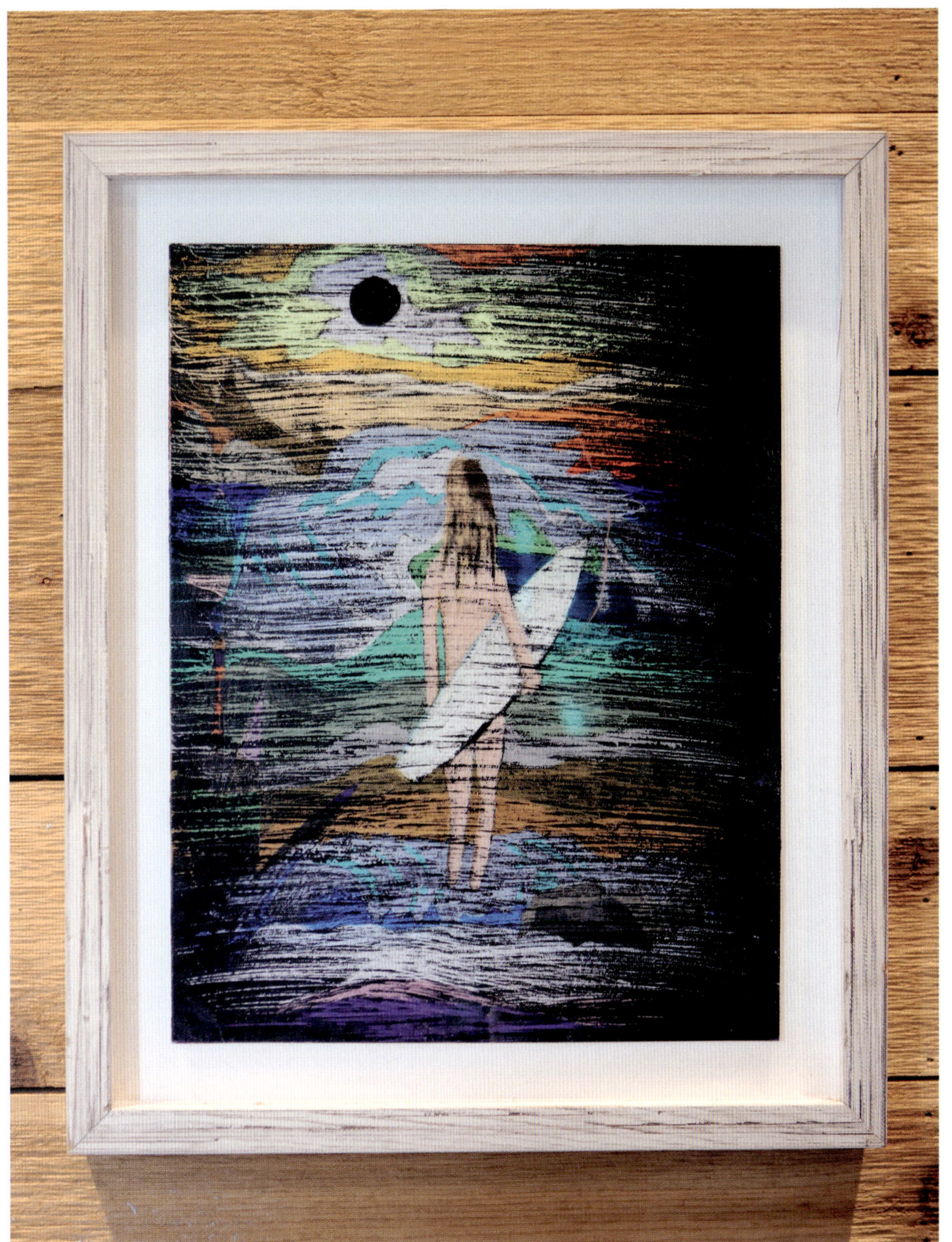

"I moved to the Hamptons in 2009, seeking an escape from the urban hustle and financial uncertainties of New York City, and turned my attention to eastern Long Island. Eventually, I stumbled upon a unique place in Sagaponack. The property, with a house and studio, was previously owned by David Porter. It felt like something you'd find in Vermont, though it was just one mile from the ocean. I was struck by the sense of wildness and seclusion it offered. I finally convinced the owners to sell me the property and embarked on a years-long renovation. The environment here has allowed me to reconnect with the natural world. Whether I'm surfing or painting or walking or sculpting or riding, it all is reflected in the works I make."

OPPOSITE A lifelong passion for surfing and skateboarding is ingrained in Curry's art, which also expresses his passion for exploring materiality.

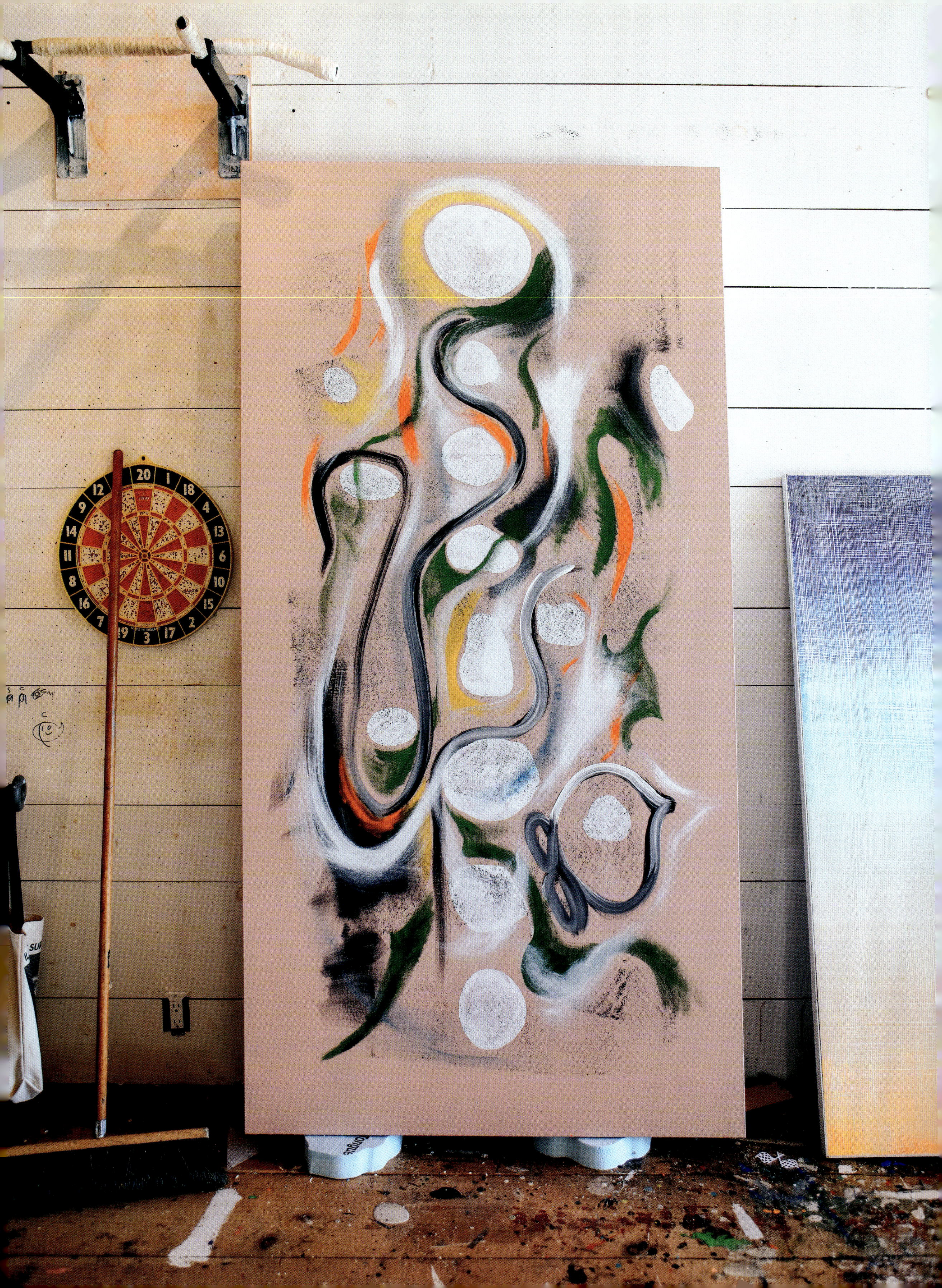

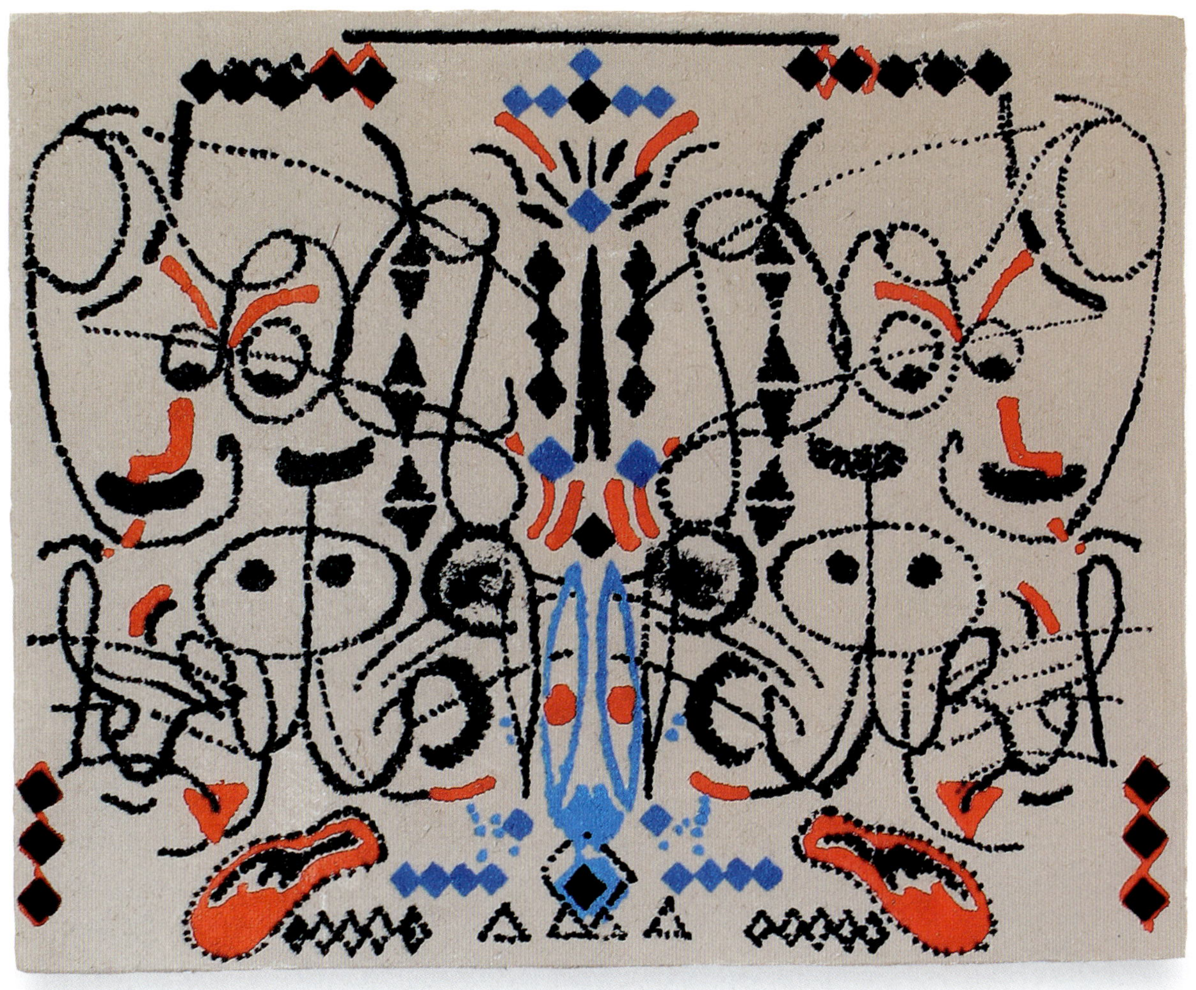

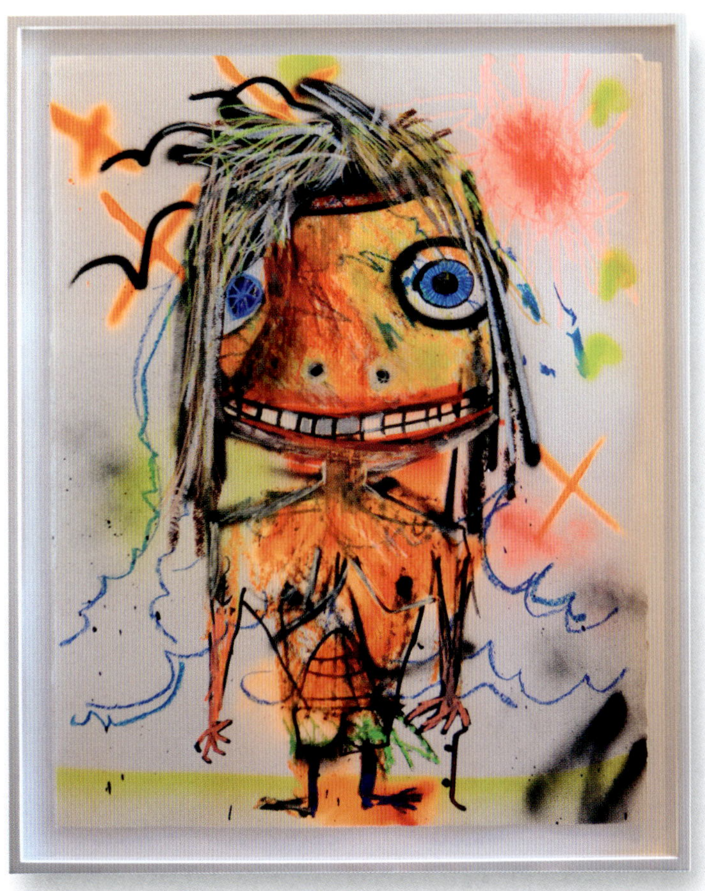

Curry trained at Bard College and the San Francisco Art Institute. "I've always toggled between abstraction and figuration and the small thoughts in between. My early works, created with stone dust and oil paint, and characterized by textured, semi-abstract landscapes, laid the foundation for my later exploration of more freehand and primal approaches to painting." His surf paintings, with their bold colors and expressive brushwork, evoke the sensation of riding the waves with paint. Curry's sculptures offer a tactile exploration of materiality. "By repurposing man-made building materials into rock-like structures, I blur the line between natural and artificial, ancient and modern."

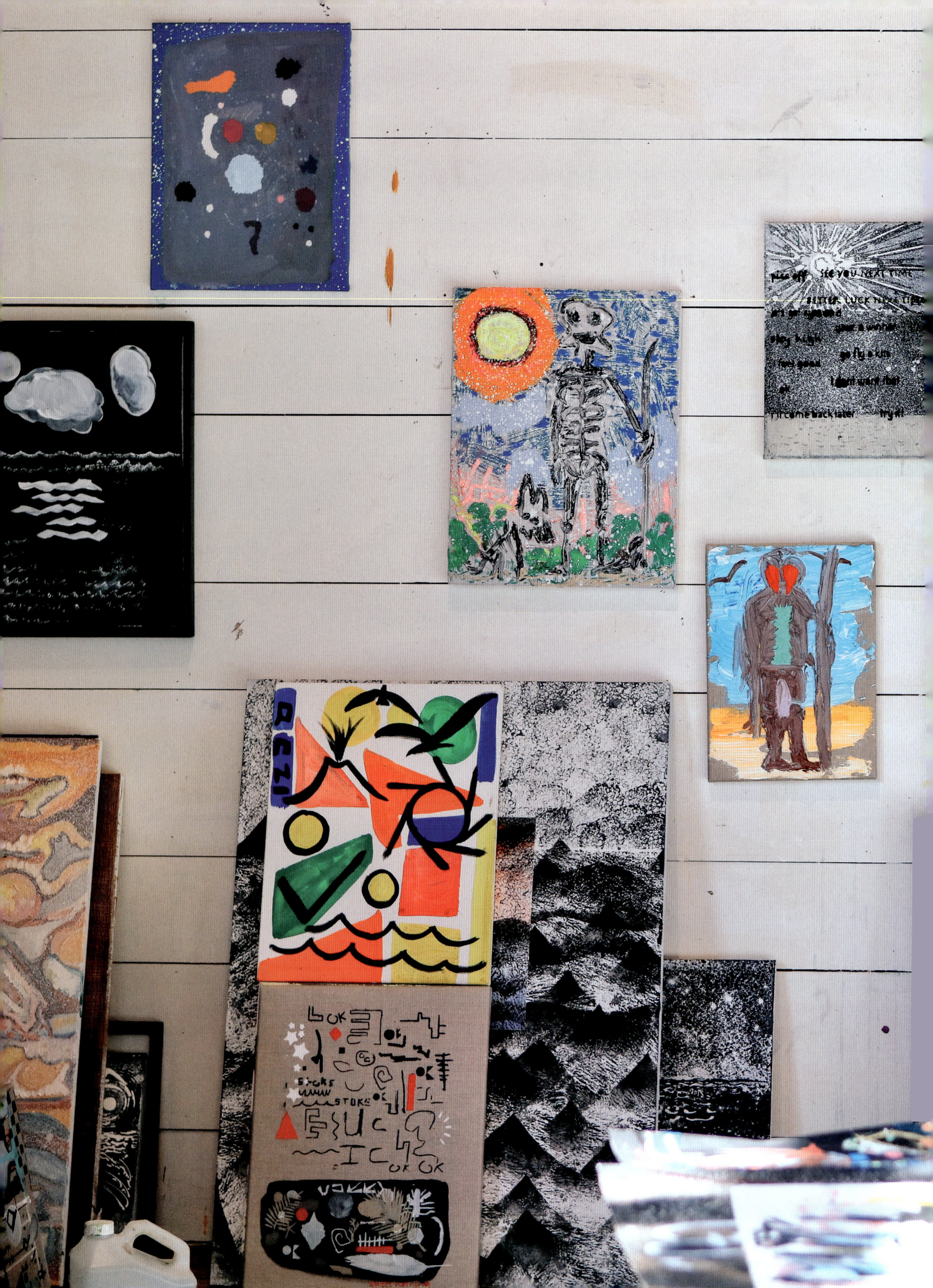
Piss off
SEE YOU NEXT TIME
stay high
I feel good
go fly a kite
ok
I'll come back later
try it
OK
STOKE
OK OK

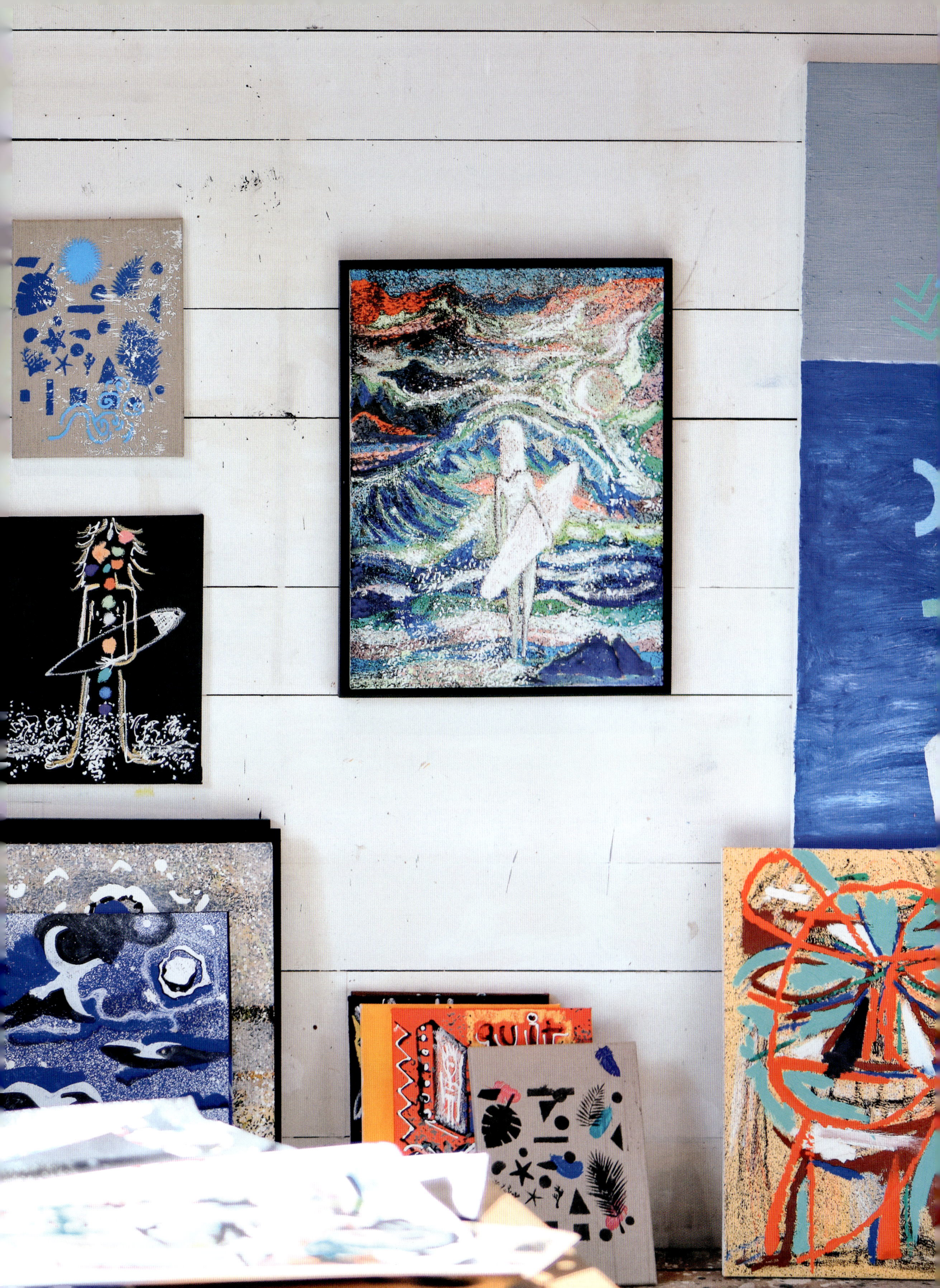

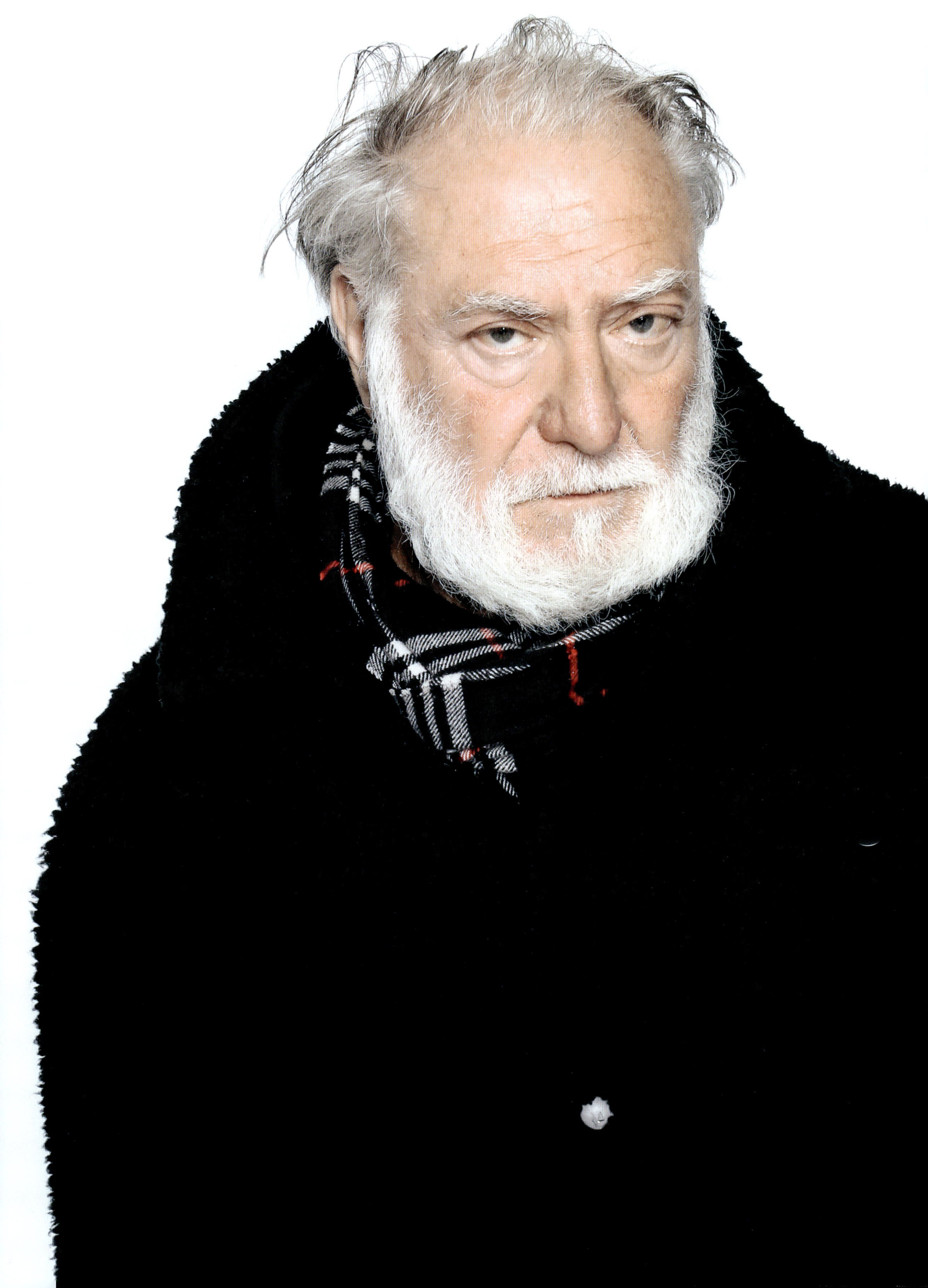

For me, a painting has to be at least the size of a door so you can go through it, so you can have an intimate mind-and-body experience with that piece of art.

EUGENIO CUTTICA

"I love to paint people because I love people, even though I'm kind of an introverted person. My way to make a connection with people is by making portraits. When I was living in New York City, I would stop people on the street and take a series of photos and then paint from those photos. When I finished the portraits, they were all the same size. I felt the humanity of that, like they are part of a big family, my big family."

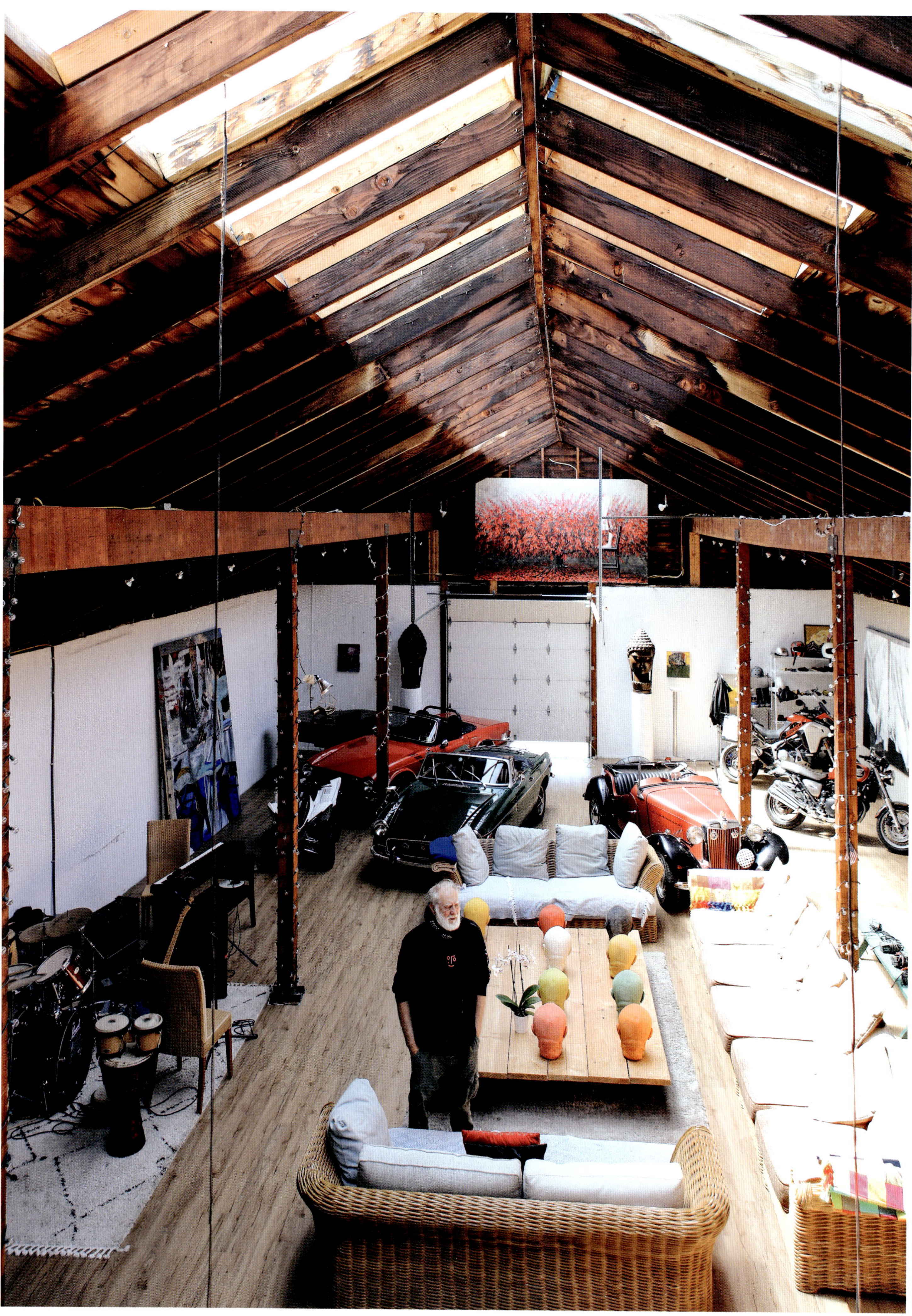

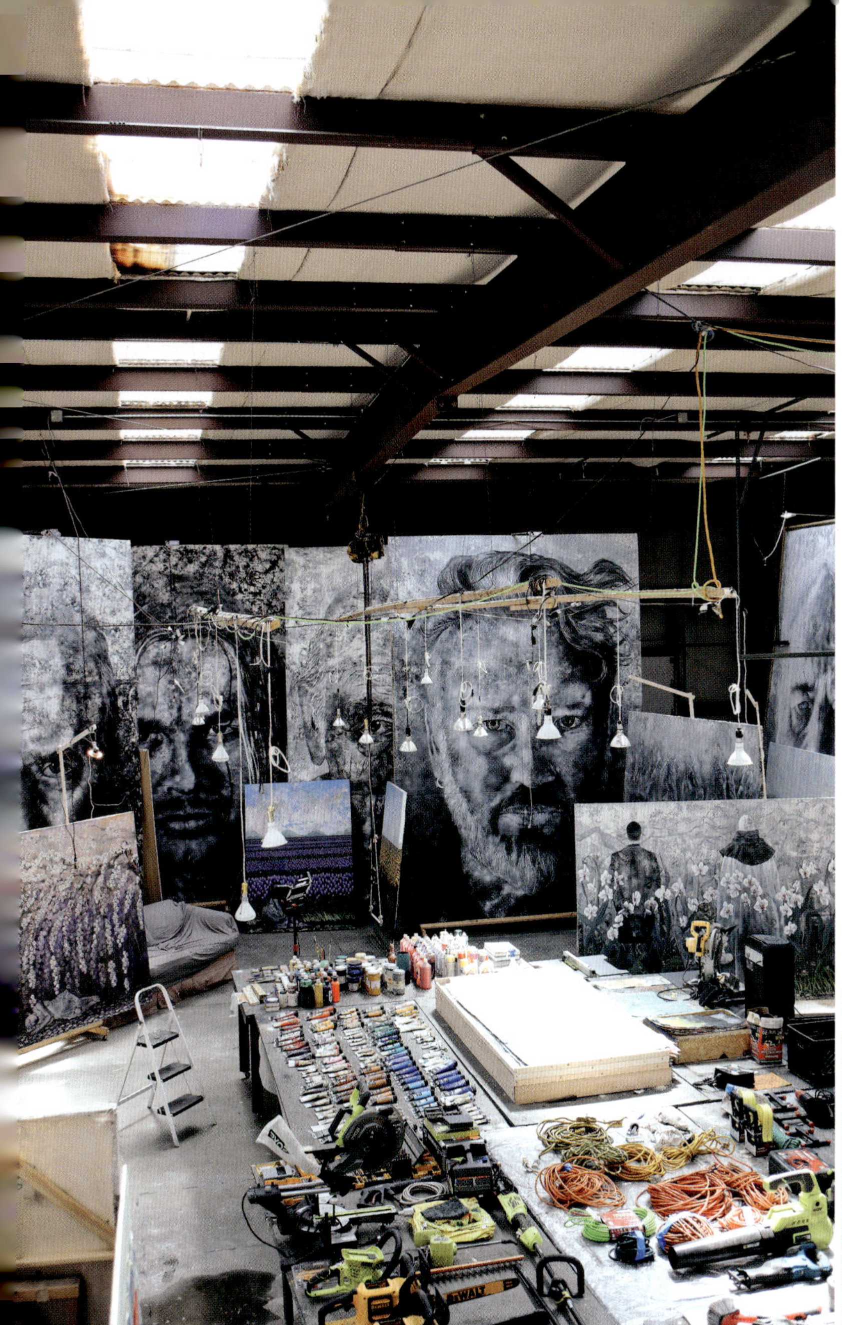

OPPOSITE AND THIS PAGE
Music, vintage sports cars, and motorcycles mix with art in this lofty space, one of many buildings in the "Camp Cuttica" compound. Friends and family often gather for meals and art soirées here.

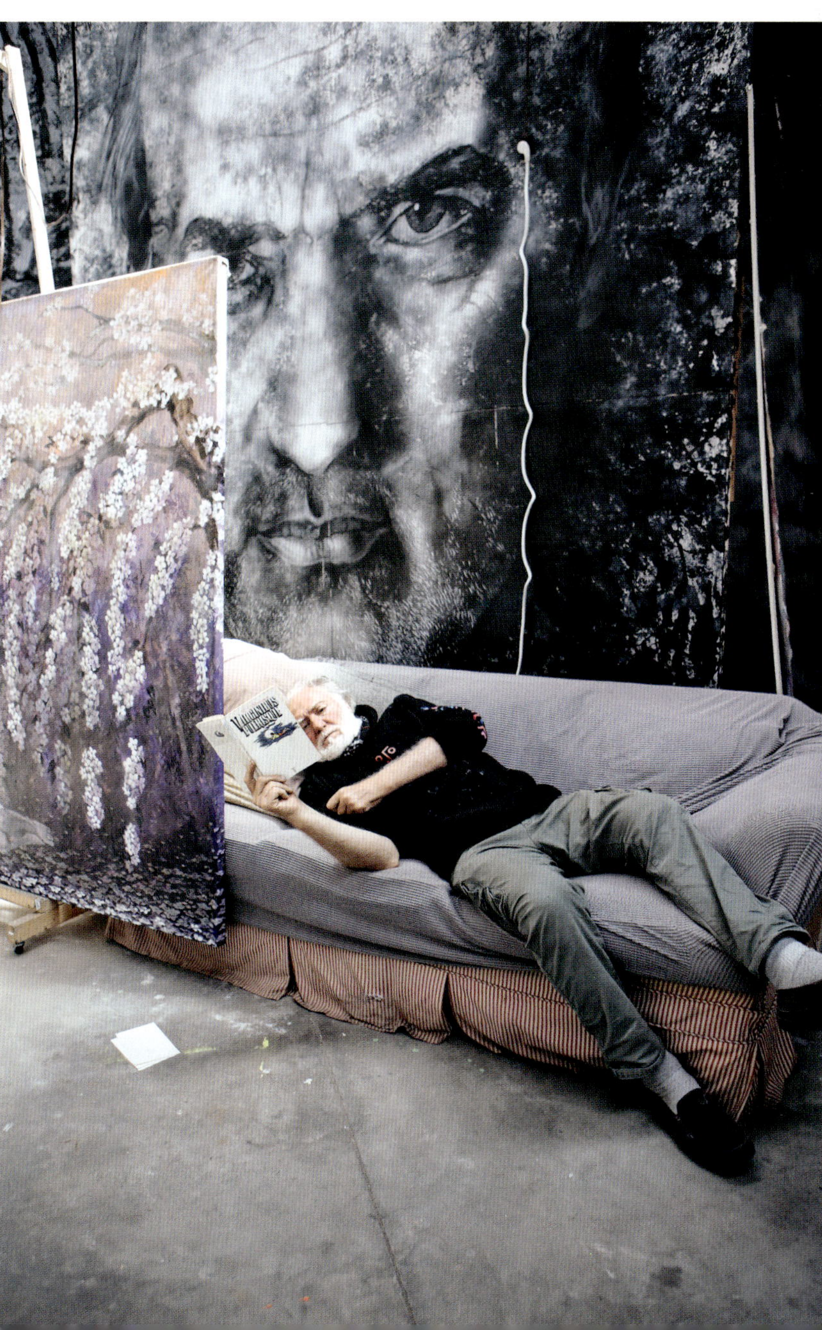

Born in Argentina, Cuttica was already well known in Buenos Aires when he moved his family to New York City in 1996, and from there to East Hampton several years later. In 2019, he created a family art compound in Flanders on a forty-acre former duck pond. It became known as Campo Cuttica, with studios for himself, his two sons, and a daughter-in-law—all artists. "We are a family of artists. I love going to their studios to see what they're doing and give them some advice. And they come to my studio and give me their opinions, so there is a constant dialogue between us."

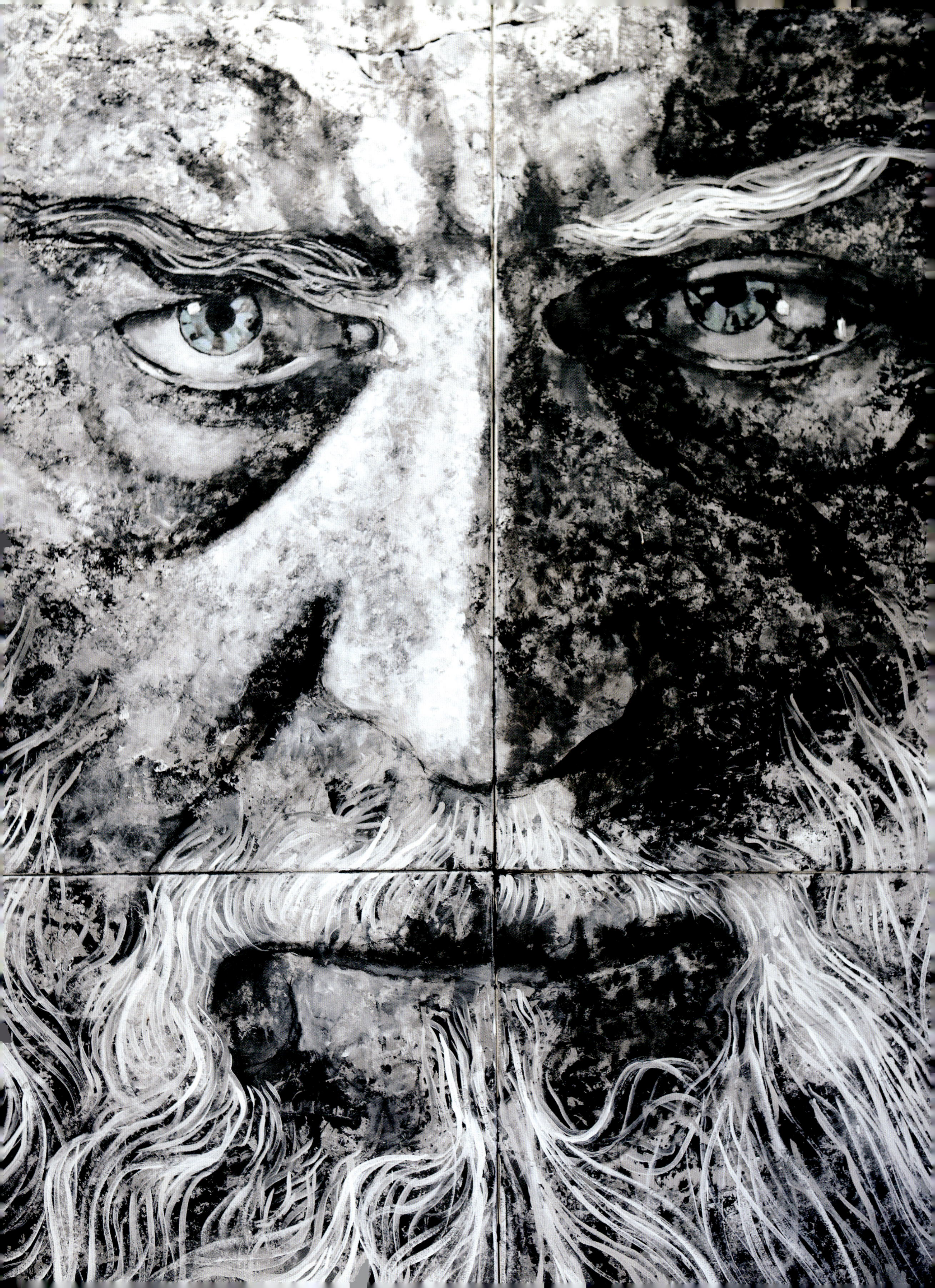

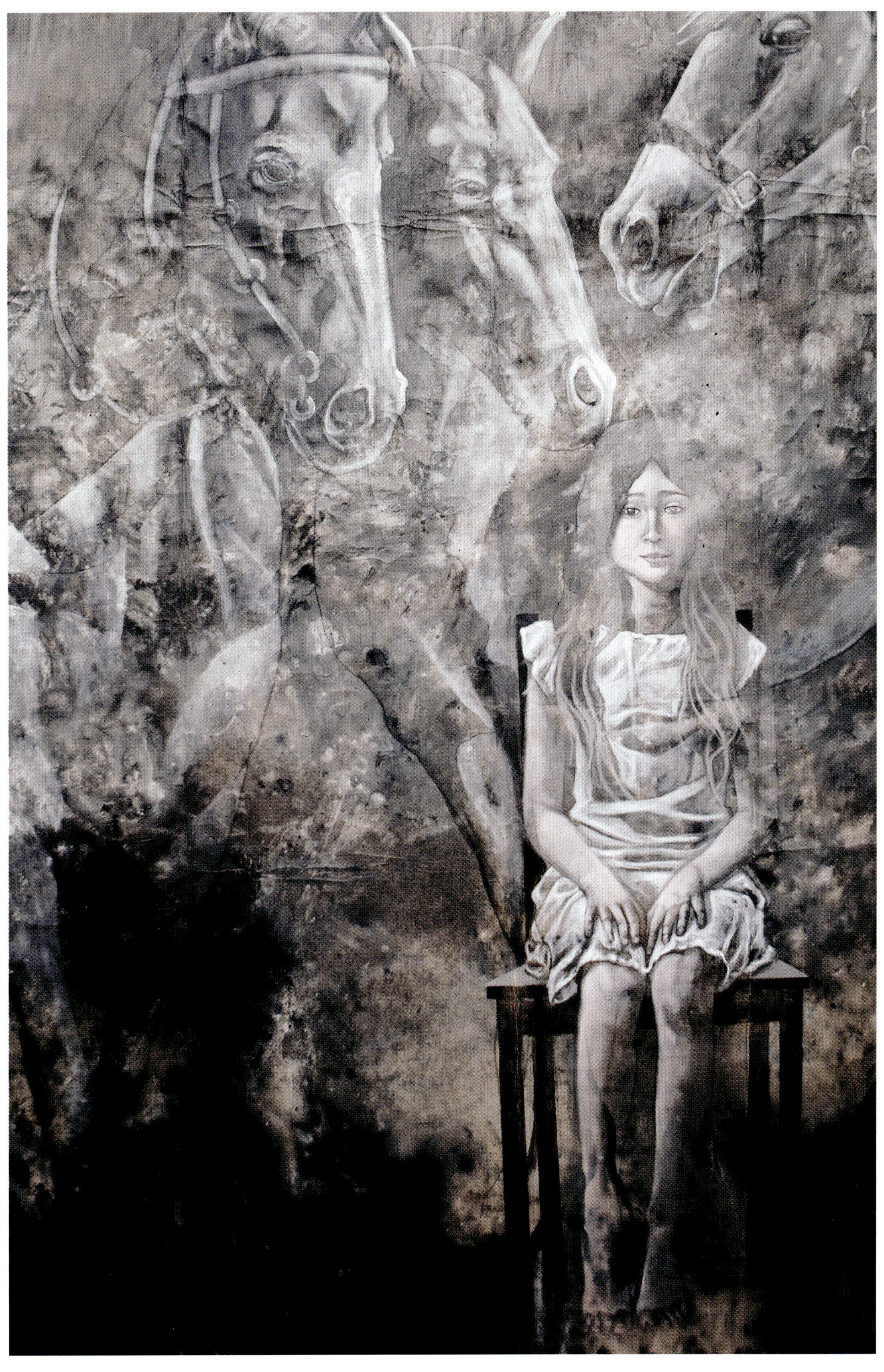

Cuttica's paintings have a mysterious, dreamlike feel that is distinctive to his work. Asked how he achieves this, he says, "Technique doesn't matter. We see beautiful drawings made in caves thousands of years ago—made with a piece of chalk or carbon on the rough walls. They look like modern art. So I don't care about the technique. I make my own paints, using various tests of durability, in the hope that my work can survive a hundred years. But I don't want the technique to put any limitations on my creativity."

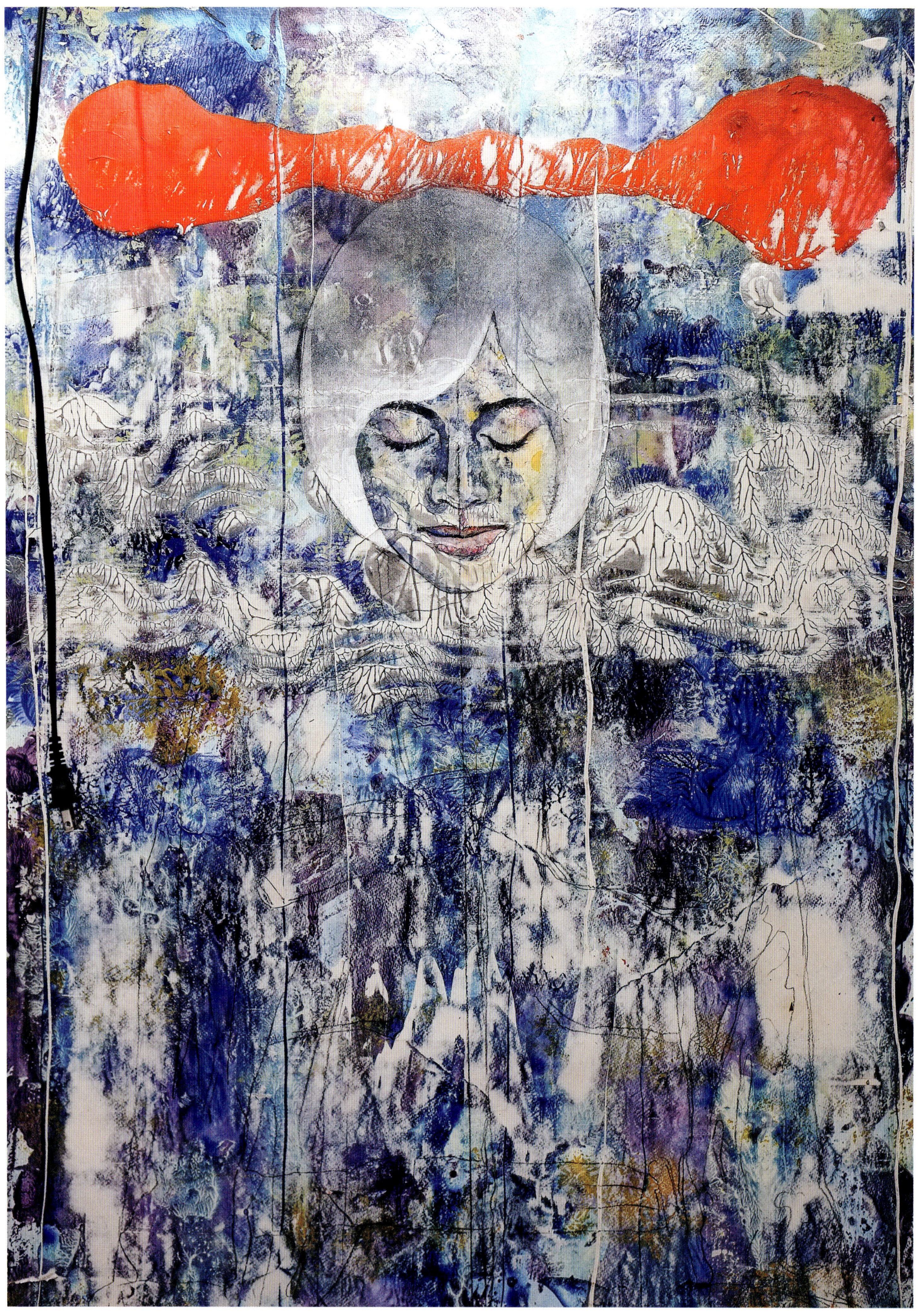

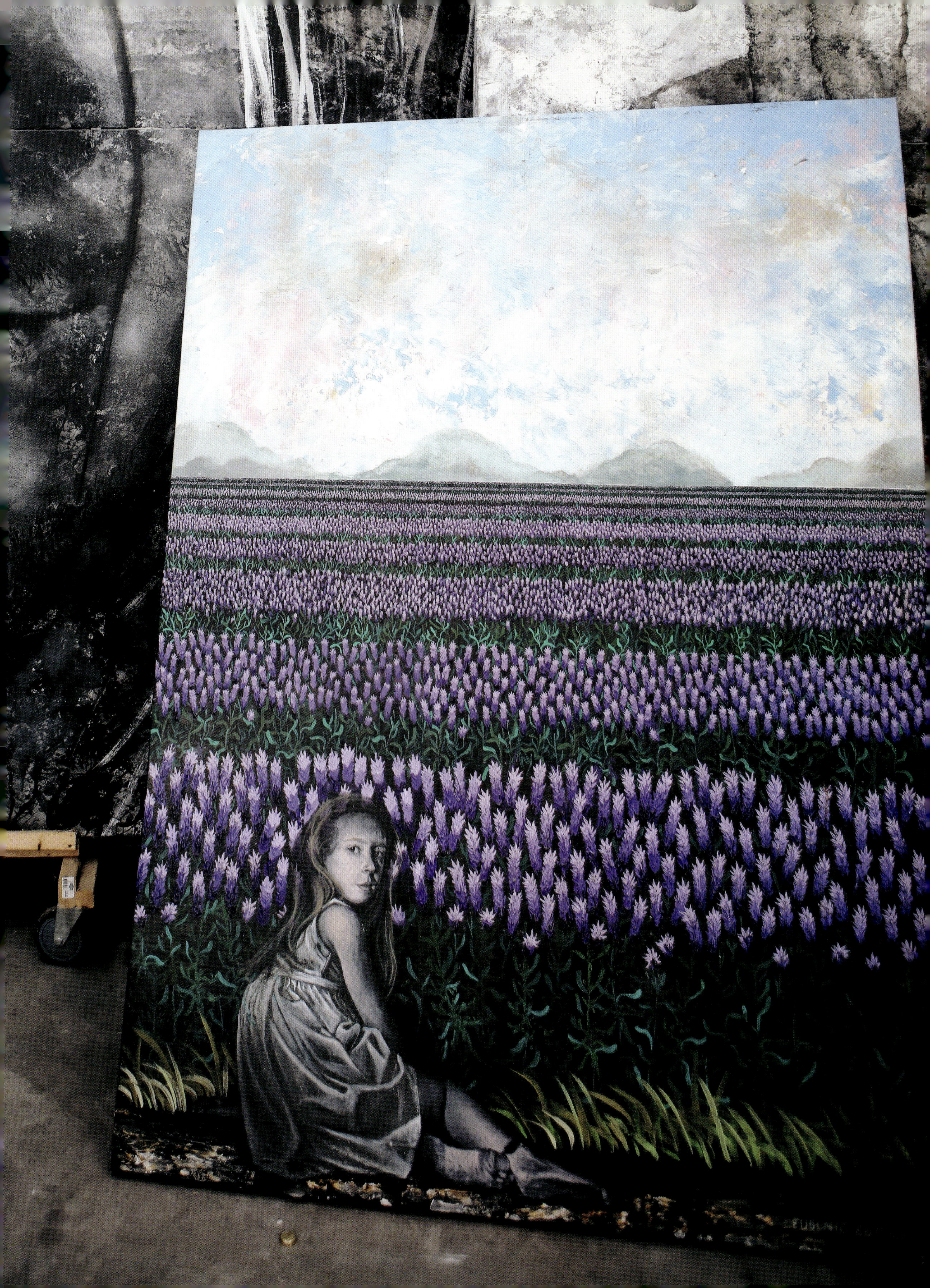

I planted this garden, and like every plant, each painting becomes a friend and a revelation.

ERIC DEVER

"I have always self-identified as an artist. By the time I was in high school, I was studying drawing in an artist's studio in Venice Beach. I let my family know that this was going to be my profession, and as soon as I could drive and could afford a used car, I began visiting galleries and museums." Born and raised in Los Angeles, Dever got his MA in painting at New York University in 1988. "My paintings during this time were influenced by the urban landscape and were elegiac as well; the AIDS crisis concerned everyone." By 2003, Dever had migrated to the East End to focus more deeply on painting. He established a studio in Water Mill, pulling color from the landscape elements, including plants, sky, and water. A yoga devotee, Dever's examinations of color blend into his understanding of nature. "When I paint, I have a sense of mixing matter, energy and lightness."

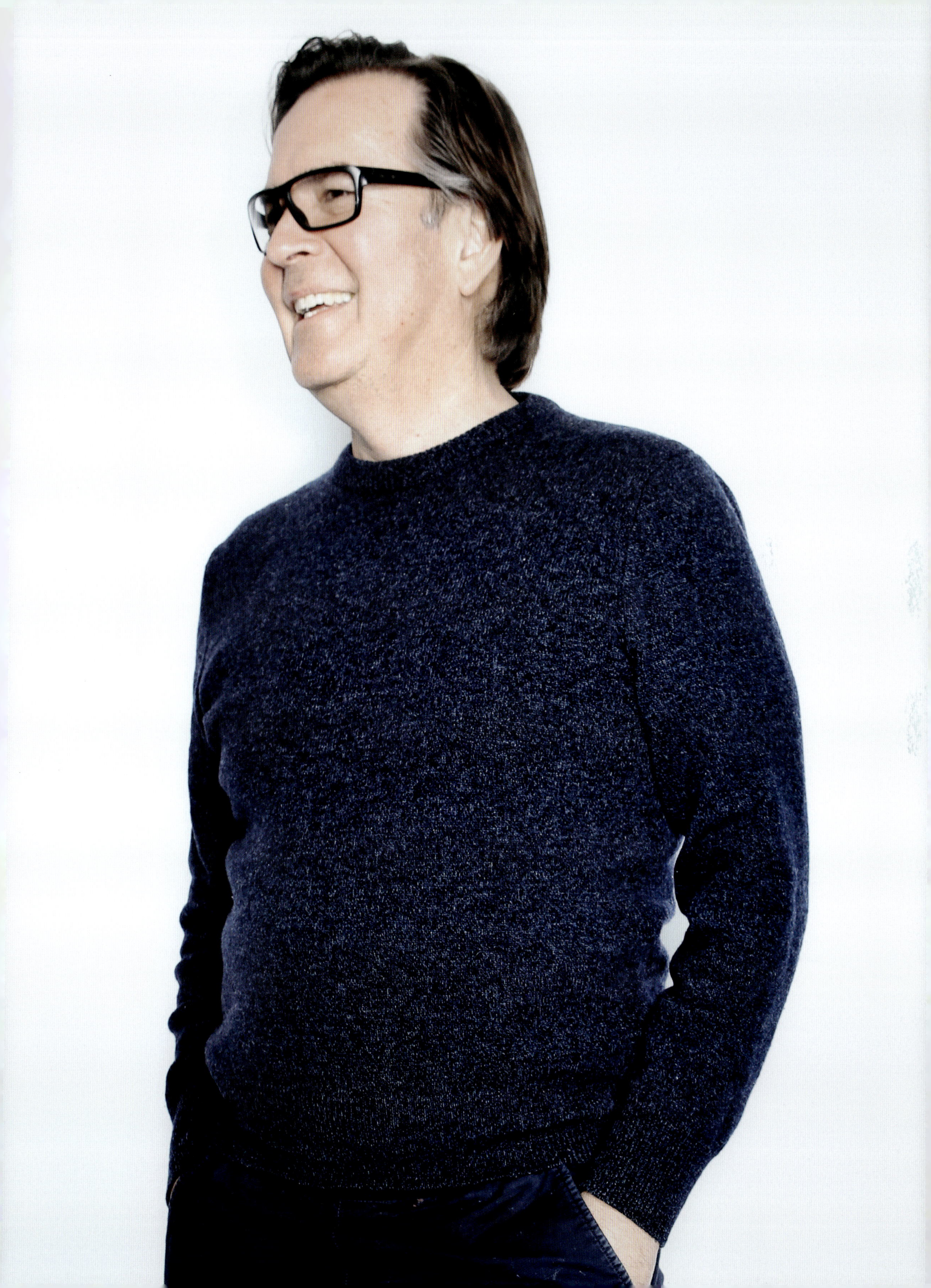

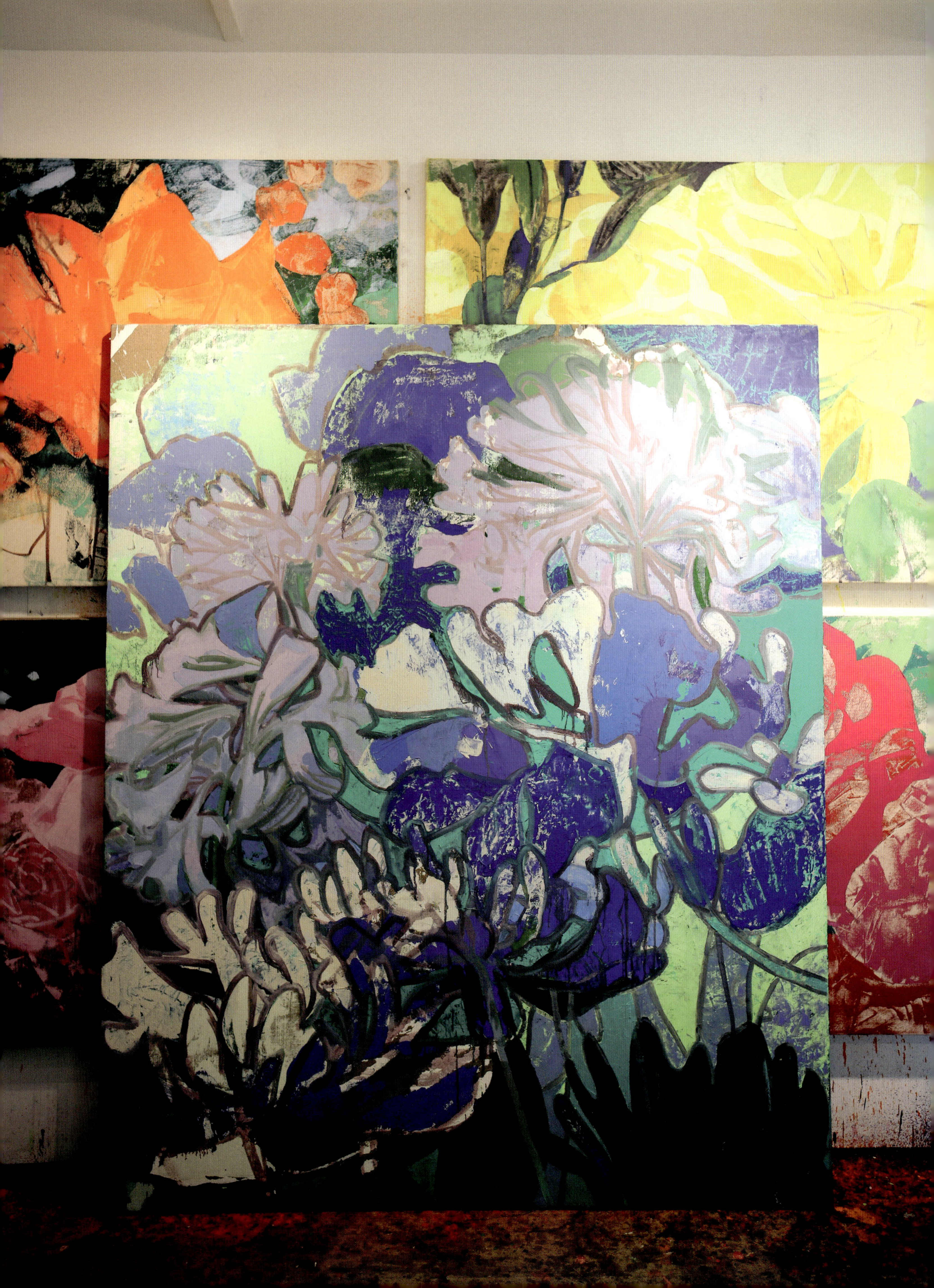

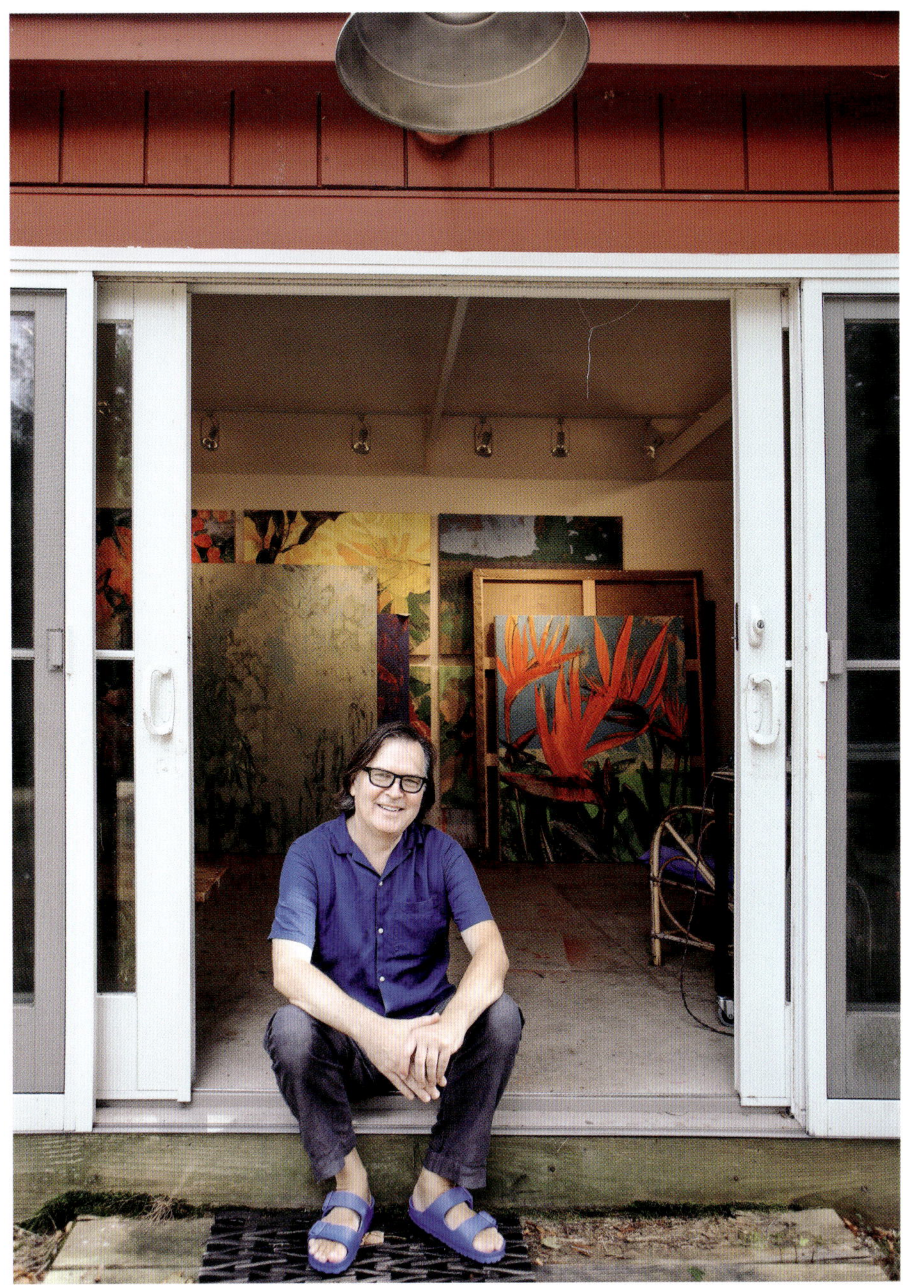

Moving between representation and abstraction, Dever finds meaning in the natural world, including its cycles of decay and the possibility of regeneration. "In 2016, I planted a garden and found myself taking cues from flowers as they blossomed, their color entering my paintings. I don't paint nature; I paint my experience of it." Dever tracks the plants' progress, uncovering patterns and rhythms throughout the year. "My work embraces a history of shared growth between the artist, his garden, and painting. I also pay homage to my hometown, recalling bird-of-paradise flowers thriving on urban traffic islands or agapanthus and calla lilies growing along driveways. The subtropical climate of Los Angeles contrasts with the colder, wetter climate of eastern Long Island."

ABOVE Dever's Water Mill studio is an oasis of floral inspiration, both inside on the canvases and outside in his gardens.

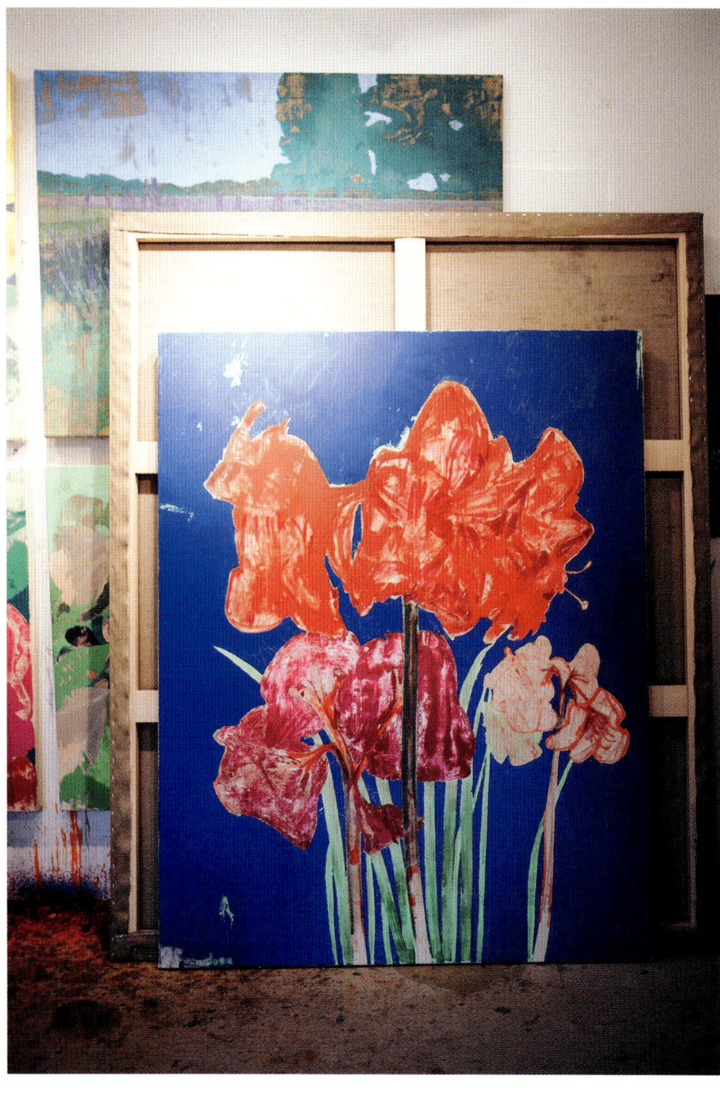

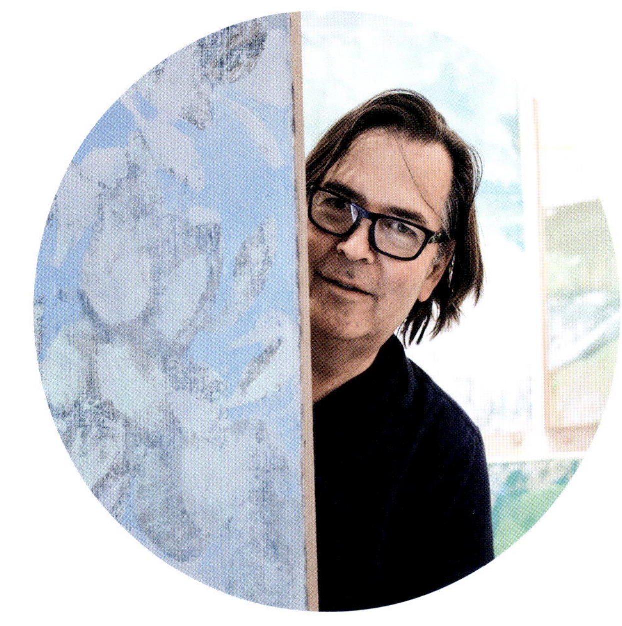

THIS PAGE AND OPPOSITE

Flowers are a main theme of Dever's work, but not just when they are in bloom. He tracks his own flowers' growth, decay, and regeneration.

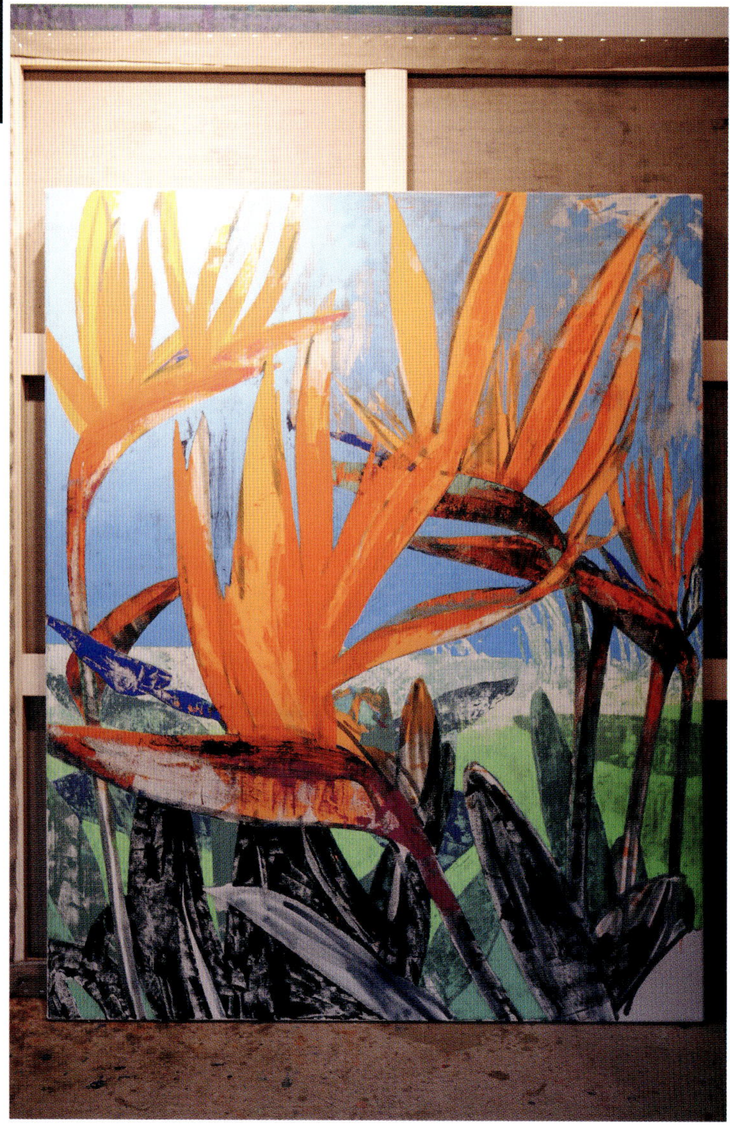

"Inspiration seems to arrive when I'm ready. It comes out of curiosity or a persistent thought—something I'd like to see or try in a painting. I prefer oil paint, emulsified wax, turpentine. These are largely organic materials and take time to dry. The pause between layers and range of consistencies suits me, and the results are satisfying, lustrous, and luminous. I usually work on several paintings at a time, so the studio is always in perpetual motion. I have a good idea each day of what I'd like to do or try. Of course, results are often unexpected, begging new questions, but that is part of the excitement of the new."

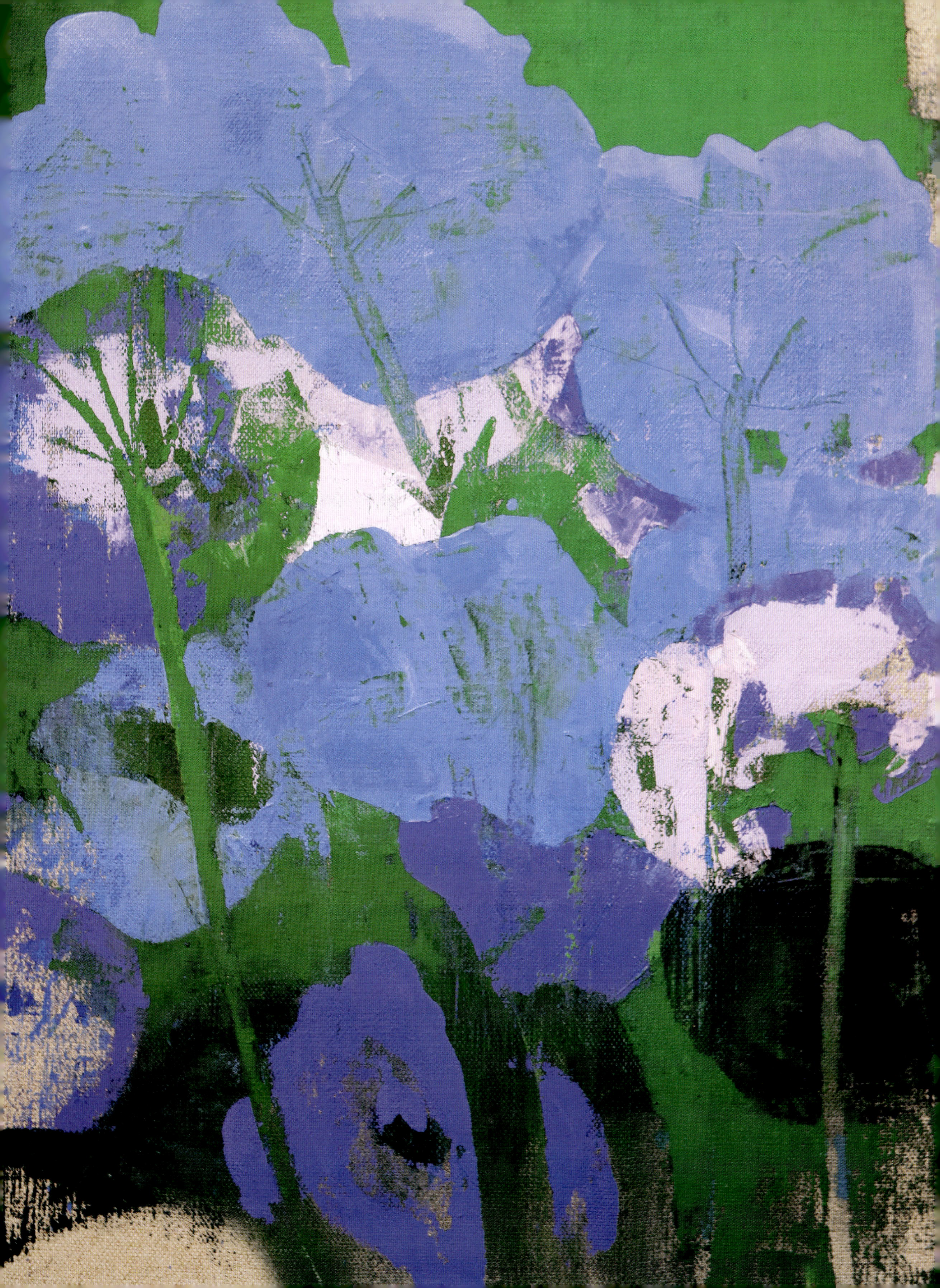

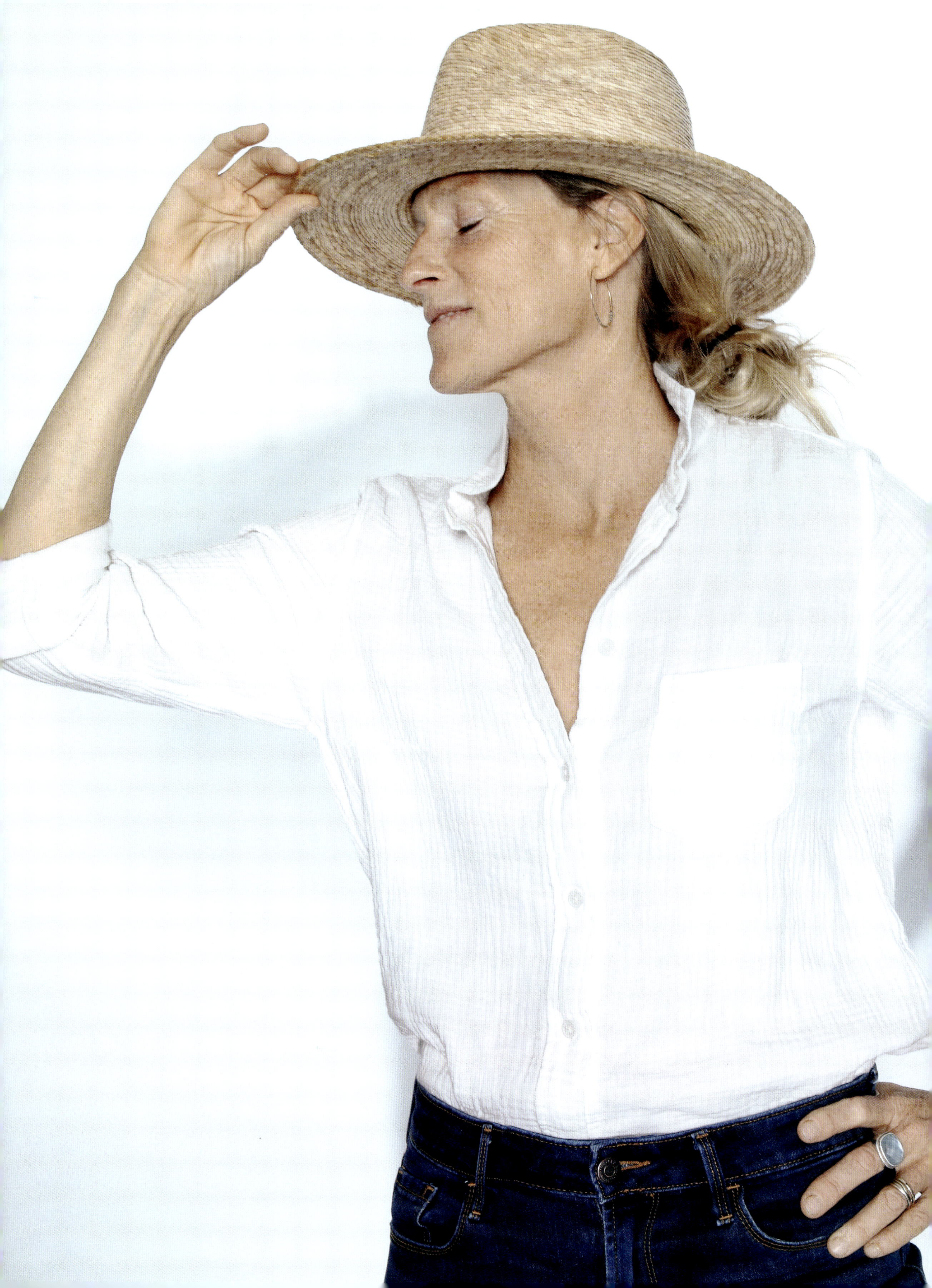

Making art is the greatest form of escapism. For me it's a portal into a different world, where I can envision a better place. Whether I'm working on an abstract landscape, the details of an intricate leaf, or a fantastical tree of life, I get to be in that place for as long as I'm painting.

IDOLINE DUKE

"I grew up out here as a summer kid, spending entire, idyllic days by the ocean, biking to Main Beach for saltwater taffy and painting rocks and shells on rainy days. I come from a family of artists, so any creative pursuit was always encouraged. I studied art history and art in college and went on to study landscape design in London, with the idea of starting my own garden-design company in East Hampton. After ten years running the business, the stress and ticks finally got to me, so a move to Vermont and a turn back to visual art seemed the obvious next step." In 2018, she and her family returned and settled in Springs.

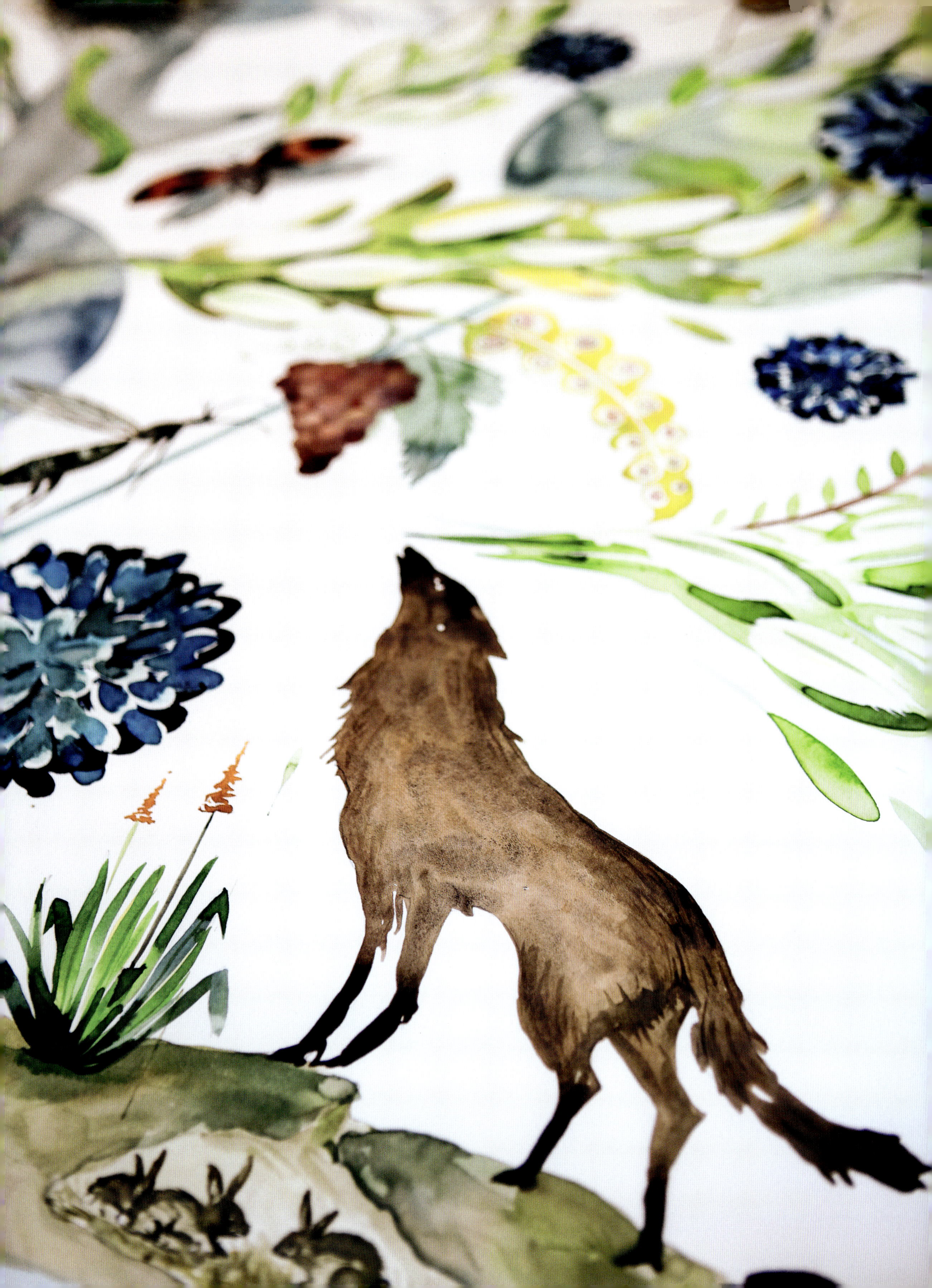

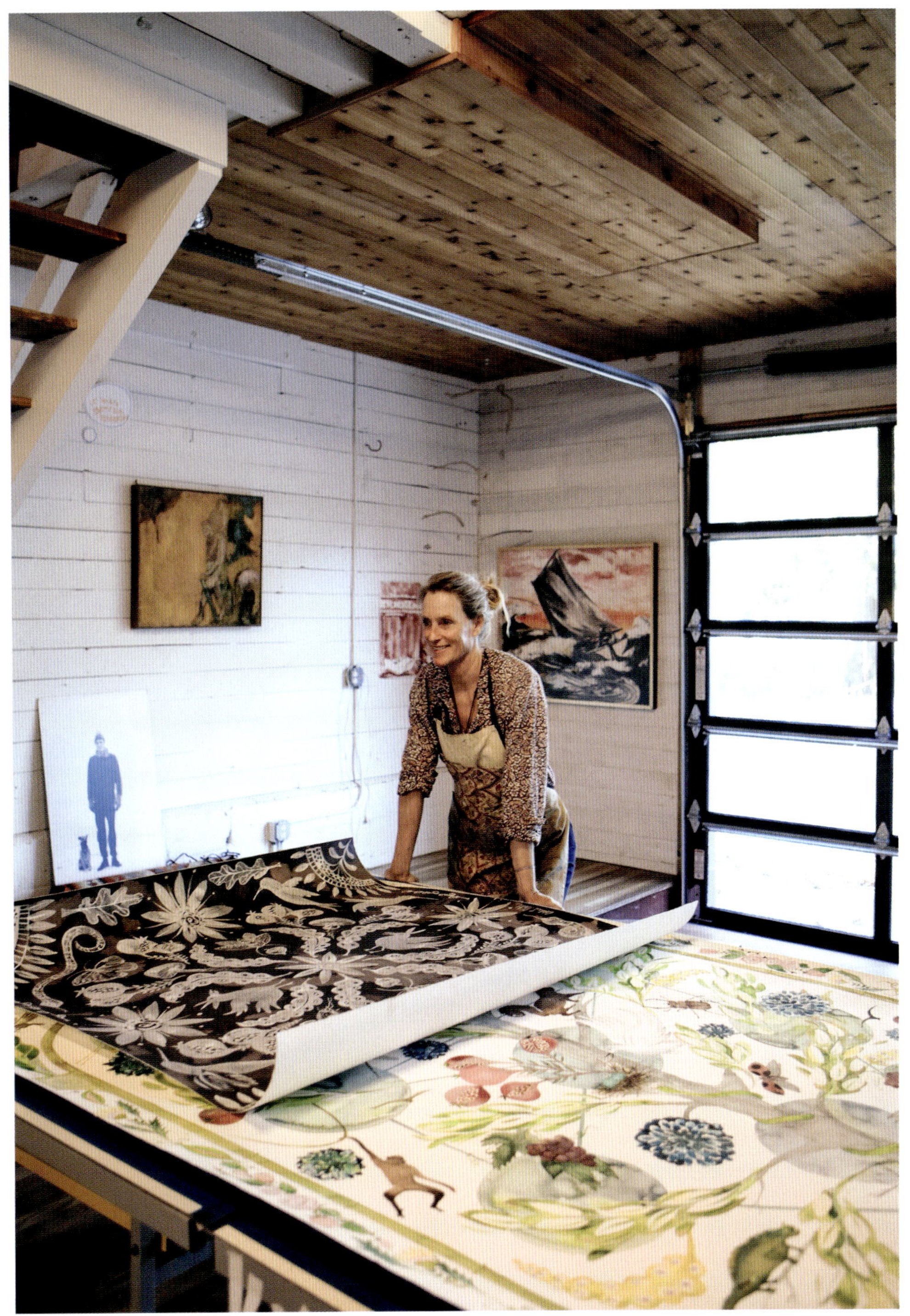

"The art community here feels incredibly vibrant and supportive. I'm so lucky that I've fallen in with this eclectic, curious, ambitious, talented, kooky bunch that brings so much energy and creative spirit to my life. My studio faces Accabonac Harbor, which has been an inspiration for so many artists before me." Duke often paints large-scale watercolors, which require her to work on a horizontal surface. She lays oversize paper on a Ping-Pong table. "Getting it to lie flat is like wrestling an alligator."

ABOVE Duke works on a flat surface when she's painting her large, nature-inspired, fanciful watercolors.

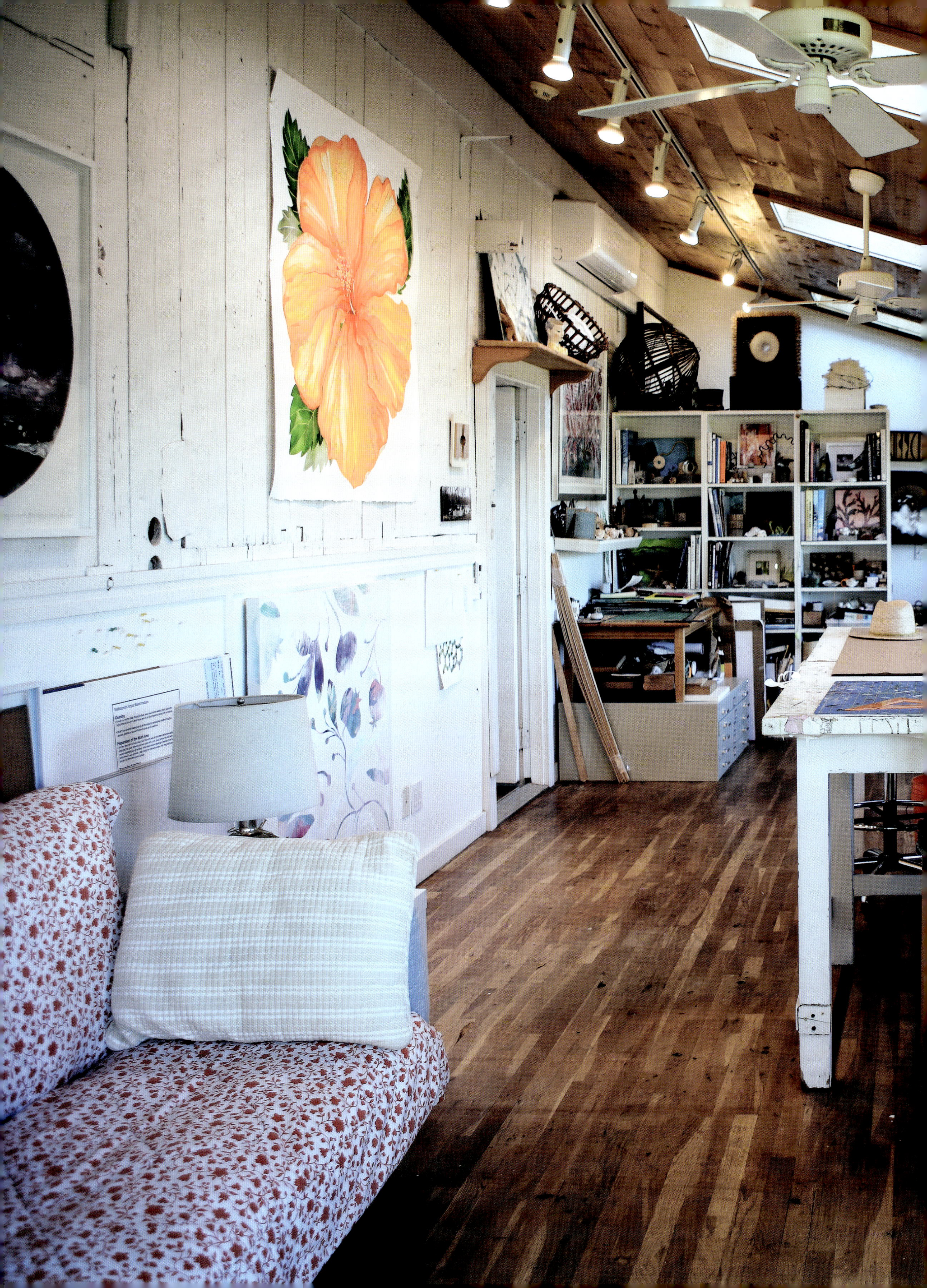

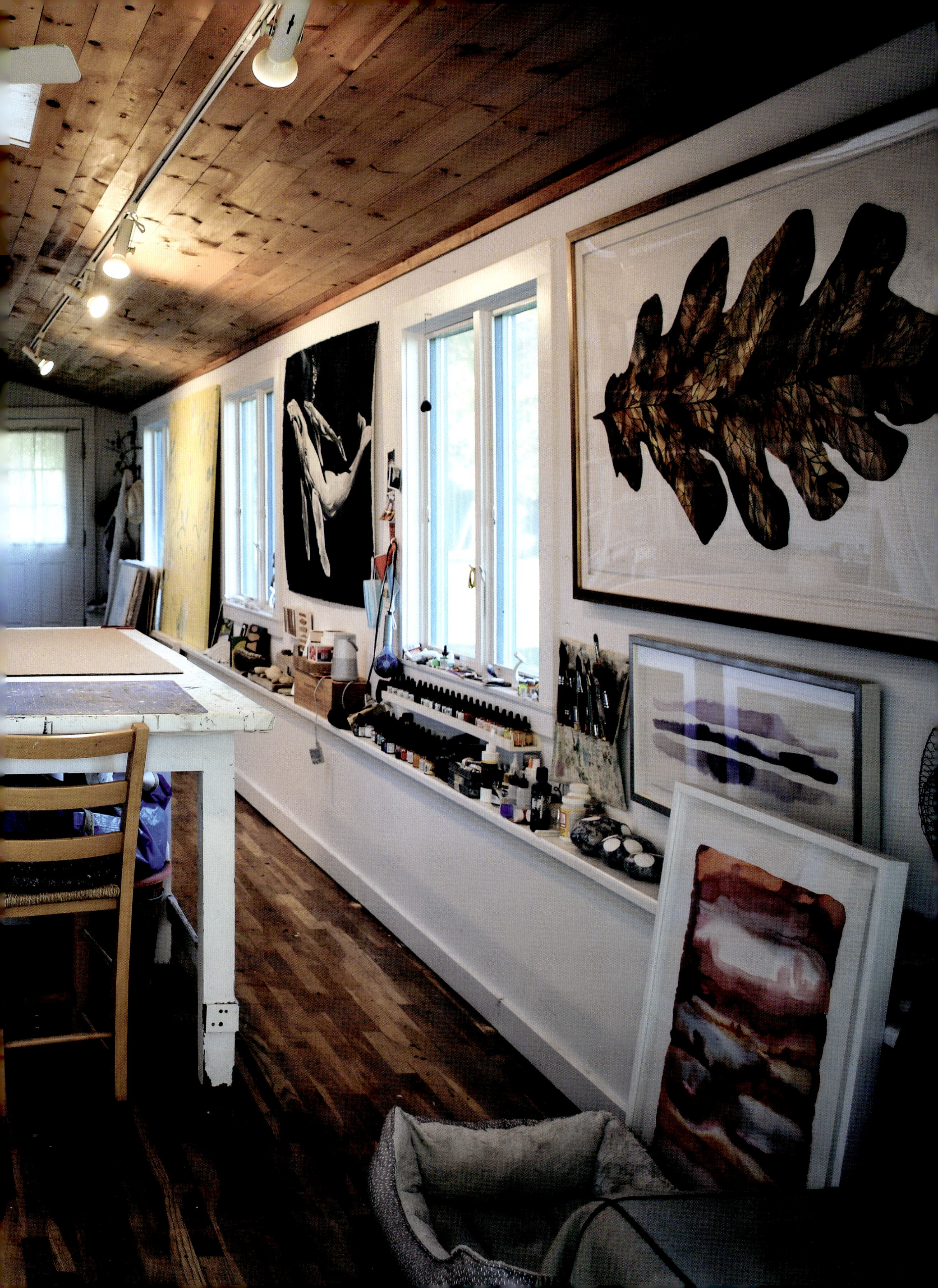

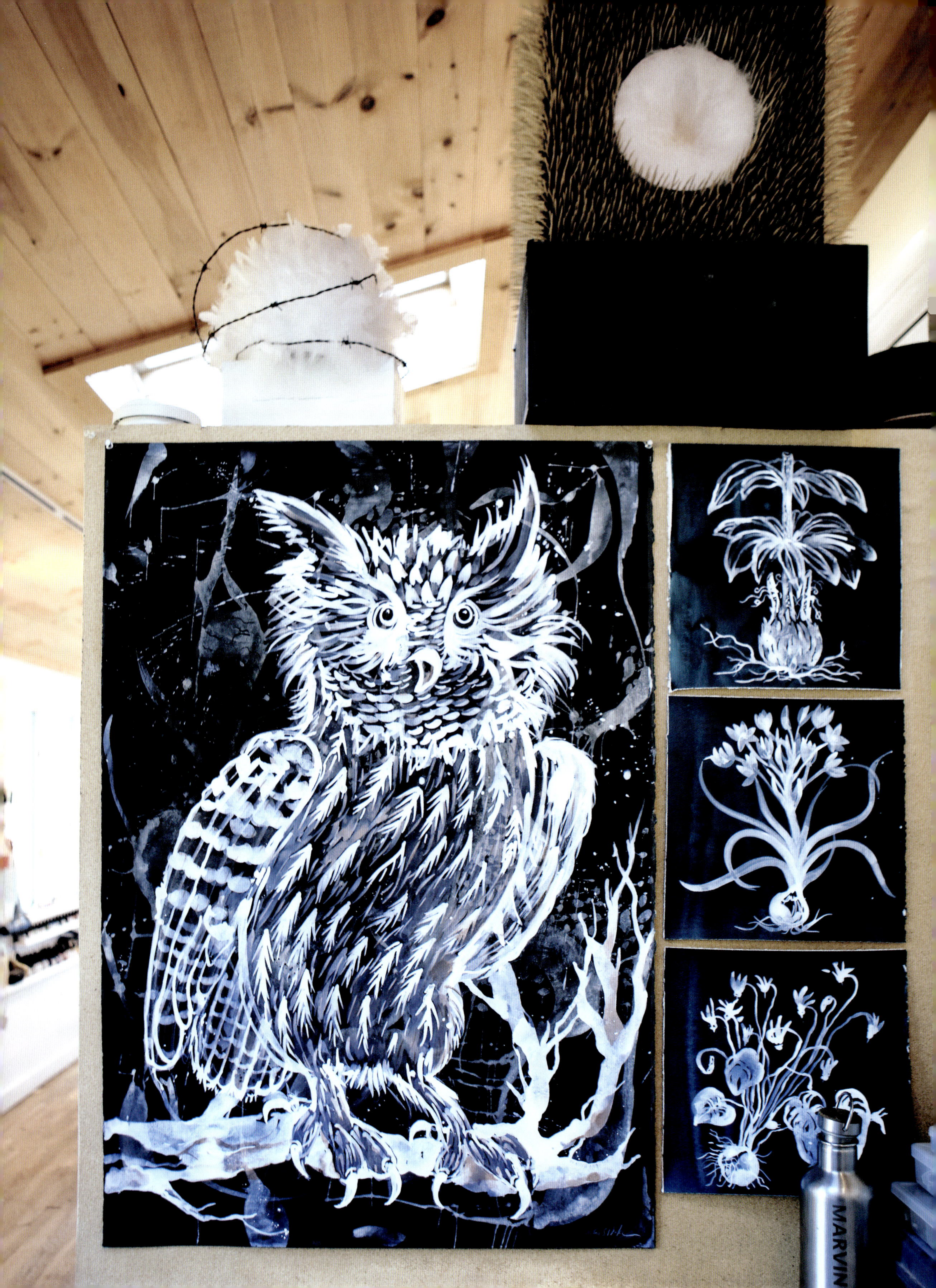
MARVIN

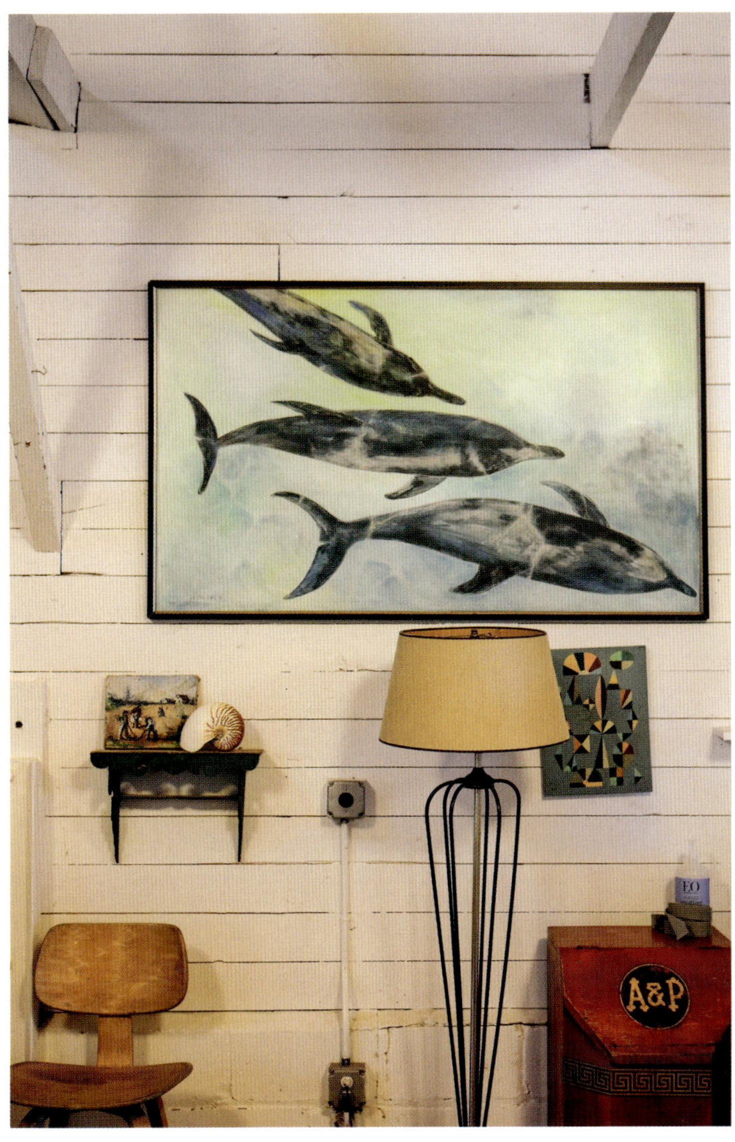

LEFT
Birds, animals, fish, and flora all show up in Duke's work and in her home, where she has an eclectic collection of found objects and art.

BELOW
The view from Duke's backyard—the marshlands of Accabonac Harbor in East Hampton—is endlessly inspiring for the artist, whose work is deeply rooted in nature.

Duke's main medium is watercolor. "It makes sense since I'm in love with the water and have always spent time in or near it—surfing, swimming, oystering, walking, or just staring. But I'm also forever playing with whatever natural or found material I get my hands on—charred driftwood, old shingles, rocks, clay, odd stuff from random dumpsters. I love creating objects that defy their common perceptions: wood painted to look like rock, feathers wrapped in barbed wire, limpet shells stacked and gracefully curled. This endless play keeps me connected to nature and is a great counterpoint to my two-dimensional watercolor and ink paintings."

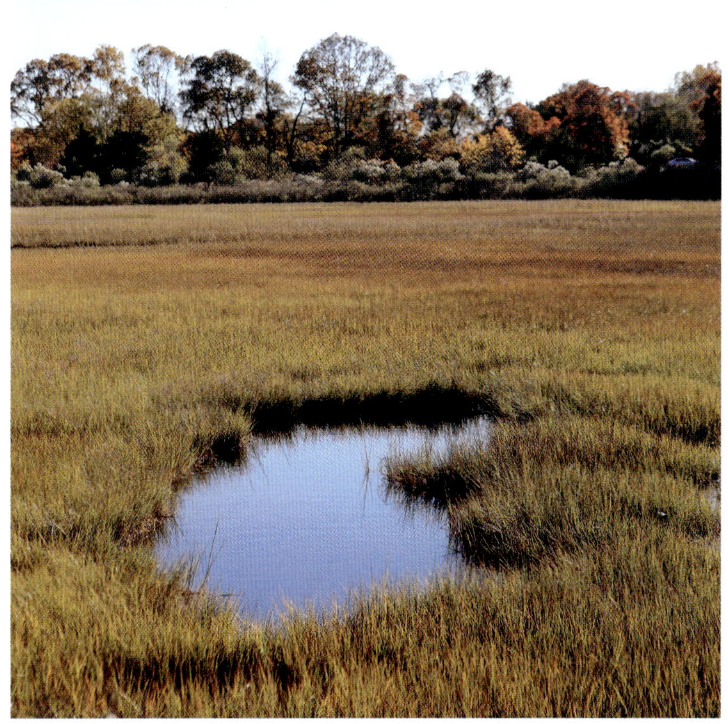

Since childhood, I have been fascinated with bubbles, and I often work with circular patterns as a means to create organic fields in the work.

EVA FAYE

Faye was born and grew up in Norway on the outskirts of Oslo, surrounded by nature. "My art education began in Paris, where I received classical training in a very academic environment, which gave me a solid foundation in drawing. I continued at Parsons School of Design in Paris, which led me to New York, where I studied at Parsons [BFA] and Hunter College [MFA]. My work changed during grad school, moving from figuration toward abstraction. It was a very natural transition, and my work has remained abstract ever since."

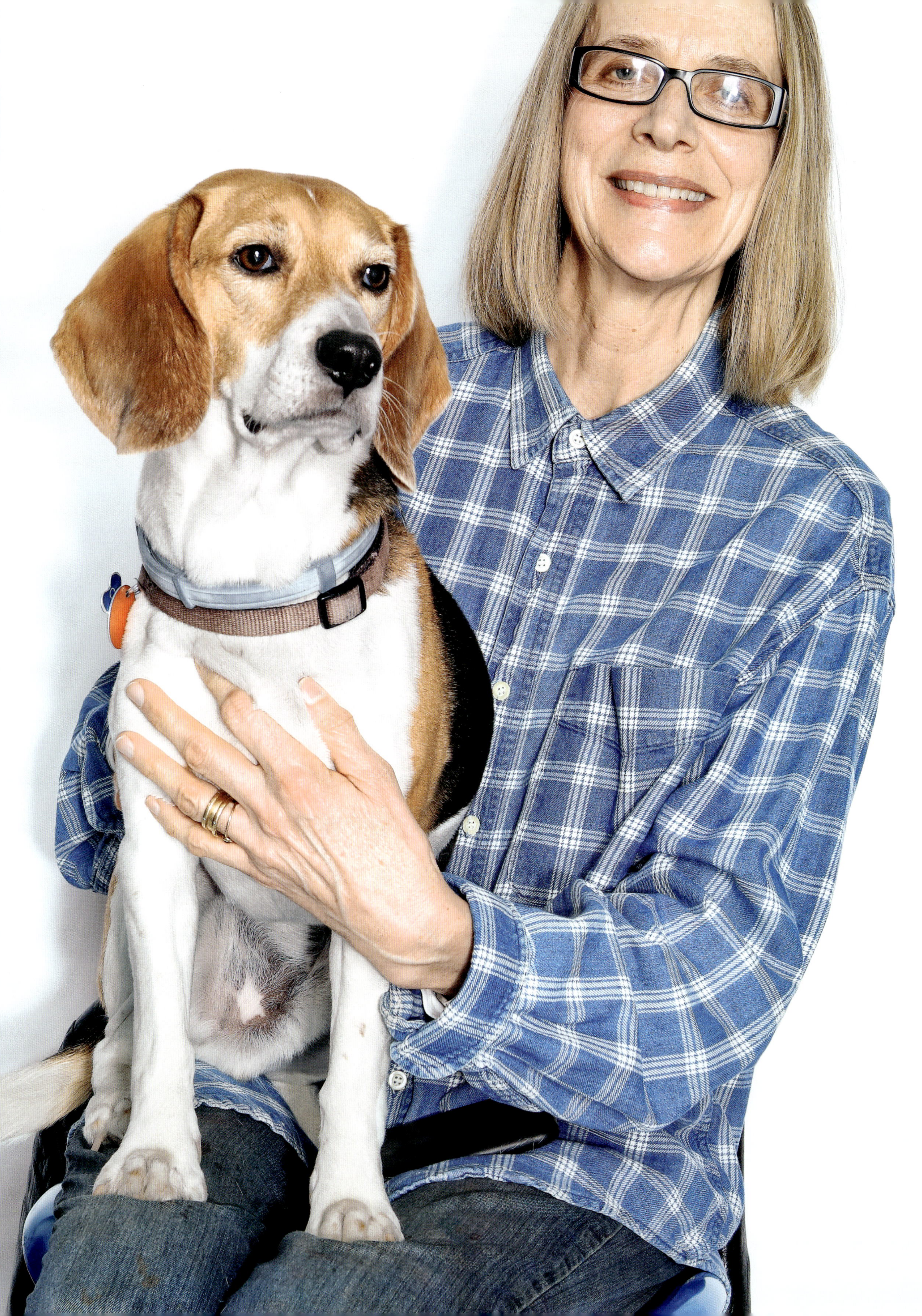

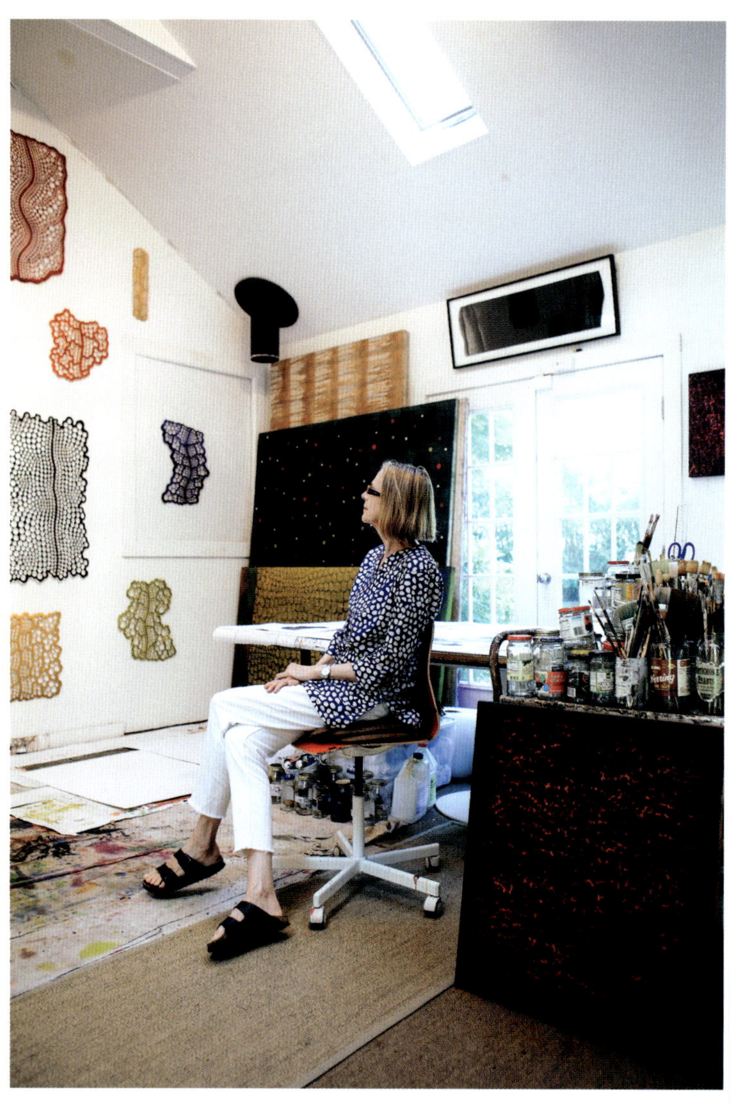

LEFT AND BELOW

The walls of Faye's Bridgehampton studio are filled with the artist's colorful abstract works, including her signature vellum cutouts, oil paintings on linen and wood, and watercolors, which she paints in thin, luminous layers.

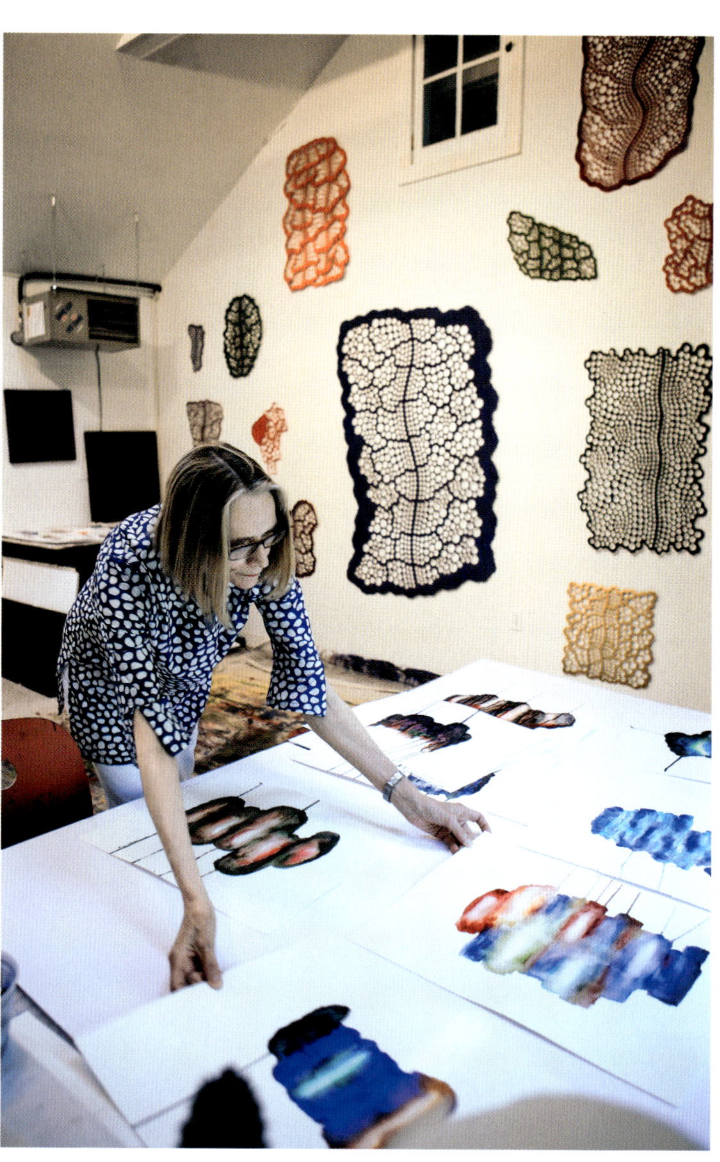

"I work both with oil on hand-cut vellum and with oil on linen and wood. I make organic patterns to create translucent, membrane-like works. Color and light are very important to me, as I paint in thin layers and experiment with adding different patterns within the paintings. By puncturing, cutting, painting, and layering, my goal is to achieve moments of visual time and experience."

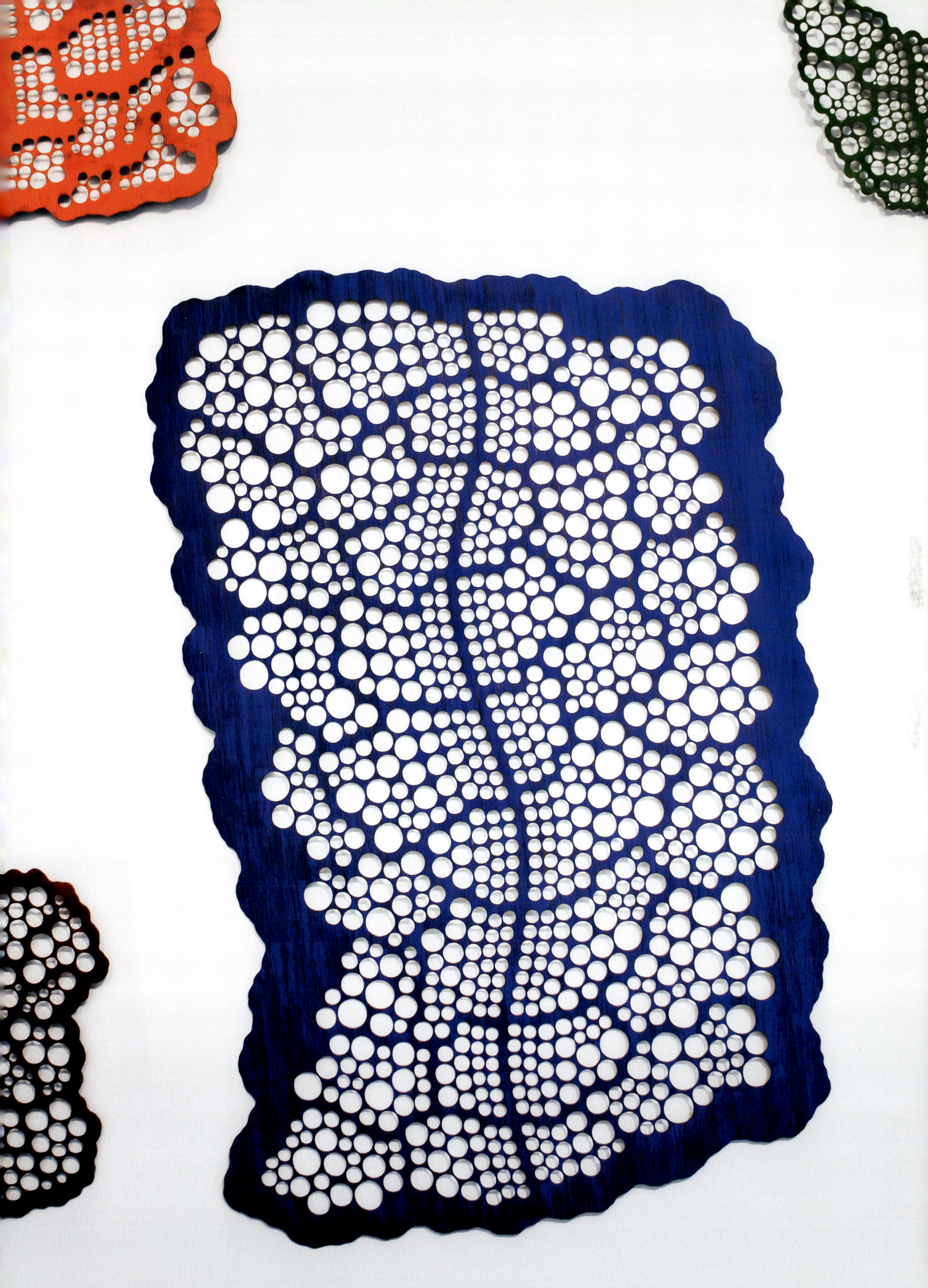

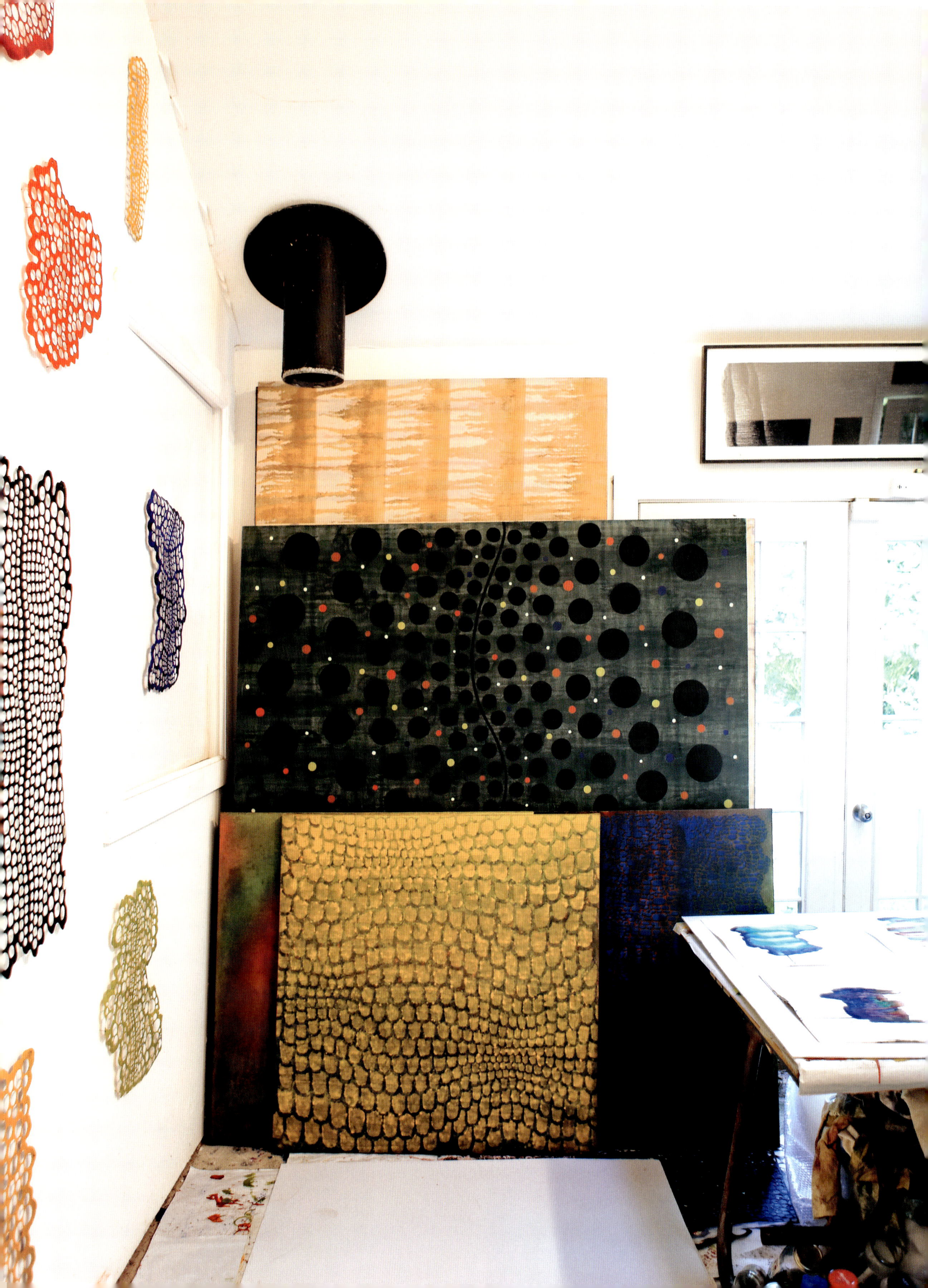

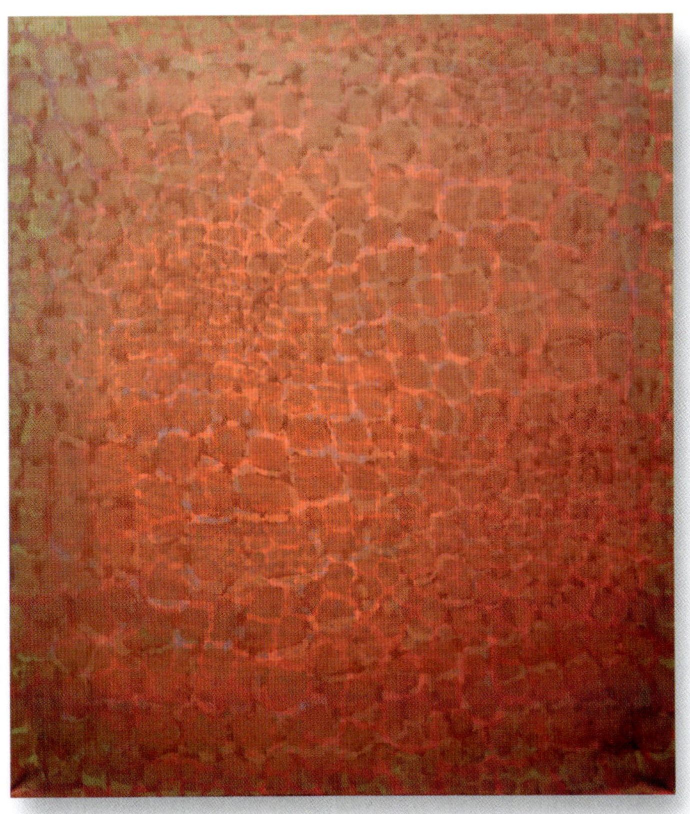

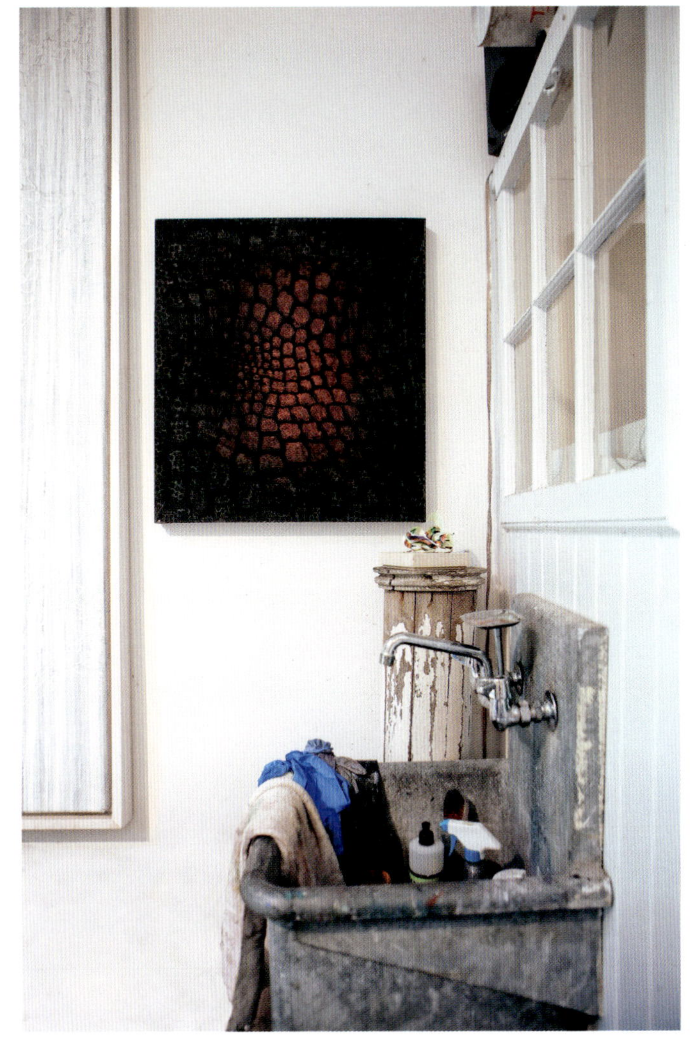

Faye has been coming out to the East End since the mid-1980s. "In 2019, my husband and I decided to make our country home our primary residence. I love having a studio right on the property and consider myself lucky to be able to live and work here. It is easy to understand why artists have been drawn to this place, surrounded by nature and the elements. My studio is my private, calm space where I can just be, uninterrupted."

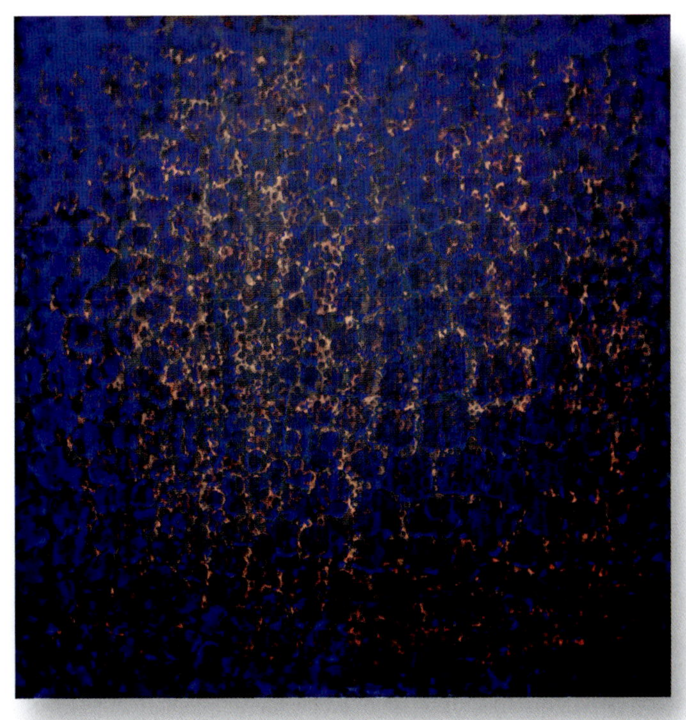

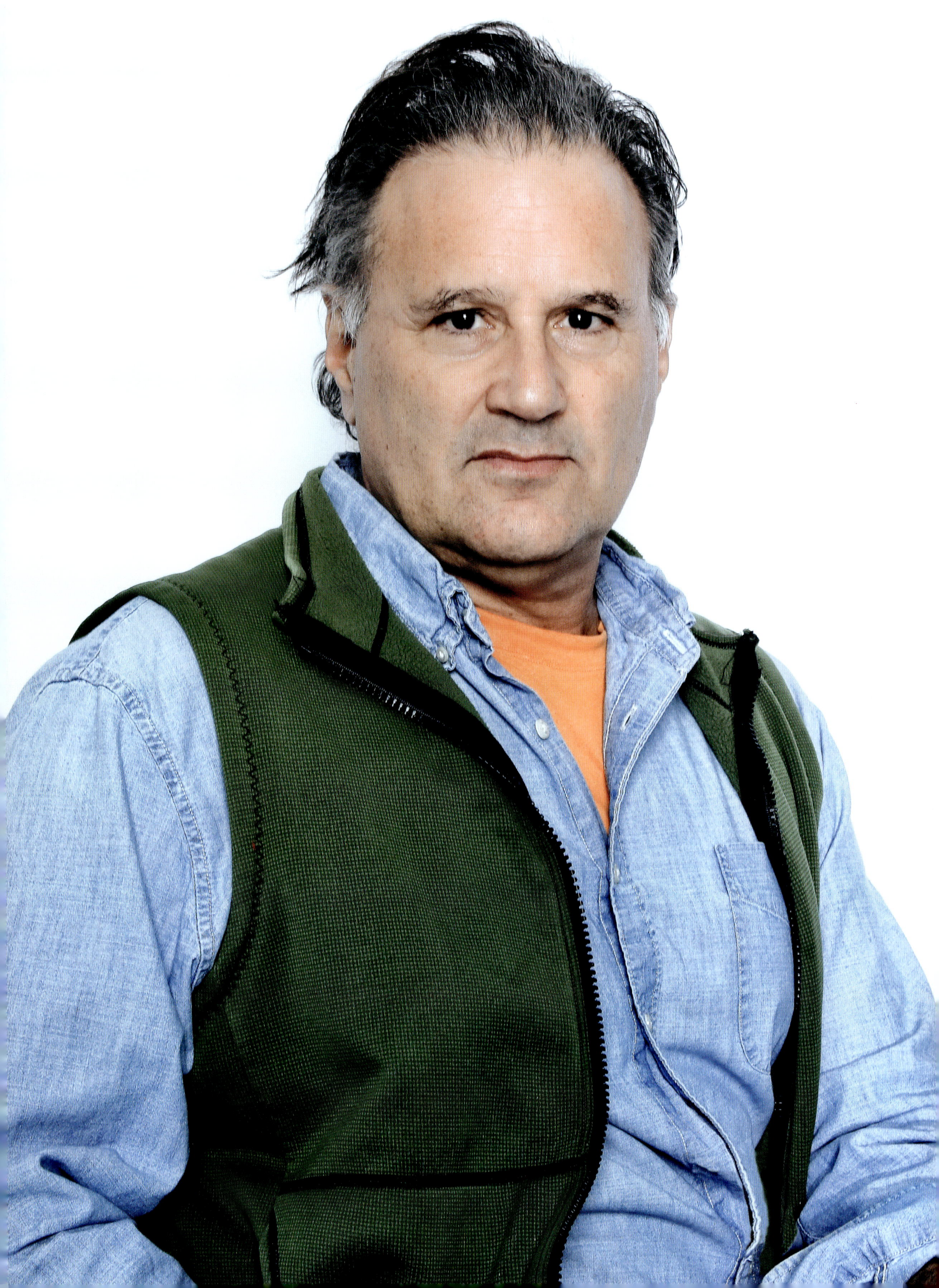

My paintings are usually—and peculiarly—painted in a kind of backwards fashion, where I paint over the painted ground I've put down. Then I like to remove material like a sculptor. So I add by subtracting.

CAIO FONSECA

Fonseca began his artistic studies in Barcelona, where he worked primarily in a figurative vein, painting and drawing landscapes and portraits. "Slowly, my work evolved to the abstraction I now practice. But it evolved *from* that early work, not *away* from it." Fonseca paints in many mediums. For his canvas works, he uses oil and acrylic; for paintings on paper, gouache "because of its great opacity." He finishes his artwork using a variety of techniques. "I often rub the surface with wax and powdered pigments. And I have a kit of tools I've collected from many different crafts—cooks, dentists, engravers, mechanics—that I use in the last stage of a work while the paint is still wet, scoring the surface to make connections and create the textures."

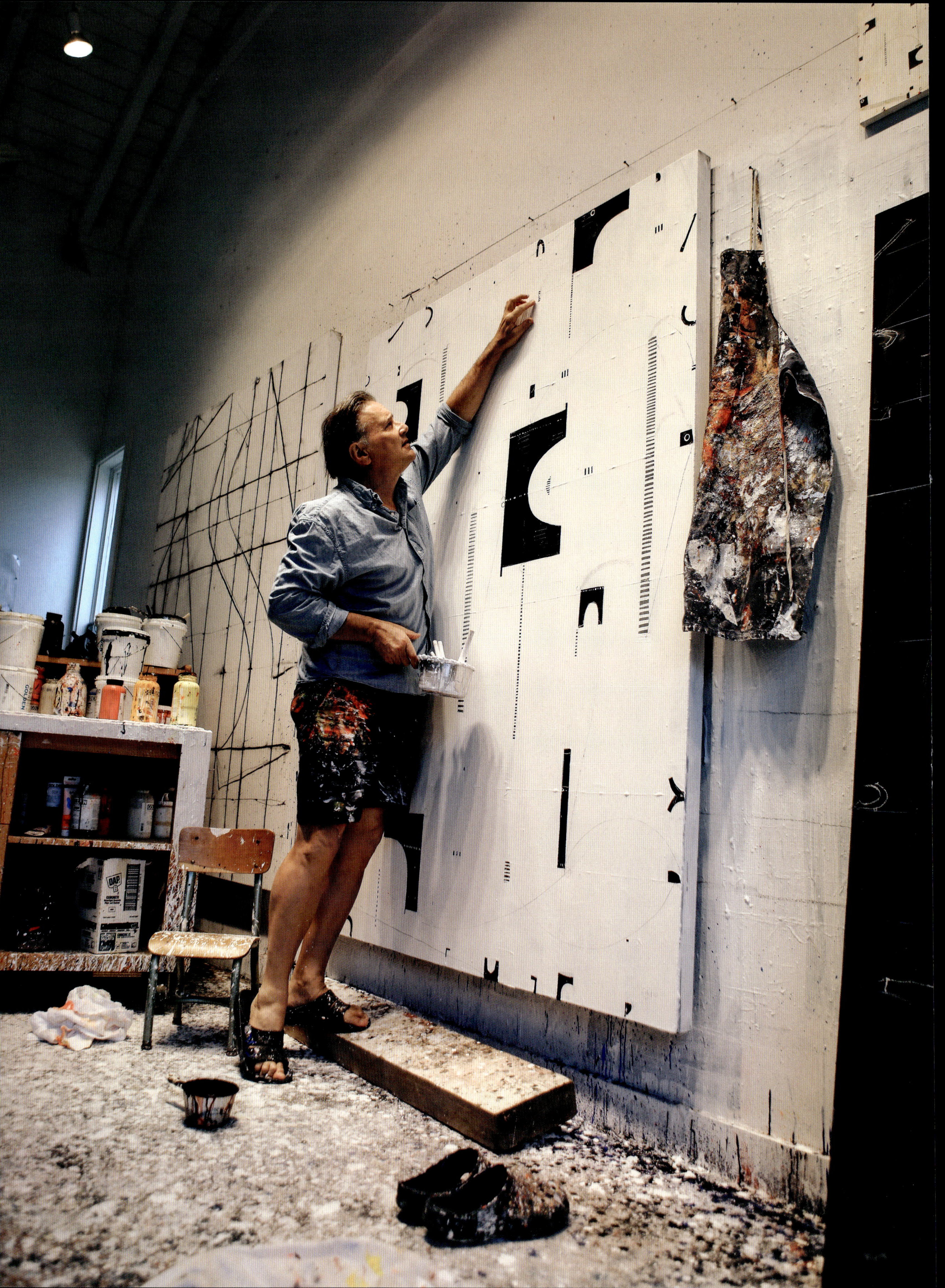
GOLDEN
DAP
CONCRETE

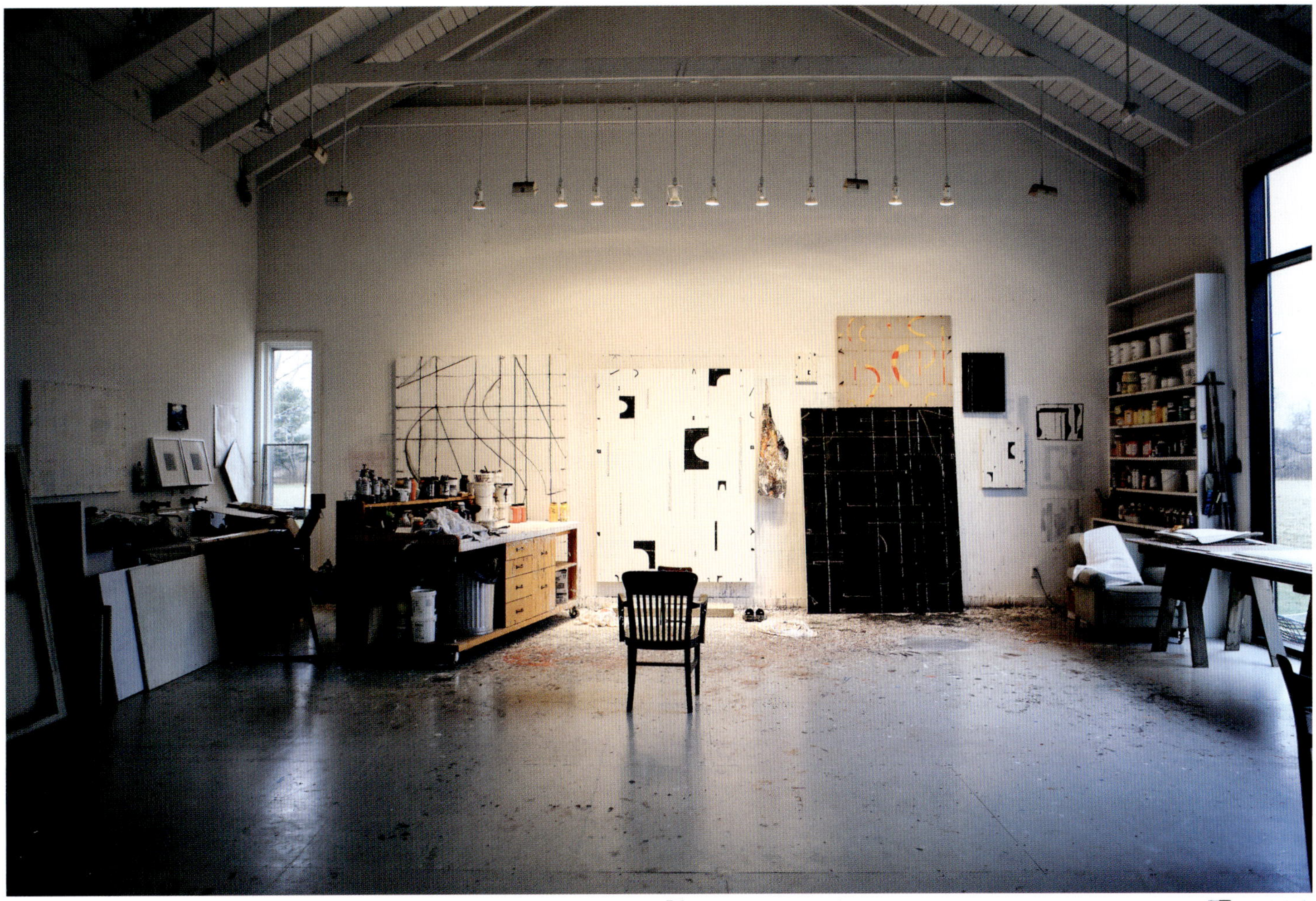

Fonseca's connection to the East End is lifelong and multigenerational. "My grandparents acquired the old Judge Seabury house on the Sag Harbor Turnpike in the 1940s. My siblings and I grew up coming here as a family. My father, the sculptor Gonzalo Fonseca, maintained a studio here. My parents were good friends with the Nivolas, the Steinbergs, and that whole group of artists, many of whom were living in Springs. I do feel part of the history of generations of artists."

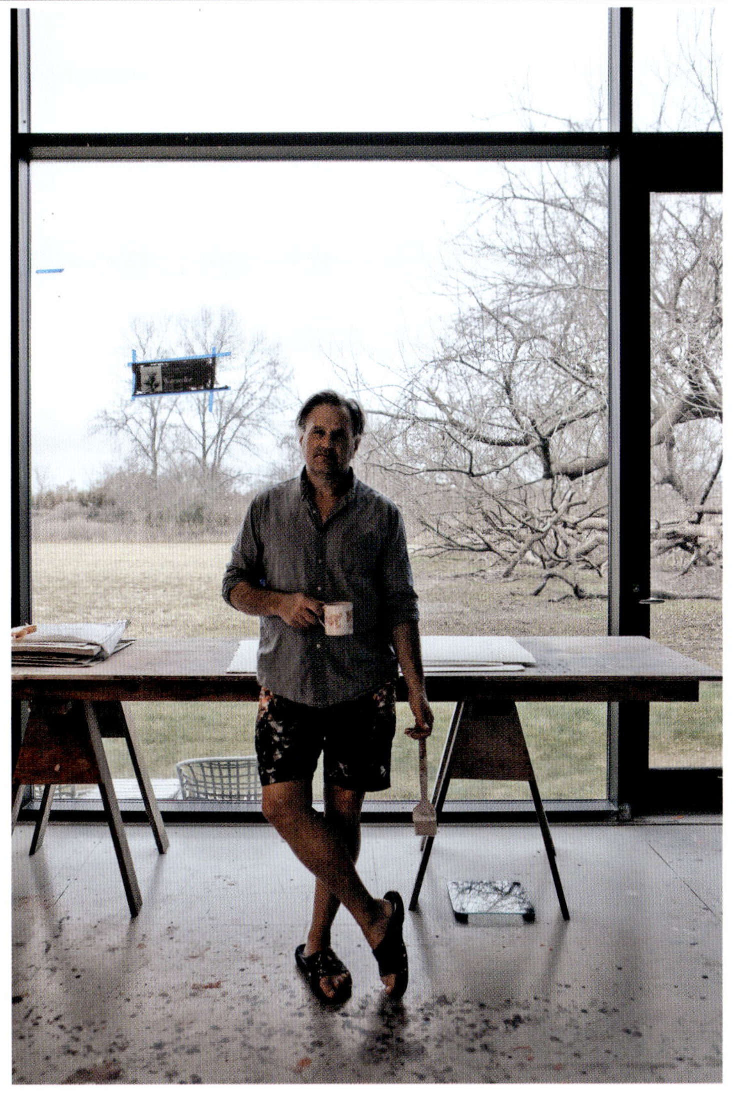

OPPOSITE AND THIS PAGE

Fonseca's lofty East Hampton studio overlooking an open field both feeds his creativity and allows him to work large-scale. For his paintings, which evolved from figurative to purely abstract, he uses a myriad of finishes—oil, wax, powders—and a variety of utensils, from brushes to engraving tools.

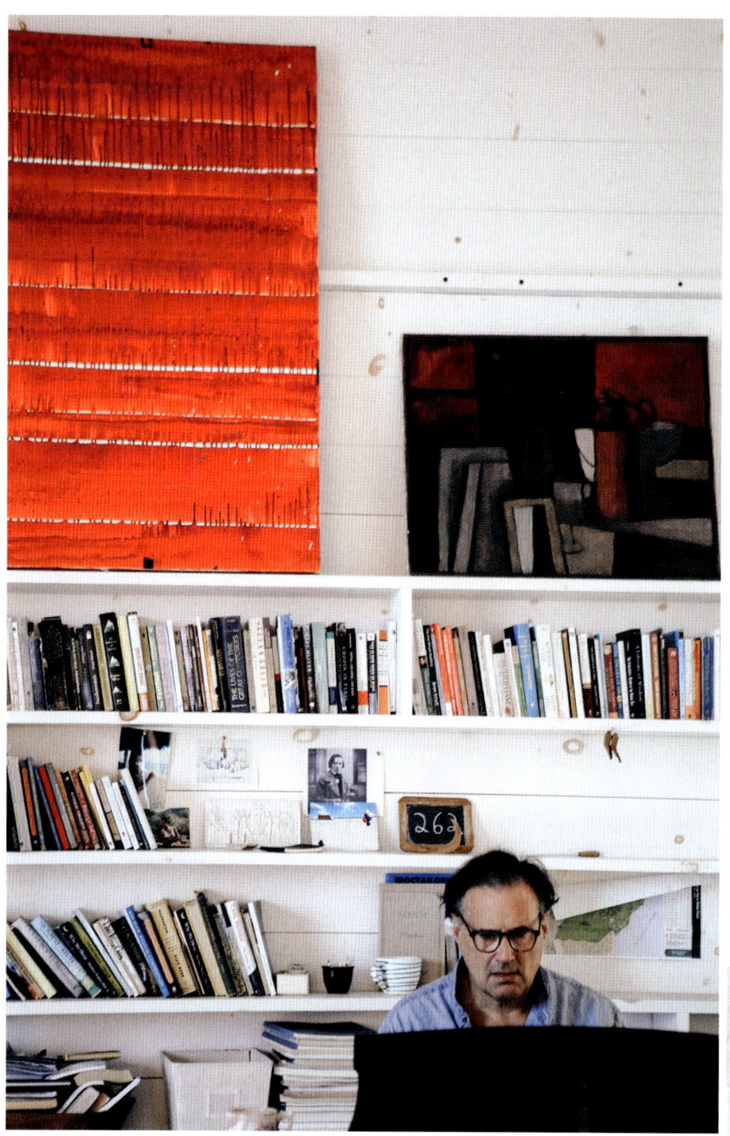

Fonseca's East Hampton studio is a large, shingled building set in open fields, an environment that inspires and informs his creativity. "As I imagine it is with most artists, there is no greater influence on my work than the quiet here, especially in the off-season. And that view! In my studio there is a fifteen-by-fifteen-foot window that looks to the north, and it's like an IMAX view of the fields, so even when I'm working, I get to witness nature around me. The horizontality of this landscape also seems to dovetail with my horizontal canvases."

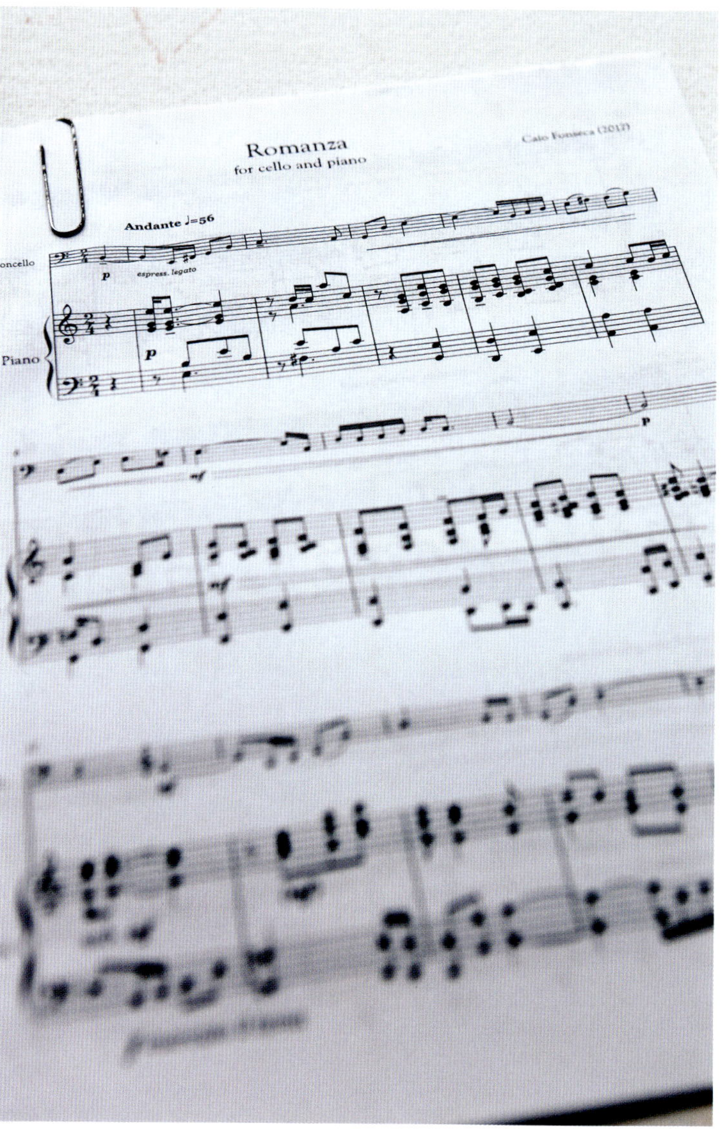

Music is another key part of his studio practice. "I have always played classical piano, and for the past twelve years I've been composing music as well. My piano is in my studio, so there is quite a bit of back and forth between my music and my art—as evidenced by a bit of paint on the keyboard."

ABOVE AND RIGHT

An accomplished pianist, Fonseca takes breaks from painting to play and compose. Visual echoes of musical scores sometimes appear in his canvases as rhythmic lines and shapes dancing on the surface.

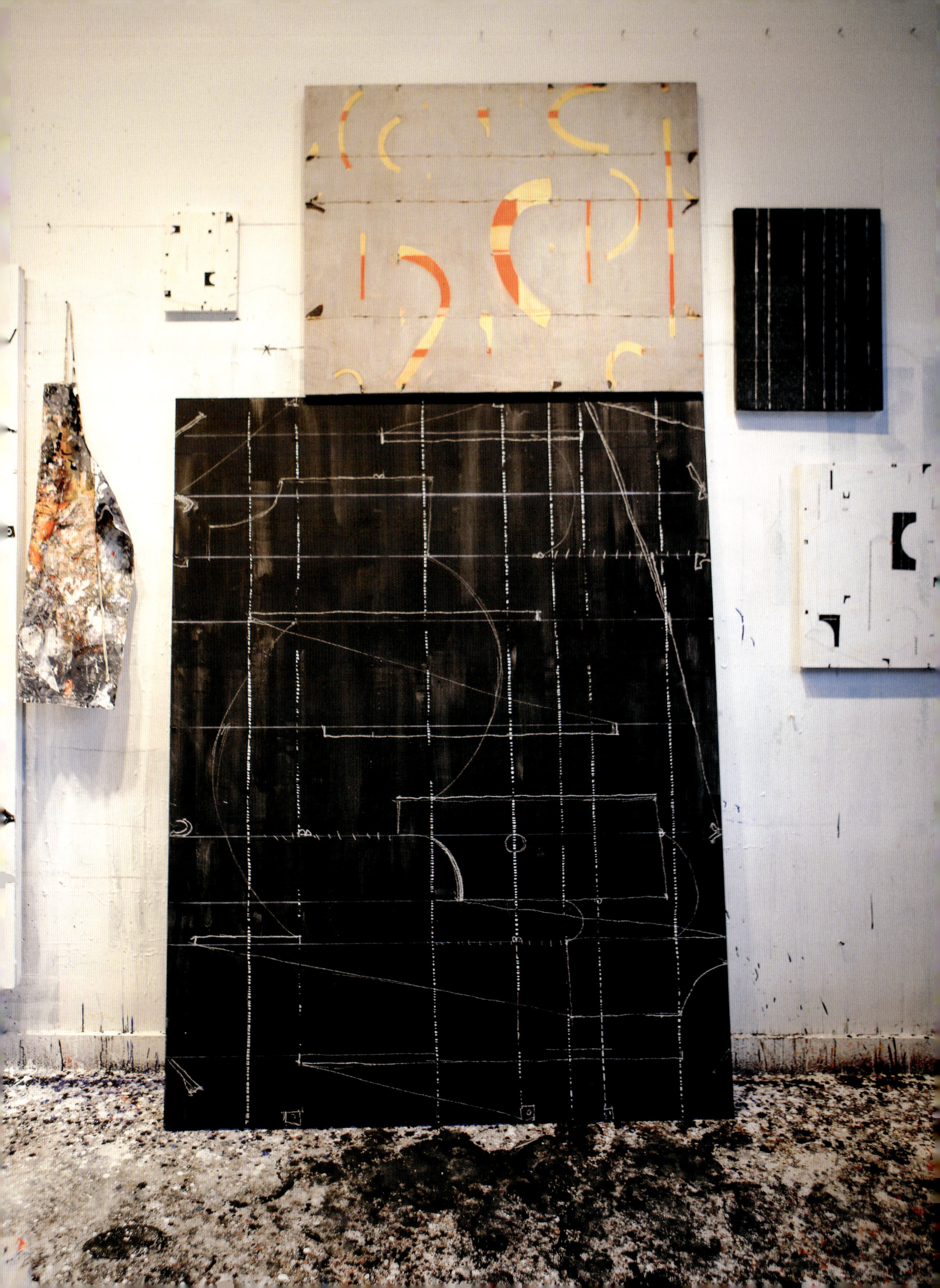

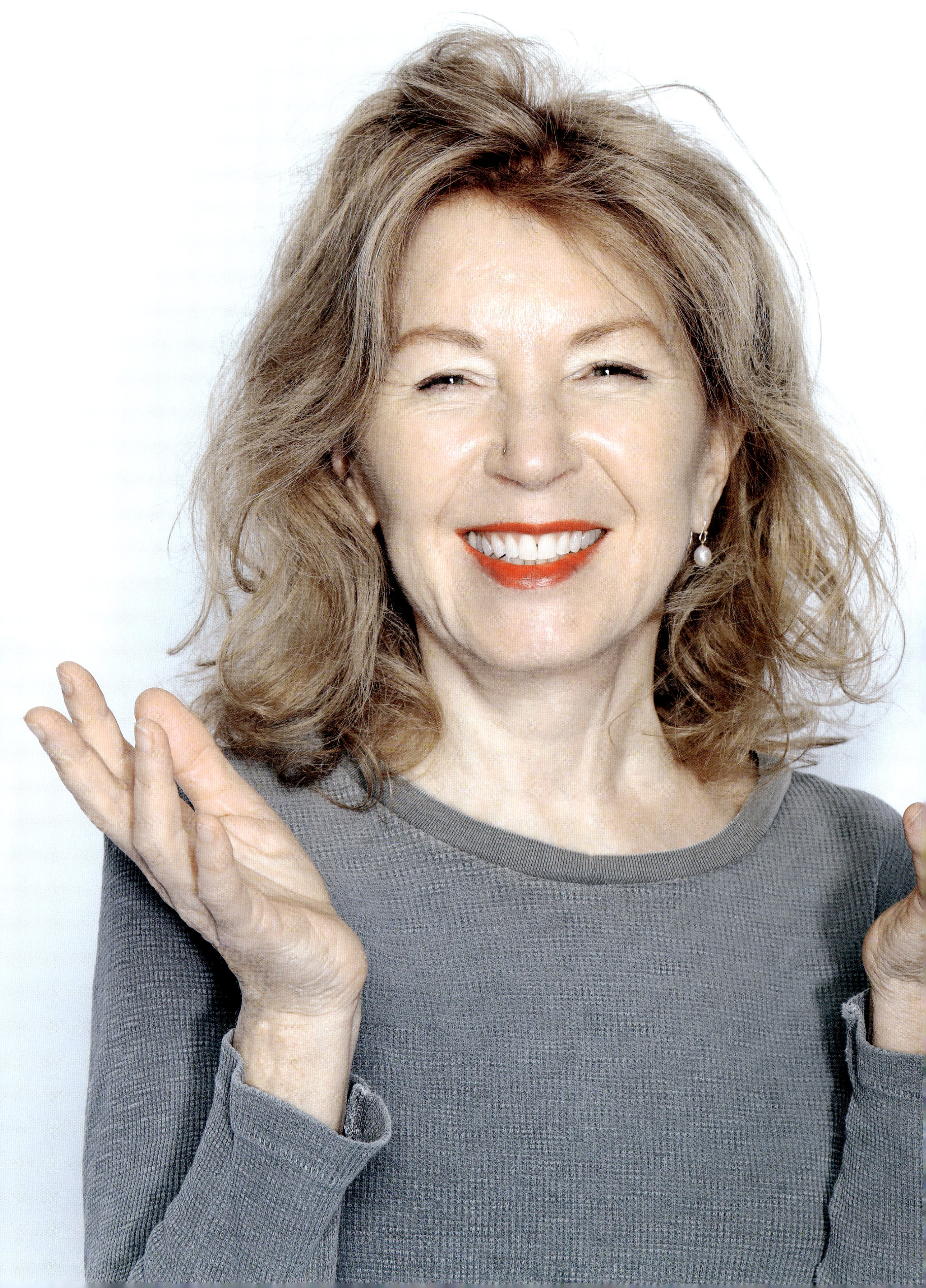

The best part of painting for me is toward the end, when it's a conversation and a dance and my eyes are on automatic, seeing what's right and what's wrong with it, going back and forth from my palette table to the surface of the painting. I can see it start to activate, become what it needs to be.

APRIL GORNICK

"We came out here in 1985 and found an affordable house in Sag Harbor that could accommodate two studios with a little renovation. It was an old farmhouse and we loved it. Then, in the late nineties, Eric wanted to build a house and found property in North Haven. At first, I was reluctant because I'd started gardening and had literally packed our little property with flowering perennials and herbs. But I loved the idea of more space. Once we built our dream house, we realized that we didn't want to go back to the city, period. I absolutely love living at the edge of somewhere—the bays, the inlets, the ocean—although I find the ocean inscrutable and frightening."

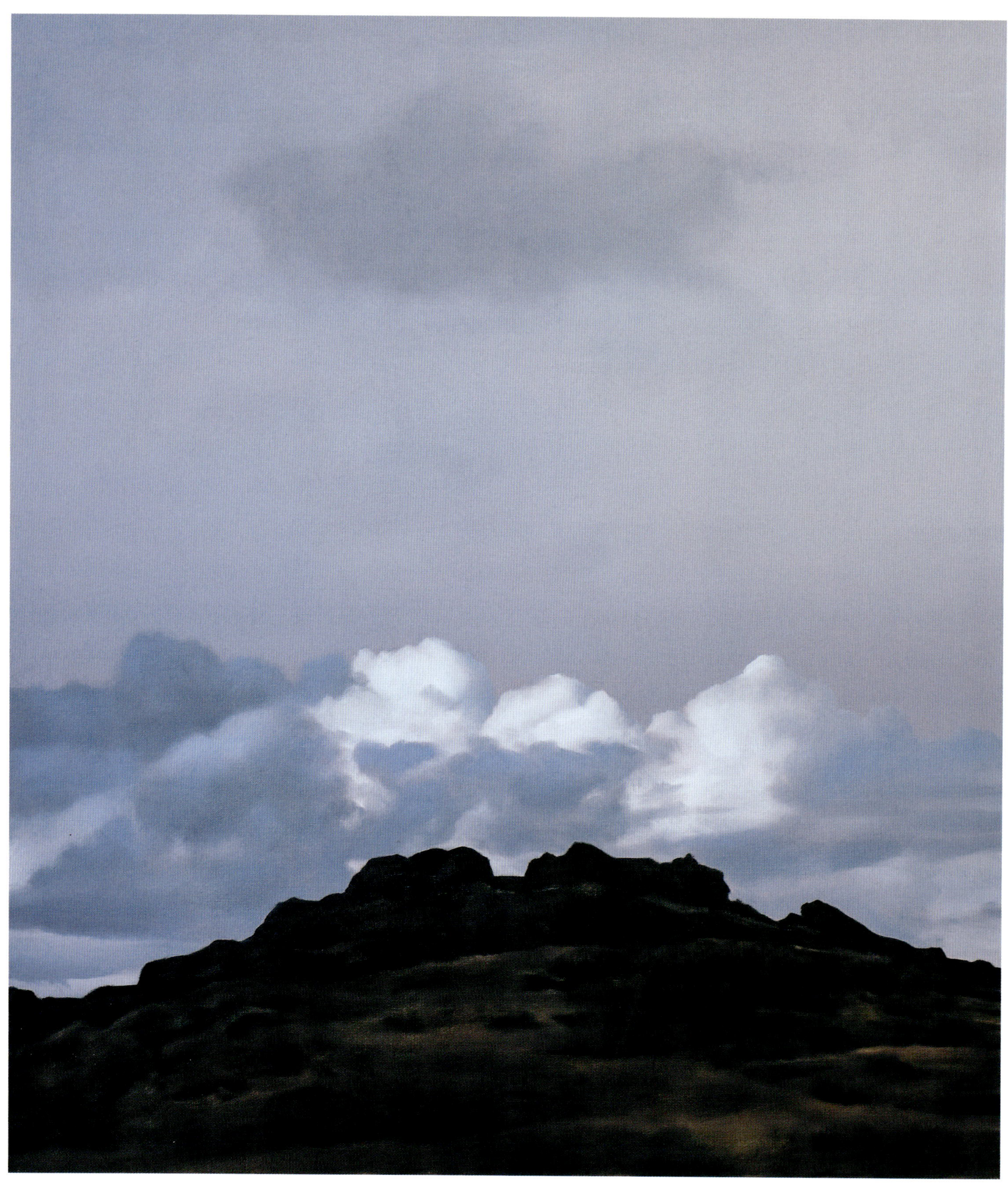

OPPOSITE Gornik ponders which colors on her giant rolling palette to work with. To create her light-filled landscapes, she uses oils and brushes of different sizes to build up layers on top of an underpainting.

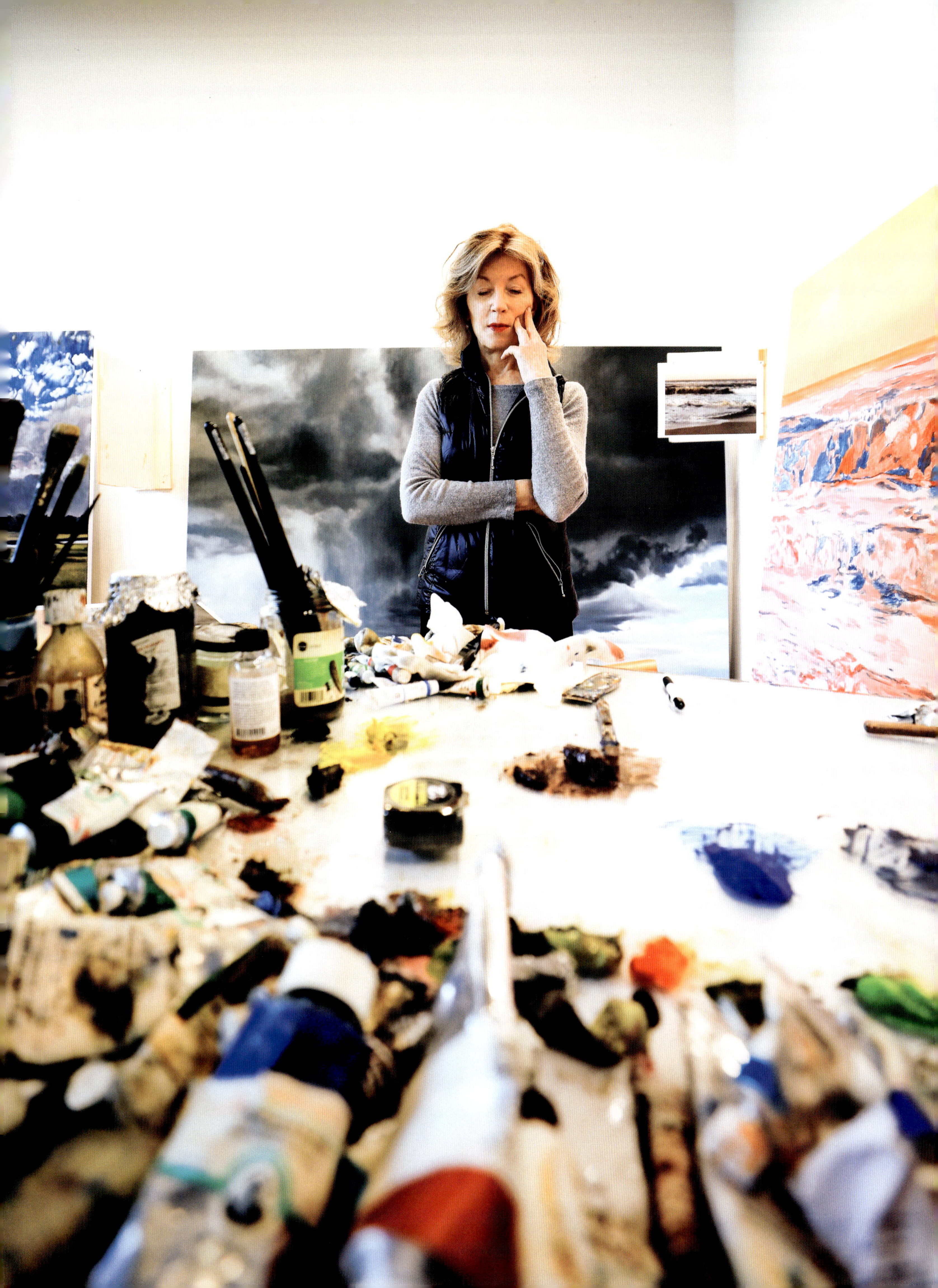

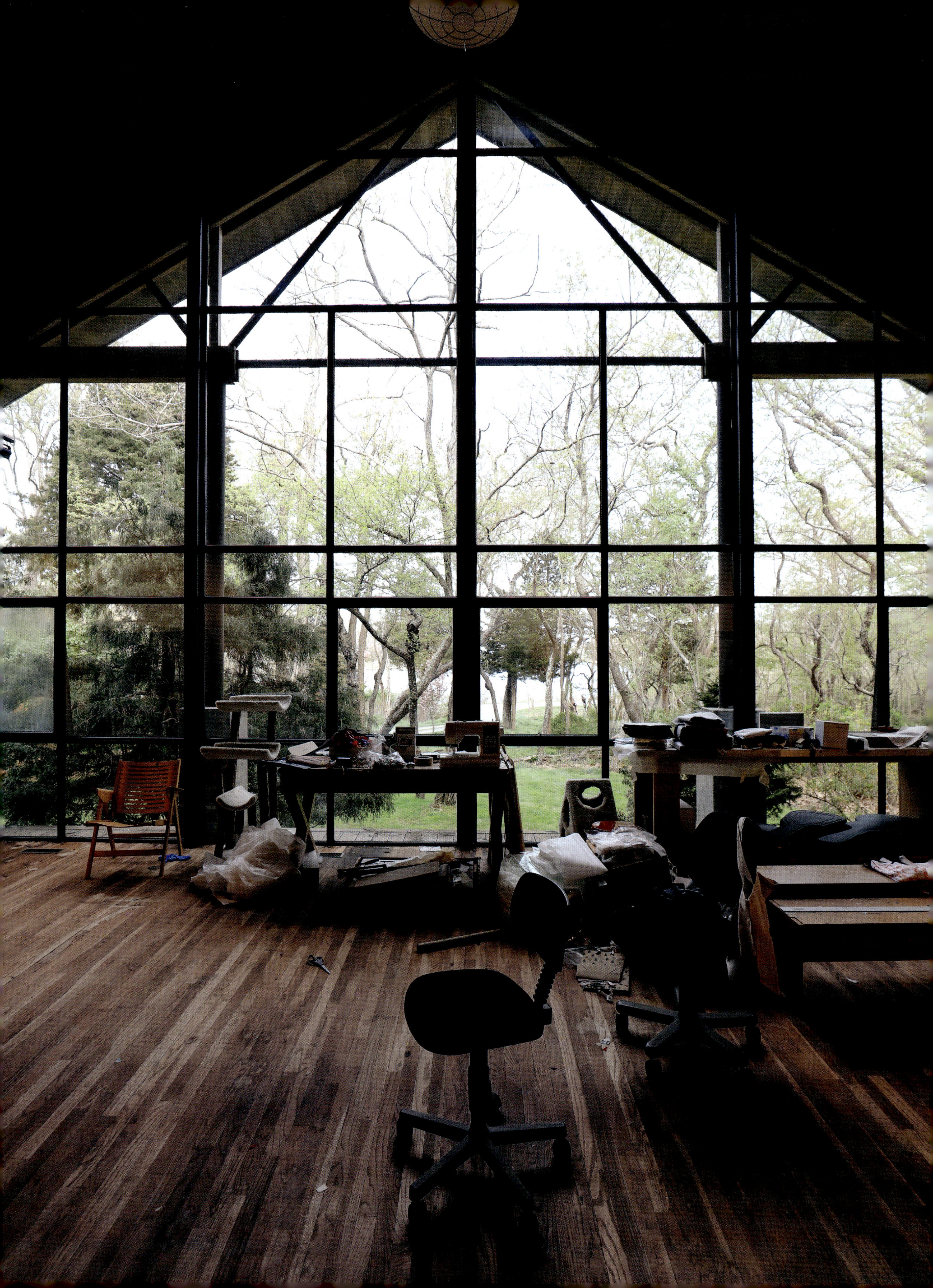

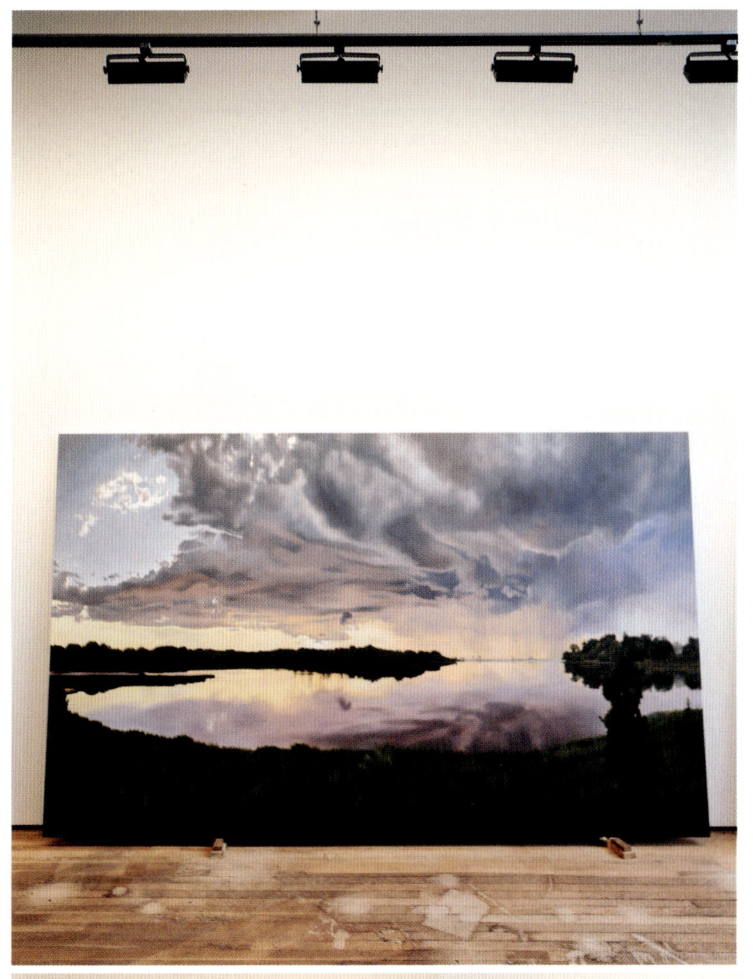

April's luminous landscapes are inspired by both the imagined and the real. Though her work is emotional and interiorized, there are recognizable places in the paintings. "I work from photos all the time, which I sometimes collage together—a piece of land from the North Fork and a sky from Rome. I used to think I had to make up everything or it wouldn't count, wouldn't really be creative. Now my computer is my favorite sketch tool." In all her paintings, Gornik incorporates light. "As a dealer once said, light is the protagonist in my work. And there are so many spots of bliss out here that I find transporting, like the marshes near the sea. Any kind of double-reflective situation like that feels transcendent to me. And I love to paint the ocean and its amazing fractal chaos. I love still and I love chaotic."

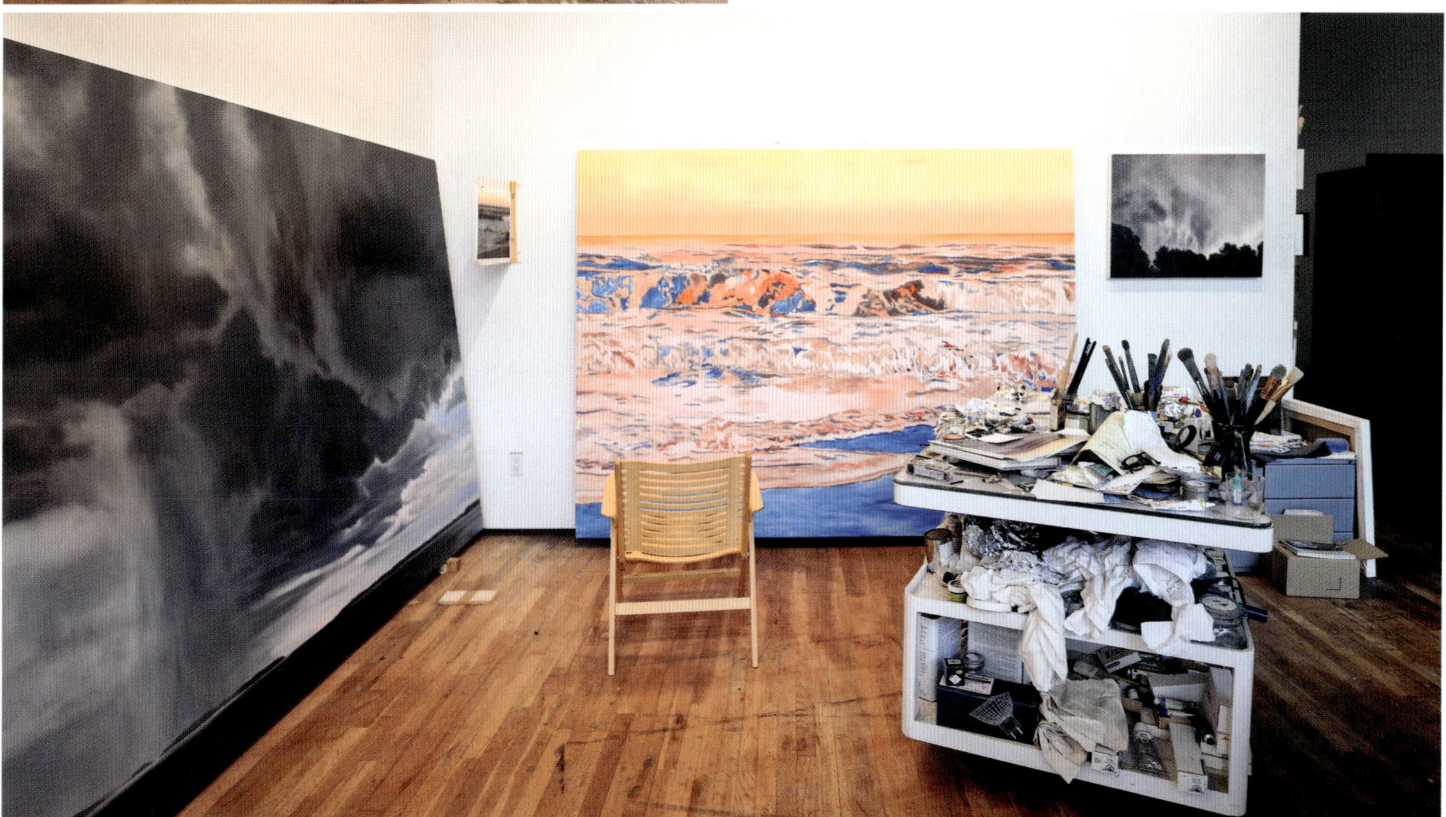

OPPOSITE Gornik's studio—also a cat playground, a recycling center, and a place for her sewing machine, which she uses for hemming her pants—has beautiful views of Fresh Pond in North Haven. Water and light are always at play in her work.

"Painting is such an immensely complicated thing to do. Between inspiration, preparation, adjustments that happen in sketching it out on a big canvas, starting to feel the weight and balance of the piece while underpainting it, then building it up in layers, and working with the tiny but important dimensionality of the surface. All that involves imagination, memory, a battle with intent, and a truce with what the painting seems to want to become. And then there's the joke that the universe usually makes when you get near completion of a painting and realize that the part you felt proudest of is now the part that has to go."

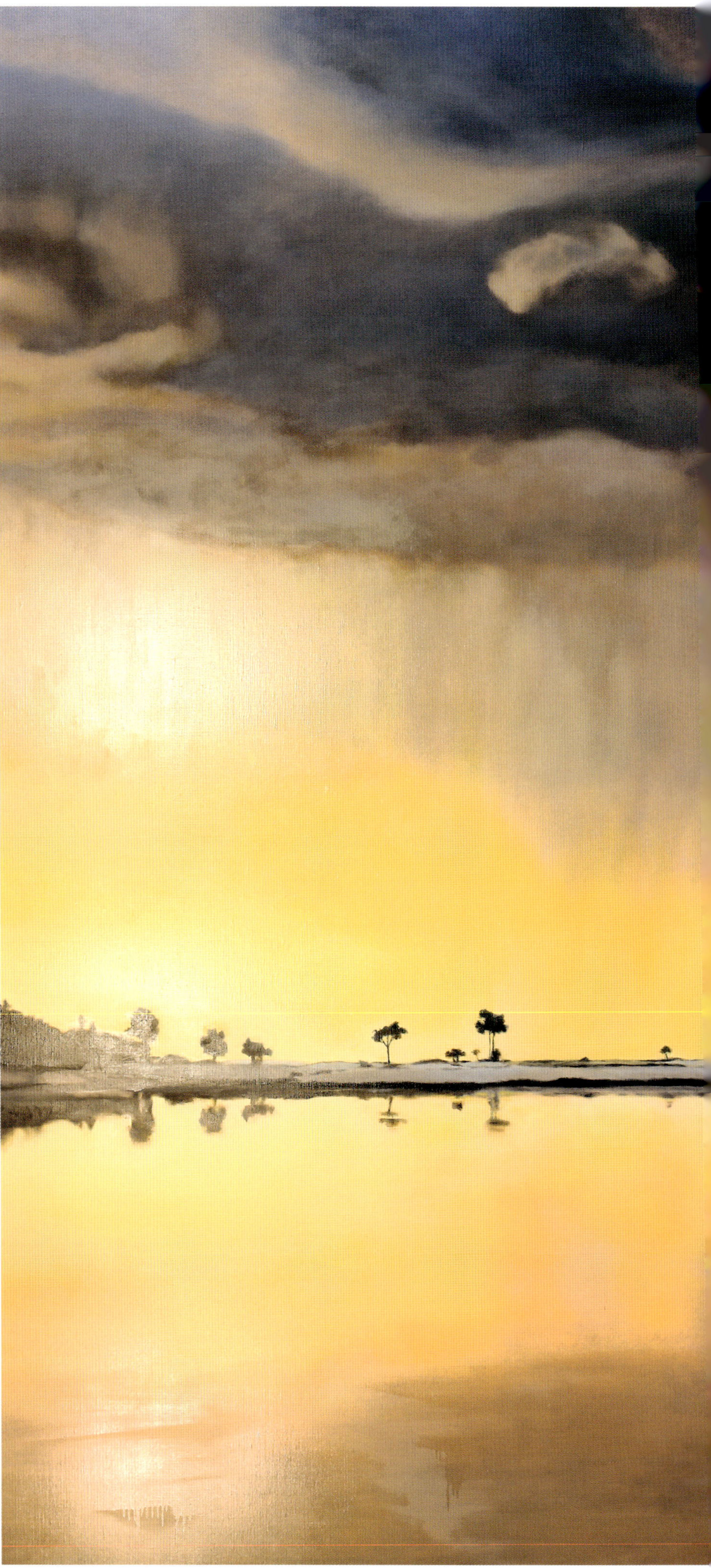

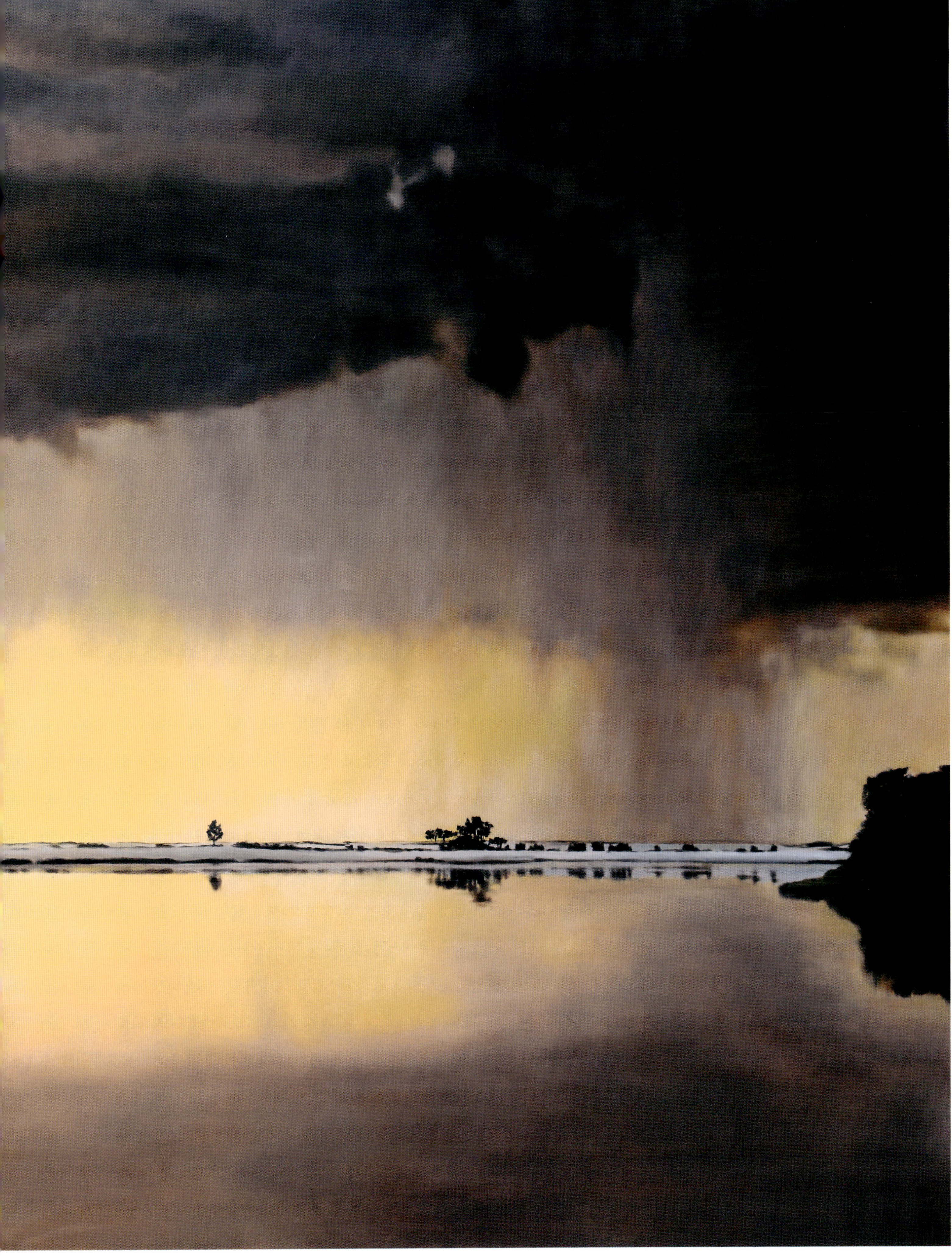

My intention is that the viewer sees the object I create for its form, not for its original purpose.

ELAINE GROVE

Grove, a native of Oklahoma, went to the University of Dallas, then worked for a year in a small advertising firm. "Walter Ender was an award-winning illustrator, and I took a commercial art class from him while at UD." In 1967, she moved to New York, where she met the artist Dan Christensen at Max's Kansas City, a bar near Union Square Park where artists and musicians hung out. "We started dating, broke up after several months, and got back together ten years later. We moved out to Springs around 1977." She still lives in the same house and works in the same big studio they built on the property. "I do my welding outside on a cement slab in full gear—helmet, heavy gloves, boots, and leather apron. I construct and paint smaller sculptures inside."

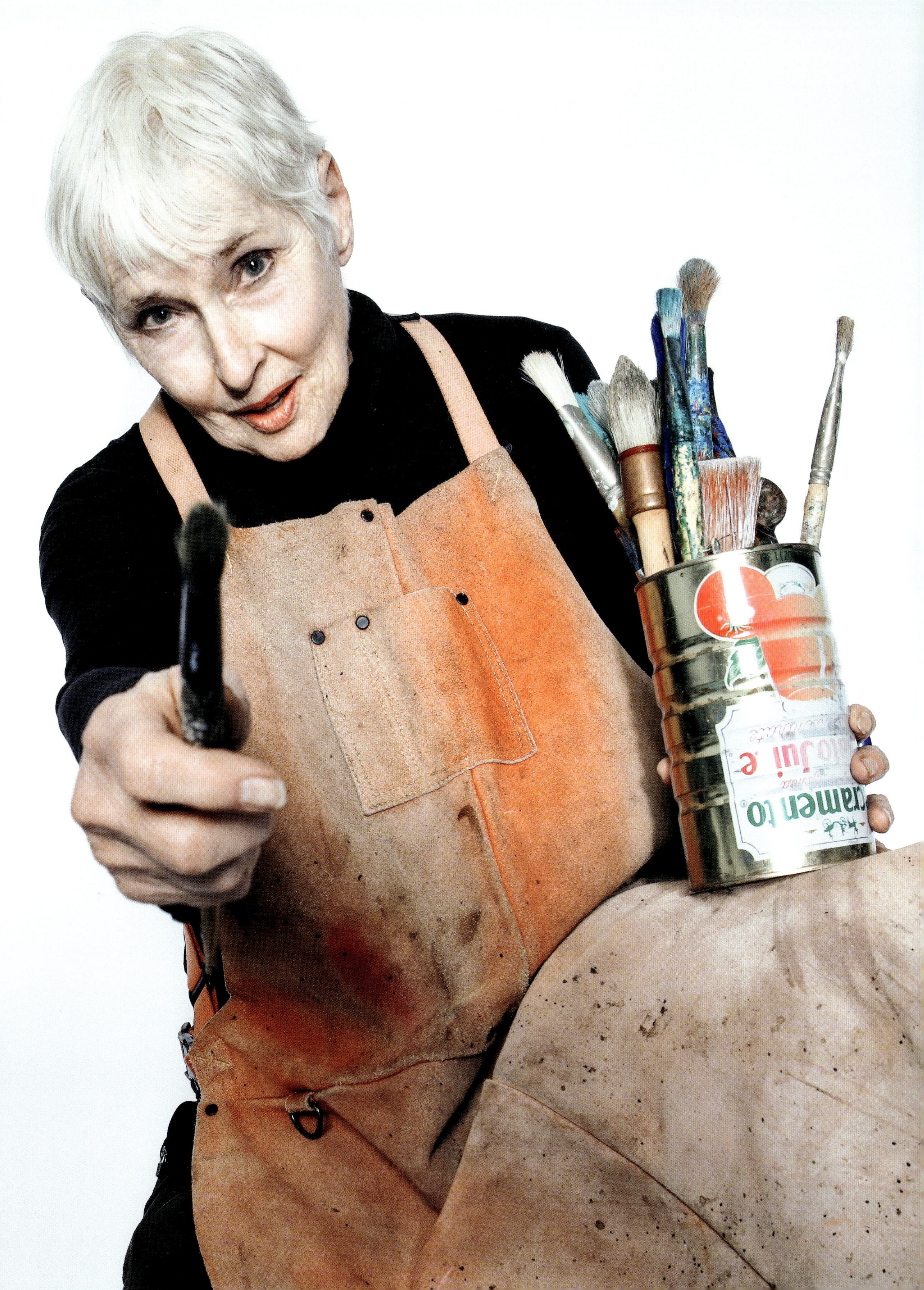

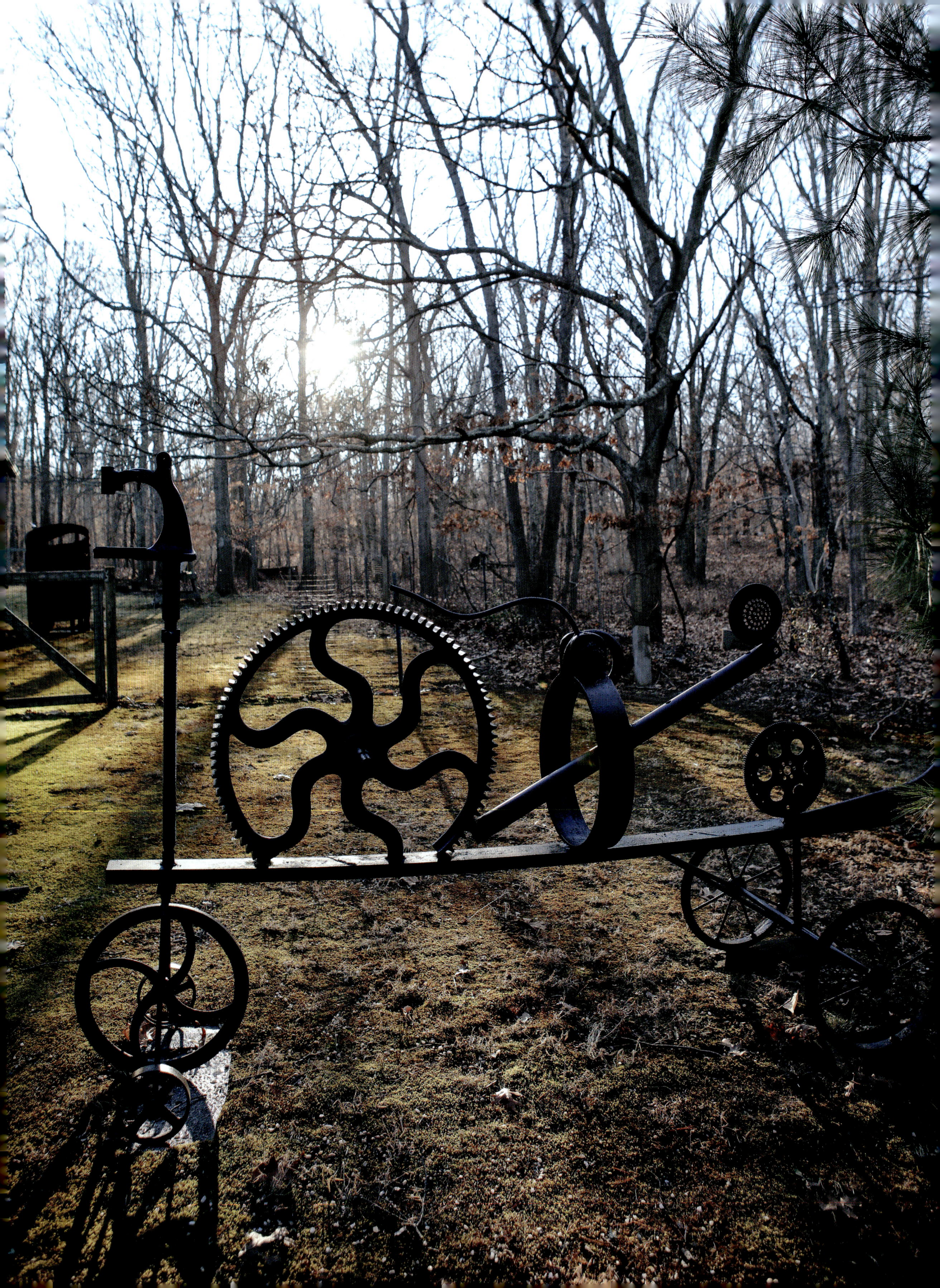

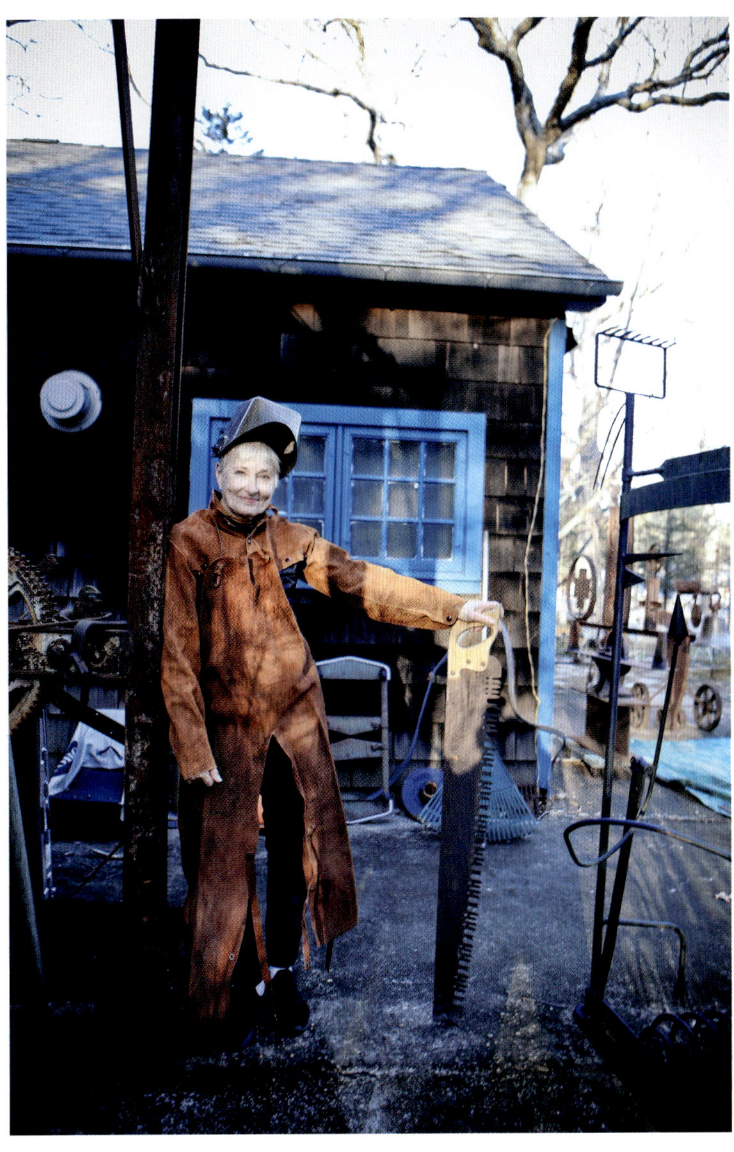

OPPOSITE

Grove has ample room in the yard outside her Springs studio to work on her large, welded-steel sculptures, which often include found objects. She likes to work in series, including her assemblages of wagon wheels.

LEFT

Grove, a former model, strikes a pose in her protective welding gear, including her well-worn leather apron.

Though trained as a painter, Grove has focused her creative output for the last twenty years on welded-steel sculpture. "I work in the classic constructivist tradition, incorporating found objects into the work." She creates series, such as one she did that revolves around war wagons. "I thought about different types of war—political, sexual, class, guerrilla. And from there, the types of 'war wagons' I could create. This lends itself to symbolism, which I use as a framework for art that can hold up on purely aesthetic grounds."

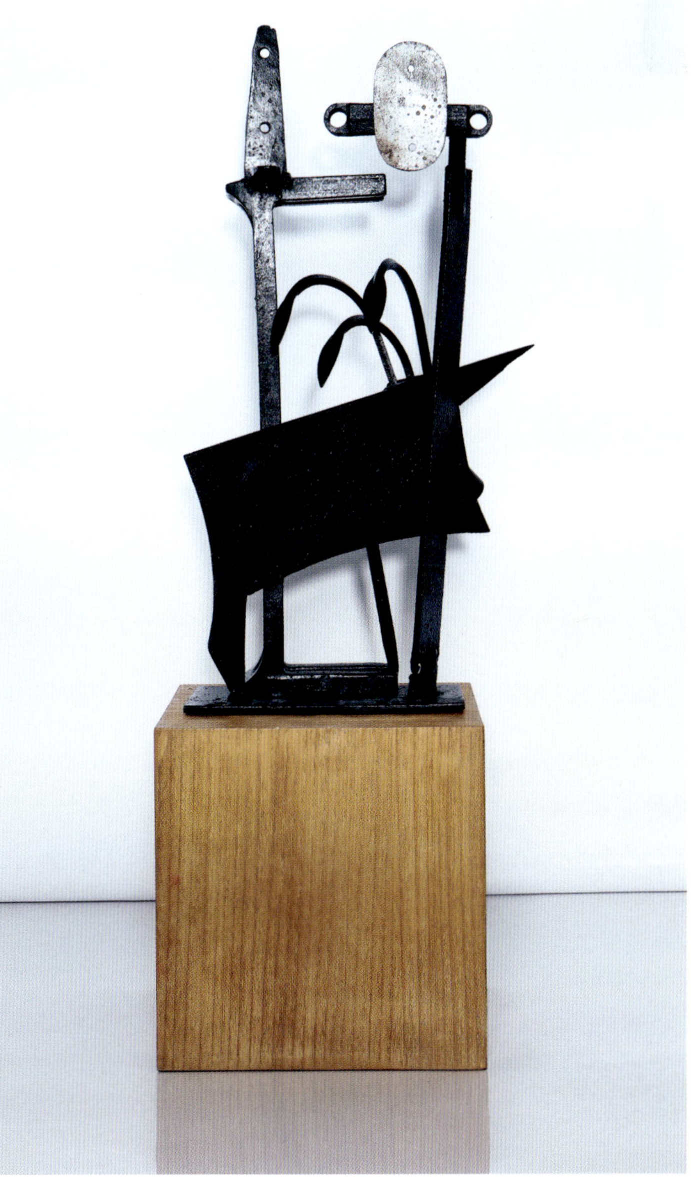

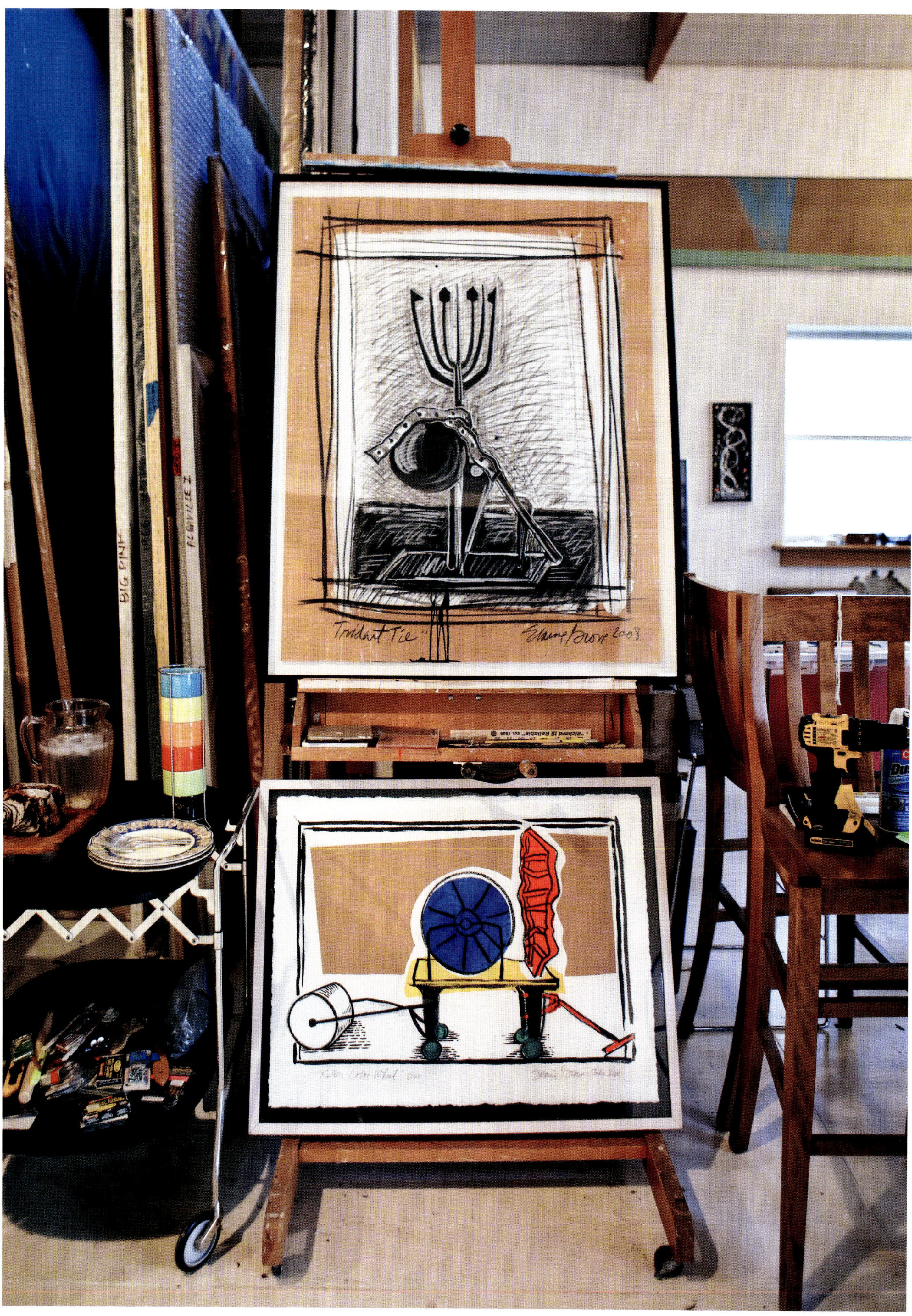
"Trident Tie"
BIG PINK

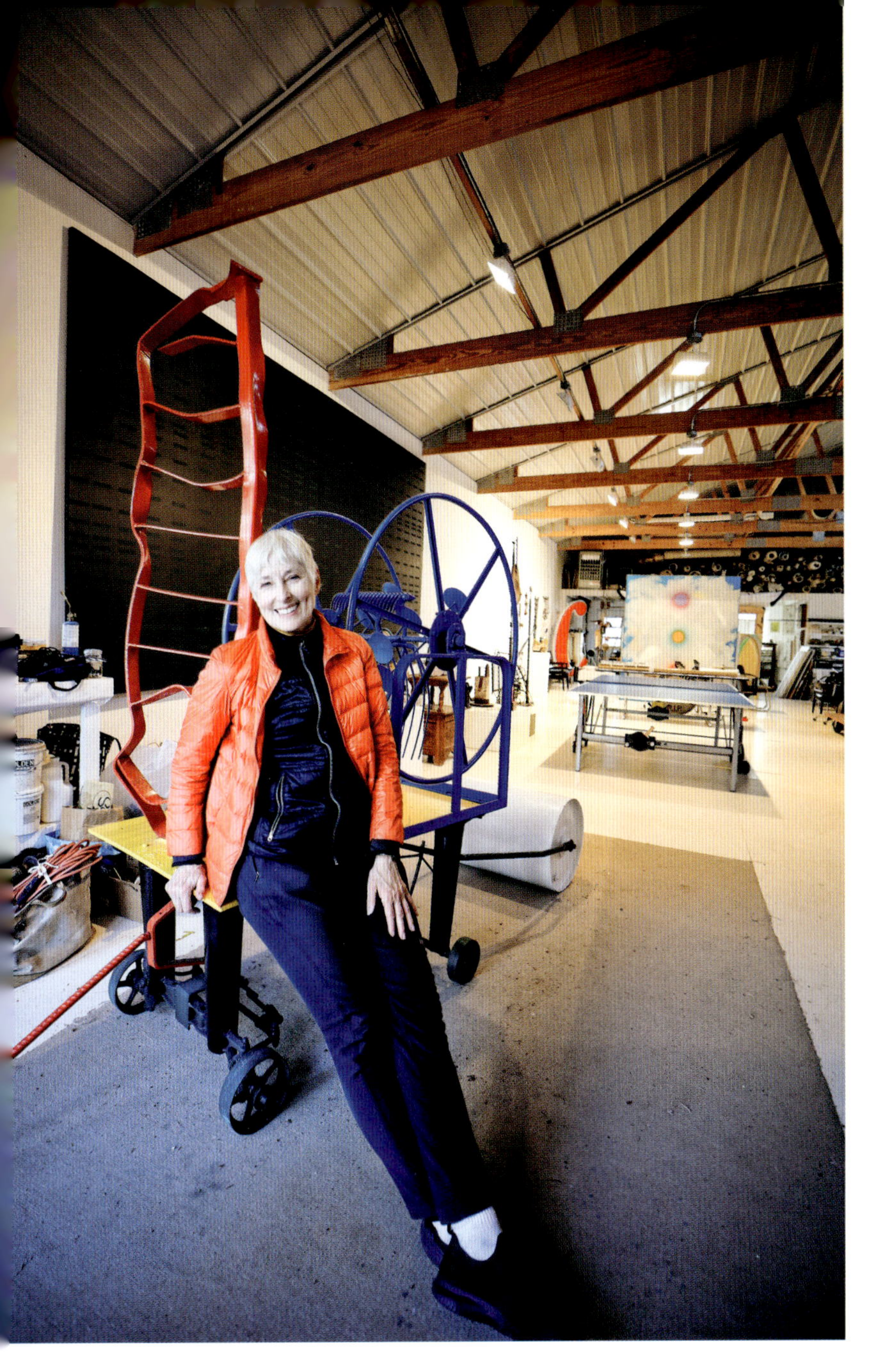

The subjects of Grove's paintings range from lizards to landscapes. She uses a variety of mediums: acrylic gel with mica particles, gesso, watercolor, oil sticks, acrylic paints, and ink. "The landscapes become lighter or darker depending upon how the light moves across it or how the painting is tilted." Her small sculptures incorporate some of the wooden blocks that her late husband would prop paintings on while working so that the paintings wouldn't be sitting in pools of paint. "I use these blocks, along with some of my own materials, to make sculptures that incorporate both of our works—a makeshift homage to Dan."

ABOVE

The artist in her warehouse-size studio, which she and her late husband, the painter Dan Christensen, built on the property. This is where Grove constructs her smaller sculptures and also paints—her first artistic mode of expression.

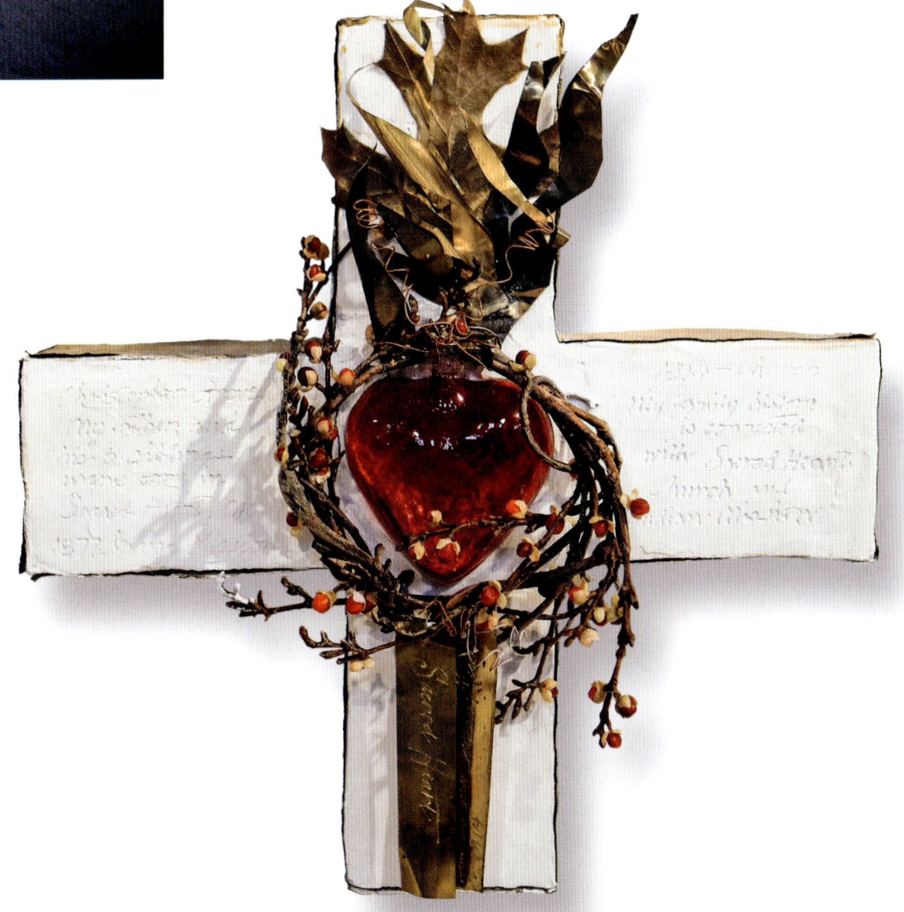

I spend a lot of time meditating and thinking about a painting before I start. A big part of my practice is contemplation. I write, too, and often include stories from my life. That dialogue is inside of the paintings. If you look for a while, you can feel the backstory.

MARY HEILMANN

Abstraction has been part of Heilmann's thinking and her work since she began creating art—first as a potter, then as a sculptor, and then as a painter. "I've always been interested in geometric abstraction—more in terms of shapes and free-form brushwork than fine-tuned geometry. And I'm interested in seeing how colors next to each other have an effect, how they shiver when you look at different combinations. But the choice of colors is always arbitrary." And as she sees it, nothing has changed or will change in the way she makes art. "My mantra is 'no linear time.' My entire body of work over the last fifty years is all of a piece."

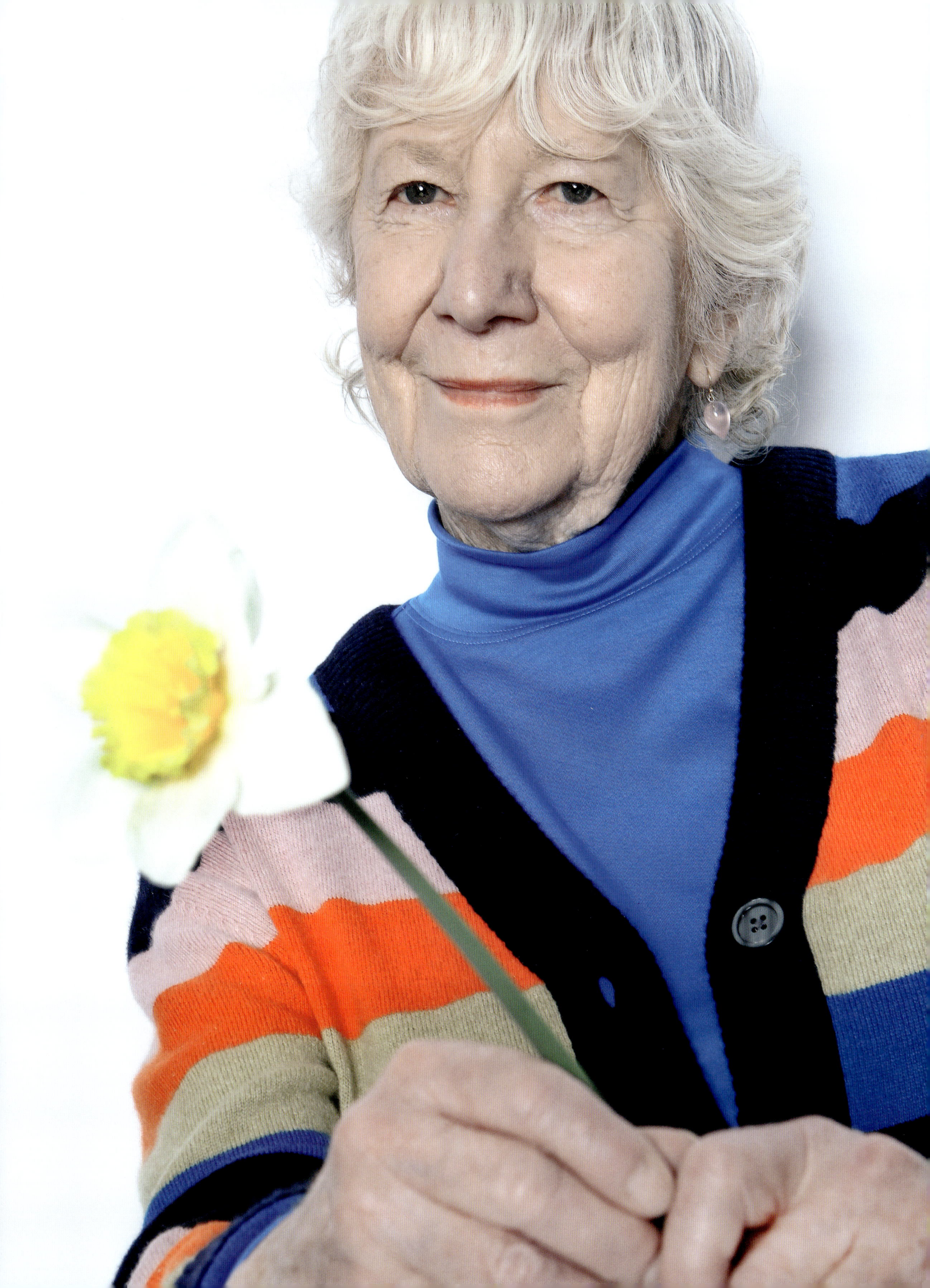

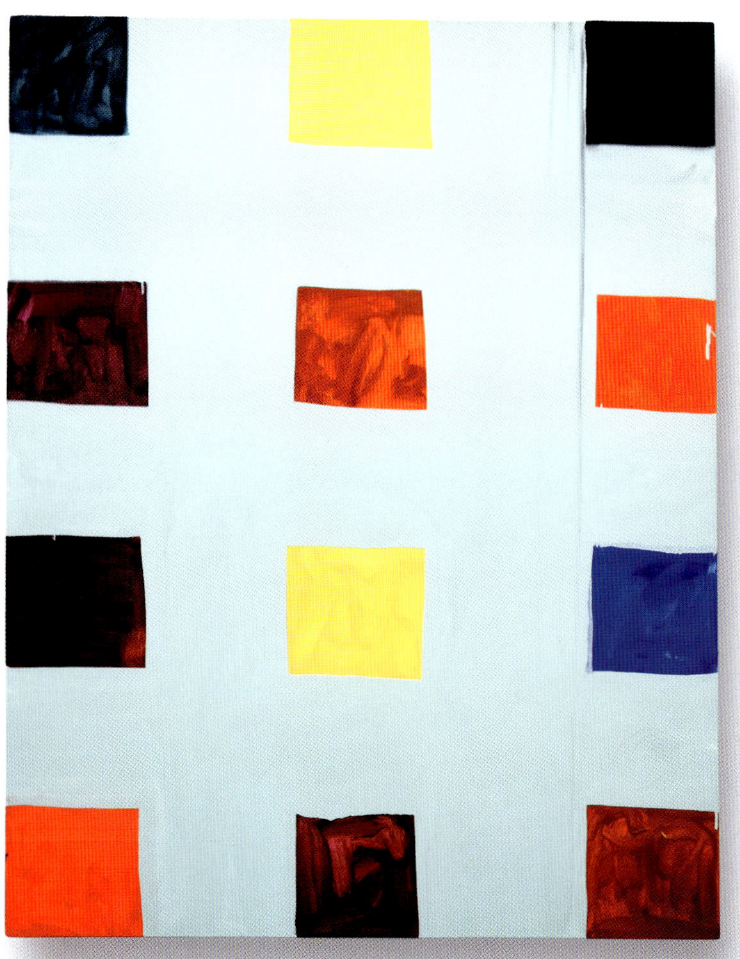

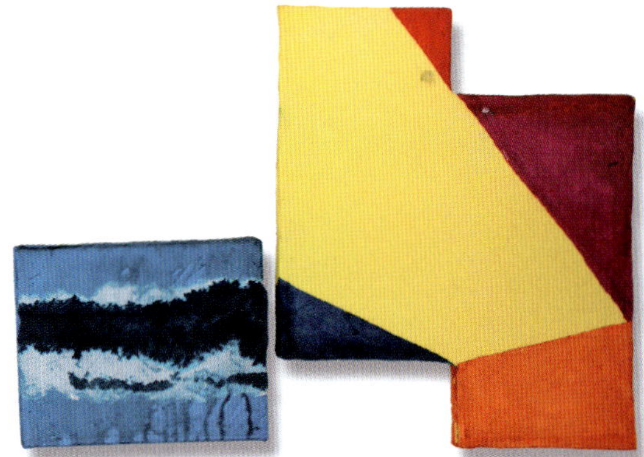

In the late 1960s, after graduate school at Berkeley in California, Heilmann moved to New York City, where she found a studio and met artists like Eva Hesse ("That was exciting!"). She started coming out to the Hamptons part-time in the 1980s. "I didn't know anyone, but I knew what was going on out here." In 1994, she bought a house in Bridgehampton and built a studio with barn doors that open wide onto a field. "This is my main place. I spend a lot of time looking outside, watching the sun move. And I love the noisy birds." After a day in the studio, she is often out socializing, going to openings. "I feel really connected here. Since I first moved to the East End, the art scene has grown even larger. There are just so many artists out here now!"

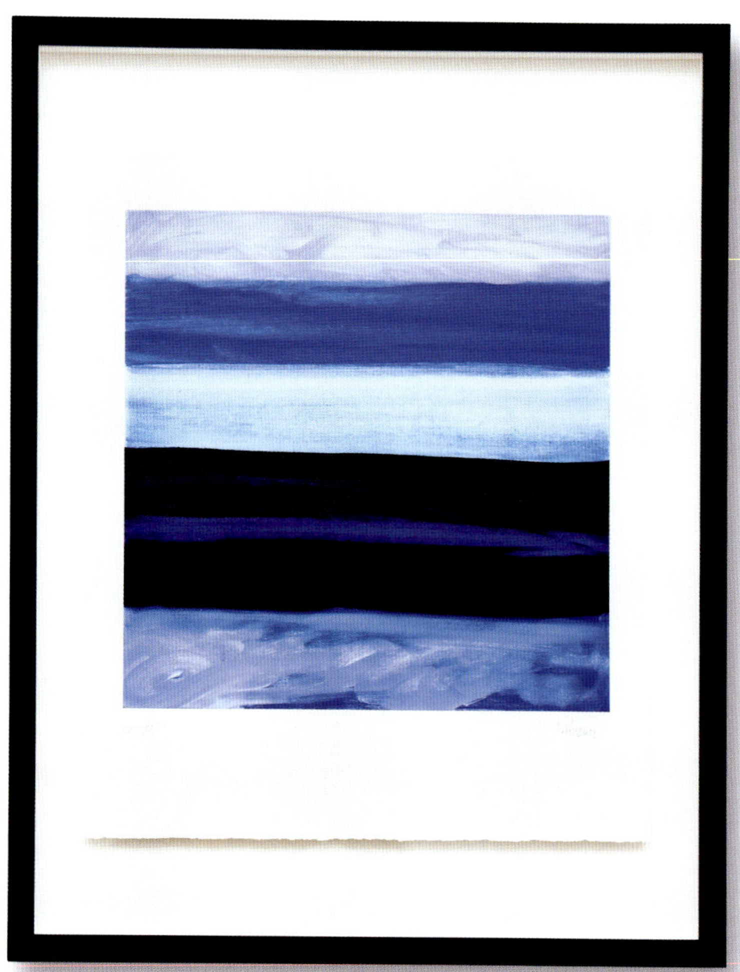

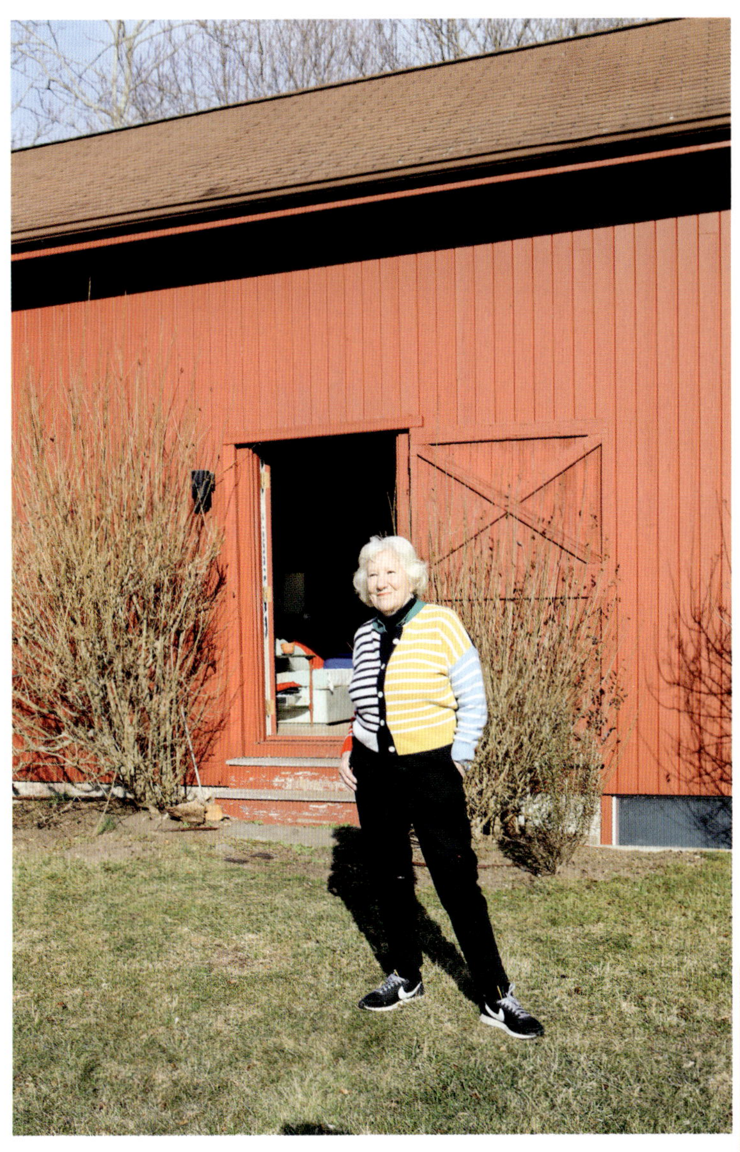

A native Californian, Heilmann has always had a fascination with surfing. "I used to surf a bit myself, but the main thing was always watching it." She brought that love of Cali culture with her to the East End. She regularly goes to Montauk to the surf beaches. "I get a lot of inspiration from the geometry of the waves, the pulls and the shapes of waves, and watching how people, the great surfers, deal with that."

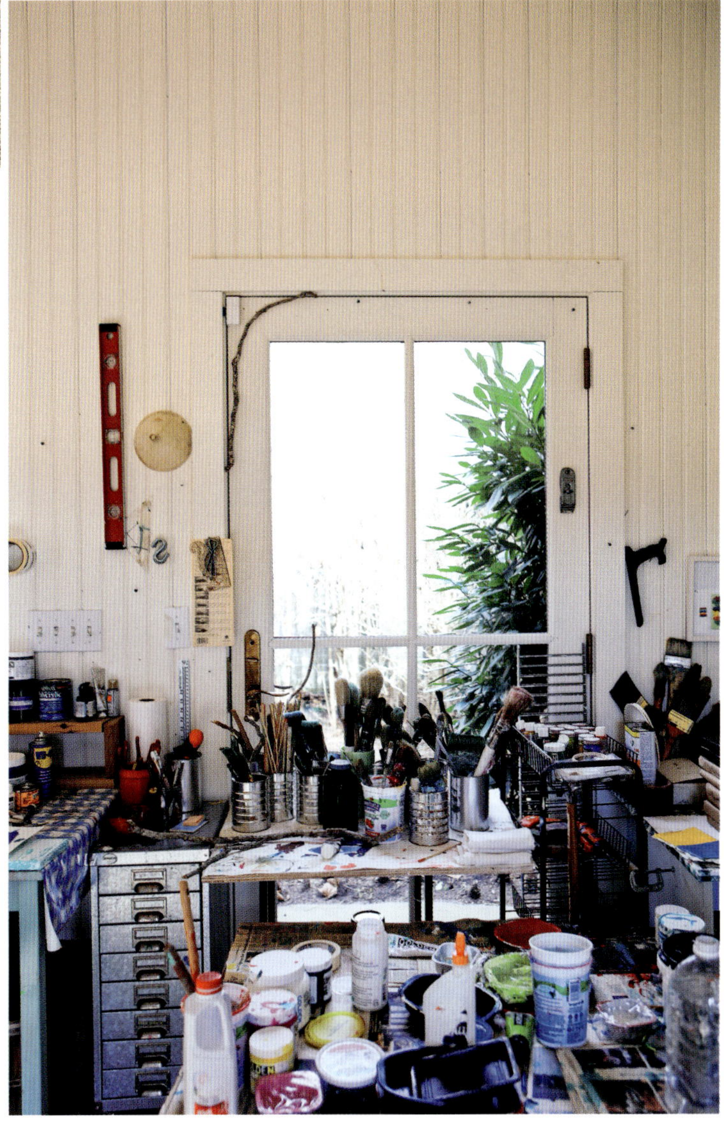

ABOVE

Heilmann built her Bridgehampton studio with barn doors that open wide to a field across the way. She loves gazing outside and listening to the birds while she works.

RIGHT

A die-hard abstract painter, Heilmann has both oils and acrylics at hand in a wide range of colors. How she uses the colors, she says, is completely unplanned.

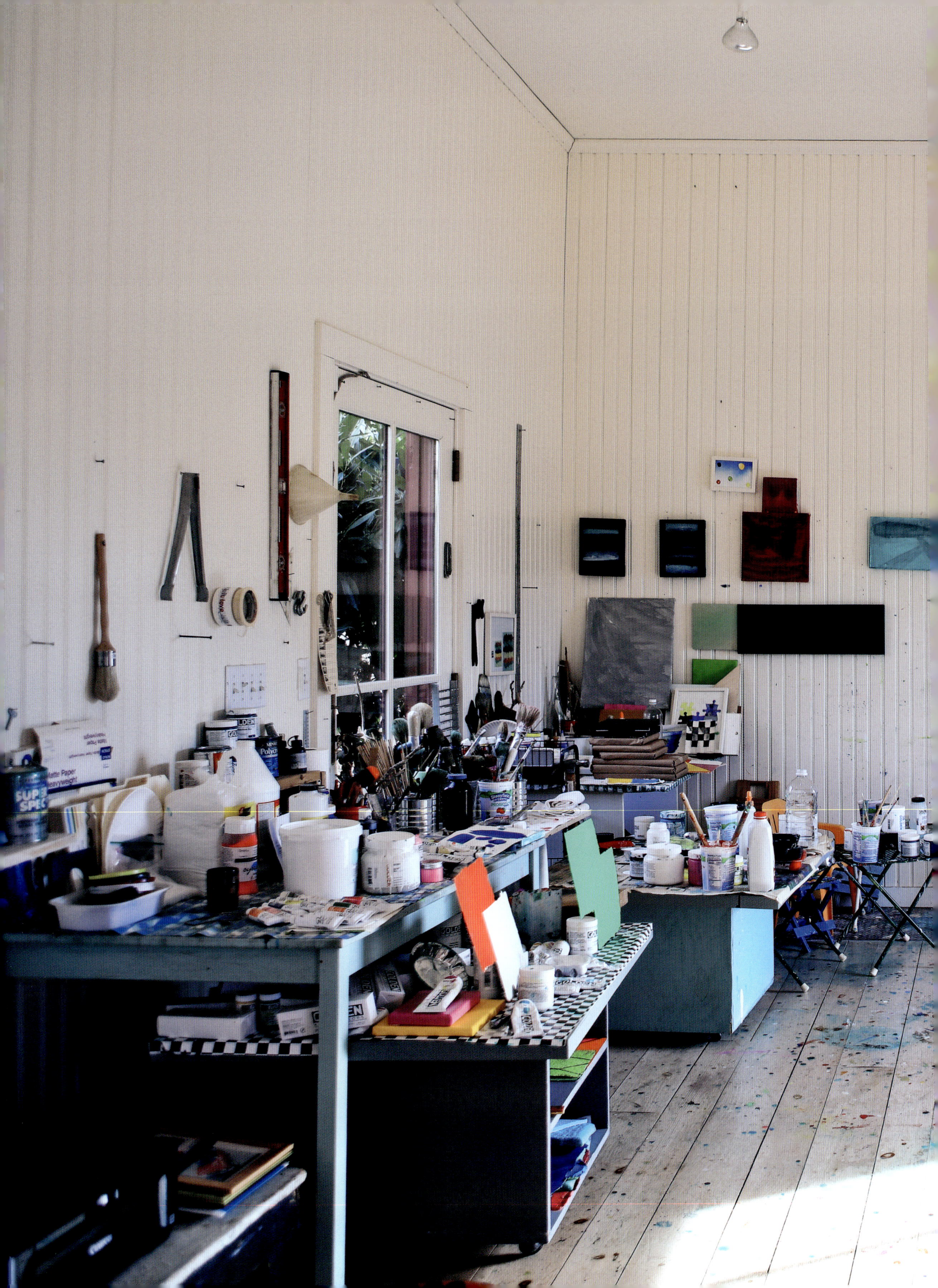

GOLDEN

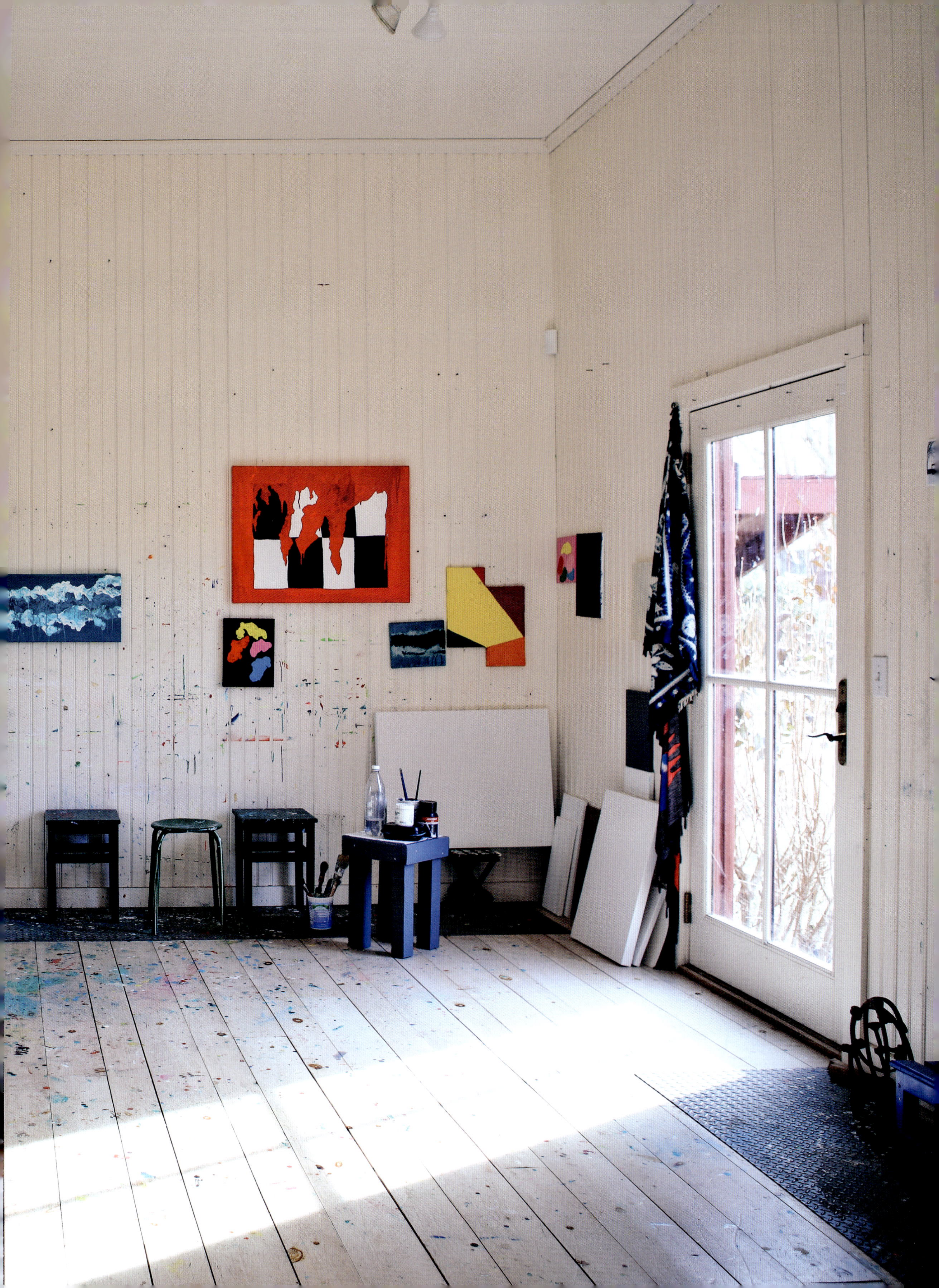

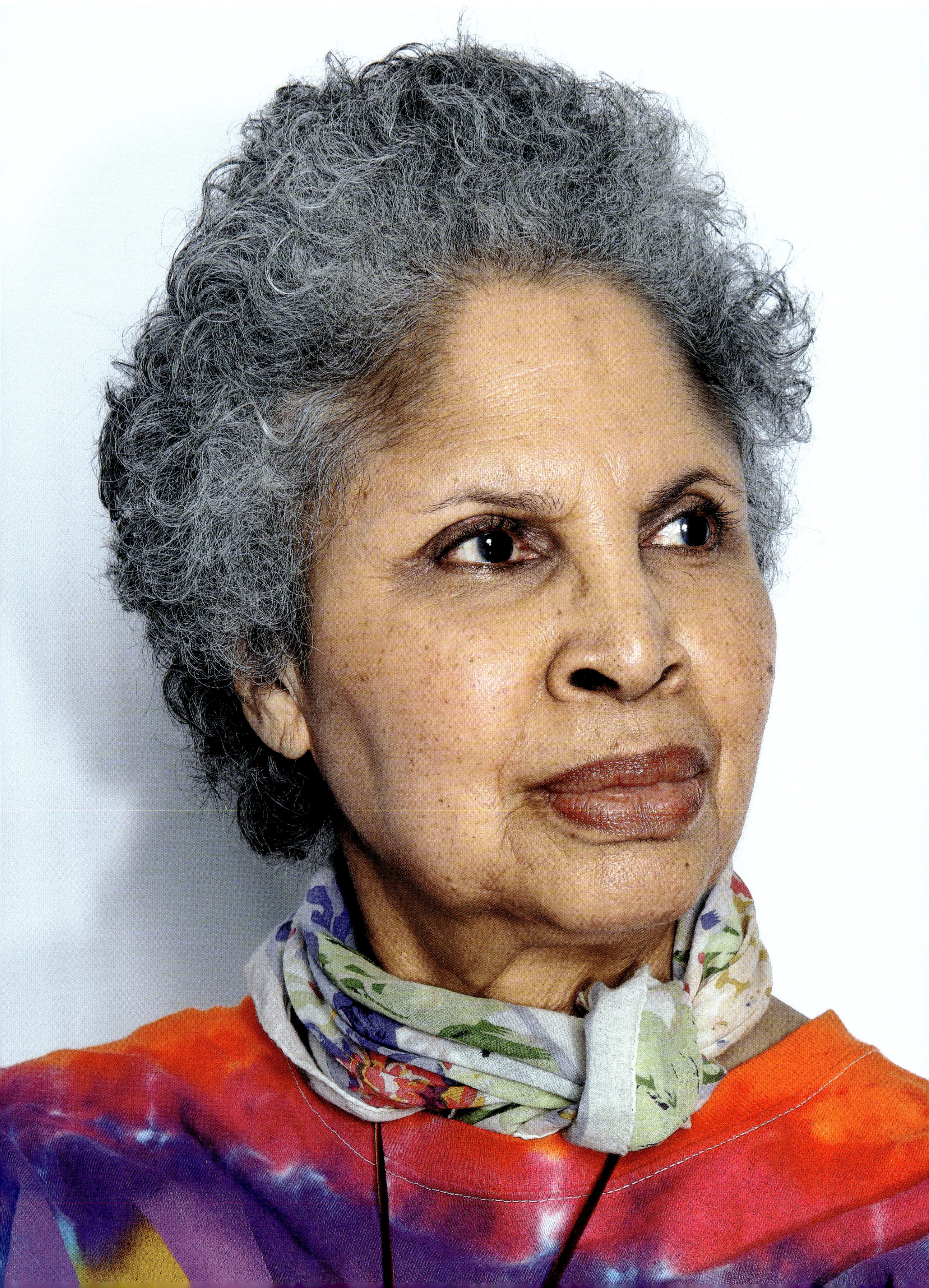

I write poetry in the morning. I paint or draw in the light of day. I weave at night. I used to listen to music—jazz or classical—but now I work in silence.

CANDACE HILL MONTGOMERY

Hill Montgomery says she's always known she was to be some kind of artist. "It's in my blood. My mom's mom taught me knitting and my Southern grandmother made quilts. I was always around women who made clothes and household lace designs, such as doilies, from scratch." Her art training began at about eleven years old. High school art classes were followed by graduate degrees in art and art history. "Everything one does has an influence on one's art, but the great museums of the world, I'd say, have been my strongest influences."

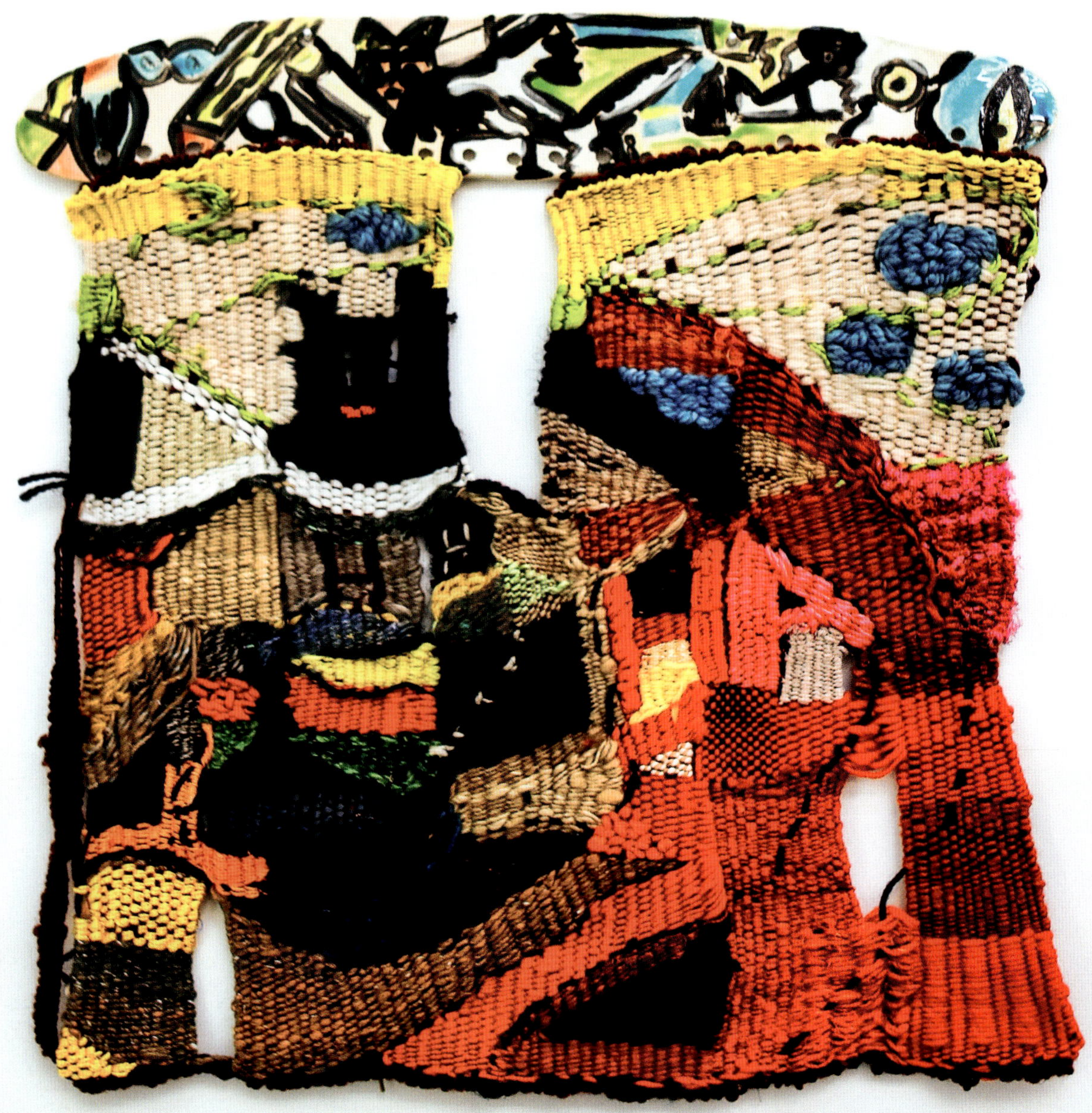

"I began living in Sag Harbor during my childhood summers. I grew up in a big, old rambling house with sloping floors and a wood stove in the kitchen—a magical life for the children of the many different families who came out here, all of us swimming at Havens Beach and sharing family-style dinners with the catch of the day." Hill Montgomery now lives and works in Bridgehampton, in a house with a similar vibe. "Fortunately, the house I'm in now enjoys the leftovers from the love that was given in it and to it. We enjoyed the sloping floors as kids, and I live in a house today that also has its insults."

OPPOSITE The artist props and stacks her paintings in every nook and cranny of her home. No surface is off-limits. **OVERLEAF** Hill Montgomery works where she lives and lives where she works. Her Bridgehampton house is brimming with her personal and artistic history.

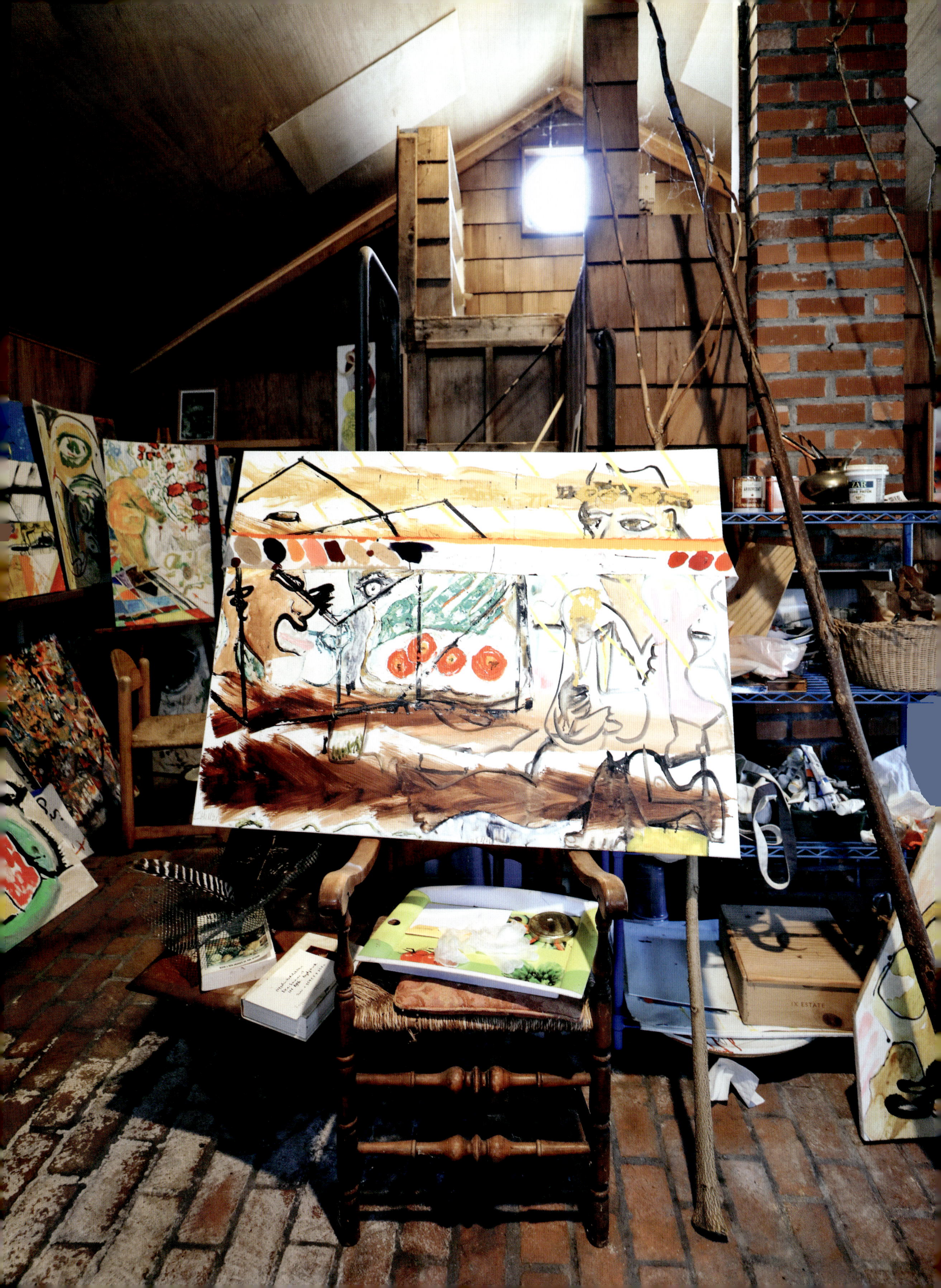

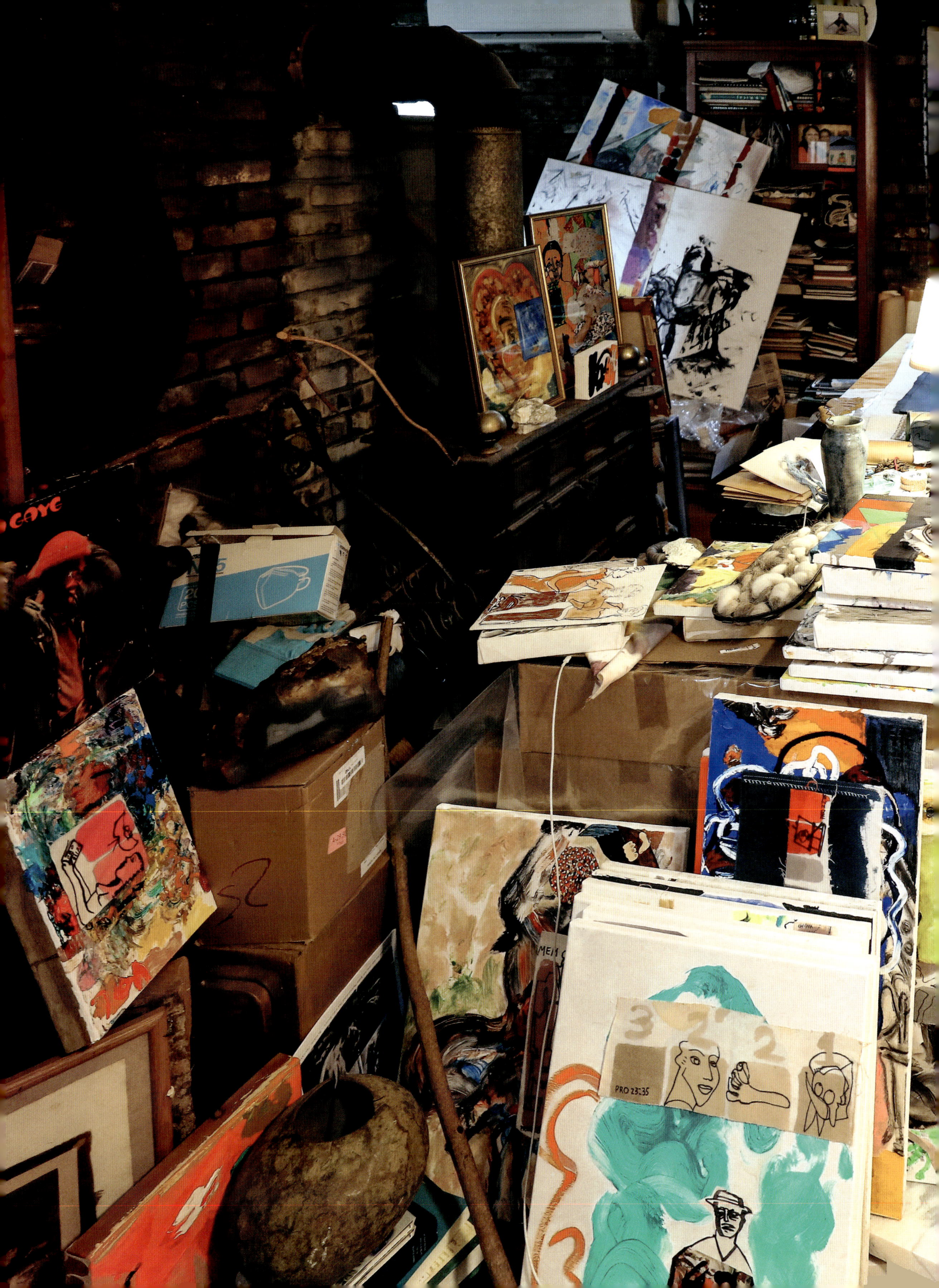
PRO 23:35

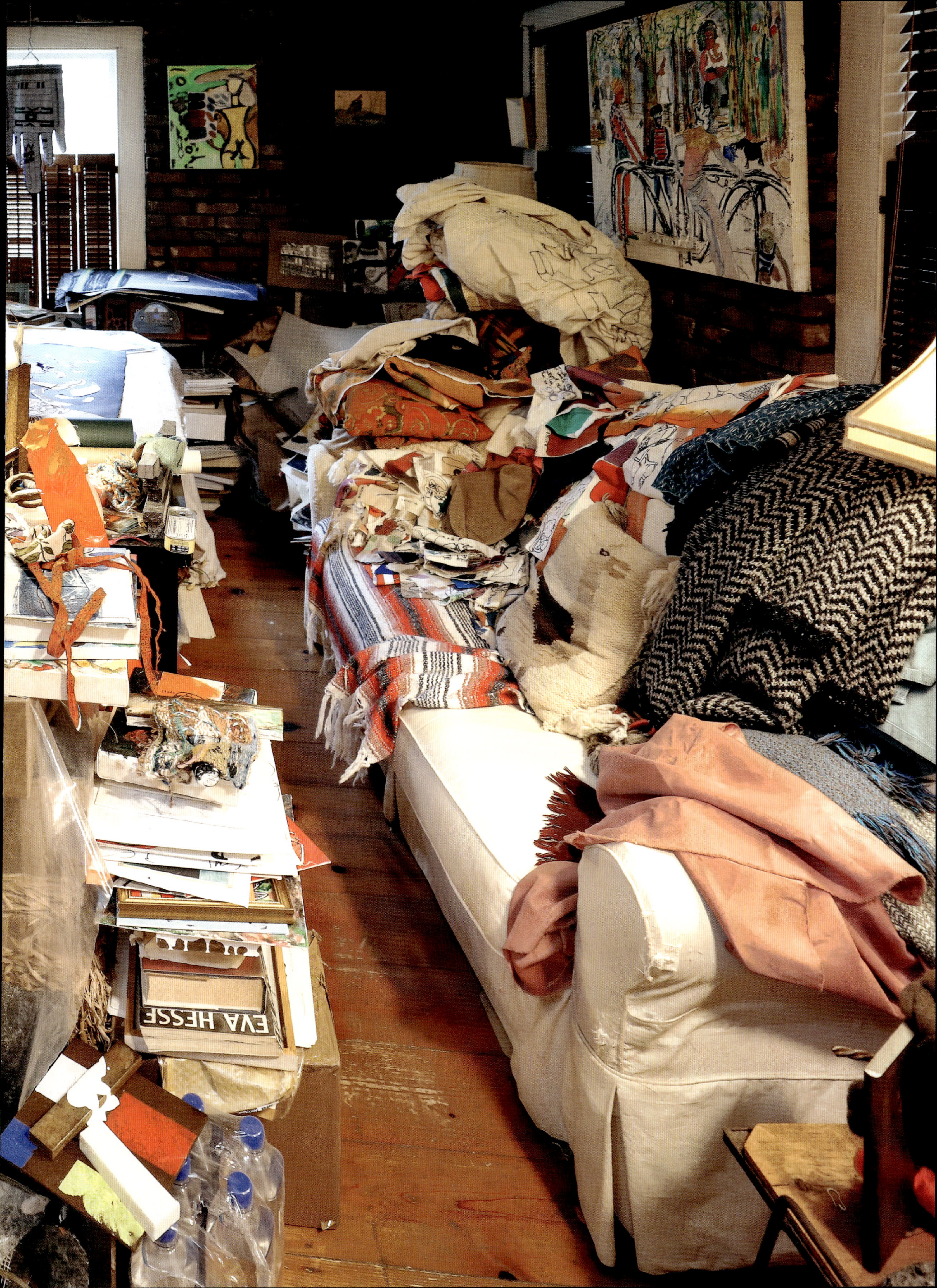
EVA HESSE

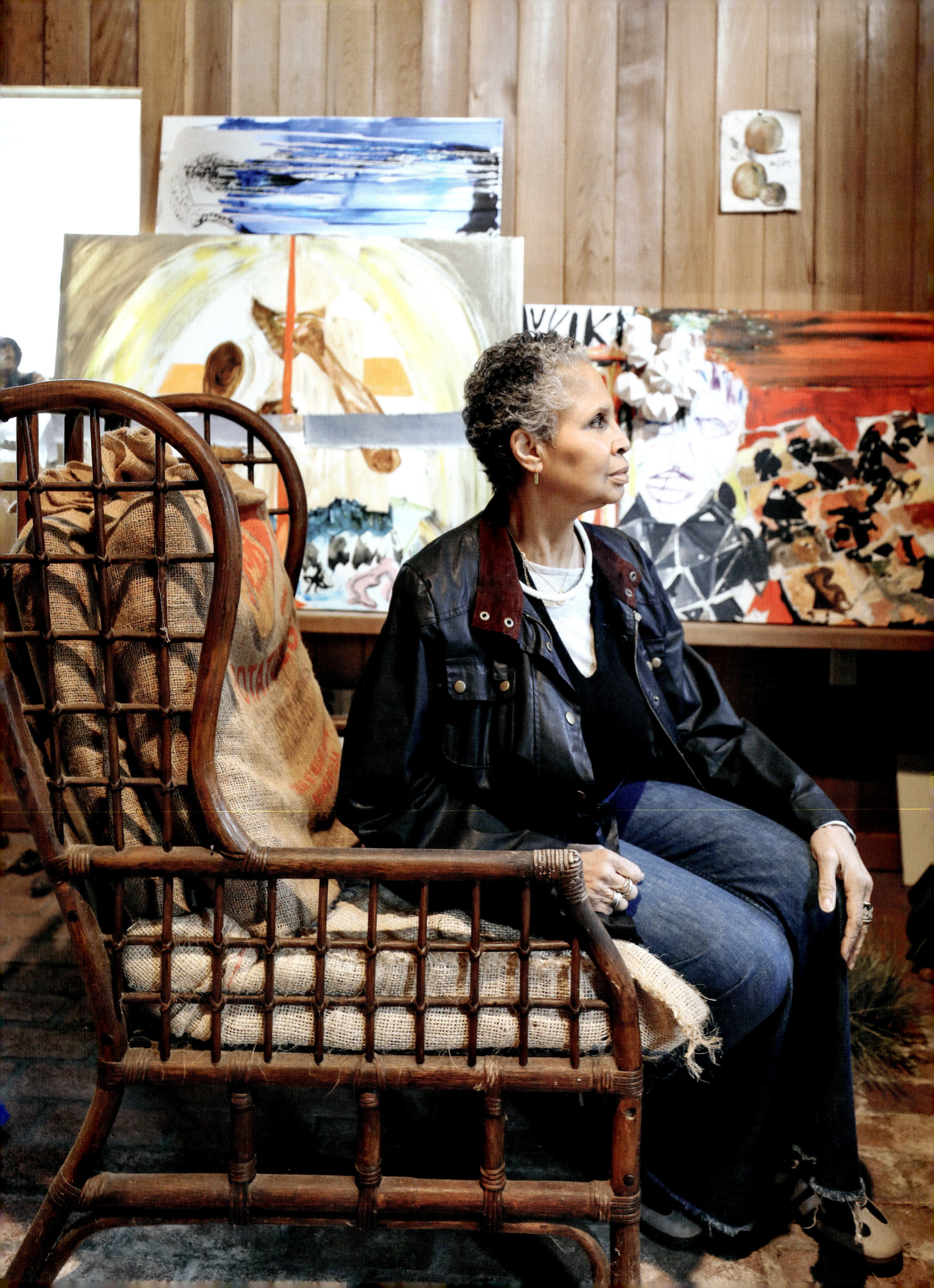

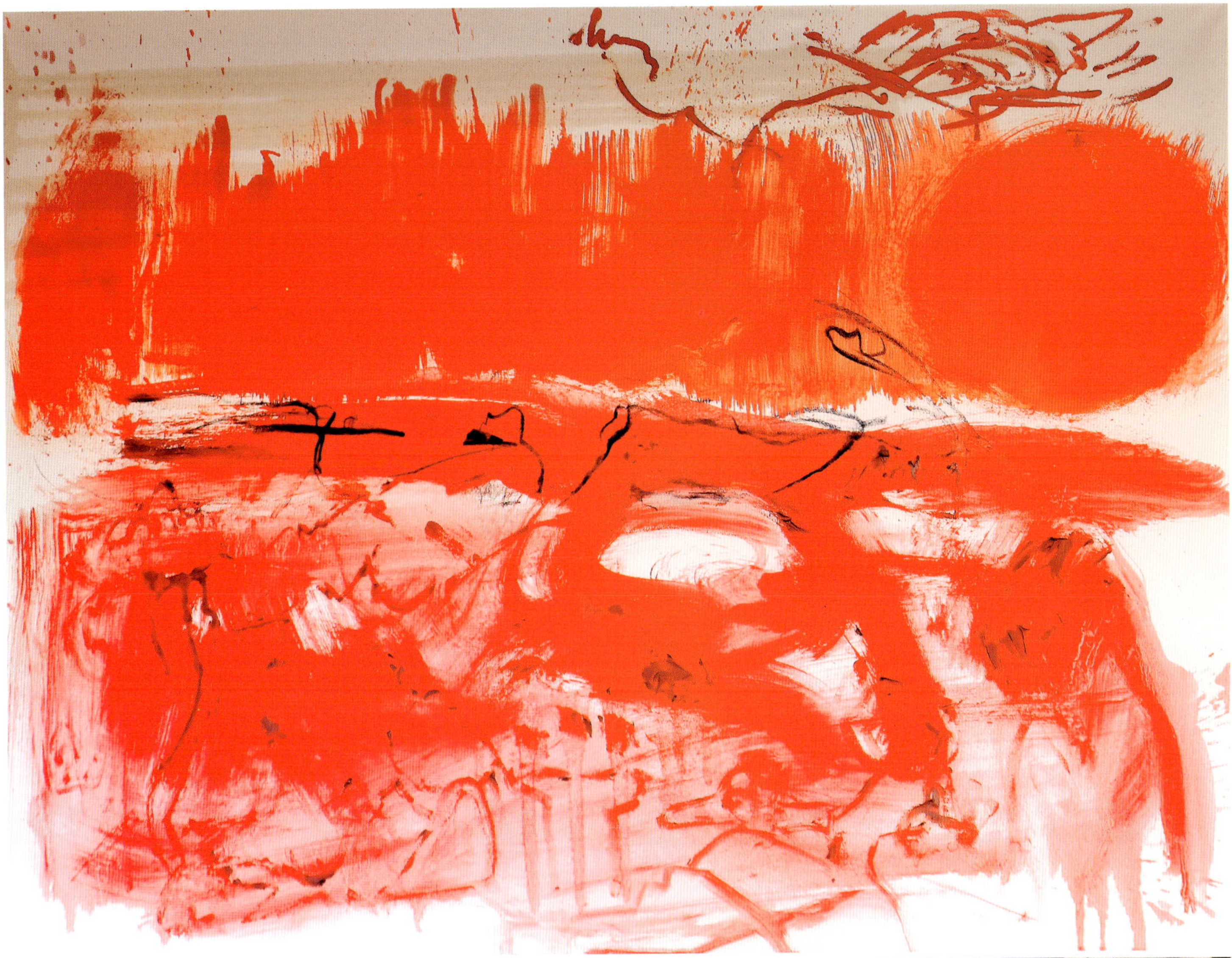

"All of my friends out here are seasoned artists for whom I have great respect. We help each other puzzle things out in the ways of pure abstraction, which keeps diverting me from figuration. I mean, Mary Heilmann is my neighbor. It doesn't get any better than that." With all the various mediums Hill Montgomery uses to create her art, how does she organize her workday? "I have a schedule, which I pretty much stick to. I write in the mornings; I do watercolors, drawings on paper, and prints for textiles in the afternoons until early evening. The late evenings are for weaving. And I only do large-scale painting in summer, when my studio is warm, since it's not heated."

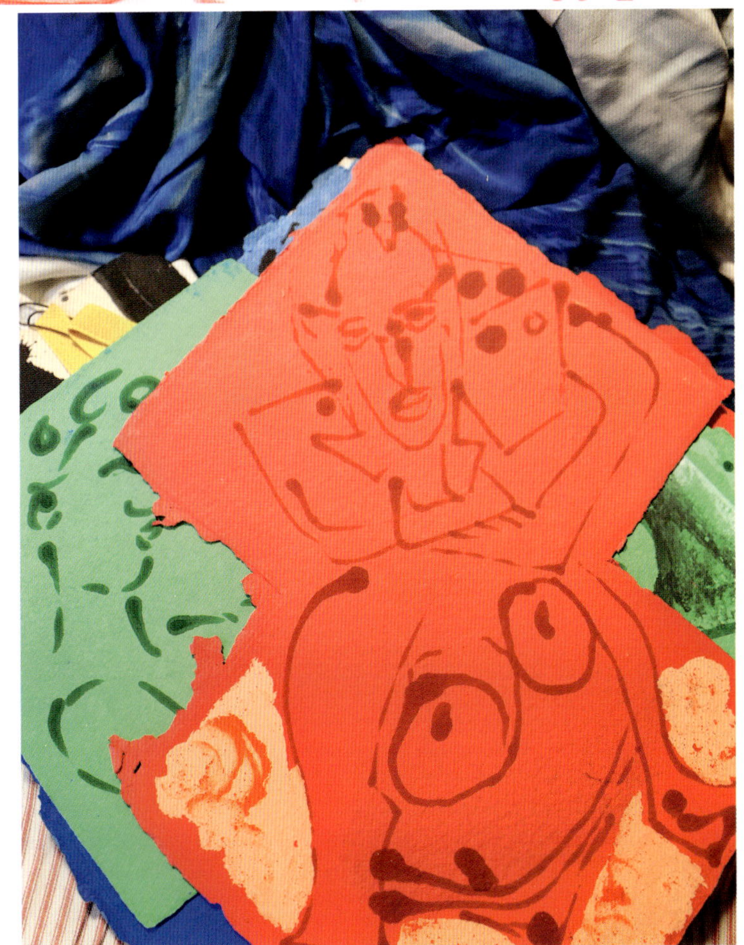

OPPOSITE The artist (and former model) poised on a chair imported from Barbados with pillows that she made out of coffee-bean and Long Island–potato sacks.

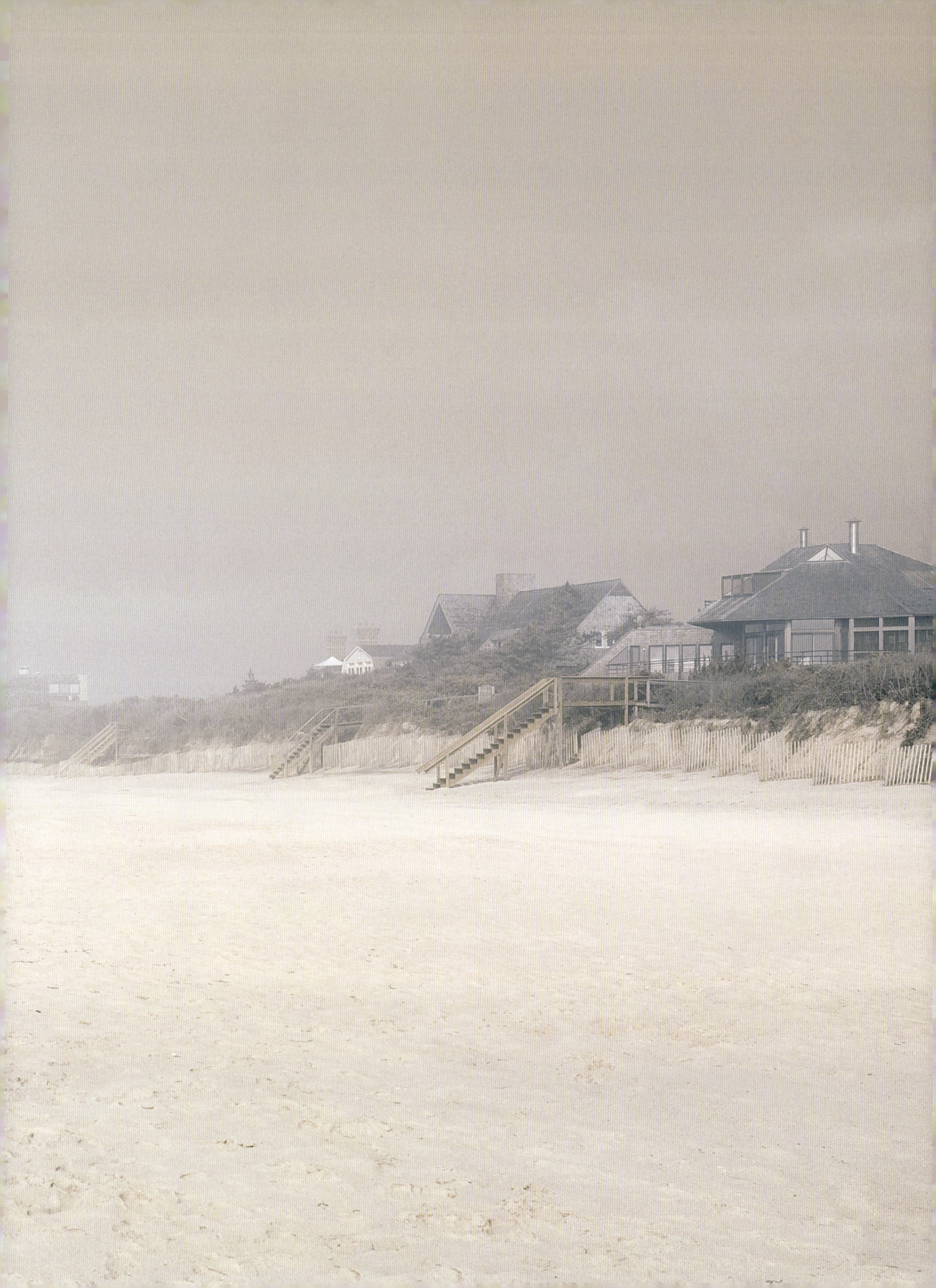

I go to the studio to test myself and see if I can surprise myself one more time. If I begin a studio session with a set idea or goal in mind, I'm bound to fail.

VIRVA HINNEMO

Hinnemo, who was born in Finland, came to the Hamptons via New York City, where she studied at Parsons School of Design. She and her husband, George Negroponte, also an artist, used to visit friends in East Hampton. "It was always a special getaway. Many of our friends were connected to the museums, to the Pollock-Krasner House and to LongHouse Reserve. I met many Swedes, as well as some Finns, who'd made their homes here." She and her husband settled in East Hampton in 2012. "I think many of us Northerners feel a connection to nature and the ocean, not because the landscape looks like Sweden or Finland but because nature is so plentiful, and we are very outdoorsy people."

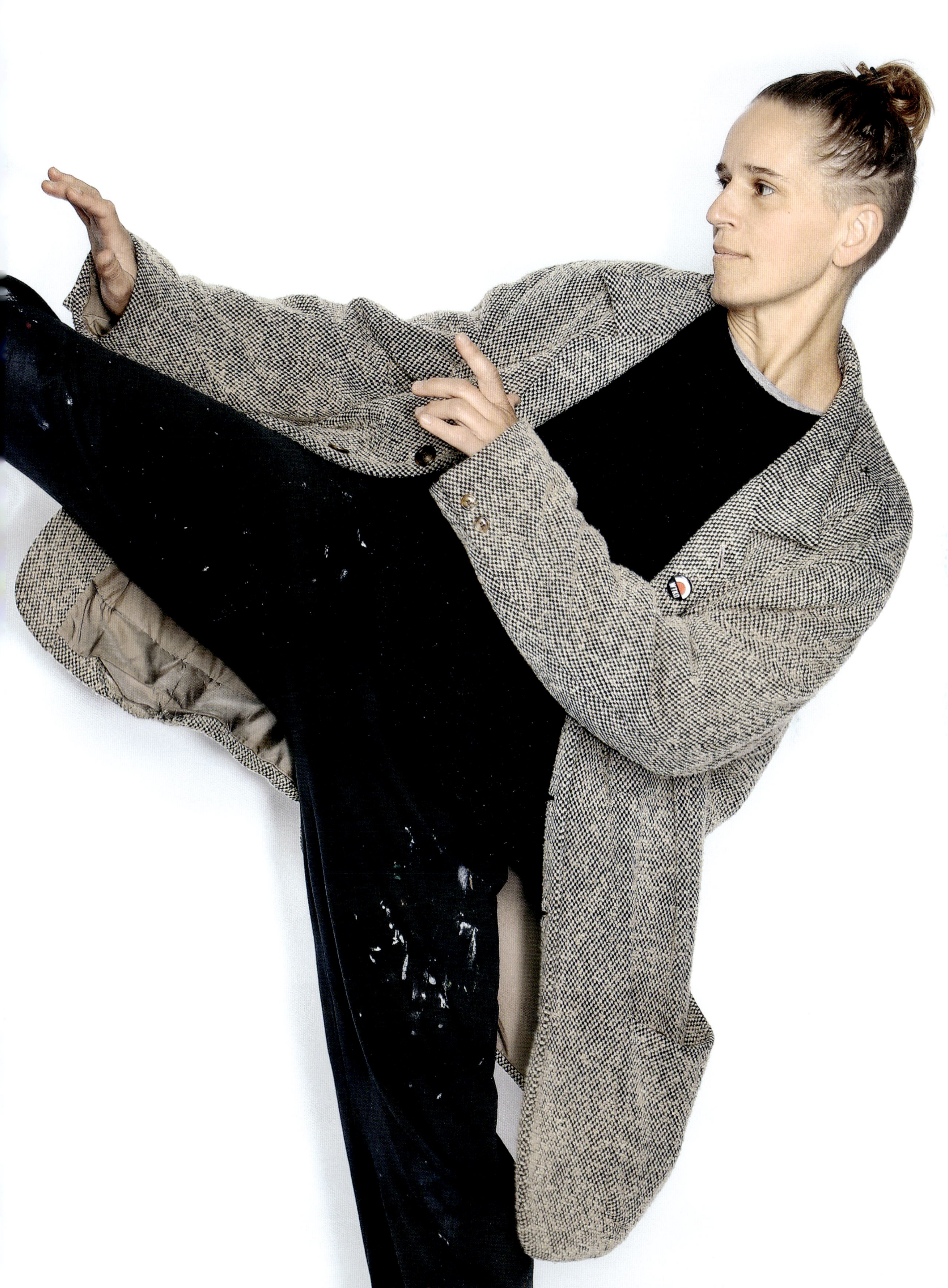

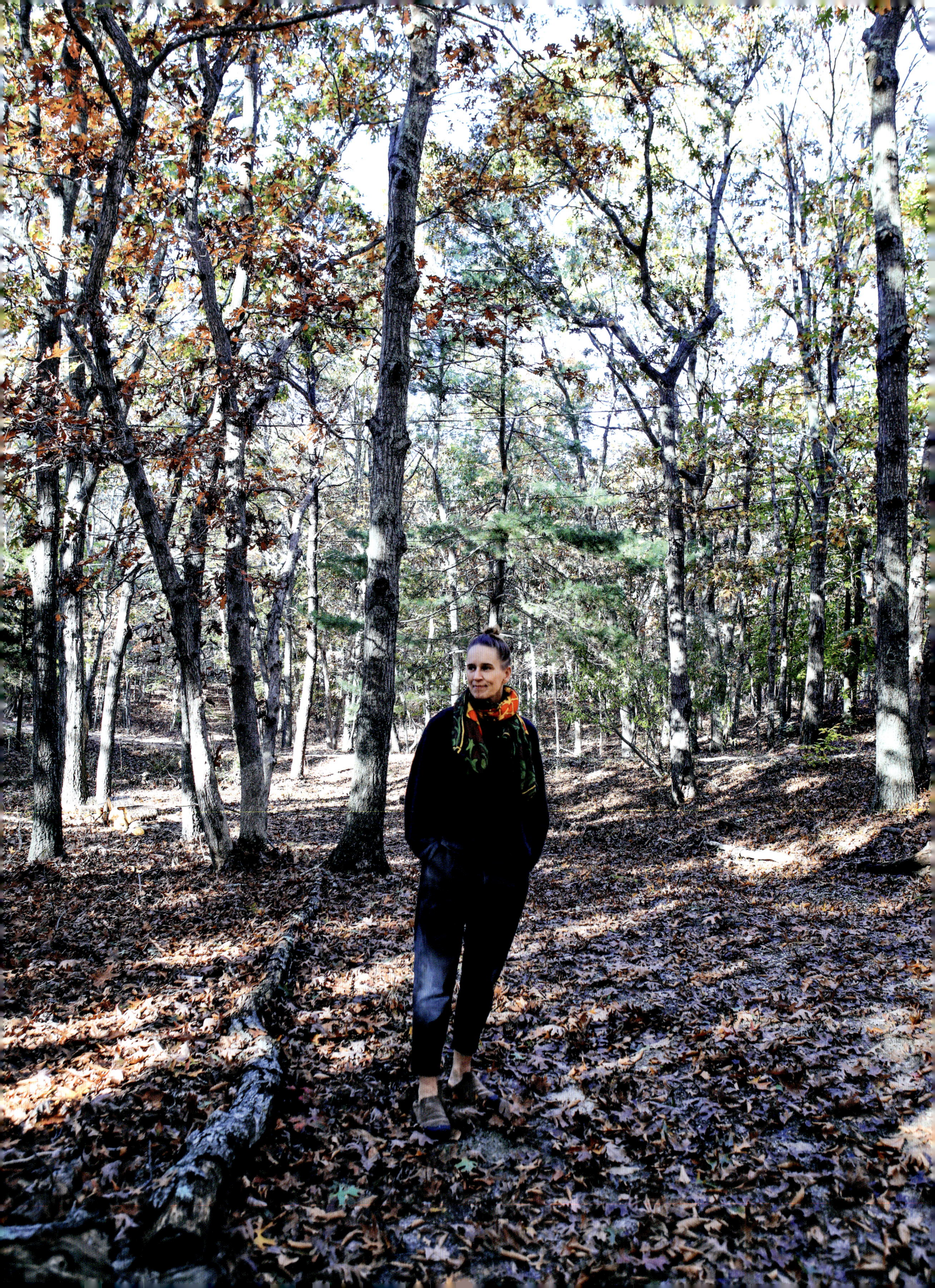

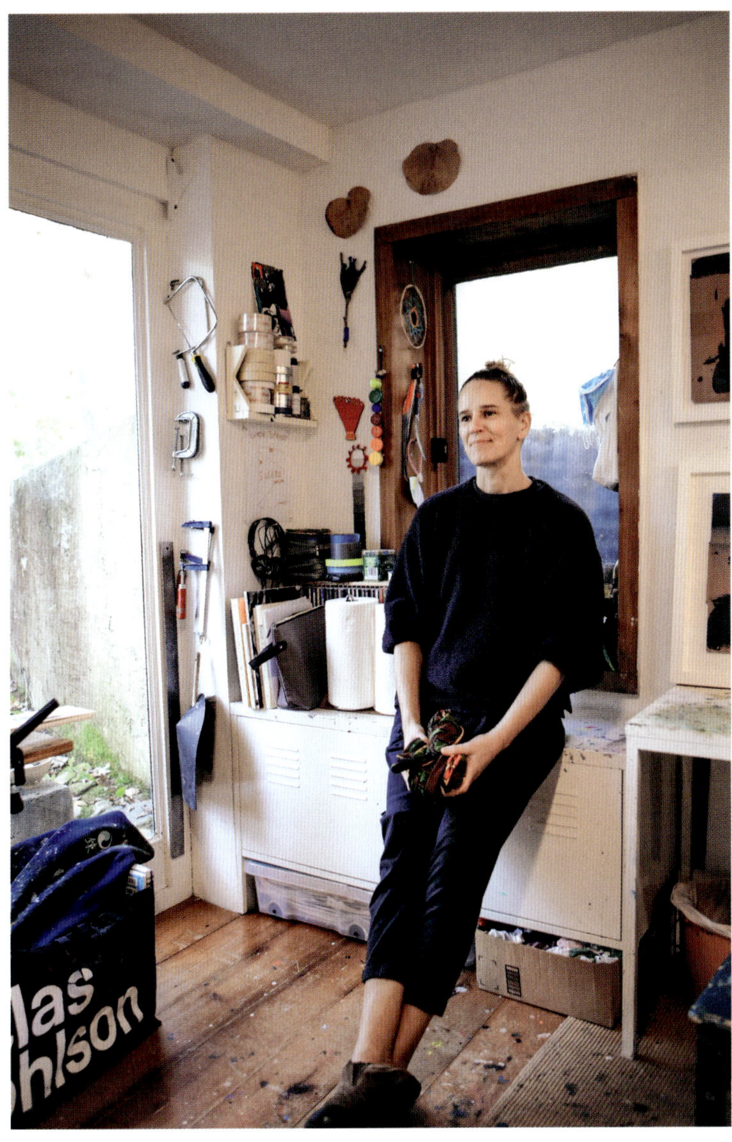

OPPOSITE

A self-described "outdoorsy person," Hinnemo, originally from Finland, is perfectly at home in East Hampton, where she and her family are surrounded by nature.

LEFT AND BELOW

Because her works are mostly small-scale, the artist needs little space for her studio, which occupies half the former garage. The other half is used by her artist husband, George Negroponte.

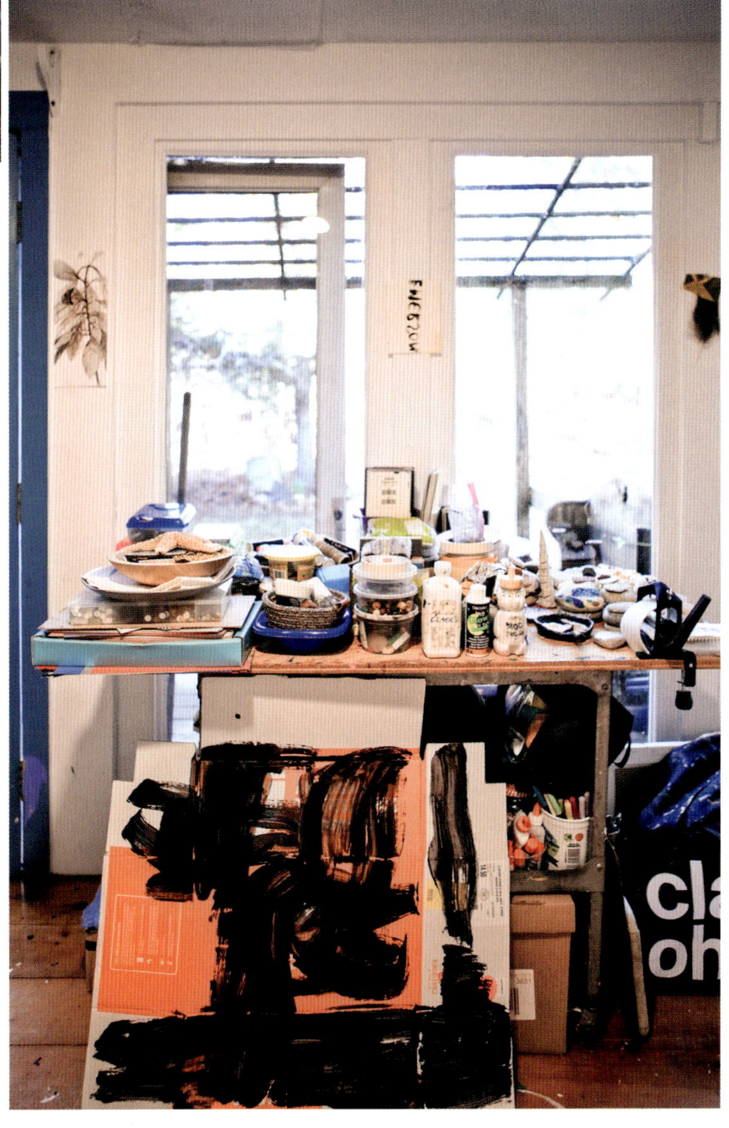

Though Hinnemo's paintings read as abstract, they also contain figurative elements such as trees. "There is always a connection to the 'seen'—to the view, the landscape, and my surroundings. So much of my work seems to be a fusion of how I see and what I see. I do consider myself an abstract artist, but perhaps that is an easy label. I'm not sure I care what label is placed on me. One word doesn't describe very much. It's a big clue, but one needs so many more words to give nuance to the work."

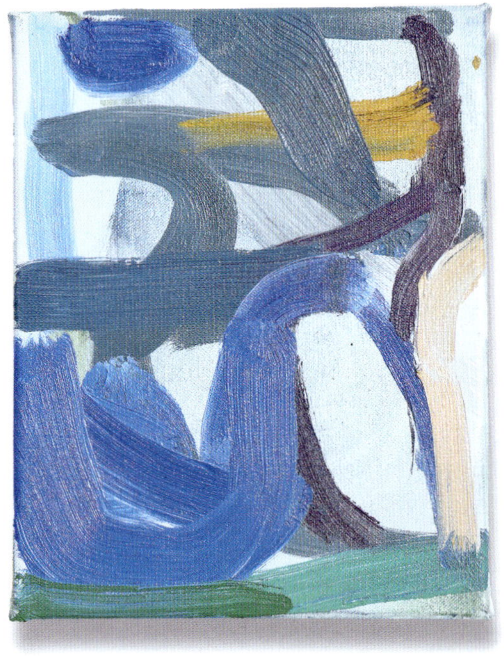

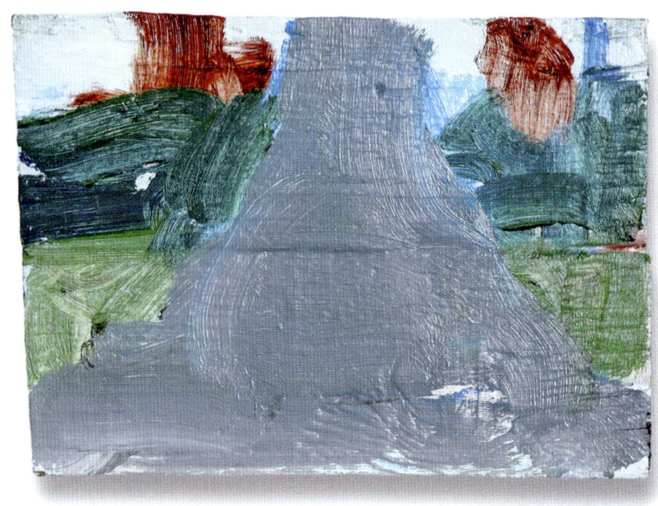

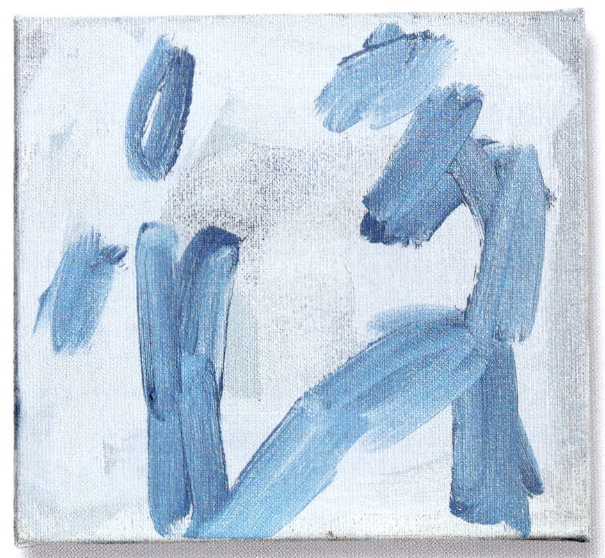

Hinnemo's main mediums are acrylic on cardboard and oil on linen. "Cardboard is a great support, and I've come to love some of the strange shapes and designs in found cardboard boxes. I've been using oil for over twenty-five years. The brush and paint glide across the surface with little friction, leaving a fresh mark that looks like it was just made, even many years later." Hinnemo mostly works small. "There's something about the relationship of the scale of the brushstroke to a small work that is difficult to mimic in a large work. A small work offers an intimacy I don't find when viewing very large works. A small work draws you in and surprises with its toughness and its power because it doesn't show off."

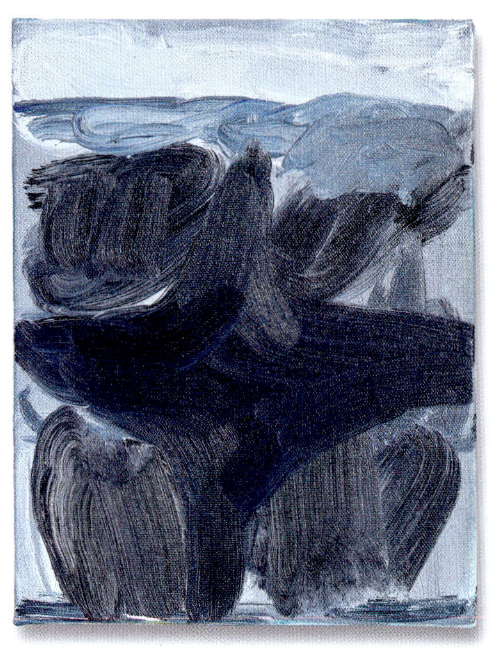

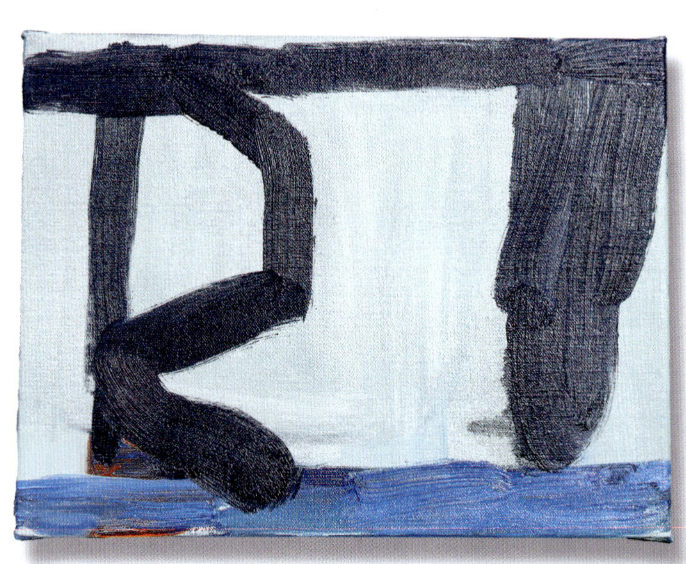

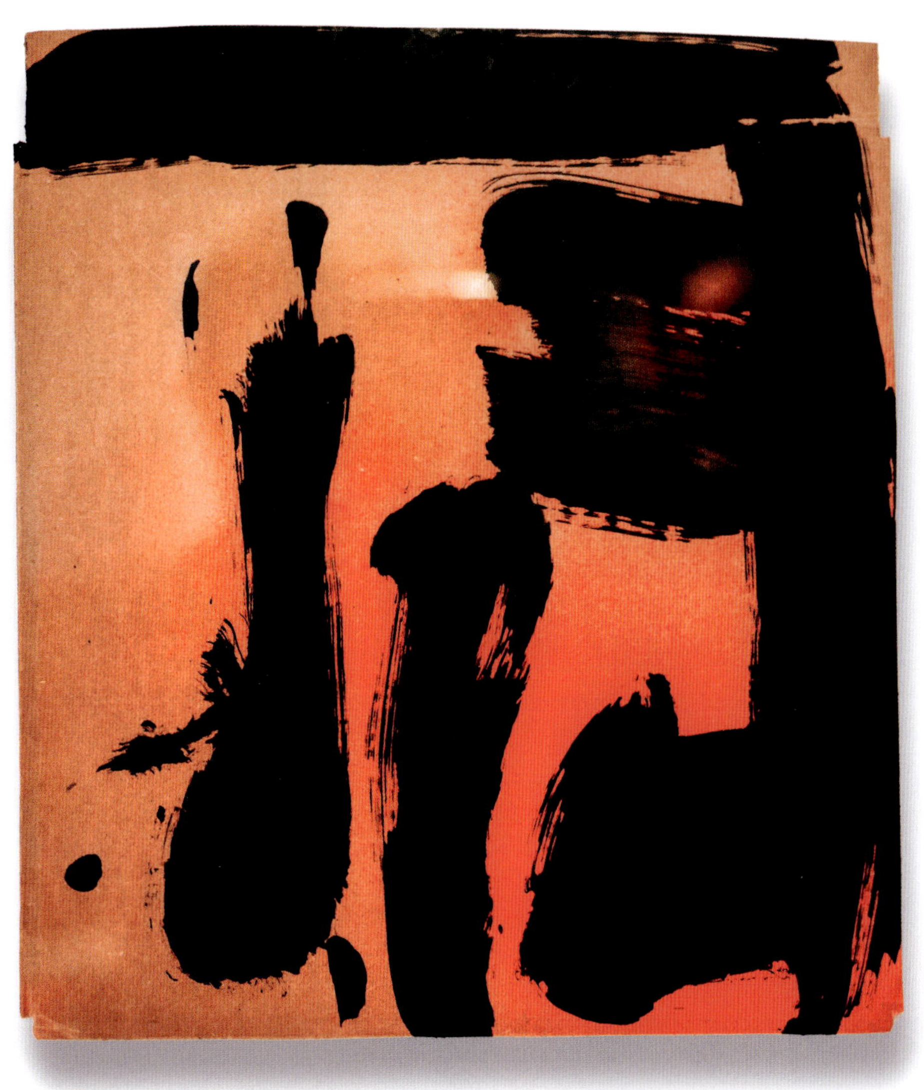

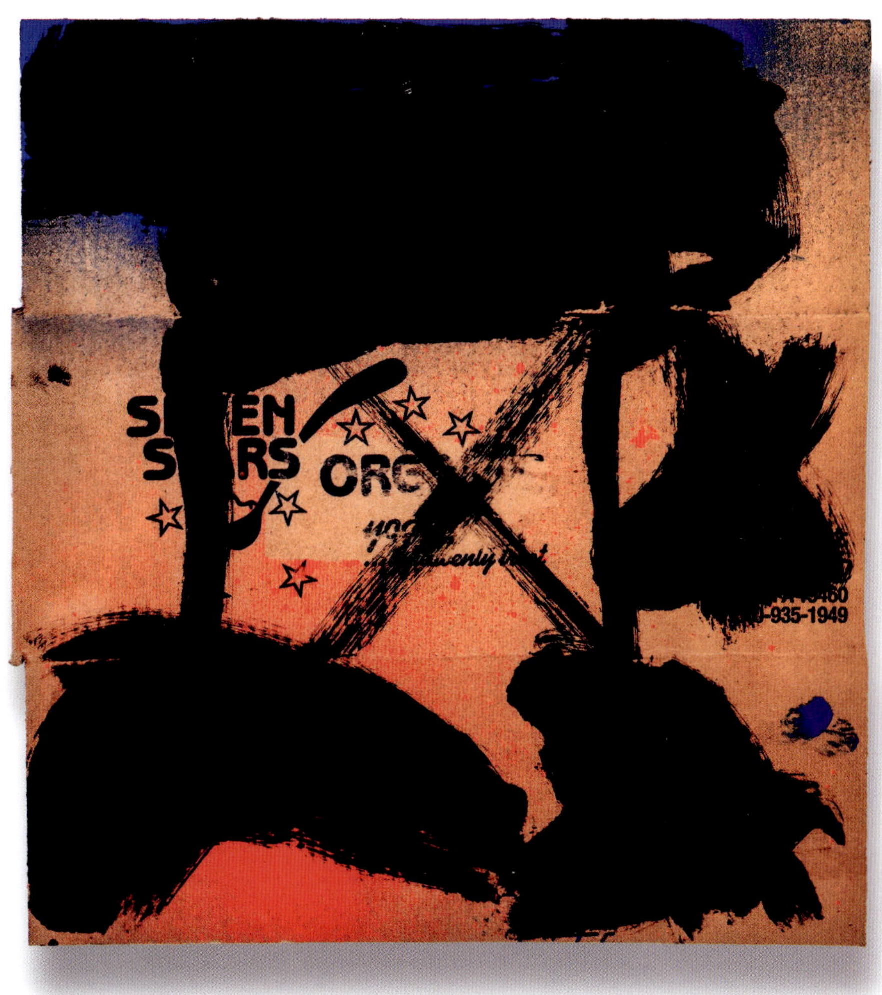

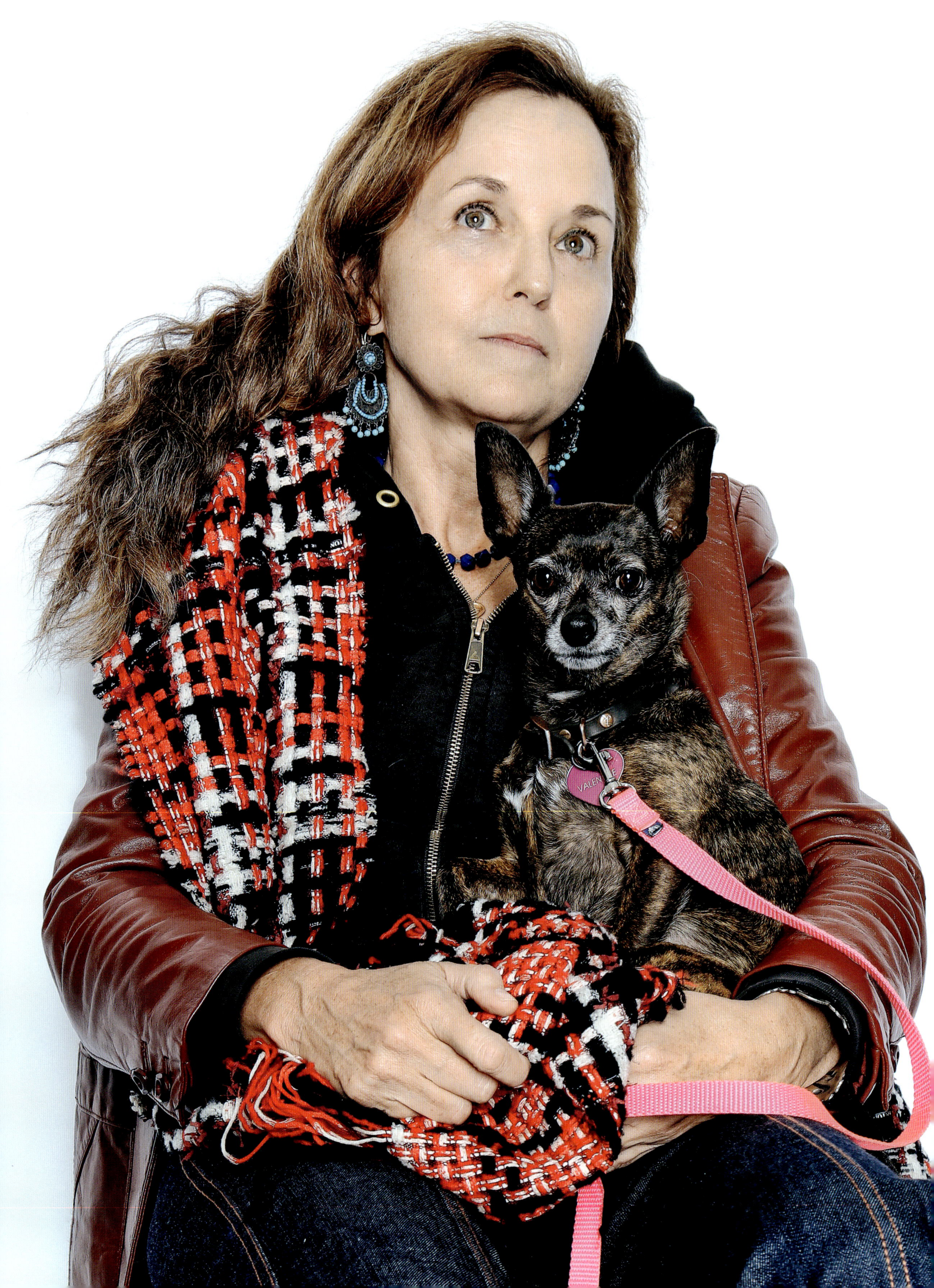

I like it when my materials have cultural references as well as an everyday use.

ALICE HOPE

"I moved here, to Springs, from another part of the country where being an artist wasn't considered a real thing. But on the East End, being an artist is practically mainstream. Art is in the water of this place, and that acceptance makes it home. My favorite time to work is before sunrise. I don't have to go far to start working. My studio has taken over my house, and I've had to kick out most of the furniture to make room for projects." Three-dimensional creations hang and drape all over her studio/living area. "I try to keep things organized because of the hundreds of thousands of small parts, but way too often I'm looking for something I can't find—most often scissors, despite having a pair on every surface."

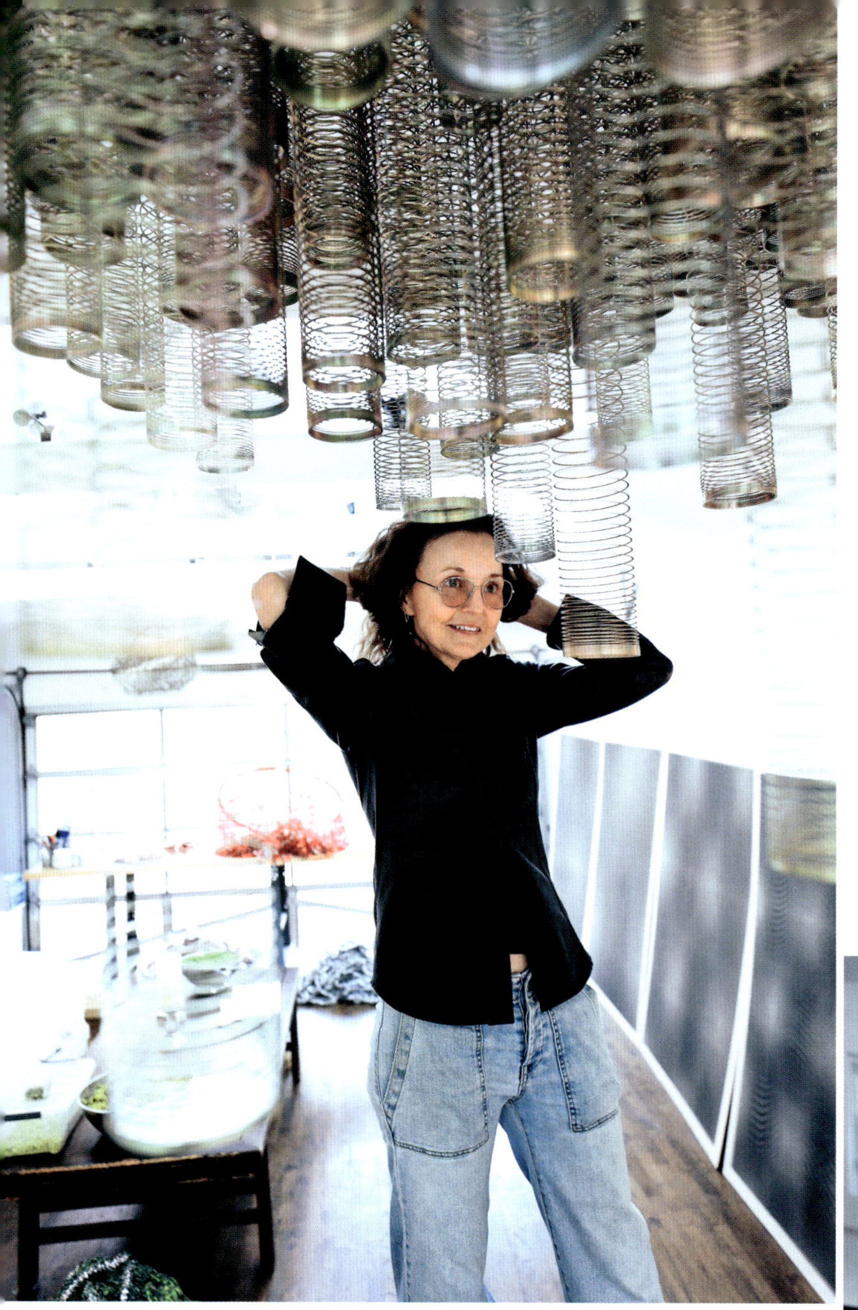

Hope uses a variety of everyday materials in her artwork, from blue painter's tape to commercial fishing nets. "The net is a global and ancient tool, and painter's tape can be found in almost everyone's utility drawer." For the last ten years or so, her main material has been the used can tab. "It can be looked at from many perspectives. It's an anti-phallus with its equal negative and positive space. It's obsolescence. It's a tool, a lever. It's trash. It's an icon."

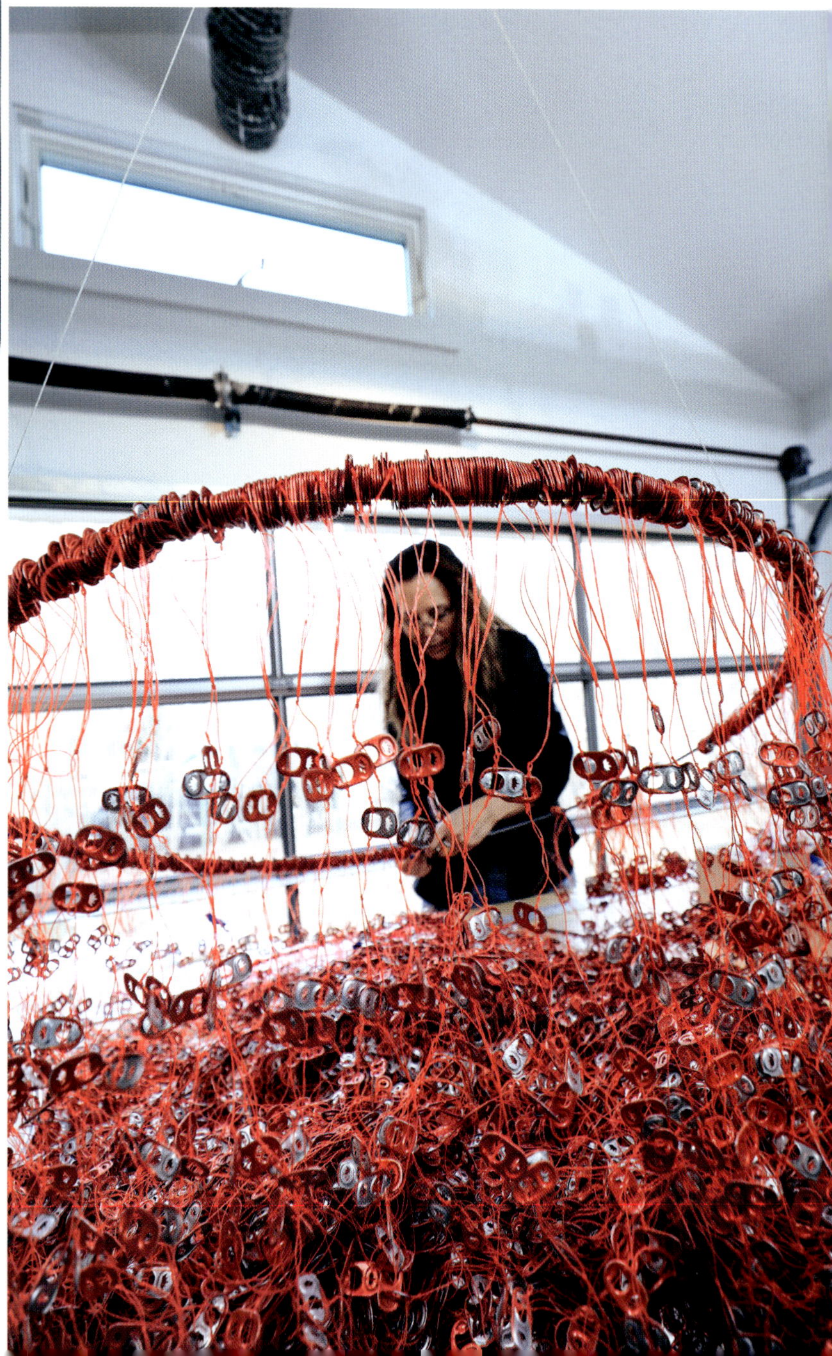

ABOVE

Hope's sculptural assemblages hang from the ceiling of her Springs home, which doubles as her studio space.

RIGHT AND OPPOSITE

The artist at work on one of her three-dimensional projects. Baskets and containers hold her numerous collections of found objects, such as can tabs, which she repurposes for her creations.

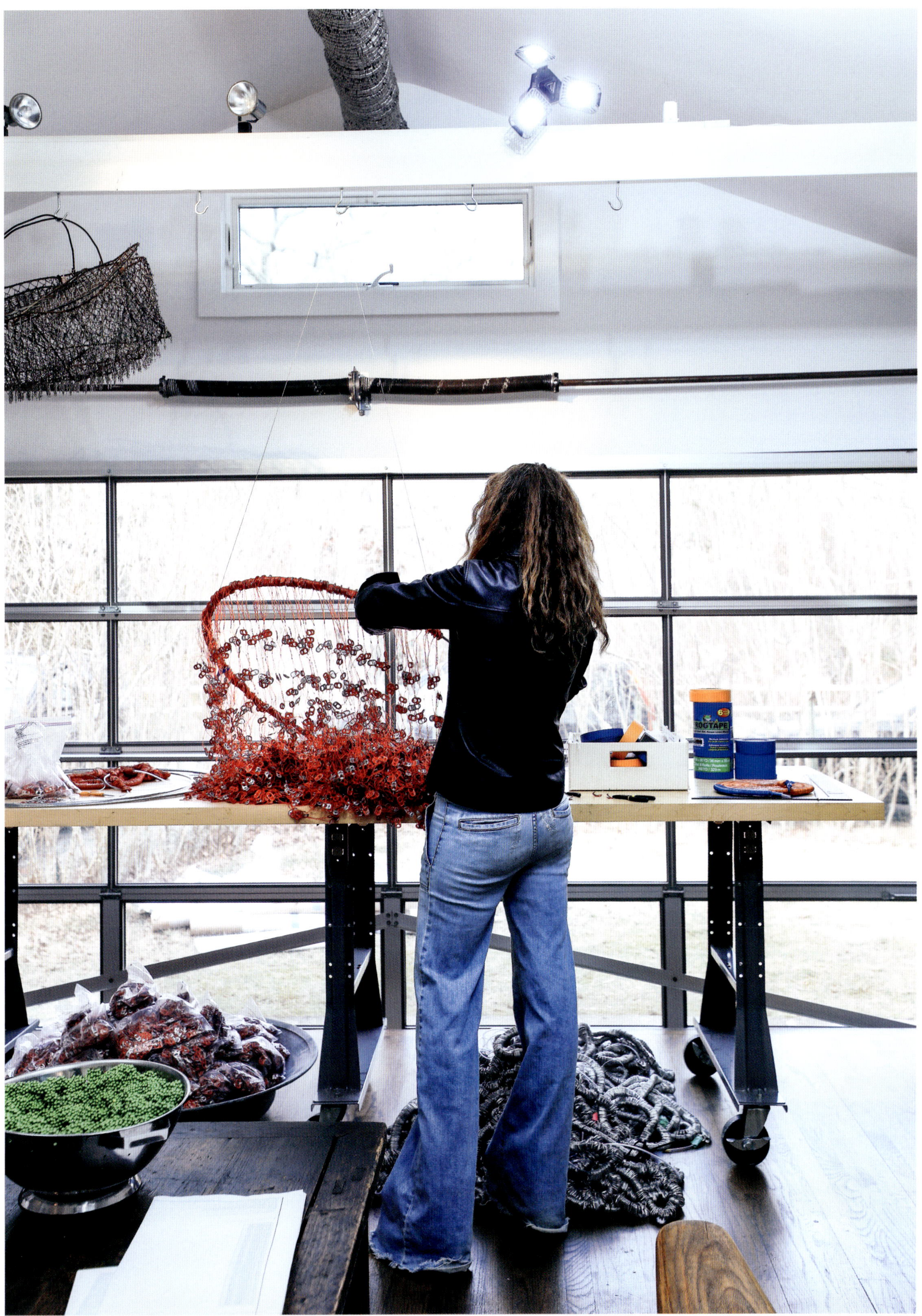

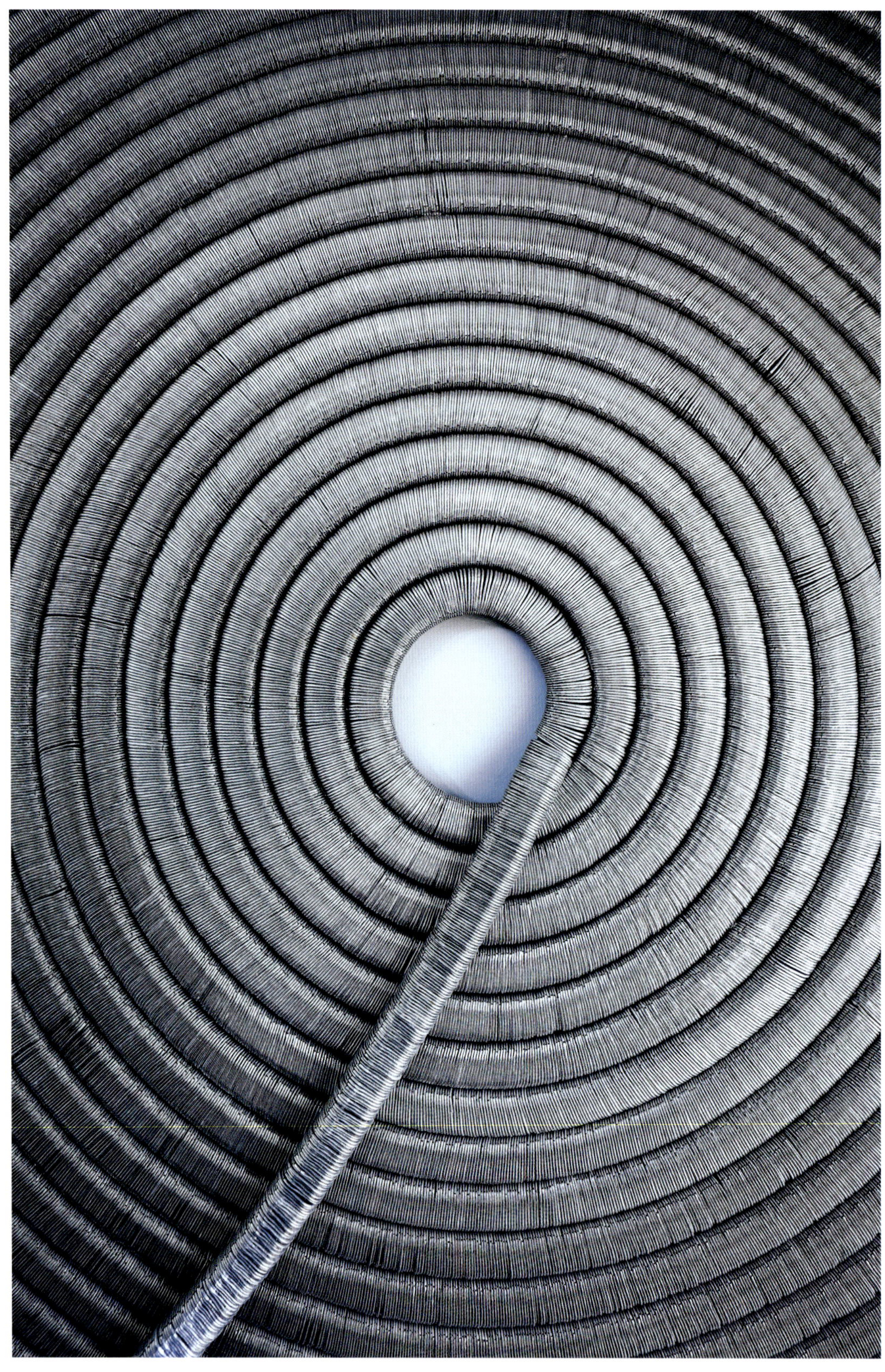

"Each of the used can tabs in my sculptures represents a moment of time when a soda or beer can was opened by someone somewhere. And each of the can tabs represents a donation, since they were collected and redeemed for charities. I see my works as a meta-hand-holding collaboration because of the tens of thousands of hands involved. My primary tool is my hand, as is theirs, in the collective gesture of opening cans and collecting tabs."

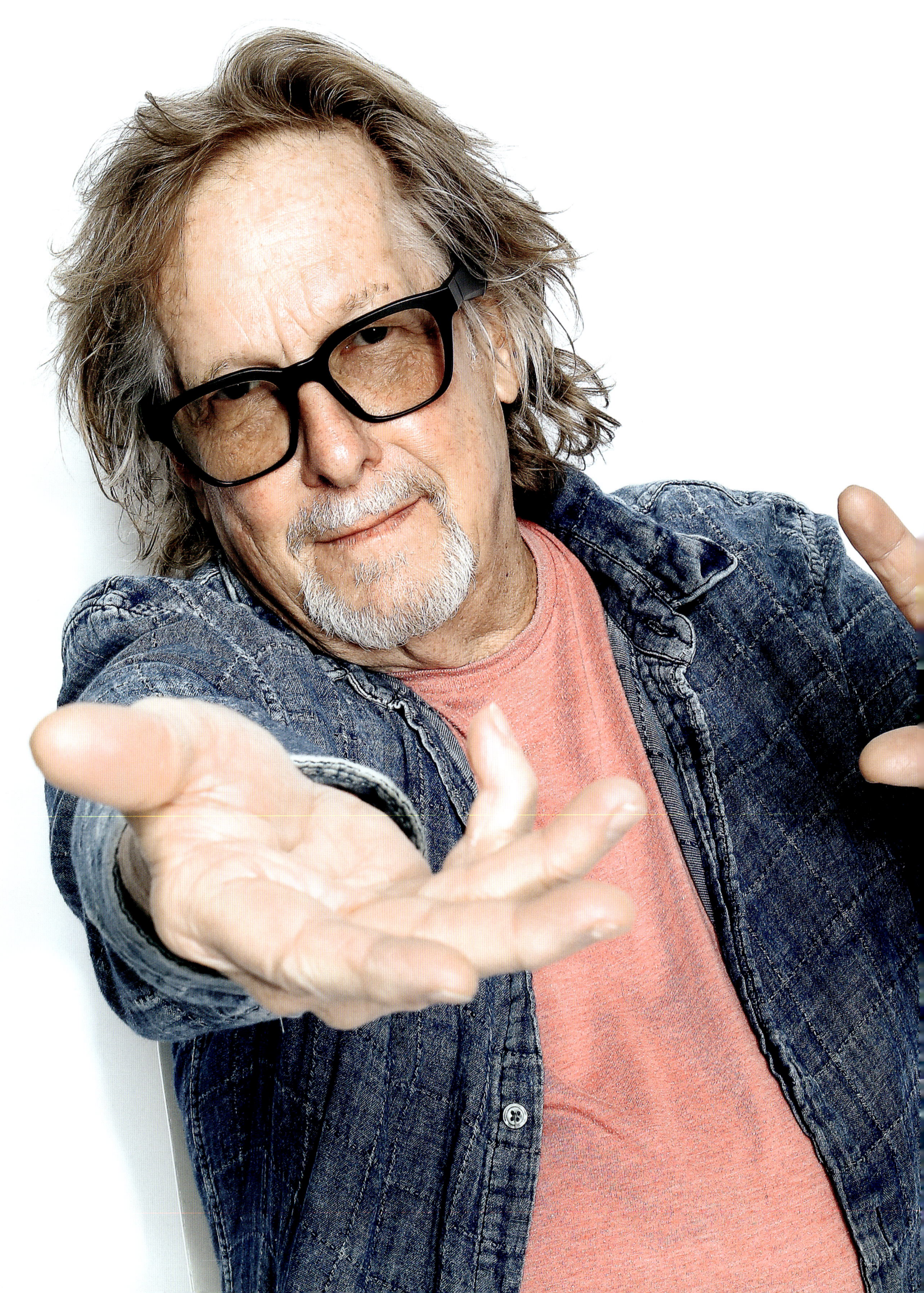

If there is a continual thread in my work,
I hope that it's an openness to discovery and
the delight in seeing things in things.

BRYAN HUNT

In 1991, after twenty years in New York City, Hunt moved to Wainscott. "I wanted a change, to be outdoors." He found a spacious studio near his house, across from a farm field and the ocean beyond. "That sublime view is my meditation and a good part of why I'm here. The seasons and the wildlife are inspiring." And the studio itself? "Also inspiring, with its high ceilings, big doors, natural light, and a decent sound system. I do like music playing to fill a mood."

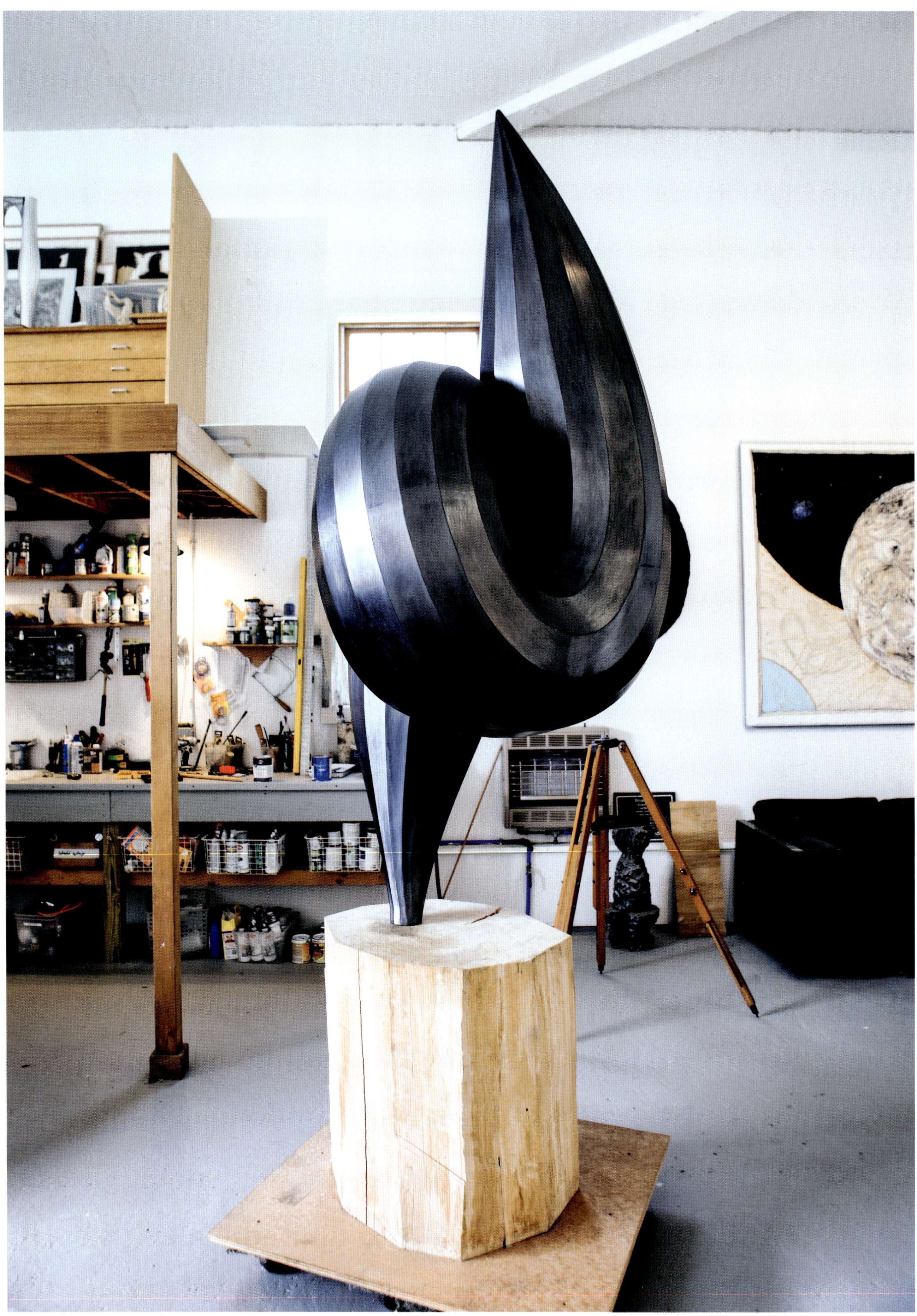

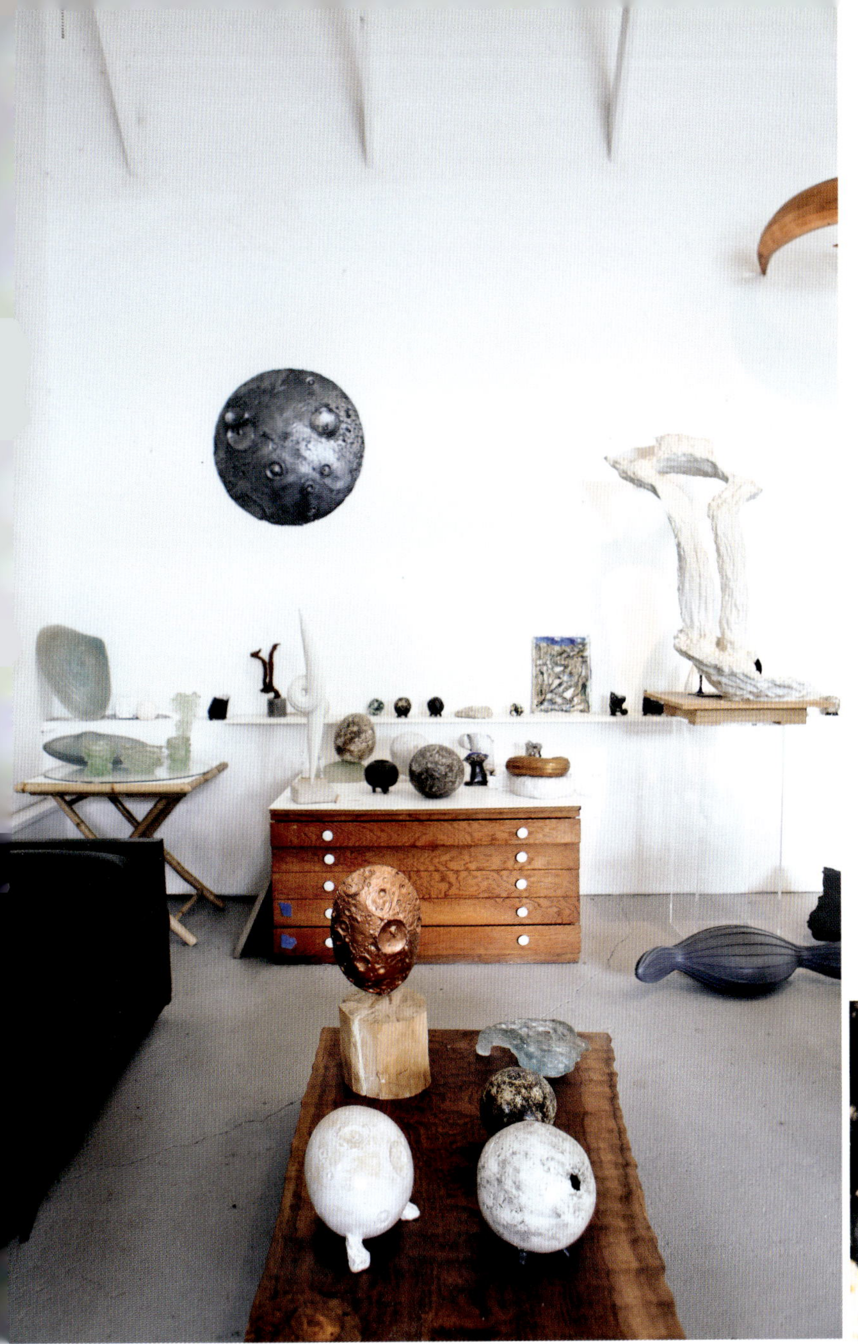

OPPOSITE

Hunt's sculptures and wall works—in a variety of materials and on a scale from small to tall—are visible from every angle in his lofty, light-filled Wainscott studio.

LEFT AND BELOW

The artist's abstract works, which often evoke elements of outer space or ocean life, fill his studio with color and biomorphic forms.

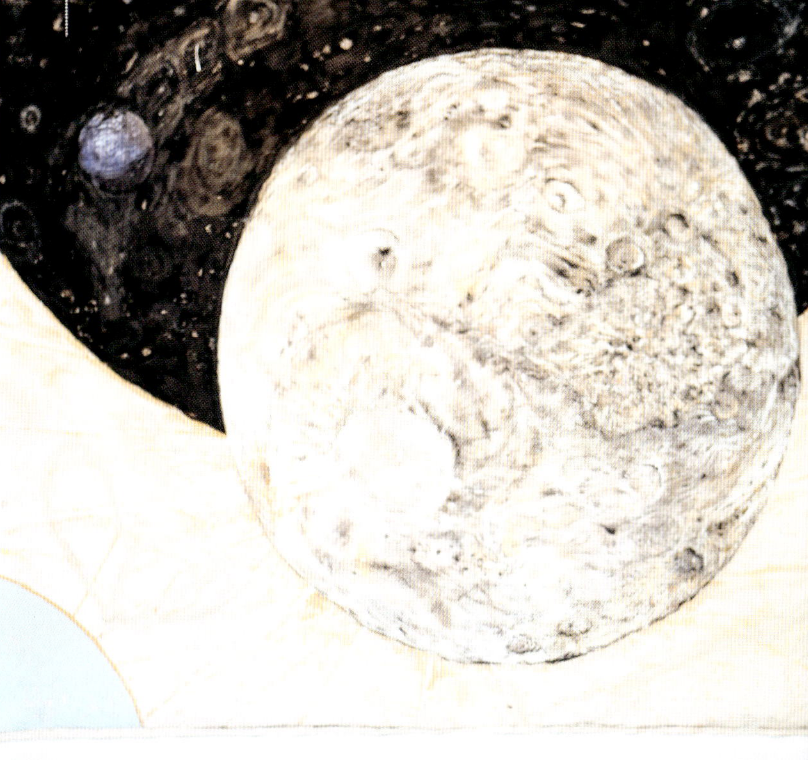

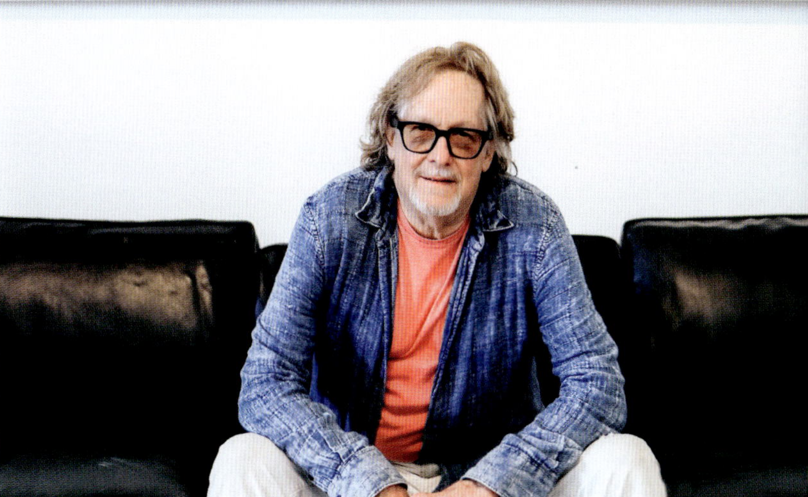

Hunt's fascination with outer space began with a job as an engineer's assistant at NASA. "I was twenty years old, at college in Tampa, Florida, where I grew up. I decided to take a year off and follow a fantasy. I moved to Cocoa Beach to look for work at Kennedy Space Center and was hired by Grumman Aircraft because I had taken drafting courses. Grumman built the lunar module that landed on the moon. It was the most fantastic job imaginable. I had clearance to the launch pads, to the vertical assembly building. I ended up working for NASA for two years while I saved up enough money to go to art school in Los Angeles."

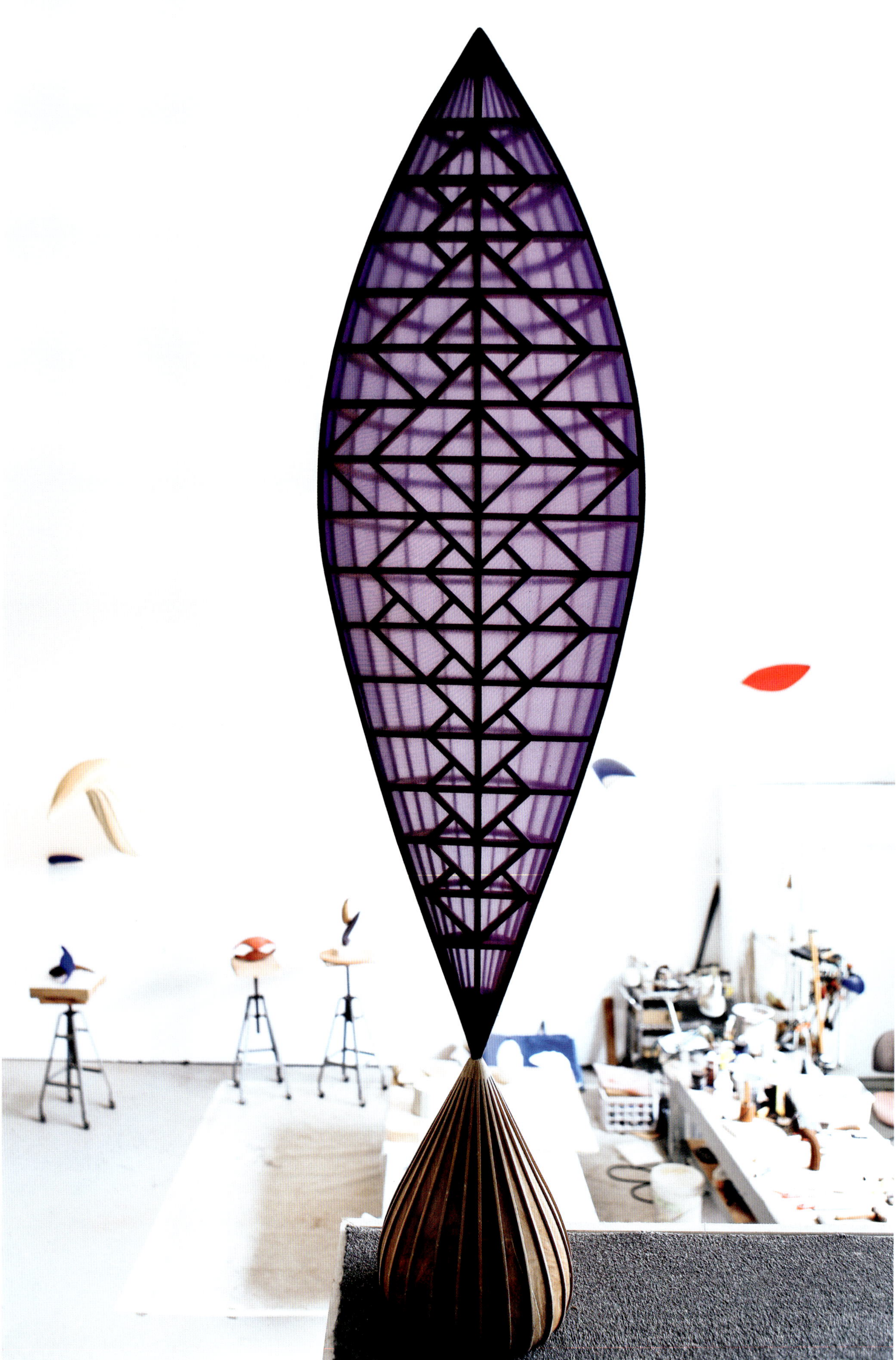

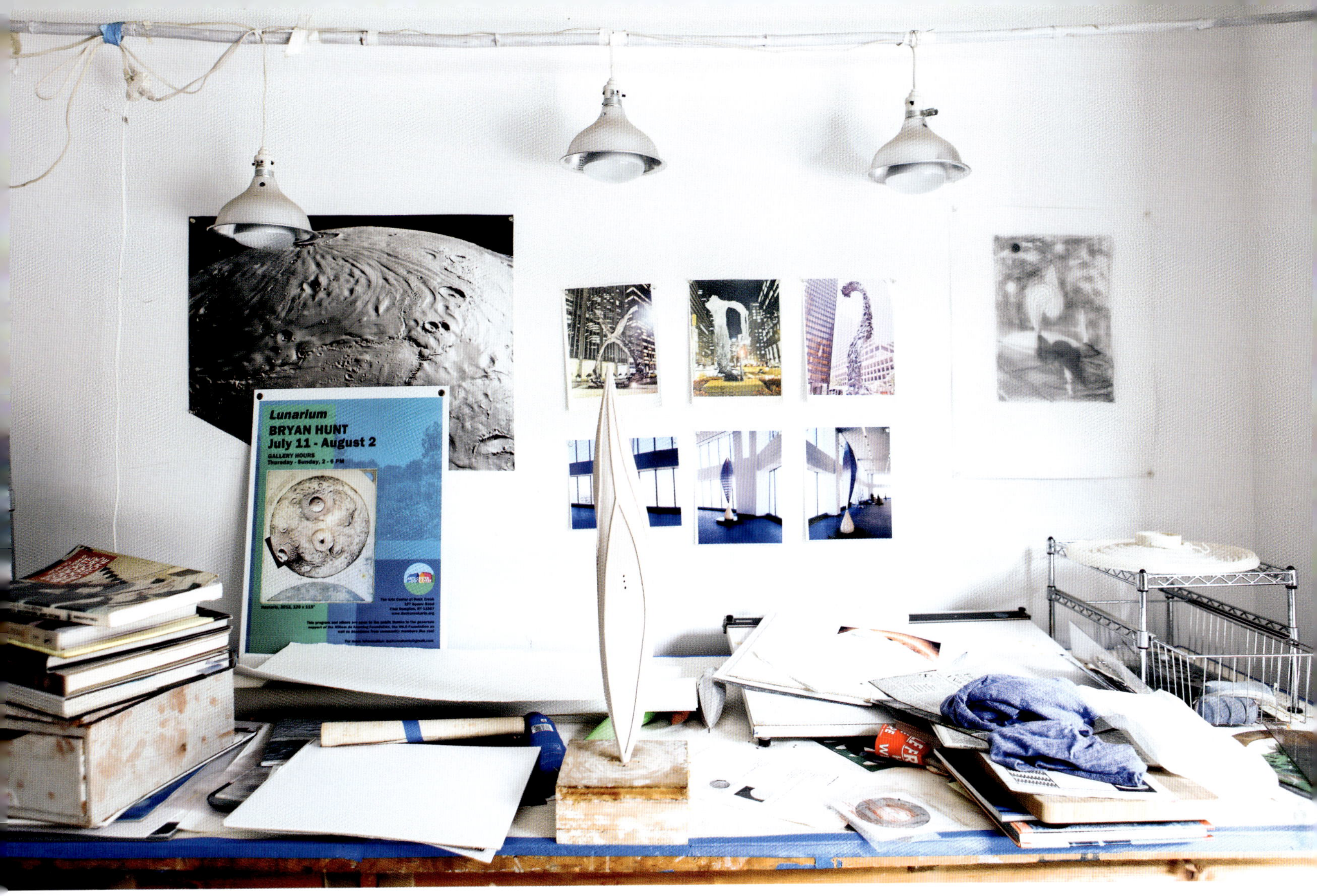

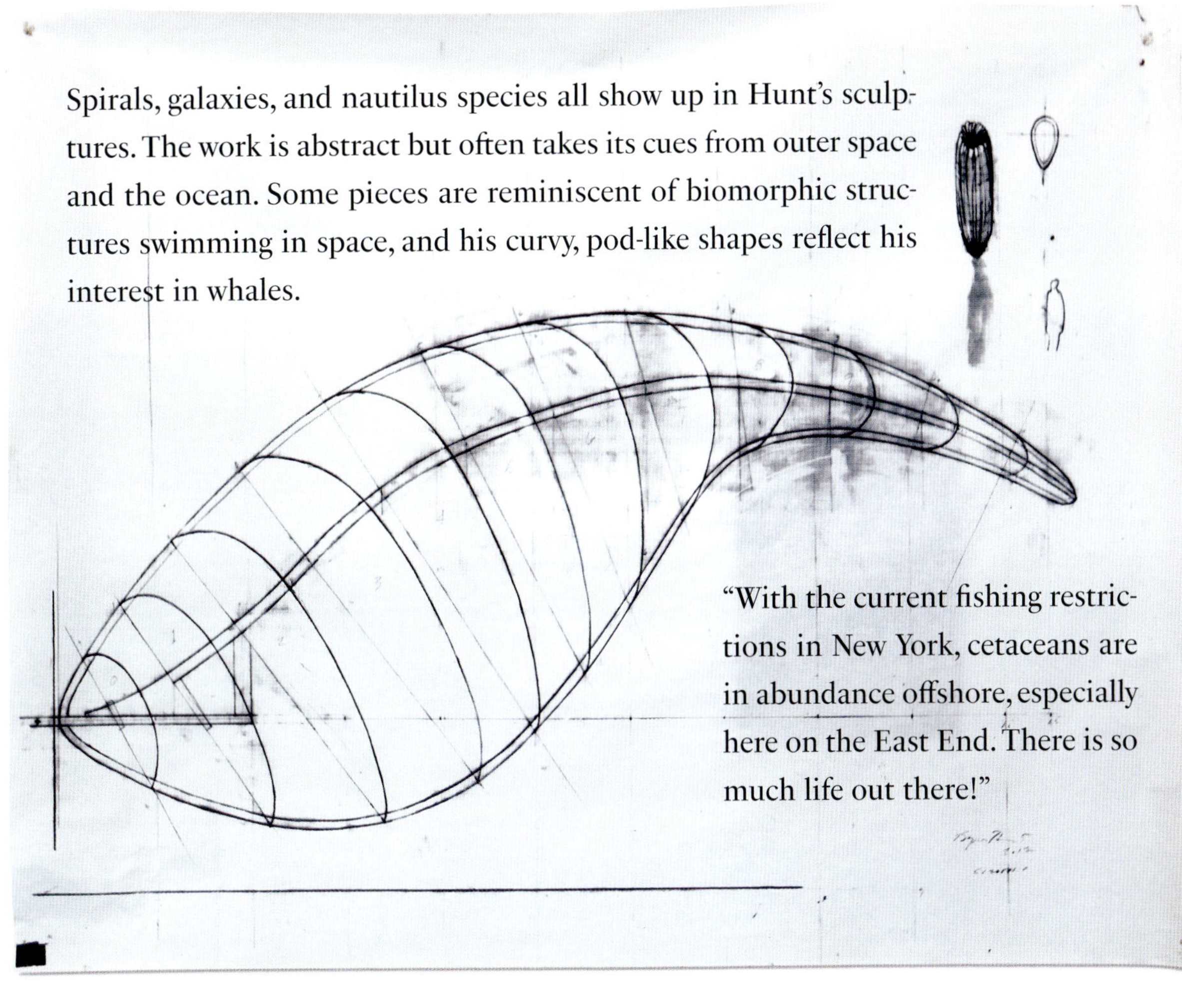

Spirals, galaxies, and nautilus species all show up in Hunt's sculptures. The work is abstract but often takes its cues from outer space and the ocean. Some pieces are reminiscent of biomorphic structures swimming in space, and his curvy, pod-like shapes reflect his interest in whales.

"With the current fishing restrictions in New York, cetaceans are in abundance offshore, especially here on the East End. There is so much life out there!"

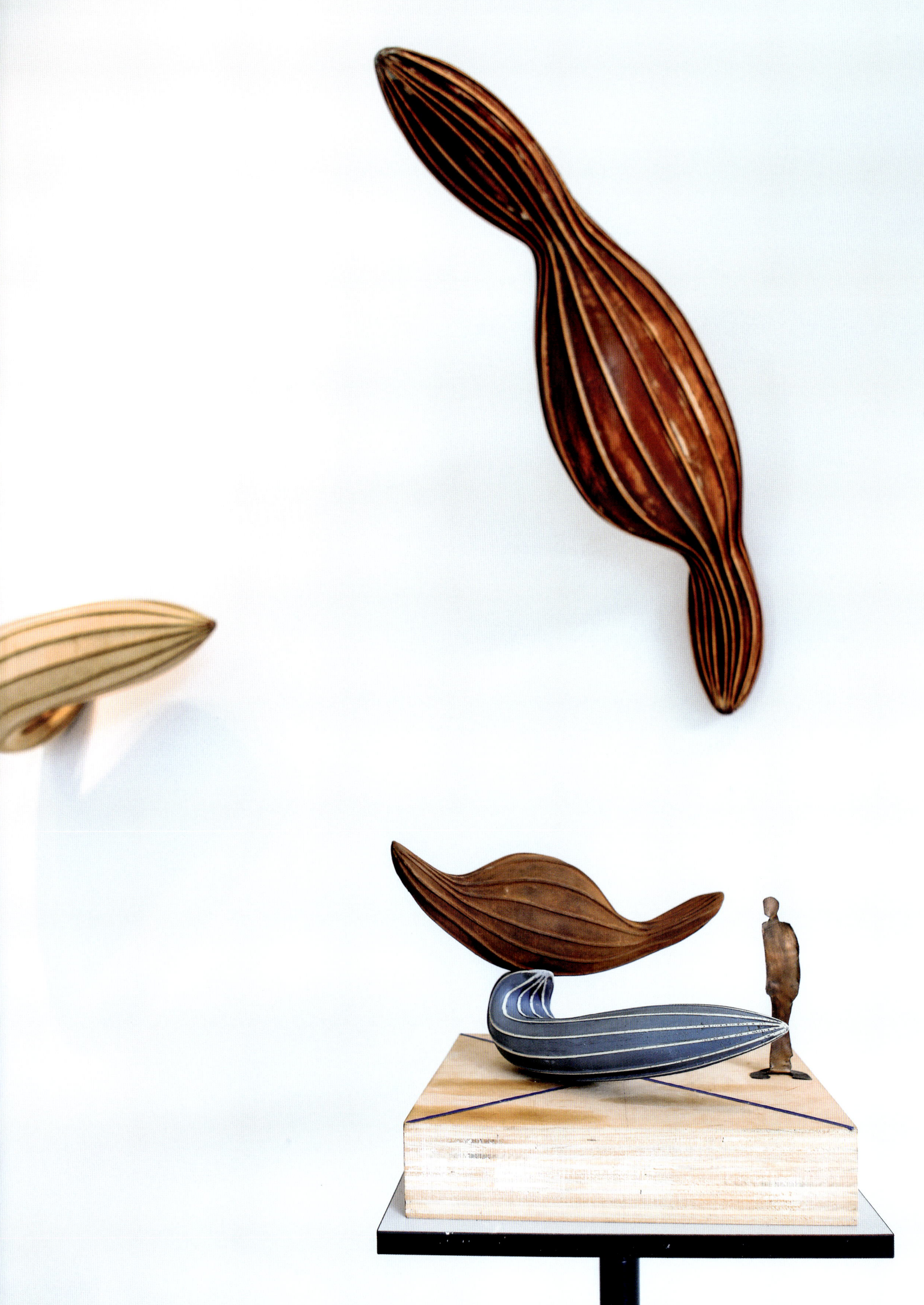

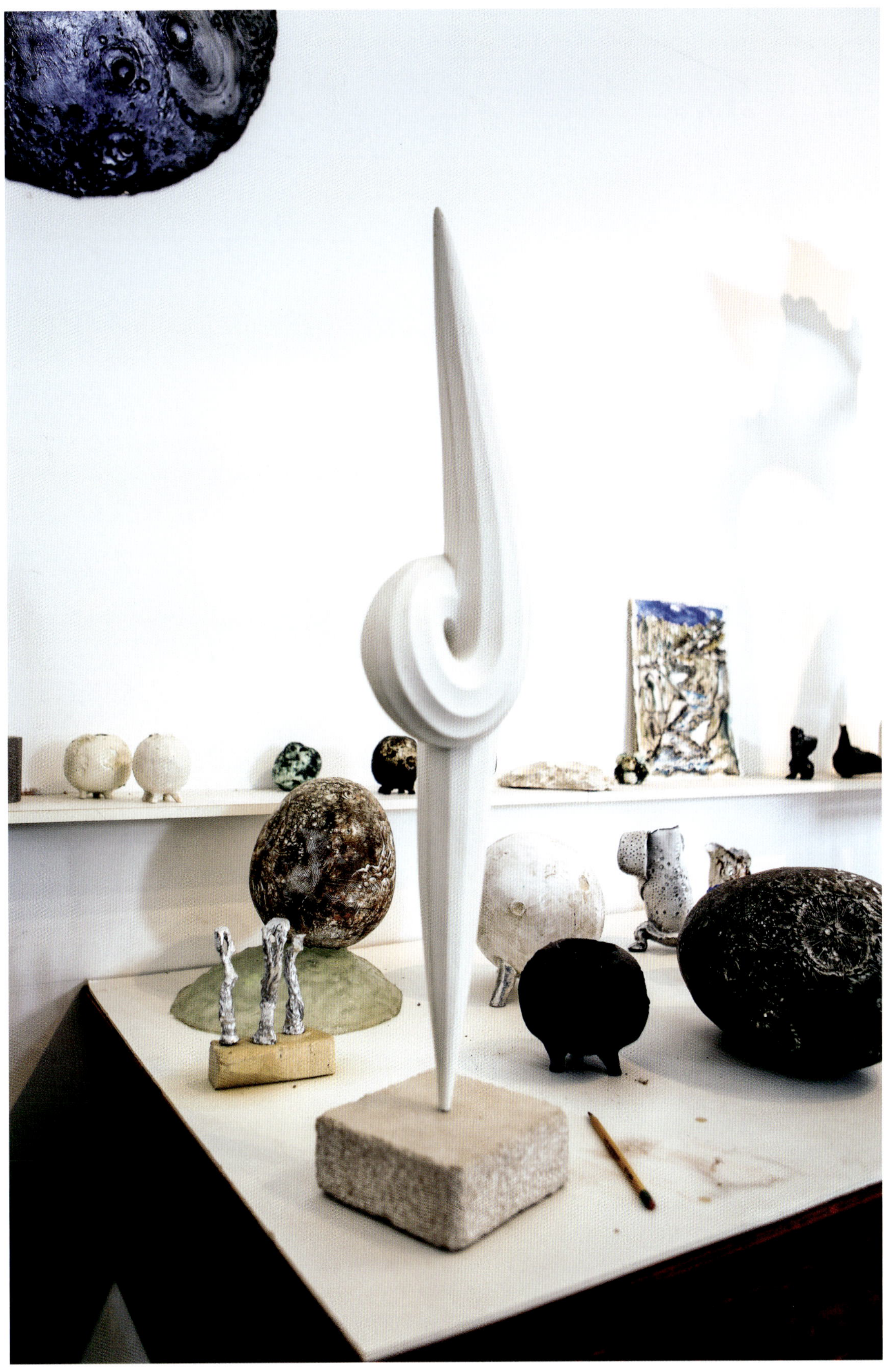

While Hunt identifies as a sculptor, he also paints. "I like to think that my paintings are a lens with which to see through things—to see line and shape flattened in space, to discover intended and unintended connections in natural forms within a rectangle."

The two threads running through my work are a reverence for nature and a creative dialogue with artists past and present.

LAURIE LAMBRECHT

Lambrecht was born in Southampton and raised in Bridgehampton, "back when it was very much a small farming community," as she puts it. She left to go to college but always came home for vacations and summers. "While home one summer during college, I worked as a hostess at [the original] Bobby Van's, a jazz venue on the weekends. Well-known authors and artists would hang out there. I now know that it was special, but I had nothing to compare it to. It was normal to me, at eighteen!" After college she moved to New York City, where she lived for three decades, going back and forth to Bridgehampton. She finally made the move to live here full-time in 2010. Her studio, which was built on the footprint of the garage, is her "happy place." "Of course, it's too small, but it has lovely, familiar light from the area where I grew up. It's my sailboat, my VW camper, my wilderness tent, my sandbox, my mountain cabin, my sanctuary."

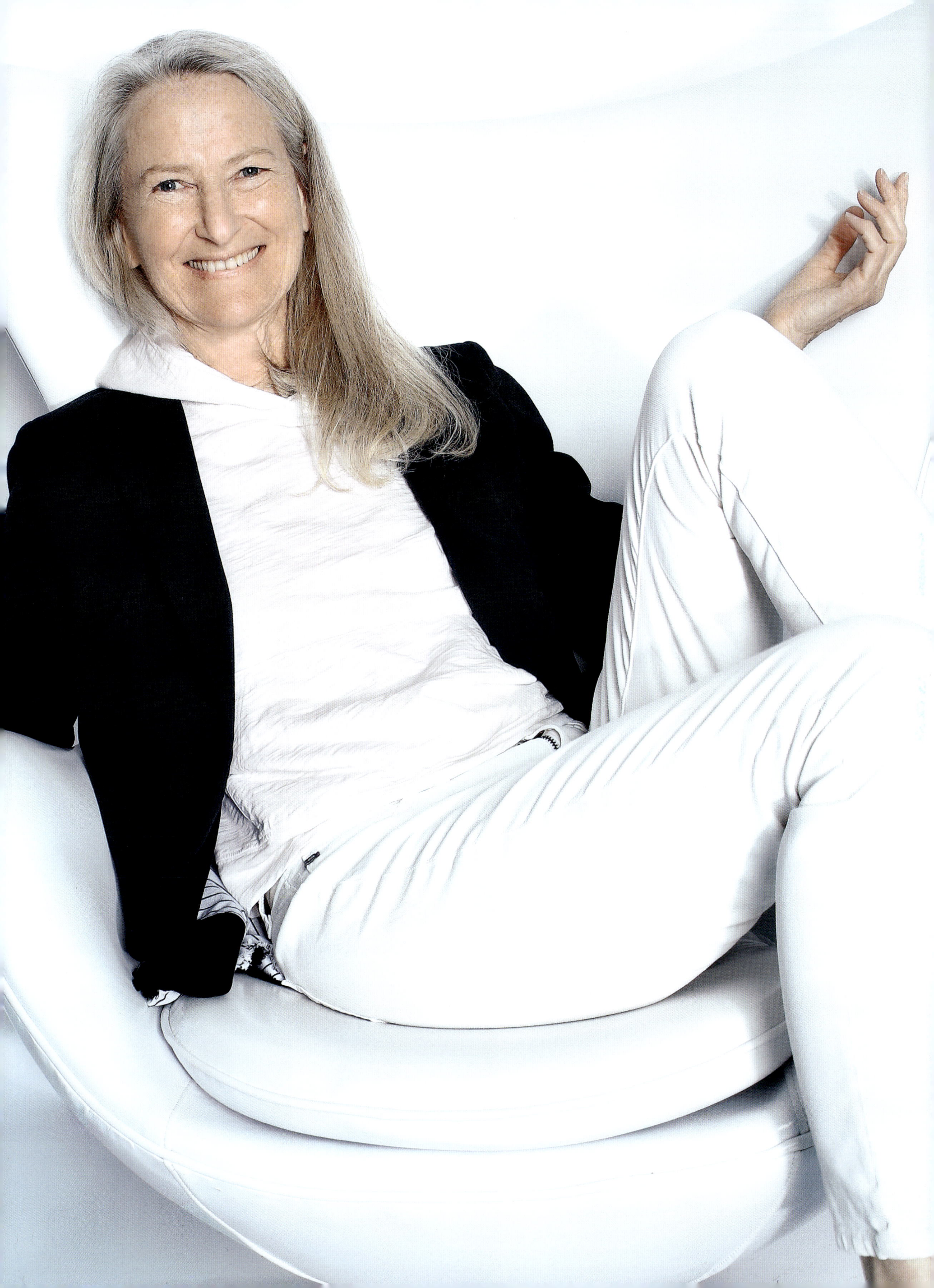

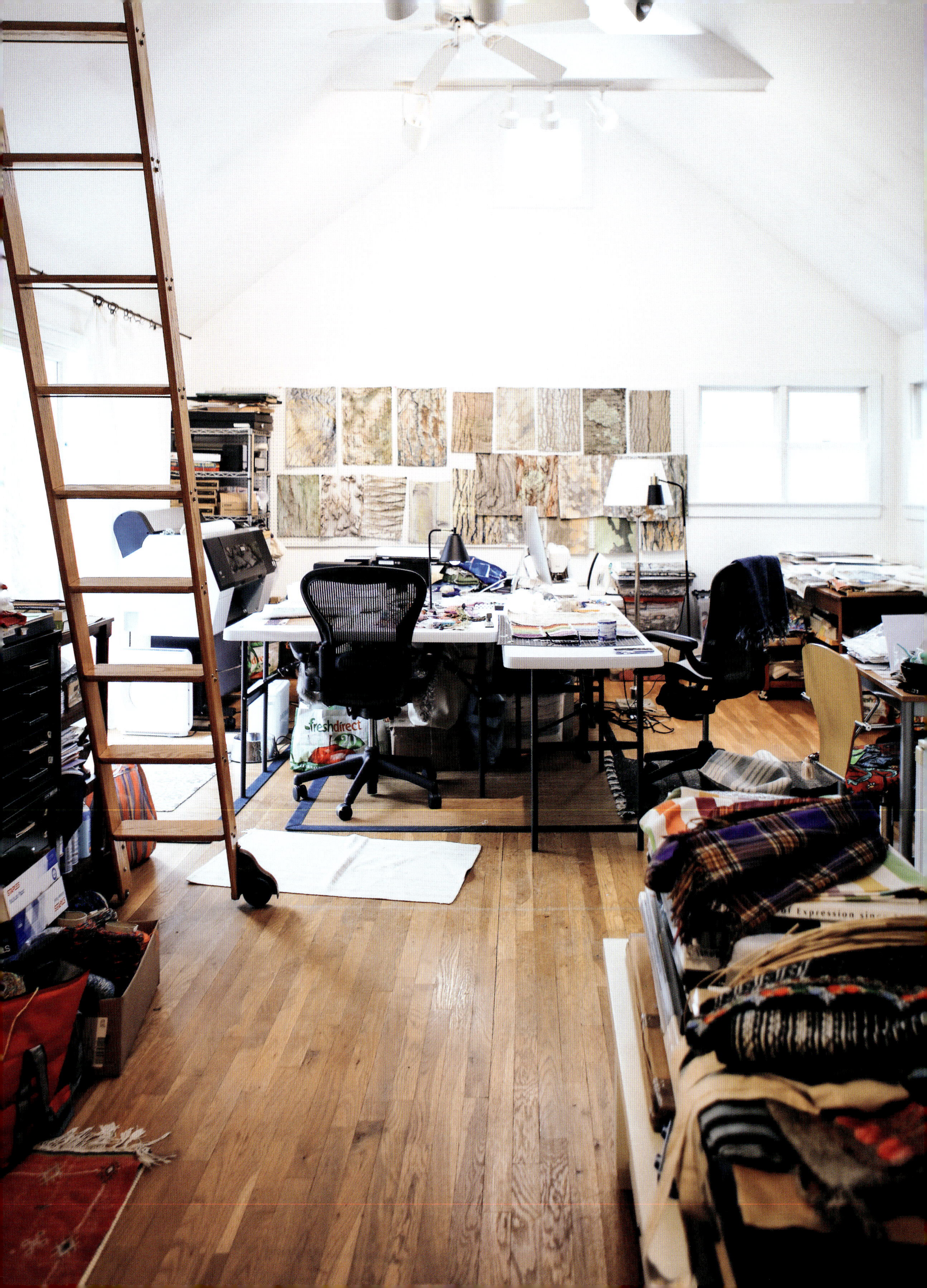
freshdirect

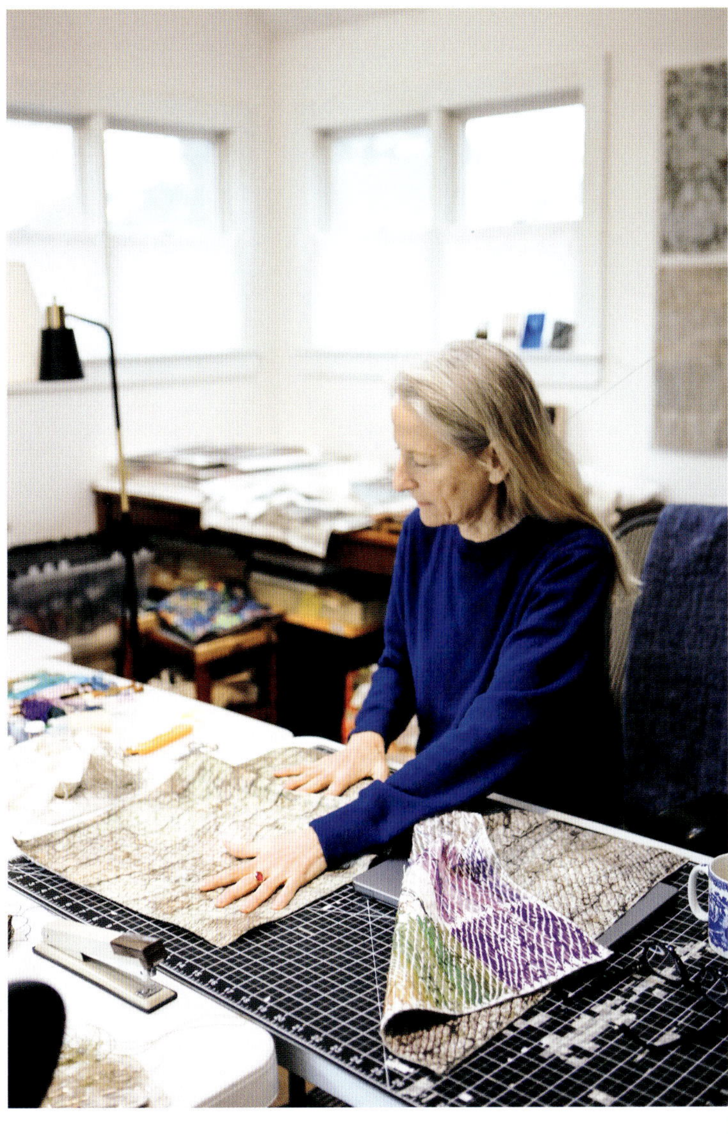

OPPOSITE
Lambrecht's studio is built on the site of the former garage of her house in Bridgehampton, the town in which she grew up.

LEFT
The artist's linen pieces are imprinted with images of tree bark. A former sweater designer, she focuses on creating works with a tactile appeal. She says the sense of touch evokes memory.

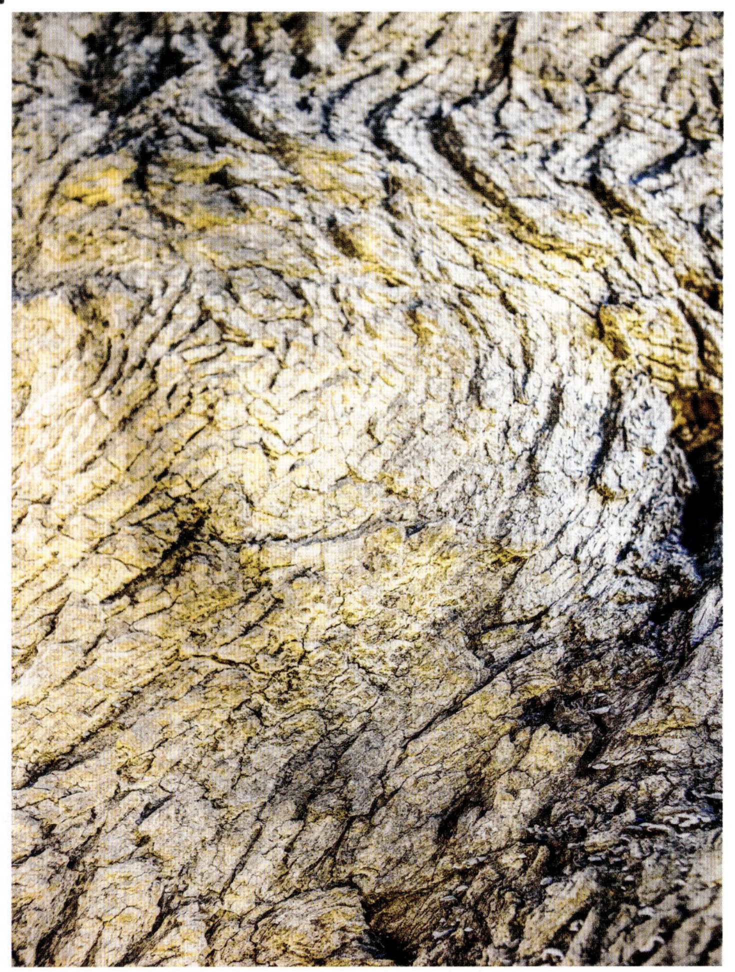

"As a young person, I was spellbound by sewing, embroidery, and knitting. My mother was very creative and loved color. We had beautiful handmade quilts on all the beds in our home. Incredible wallpapers and tablecloths were very much a part of my surroundings." Lambrecht became a sweater designer while in graduate school studying photography. "I went back and forth between my two ways of exploration and expression but didn't fully combine them until the past decade. Now the way something looks or appears is no longer enough. I need to touch and relate with senses beyond my eyes; hence photography and the tactile nature of fiber work."

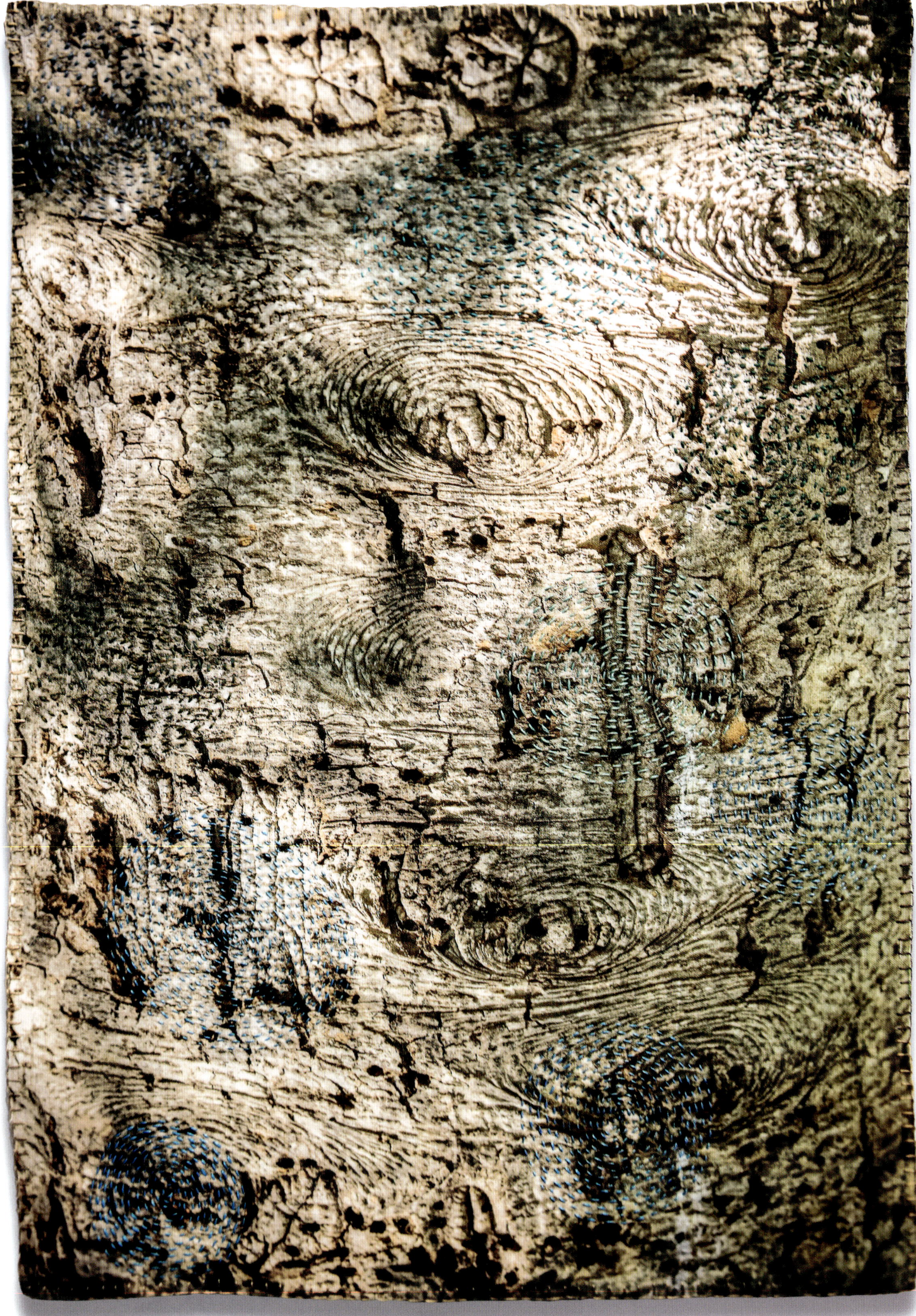

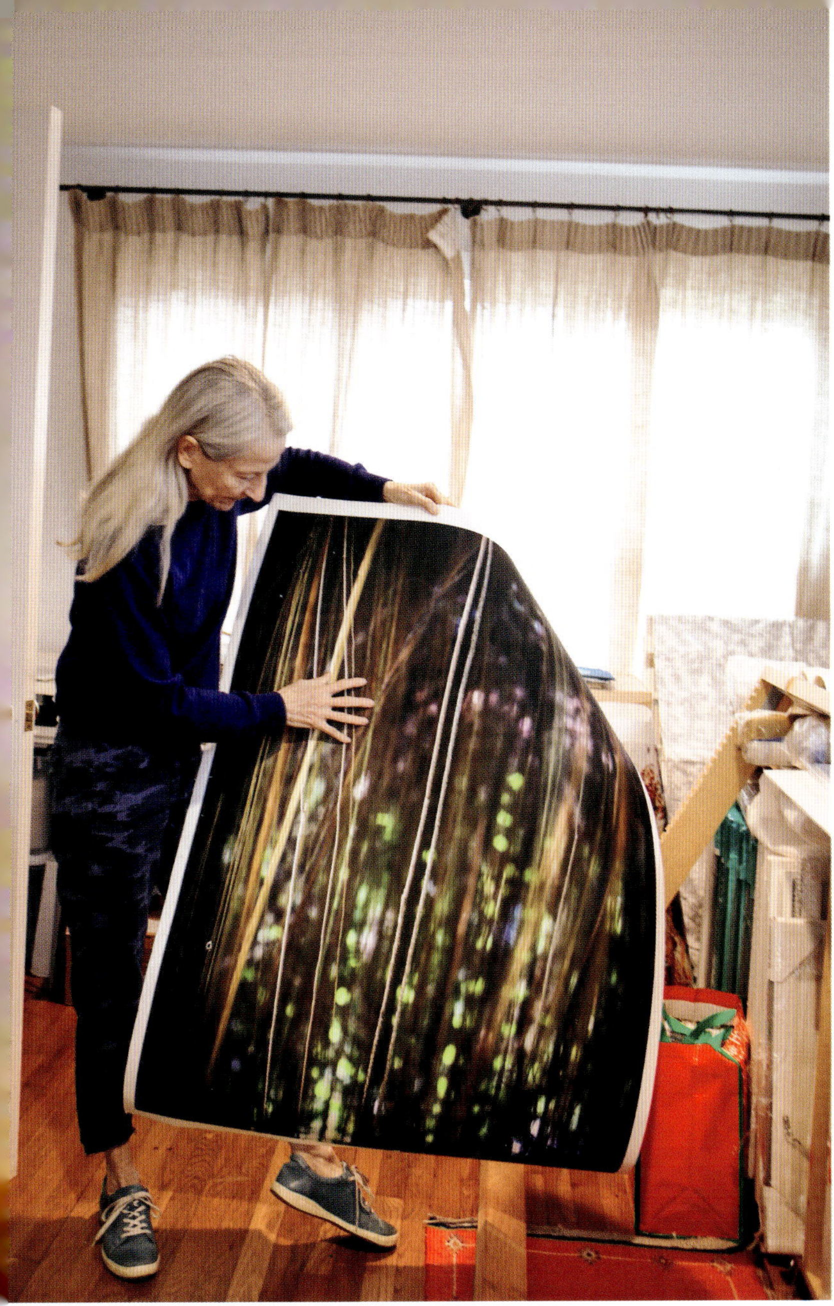

LEFT

Lambrecht expresses herself in many mediums, including photography, one of her first artistic endeavors. Light is always a factor in her photographs.

BELOW

From the time she was a child, Lambrecht has been fascinated by knitting and embroidery, which are an integral part of her artwork.

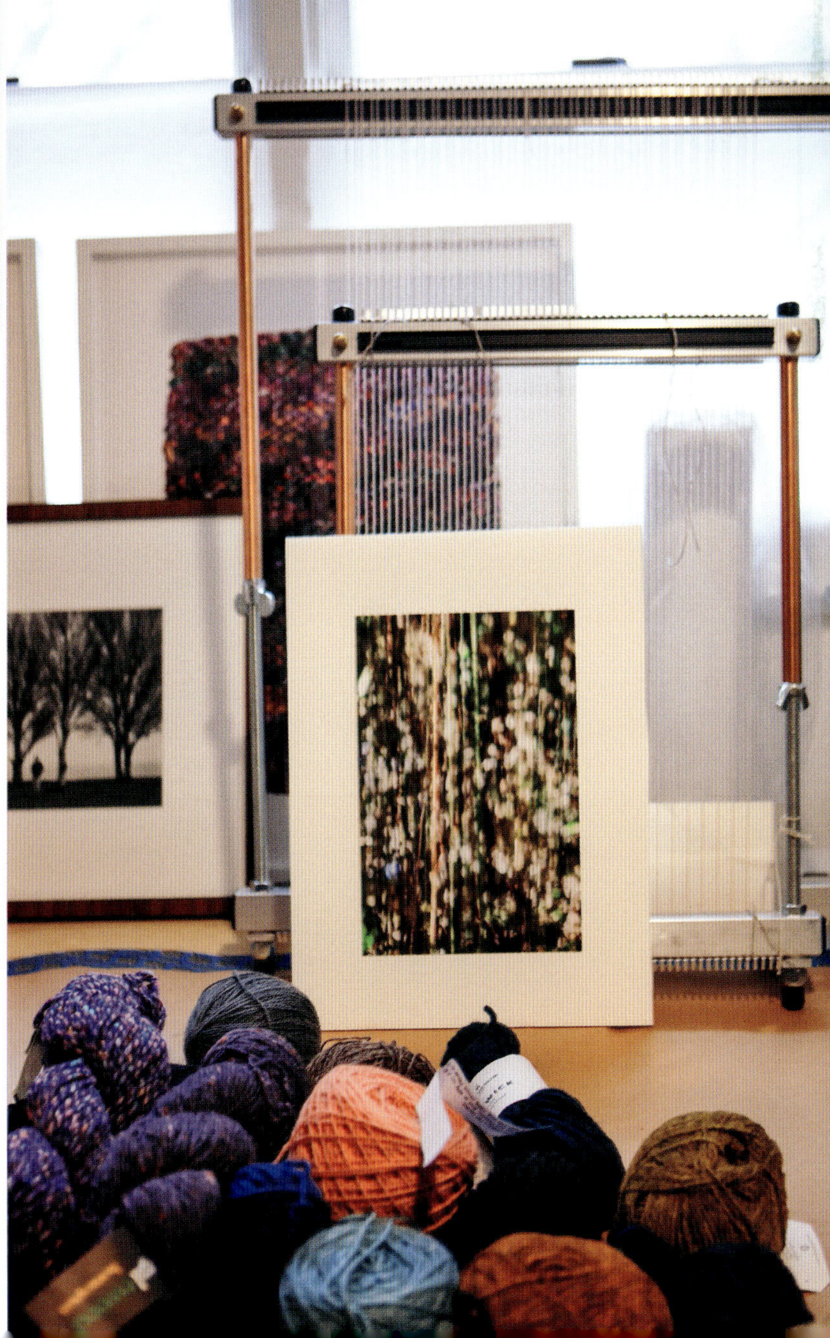

Lambrecht, who studied art, photography, and design, continues to find creative outlets in many mediums, including photography, printmaking, and such fiber arts as knitting, embroidery, and weaving. "With photography, I consider what's visible and how light influences the object or situation. Capturing light is a bit like holding breath or time. Working with a camera has guided how I see and has shaped my vision. Printmaking is and has always been an important part of my expression, and working with fiber involves touch, which is filled with the sensation of memory."

I'm an abstract person who paints.

CLAUDE LAWRENCE

"I first came to live in Sag Harbor in 1994 with a girlfriend. After we broke up, I moved to Philly and worked as a house painter, then went to Chicago—where I had grown up—because I hated Philly. My music and art then found me in Mexico, where I earned a living and took tango lessons. I returned to Chicago, where I met Leslee Stradford. After a stint in France, we came back to Sag Harbor together and have been here since."

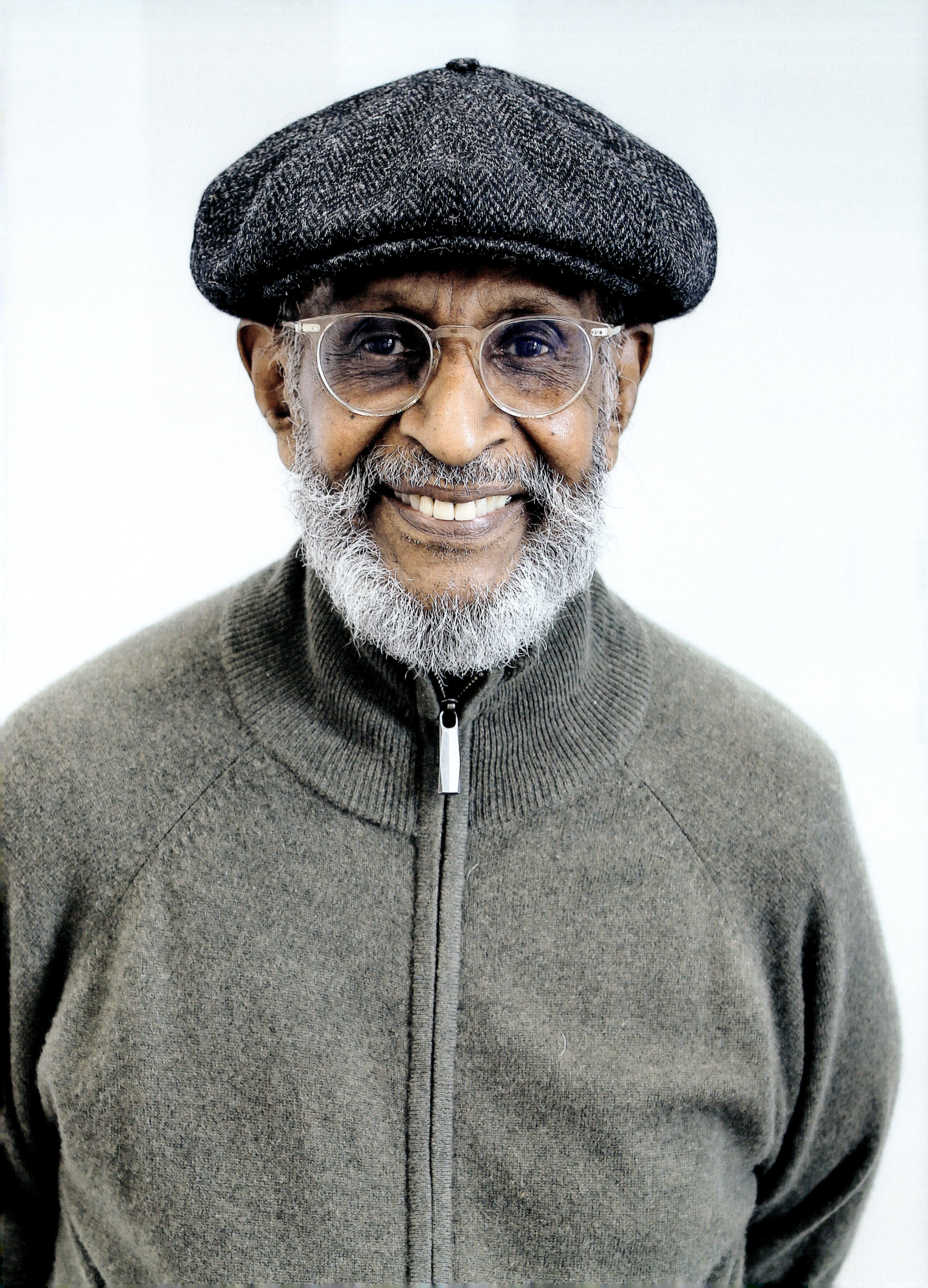

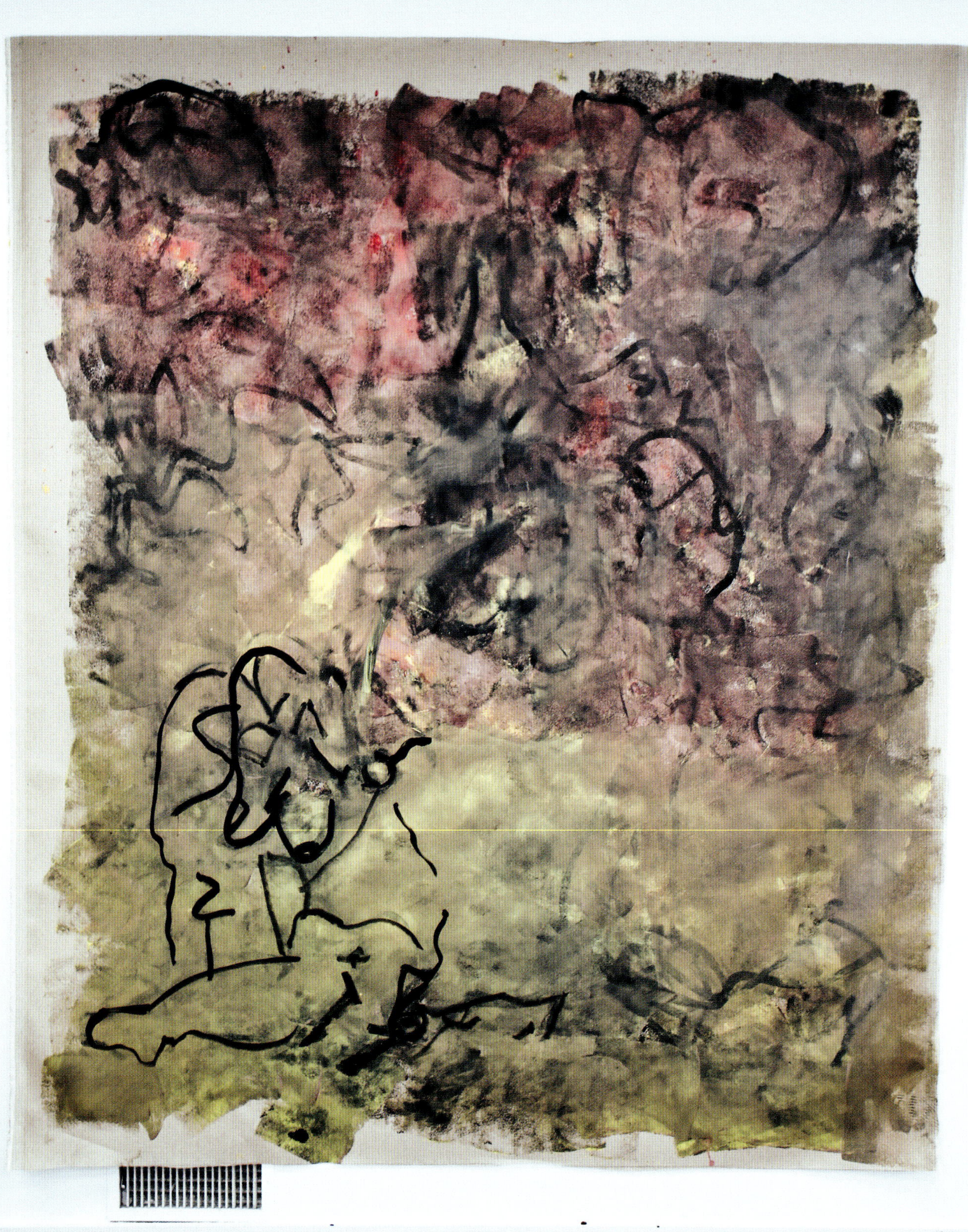

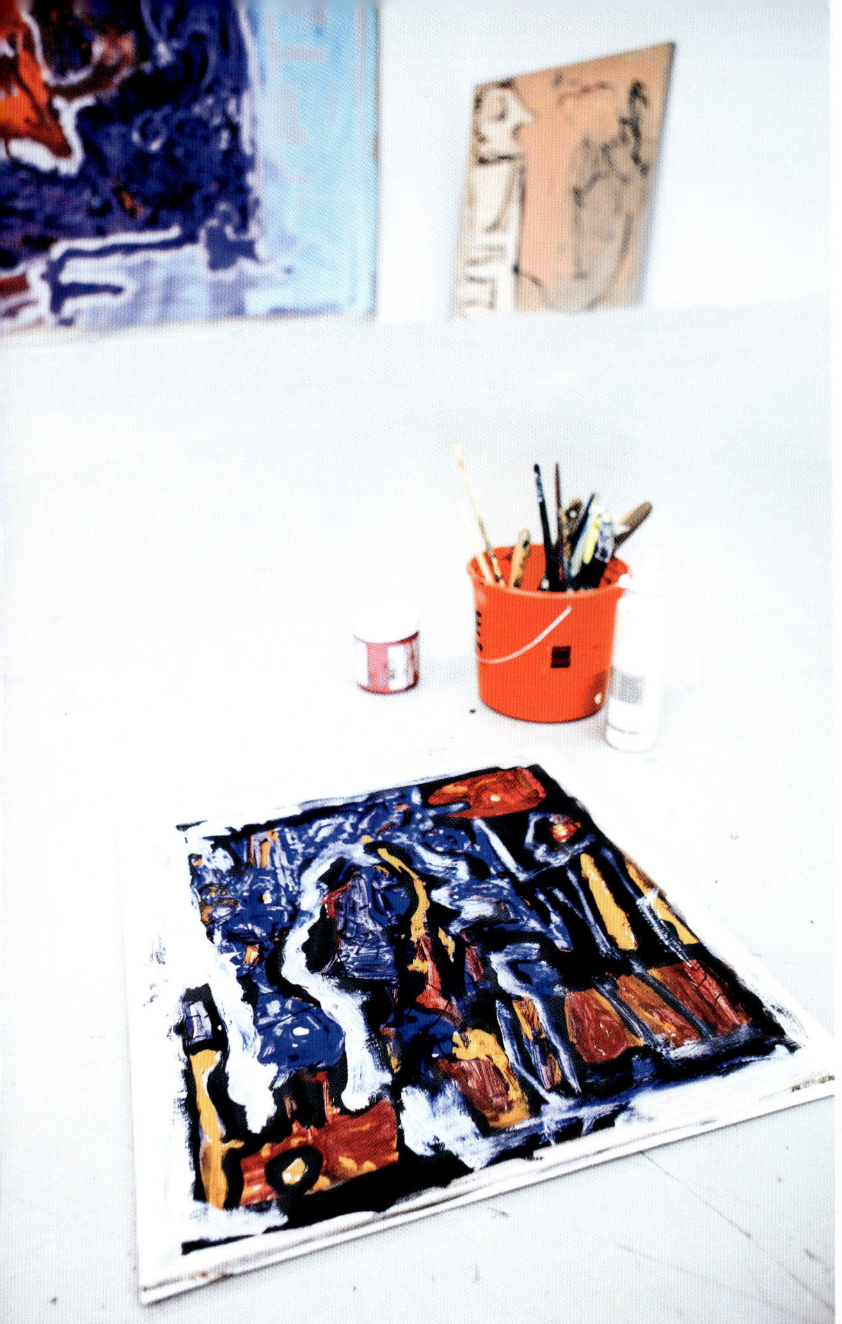

Lawrence's colorful, densely painted, bold canvases have an improvisational, rhythmic feel that is clearly rooted in jazz. Lawrence is a musician himself. He played the tenor saxophone in high school and worked the Chicago jazz club circuit in the fifties and early sixties. In 1964, he began performing in clubs in New York City and hanging out with artists who moved in jazz circles. "Music is my inspiration."

BELOW

Self-taught, Lawrence paints with oil and whatever tools come his way. His abstract works have a musical energy, born of his longtime love affair with jazz.

Though Lawrence never had formal art training, he was always drawing and painting as a child. "I considered myself a naive, abstract artist. Since I was always painting, I finally decided to do it full-time at the ripe old age of forty-three." Lawrence prefers oil as his medium, and as for tools, "just brushes and whatever comes along." After his late start in the art world, Lawrence quickly gained attention, and collectors began buying his work. In 2013, the Parrish Art Museum in Water Mill, New York, acquired three paintings, followed by several museums in New York City, including the Metropolitan Museum of Art and the Studio Museum in Harlem.

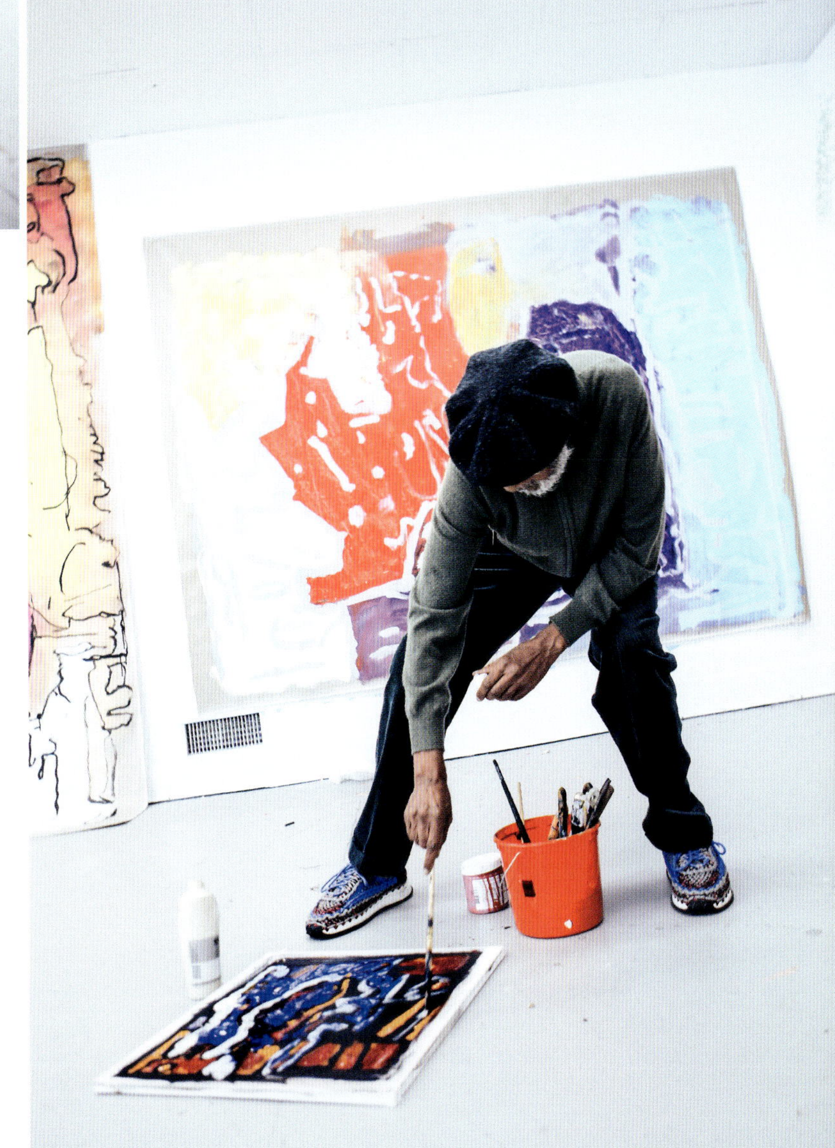

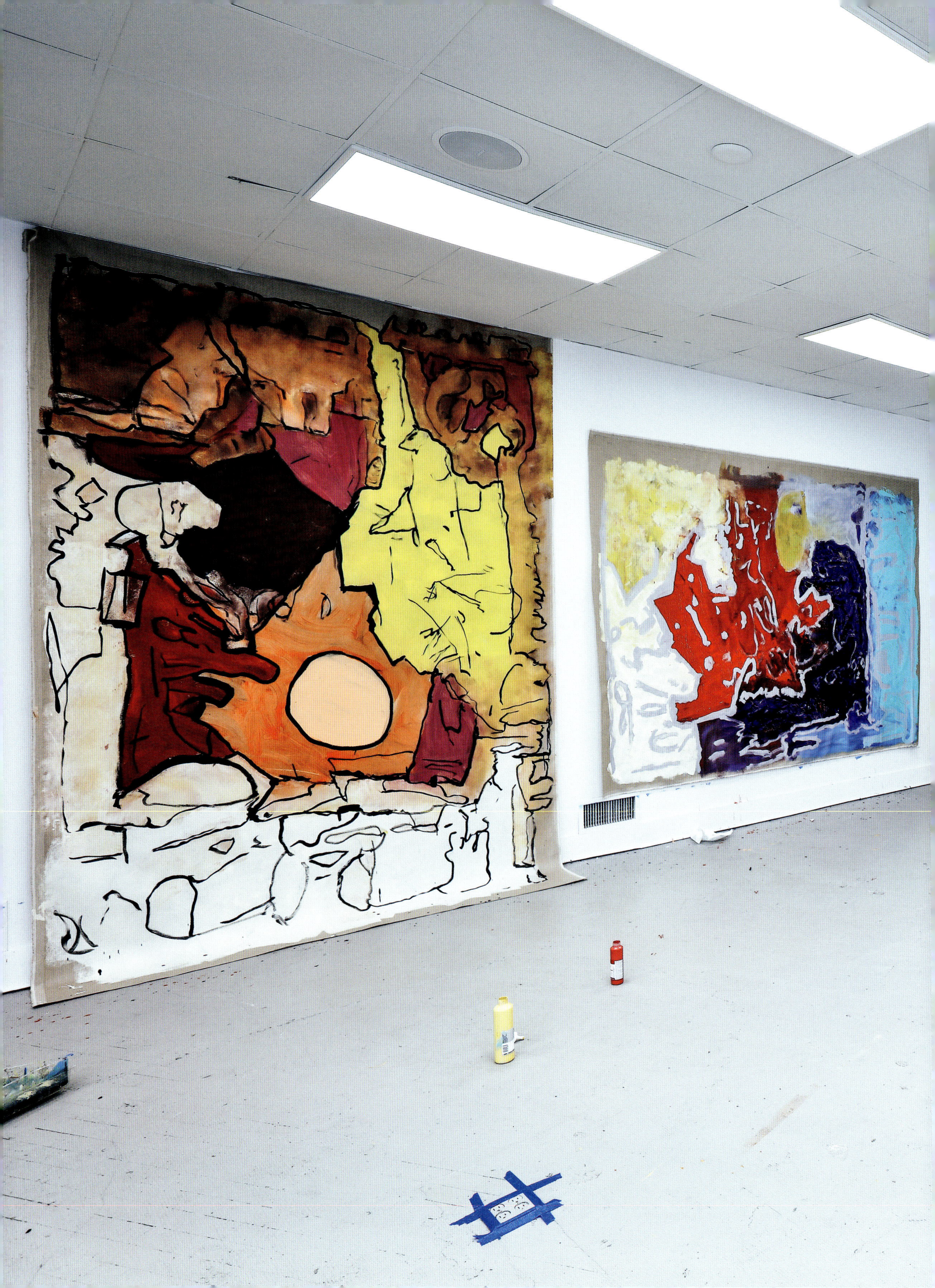

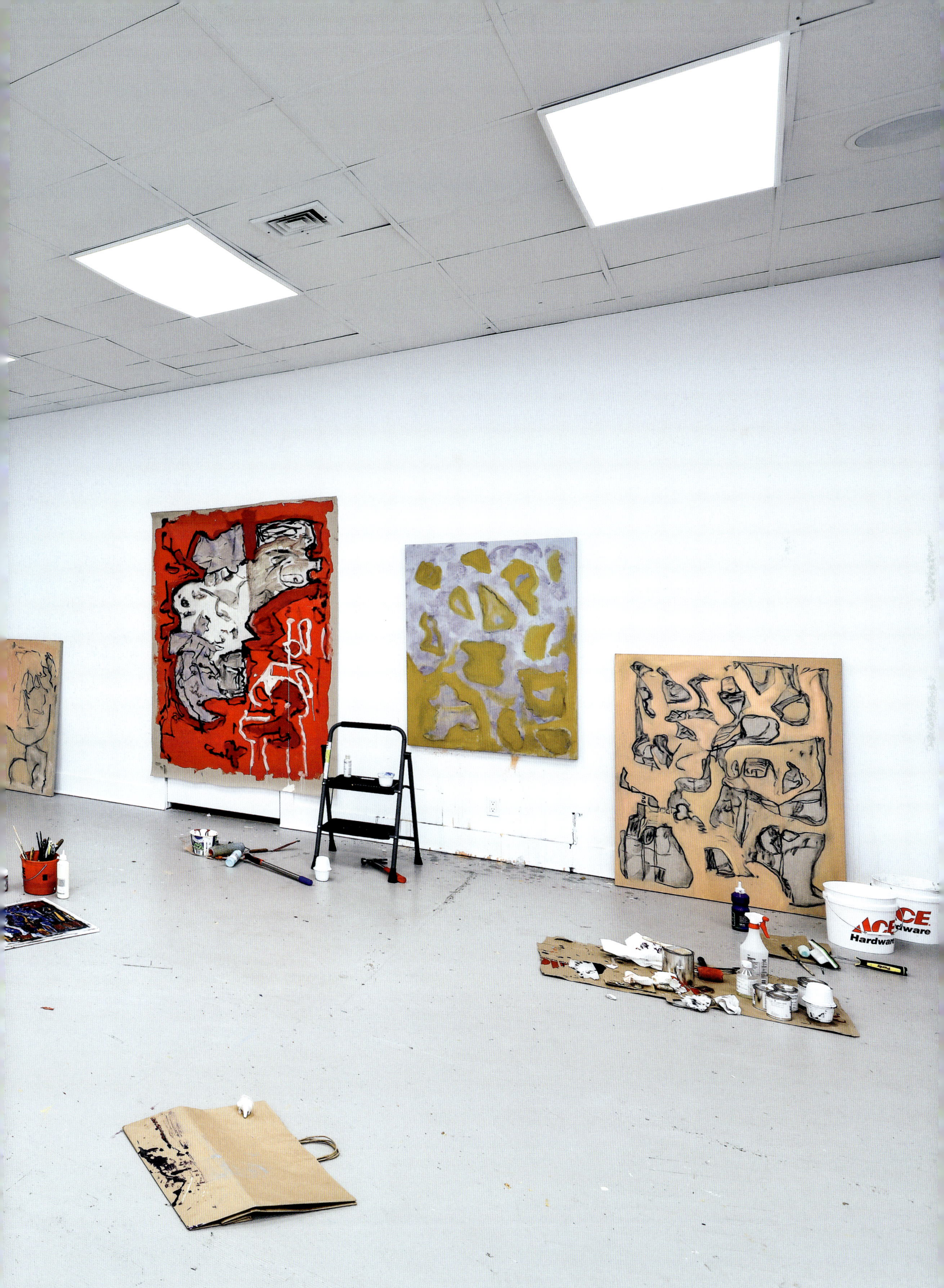
ACE
Hardware

I've done portraits of artists, actors, politicians, adolescents, and dictators, as well as images related to climate change, endangered species, and war. And cats—I have two.

CHRISTA MAIWALD

Born in a suburb of Philadelphia, Maiwald knew from the age of five that she wanted to be an artist. At seventeen, she went to the Tyler School of Art in Philadelphia and from there to the School of the Art Institute of Chicago, earning her MFA in 1973. She moved to New York City for the next eight years and worked as a video artist, exhibiting in galleries and mounting a solo show at the Whitney Museum, where she met her future husband, who was working there. They were married in East Hampton and moved to Springs in 1985. "Living near the ocean is a dream, and the art scene keeps getting better and more interesting every year. I love it here and will never move away."

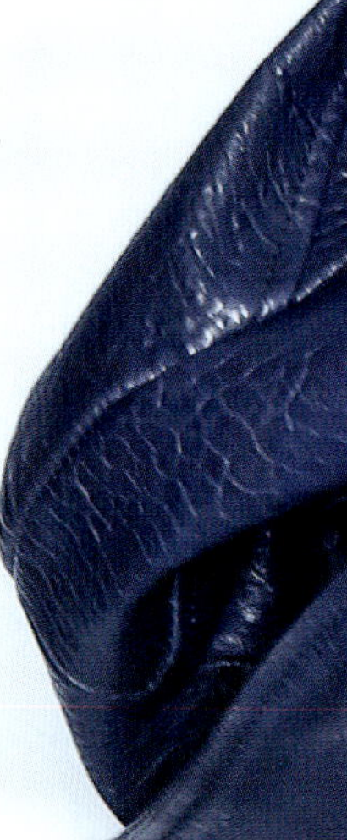

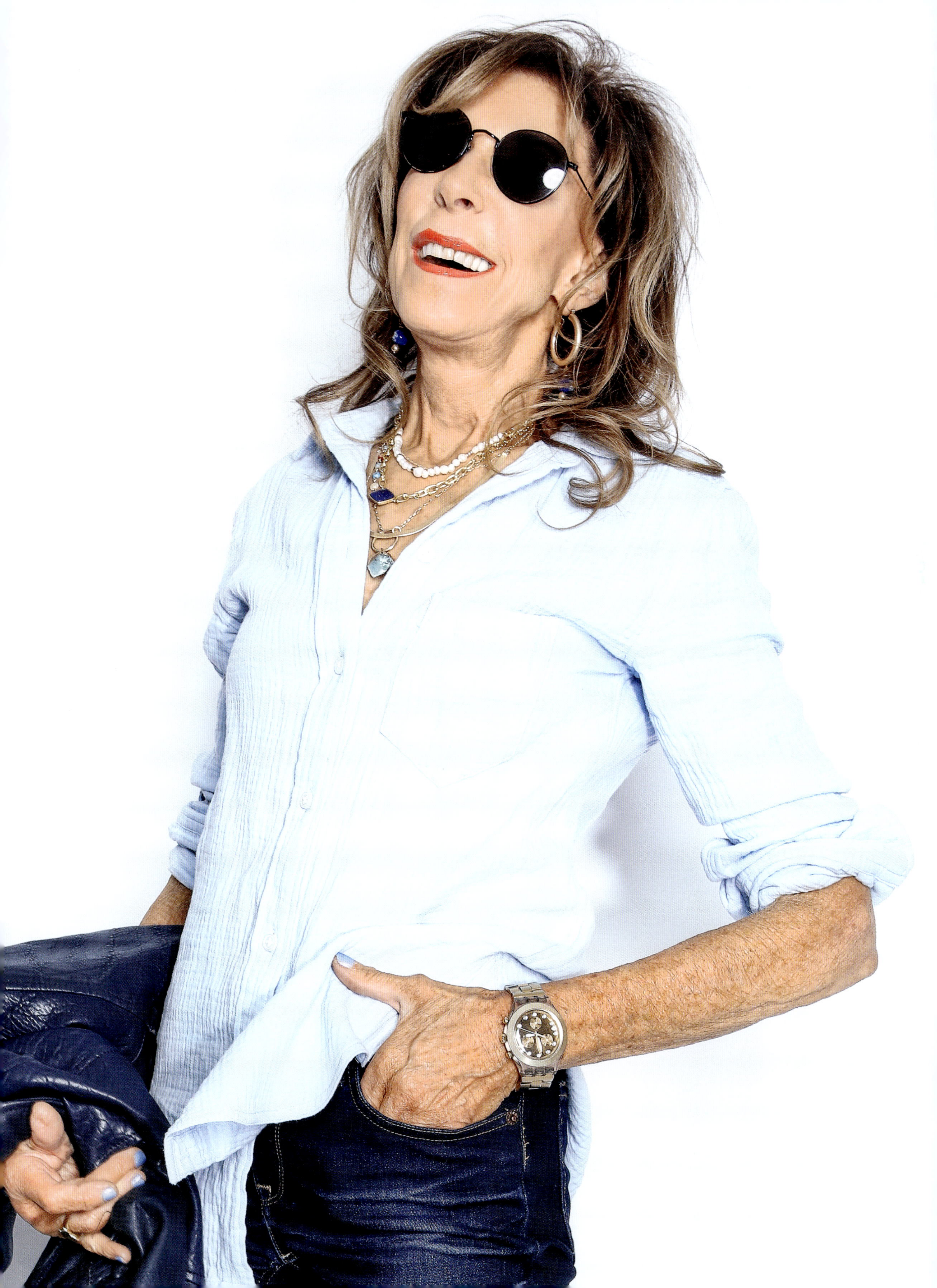

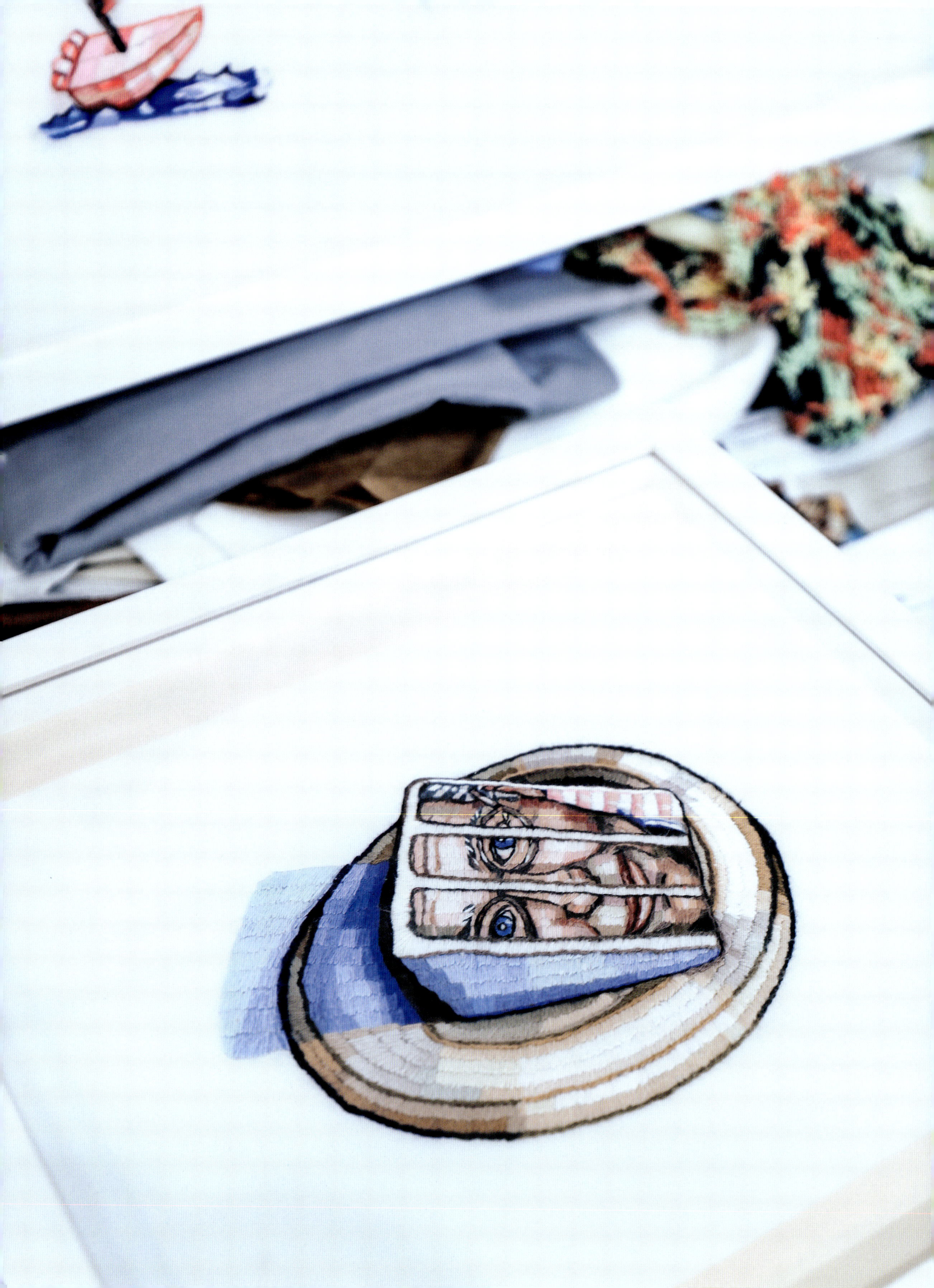

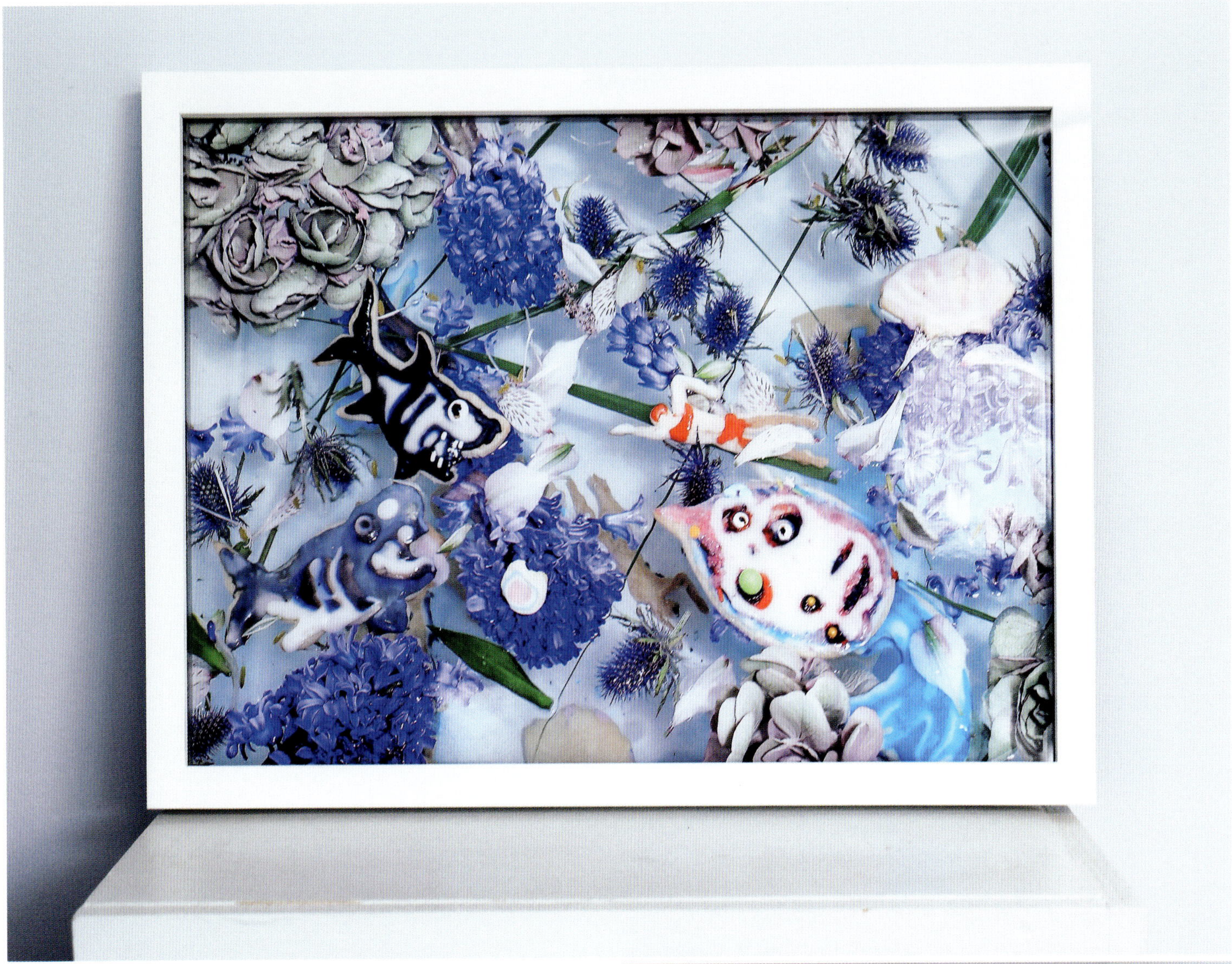

"I work mainly in photography and hand embroidery. Because embroidery is such a slow process, with one piece taking weeks to months to finish, I also do photography for instant gratification. Ideas propel my work. Each idea generates a series, sometimes in both mediums. I glean my images from newspapers, magazines, and photographs I take, but, most of all, from the internet. If I'm embroidering, I make outlines of the images and start stitching. With my photography, I don't plan or manipulate. What you see is what was there."

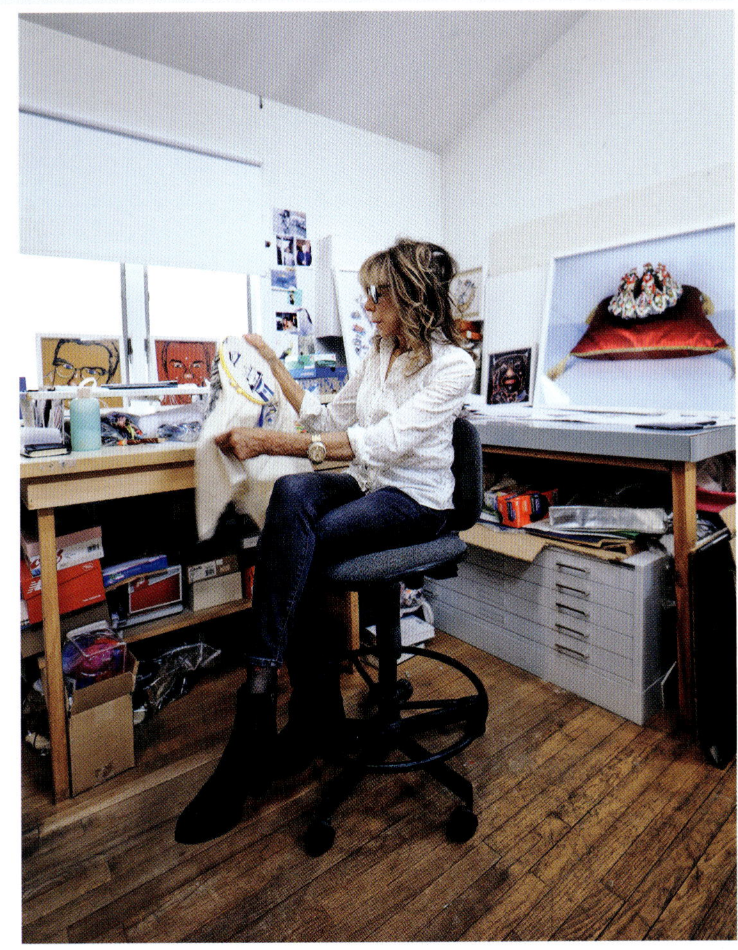

RIGHT Maiwald in the upstairs studio of her East Hampton house. Her highly detailed embroidered works take anywhere from three weeks to four months to finish.

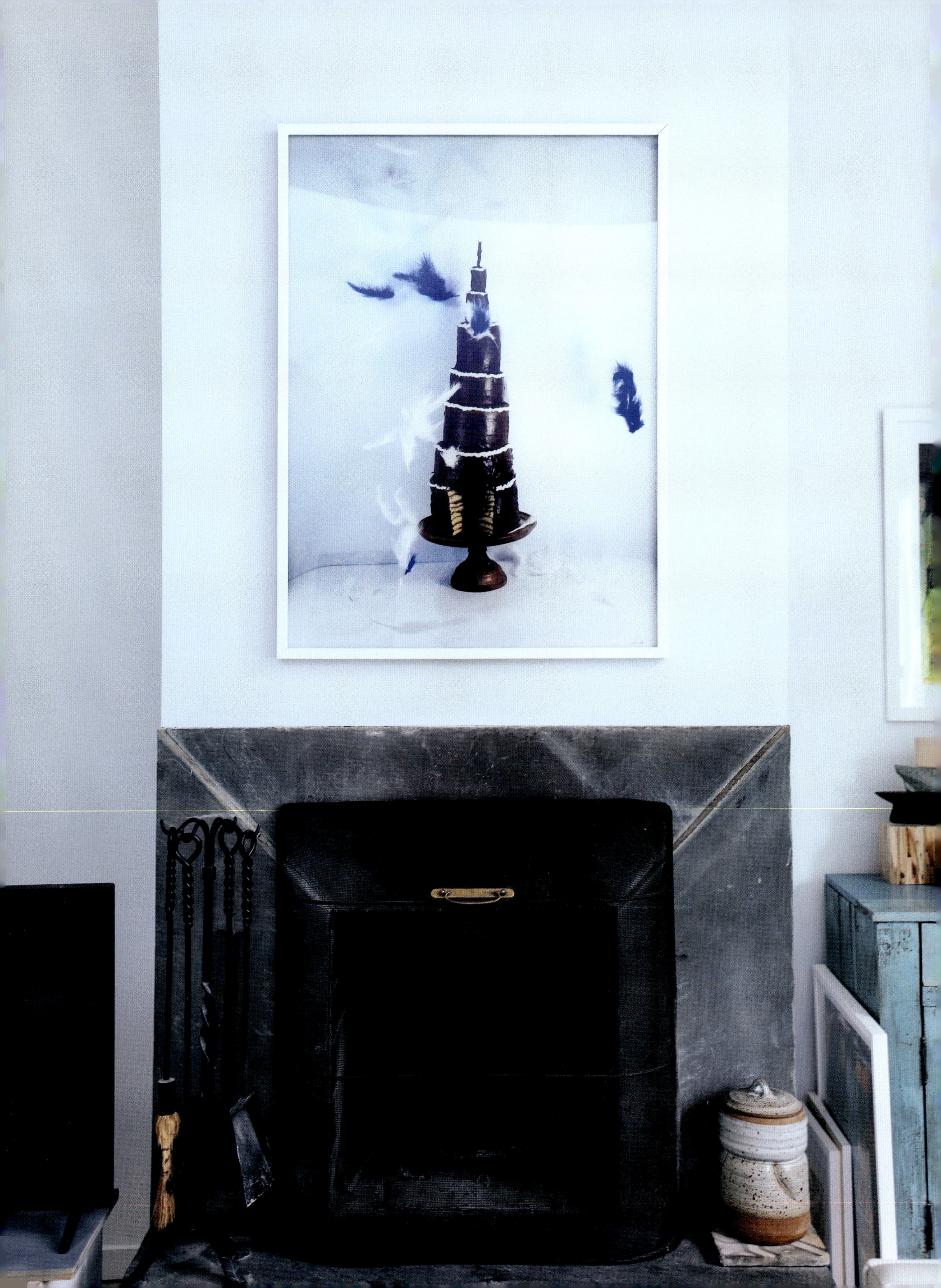

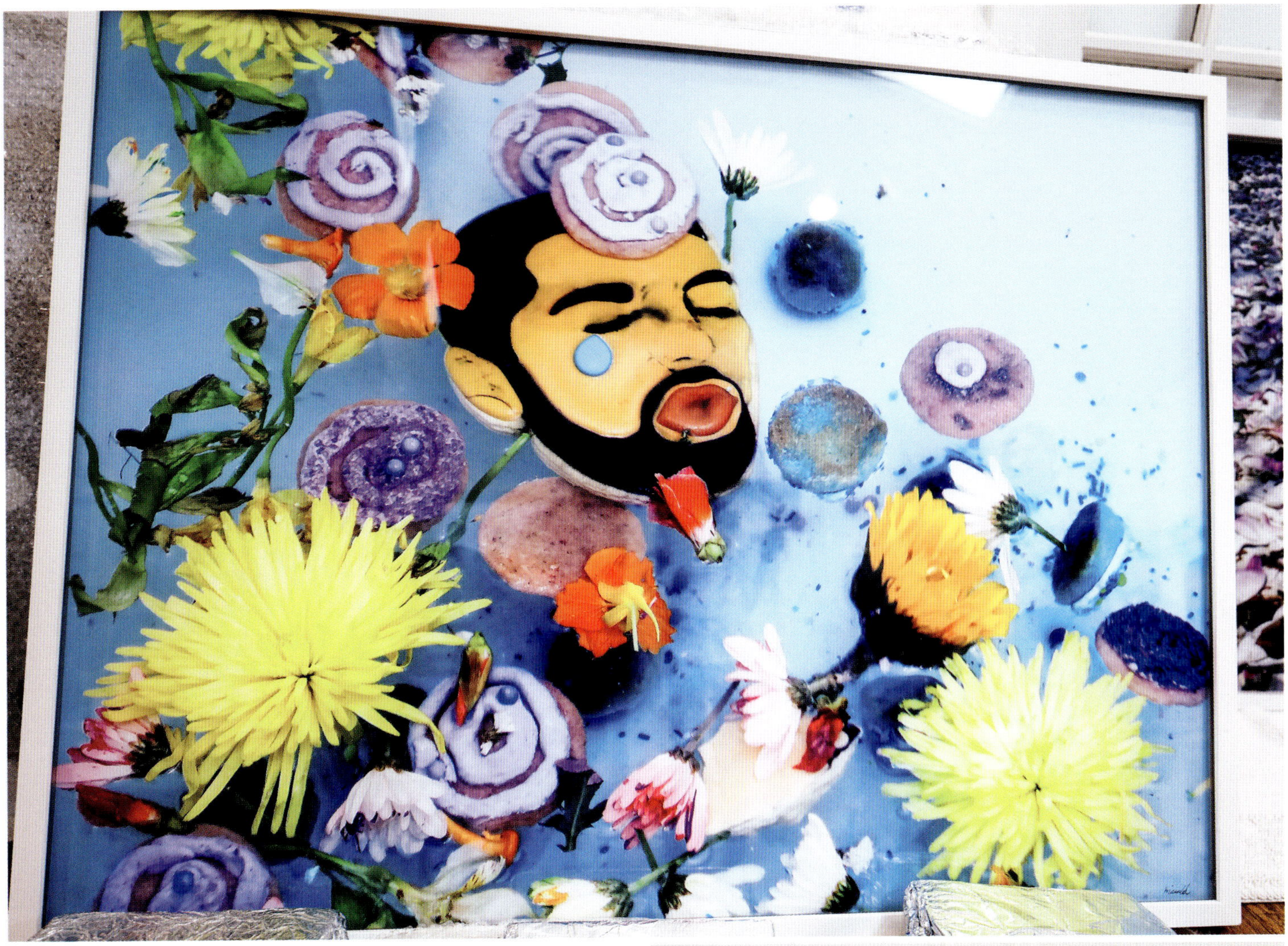

Maiwald's love of baking often shows up in her work. "For a series of photographs called Landscape Cakes, I baked and decorated cakes shaped as birdhouses, clams, and boats, then photographed them in their natural environments. This led to the Floating Cookies series, for which I created hundreds of cookies with themes like overfishing, temperature rise, and wildfires. I filled my bathtub with water and various flowers, tossed the cookies in the tub, and photographed them as they swirled around, crumbled, and slipped down the drain. What took a week of baking to prepare for was gone in minutes." In the same vein, she's done fleeting portraits of famous creative people. "I use edible paper and inks to draw the faces and place them on backgrounds I create and then quickly photograph them as the portraits start to melt or disintegrate. That's life."

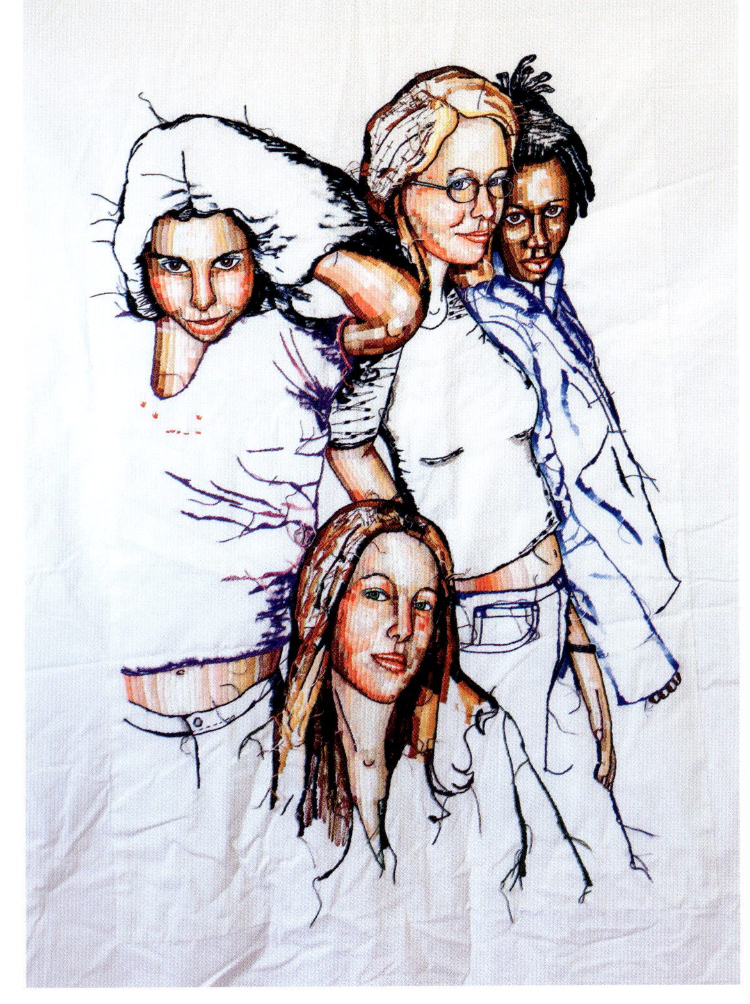

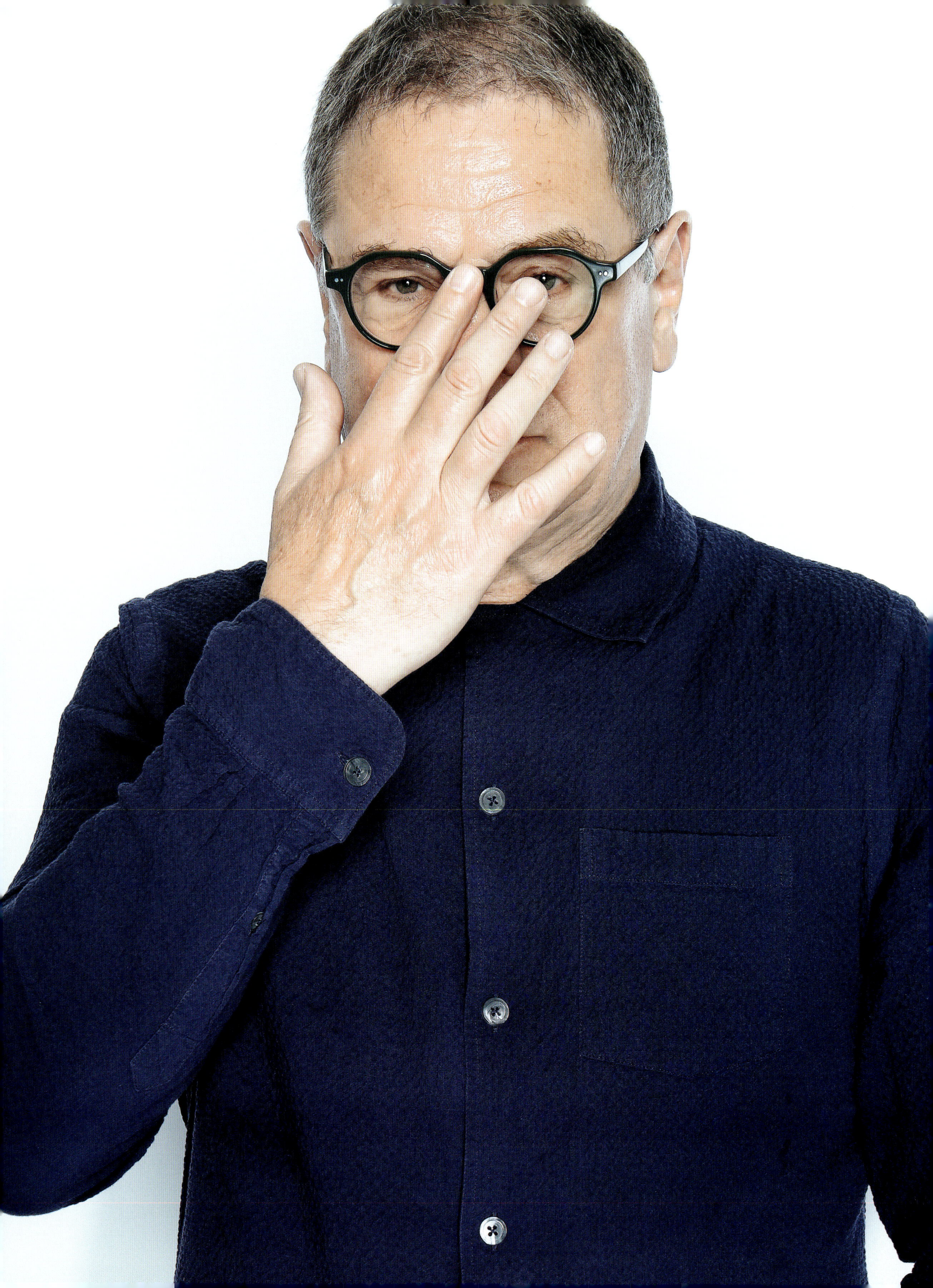

I think of my painting as a stratification of events, characterized by swift accelerations, sudden arrests, and abrupt discontinuities, evoking the ebb and flow of life.

FULVIO MASSI

Massi was born in Trieste, Italy, and moved to Milan at age four. "For as long as I can remember, art and music have been a focal point in my life. As a child, I was an obsessive drawer, almost to the point of it interfering with my academics. My teens led me into the world of rock. As I continued playing and exploring music, I felt an affinity toward jazz. That in turn steered me to New York City, where I performed on the club circuit." Massi supported himself working as a part-time carpenter, building lofts downtown—an experience that planted the seeds of his future interest in architecture.

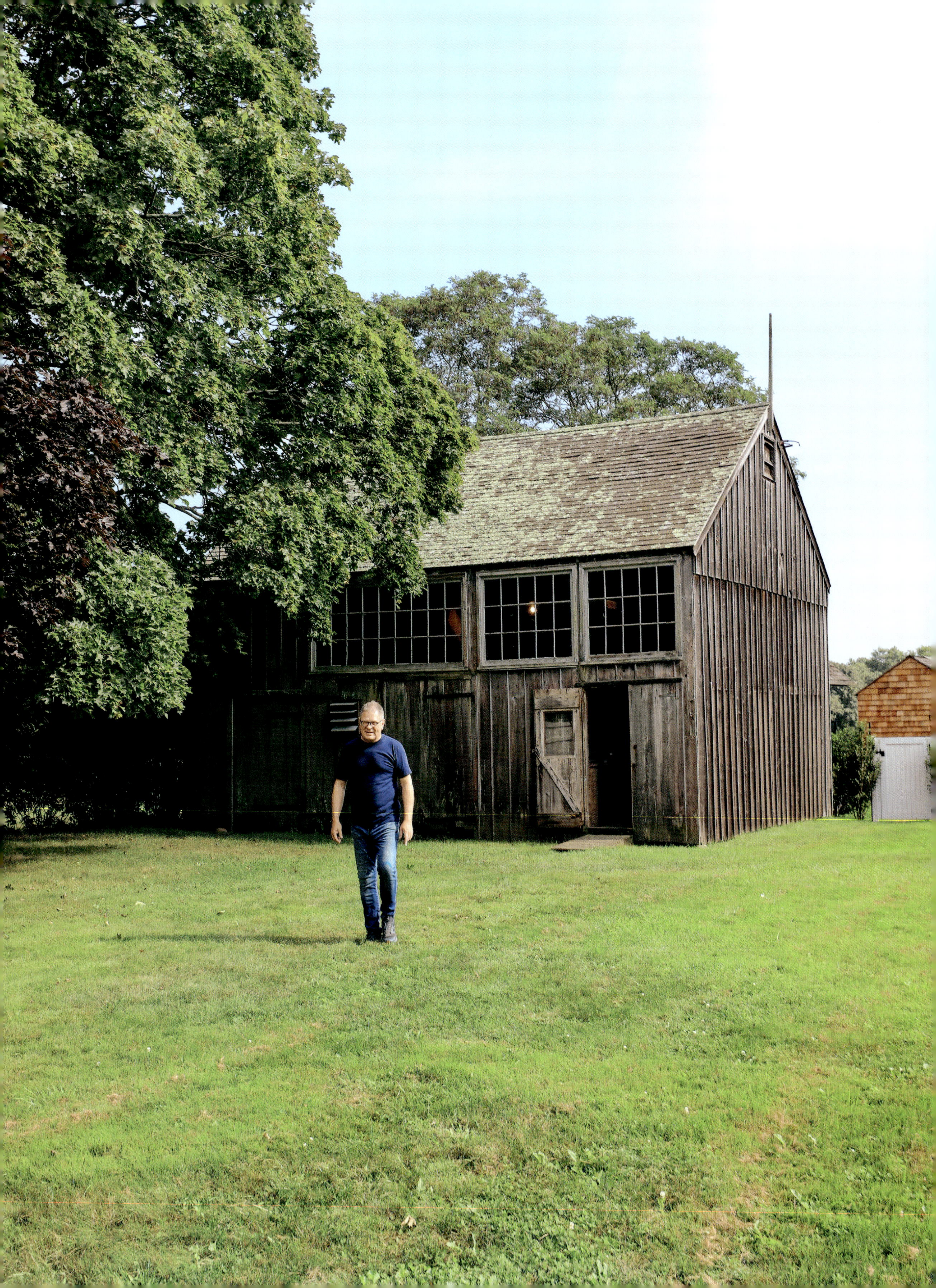

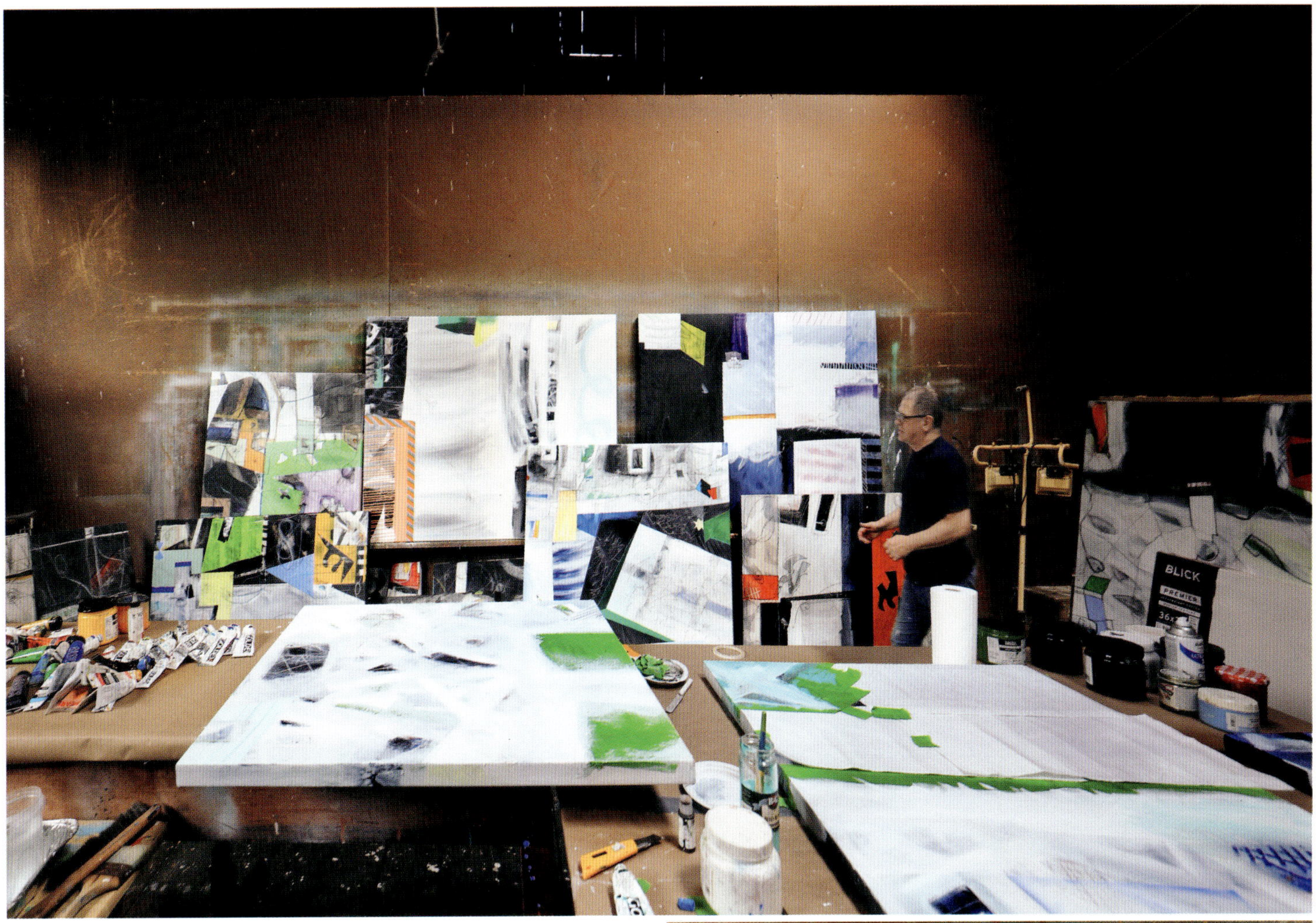

Massi knew of the Hamptons because his wife was born here. They met in Italy, where they lived together for thirty years. "We would often visit the East End in the summer and ended up moving here full-time in 2000. My first art exhibits were at Ashawagh Hall in Springs, around the corner from Jackson Pollock's and Willem de Kooning's studios." Massi's own studio is on his Bridgehampton property—a large, skylit barn that remains unaltered and, for that reason, seasonal. "I like to paint in very bright light and sometimes, purposely, in dim light, at dusk. It's surprising to see something that you painted in a specific light condition acquiring a new meaning when the light condition is reversed."

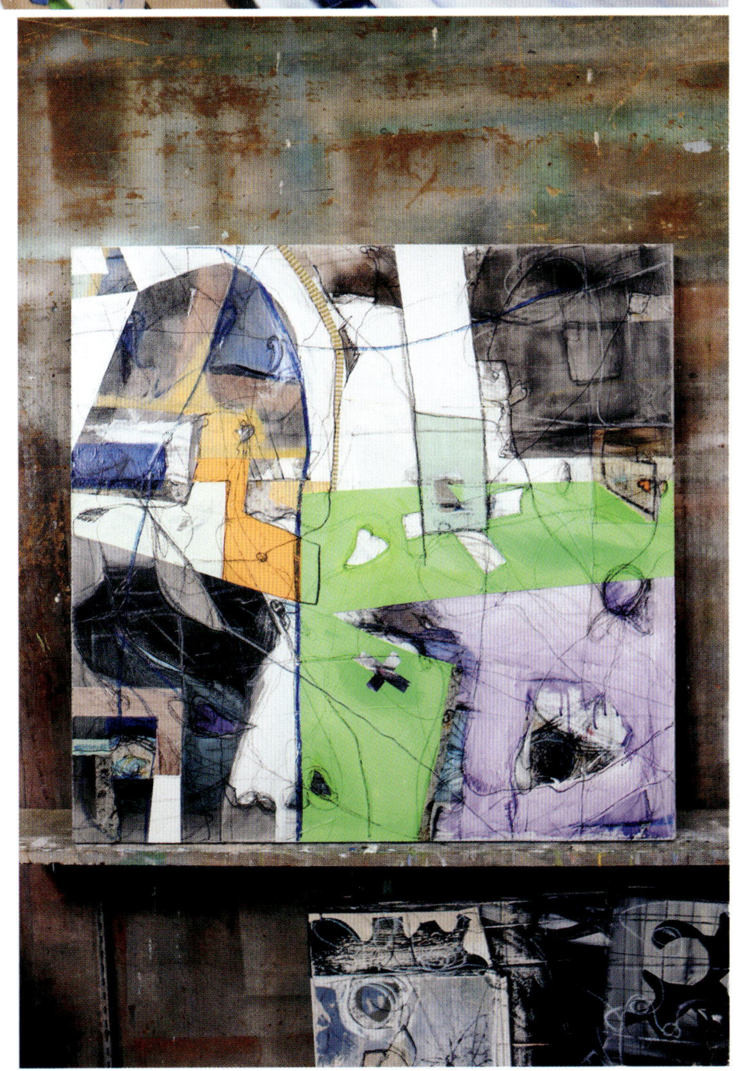

OPPOSITE AND ABOVE Massi's Bridgehampton studio space—the original barn on the property—has loads of rustic charm and light but no heat, so he uses it seasonally.

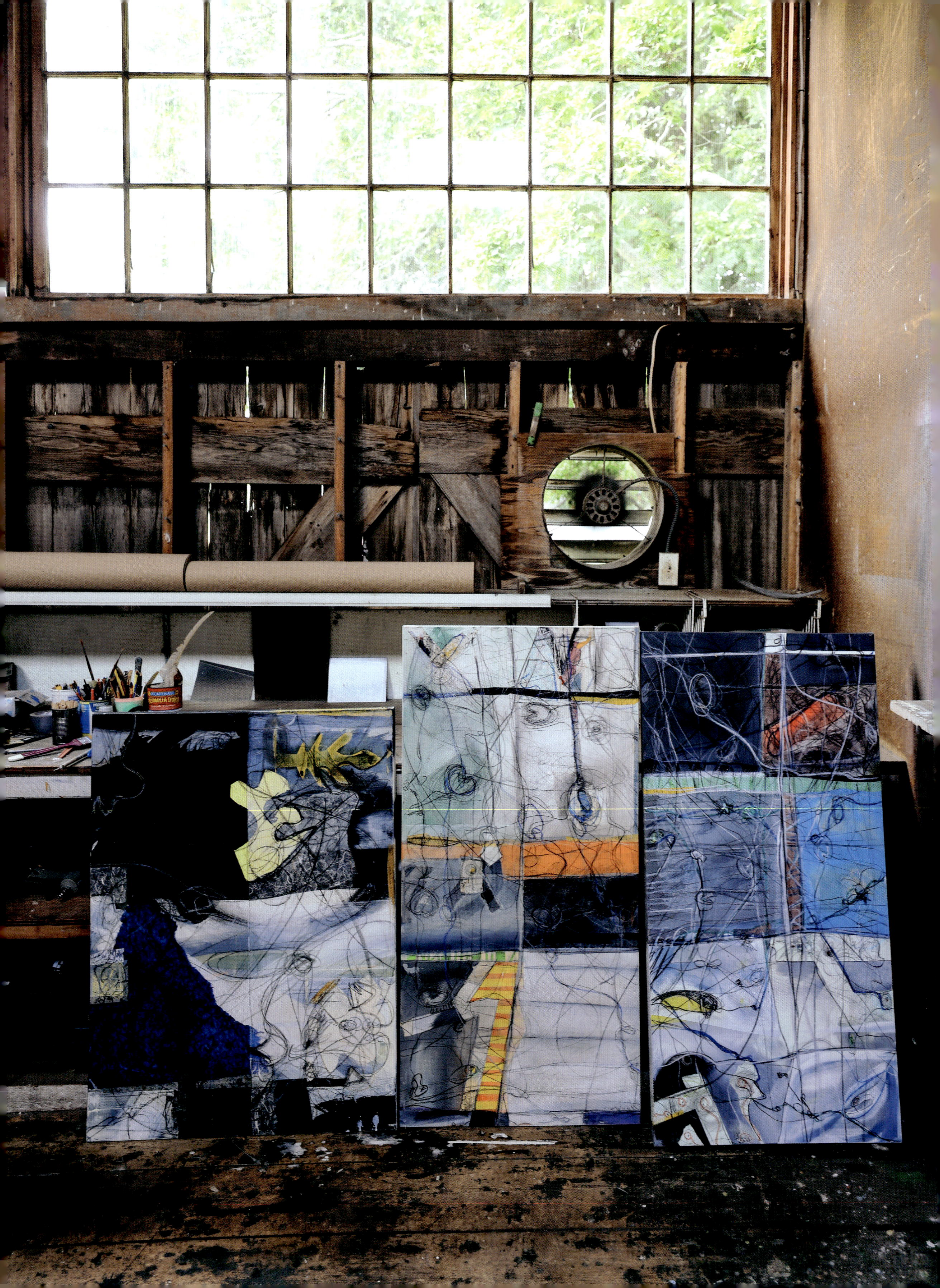

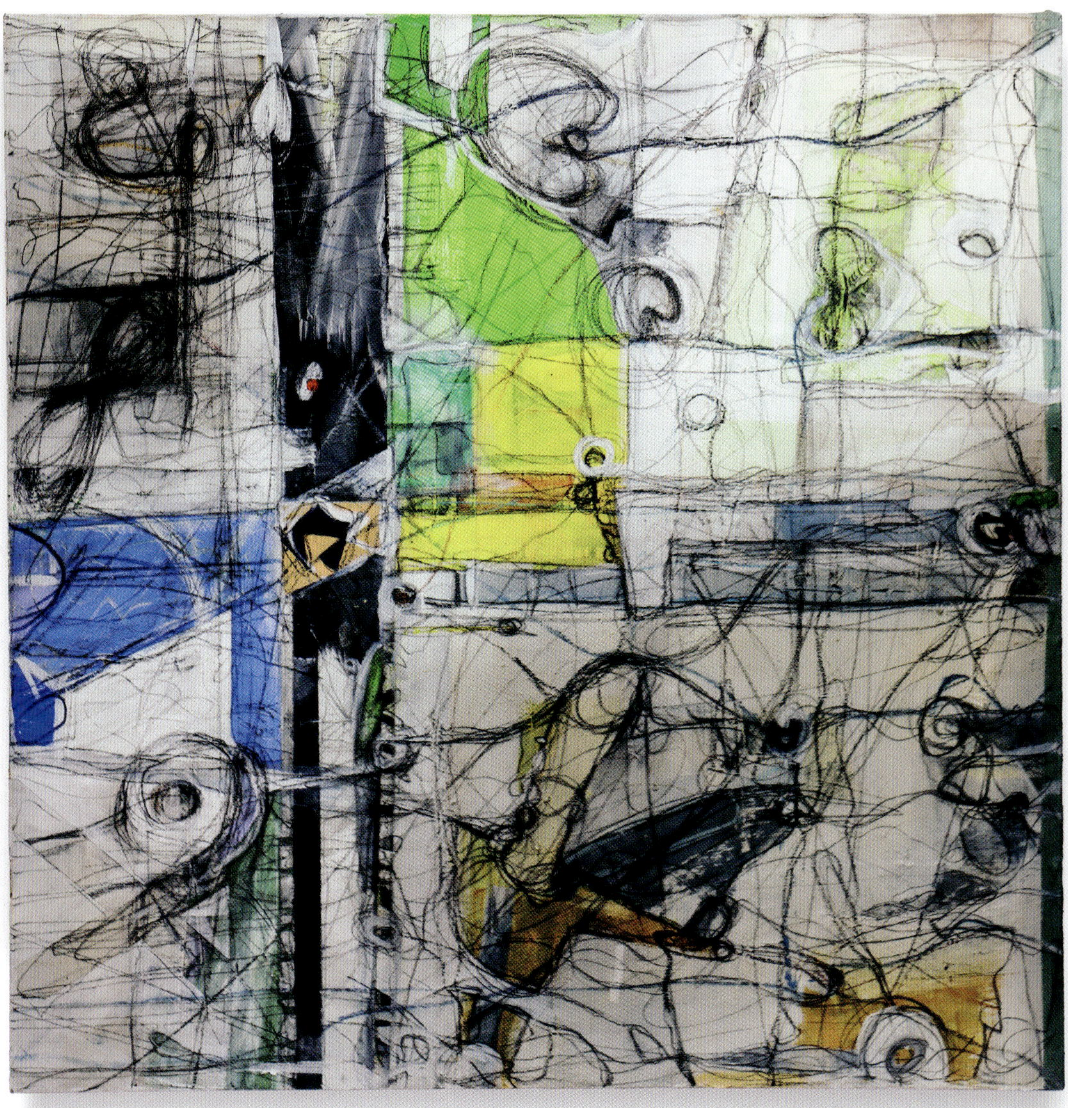

As an architect and artist, Massi works in two distinct creative disciplines, yet for him they are intertwined. "Art is a constant presence in my thoughts, encompassing informal ideas, observations, or any input that serves as a catalyst in my creative process." And while his paintings proceed from sensations, they bear the mark of architecture. "They have various entrances and exits, multiple centers and orientations. Through the frequency and variation of grids, the space is partitioned, evoking plowed fields or abstract urban diagrams with streets, avenues, and blocks, reminiscent of the built environment. The use of lines in my art is characterized by spontaneity and emotion, in contrast to the planned linear elements in architectural drawings." Massi's collage-like paintings also evoke a sense of freedom. "Sometimes I paint over layers, sand some parts, and, almost magically, new elements emerge, suggesting a new direction. It's a dynamic process like chasing shapes in the ever-shifting clouds or finding unexpected forms while gazing at the sky."

OPPOSITE When he's not drawing up architectural plans, Massi is in his studio creating collage-like paintings.

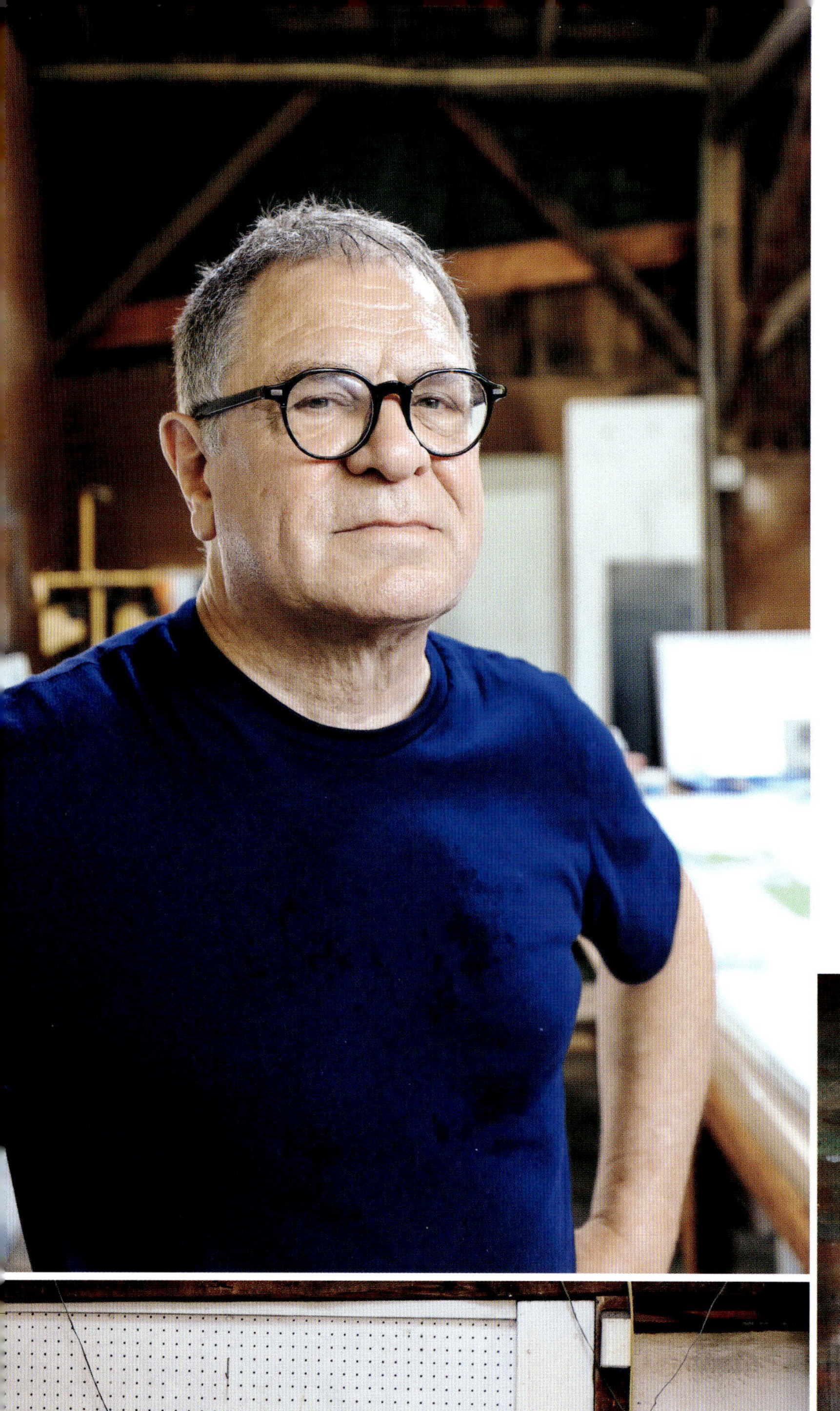

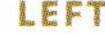

LEFT

Art and music have always been part of Massi's life. An obsessive doodler as a child, he also became a jazz musician before taking up architecture.

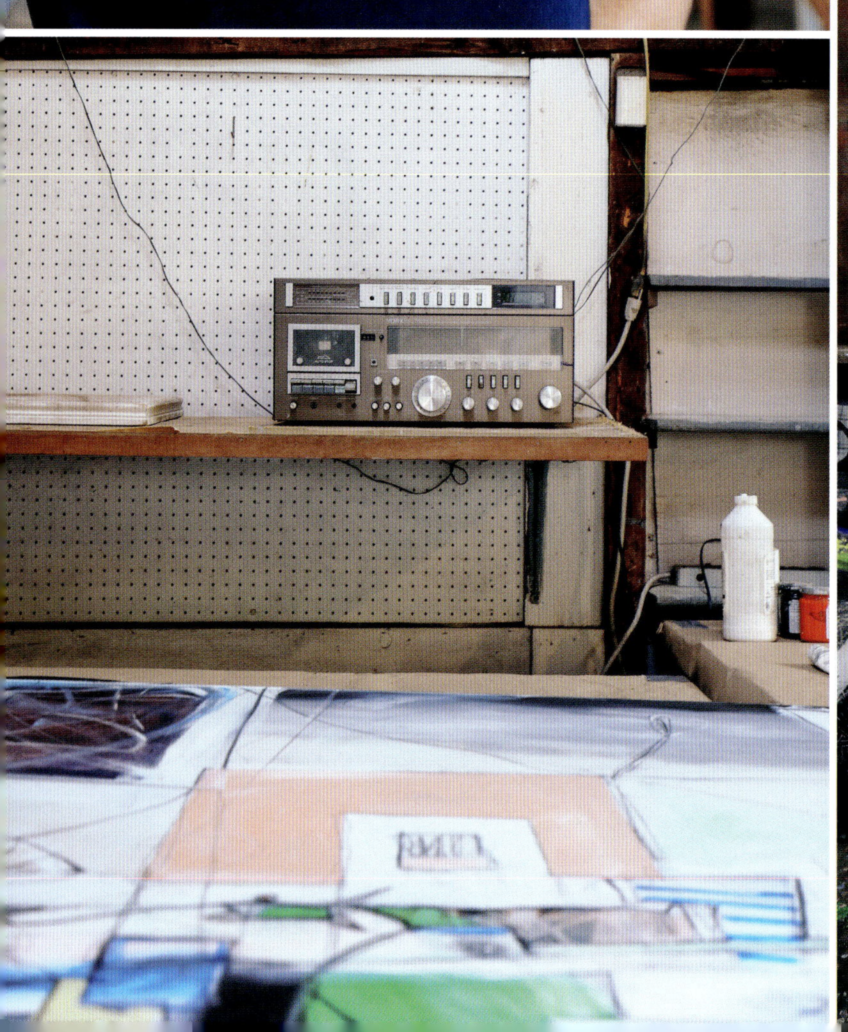

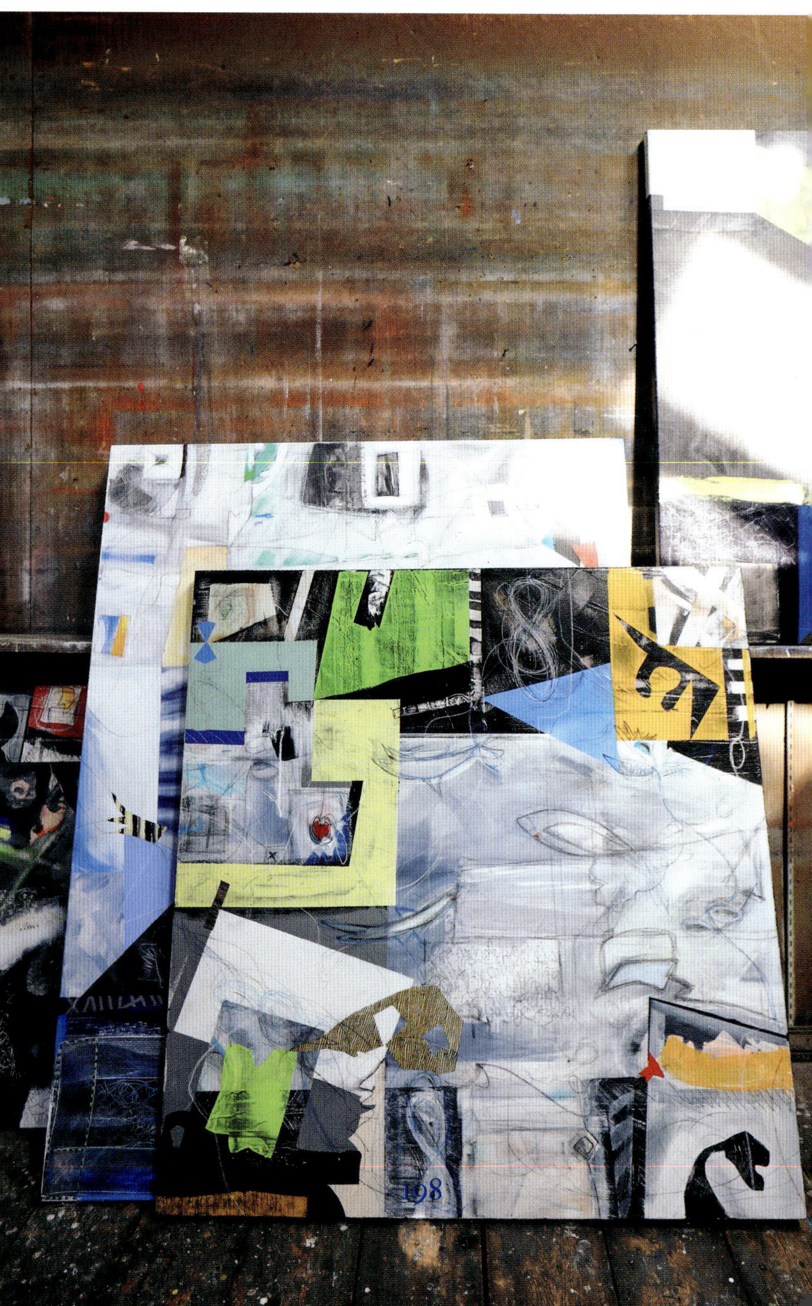

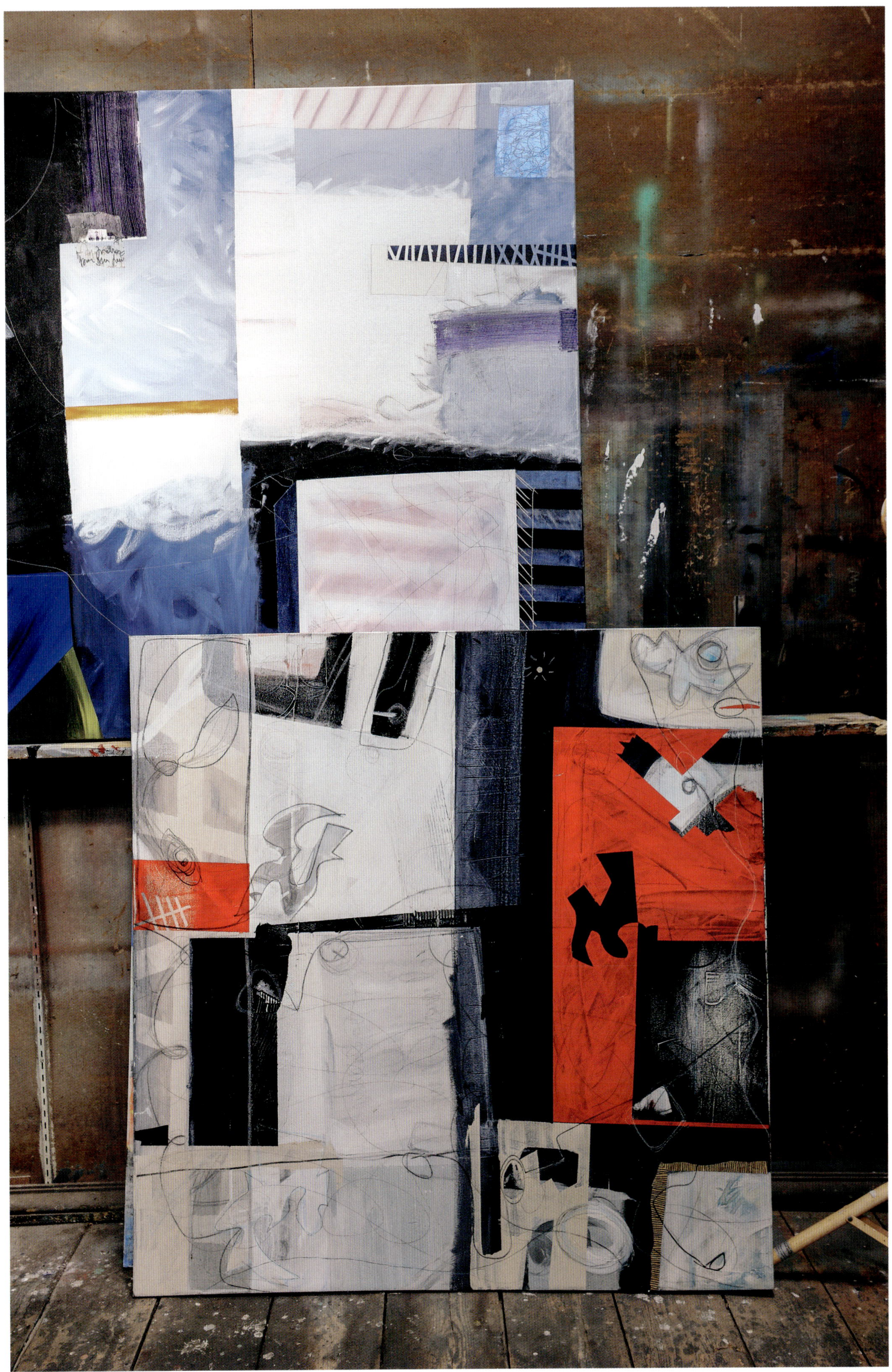

When I was a young artist, I painted the world around me. I still do that, but I also paint the stories and allegories in the box, which is my head.

PATON MILLER

Miller was born in Seattle and moved to Hawaii at age thirteen. After studying at the Honolulu Academy of Arts, he spent a year traveling through Asia and Europe, painting and drawing. Next came New York City. "While I was there, I visited a friend in Southampton. She recommended that I stop by Southampton College, where I met the director of the Fine Arts Department. The artworks I'd made while traveling earned me a scholarship, and after graduating in 1978, I started exhibiting in the city and on eastern Long Island." After a brief move back to Hawaii, Miller returned to Southampton. "I've been here ever since."

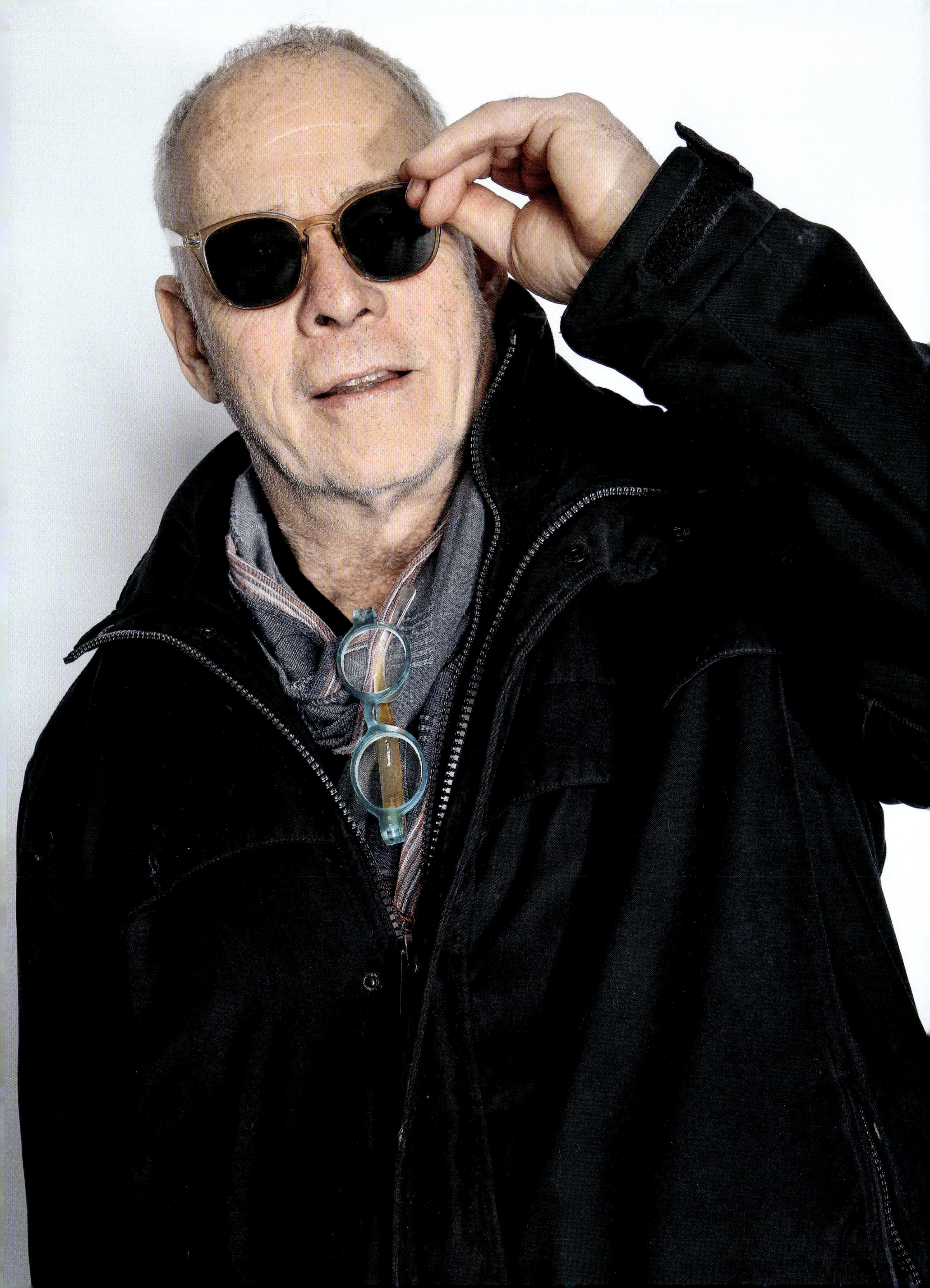

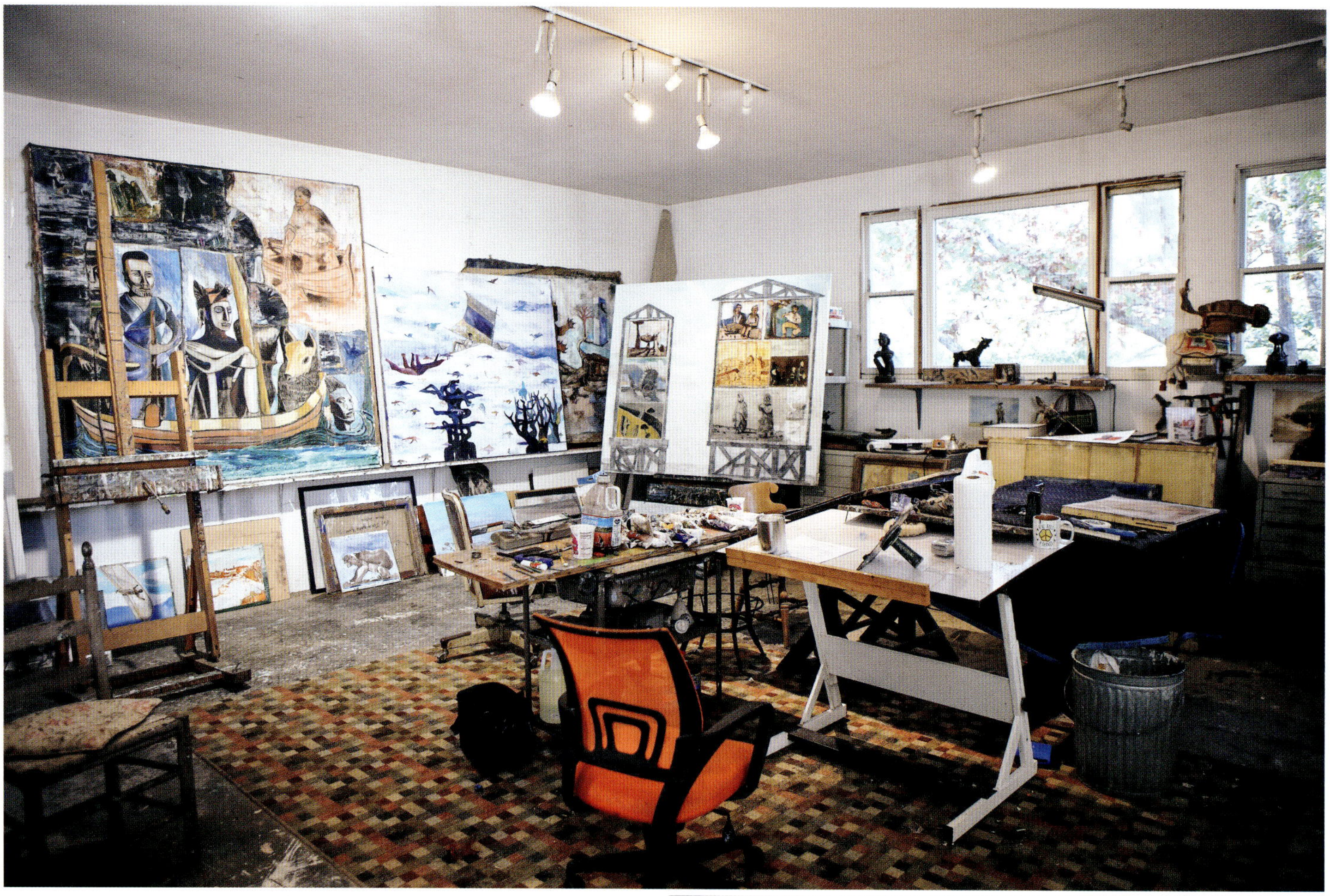

"I am a narrative painter, and I'm attracted to just about anything around me and the stories that hitch a ride. My work is representational of my life." Miller paints and draws in a 1,000-square-foot barn on his property. He uses oil, gouache, and all sorts of pencils and charcoal. "New pieces can start in a myriad of ways—as a reaction to nature or an idea spun from whole cloth. When I was young, I didn't work that much from my imagination. As I grew older, with more experiences, my work became more about an inner dialogue."

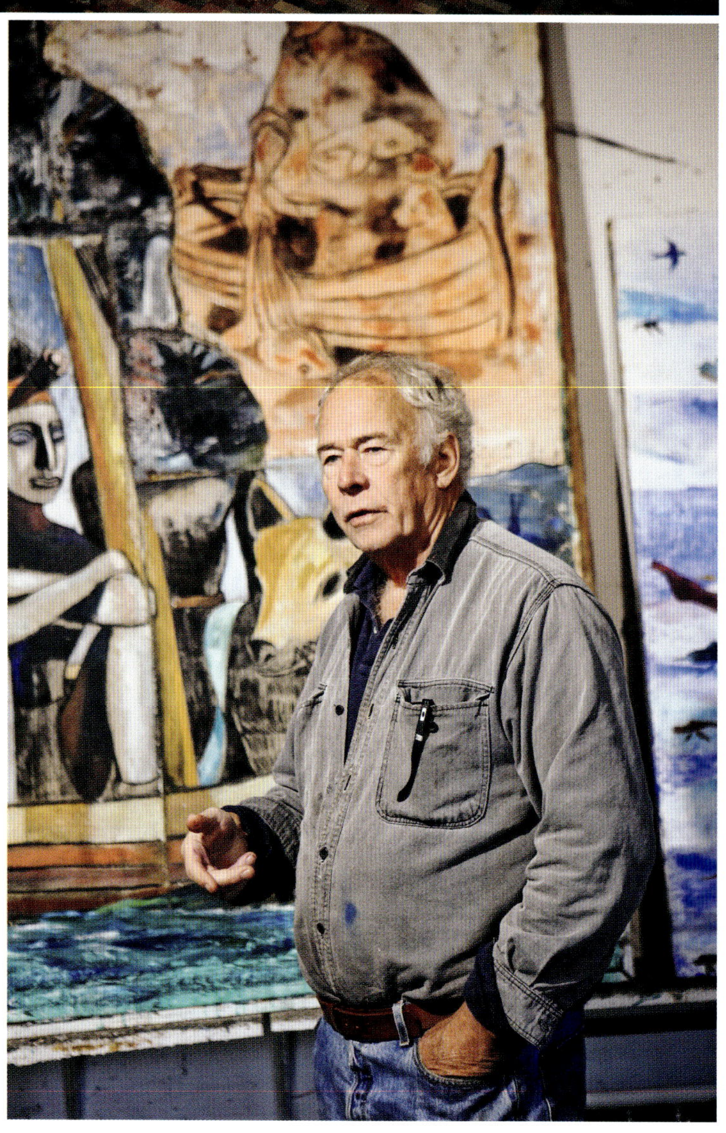

ABOVE AND RIGHT

In Miller's spacious barn studio on his Southampton property, his preferred mediums—oils, acrylics, and all sorts of pencils and charcoals—are at the ready.

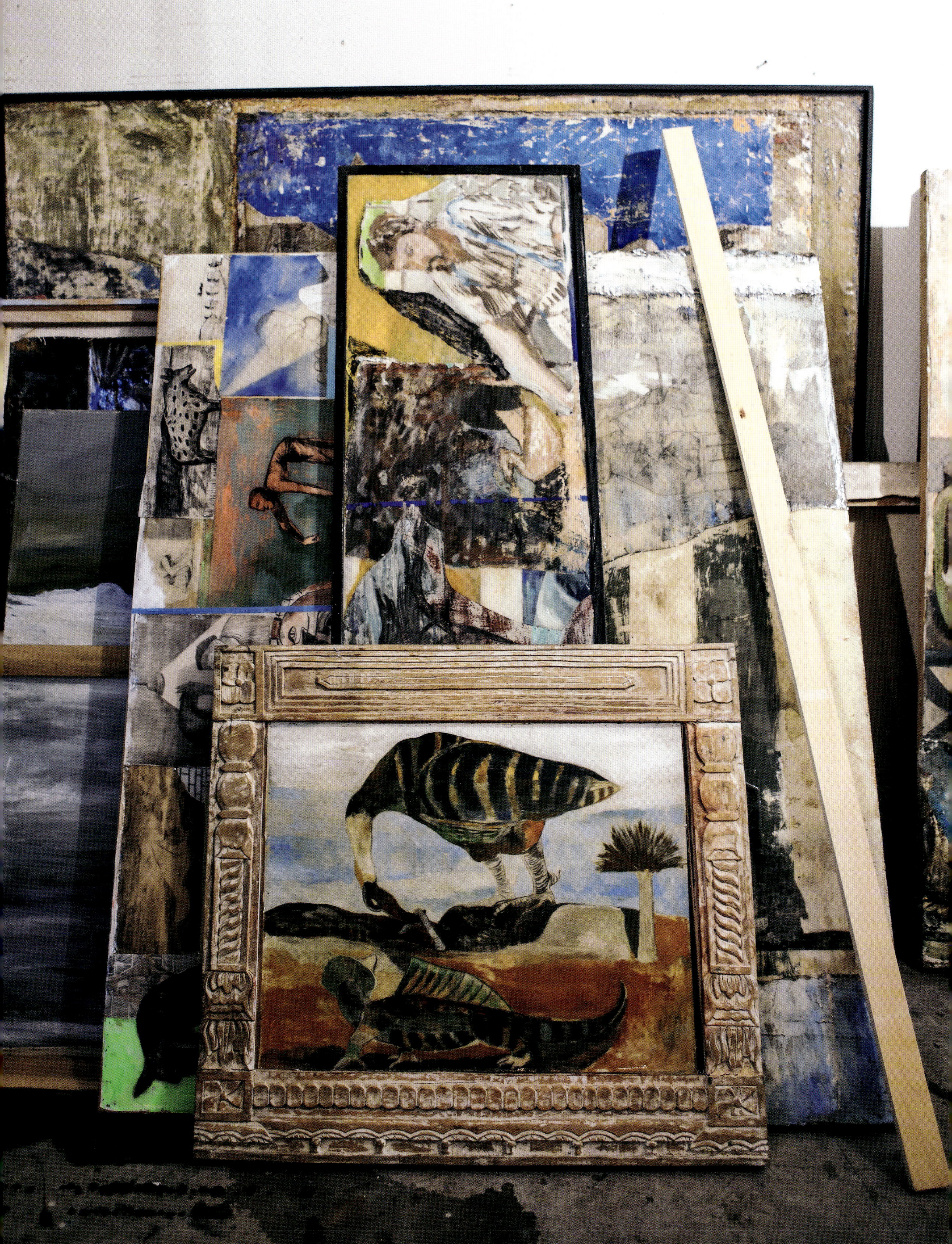

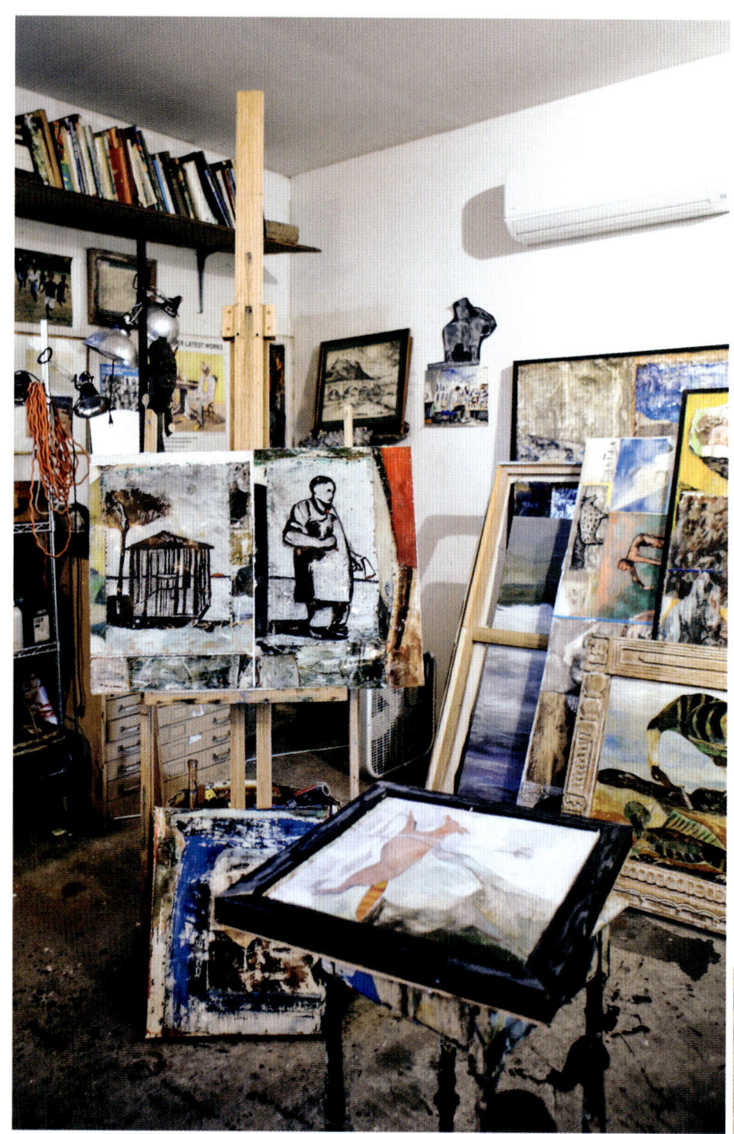

"The community here, past and present, is very important to me," says Miller, who has curated the annual East End Collected exhibition at the Southampton Arts Center for more than a decade. "It began when I was invited to a meeting of village residents in Southampton to discuss the future of the Samuel Parrish building. I suggested that a new arts center would have a chance to succeed if it mirrored our artist-rich area. A few months later, I was asked to curate an exhibit reflecting that mission." Since the first exhibit, the show has grown to include more than two hundred artists each year. The goal is simple: Us Here Now.

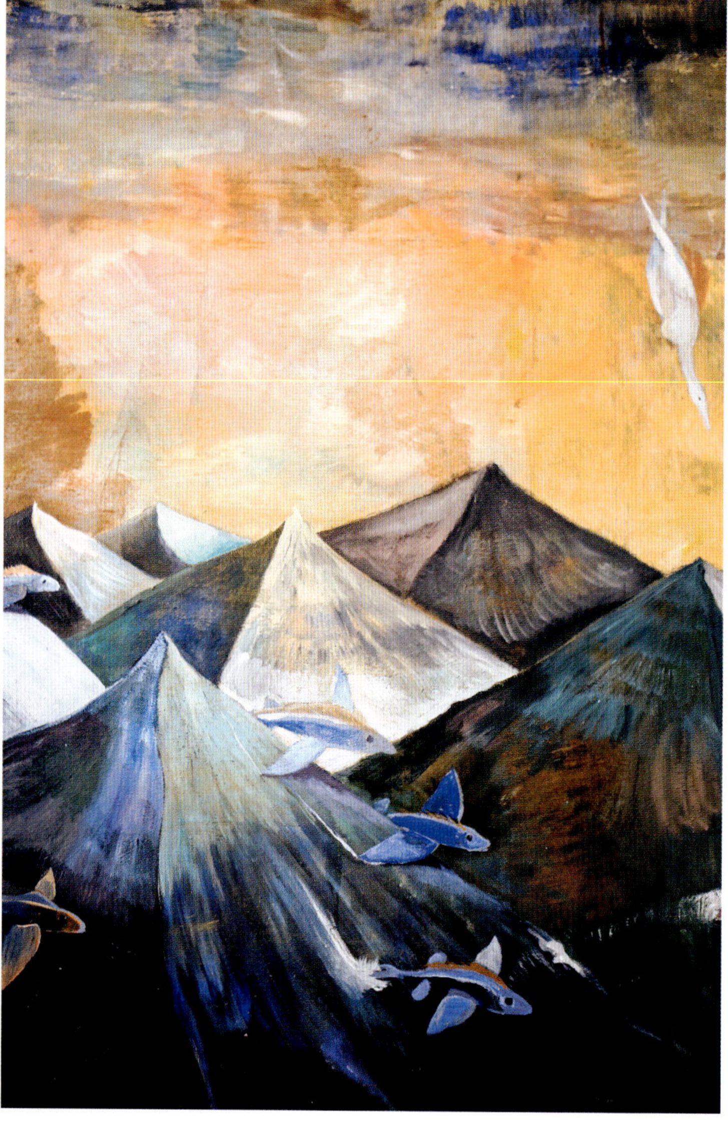

ABOVE

The artist tells stories with his paintings—tales of his travels in Asia and Europe as a young artist, and those of his imagination now, as an older artist.

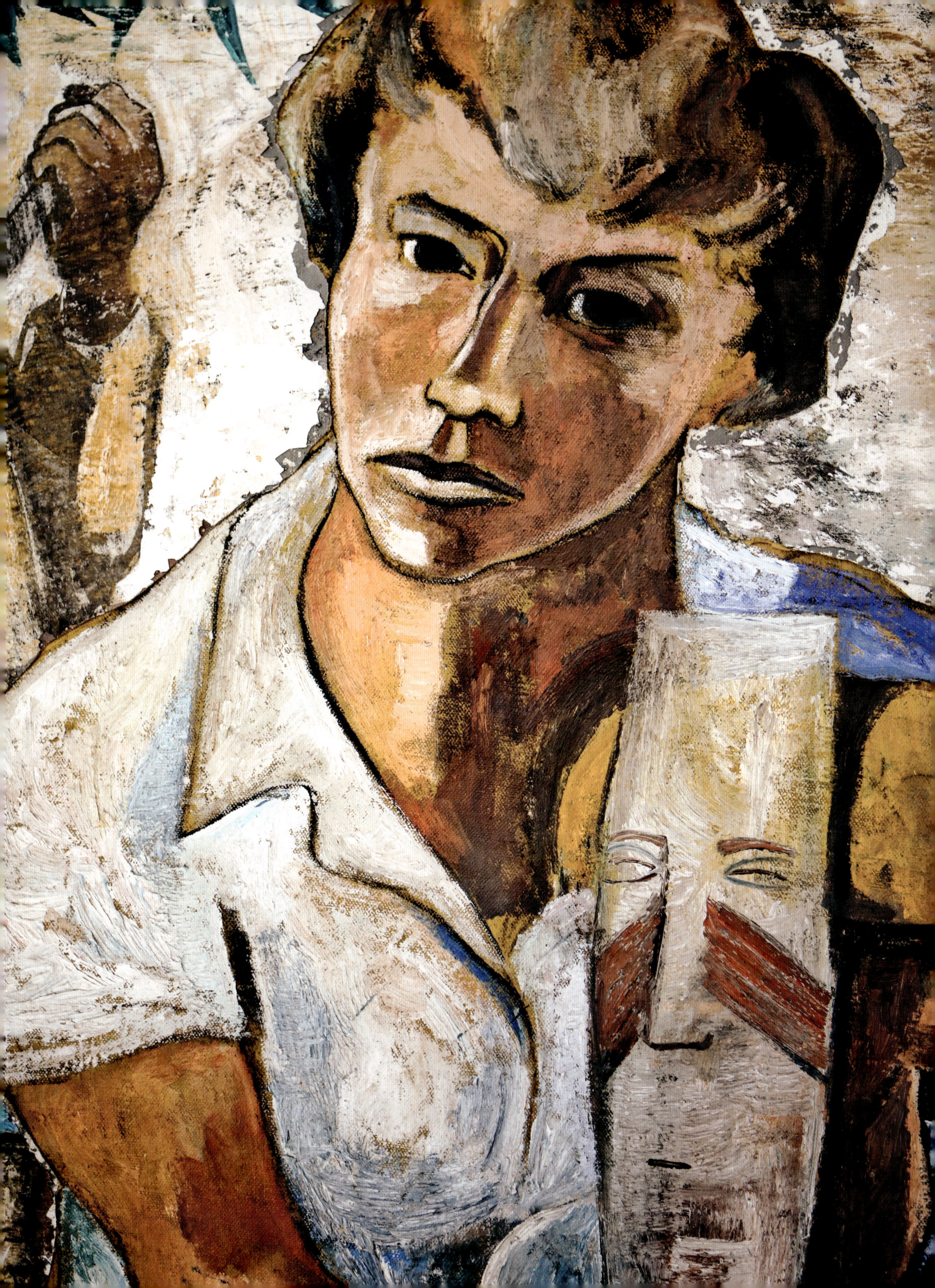

Jazz has been a key element in my work environment since I first saw Keith Jarrett play with Charles Lloyd when I was a teenager. The risk-taking of musical improvisation is an inspiration to my process, to the search for an unexpected result in my art.

STEVE MILLER

Miller first came to the Hamptons in 1978. "I chased a relationship with someone who was part of a share house in Southampton. We ended up loving it out here and eventually rented a dune shack in Sagaponack. It was a dream to live at the beach and watch the sunset over potato fields from our porch, listening to jazz. A few years later, I bought Frank Stella's Sagaponack studio—and am still there today." Another motivation for the move out east: "The intrigue of Pollock and de Kooning was always in the back of my mind. I grew up in Buffalo seeing Pollock's *Convergence* at the Buffalo AKG Art Museum, and that painting changed my life. The fact that those two artists lived out here was a definite incentive."

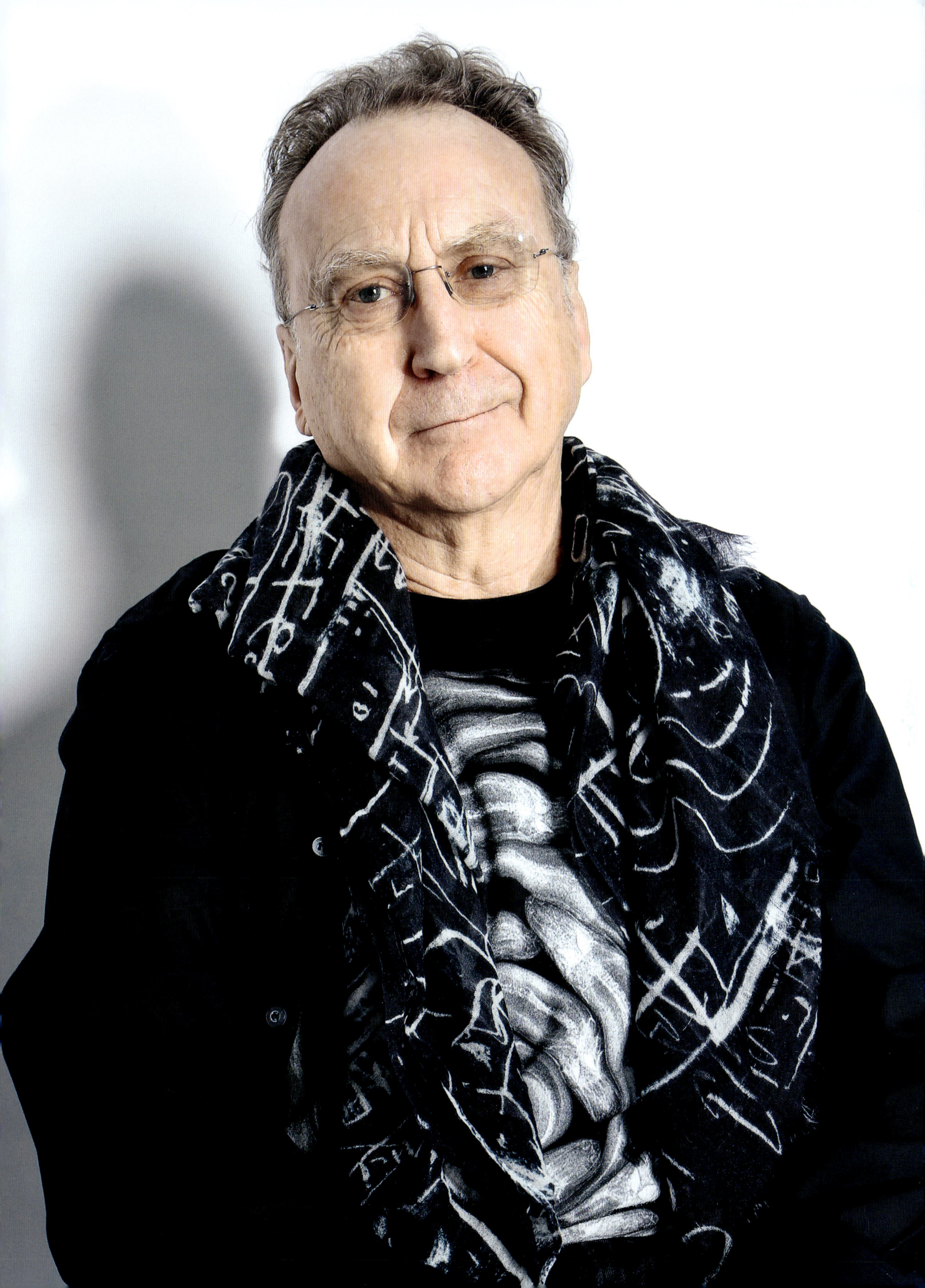

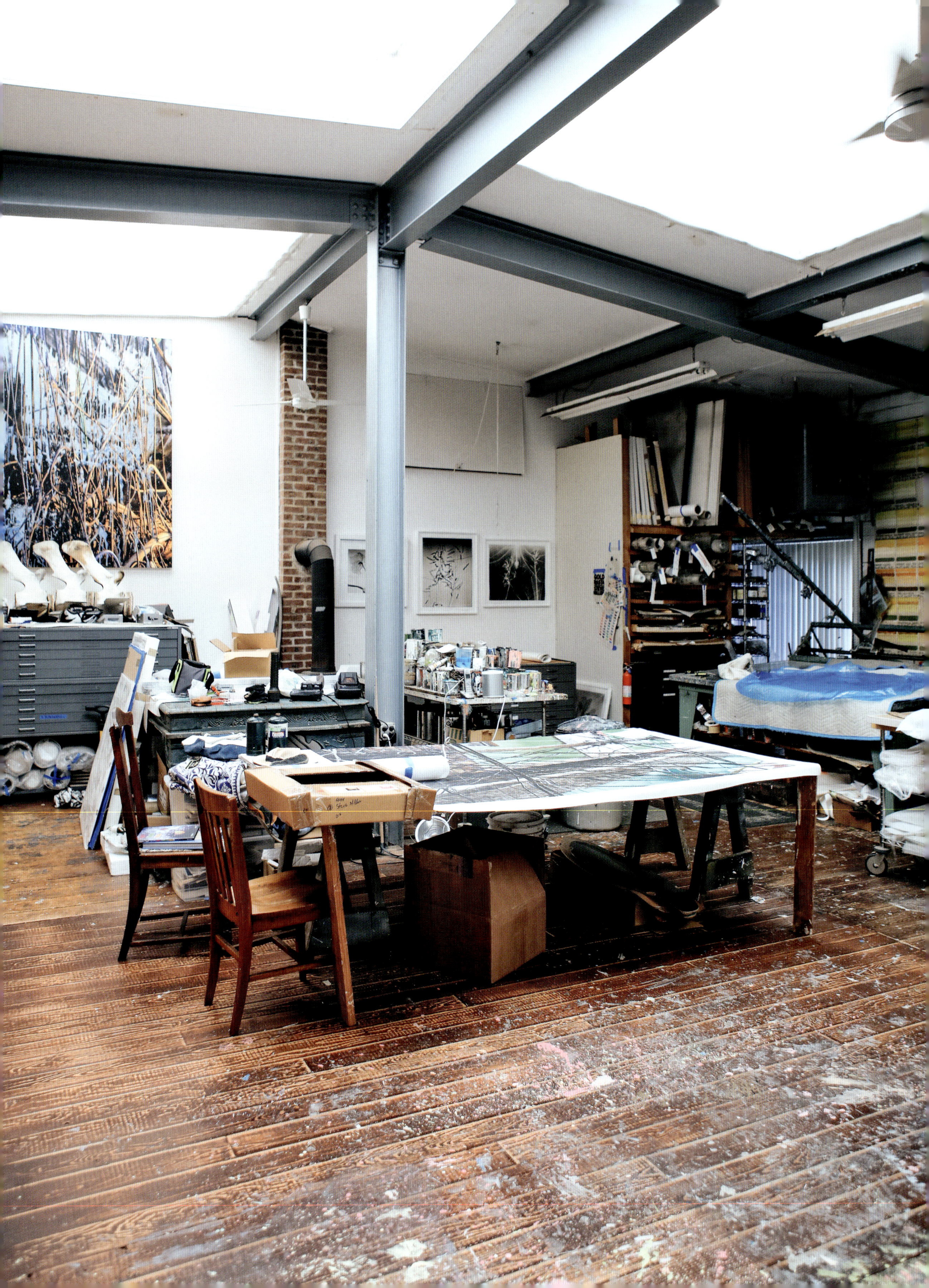

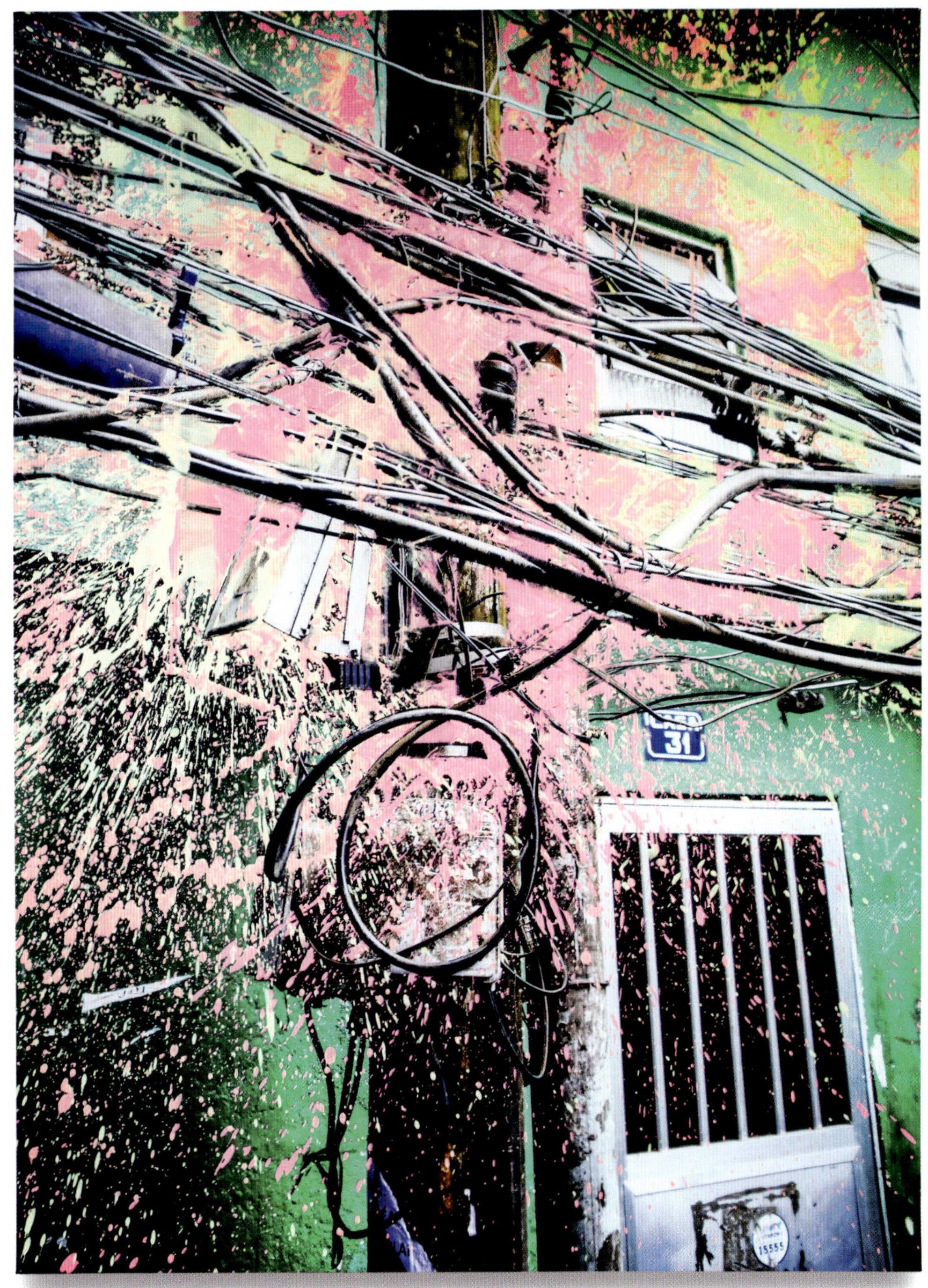

Miller likes to use a range of mediums and materials, from cashmere to cotton duck. "The freedom to play with sculpture, silk screen, surfboards, skate decks, traditional painting, books, and fashion allows me to communicate content to different viewers." Miller's work habits are equally free-form. "I have no regular hours. My living room is my studio, so I enjoy the luxury of living with my work and dropping in at odd hours to explore a visual connection. I can walk into the studio, look at a composition, and make some color decisions or make some work happen quickly, like one of my book pages with silk screen and paint."

OPPOSITE The multimedia artist lives and works in a converted potato barn in Sagaponack that was formerly Frank Stella's studio.

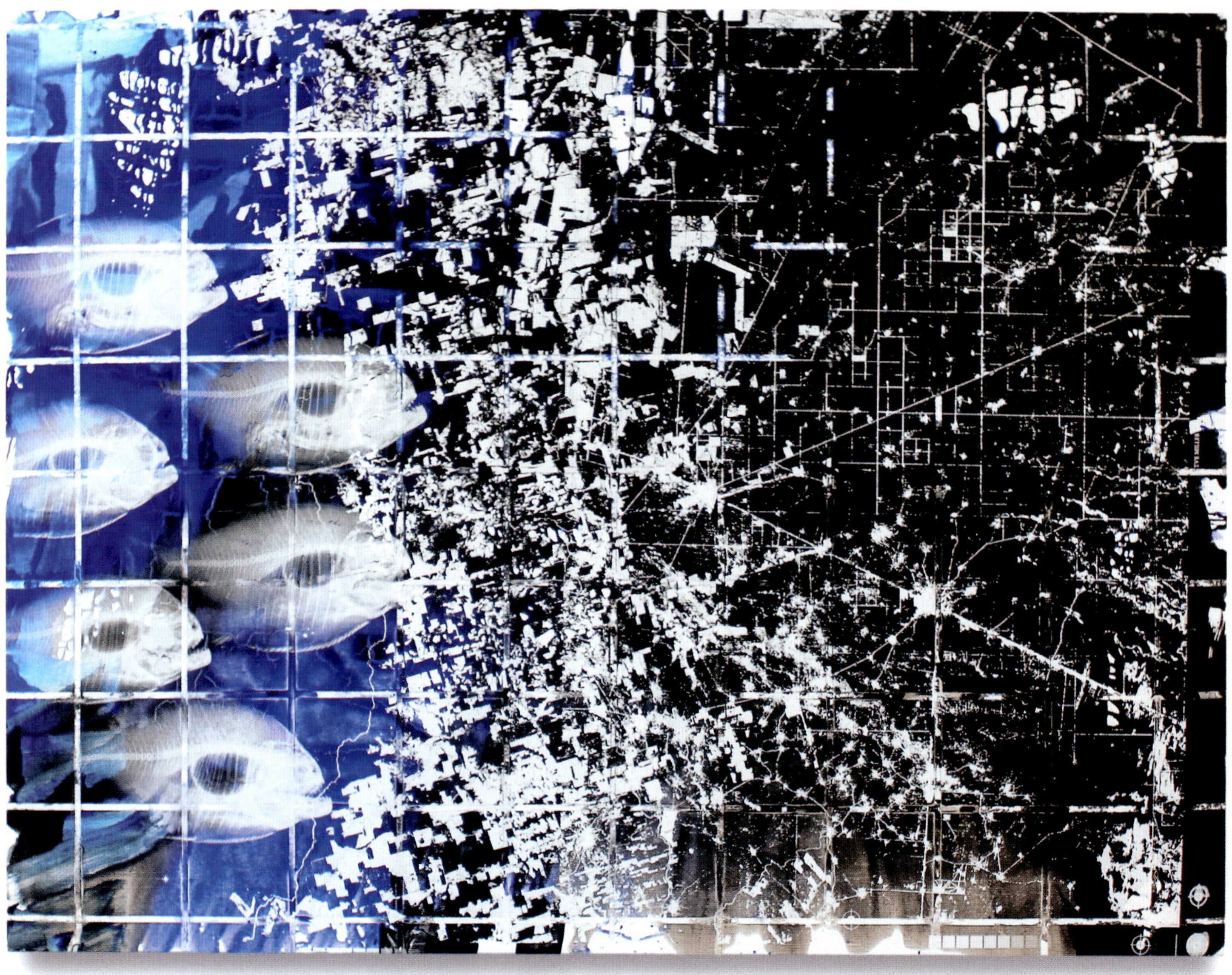

Why the reptilian images on surfboards that Miller has become known for? "I'm creating a message about the destruction of the Amazon ecosystem and the near extinction of the caiman lizard. The animal 'trophy' is an example of an unnecessary death. Instead of killing and stuffing a caiman, I wanted to create an eco-trophy that left the animal alive. Years ago, I brought a caiman from an Amazon zoo to a nearby hospital for an X-ray and placed that X-ray onto a surfboard that mirrored the shape of the reptile. Surfboards are ubiquitous in Brazil. I thought of this object that moves through the water as both a functional thing and a purveyor of an environmental message about the fragile beauty of nature—a way to communicate art and ideas beyond the confines of a gallery."

OPPOSITE Miller in his living room/studio, surrounded by his work (the pillows and surfboard) and part of his significant collection of Neolithic Chinese pottery, 4000–200 BCE.

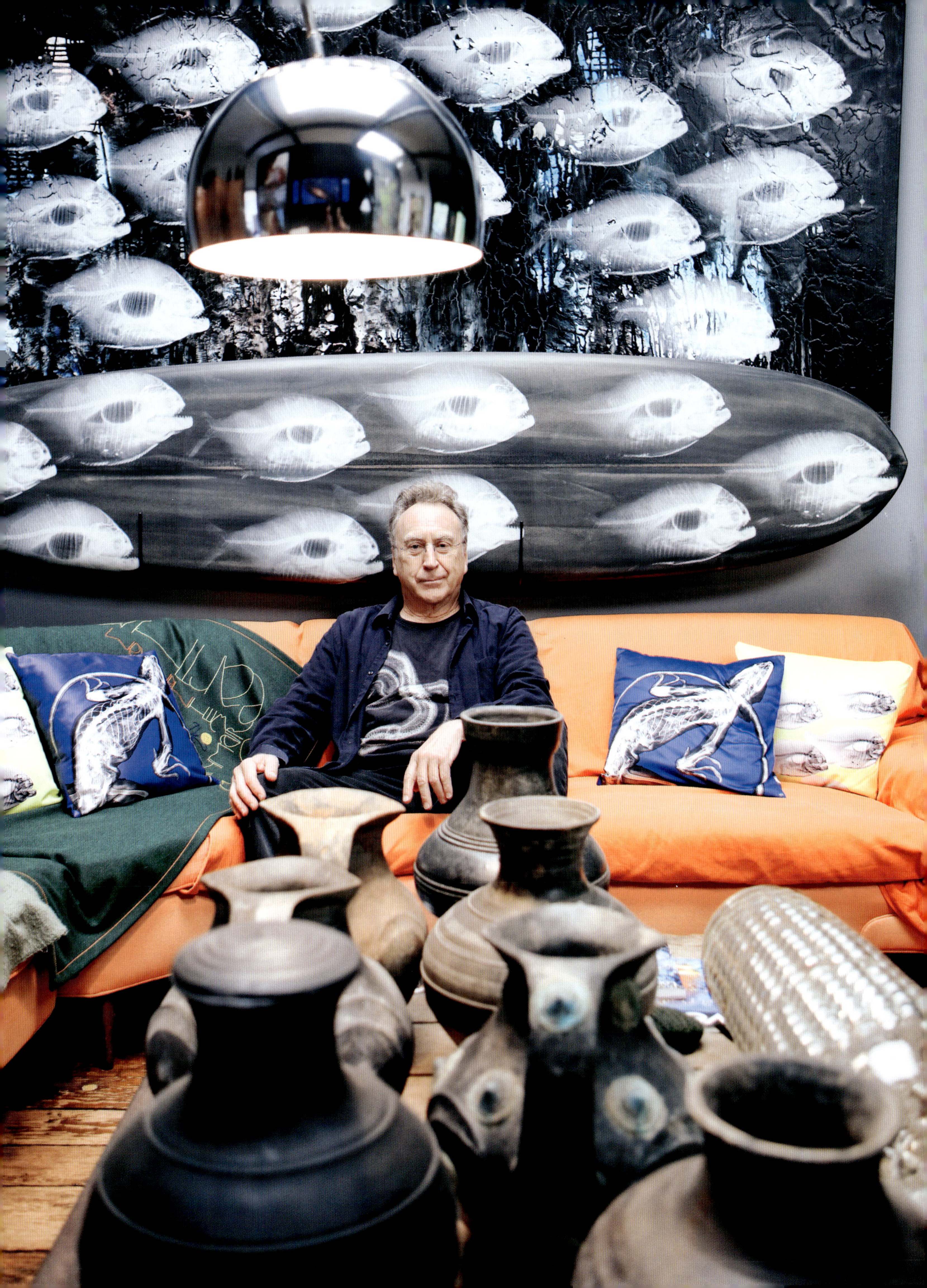

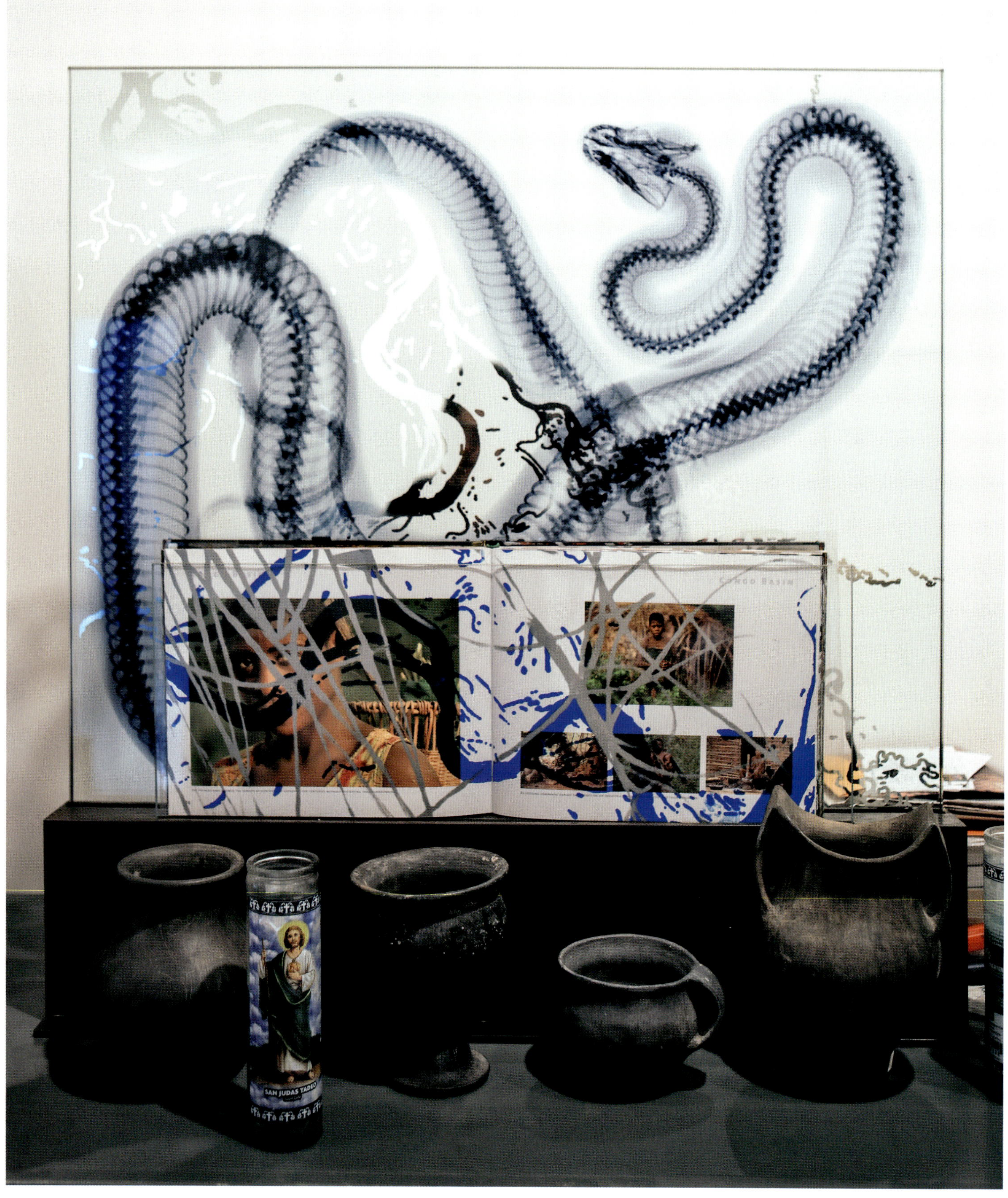

ABOVE AND OPPOSITE Much of Miller's artwork sends a message about the fragility of nature, often through motifs of X-rayed oceanic and reptilian creatures. He also explores pure abstraction with his silk-screen paintings.

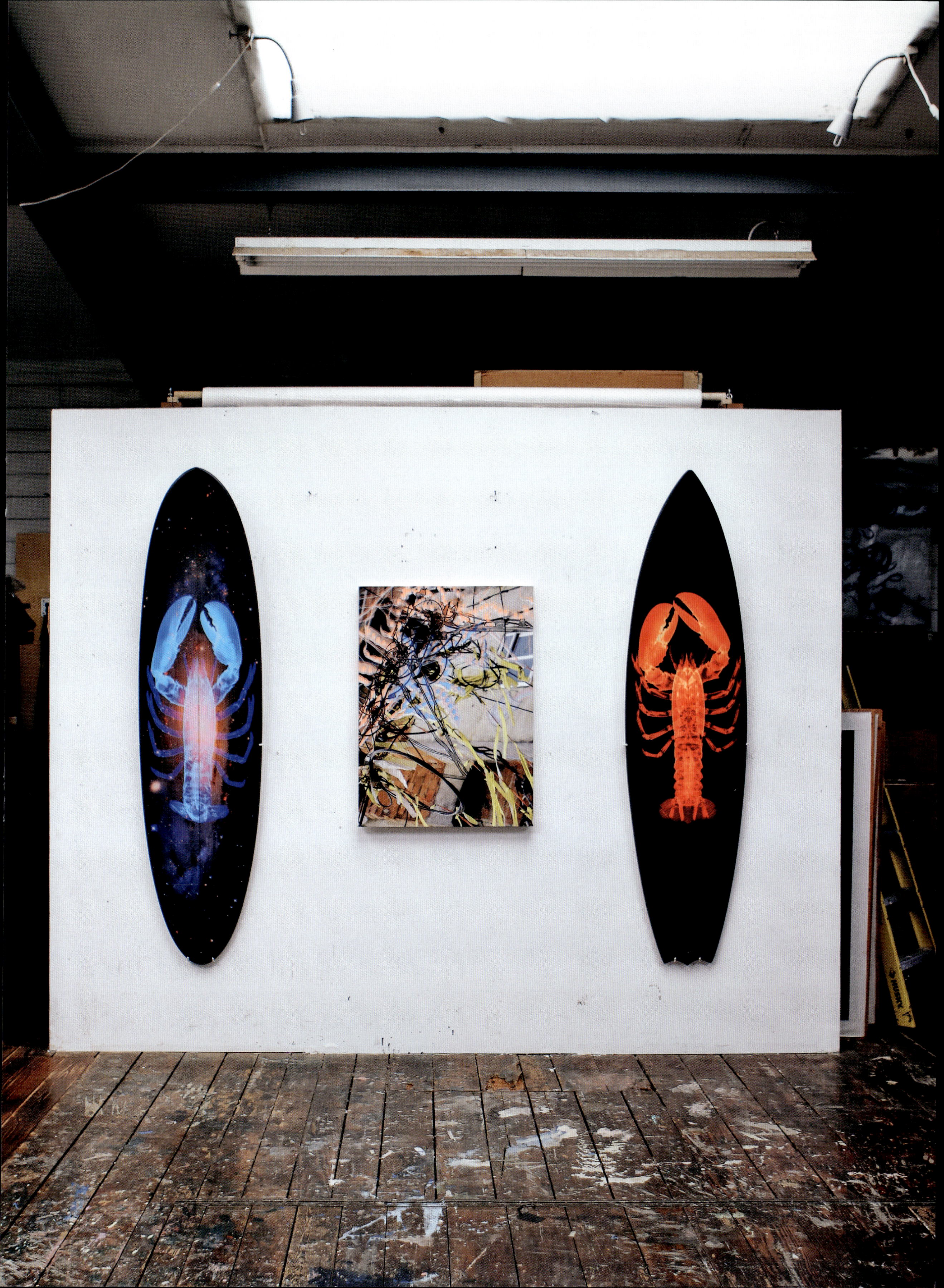

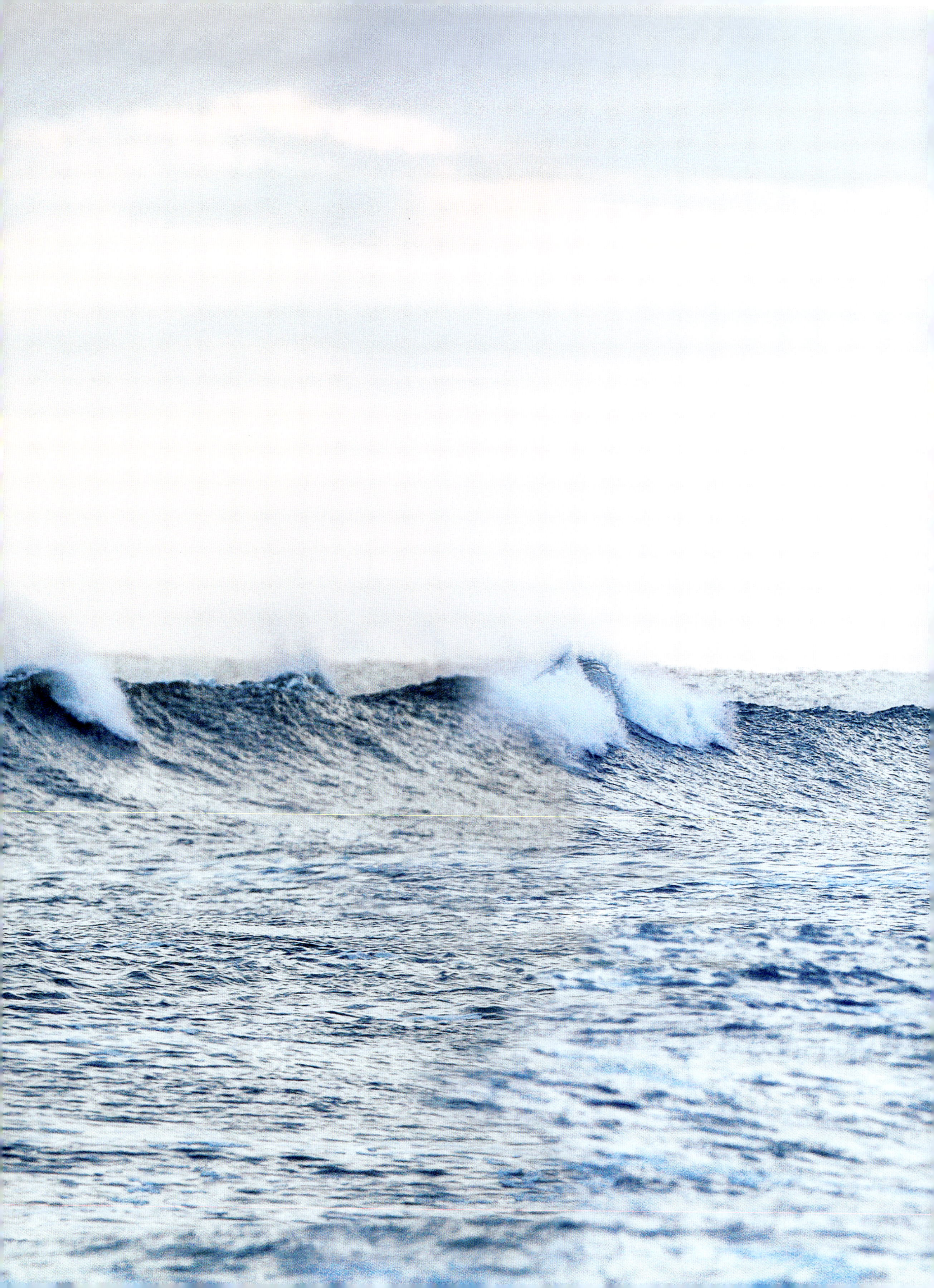

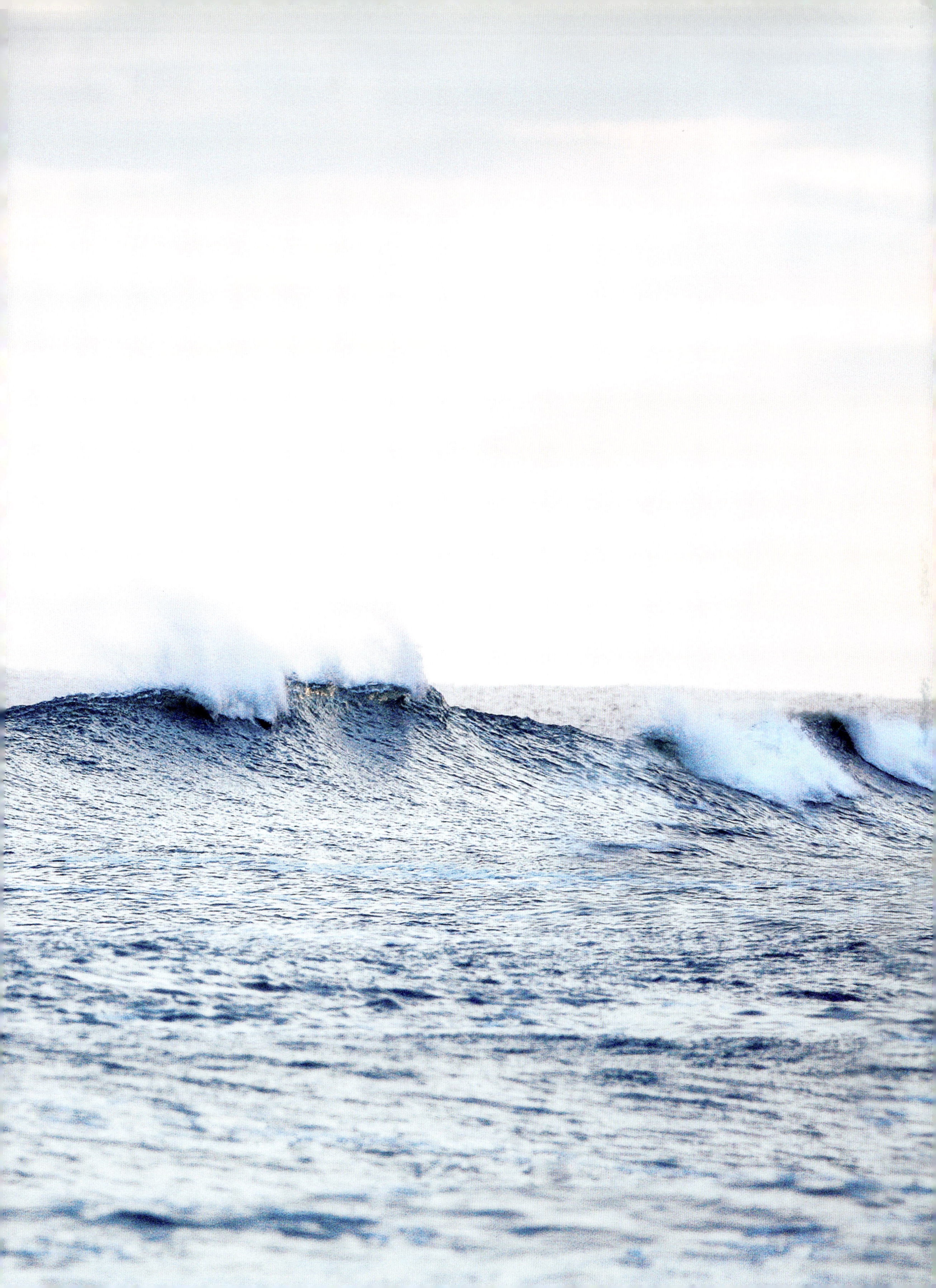

I love the studio I built out here. It has changed the way I work and the work itself. The landscape, the sea, the light have all taken hold of me. Walking along the coast every day has brought clarity and focus to my painting life.

JILL MOSER

Born in New York City, Moser received her BA in cultural anthropology at Brown, came back to New York City to study painting at the Brooklyn Museum, and earned her MFA in painting at Hunter College. She has taught at Princeton University, Virginia Commonwealth University, SUNY, and the School of Visual Arts. "On a summer visit to the East End in 1996, I met my husband and for the next fifteen summers we lived on our sailboat, *Blue*, moored off Shelter Island. In 2012, we built a house on the island and came here on weekends for work retreats. The landscape, with its shifting contours and colors, had such an effect on my work that I was inspired to build a studio. In the fall of 2022, after working in the city for over thirty years, I made the dramatic move here full-time."

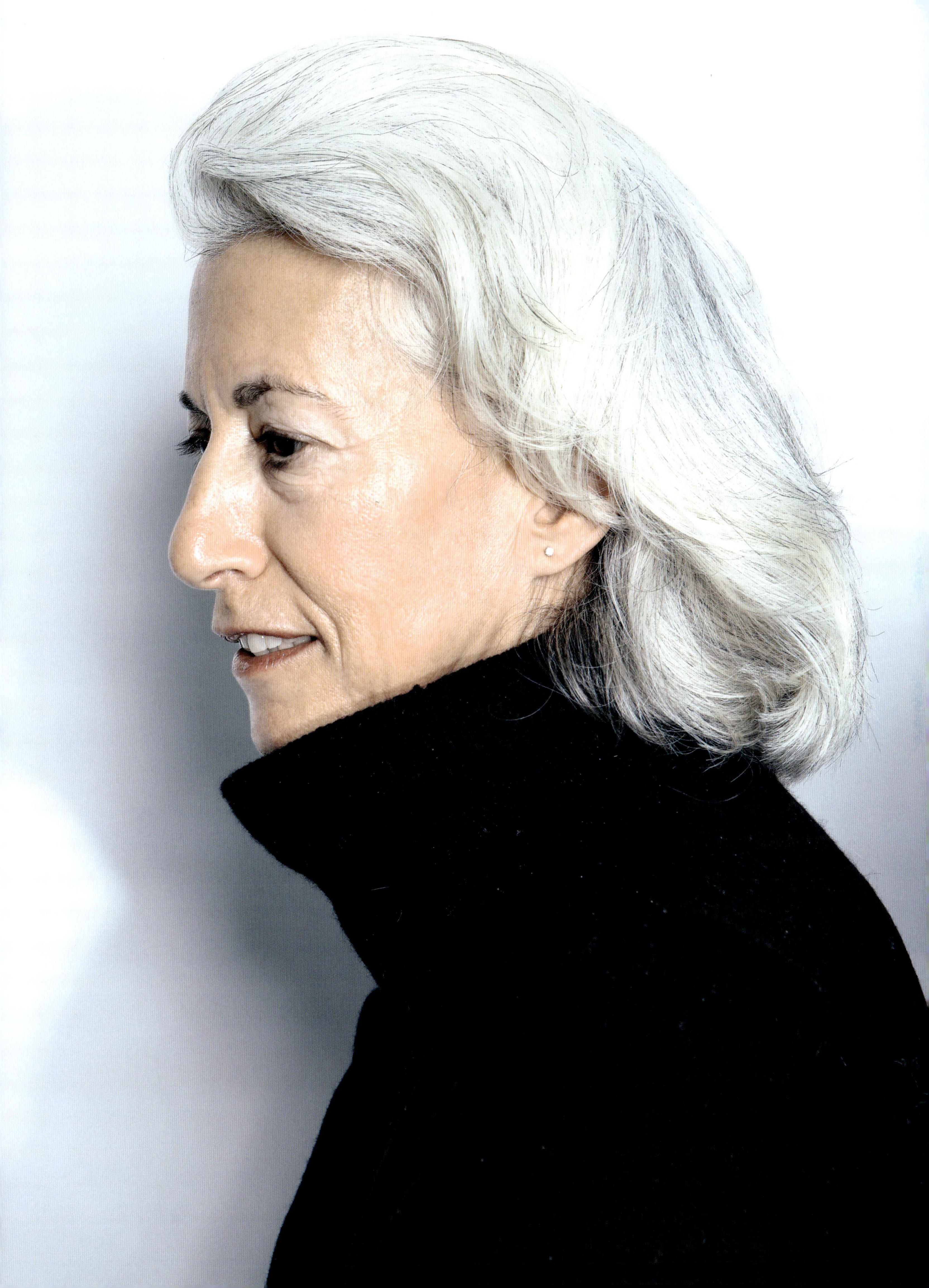

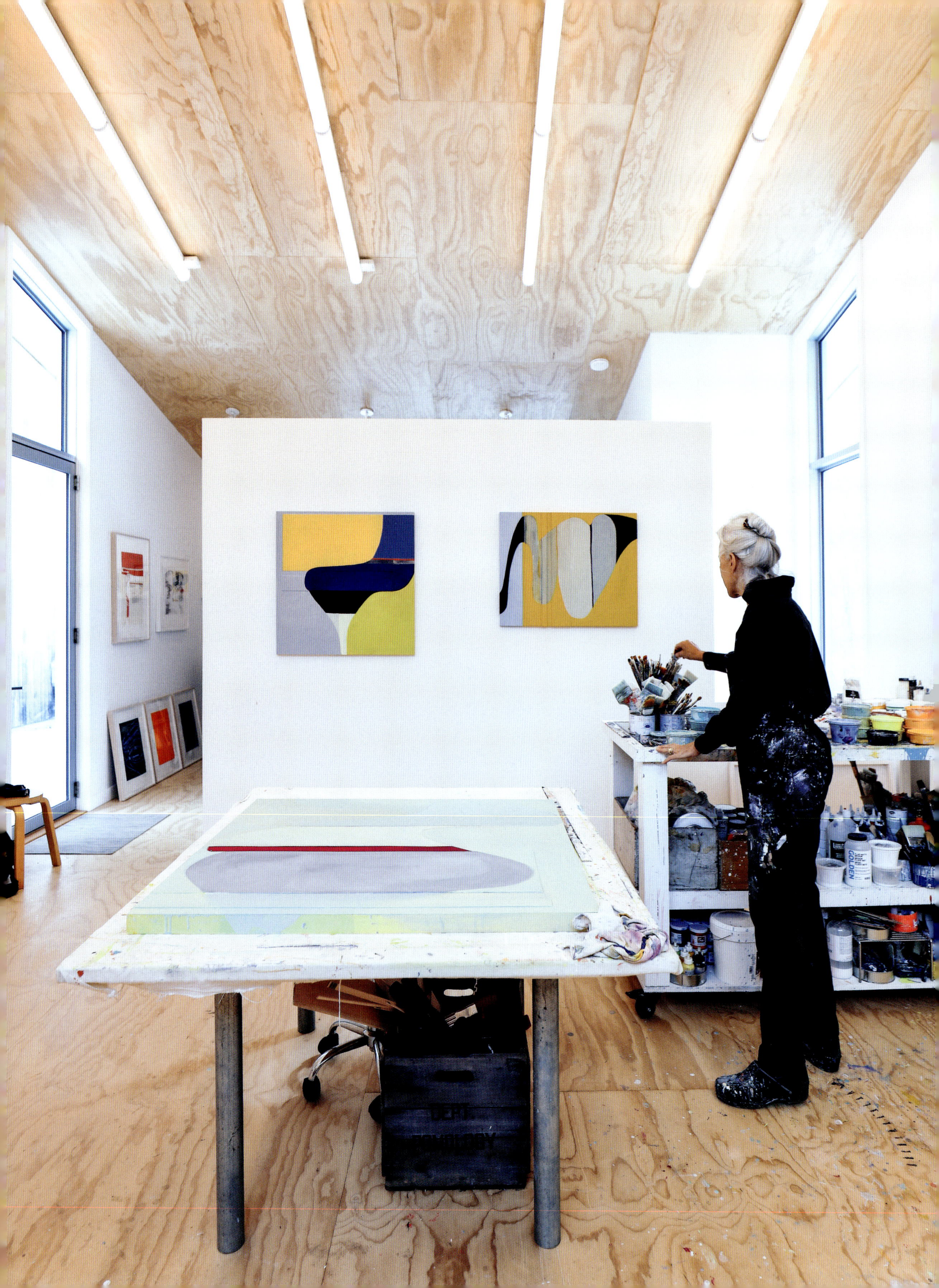

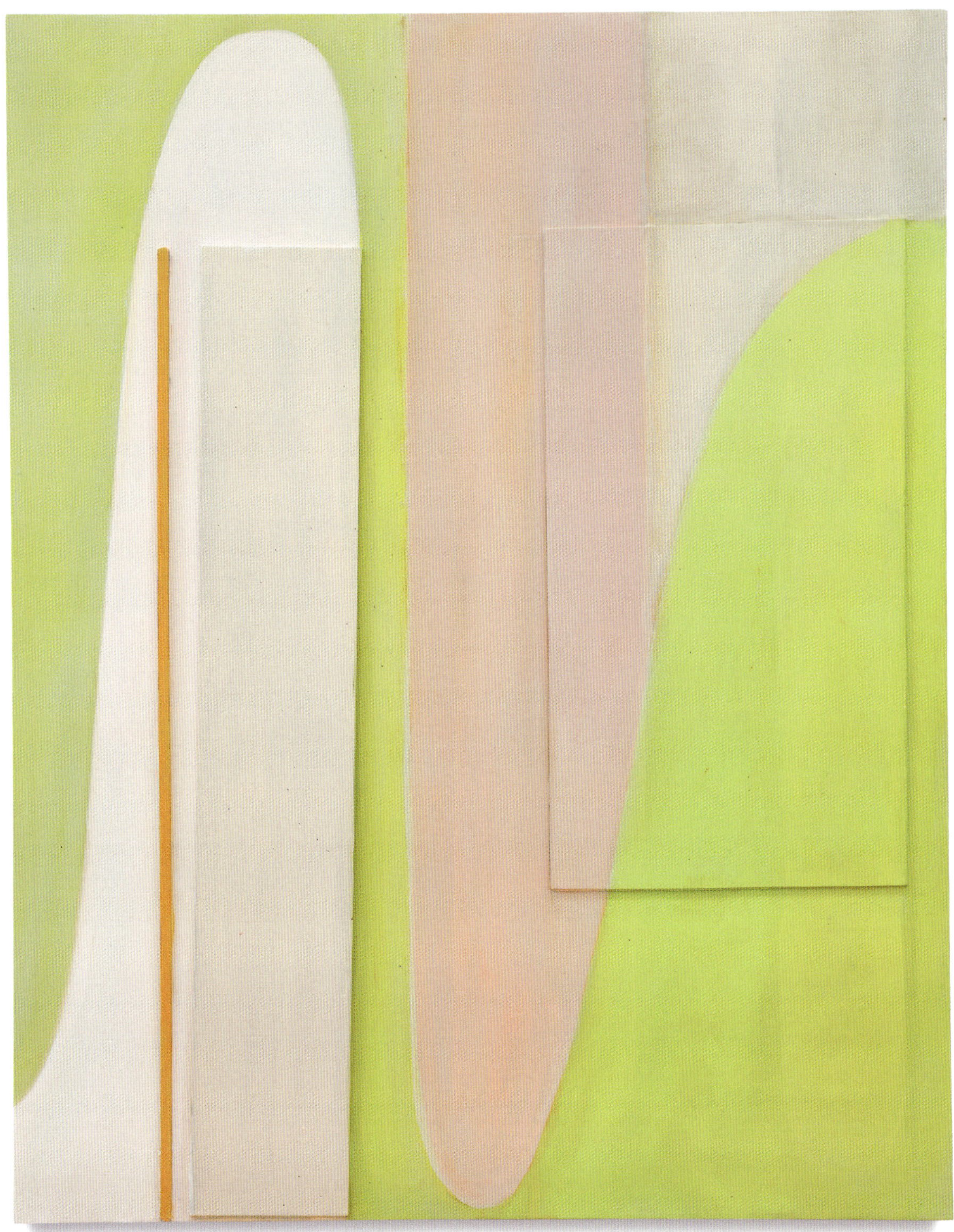

"During the pandemic, my work took an unexpected and remarkable turn. Reworking earlier prints and drawings in a search for tangible light in dark times, new ideas coalesced and led to an entirely novel set of paintings and works on paper. I delved even more deeply into color's sensorial charge and its animation of form and shape. My decades-long engagement with gesture as an arrested image found new meaning in the work."

OPPOSITE Moser in her Shelter Island studio, which she and her husband built and which inspired her to move to the East End full-time.

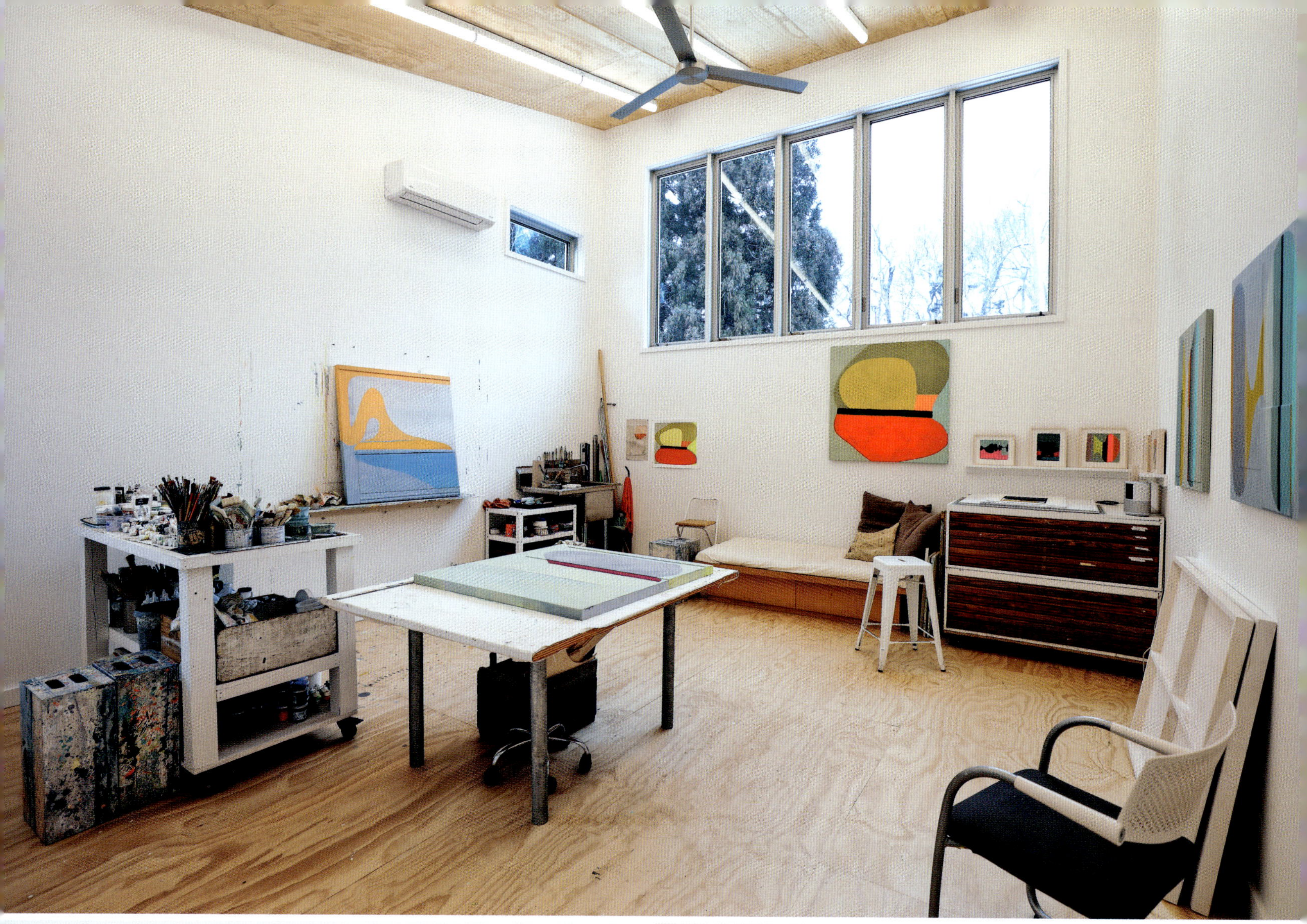

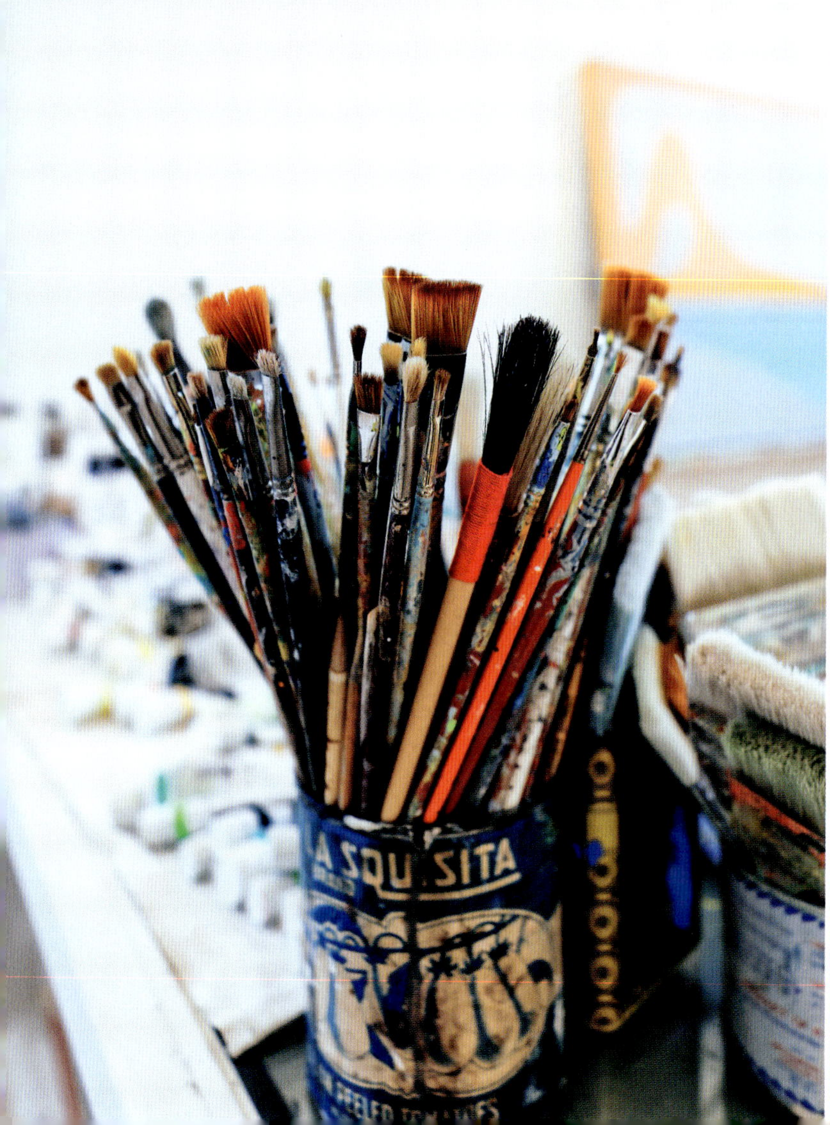

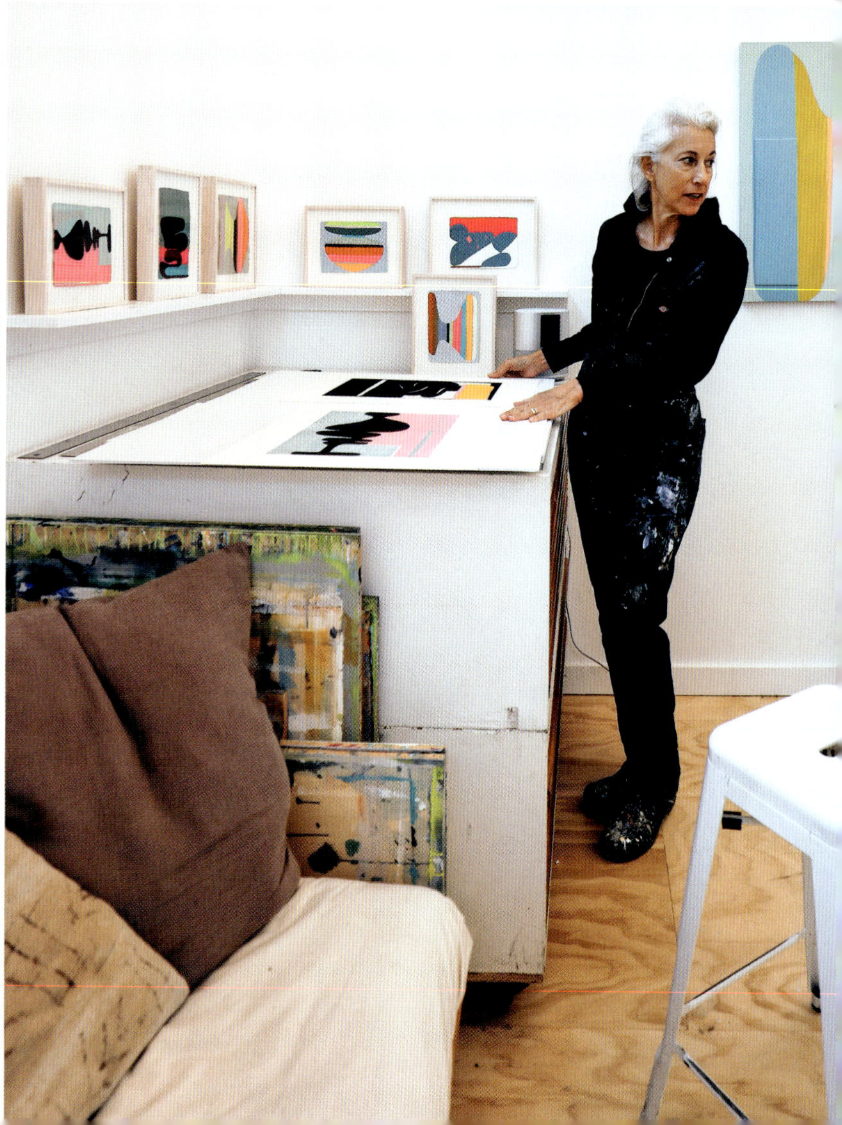

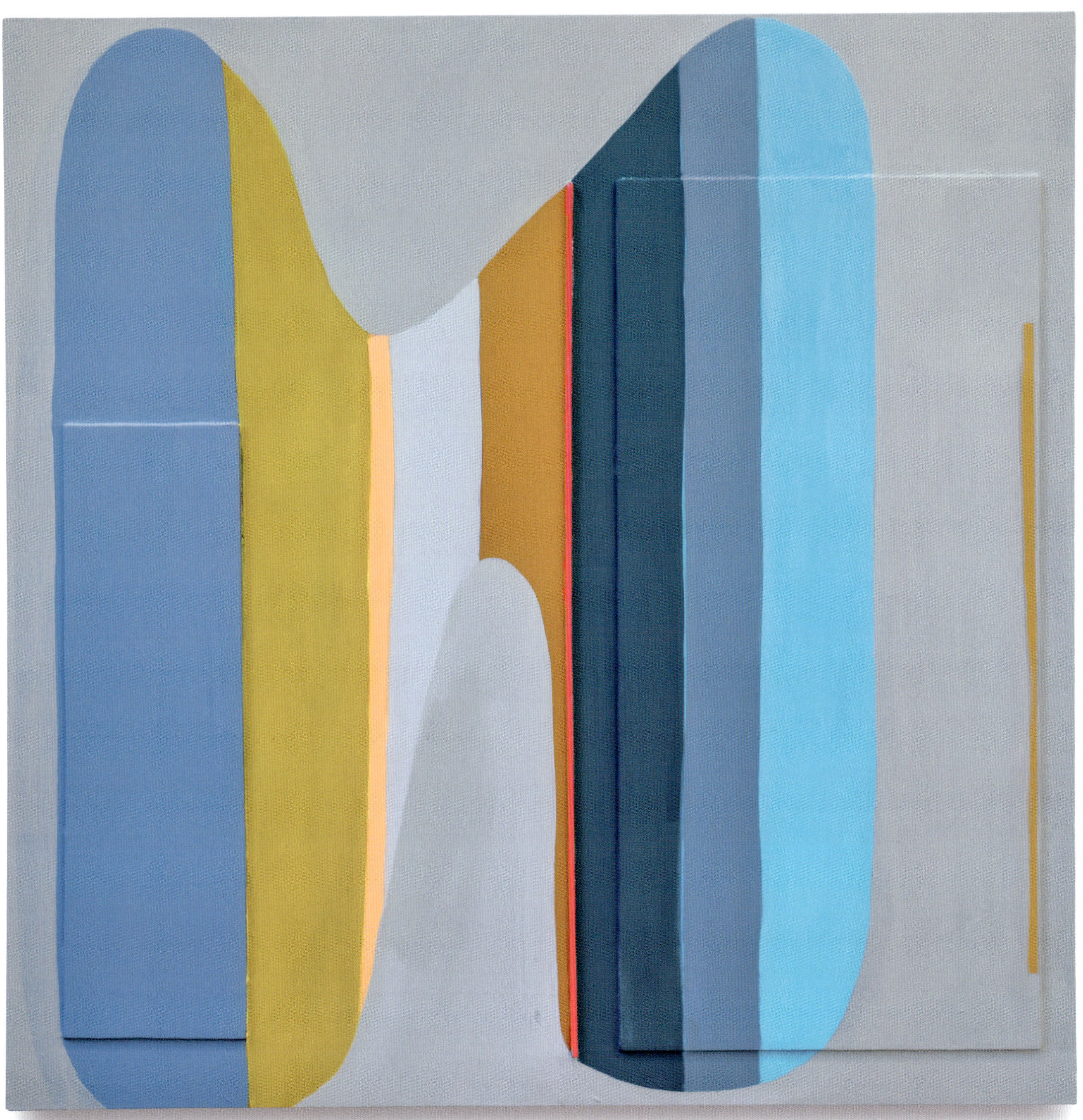

"In constructing paintings and collages with layers of wood and paper, I search for shapes with a tactility and textural vibrancy animated by color. Forms I once teased out with lines and held in suspended animation are now embodied and held in buoyant spaces—fragmented references to bodies and nature, lush and verdant. My palette, borrowed from the history of painting, is now also informed by the saturated light of the East End."

OPPOSITE The juxtaposition of vivid hues is the driving force behind Moser's animated abstract paintings, which pop and vibrate on her studio walls.

If I'm asked about my abstraction, I say it's about accepting my reality as fractured. I'm an abstract mark in space and want to claim it.

GEORGE NEGROPONTE

"I grew up in cities, New York and New Haven mostly, so my frame of reference is limited to sidewalks and concrete." Negroponte and his wife, Virva Hinnemo, also an artist, moved to East Hampton in 2012. "I was mesmerized by Pollock and de Kooning and hoped that their work would rub off on me. Impossible task." Still, the landscape triggered his imagination. "I liked to think about Pollock putting his nose into a bush and having a look. De Kooning loved Louse Point. The same goes for James Brooks, Charlotte Park, and Robert Motherwell. Their work was based on and by nature, so they soared here. I admire so many of the artists in my community and the artists I write about."

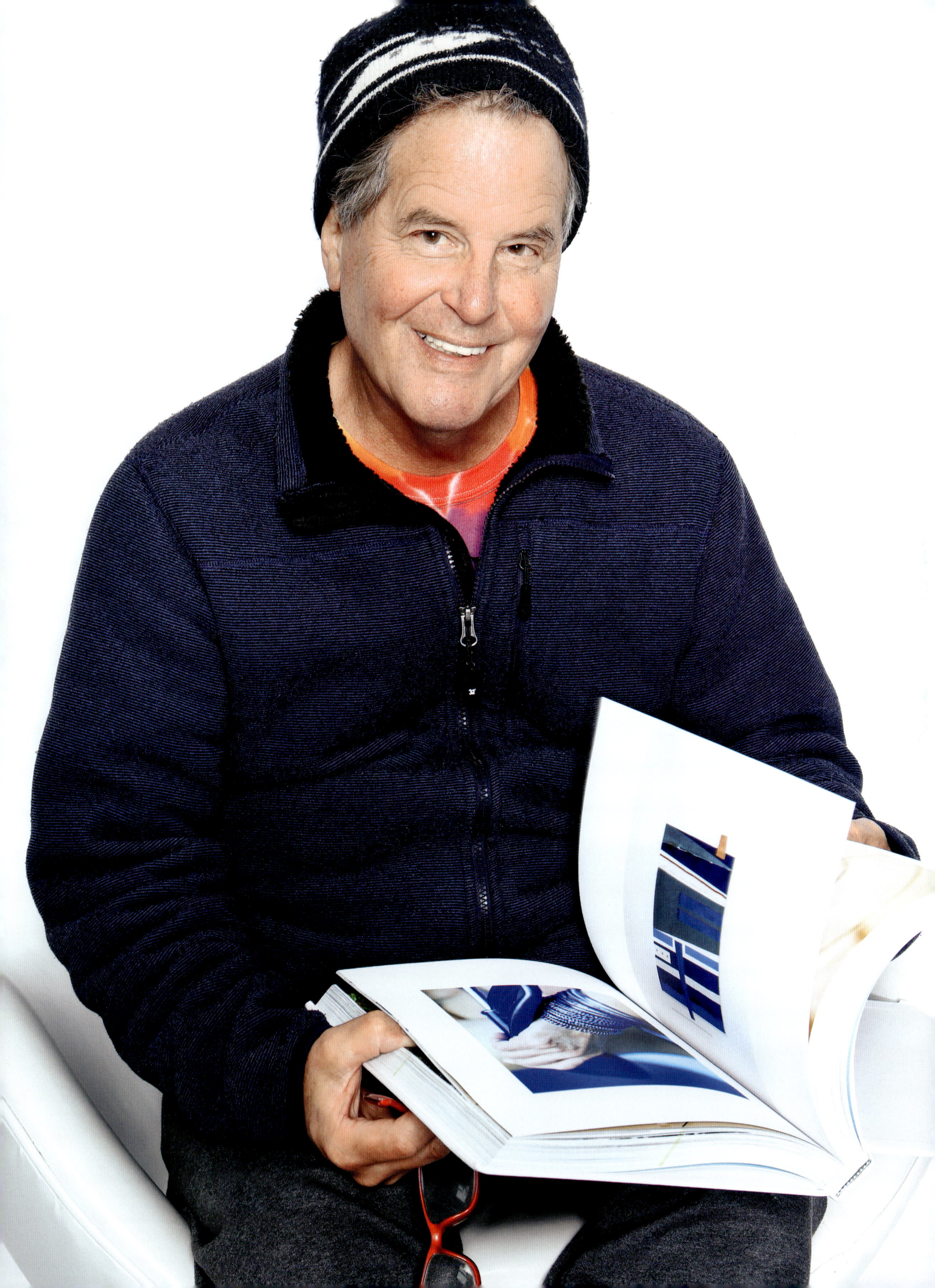

Negroponte's medium of choice? "House paints work well for me. I remove more paint than I put down. Sandpaper is my life's method, and I put paintings out in the rain and snow; my medium is weathered. I can work forever on a painting. I mostly sit and paint and use anything and everything. My fingers do the job for me. Touch is vital." Collage is a big part of Negroponte's work. "It's built into me by painters like Georges Braque and Conrad Marca-Relli. I want to see my seamless surface interrupted. I find it exciting."

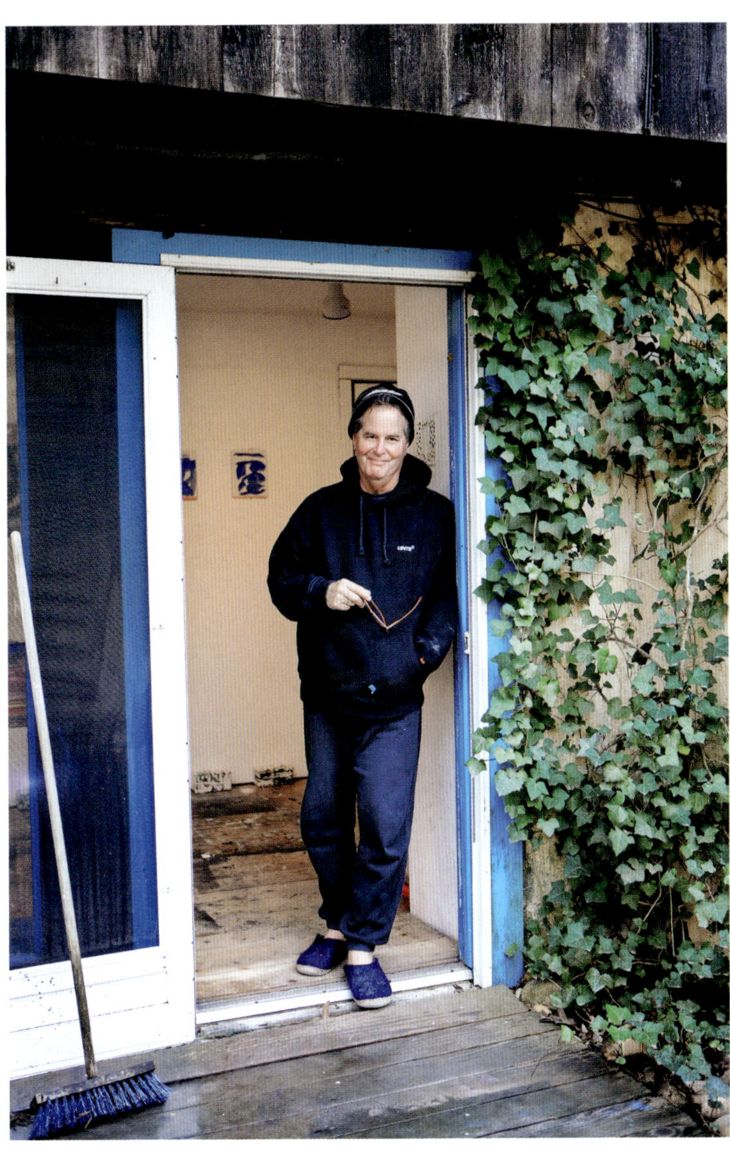

LEFT AND BELOW RIGHT

Negroponte works in his half of the East Hampton garage/studio that he shares with his wife, the artist Virva Hinnemo. A door separates the two halves, giving the couple space as well a connection—the opportunity to be inspired by each other.

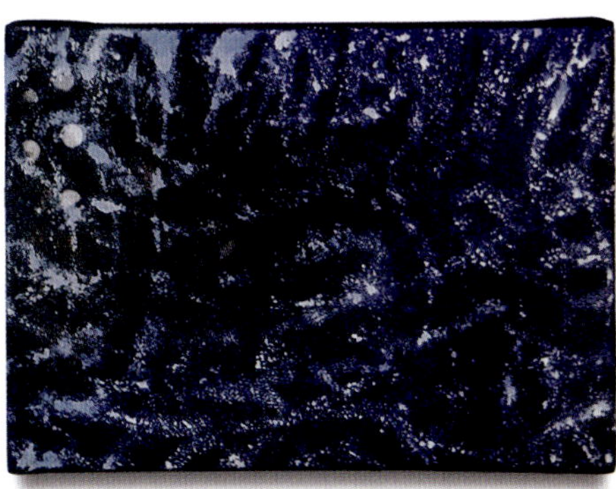

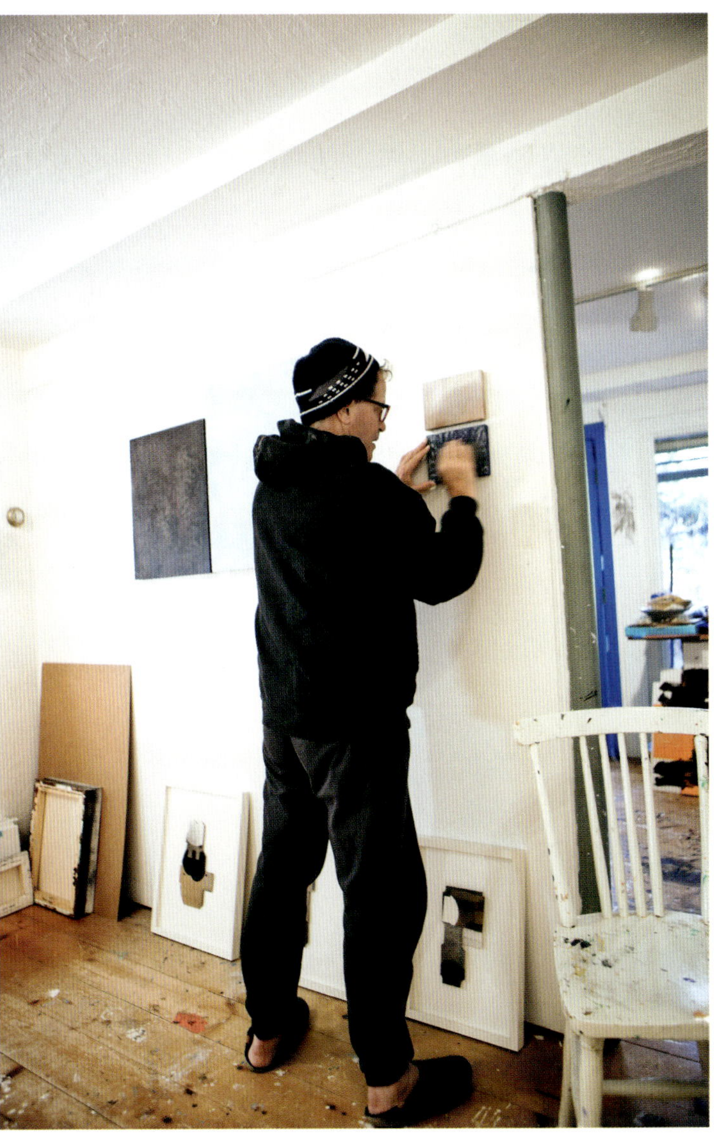

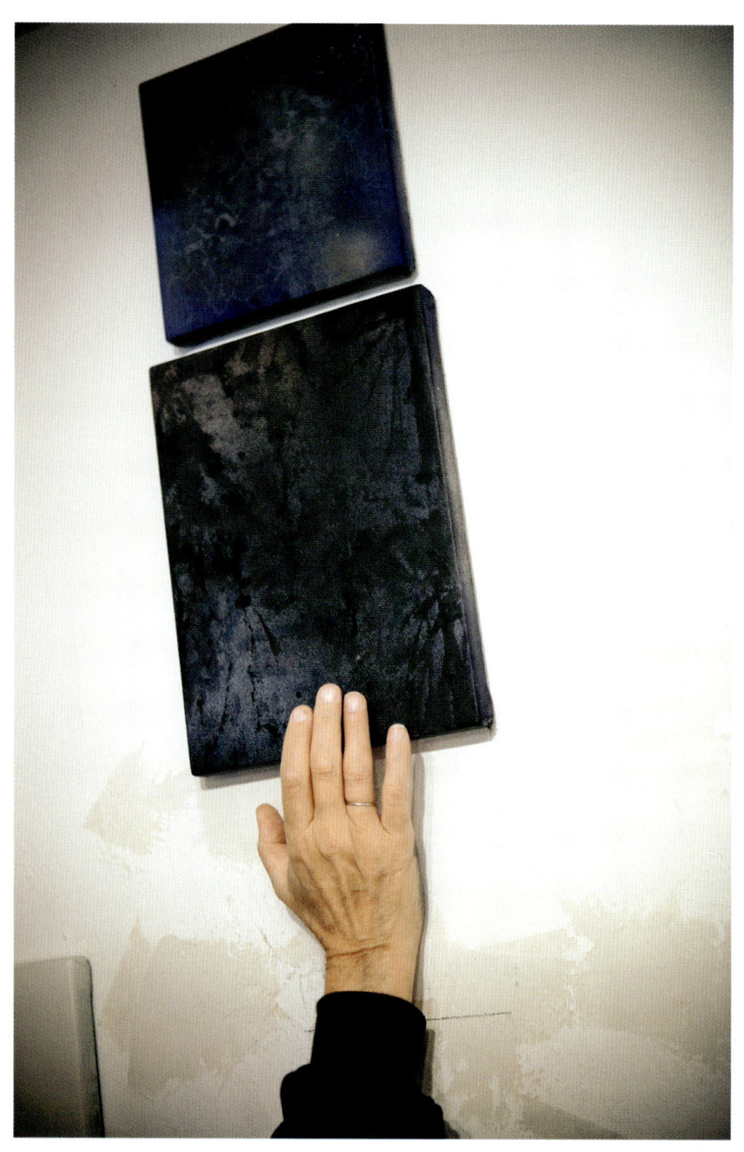

"My scale is small to medium; I arrived at it because each place I've lived asked for something unique. And since the surface is critical, a lot must be visible and manageable for me, something I can rework easily. A small scale requires the wisdom of the painting to be discrete. I like that. Byzantine icons are often small and transportable; it makes worshiping more intimate. The light is like a glimmer."

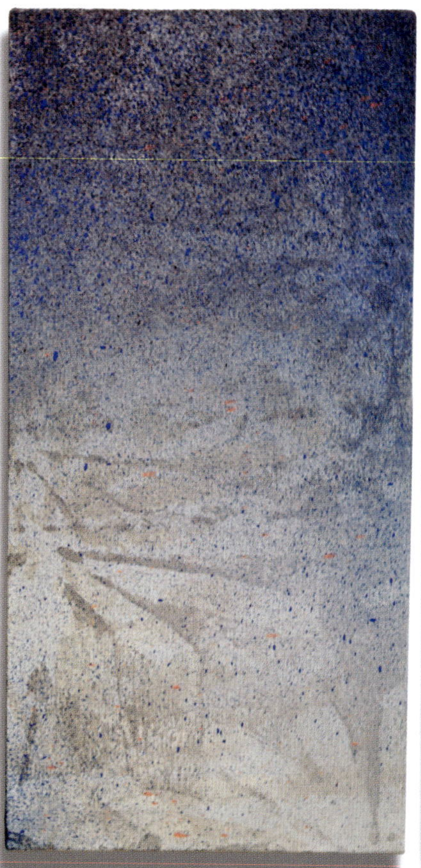

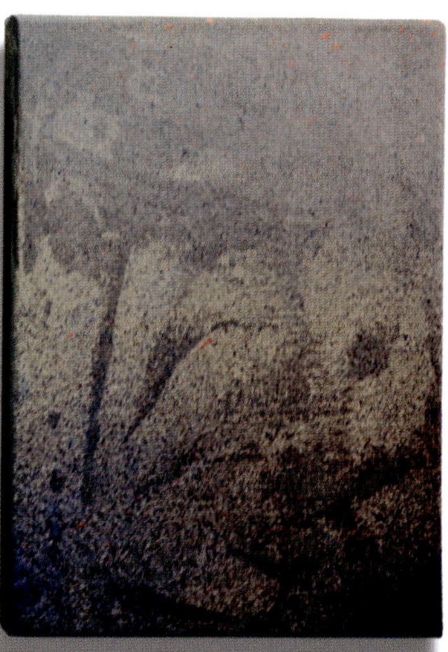

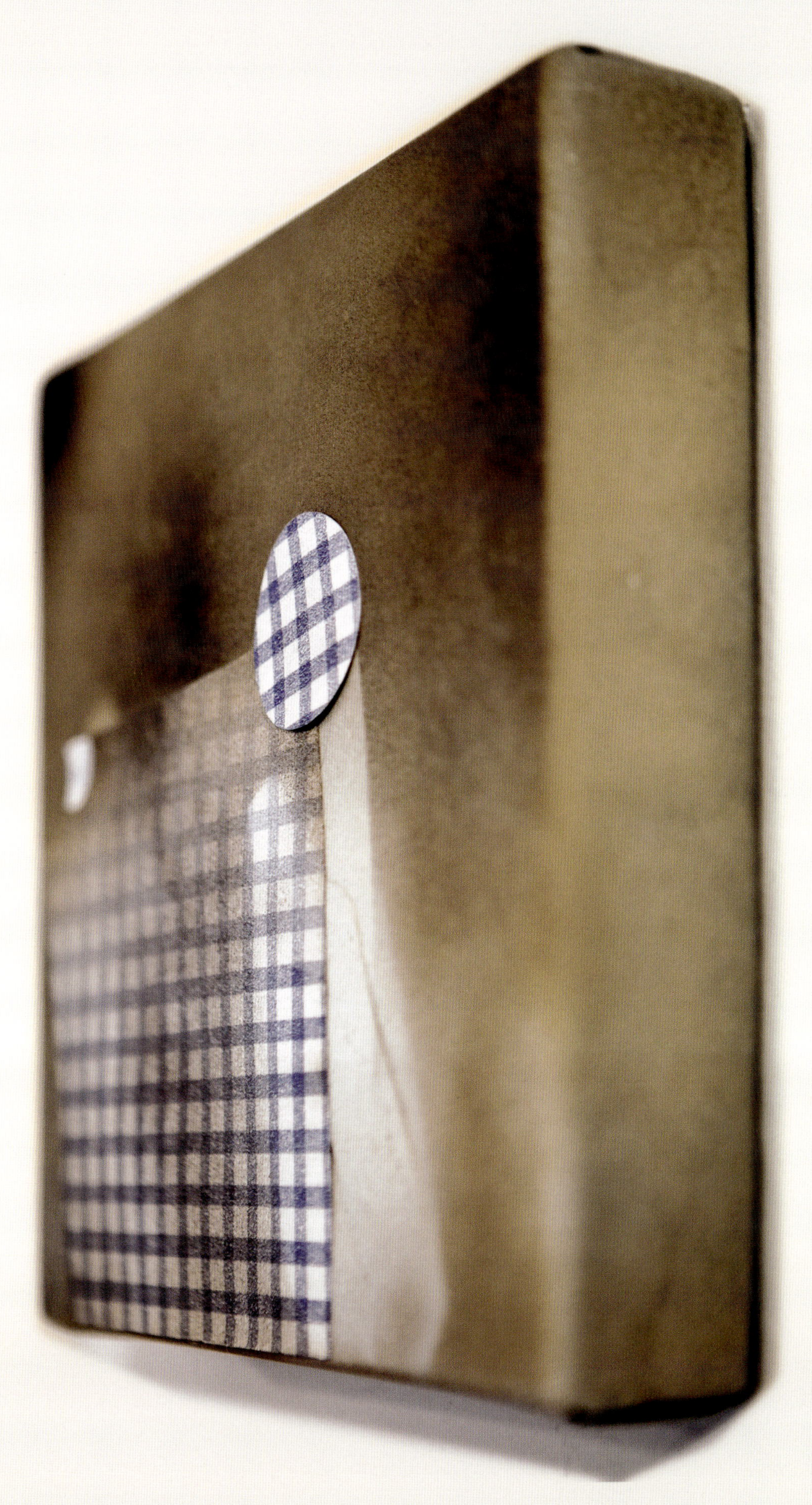

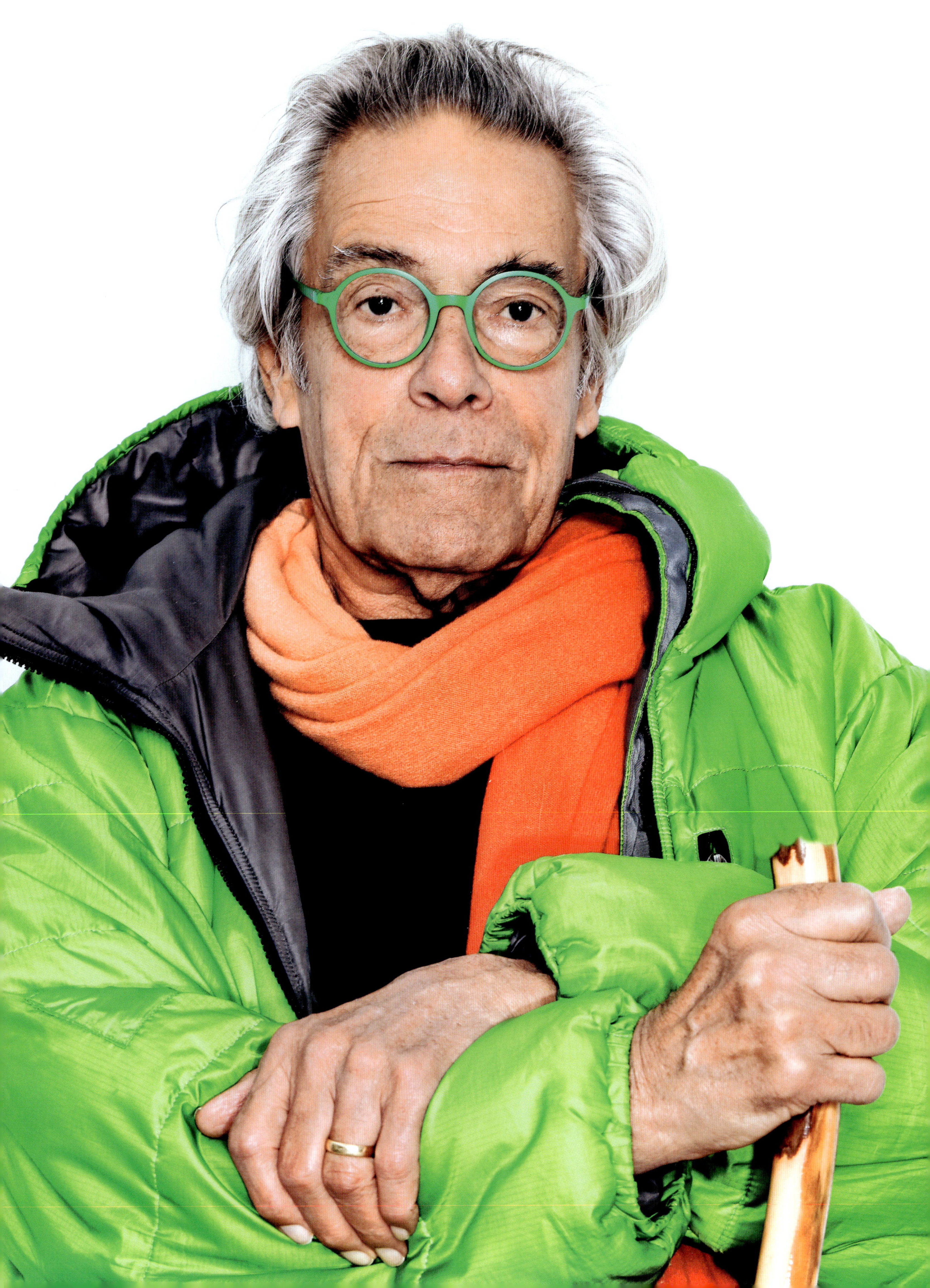

I was twenty-four when the magic and alchemy of photography took over as I watched my first image materialize itself on a blank piece of white photo paper in a tray filled with liquid developer.

MICHAEL O'NEILL

Although O'Neill grew up in Manhattan, he spent part of his childhood traveling with his parents, who were archaeologists and anthropologists—a circumstance that helped pave his future artistic path. "We lived in tents on the banks of the Missouri River in South Dakota. There were no other kids to play with, so I would sit under a big tree and watch bugs and collect them in a jar to study. When I was twelve, we lived in Trinidad in the West Indies. Free time found me dreaming in the mango groves and collecting giant, iridescent-blue butterflies. This is how I got the 'collecting bug,' which is what photographers have: they take pictures and collect images."

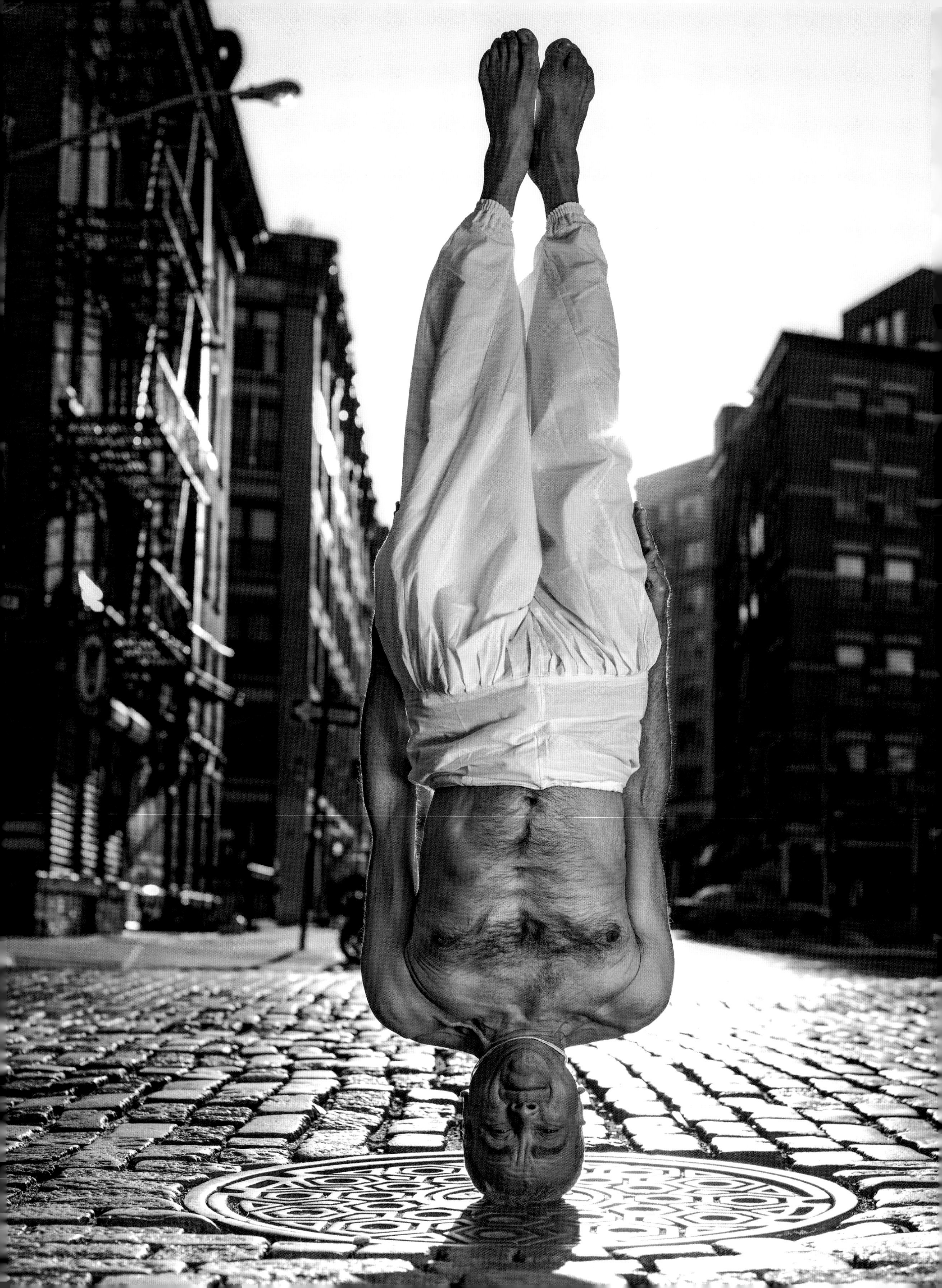

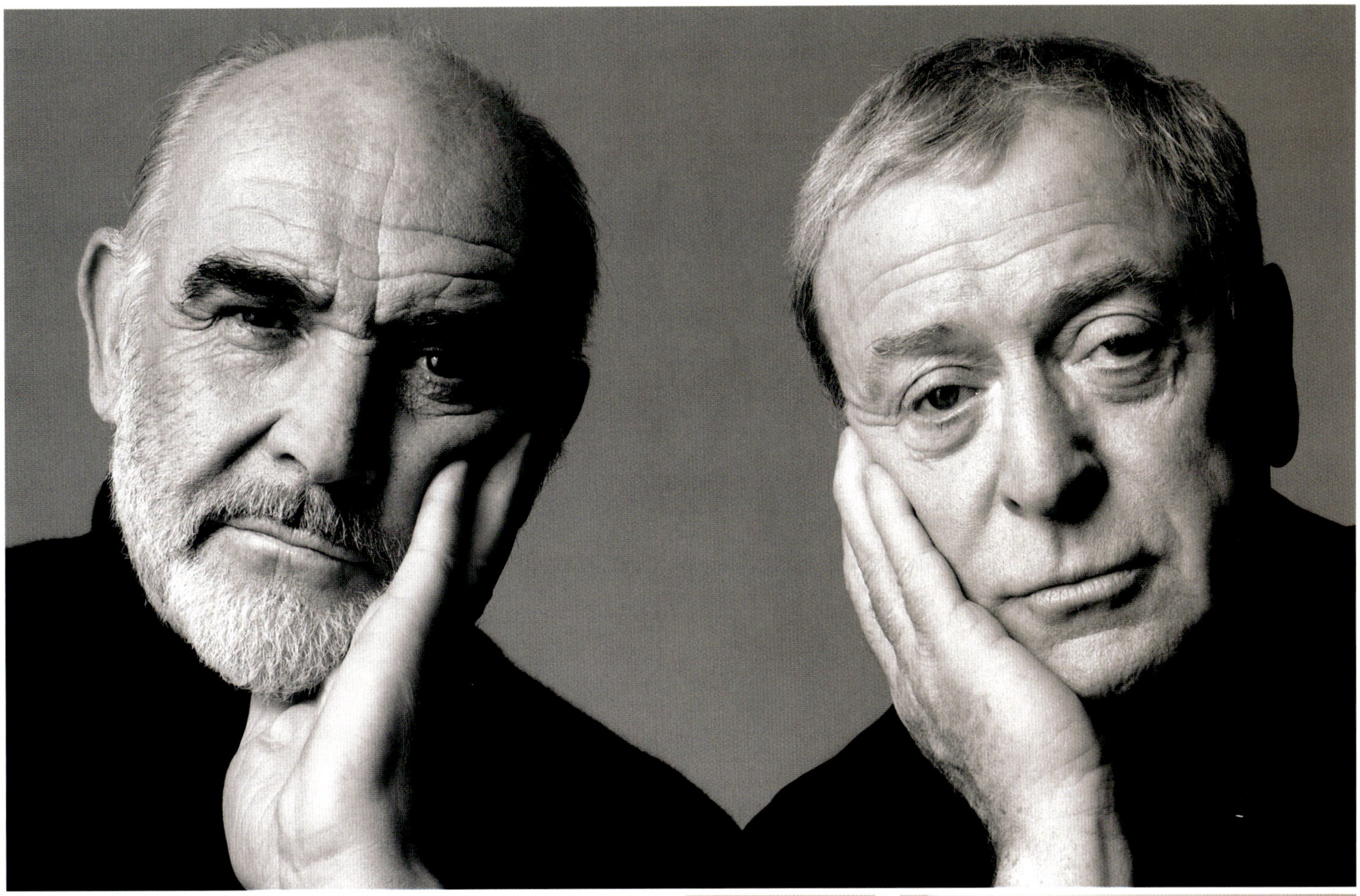

"Jacques Cousteau was my idol in my teen years. The first camera I purchased was an underwater camera. Through friends in the archaeological world, I was able to join Mexican treasure-hunting trips and dives. In 1965, I arrived at Tulum on the Yucatán coast with a companion, and we hiked the entire coast, which at that time was pure wilderness with coconut trees and a few plantation caretakers. Upon my return, some family friends who were photographers offered me a job. I went into business, getting commissions for still-life photos. It was much easier for clients to give me still-life shoots, rather than fashion shoots, with all the costs of stylists, hair, and makeup." O'Neill did eventually focus on fashion and later, travel photography.

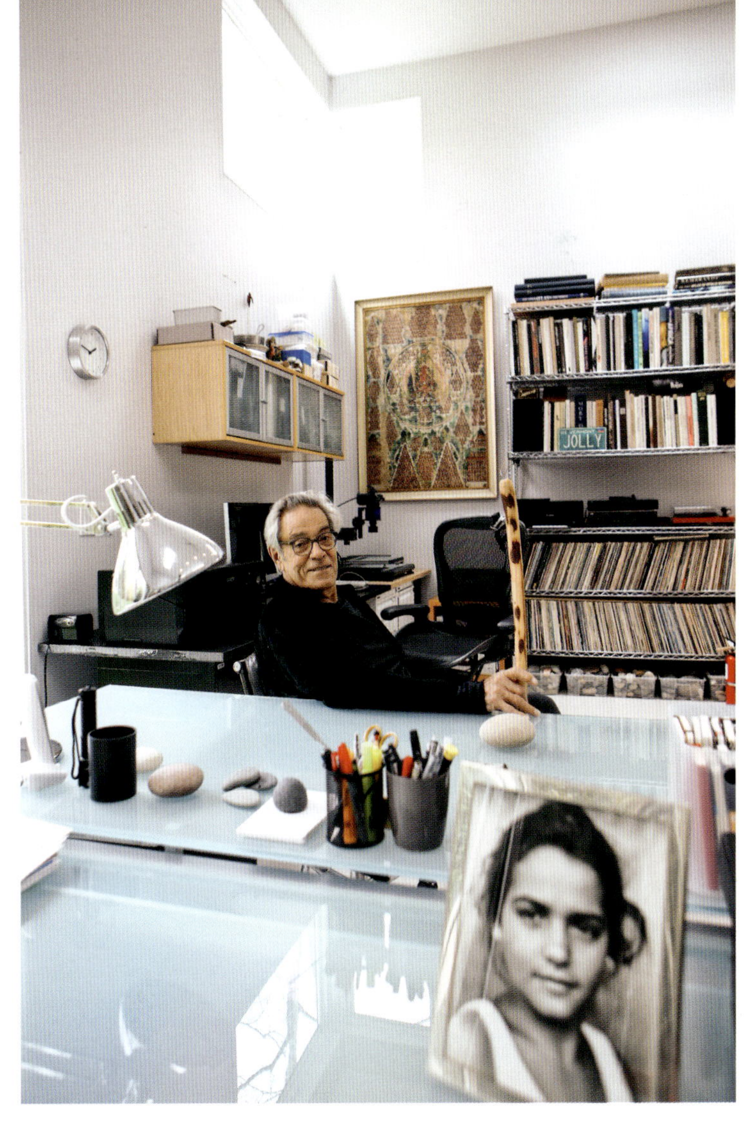

RIGHT The photographer in his studio, his refuge. Furnished with a couch for reading and daydreaming, it also houses his large archive of film in a waterproof space below.

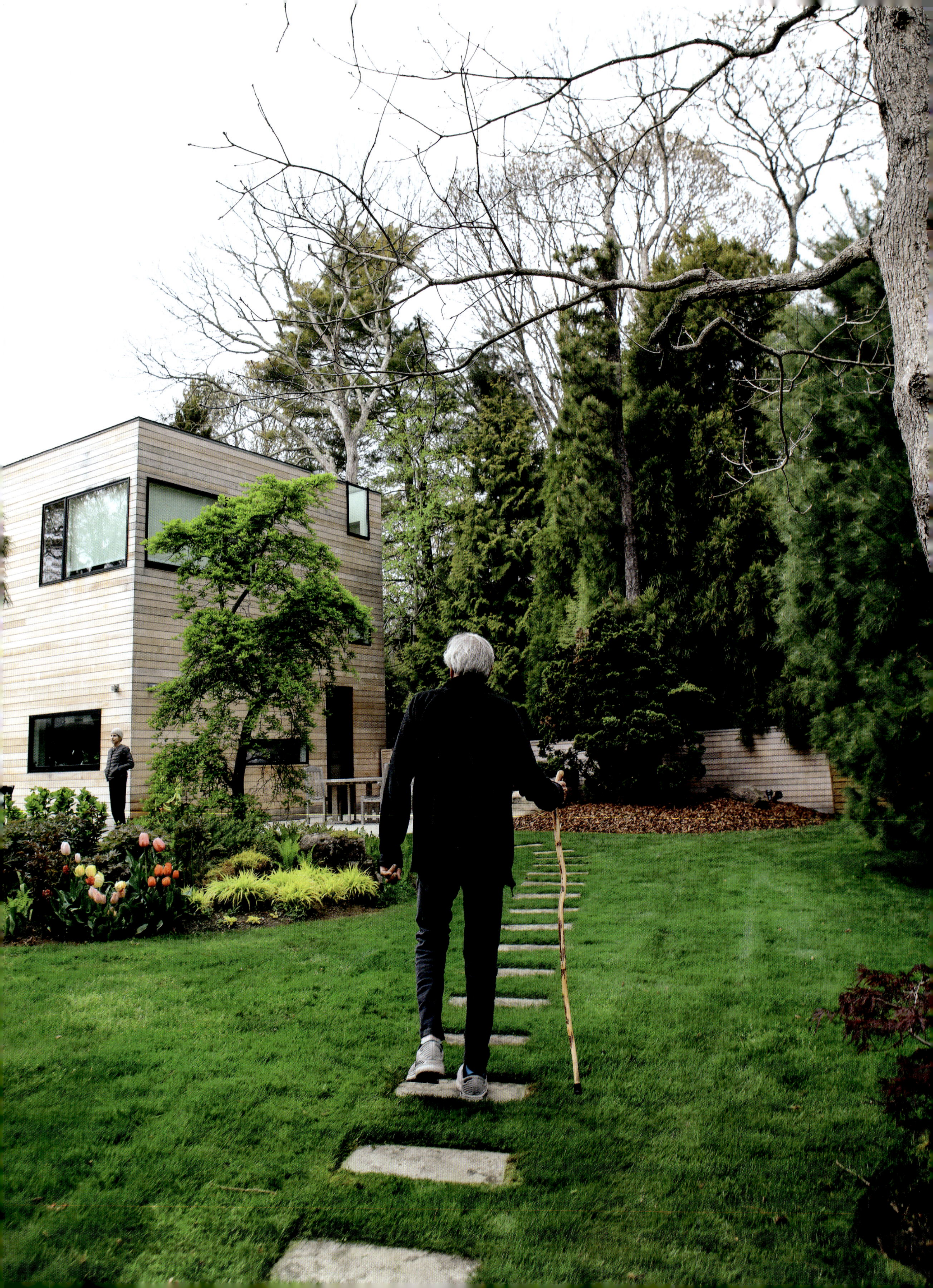

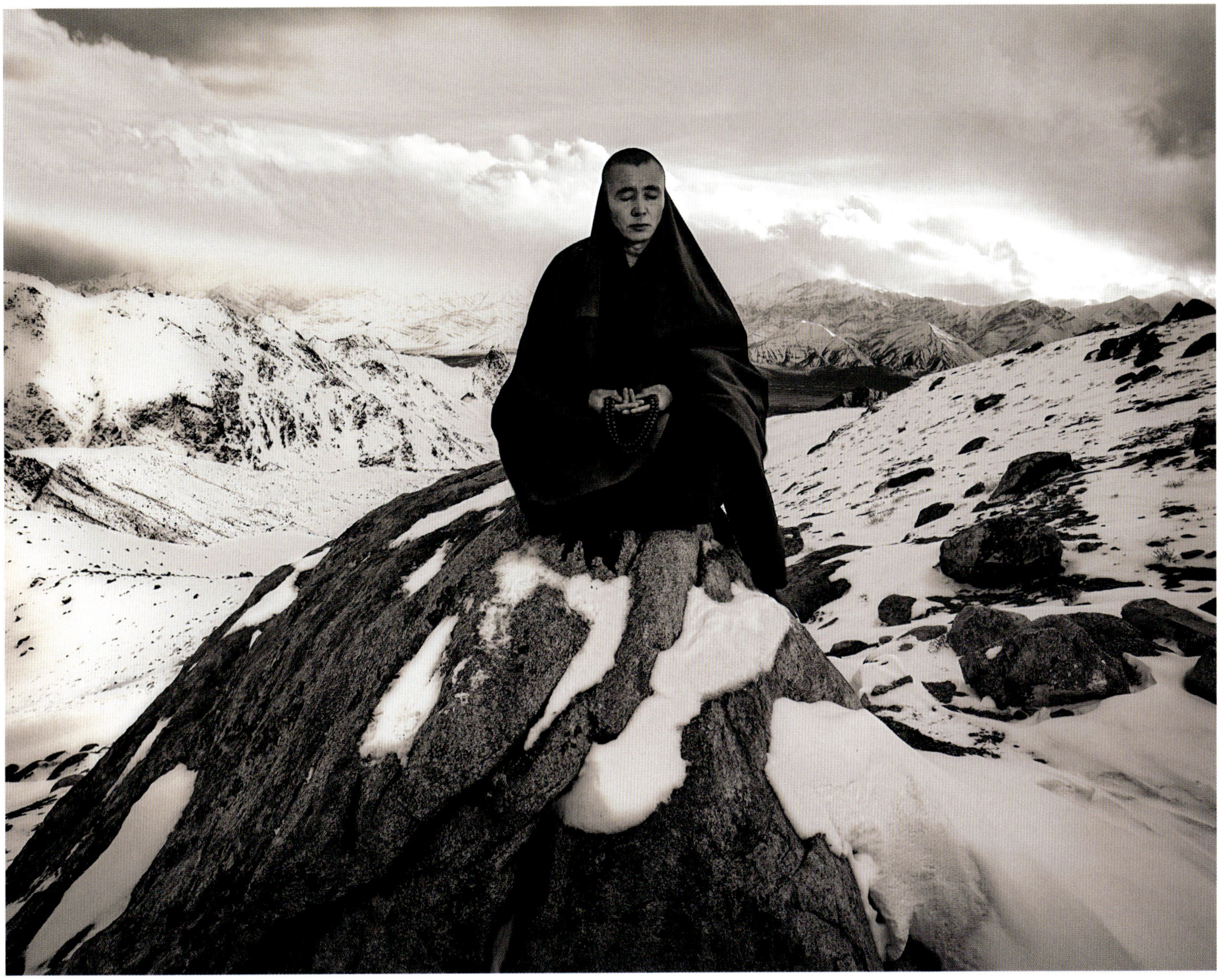

O'Neill and his wife started coming to the Hamptons in the late 1980s, and in 2011 they built a modern house in Wainscott with a separate studio building. "It became obvious that it was time to move out here permanently. The studio was built primarily to house my film archive in a waterproof location; it also serves as our daily workspace and a place for me to daydream." As O'Neill's commercial career in fashion photography was winding down after fifty years, he turned to yoga, both as a passion and as subject matter. "Over a ten-year period, I returned often to India, Nepal, and Tibet in China to build a body of work focused on recording and honoring yoga masters." He also turned to nature. "I began going for long walks on bay beaches here and collected a lot of stones. One day a stone happened to be in front of my lens, its spirit asking to be enlarged into an abstract photo."

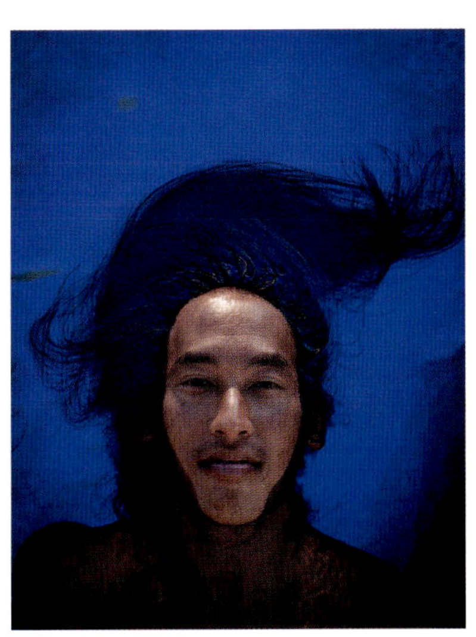

OPPOSITE O'Neill takes the short walk from his studio to his house in Wainscott, which he and his wife built in 2011 and now live in permanently.

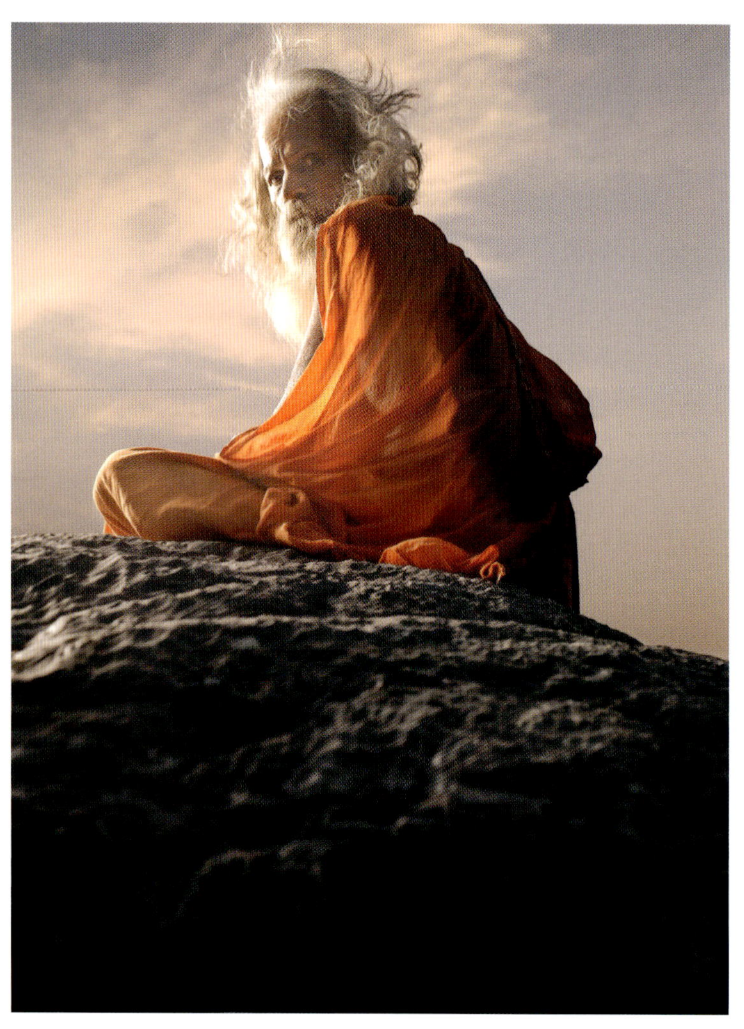

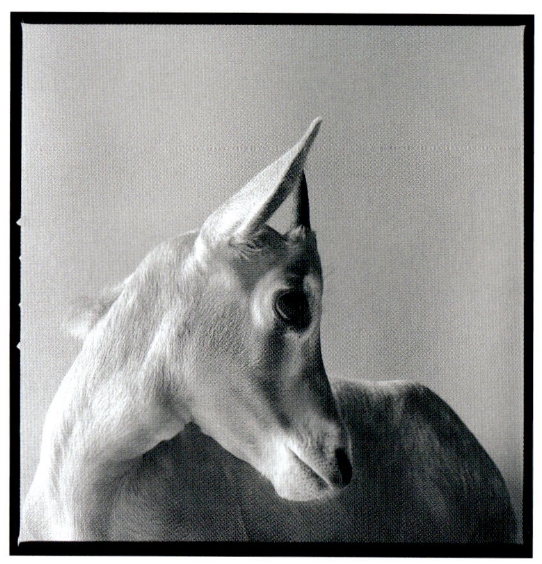

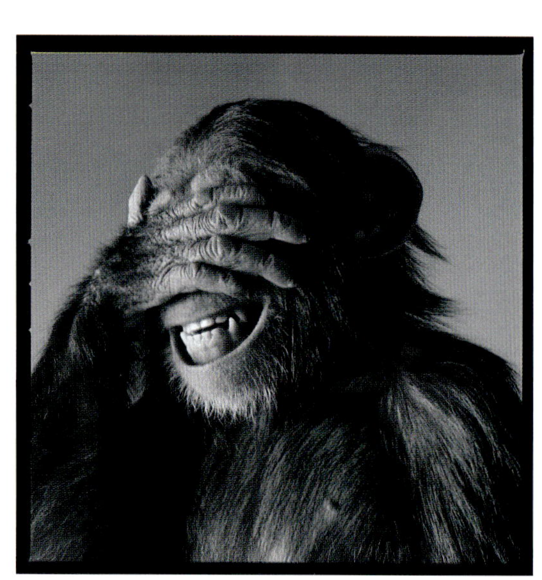

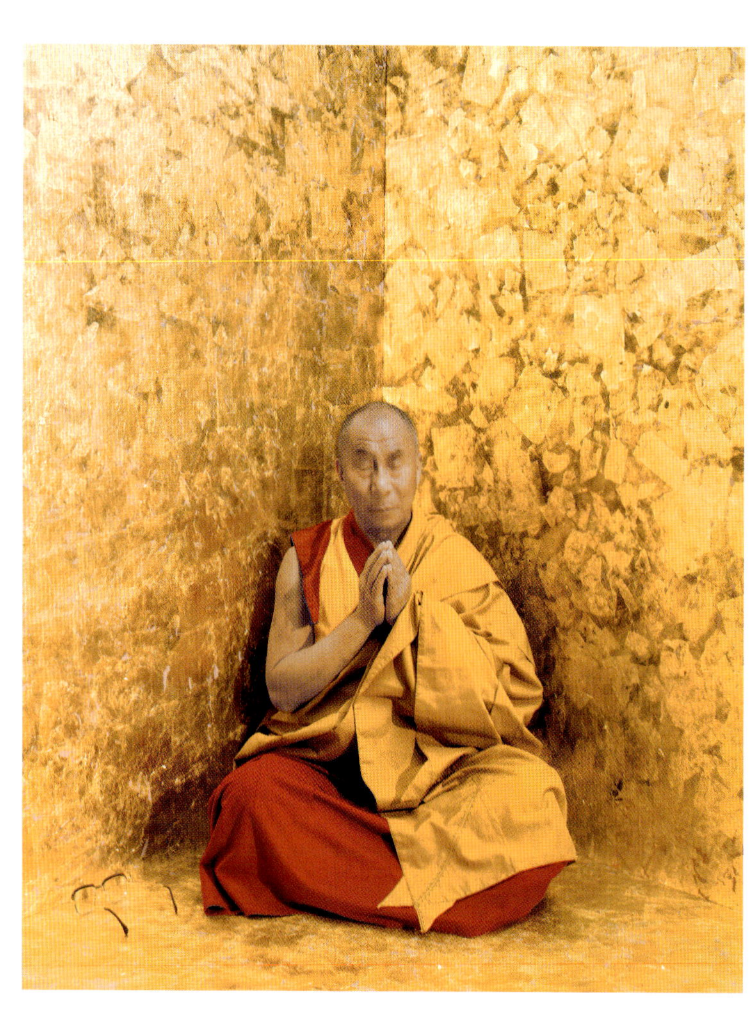

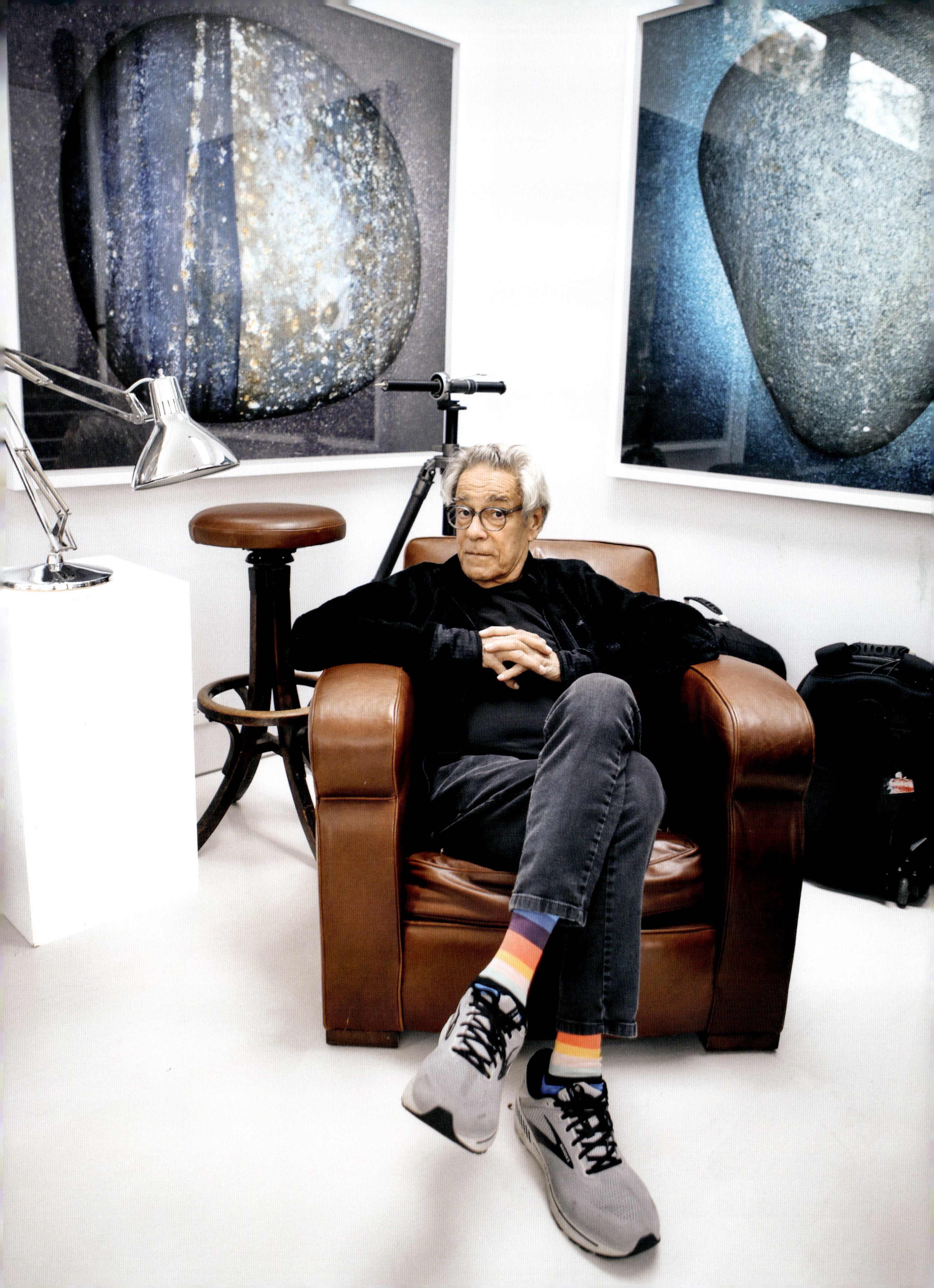

My ideas come from motorcycles, cars, construction sites—anything mechanical, anything that goes fast.

JOEL PERLMAN

Perlman's passion for industrial metal is expressed in sculptures that range from indoor to outdoor—the largest of them monumental. Though some of the shapes are linear or twisting, circular forms dominate. "About twenty-five years ago, I introduced circles into my hard-edged work and they gradually took over." Why abstract? "The material and the process lead to abstraction. I have no choice. This is who I am and what I do."

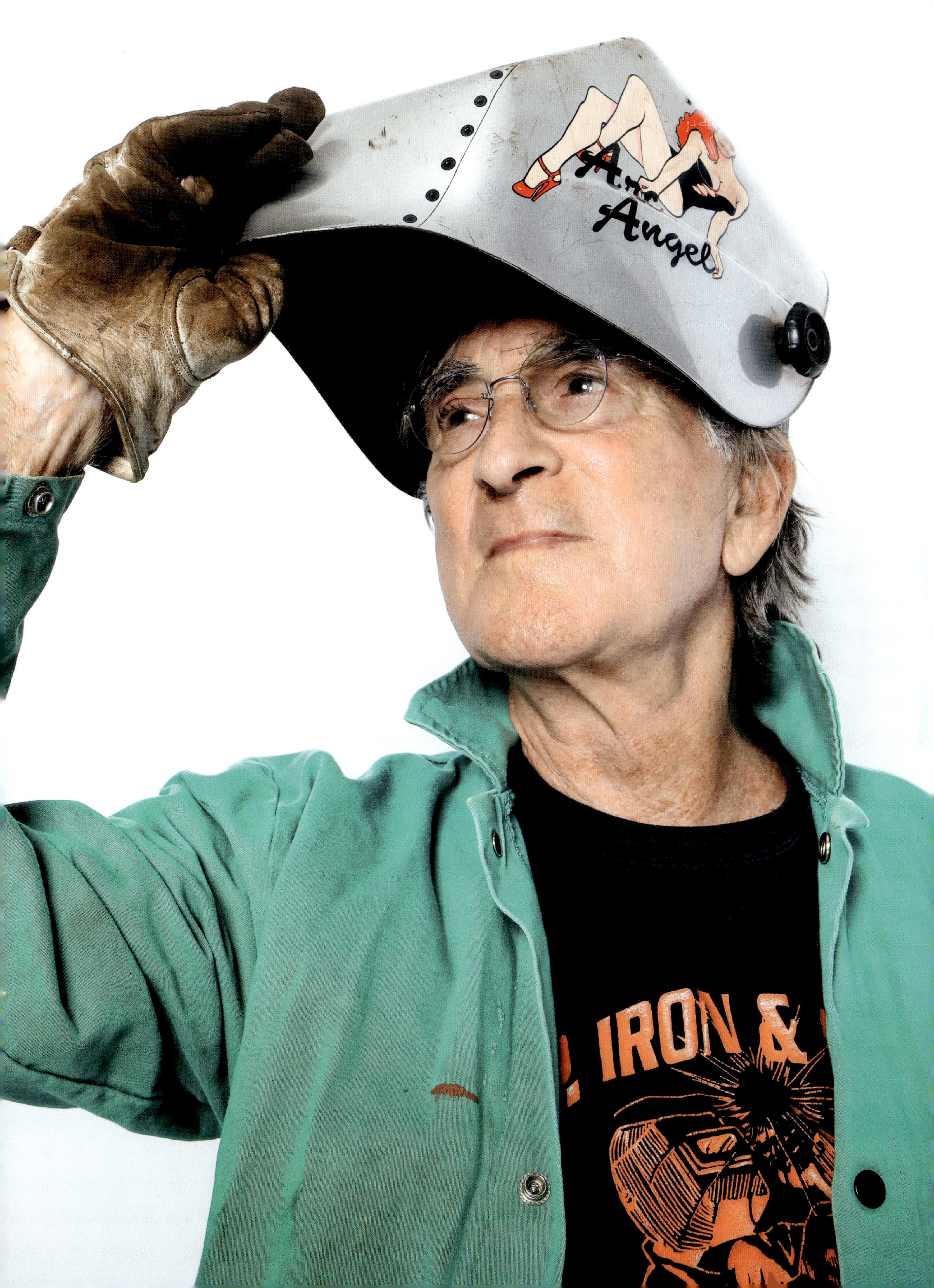
Angel
IRON &

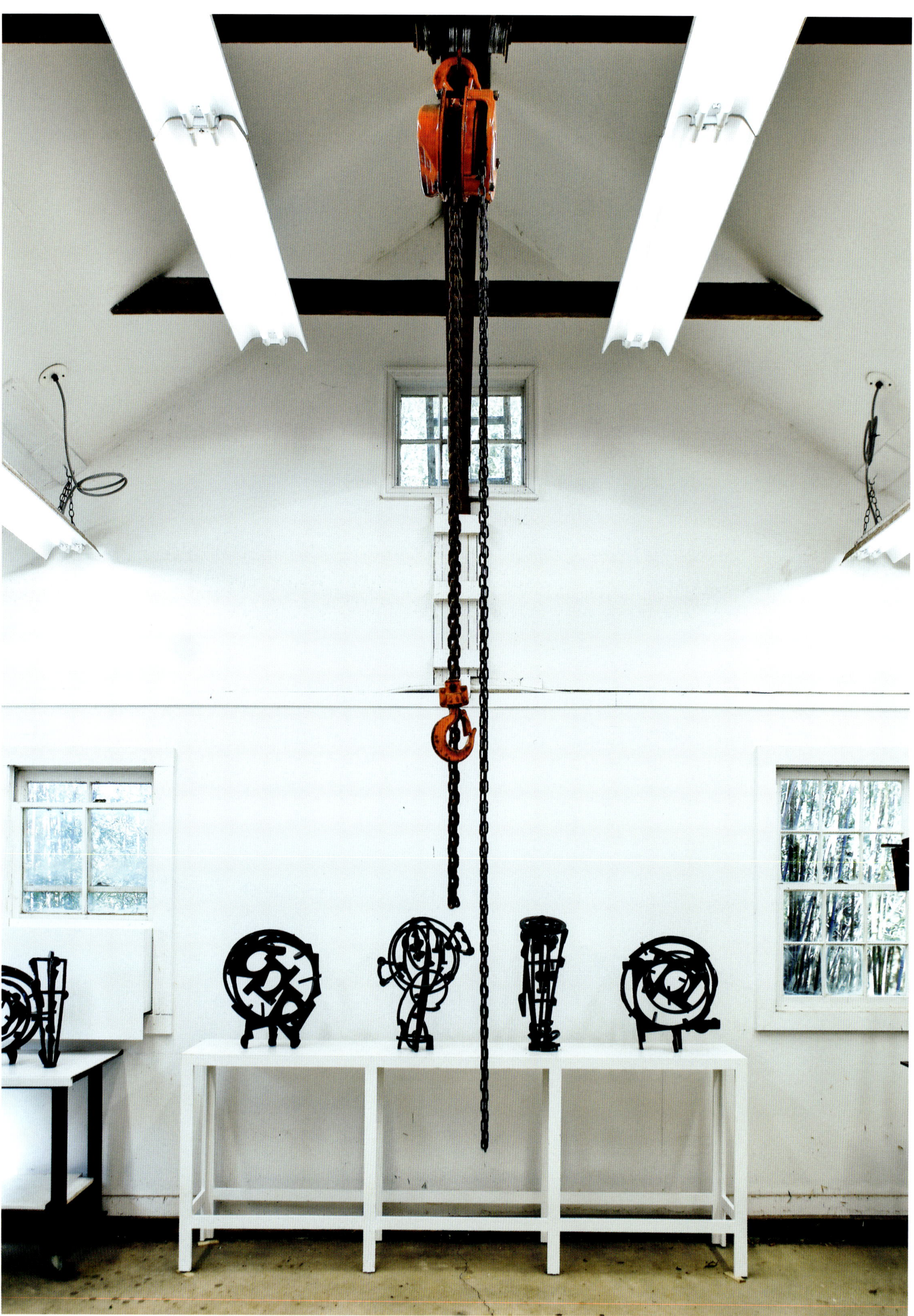

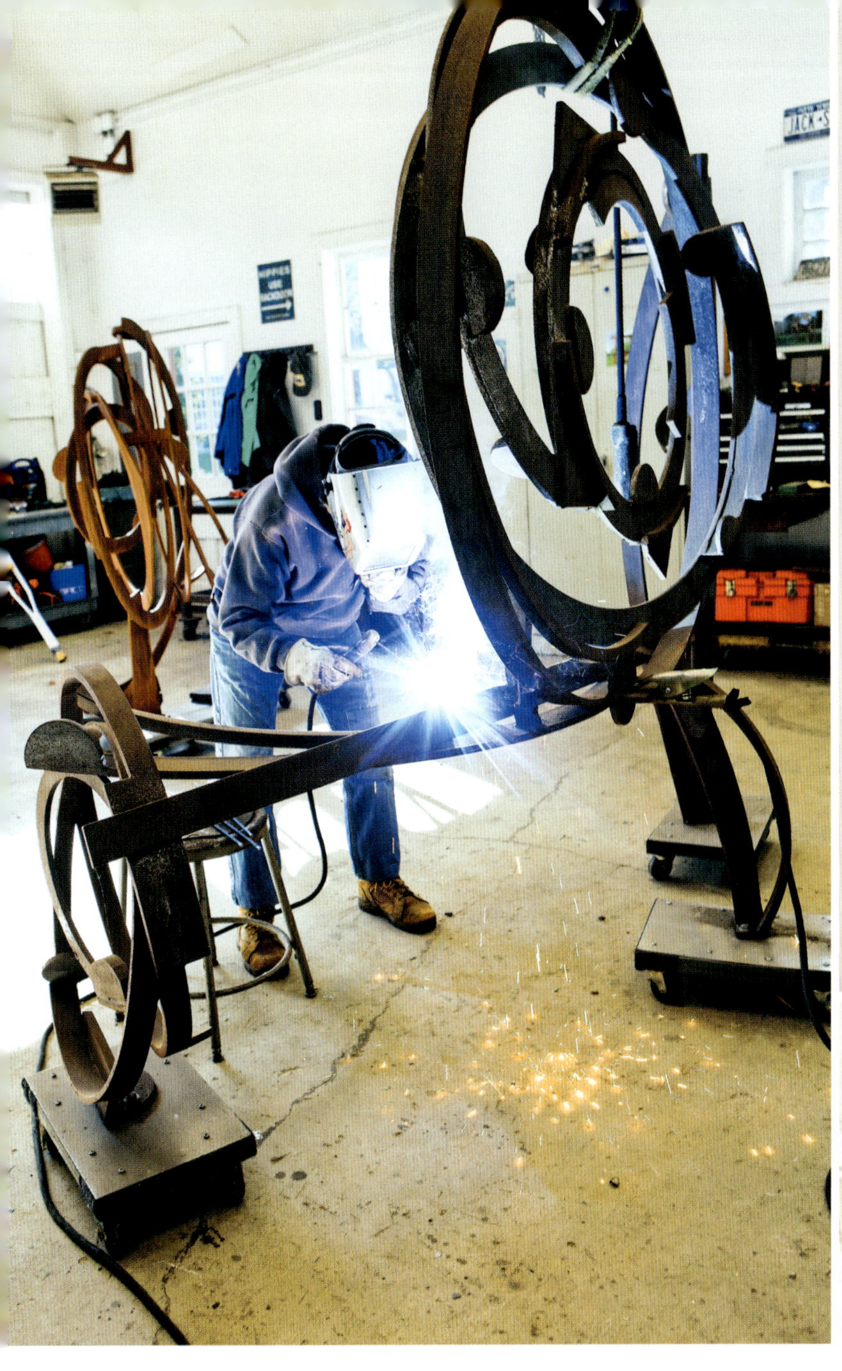

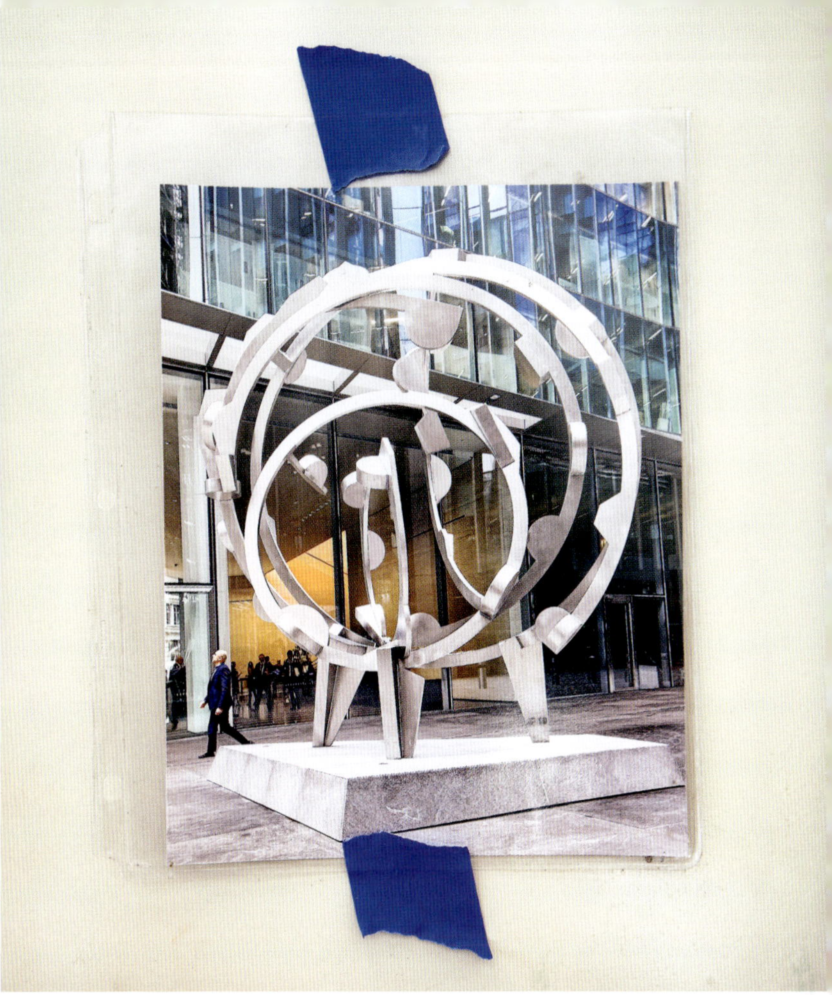

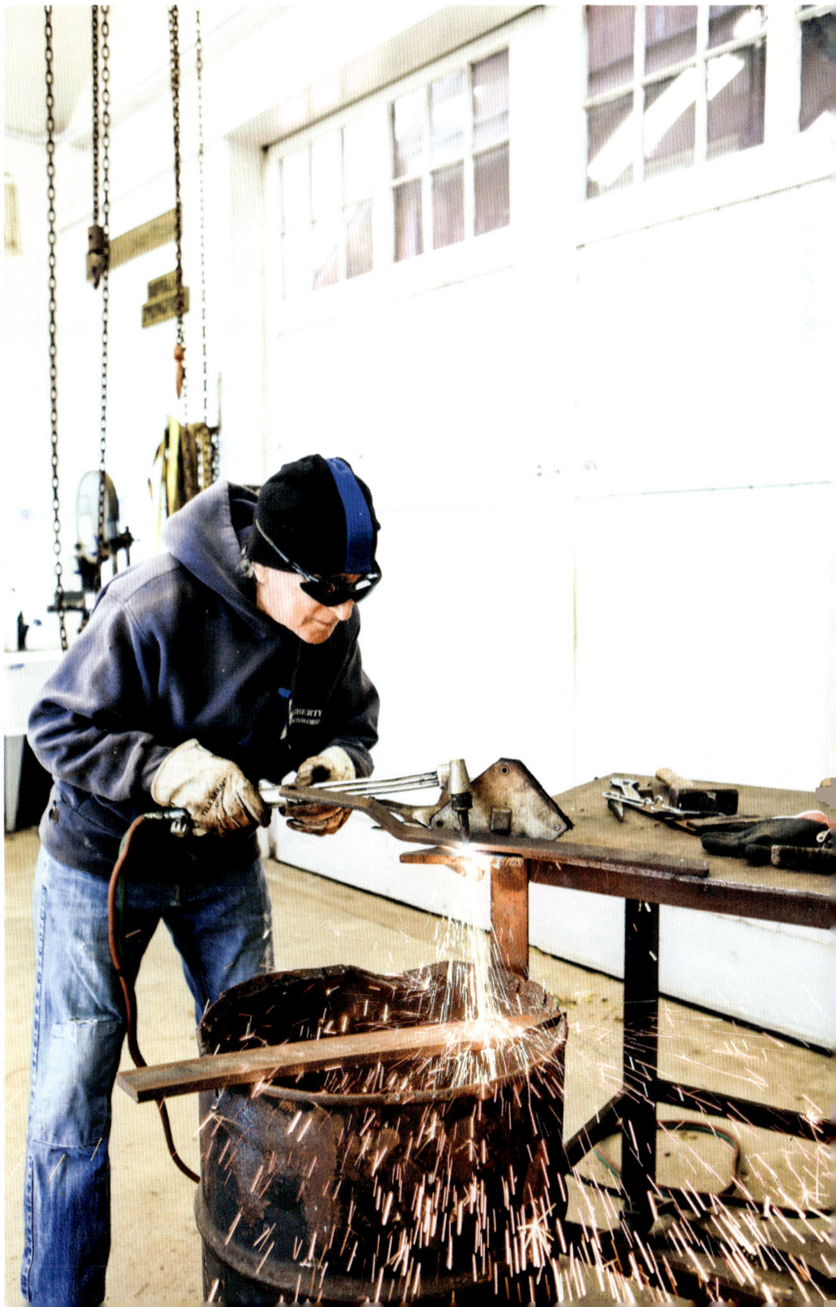

A native New Yorker, Perlman discovered the East End fifty years ago, when he was an art mover and had to deliver a painting to Baby Jane Holzer. "It was a sunny April day, and I'd never experienced such exquisite light." He came to live in Southampton in the 1970s, then bought his current Water Mill property in 2005. "I built my studio, which is where it all happens. With the barn doors open, I can drive my truck in and load it with the electric gantry cranes. That is how little guys make big sculptures!"

OPPOSITE A crane hangs from the ceiling in Perlman's Water Mill studio, ready to lift his large steel sculptures and load them onto a truck.

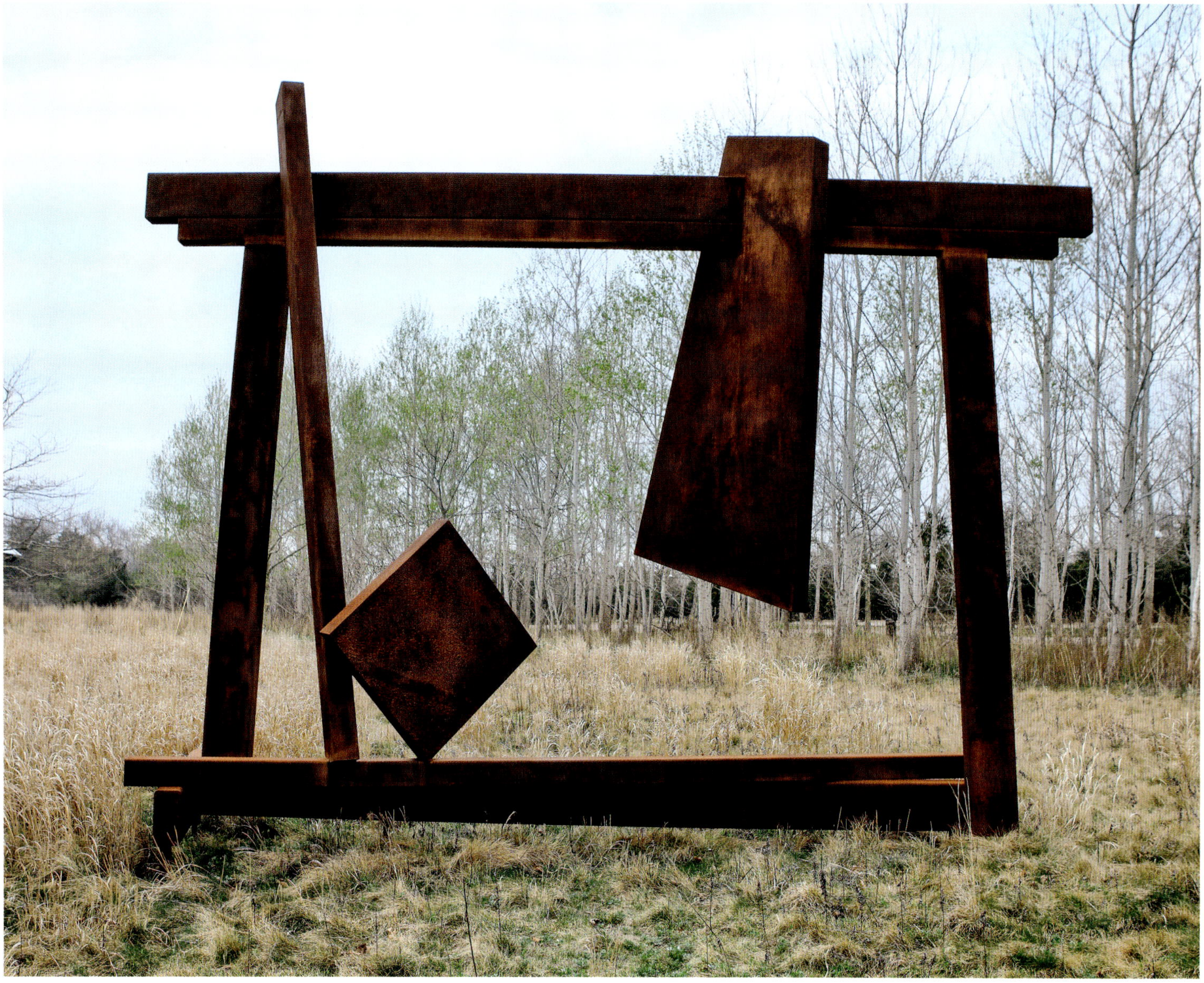

"My tools are very basic—a welder, a cutting torch, and a grinder. I am a builder, a constructor, so welding metal is the perfect voice for me." Perlman is in his studio almost every day. "Sometimes I play Springsteen or eighties' rock, but often it's too noisy to hear much. I wear a fire-retardant jacket and my oldest clothes when I am welding because everything I put on while working gets ruined."

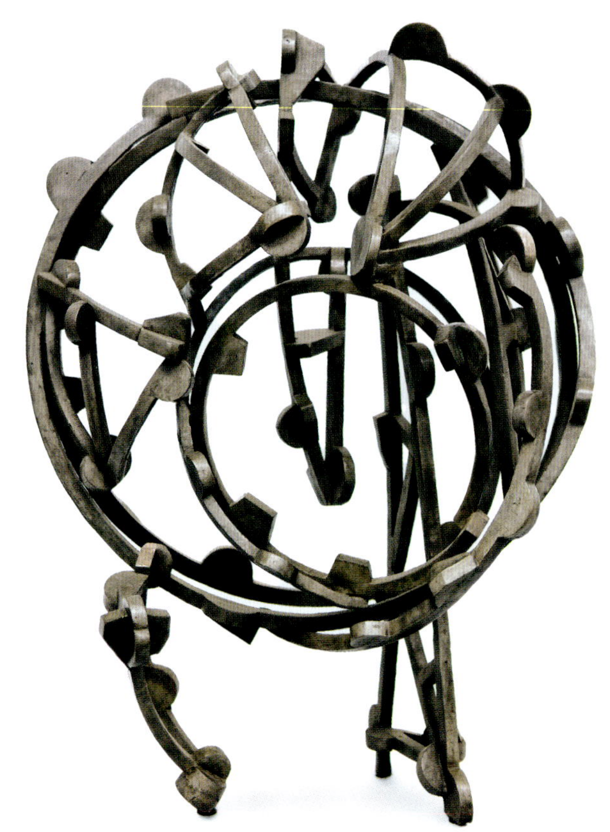

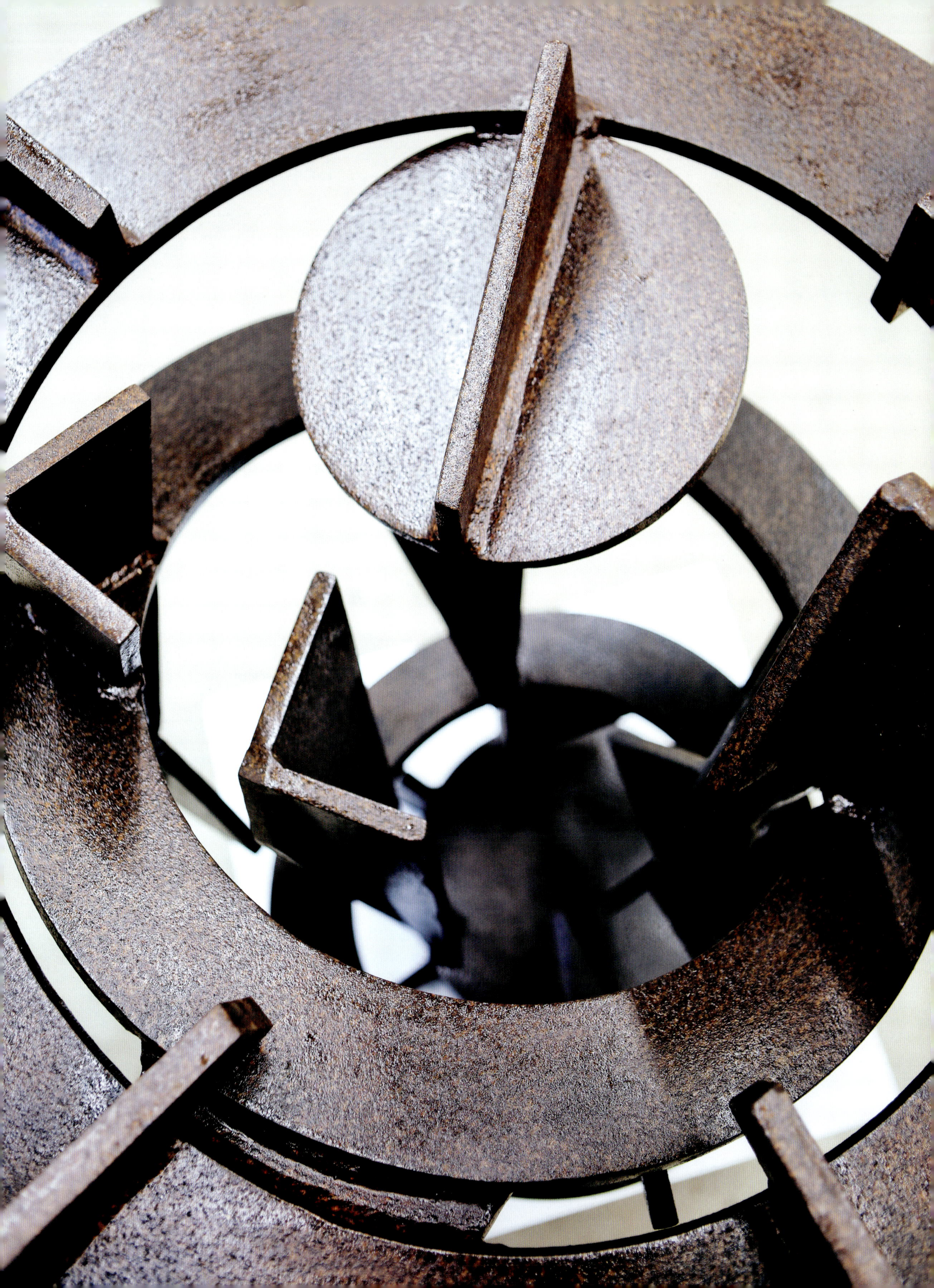

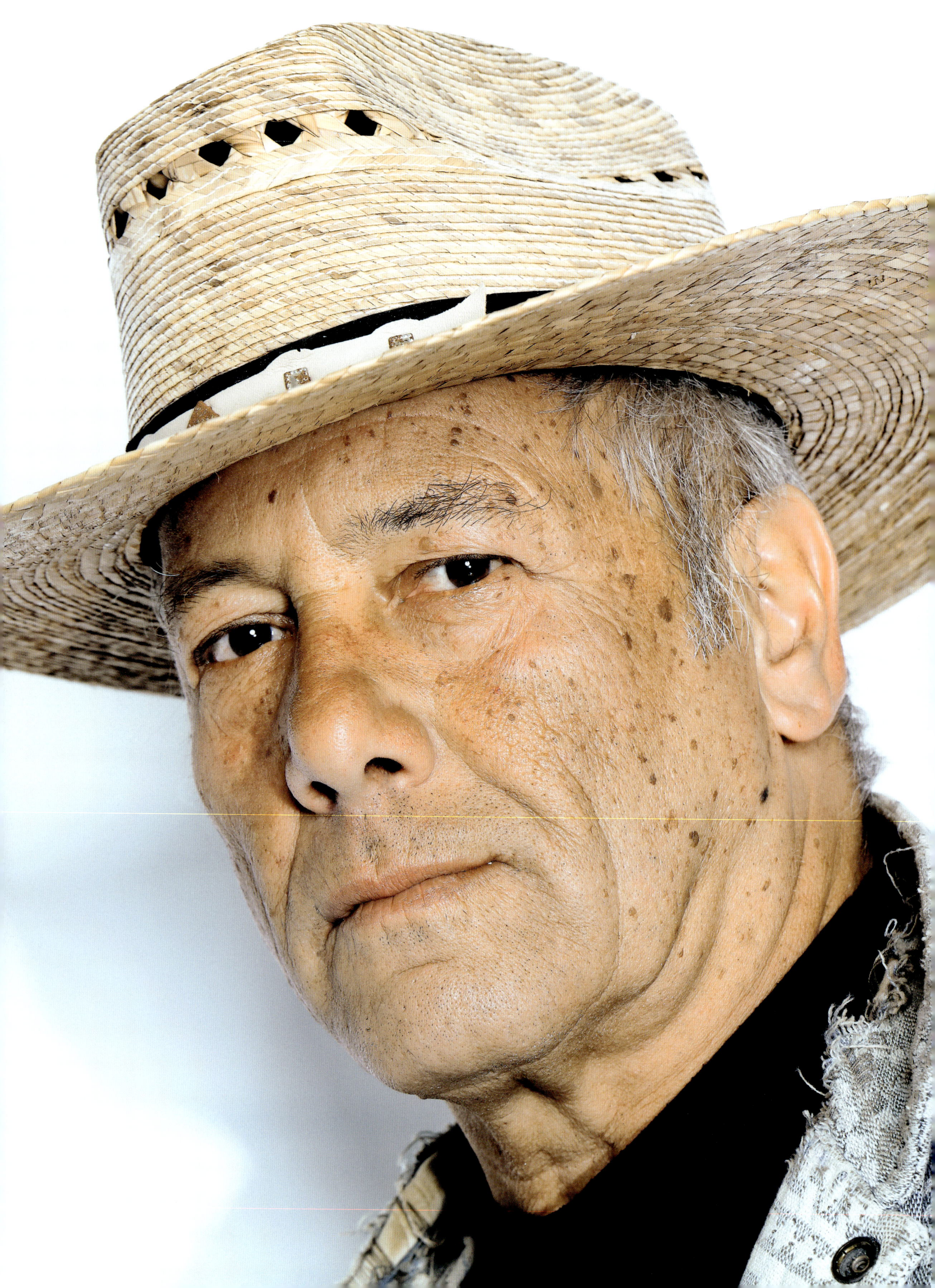

I can't adhere to a schedule. Sometimes the ocean dictates my schedule. If the surf is good, I work the night shift. If I can't sleep at night, I play guitar or tweak a painting. I sit at the drums, throw a round of darts at the dartboard, or stare at a blank canvas until it screams at me to just start.

DALTON PORTELLA

A painter first and foremost, Portella uses photography "to capture the beauty of where I live. It's what I do while I'm thinking of what to paint next. I'll go photograph scenes that bring me tranquility and joy. It gets me out of my head and out of the house." Photography also serves to capture references for his figurative work. "When people ask me what kind of artist I am, I show them pictures on my phone or website. I'm multidisciplinary. I never want to get pigeonholed into one genre. I'll leave it up to someone else to describe me."

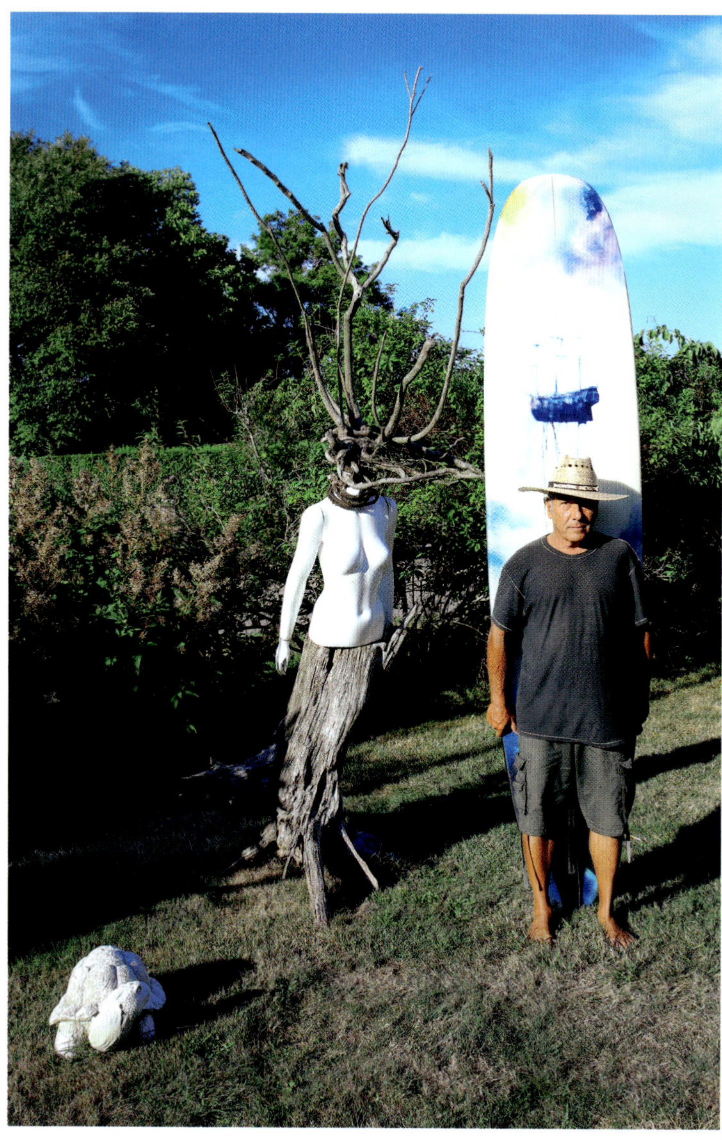

LEFT

Portella surfs, paints, takes photos, and plays music. A transplanted Brazilian, he feels right at home in Montauk, where he's lived for more than two decades.

It was surfing that lured Portella, a native of Brazil, to the East End. When he was seventeen, in high school in Rio de Janeiro, he saw a picture of a wave at Turtle Cove in Montauk in a surfing magazine. "Before that, I didn't know there was good surf in New York. I'd had my heart set on art school in California." After a few years in California, he found himself in New York City working as a photo retoucher. He saved up, bought a car, and in 1980 drove out to Montauk. He was hooked. He bought a house and in 2001 moved to Montauk full-time.

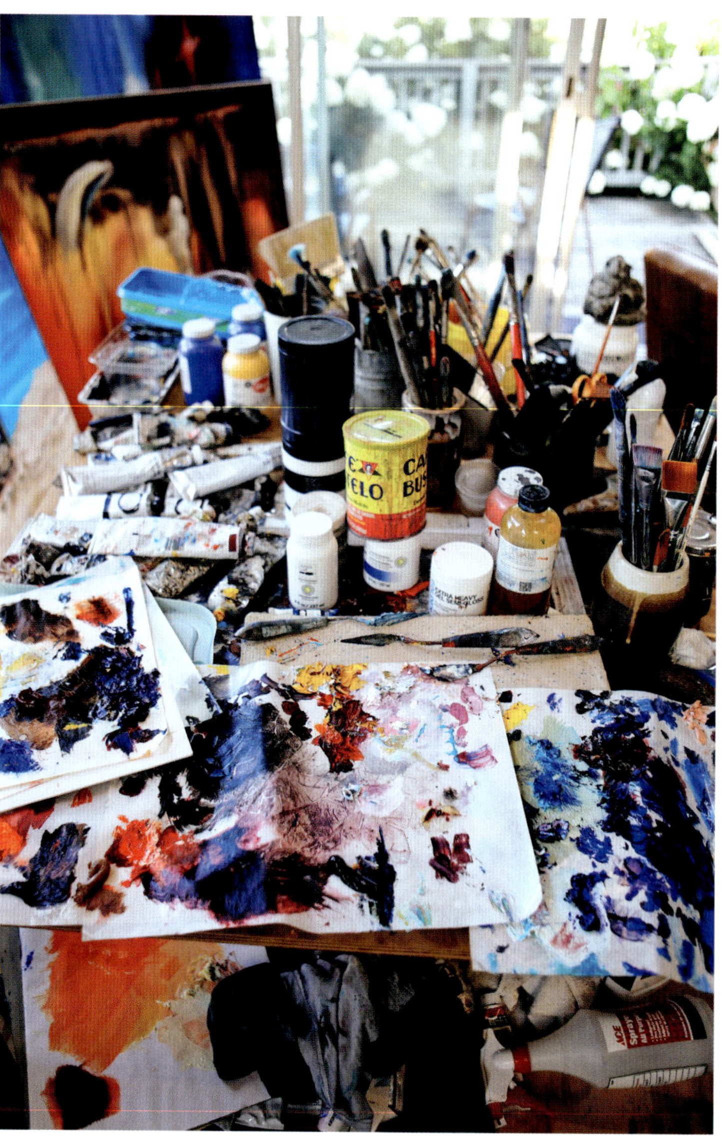

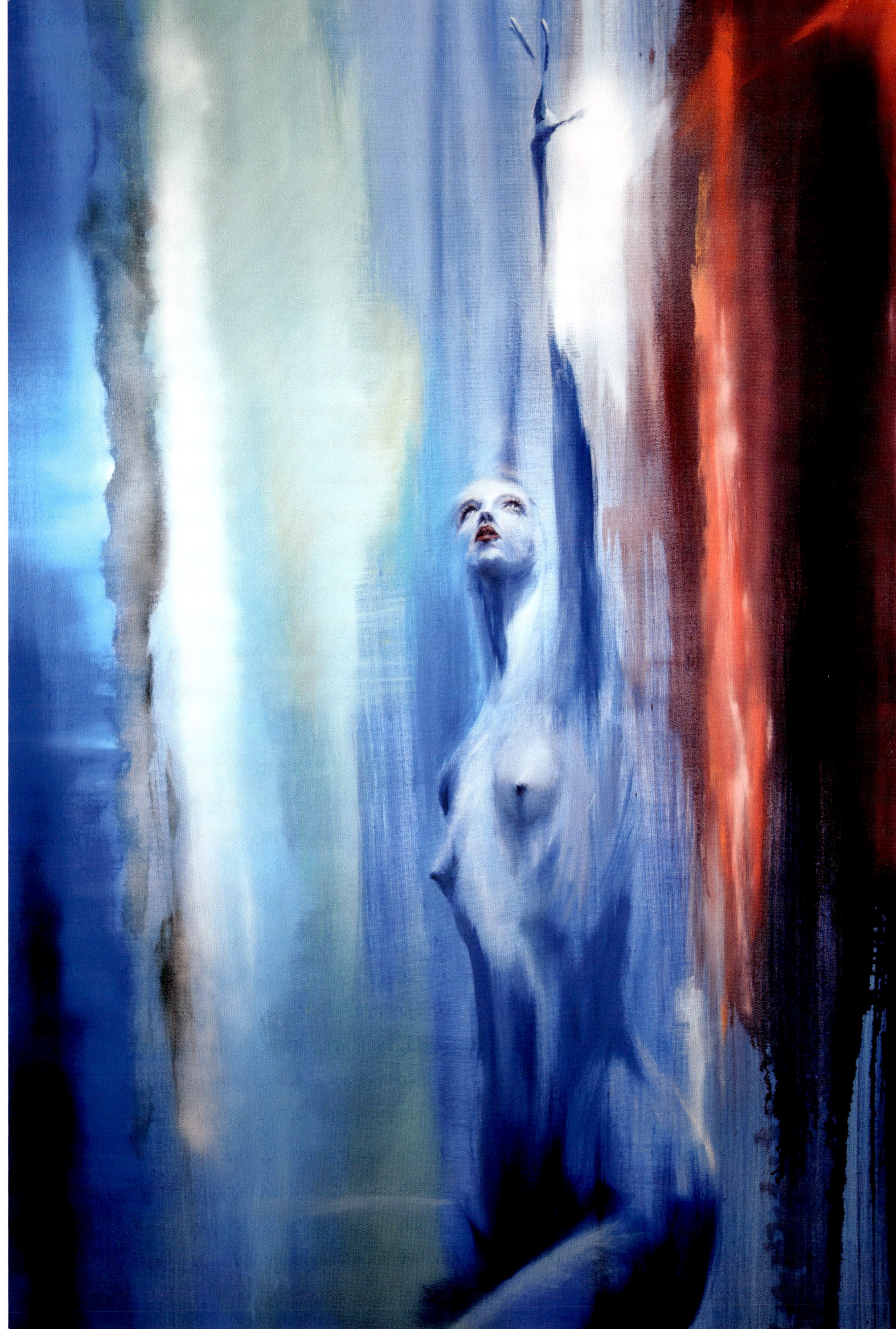

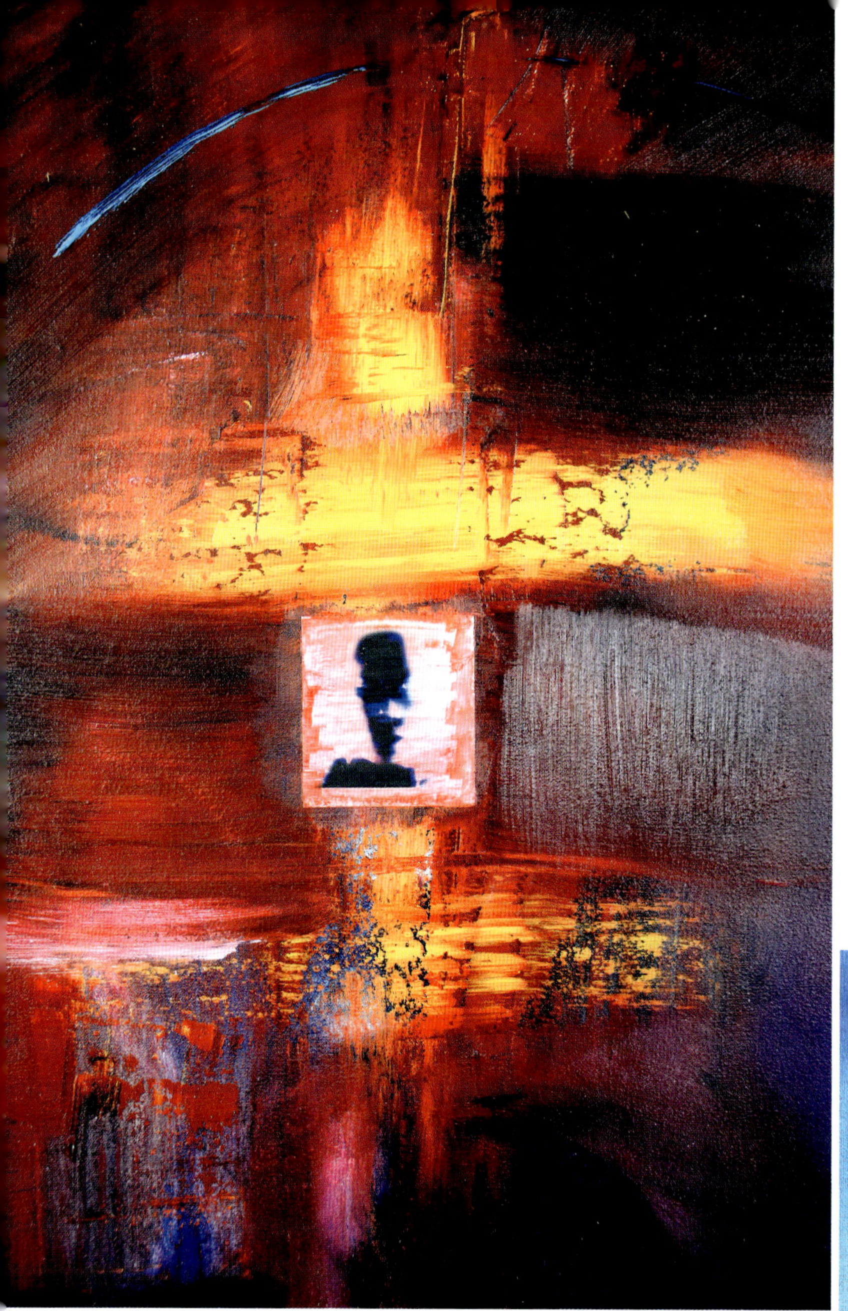

OPPOSITE
Portella's semi-figural, often dreamy or mystical paintings frequently involve water—a powerful draw for him and an unending source of inspiration.

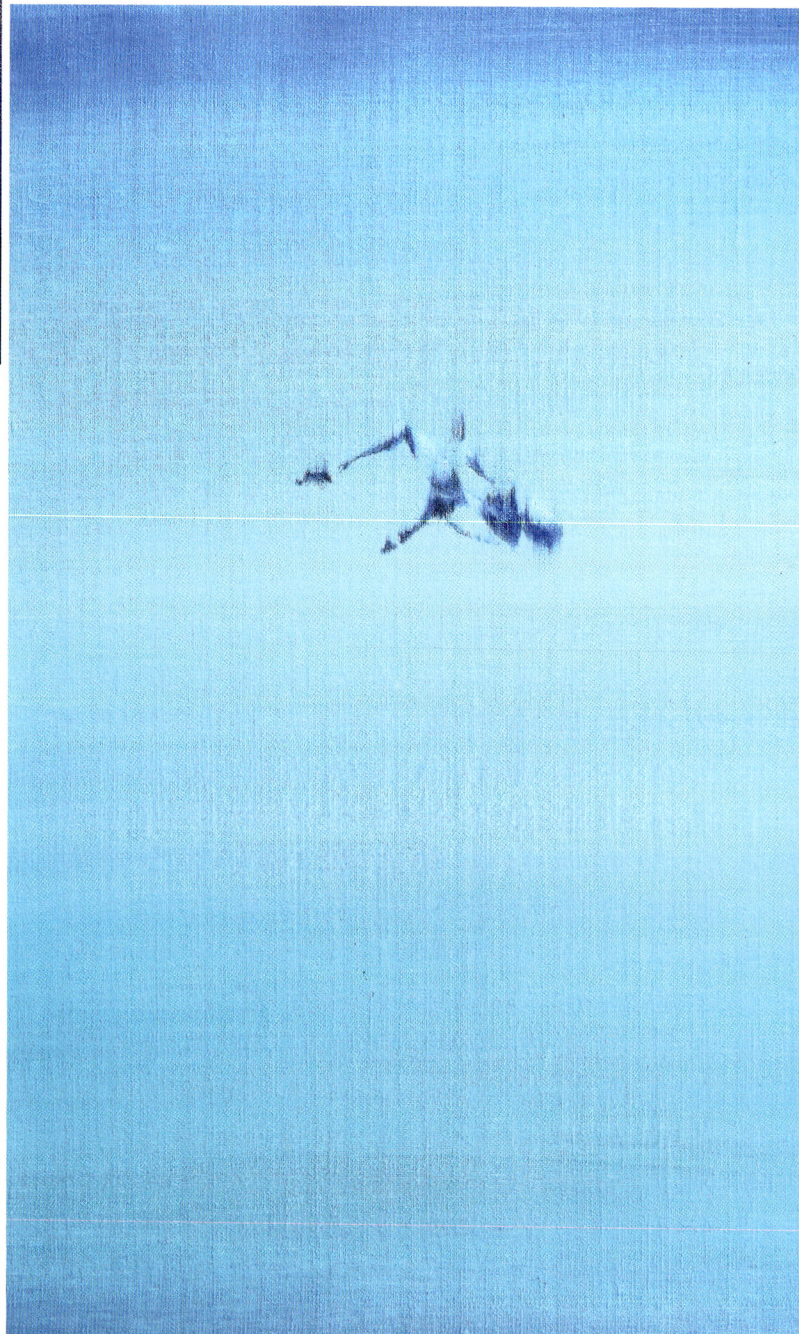

When he's not surfing the waves, Portella is painting or photographing the water—as well as what's in it, including sharks. "I was looking through some sketchbooks from the eighties and realized I had drawn my first shark back then, inspired by their beauty and form. I decided to start painting them again. I wanted to bring awareness to their beauty and the threats they face from overfishing. I wanted to first shoot them in their natural environment, so I went on a cage dive. I filmed the sharks and started my painting series. I found them to be a perfect vehicle for exploring composition and form."

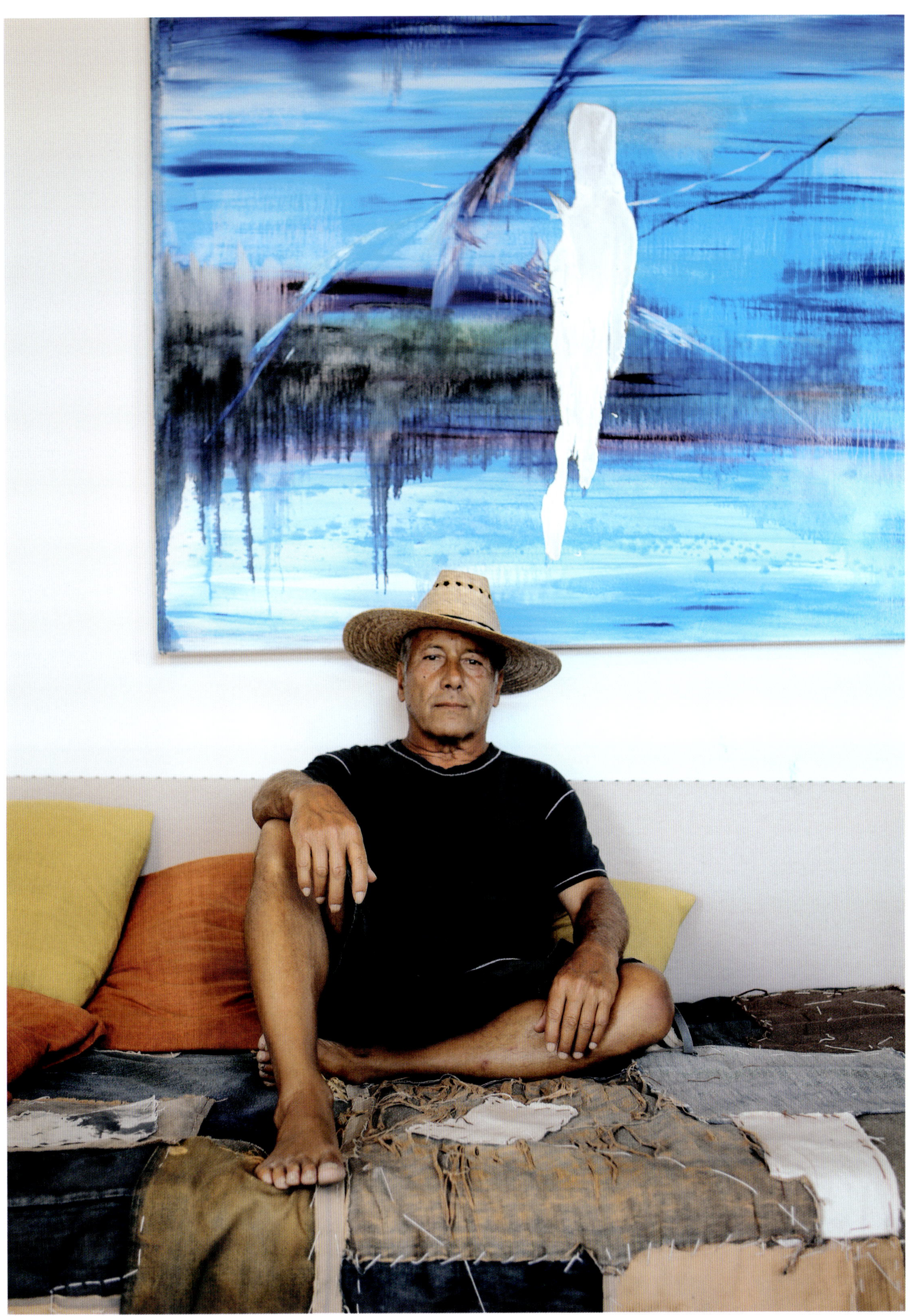

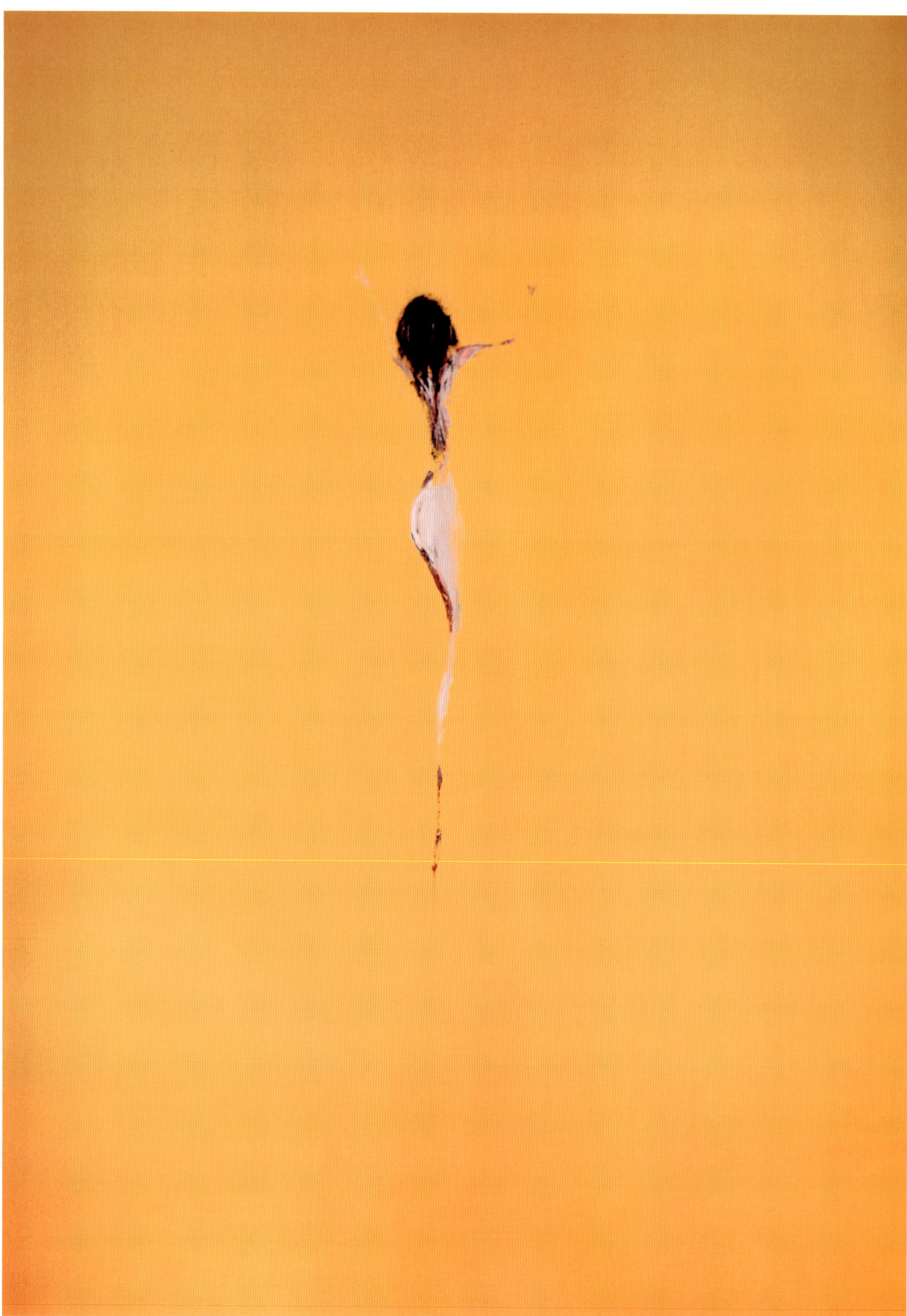

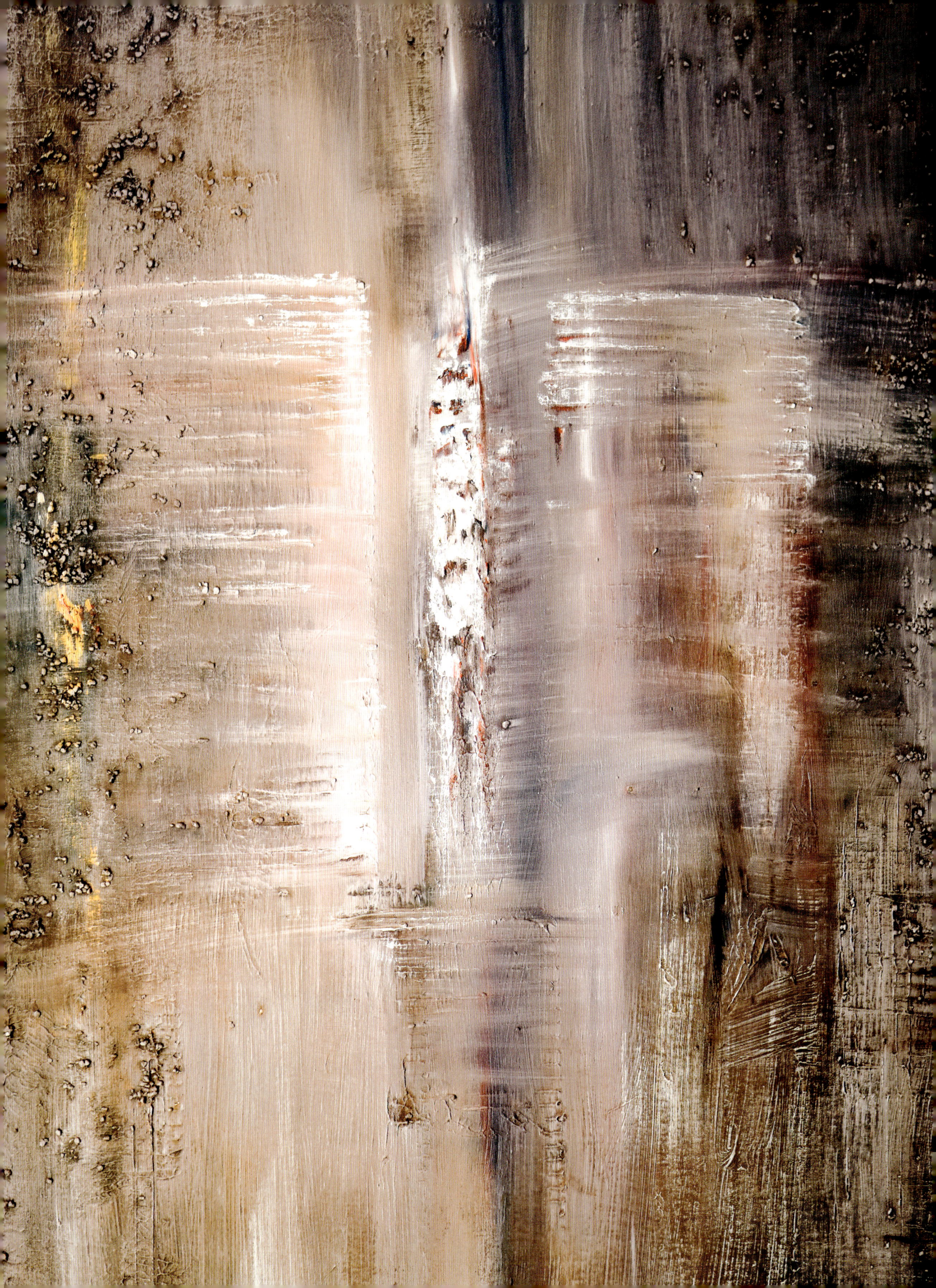

One thing I can't do is throw anything away—food, stuff—so I put it all in the paintings. At least I know I'm recycling while building the character and surface of a painting.

WILLIAM QUIGLEY

Quigley, born in a small town outside of Philadelphia, studied art at the University of Pennsylvania and Columbia University Graduate School of Fine Arts. "I was painting very abstract then and had my first shows in 1985, while still in grad school, with Warhol. By 1989, I was showing with de Kooning in Los Angeles. It was de Kooning who encouraged me to come back to New York. In 2013, I moved from SoHo to East Hampton full-time. "Where else does one have such a concentration of artists, architects, educated art enthusiasts, dealers, and collectors—and enough walls to collect and exhibit the works they covet? And I loved the freedom and quiet out here. I felt I had years of intellectual residue in my brain and could exhale all those thoughts in paint."

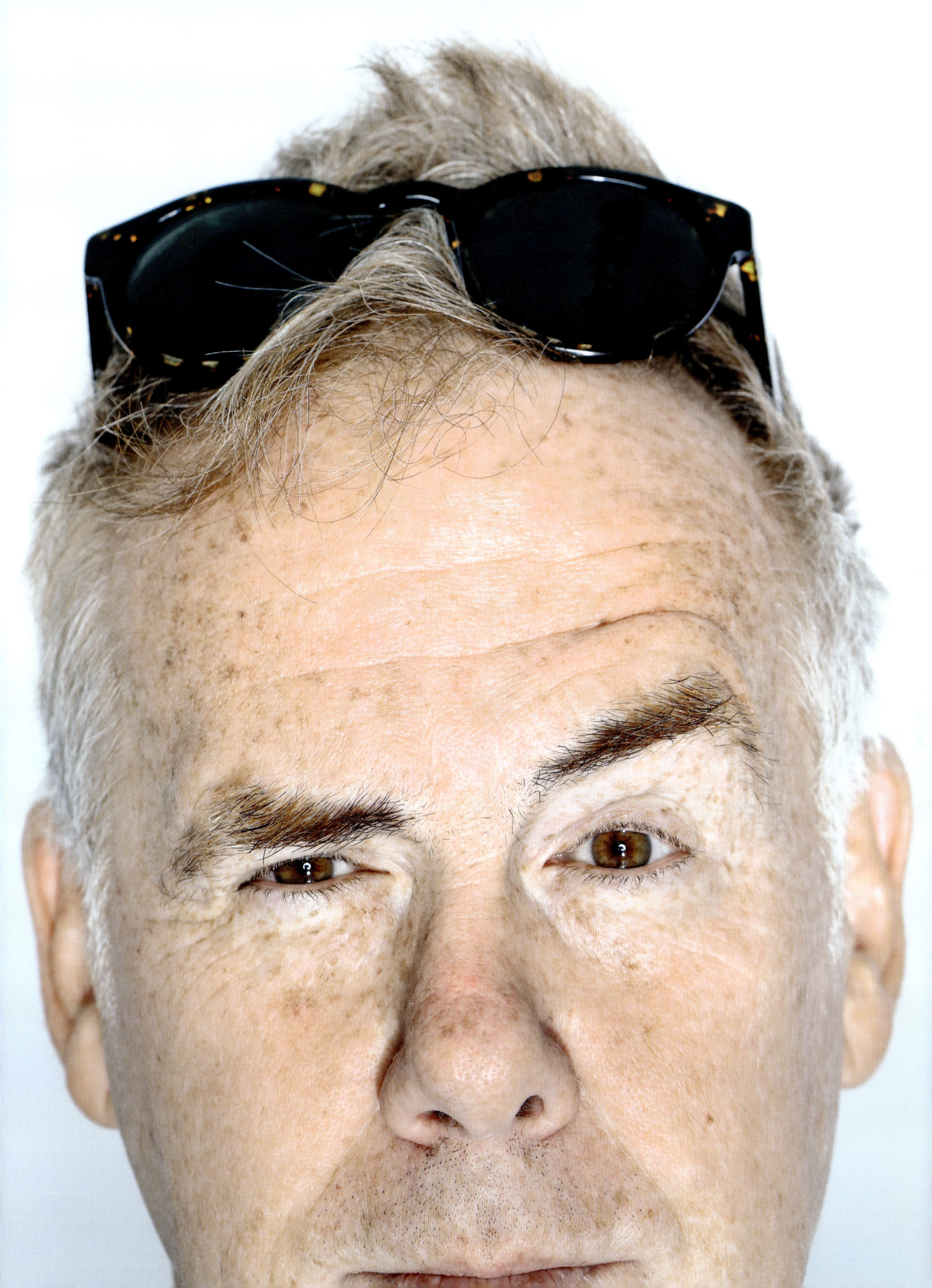

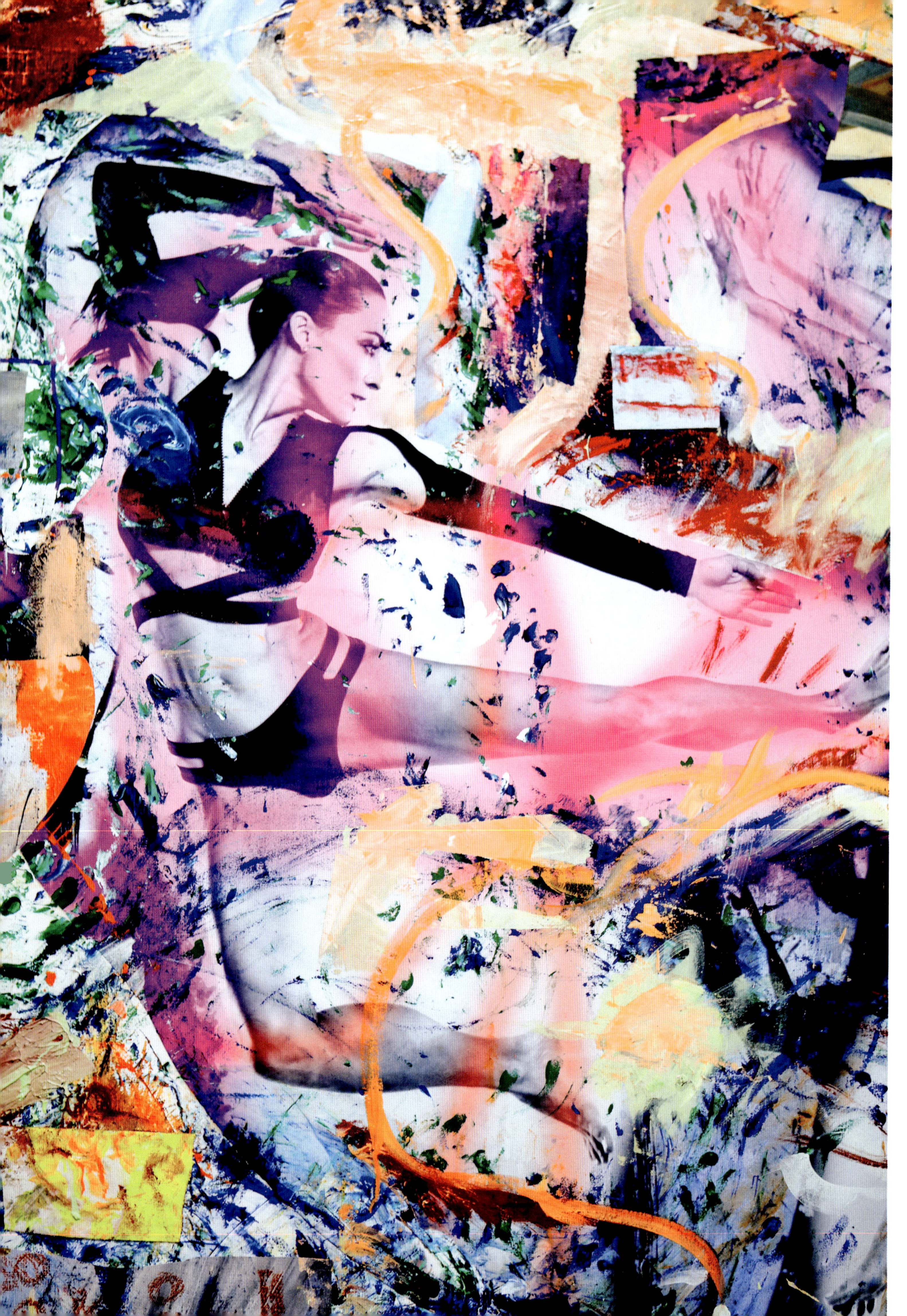

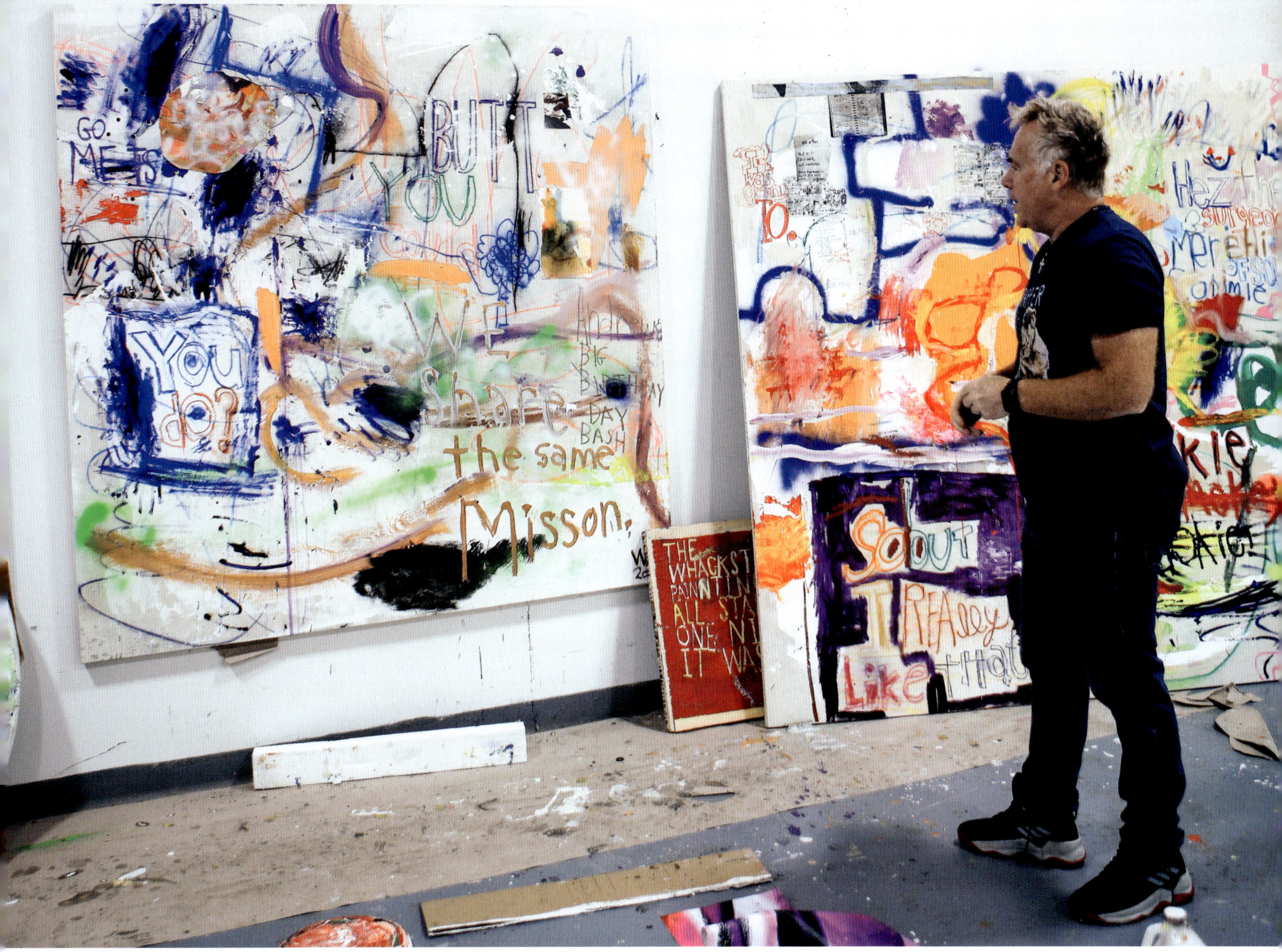

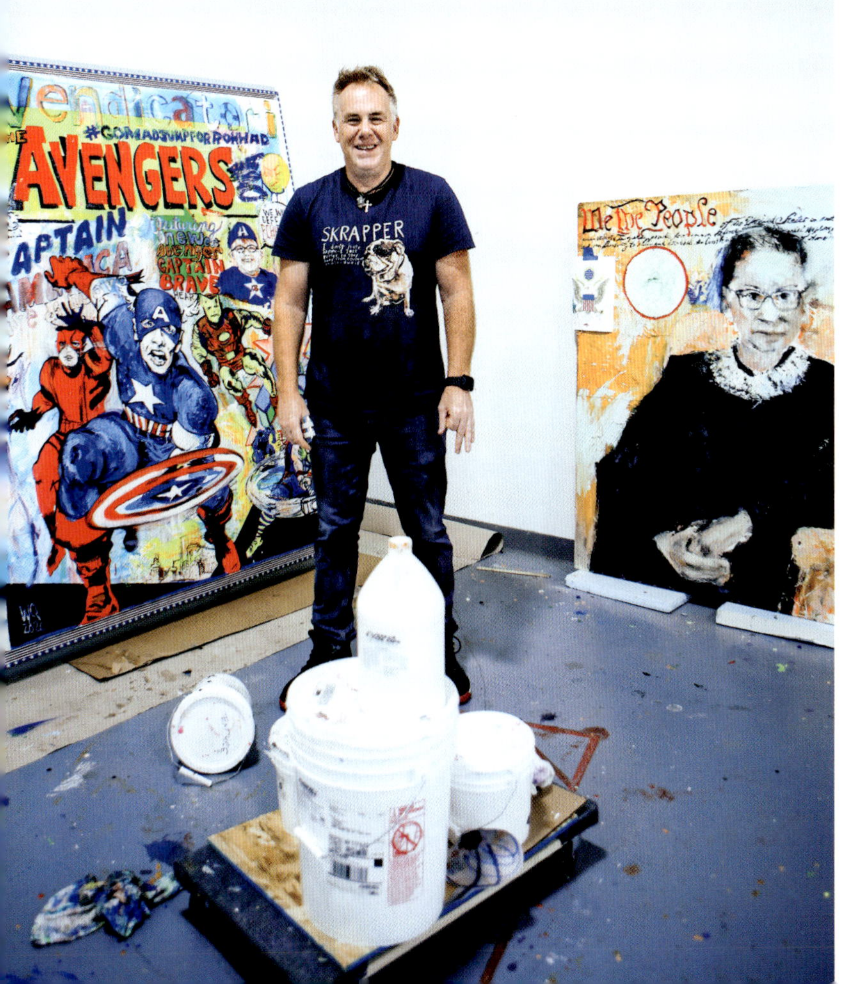

"Much like life and the advanced distractions of social media, sticking to one medium is almost boring. I do love the nostalgia and history of paint on canvas and the square, rectangle, or circle of a painting on a wall. But there are so many other directions to go. Everyone thinks I'm a sports or celebrity painter. Not at all. I paint about history and the people and events that define our history. I go back and forth between abstraction and figurative work. Exploring abstraction allows me to be a better painter. I think it's difficult to make a successful abstract painting. And being a good figurative painter is often veiled by its content and the simple fact that it's a figure. Bacon, Picasso, and Rembrandt were painting portraits of the people of their day. I am doing the same."

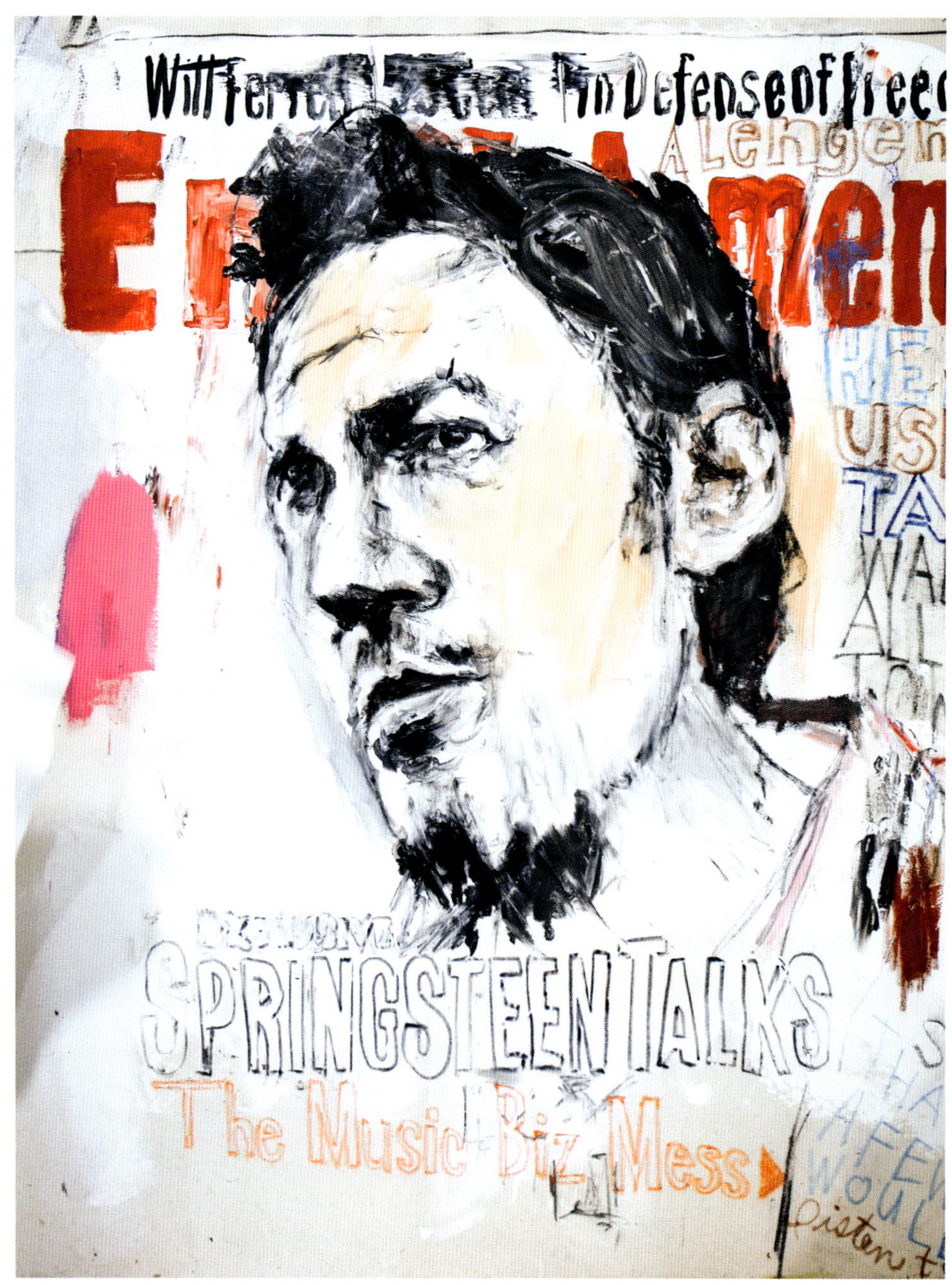

"My studio is like a sacred church with all this stimulation in it. What drives me to go every day is an intense feeling that I haven't done anything yet, that life is short, and I still have stories and memories to express. I go to the studio around noon, drink coffee, dream about going to the gym, dribble a basketball, shoot some hoops in the warm weather outside my studio, then try to work until about 2:00 or even 4:00 AM. I may read, post some stuff, eat, and dance somewhere in between." Dance? "While living and painting in Los Angeles from 1989 to 2000, I art-directed music videos to make some money and ended up dancing in a lot of the videos and onstage with Prince, Madonna, Kid Rock, Lenny Kravitz, Paula Abdul. So I started making selfie dance videos in my studio. And I'm still doing it."

OPPOSITE Quigley's cavernous East Hampton industrial space is where he paints, contemplates his paintings, cranks up the music, and often makes video shorts of himself dancing.

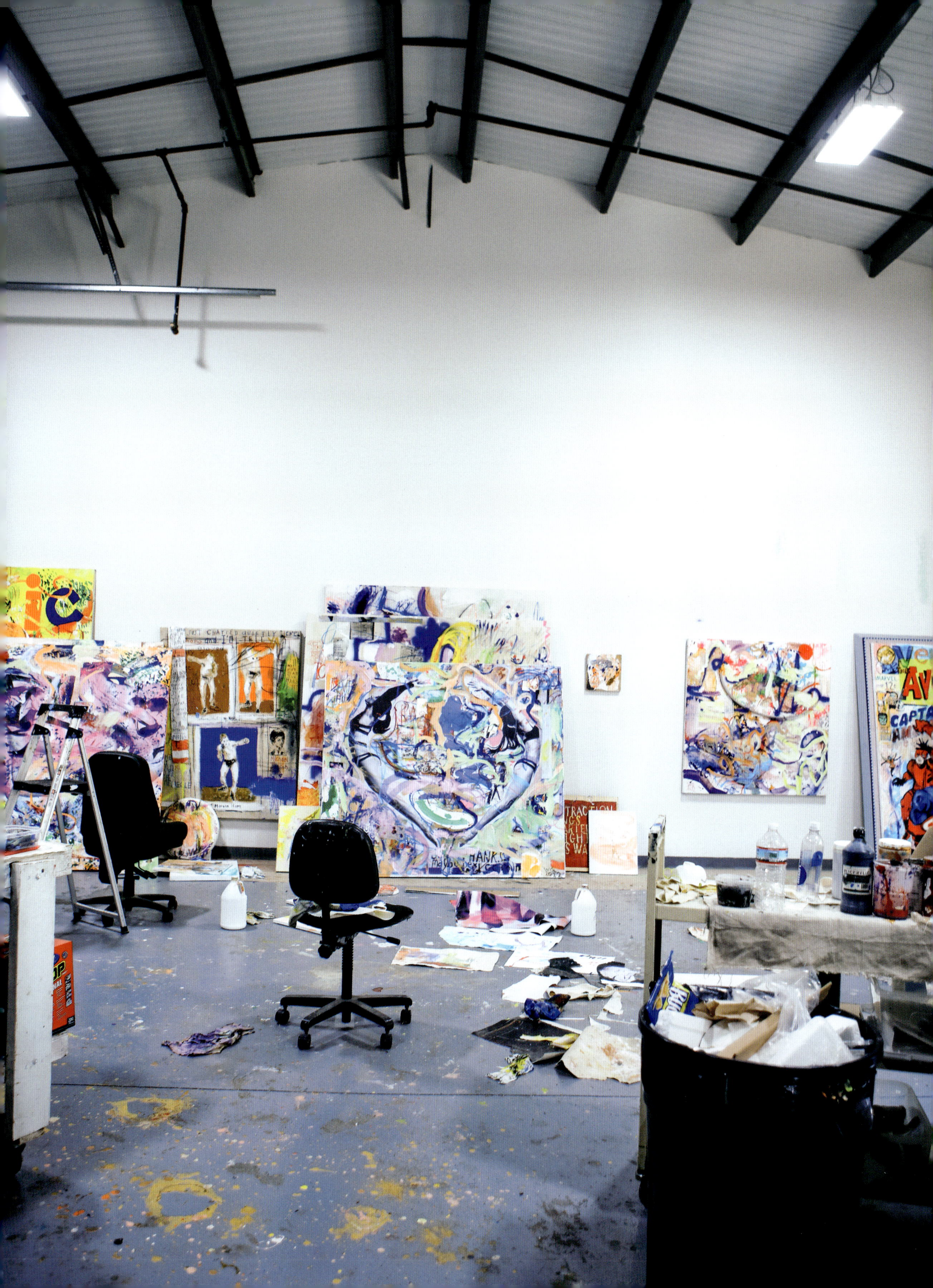

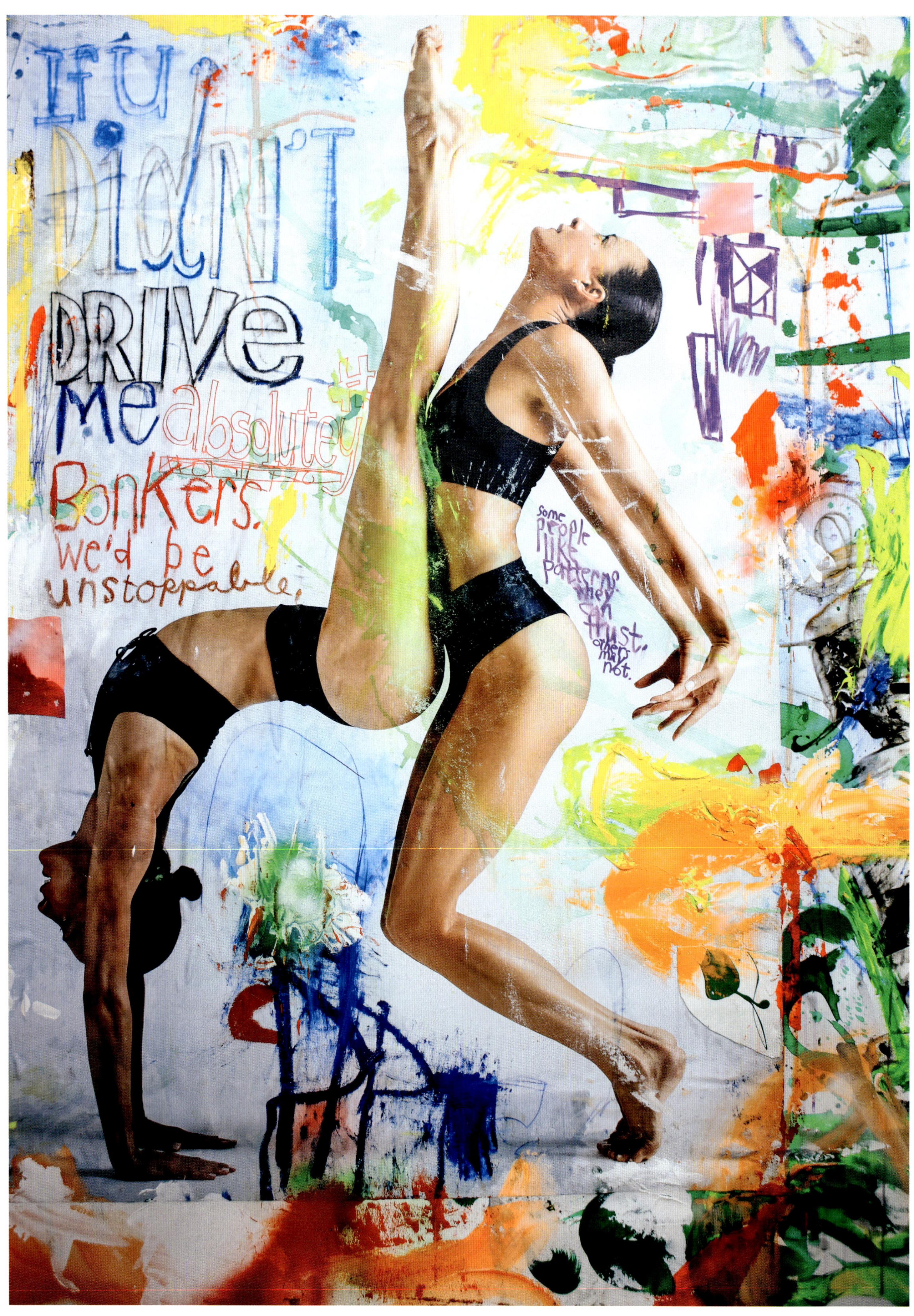
If U
DIDN'T
DRIVE
Me absolutey
Bonkers.
we'd be
unstoppable,
some
people
like
patterns.
they
can
trust.
others
may
not.

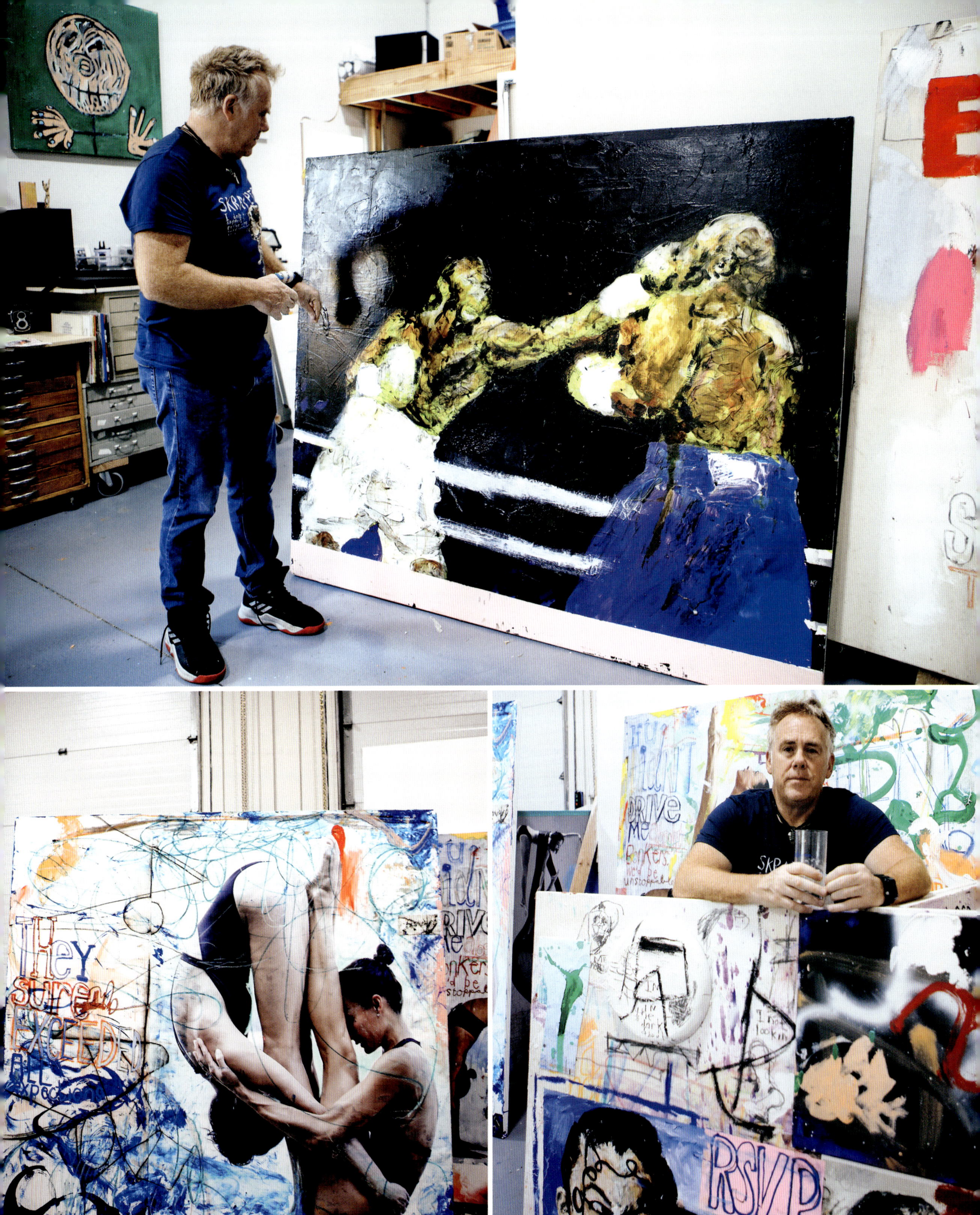
They
RSVP

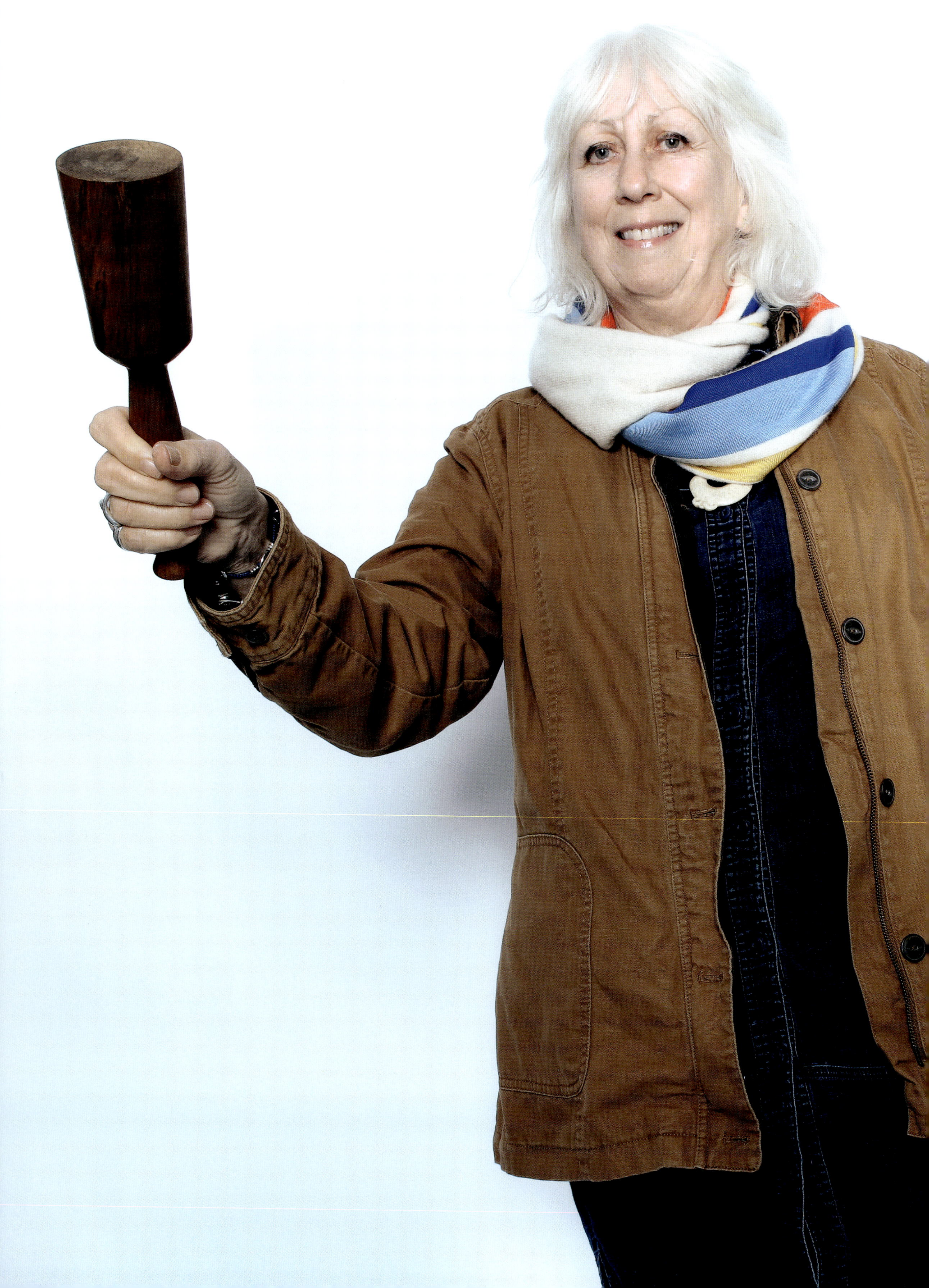

I'm inspired by human and plant-like forms. I aim to create abstract pieces that look as though they exist in the natural world.

SALLY RICHARDSON

Richardson sculpts in both stone and wood. "The process for each is quite different. When carving wood, I work with the grain horizontally, using a chisel and mallet. When carving stone, I can work on the material from any direction. The process with stone is a lot longer, as there are many stages and tools: the point chisel for roughing out, then the tooth chisel, flat chisel, rasps, and many, many hours of sanding. No power tools!"

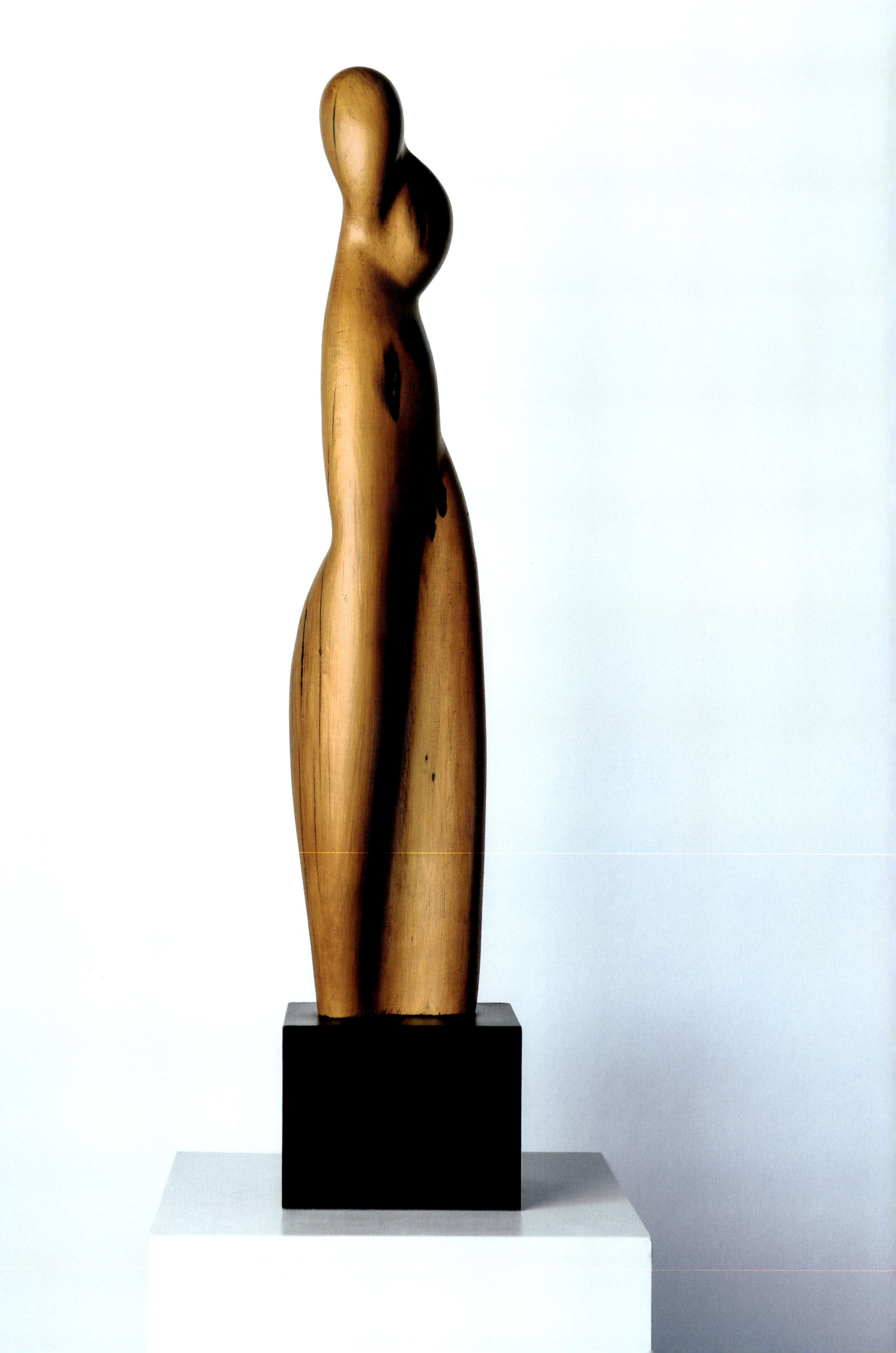

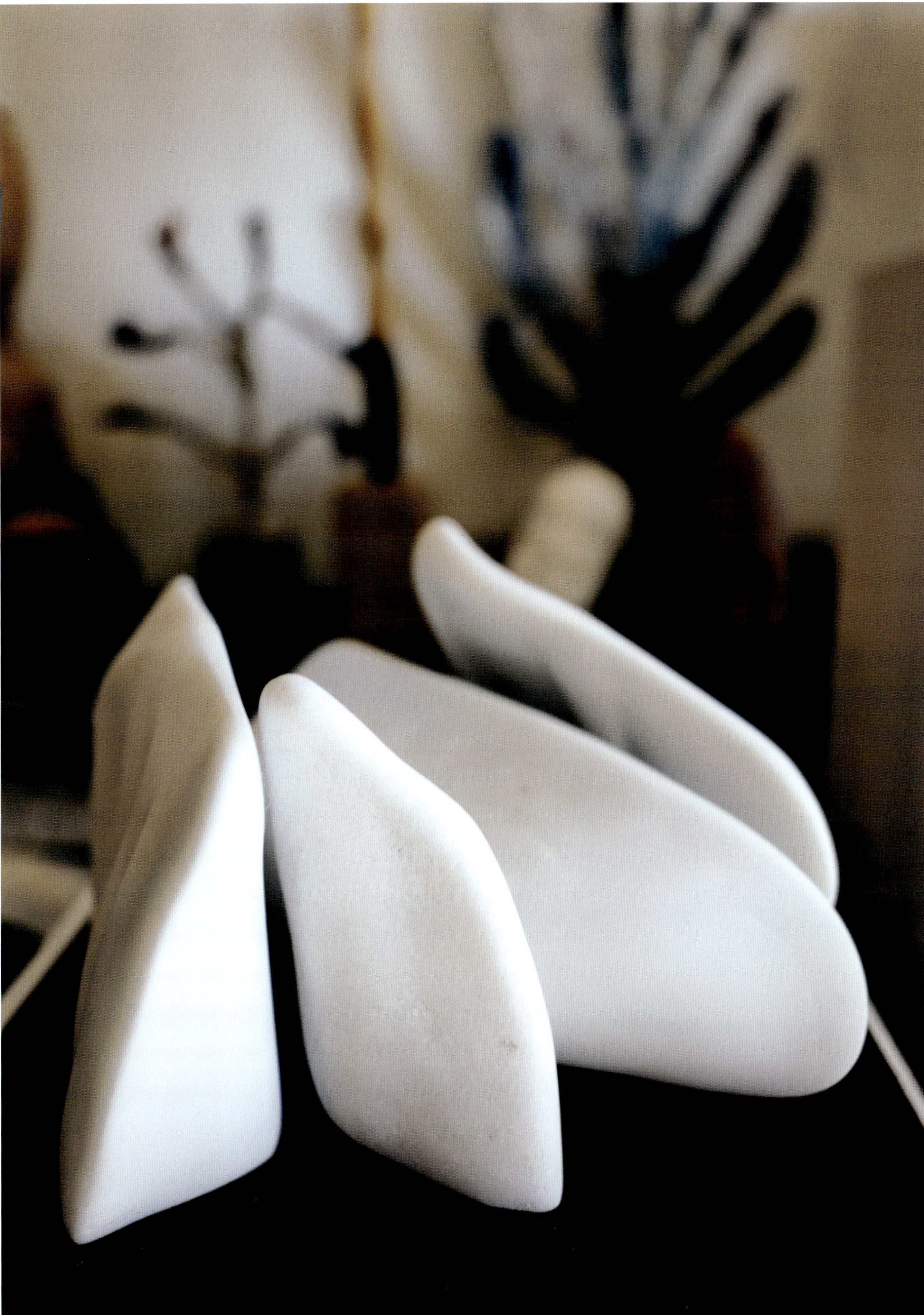

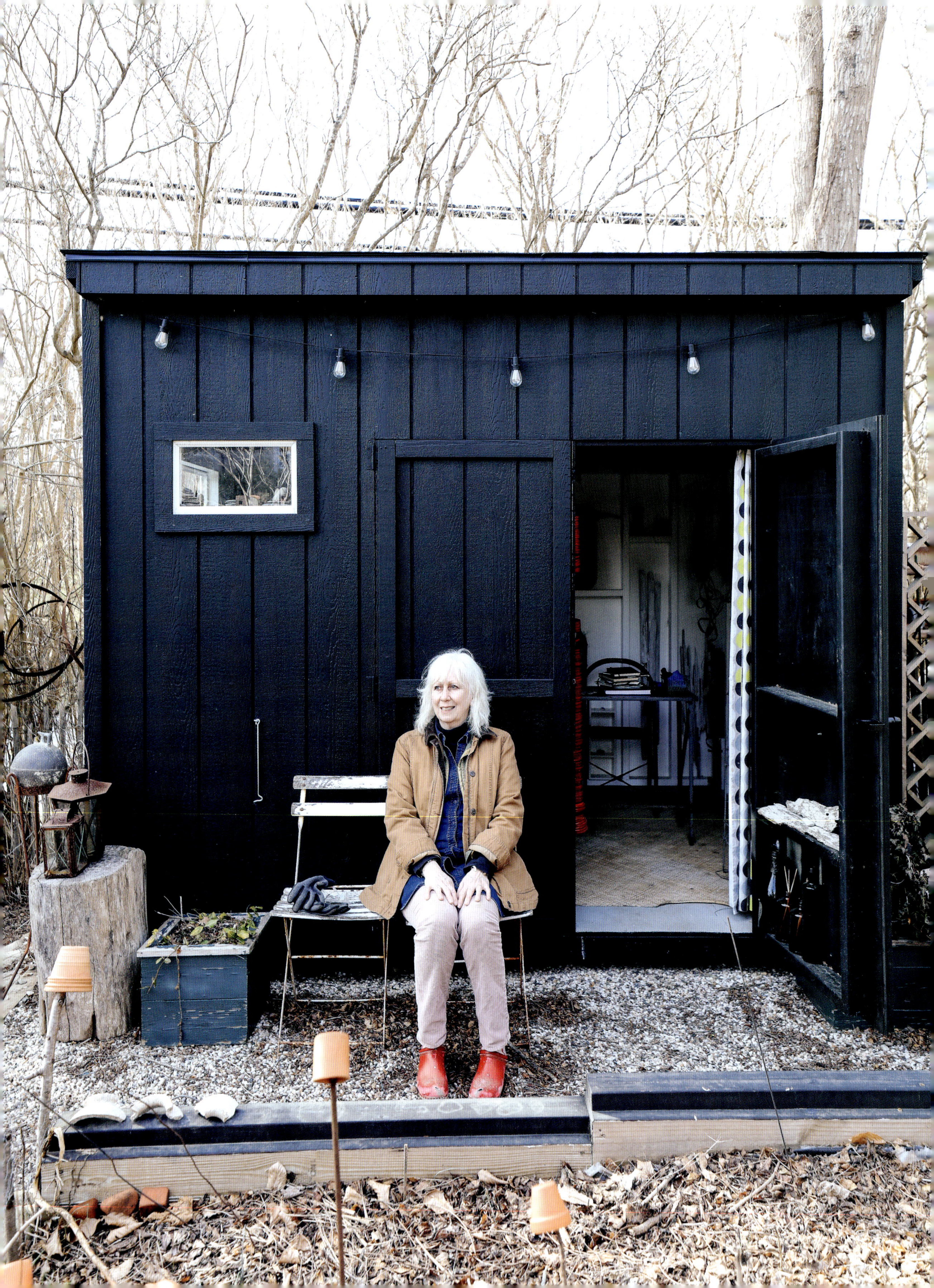

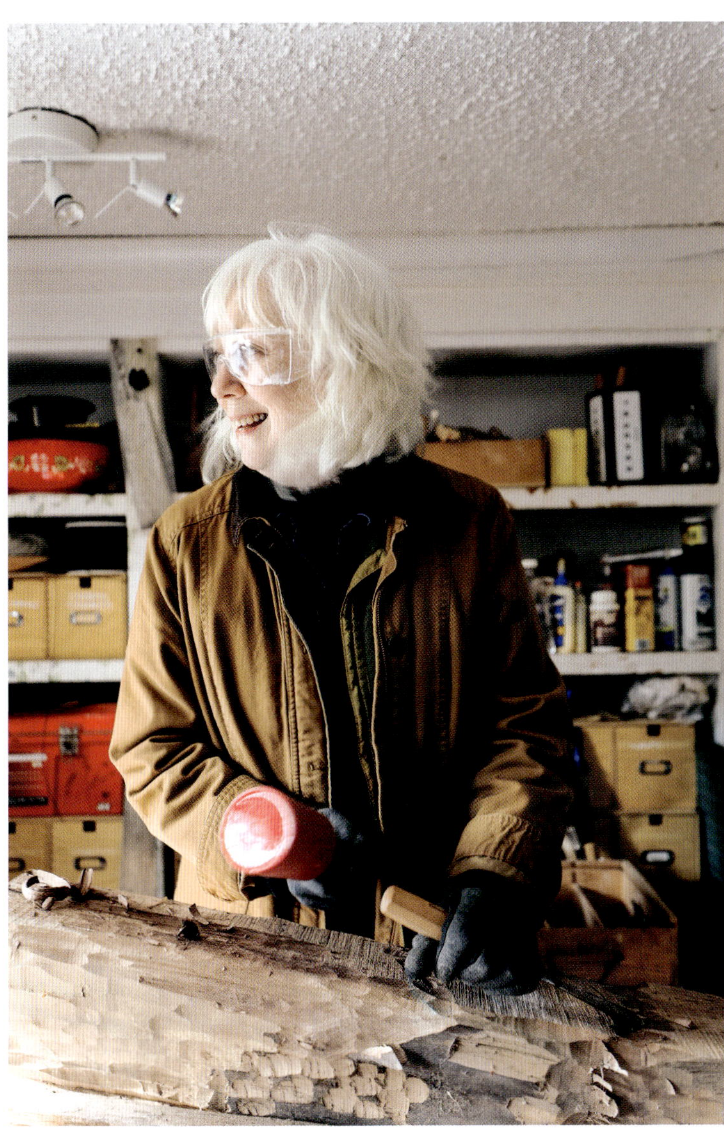

OPPOSITE

A tiny garage from the 1920s serves as the artist's studio, with just enough space for her woodworking bench and carving table. Weather permitting, she also sculpts outside.

LEFT AND BELOW

Originally from a small town in England, Richardson feels right at home in Montauk and in the charming stucco cottage she shares with her husband.

"I moved to Montauk year-round in 2003 but had spent many summers here when I was living in New York City. I grew up in a small coastal village in England, so Montauk felt very familiar to me." Her studio, originally a garage built in 1928, is "too small for today's cars but perfect for a studio. I have a woodwork bench and a stone-carving table, which is on casters so I can move it around. I work outside during the summer months, especially to carve stone, as it generates a lot of dust. I wear protective goggles. It's tempting not to, but I've learned the hard way after getting chips of wood and marble in my eyes!"

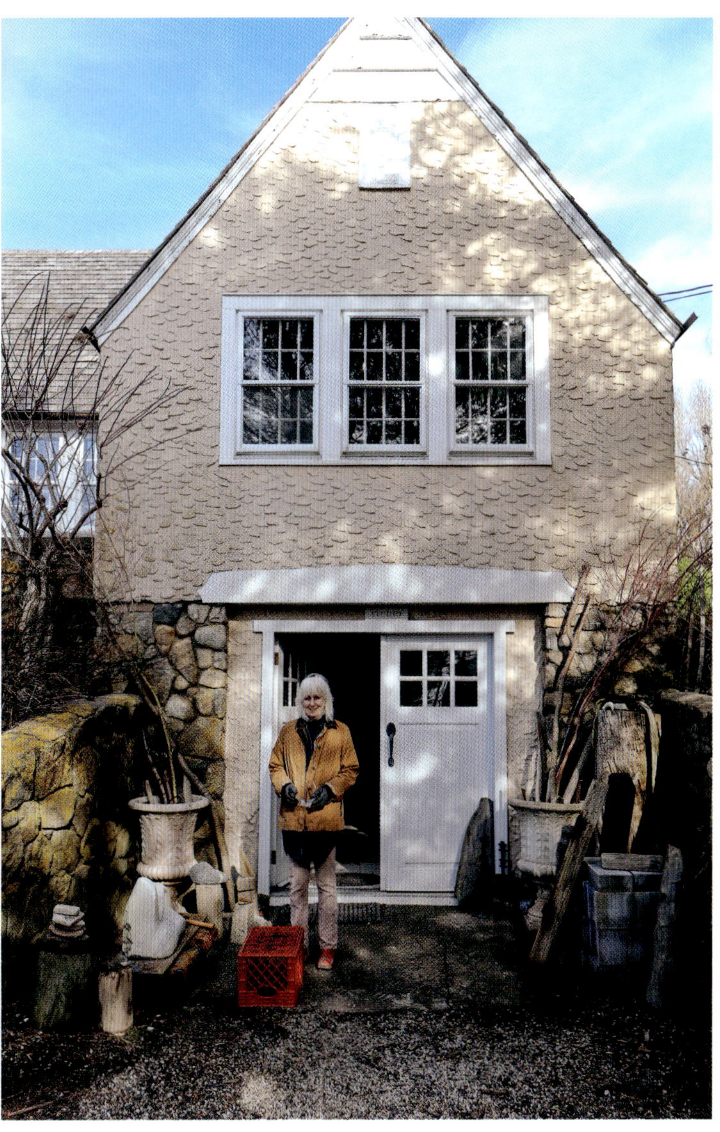

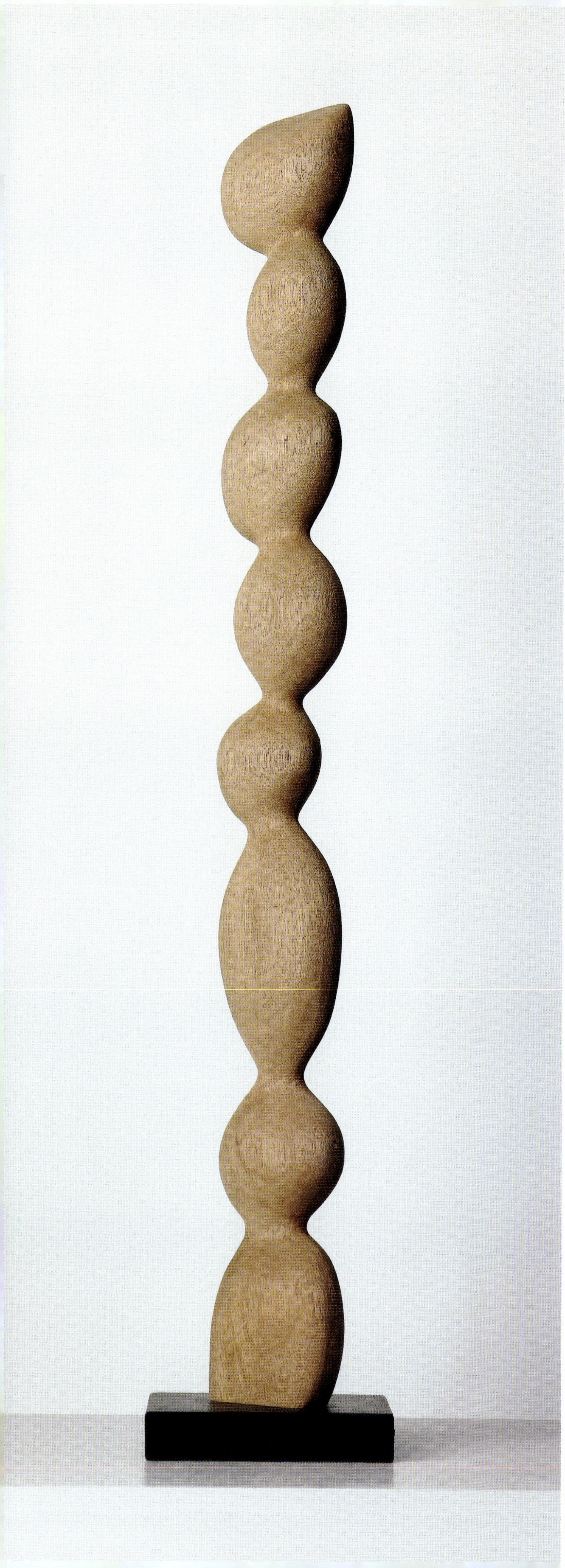

“When it comes to wood, I especially like working with cherry, walnut, and New Zealand’s native totara. Each type of wood has a unique character.” And she has quite the stockpile—“a lifetime’s worth of wood. Friends will often give me pieces. And I find materials on beaches and on trails that I also use for my assembled pieces.” She says she can carve for hours a day. “I enjoy the solitary nature of the work and find it meditative. Carving feels natural, and I become immersed in the process, although it’s very slow since I only use hand tools. Each day in my studio is one of discovery as the form within the material reveals itself.”

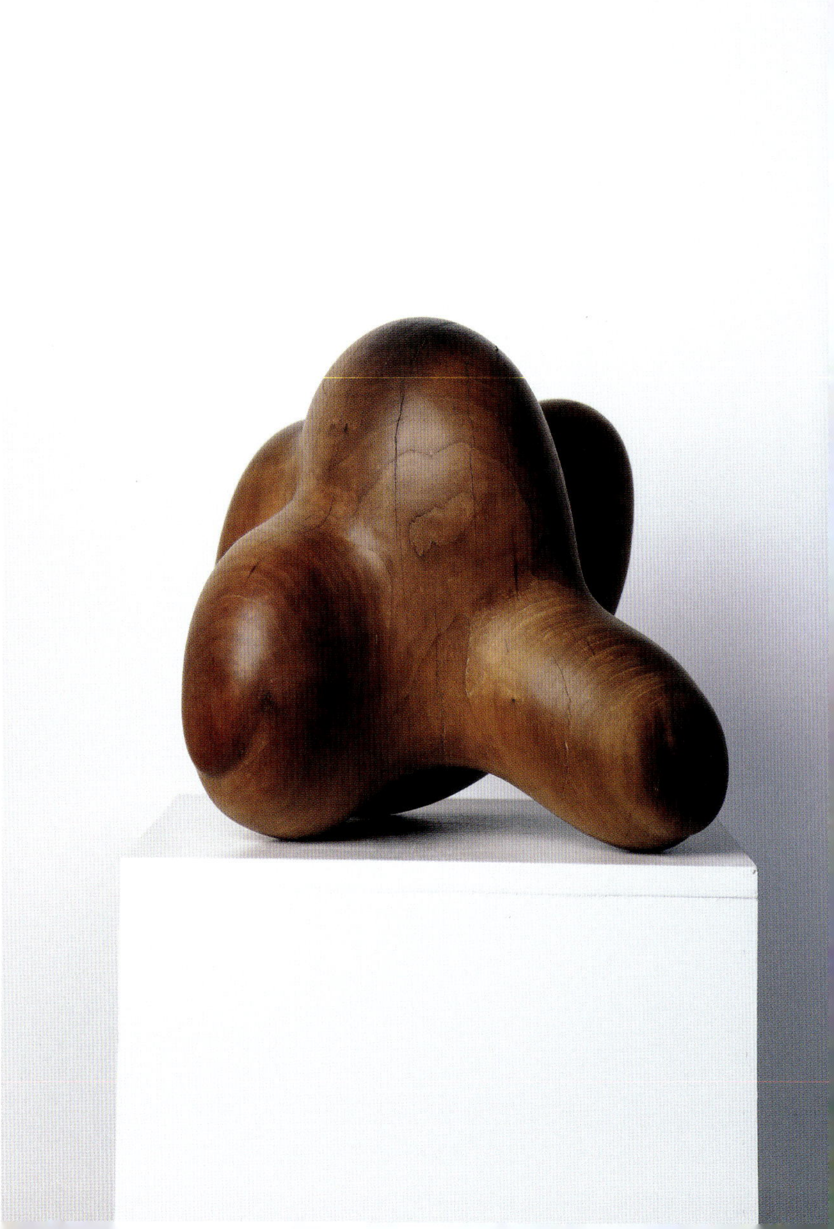

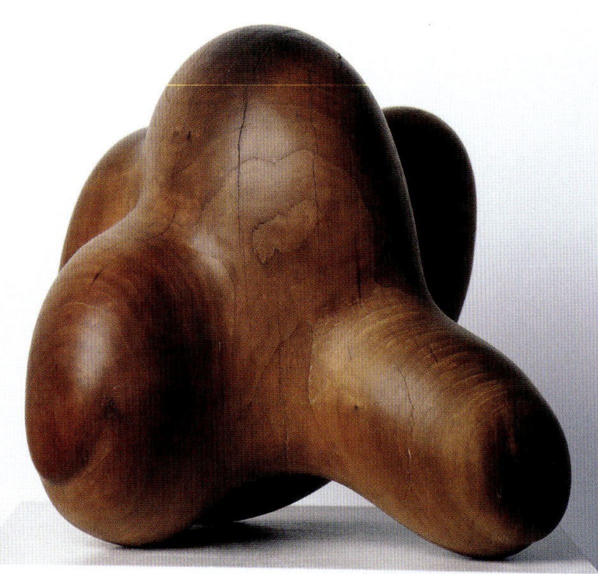

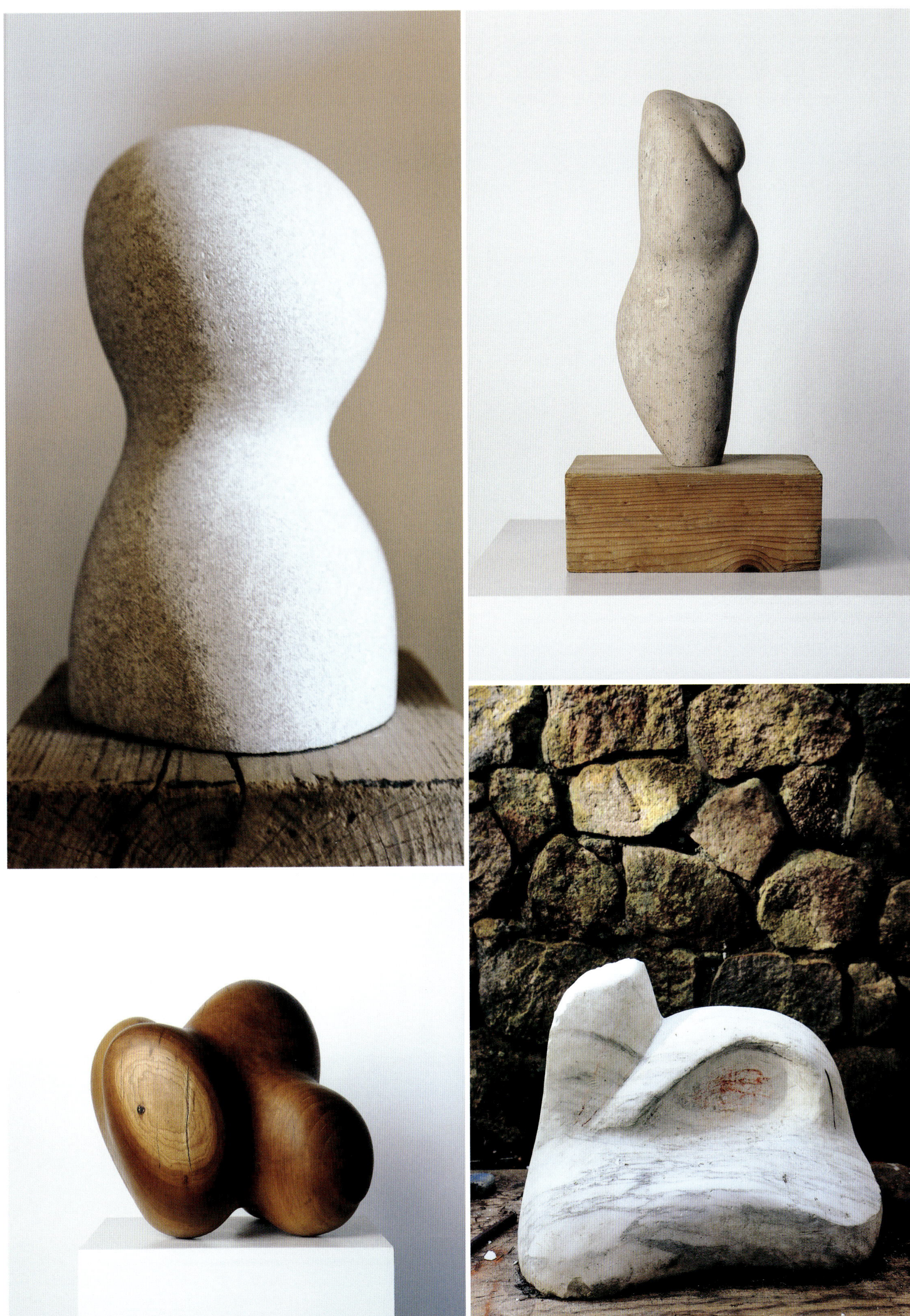

I have arrived at a set of symbols based on simple color, rectilinear form, and surface. By the arrangement of these symbols, I achieve a composition that is both asymmetrical and balanced.

DAN RIZZIE

Rizzie came to Block Island with his family in the early 1960s. "I was ten years old. I fell in love with the area and was determined to live here. I'm fortunate that Sag Harbor has been my home for the last thirty years. And I feel lucky to be a part of a group that boasts such a talented and diverse arts community." And then there is the landscape. "Suffice it to say that it's difficult to not be affected by the beauty of the East End. I try daily to not take it for granted."

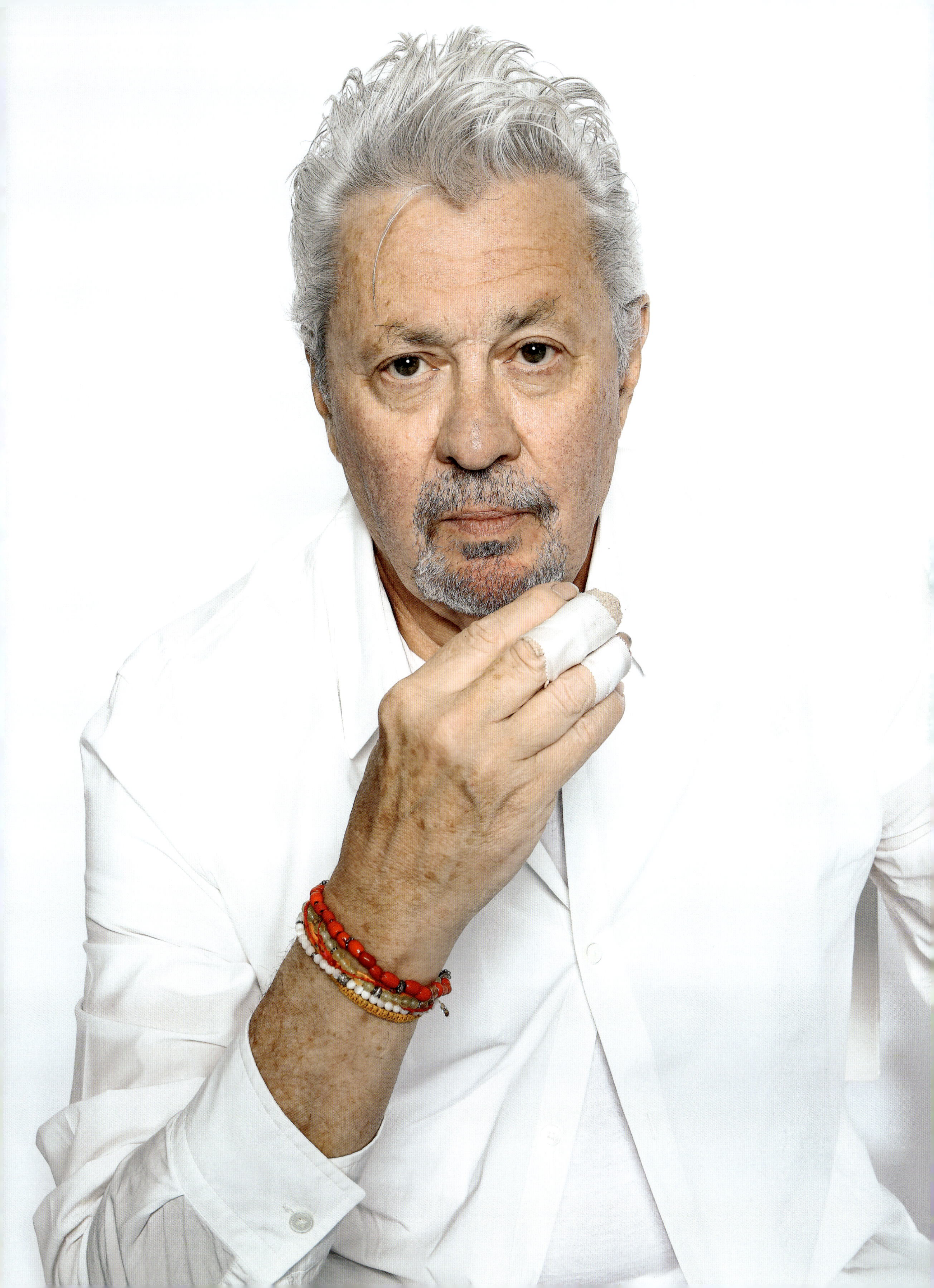

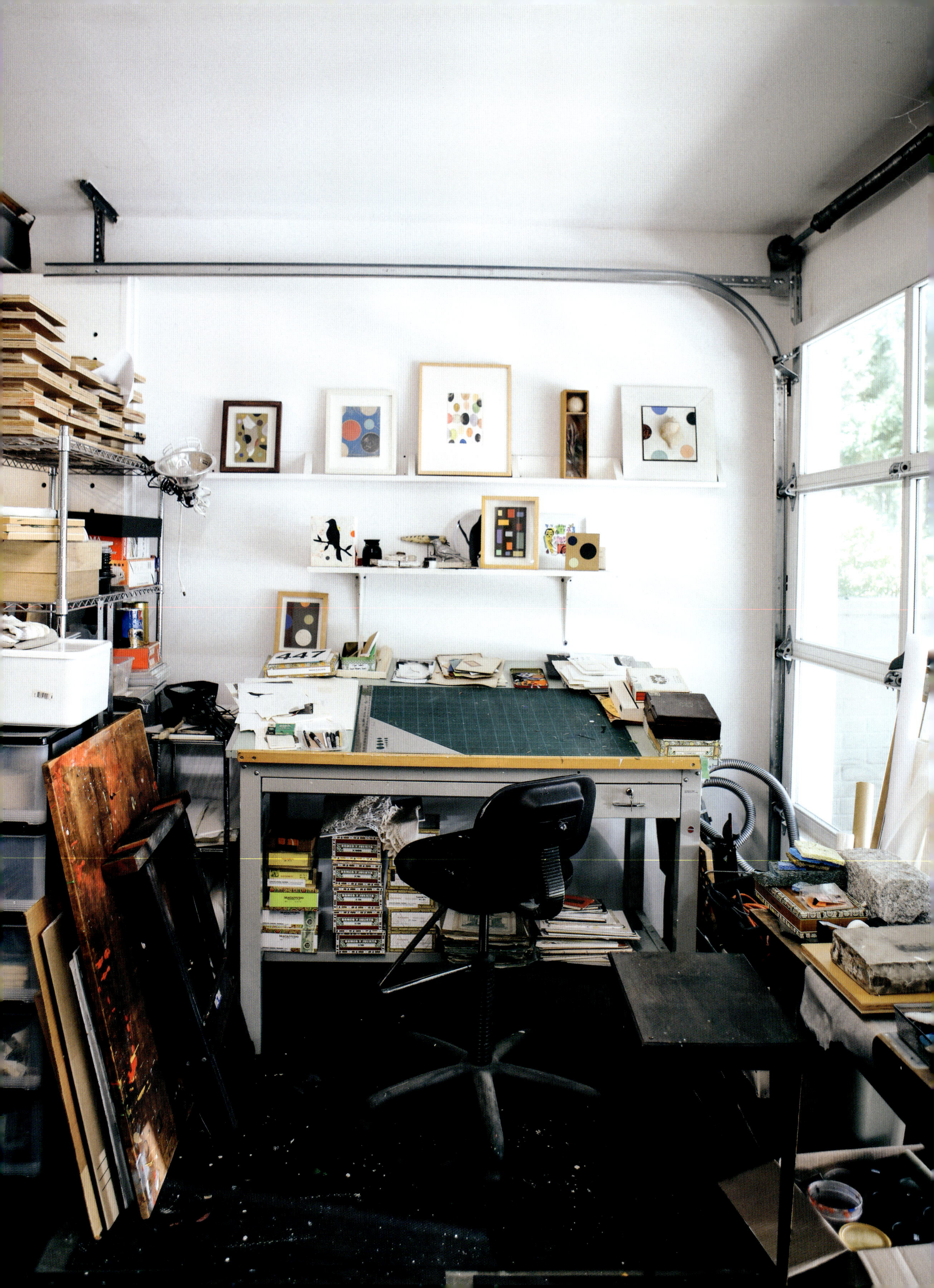
447

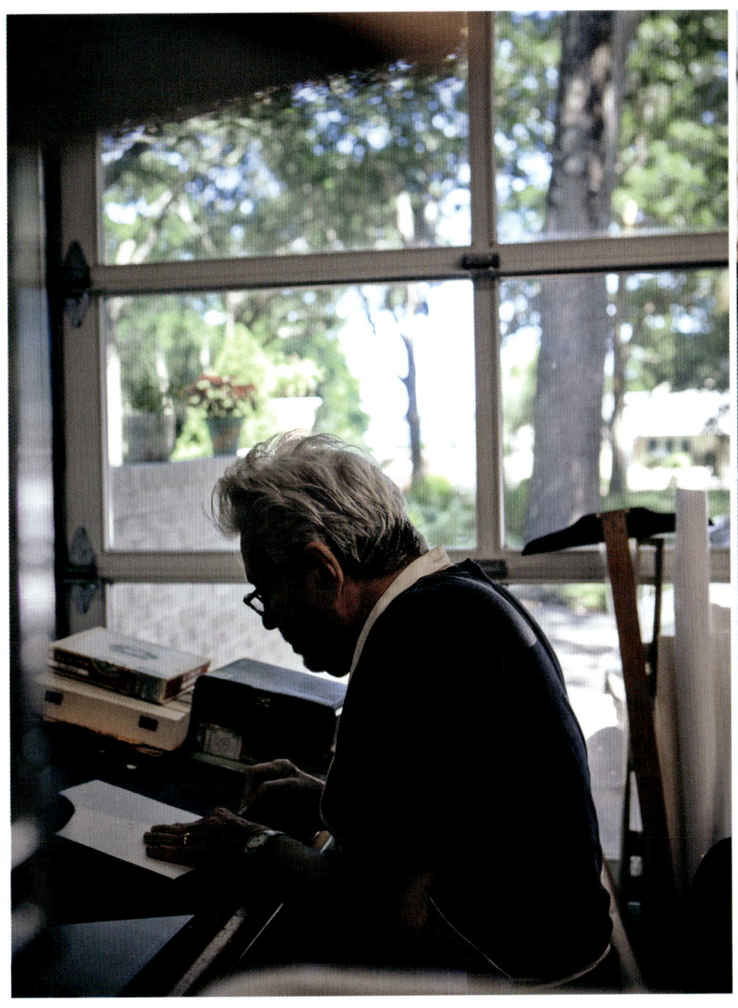

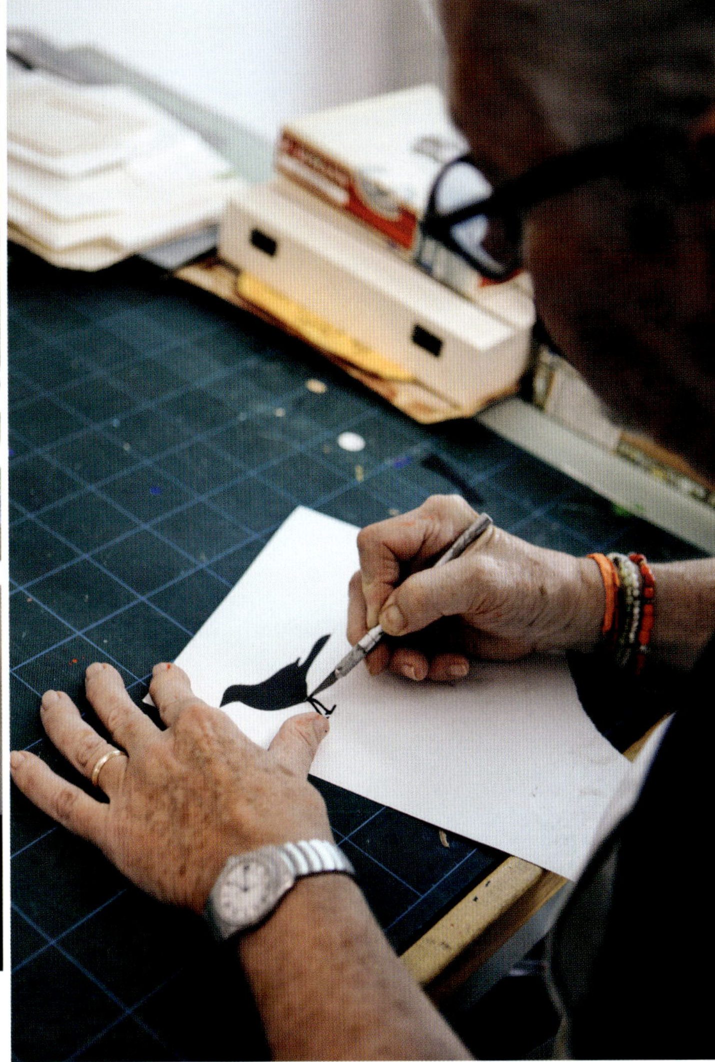

"My studio is filled with different materials, and I use whatever it takes to get the job done. I use a variety of paints, both oil and acrylic, as well as other mediums that I add to my palette like gel, marble dust, sawdust, and sand. I use different types of canvas and wood—usually mahogany—that are made into panels for me to paint on. I also have a tremendous supply of handmade papers, documents, stamps, and objects that sometimes find their way into my works. Over the years, I have collected stuff from all over the world, and it's all here in my studio waiting to be used."

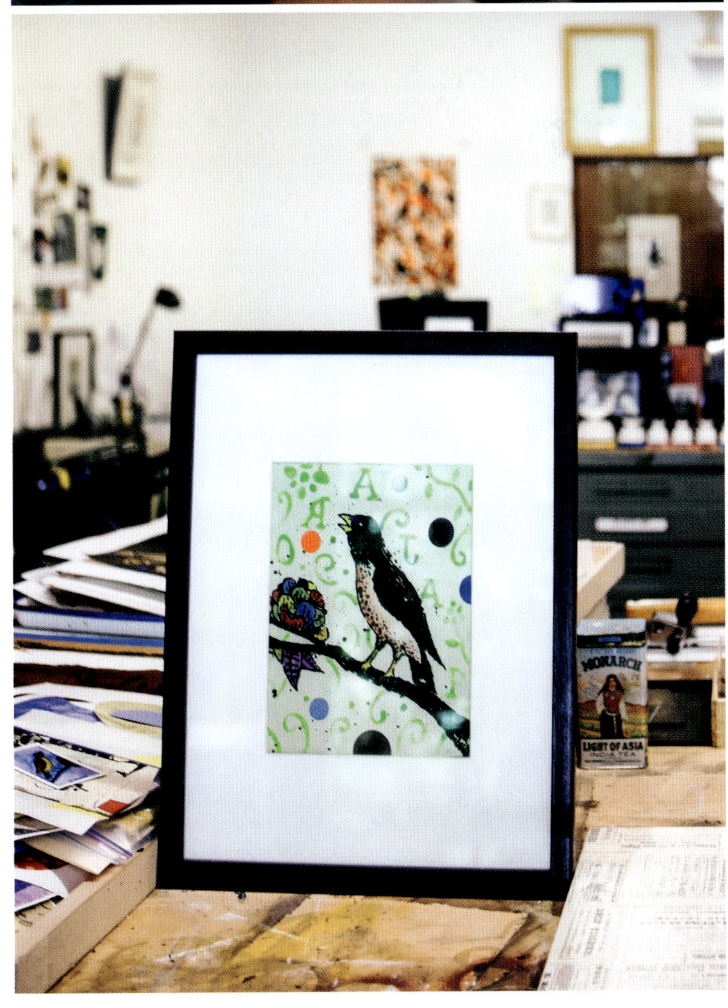

OPPOSITE AND THIS PAGE

Rizzie spends a good amount of time sketching at his desk. One of his recurring themes is birds. In fact, he feeds the many species of birds that perch in the trees on his Sag Harbor property to keep them coming back.

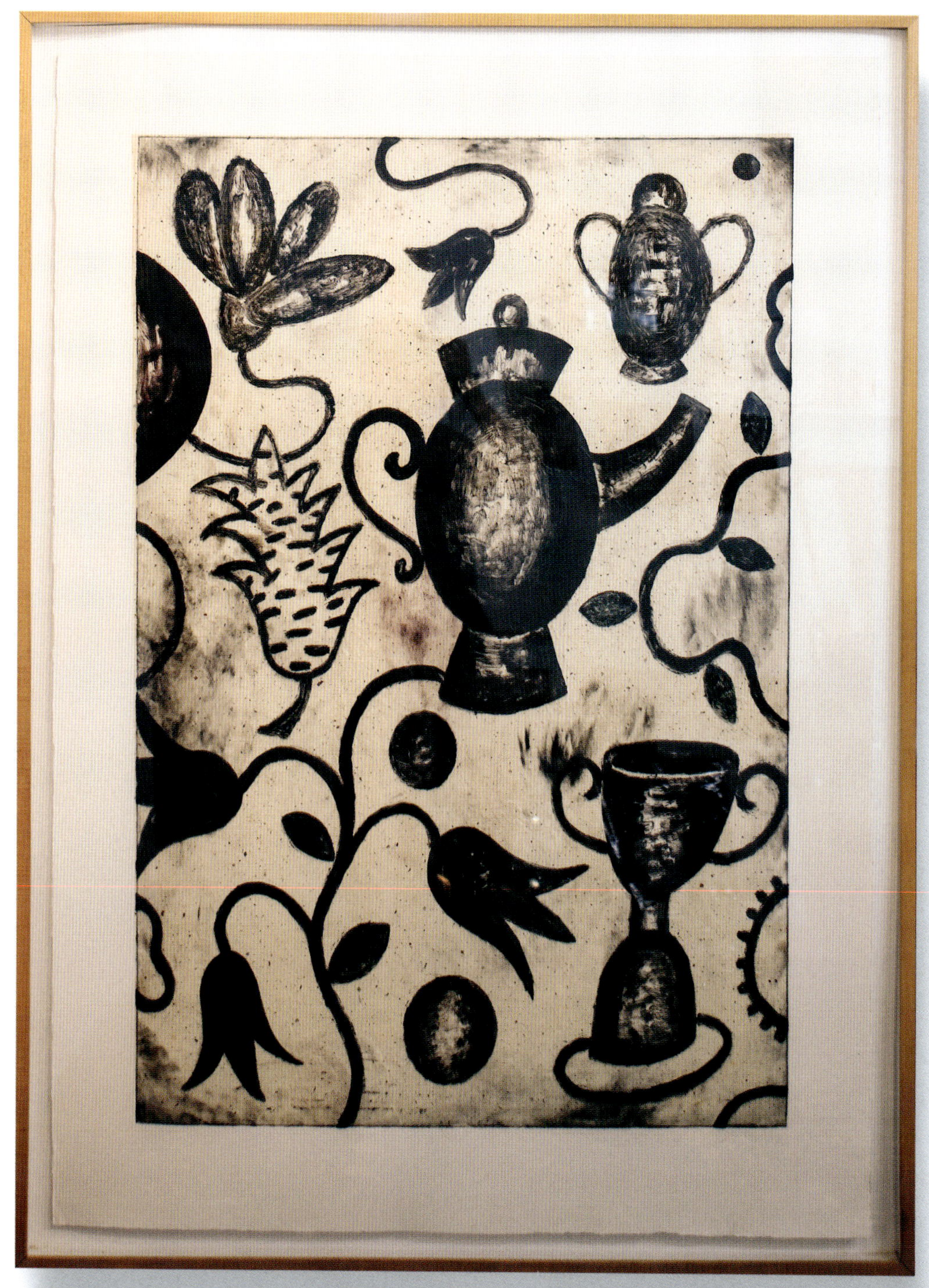

"I used to work late into the night. Now I find myself more productive in daylight. When I listen to music, my first choice is Rosanne Cash. She's a great friend and an incredibly talented artist whose music and lyrics inspire me and keep me going in the studio." As for subject matter, "Birds in particular found their way into my work because our property is filled with large old trees where ravens, red-tailed hawks, and many other species make daily appearances. Feeding them has kept them coming back." And then there are the recurring circles. "A perfect shape, just like the sun, the moon, and the earth. I arrange them in a way that is felt rather than calculated. The size, the color, and the placement are also salient in creating a composition that is balanced and compelling."

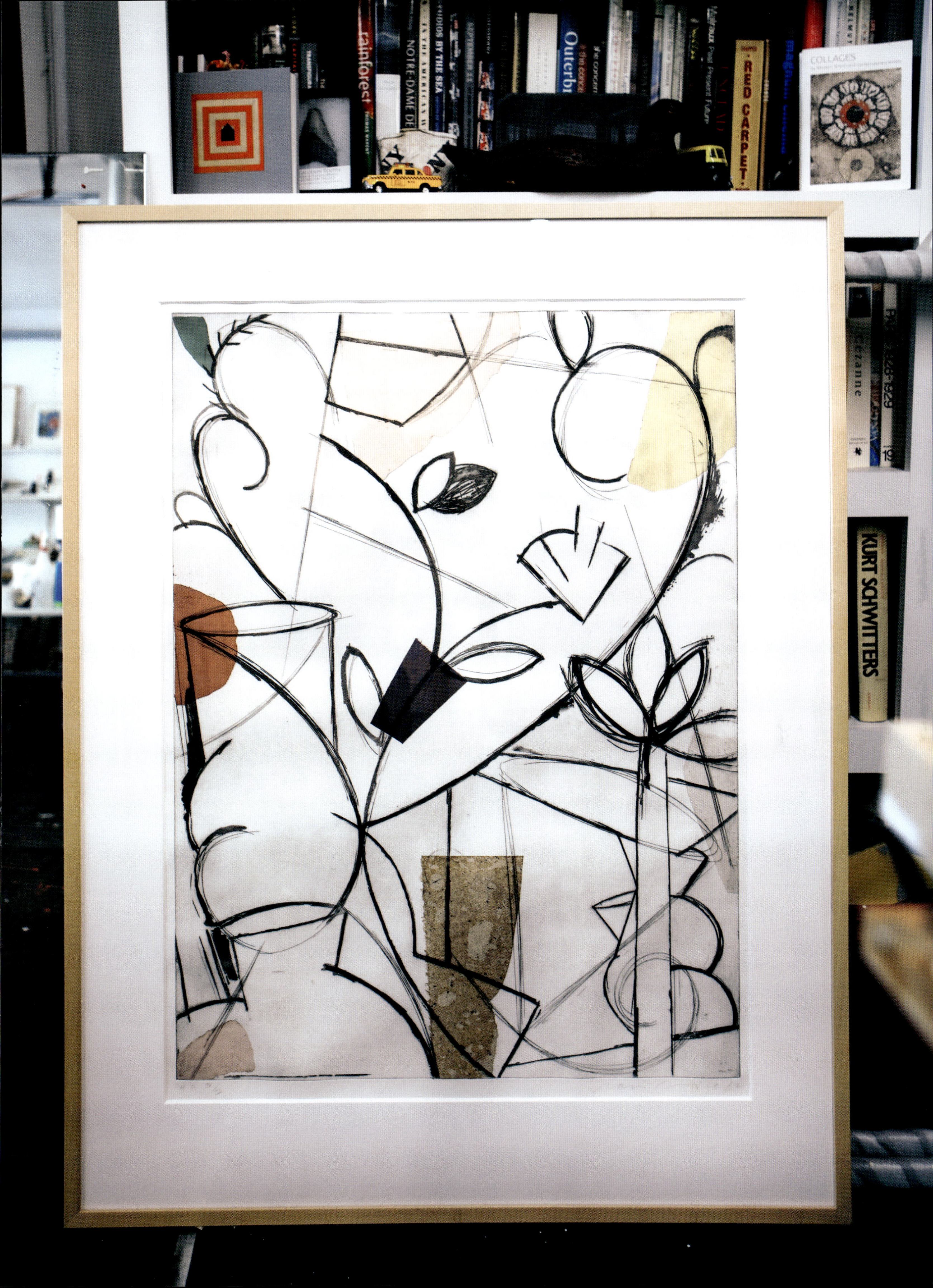

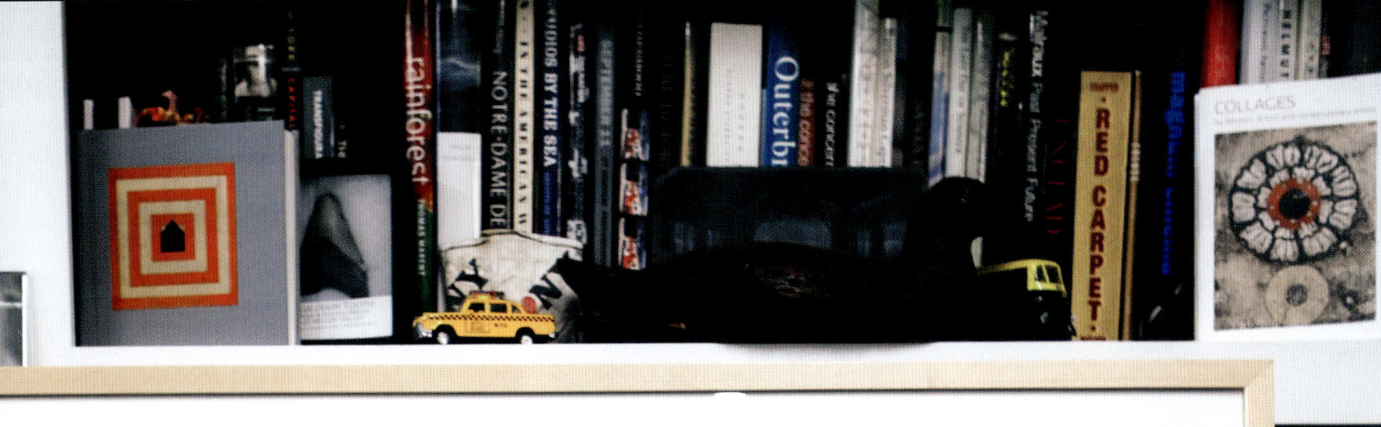
rainforest
NOTRE-DAME DE
RED CARPET
Past Present Future
COLLAGES

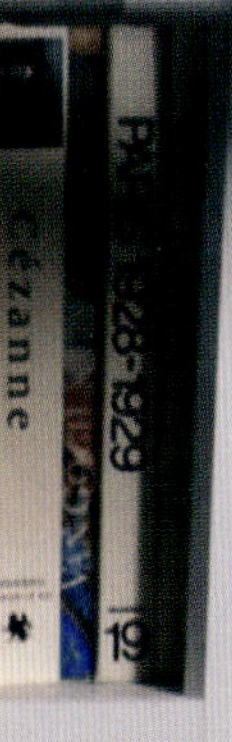
Cézanne
1928-1929

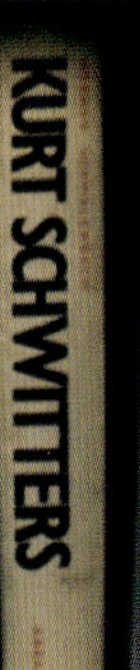
KURT SCHWITTERS

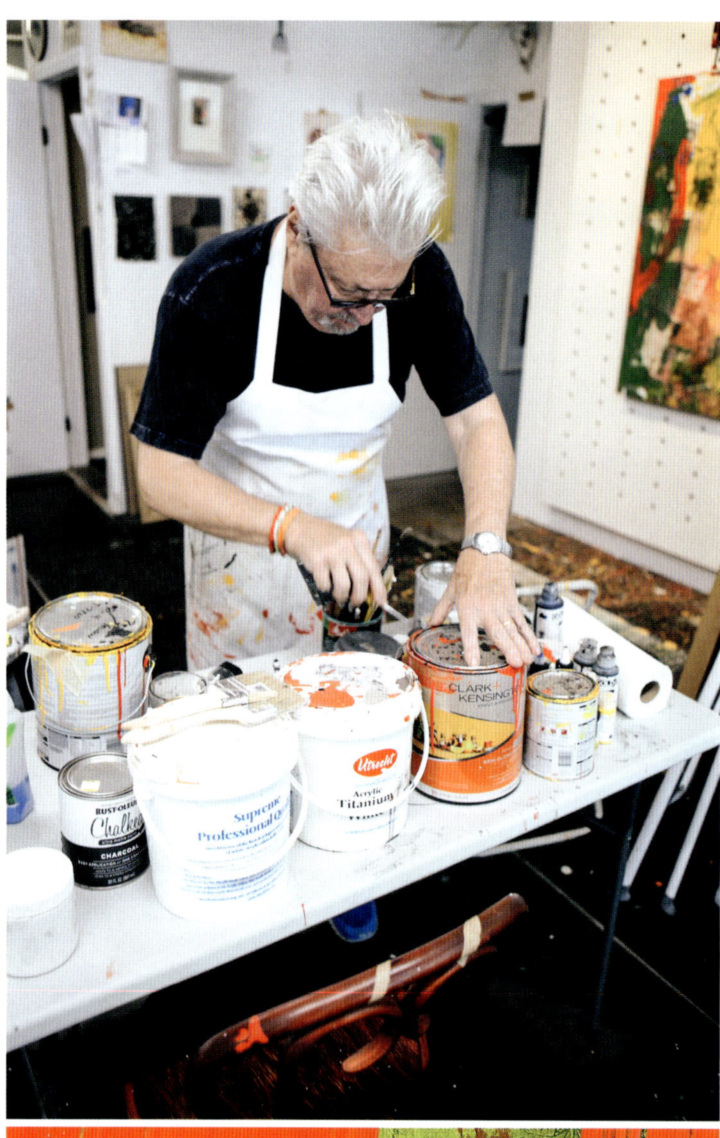

THIS PAGE AND OPPOSITE

The artist works on canvas or wood panels with oil and acrylics, to which he may add other elements, such as marble dust or sand. Tools range from brushes to his own hand, which he'll happily dip right into the paint.

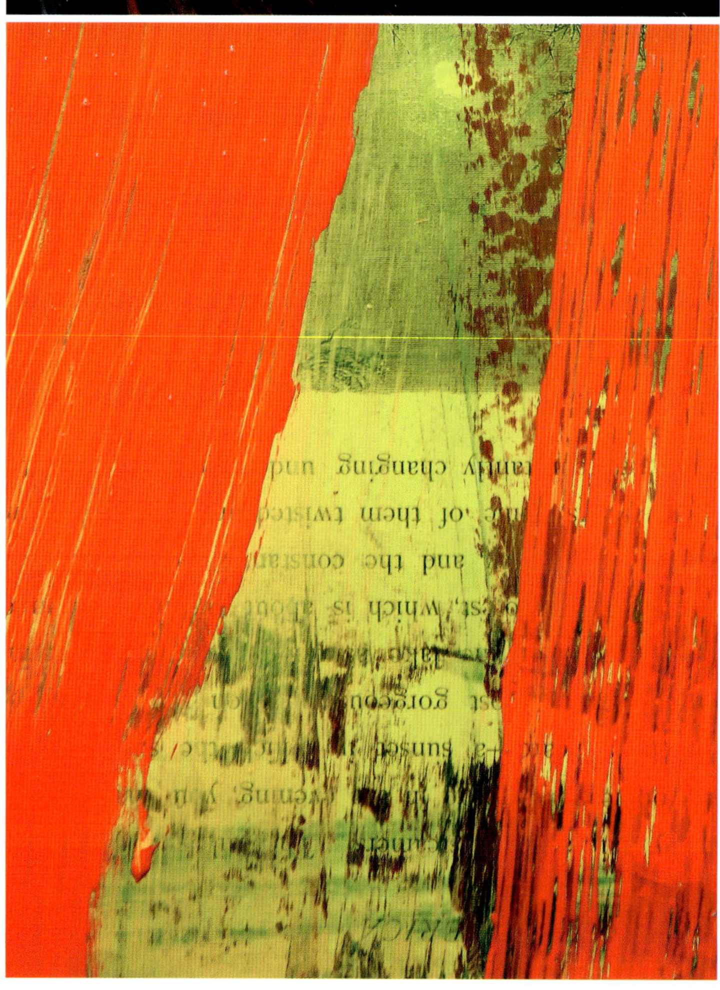

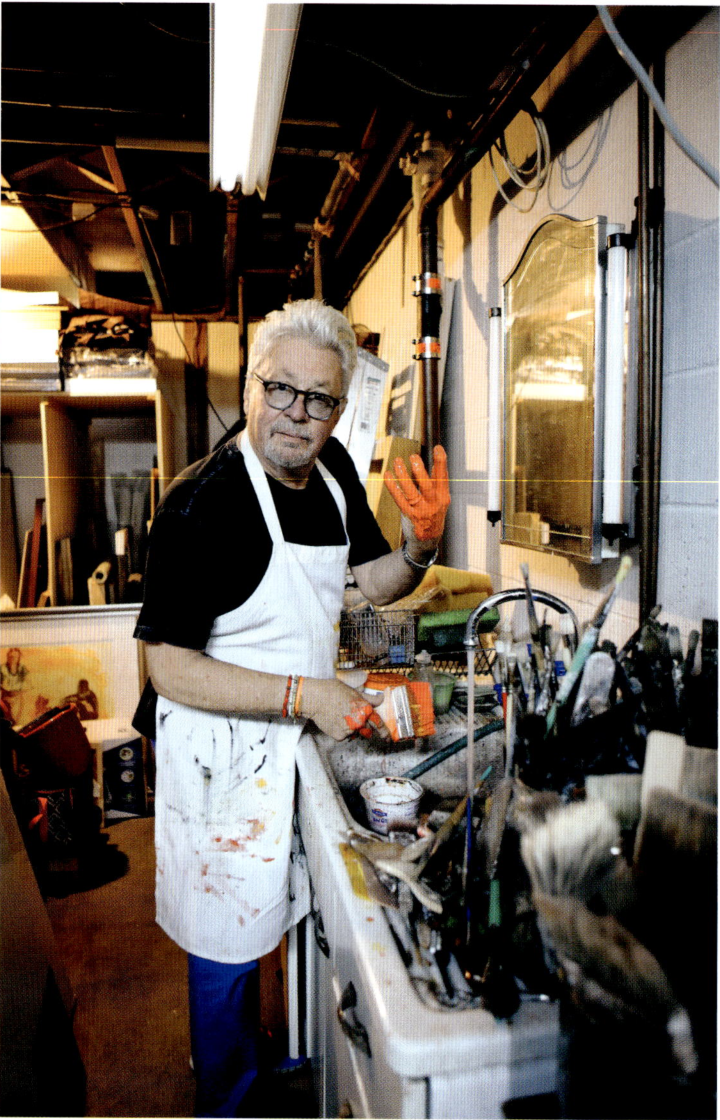

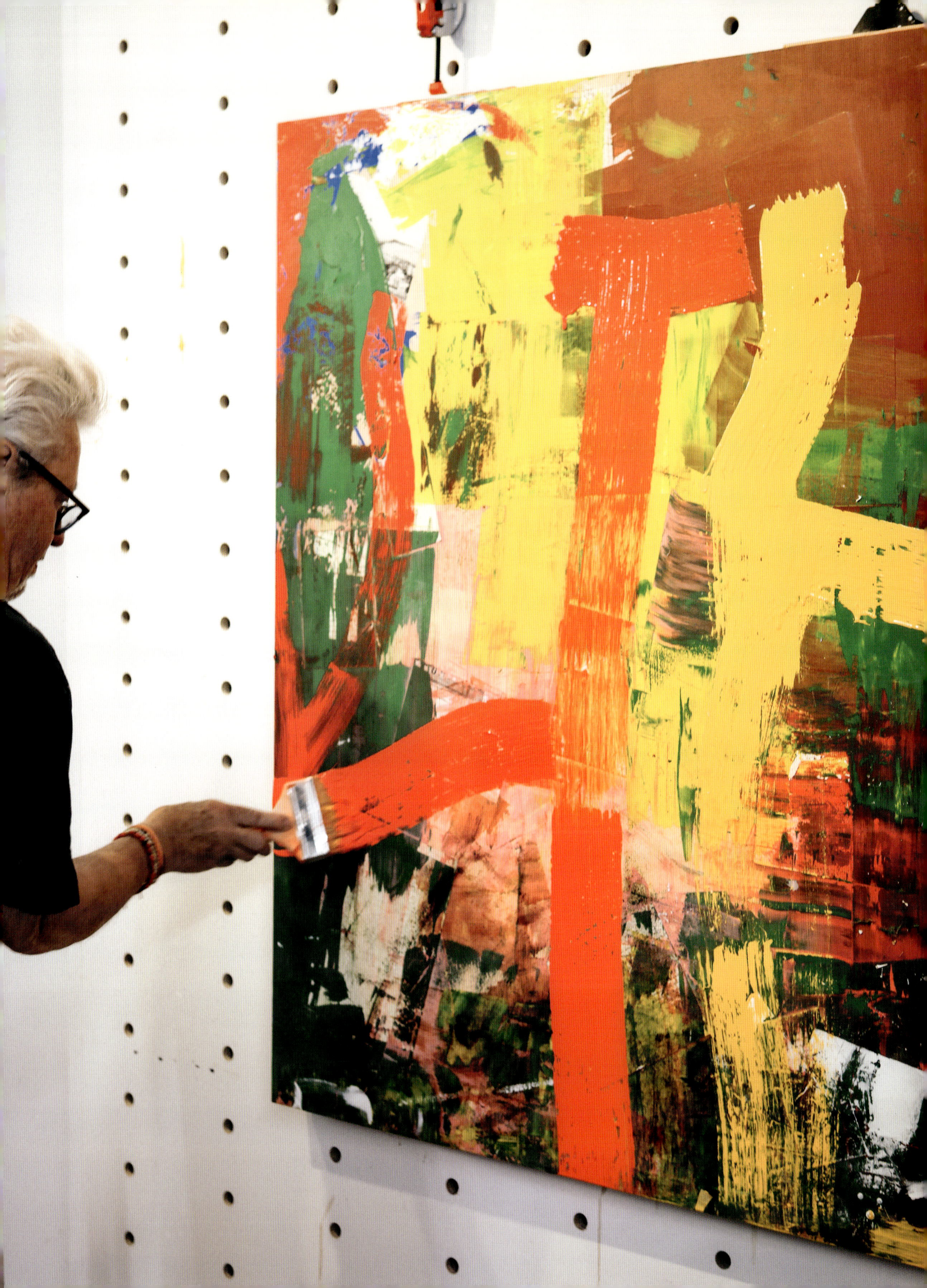

I let others define my work, but it is realism, no doubt. What's interesting is that I eyeball so much that a lot of things are slightly off. You need a better eye than mine to notice that from a distance.

RANDALL ROSENTHAL

"I started surfing on the East End as a teenager in the early sixties. In 1979, my wife and I moved from Utah to Springs and bought a house, a 150-year-old tool shed. I decided to build a bookcase. It came out pretty well, so I built a painting studio for me and a photography darkroom for my wife. Then I built a bedroom addition. I used salvaged materials and hand-dug the foundation. I was working as a carpenter and roofer for several years when Norman Jaffe, the architect, hired me to do sculptural designs—doors, windows, furniture. It was his idea that I become a sculptor, and he got me my first commissions."

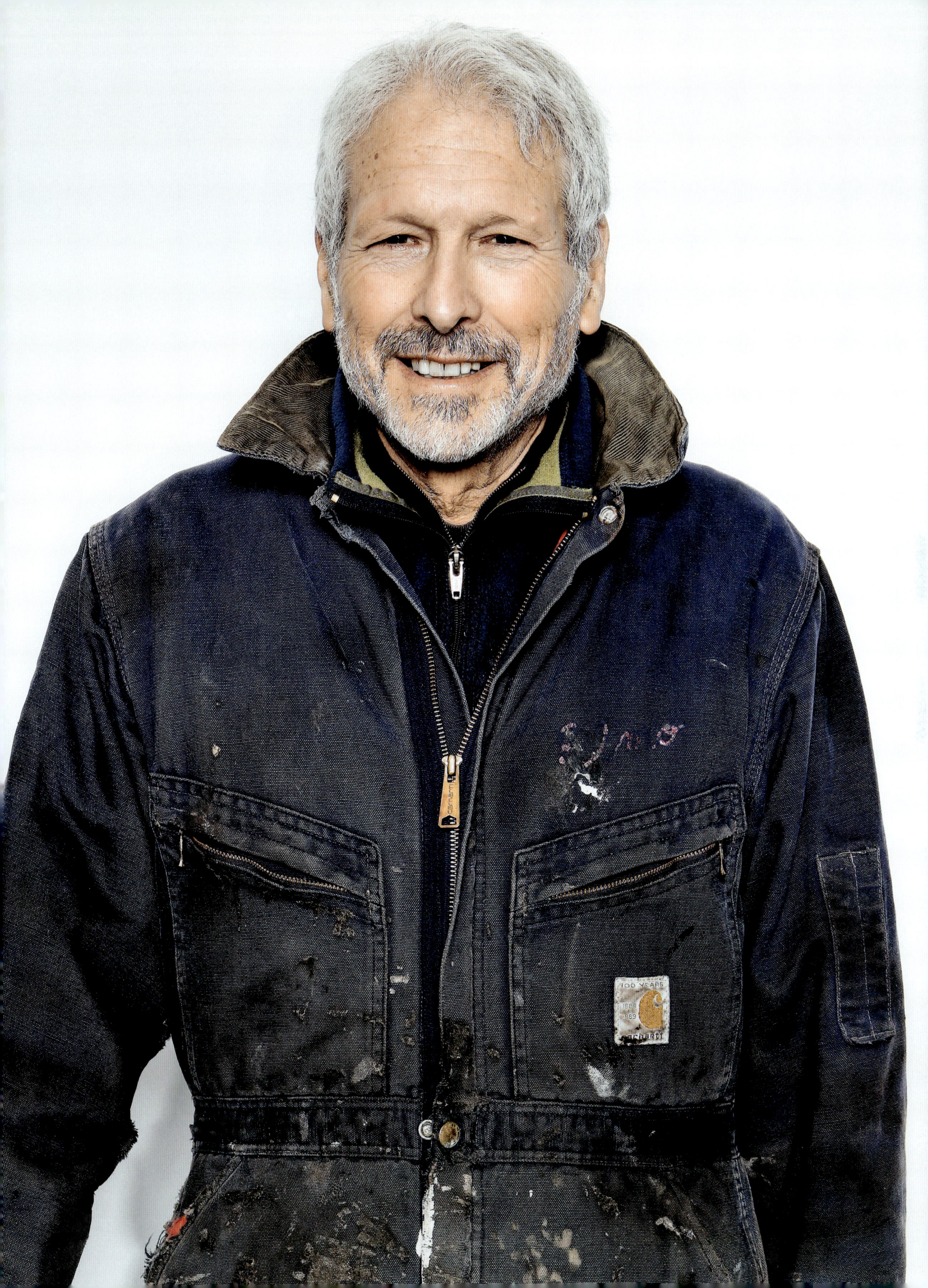

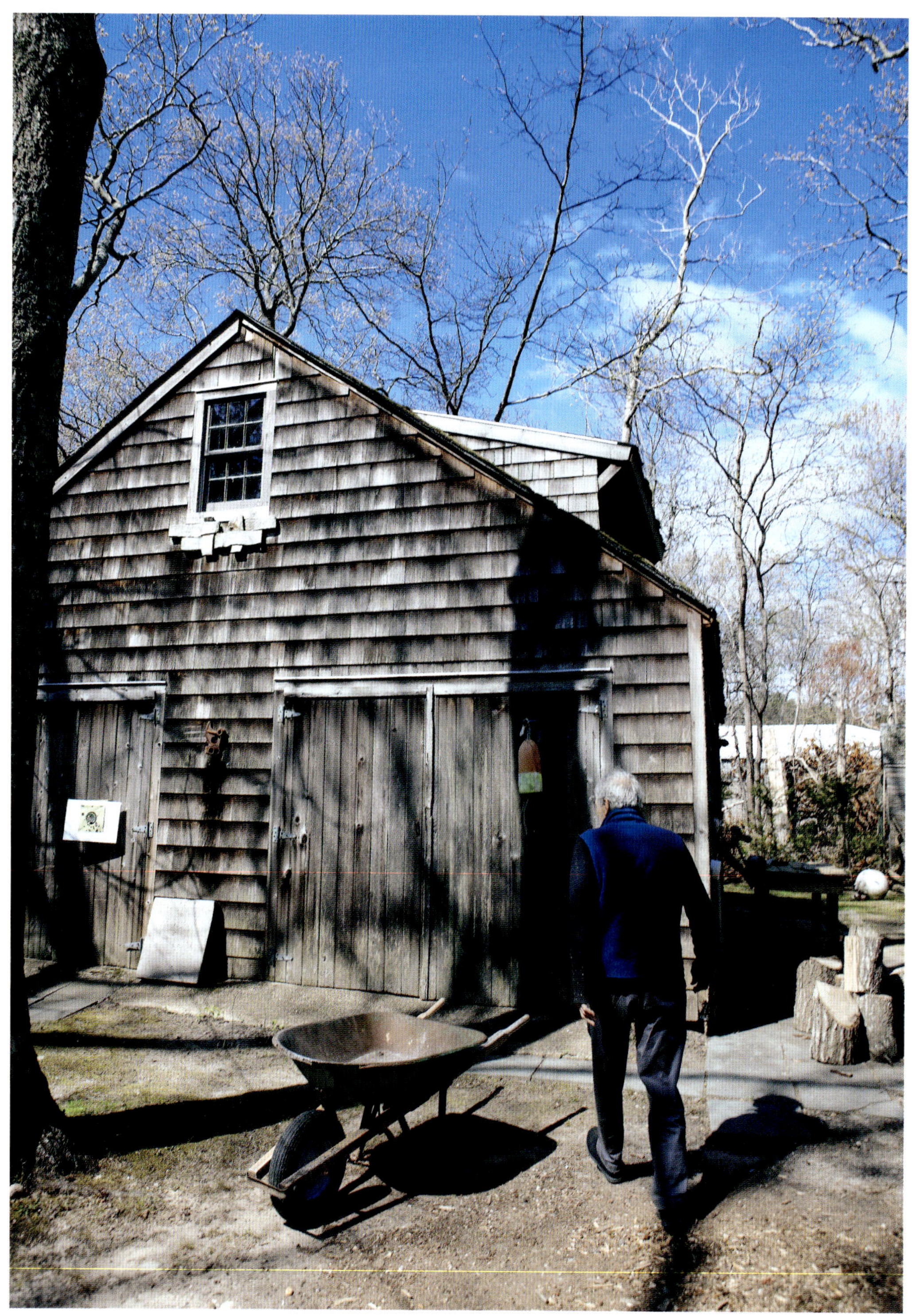

Rosenthal is known for his ultra-realistic carvings of paper objects, including books, newspapers, puzzles, nautical charts, baseball cards, and dollar bills. "I began carving paper objects because after ten years of doing architectural sculpture, I won an international contest to carve a lectern for a church in Seattle, Washington. For the bible rest, I carved an open book. Something about it really resonated with me, so I carved a few more books. Then I started doing paintings on the carved pages—and here we are." The pieces are always true to size and carved from one block of wood. "I do not do any preliminary work and try to mostly be spontaneous—in slow motion—making the piece up as I go along."

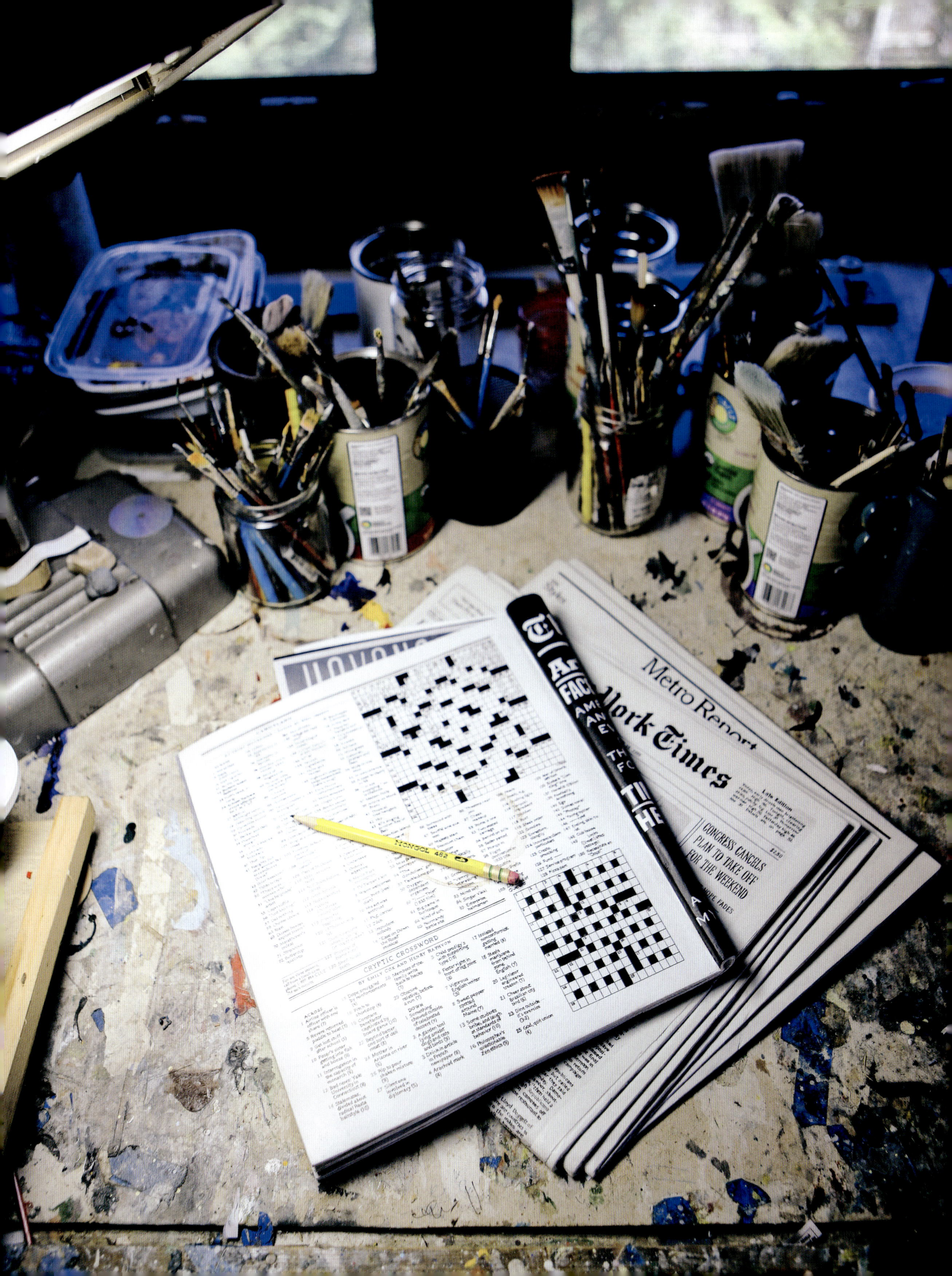
Metro Report
York Times
Late Edition
CONGRESS CANCELS
PLAN TO TAKE OFF
FOR THE WEEKEND
CRYPTIC CROSSWORD
MONGOL 482

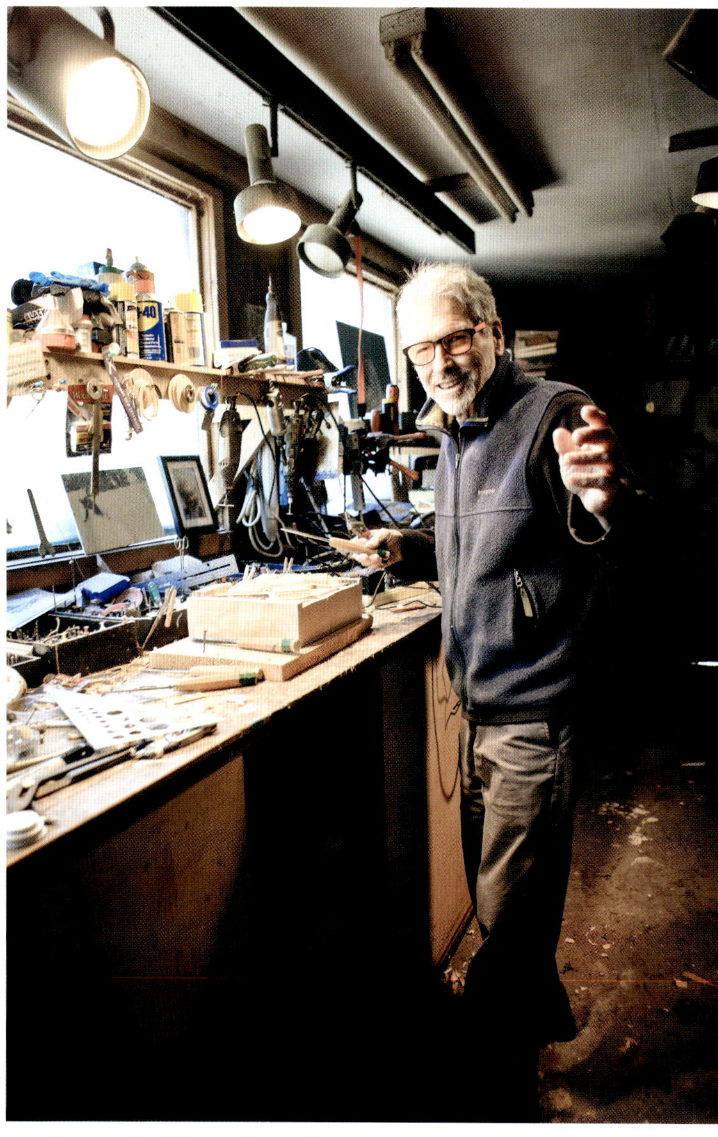

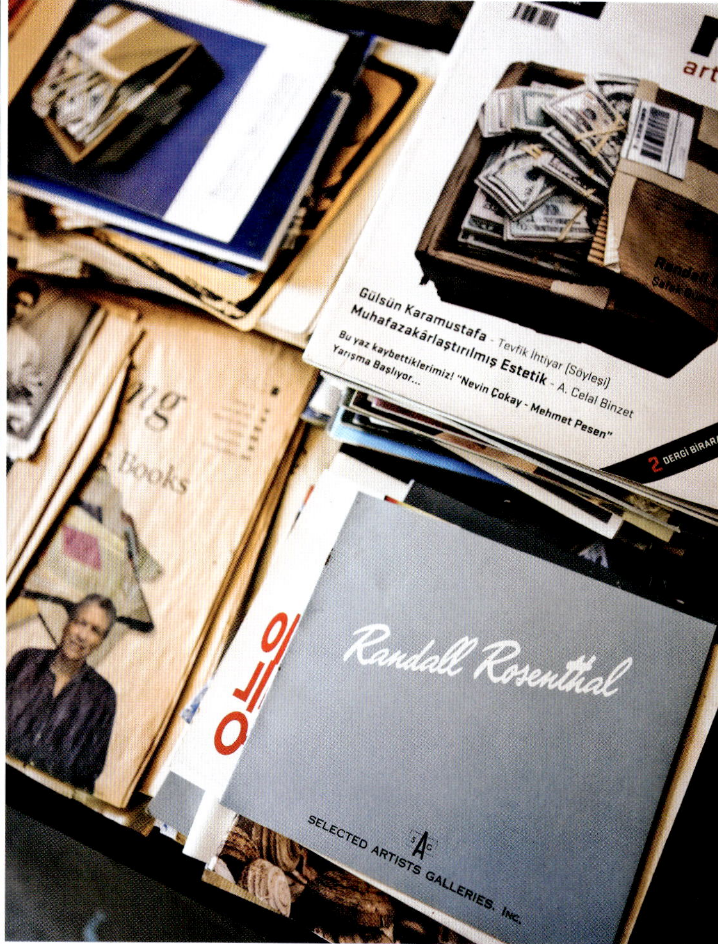

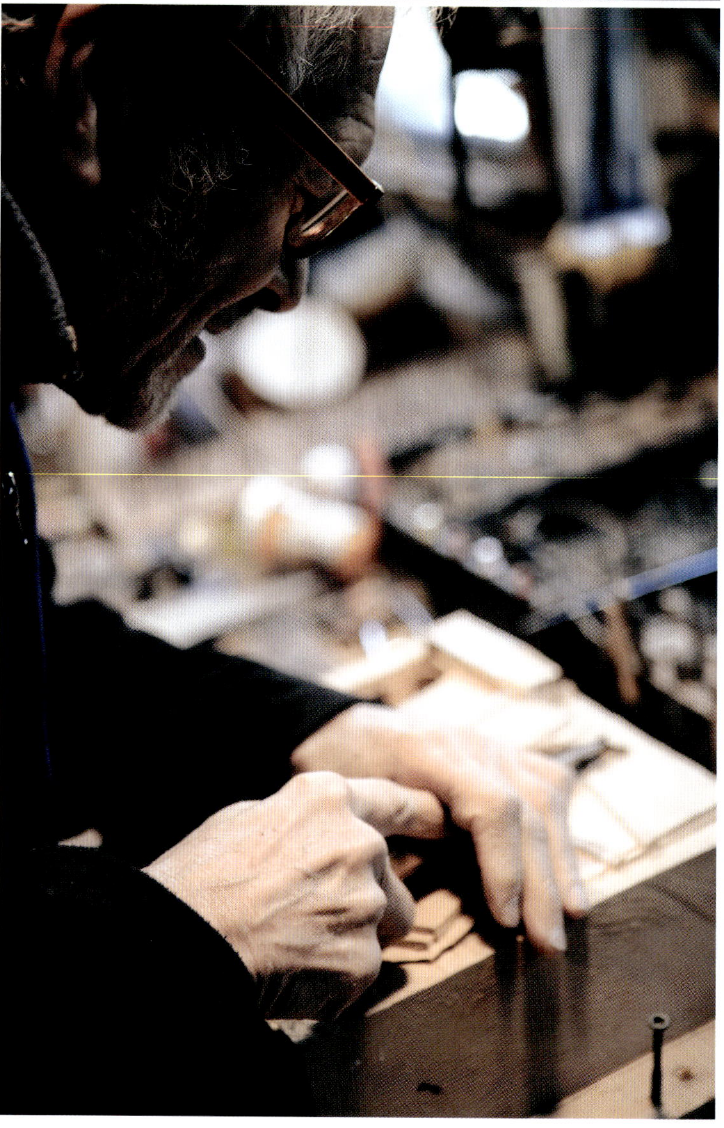

"I have traditional carving tools and prefer to do as much as possible with them. Given the choice, I will use a hand tool, but I also have an extensive collection of rotary tools and hundreds of cutting bits. I have air tools, too, but almost never use them for sculpture. I once rebuilt a classic car and a classic boat. I have lots of tools."

THIS PAGE

The artist upstairs in his two-level Springs studio. Its numerous small workspaces are scattered with carving tools (both hand and rotary), which he uses to create his startlingly realistic sculptures of everyday objects—newspapers, notepads, matchbooks—out of single blocks of wood.

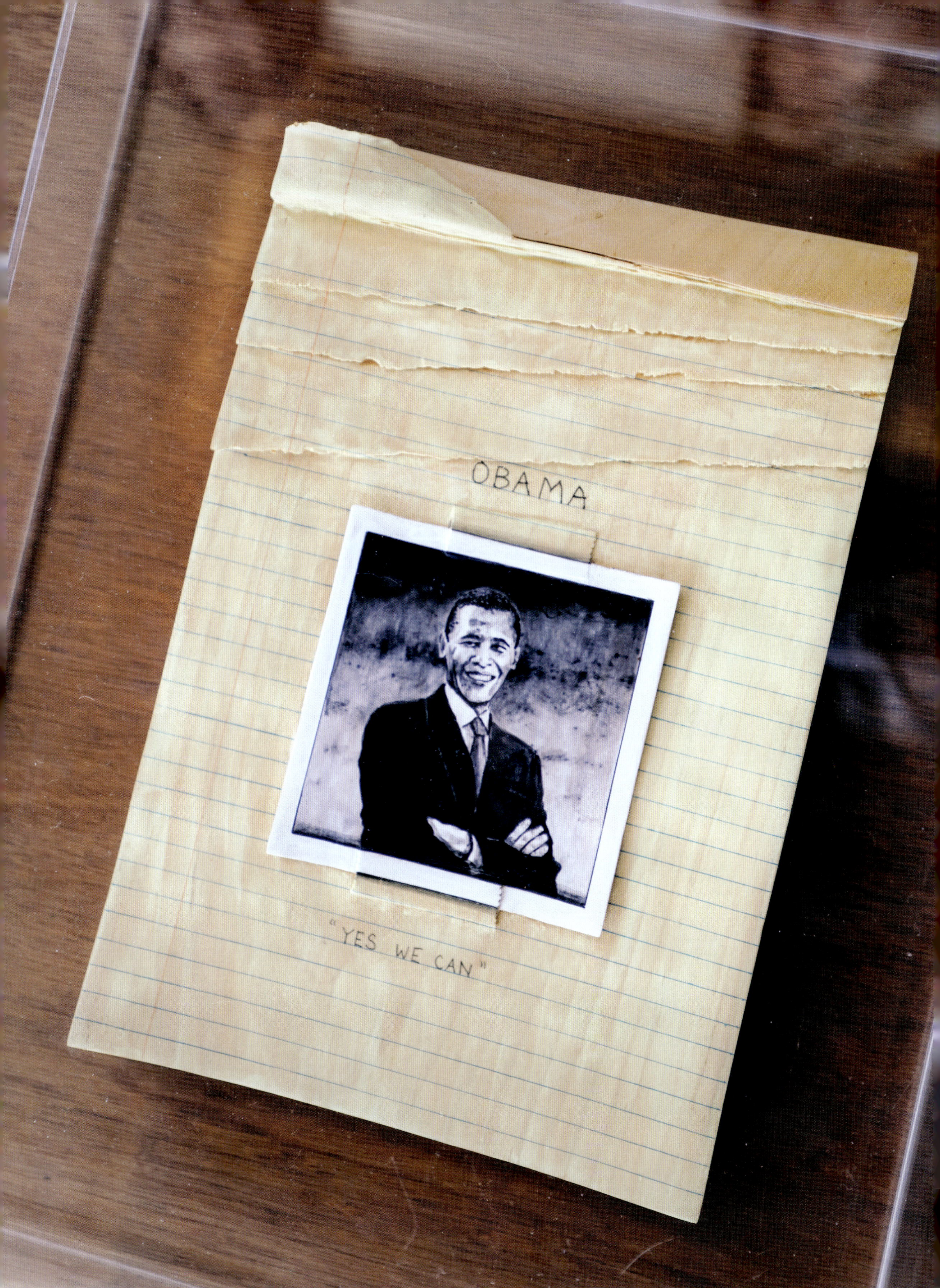
OBAMA
"YES WE CAN"

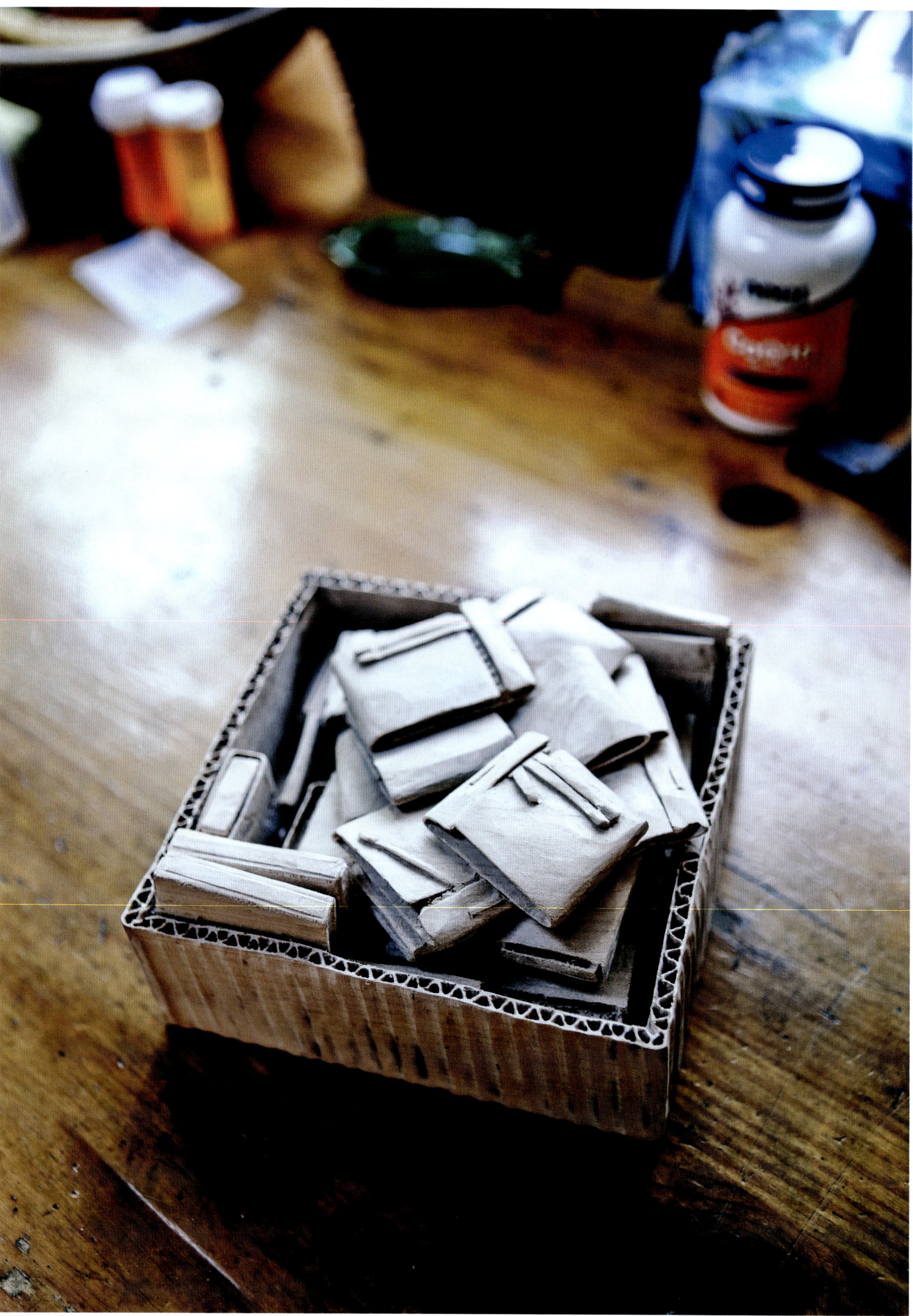

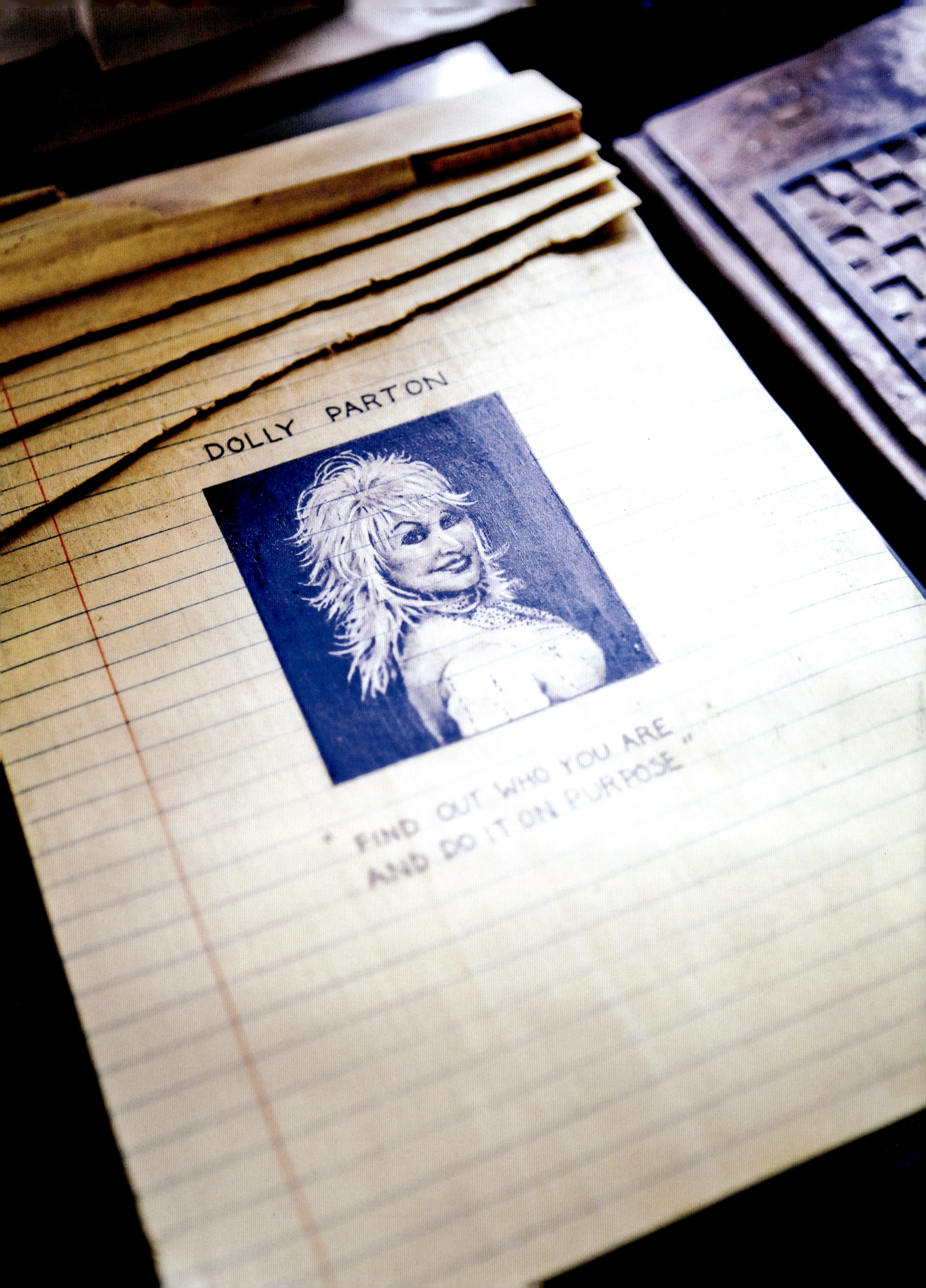
DOLLY PARTON
" FIND OUT WHO YOU ARE
AND DO IT ON PURPOSE "

I am deeply affected by landscape. I am curious about the inner life of mountains and trees, of the ocean and sand—and what lives within, what has been there before.

TONI ROSS

Born and raised in Manhattan, Ross got a BFA from Wesleyan University. When she was twenty, she met Elaine de Kooning, who became her mentor. "Elaine encouraged me to move out east. She found me a little house to rent near her house and a studio in Amagansett. She allowed me to paint portraits on an easel next to hers in her studio and invited me to live-model drawing sessions with the likes of Mercedes Matter and many other extraordinary women. After that I traveled a bit, then returned to New York to work in restaurants. In 1988, my late husband and I moved to East Hampton to run a restaurant and raise our children. The restaurant is filled with outsider art that we collected, as well as with work by contemporary local artists. We knew we'd rarely be at home, so why not have art surround us there? After some time as a pastry chef and working the front of house, I went back to focusing on my studio practice."

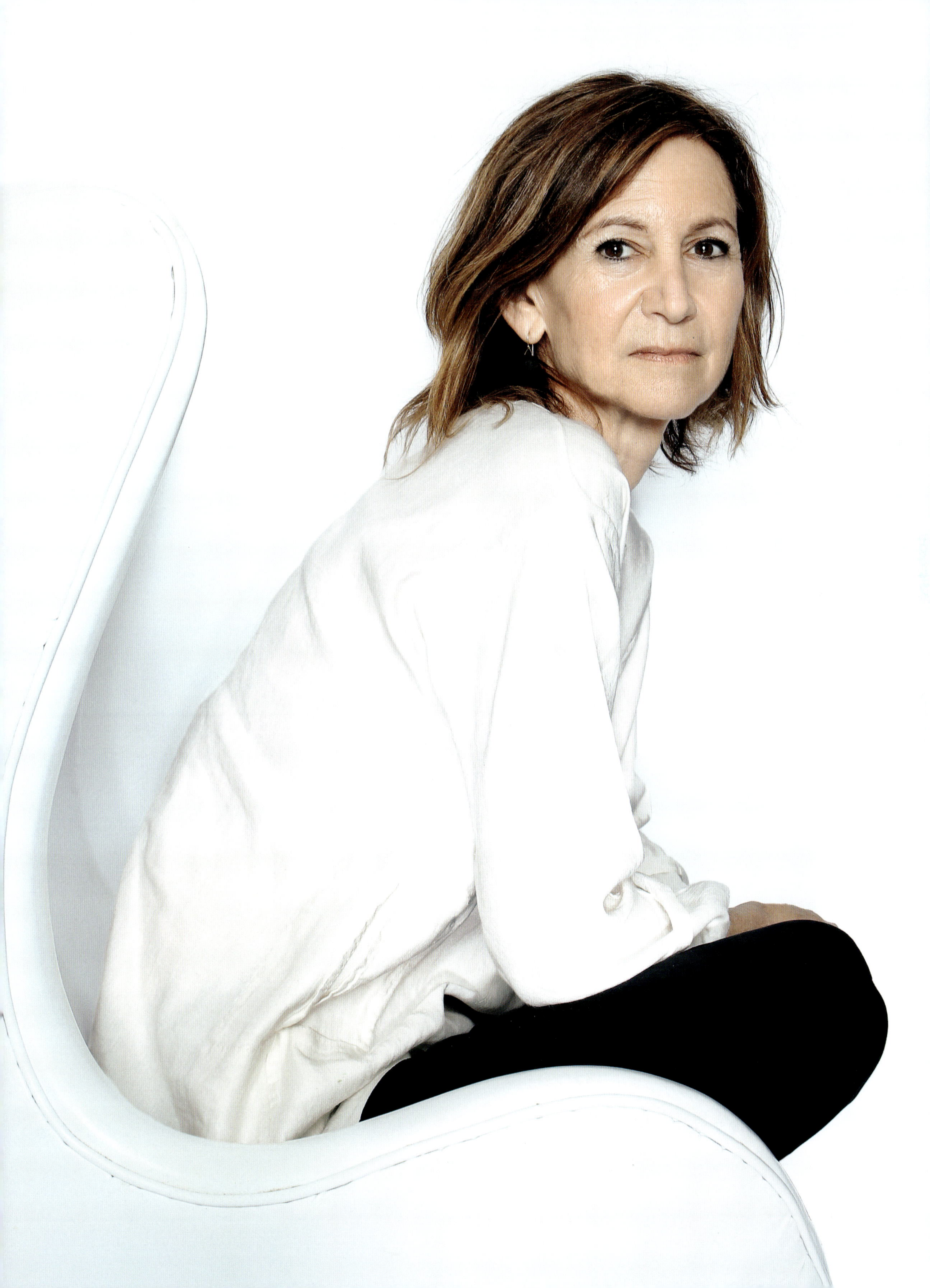

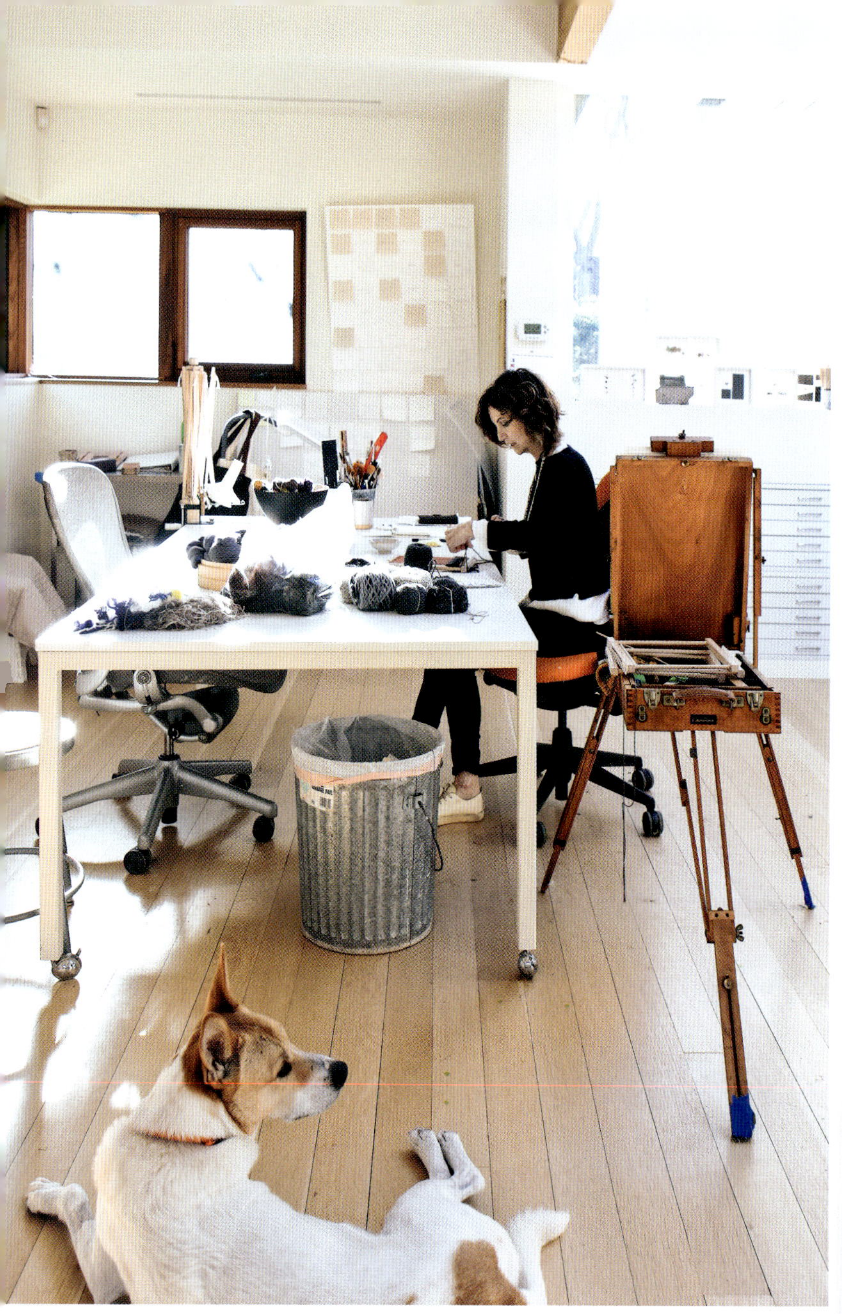

LEFT
Ross and her dog, George, a thirteen-year-old rescue, in her Wainscott studio, which is in walking distance of the ocean. As a sculptor and textile artist, she works in a range of mediums, including clay, wool, and cloth.

BELOW
Ross weaves on small looms, which she often packs in her hand luggage when she travels, so she can work on the plane.

Ross is a sculptor and multimedia artist. "I have always been attracted to natural, time-honored materials such as clay, cloth, wool, straw, and twine. Clay presents its own set of challenges, in terms of time and attention, firing mishaps—sometimes creating happy accidents—and storage. Most recently I've been working in textiles, creating several series of weavings. Textiles allow me the freedom to travel, to leave the work and pick it up another time. My main tools are weaving needles, my fingers, small lap looms, and my little fold-up scissors, which get packed away in my hand luggage on airplanes. I get quite a bit of work done on long flights."

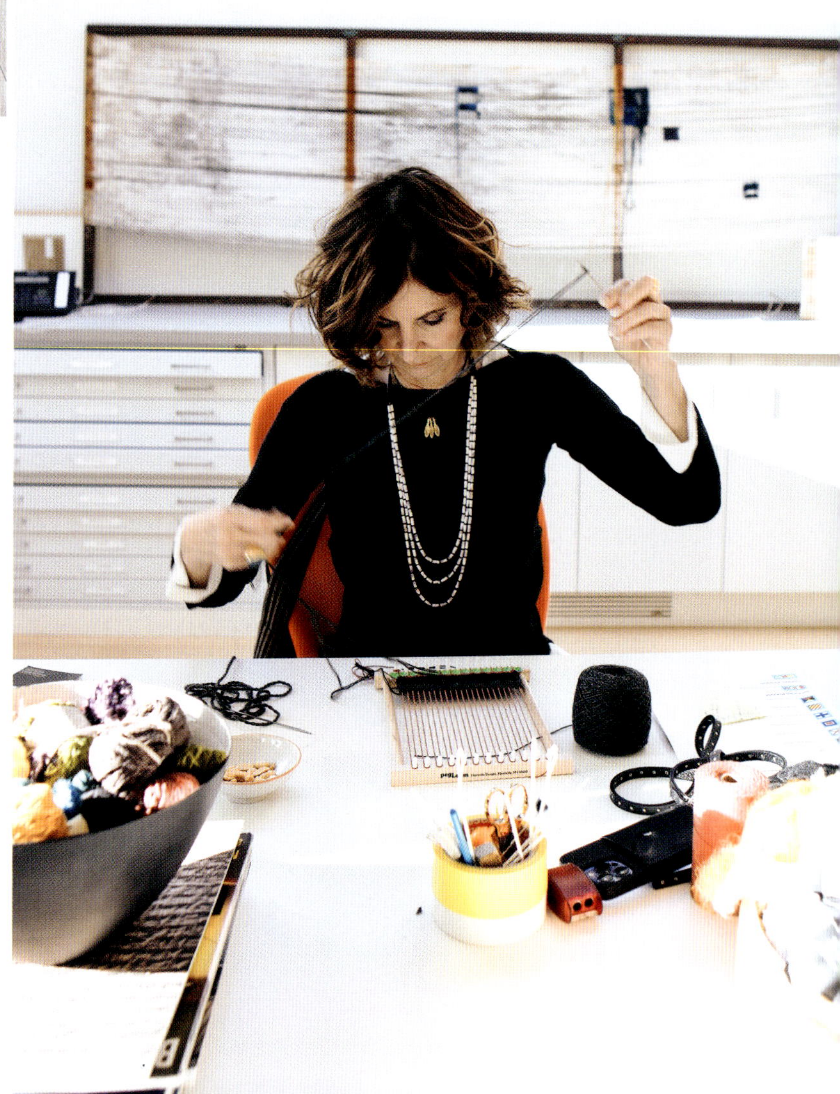

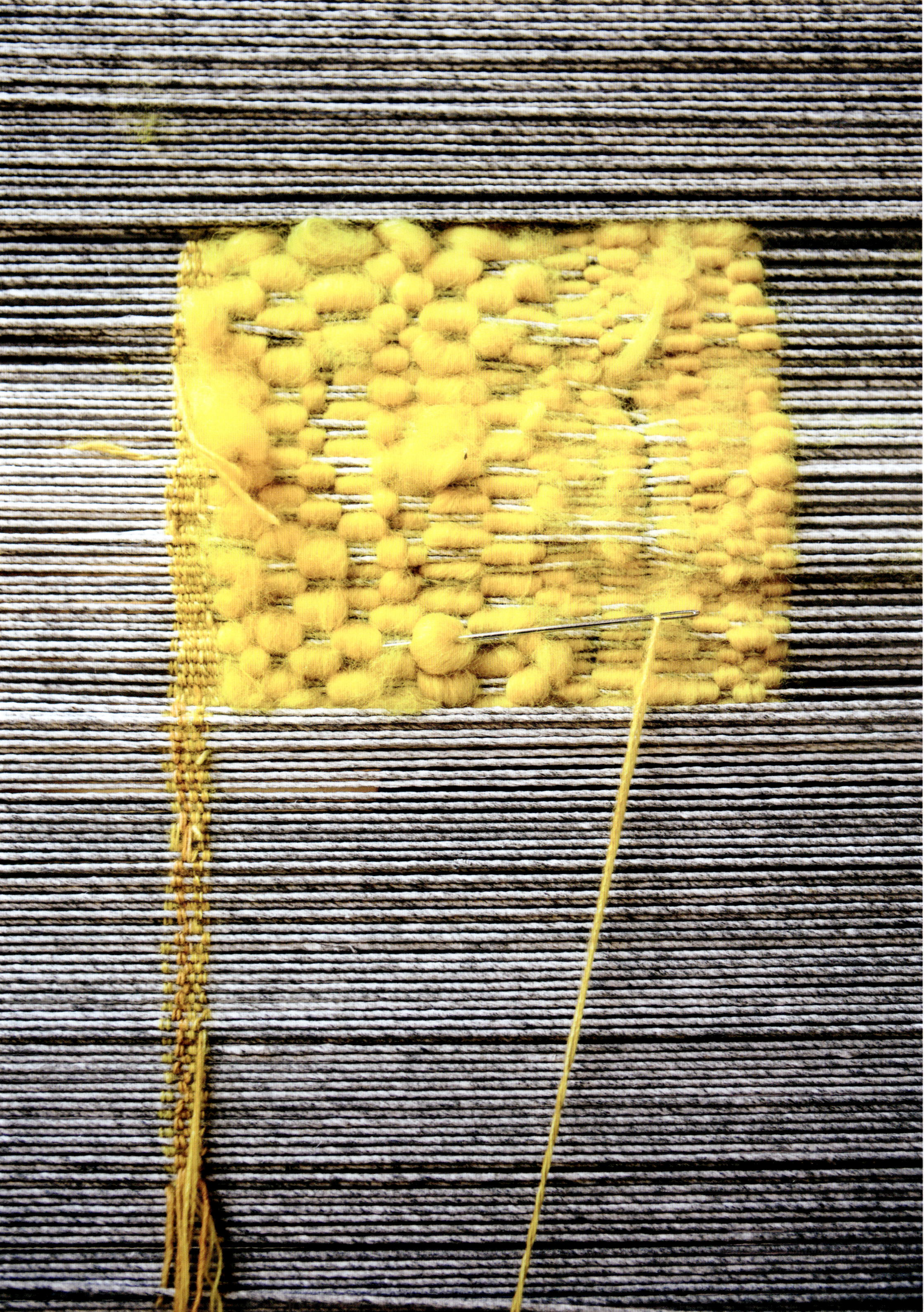

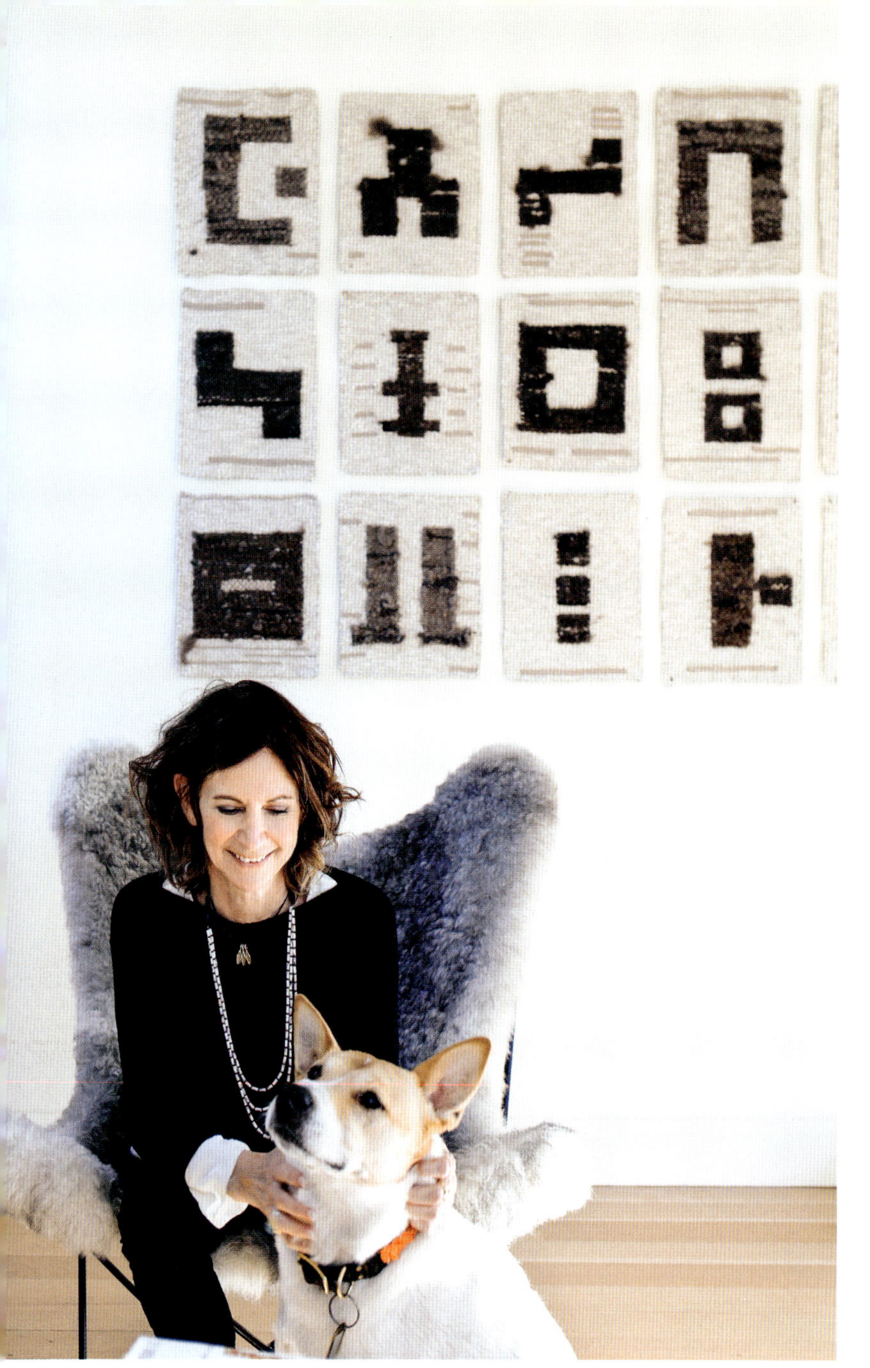

"I am inspired by so many things, people, and places. It could be a passage or a single line in a book, a piece of poetry, a landscape, a social or political challenge, Morandi, Cézanne, Olga de Amaral, Cycladic art, archaeological finds, alphabets, blackboards, or the passage of time—its effects on surfaces and its scarring." What inspires her to keep creating? "It's my meditation, my search for truths, though there are rarely answers. It's sometimes my only mode of expression, my visceral response to the world around me. Tuning out the noise of the universe."

LEFT

The artist's diverse inspirations, ranging from the landscape to poetry, archaeological finds, and alphabets, are expressed in mostly abstract works made from earthy, natural materials.

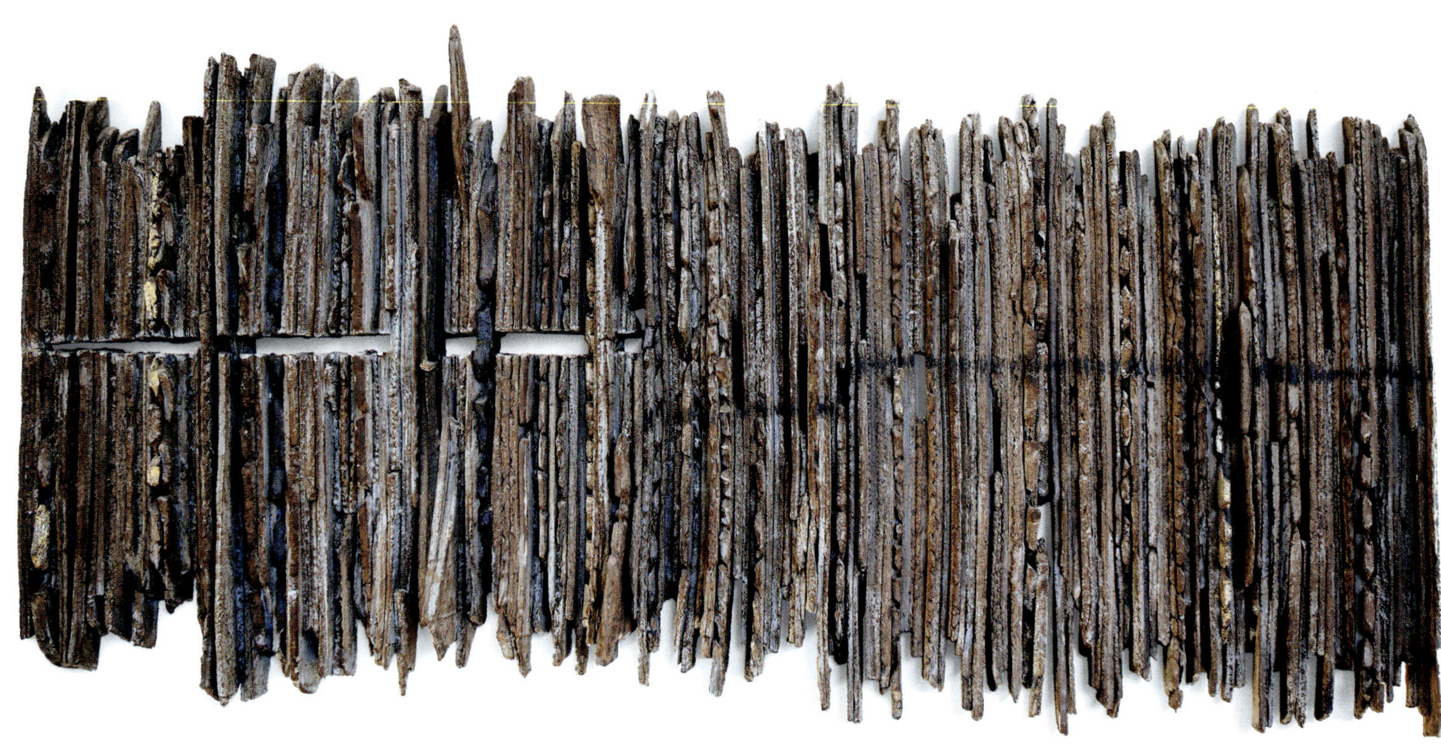

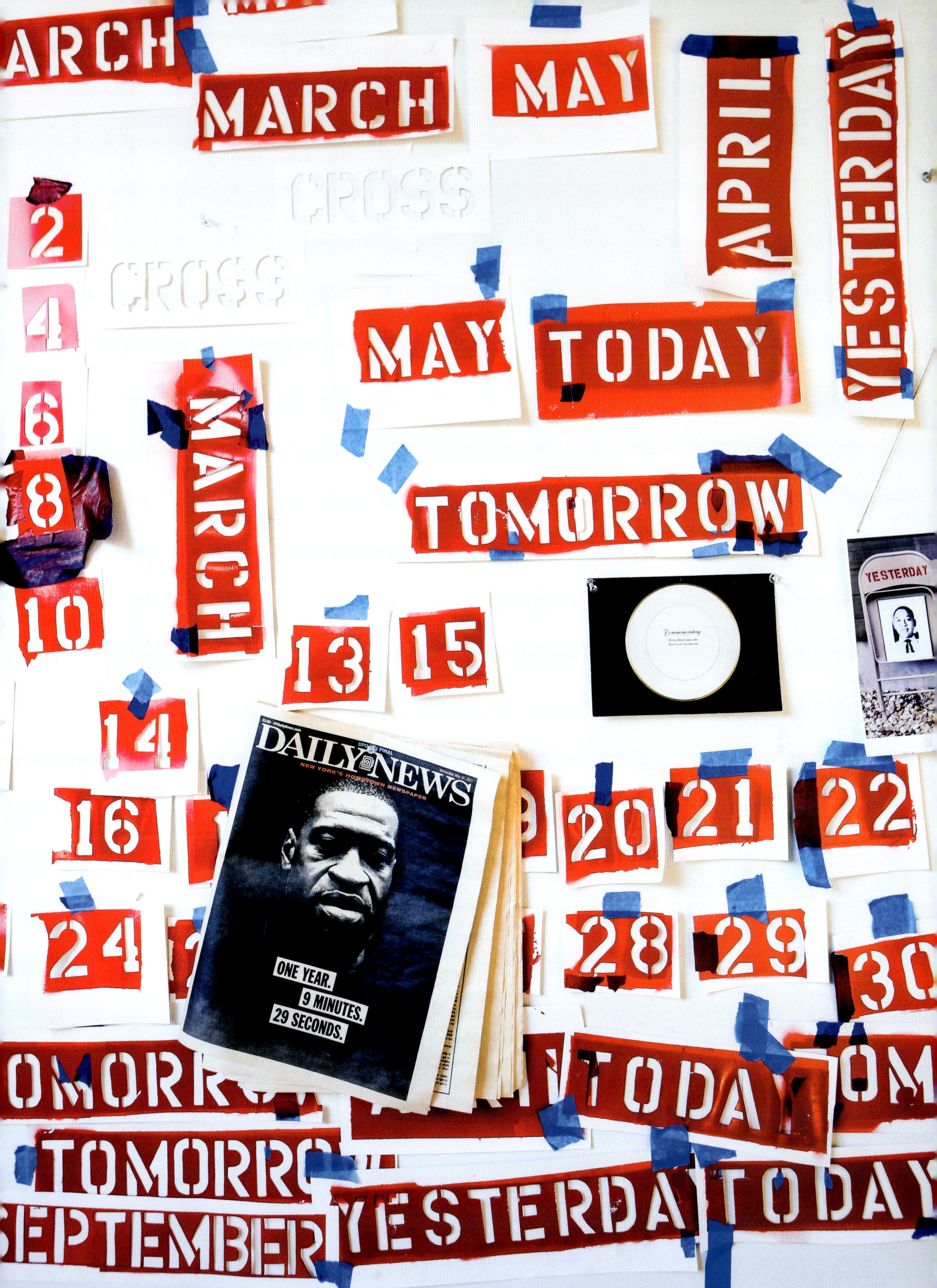

MARCH
MAY
APRIL
YESTERDAY
CROSS
2
CROSS
4
MAY
TODAY
6
MARCH
8
TOMORROW
10
YESTERDAY
13
15
14
DAILY NEWS
NEW YORK'S HOMETOWN NEWSPAPER
16
20
21
22
ONE YEAR.
9 MINUTES.
29 SECONDS.
24
28
29
TODAY
TODAY

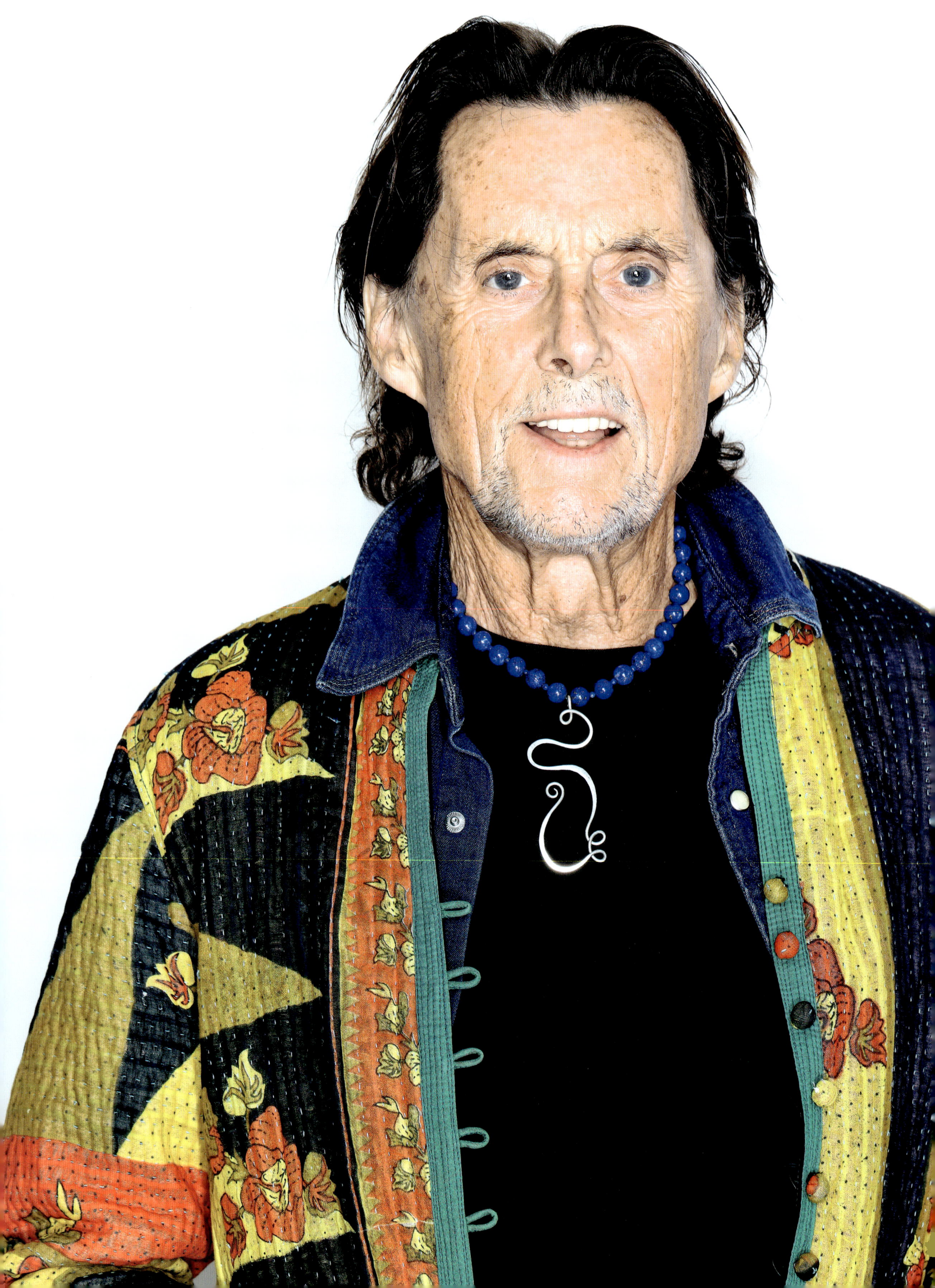

I start each work reflecting on what is moving through me. Colors seem to emerge first—often ultramarine blue and gold, deep purple, orange, and copper. As elements arise and the dance spontaneously begins, the painting takes form.

WILL RYAN

Ryan grew up in New Jersey, right across the Hudson River from Midtown Manhattan. "For my tenth birthday, my parents gave me the Jon Gnagy "Learn to Draw" kit. It was a fantastic kit that had a drawing pad, charcoal, pencils, a kneaded eraser, and a book with examples and instructions. Once I started drawing, I knew I wanted to become an artist." After high school, Ryan got a job working as an apprentice in an illustration and design studio in Manhattan while attending the School of Visual Arts at night. "At that time, illustration was waning, and photography became the medium for advertising, book covers, and movie posters, so I shifted my studies to photography and opened a photo studio in Greenwich Village."

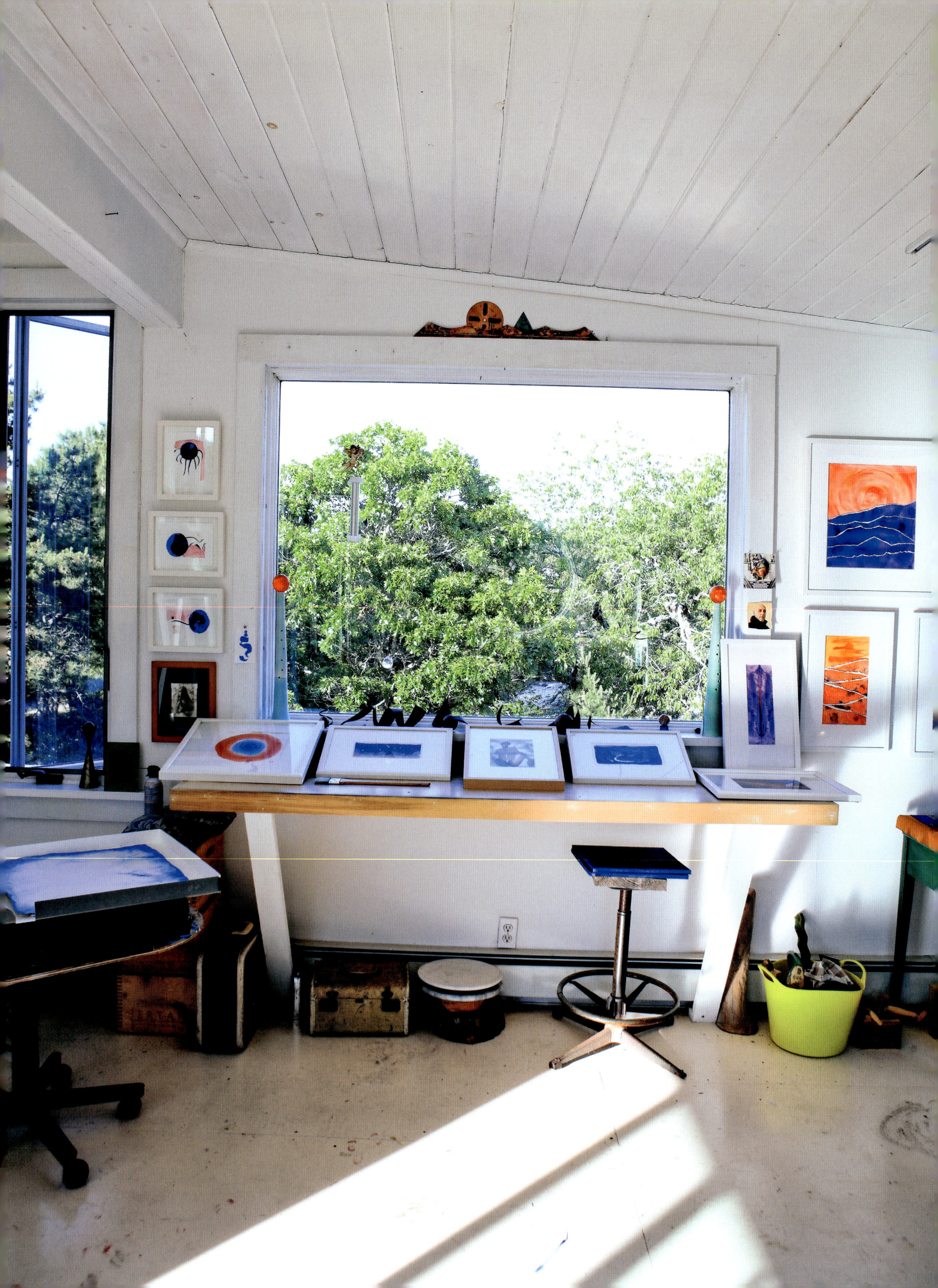

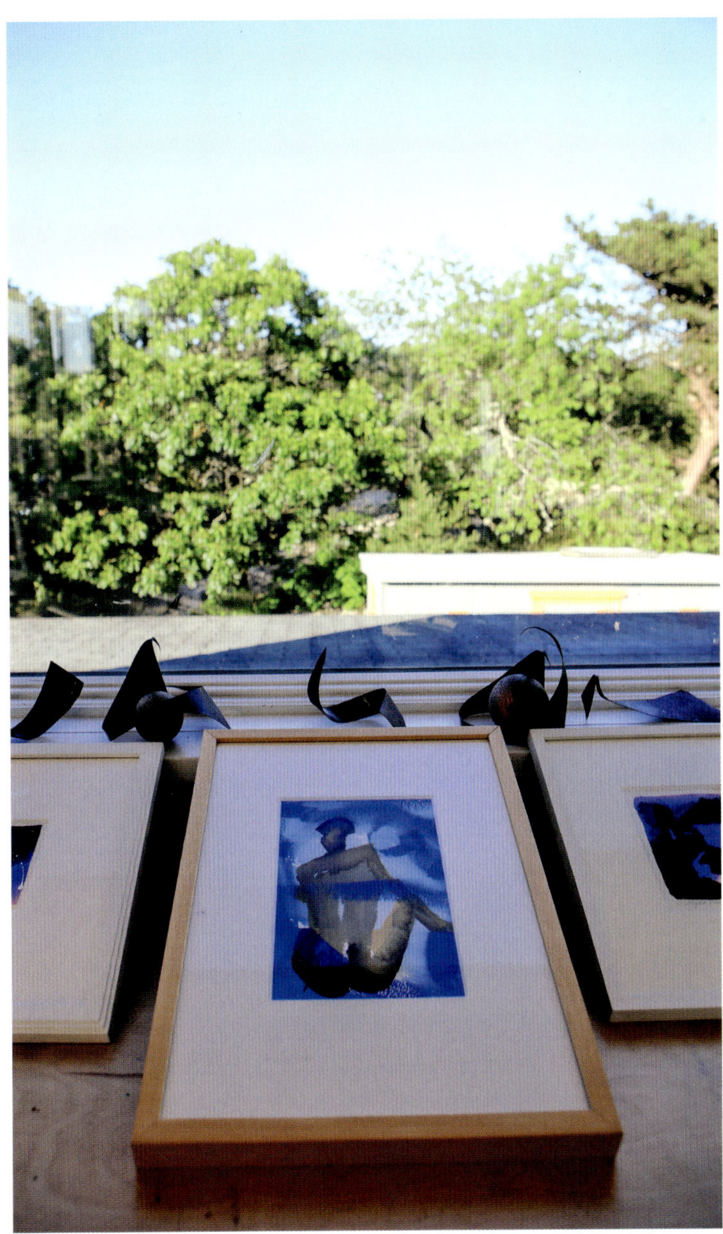

In the summer of 1983, Ryan was invited by a friend who'd rented a house in Amagansett to visit for the weekend. "I fell in love with the light and the sea." After renting for the next few summers, he bought his house and studio on Lazy Point and that first summer taught photography at the Art Barge. "Meeting [cofounder] Mabel D'Amico was life-changing. She was a true artist, and she encouraged me to start making art for myself again. My first pieces incorporated photos, copper, found objects, and pigment. It was freeing to not have any rules, and I transitioned from photography to being a full-time artist." Ryan now splits his time between Amagansett and Maui. "The dynamic landscape there, with the waterfalls, volcanoes, rain forests, and the bluest of seas, also informs my work in a big way."

OPPOSITE

To get to his light-filled, treetop atelier, which he calls his "roost," Ryan climbs a circular staircase from his downstairs living space.

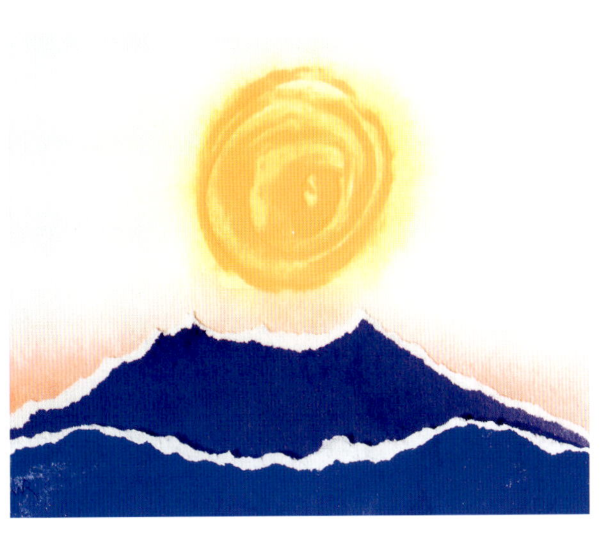

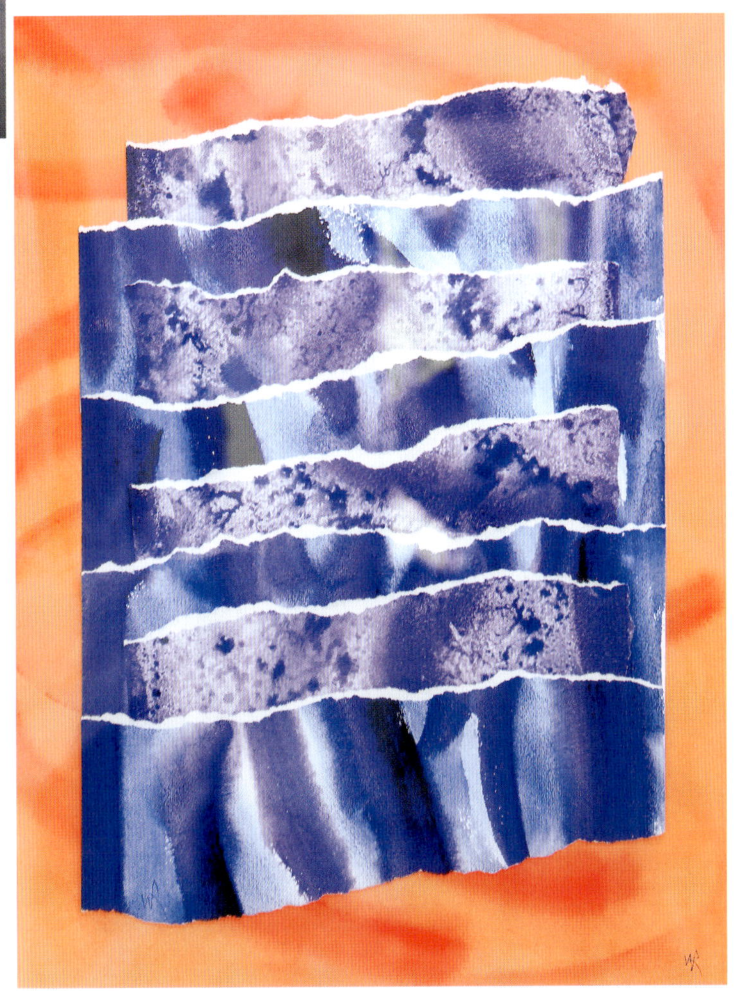

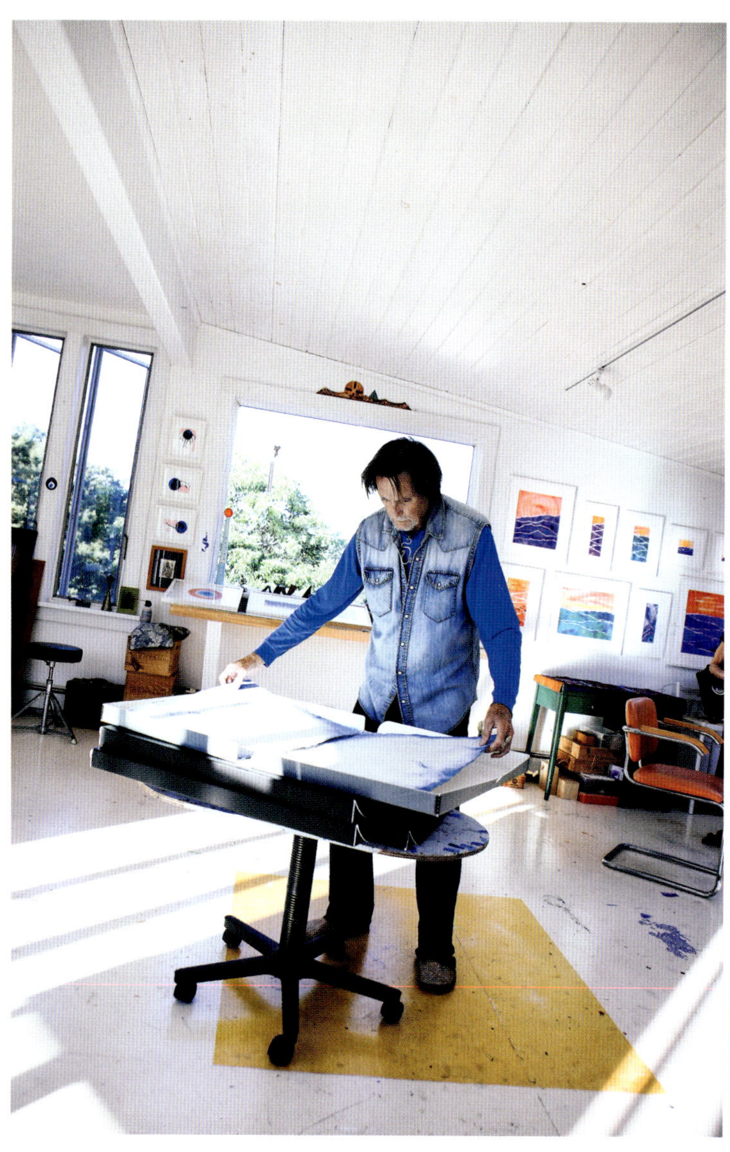

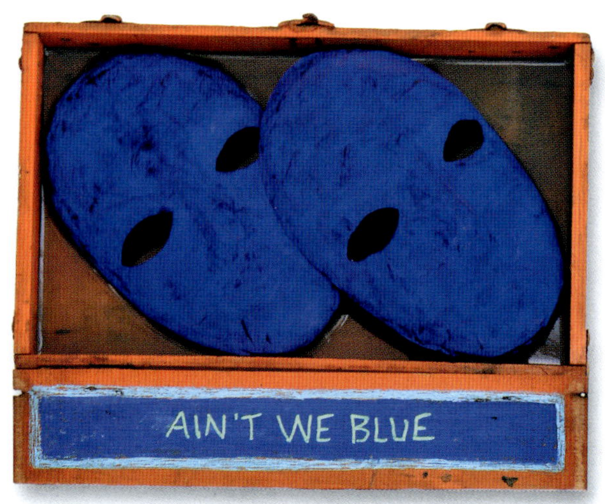

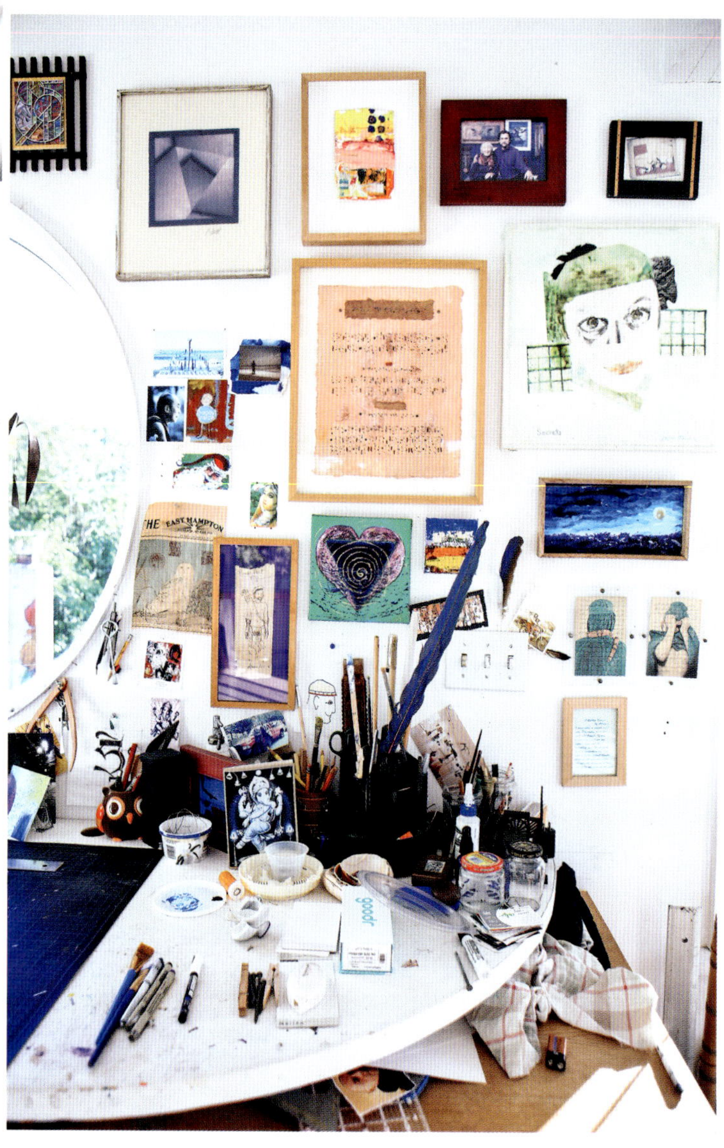

ABOVE LEFT

Acrylic and watercolor are Ryan's main mediums, though he also makes hand-hammered silver jewelry, which he sells, gives to friends, and wears himself.

RIGHT

Ryan's collection of art (his own and that of friends) ranges from nature-inspired to abstract, spiritual to witty.

OPPOSITE

In addition to making art and jewelry, Ryan meditates, writes poetry, and plays the flute.

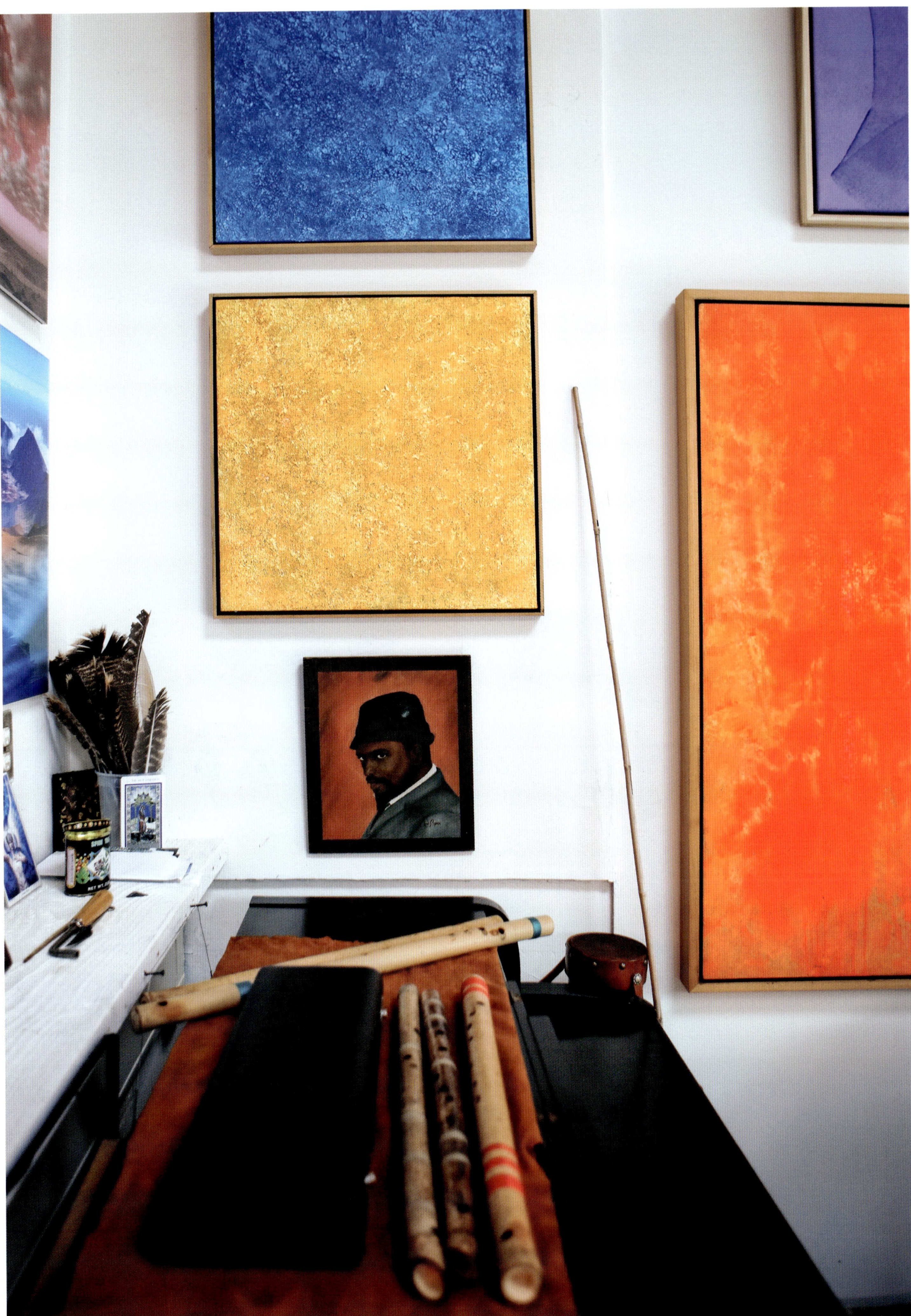

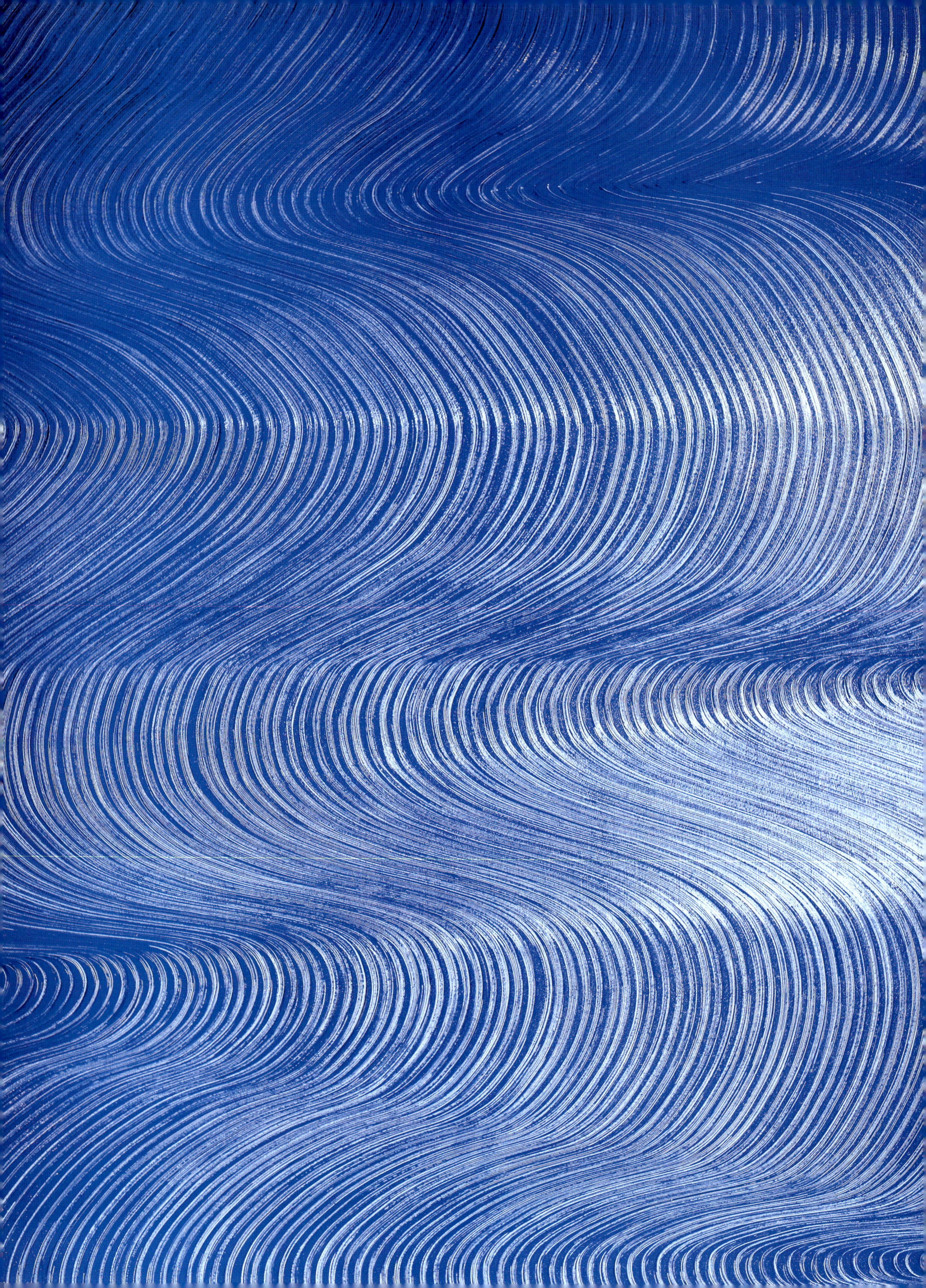

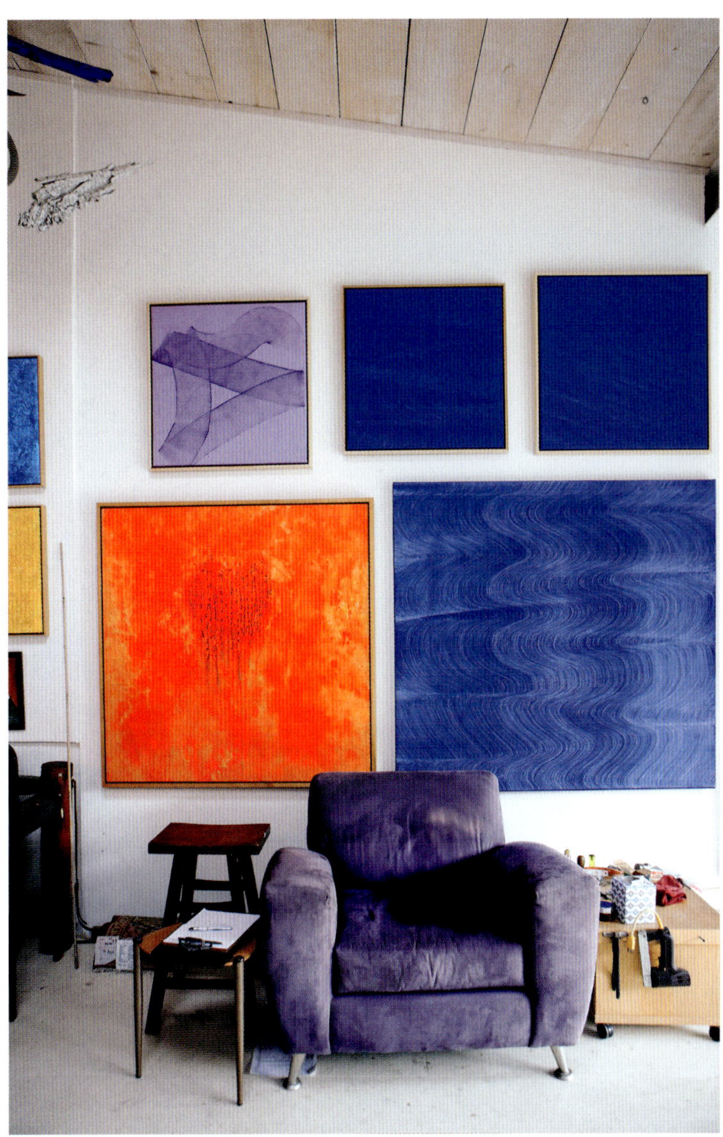

"My daily work schedule starts with a morning meditation. I have been doing transcendental meditation since 1975. I do some yoga, then it's off to the studio, coffee in hand; I turn on some music and go to work. The studio is my sanctuary. Actually, I have two in my Amagansett home. Upstairs is my roost, overlooking the dunes with lots of light flooding in. The downstairs studio has sliding glass doors that allow me to work larger, both inside and outside. I used to work in oil, but because of the fumes I now mainly use slow-drying acrylic. I also do watercolor and make hand-hammered silver jewelry. And there is always a flute lying around in the studio for me to pick up and play."

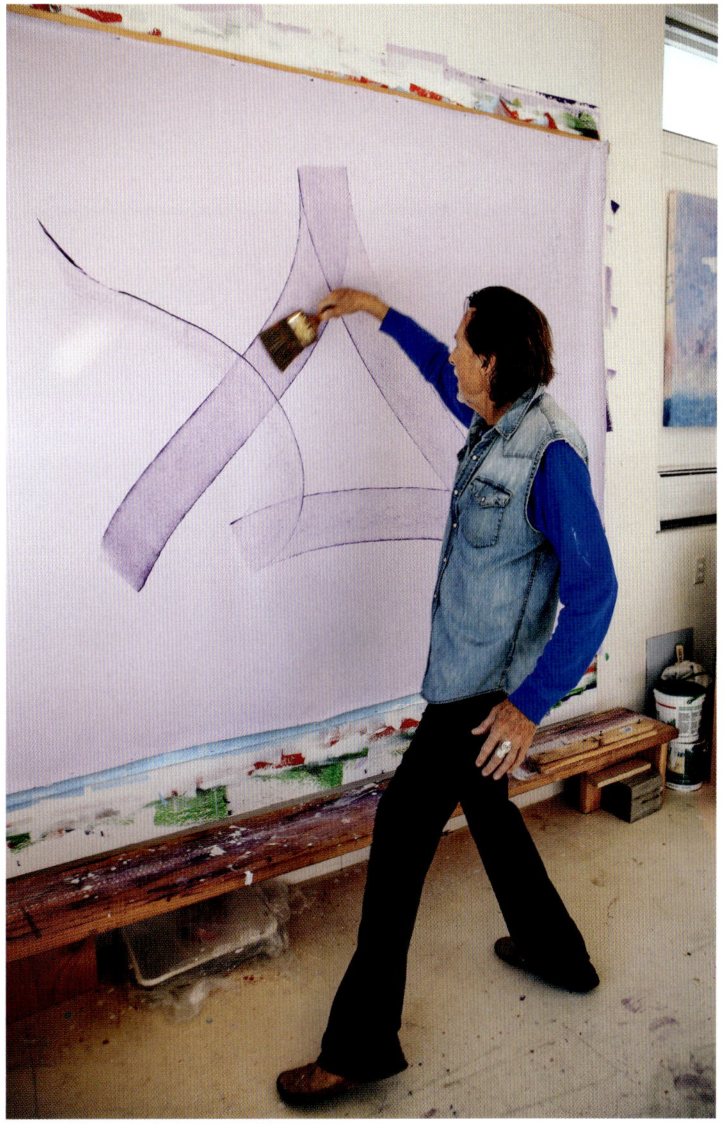

ABOVE

Bright, upbeat colors play a key role in Ryan's painting—especially ocean blues, which makes sense, given that he spends half the year here, half in Hawaii.

RIGHT

Ryan also has a large downstairs studio with sliding glass doors, so that he can work larger, both indoors and out.

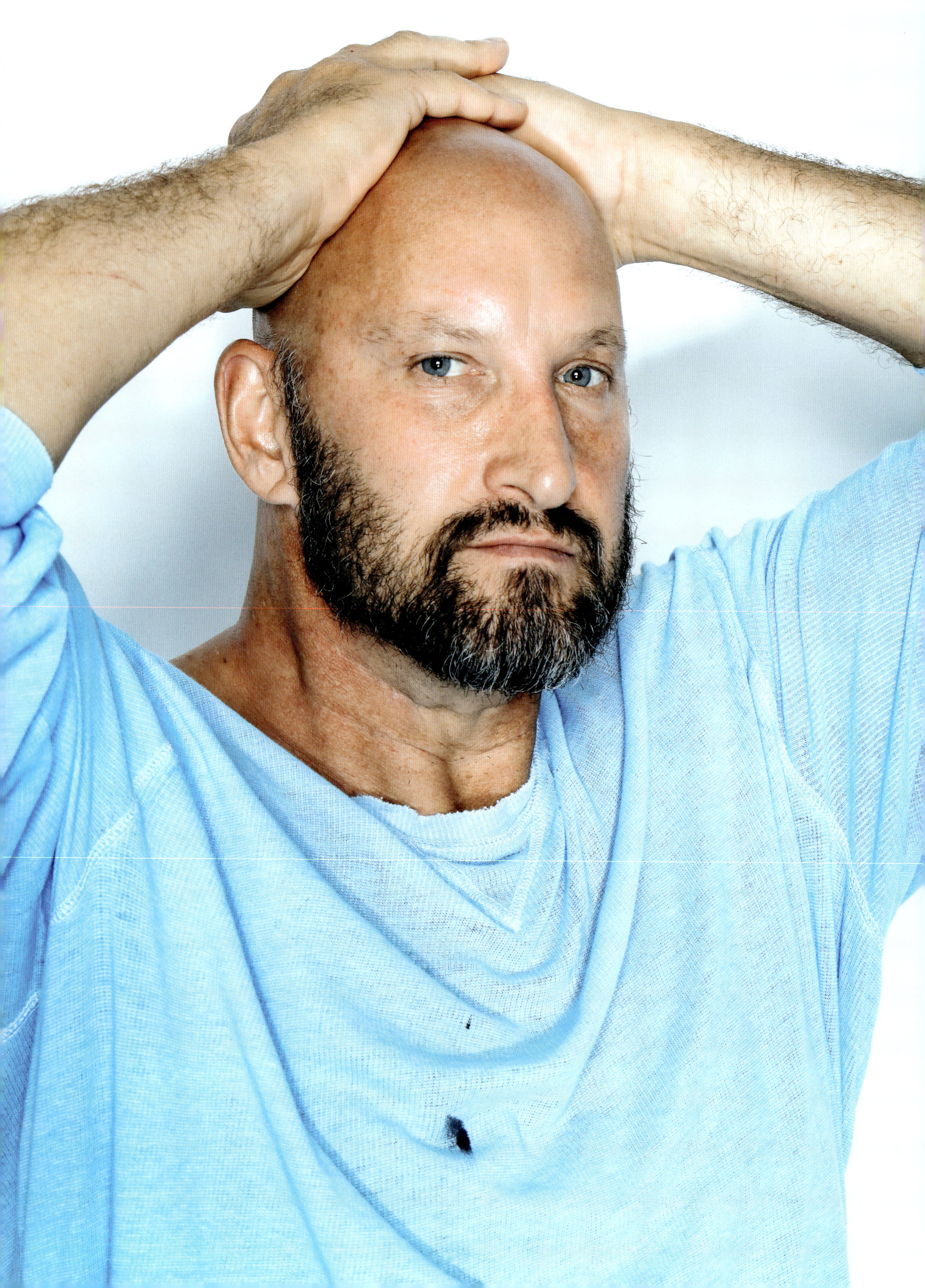

If you arrive here with integrity and character and something to offer, the community pulls you in. If you're good at what you do, there is an audience here for you. An intellectual one. A sophisticated one. A loyal one.

MATTHEW SATZ

Born in Brooklyn, Satz grew up in Huntington, Long Island. "I would come out to the East End on rare occasions with family or friends. The ocean had always been a draw, the mom-and-pop shops in those days were unique, and potato fields seemed to separate the small towns from one another and from the beach. My dad would race down the long stretches of empty asphalt blaring the Doobie Brothers. I retain vivid recollections of the sounds and sights and smells of the sea, and always felt a sense of familiarity here."

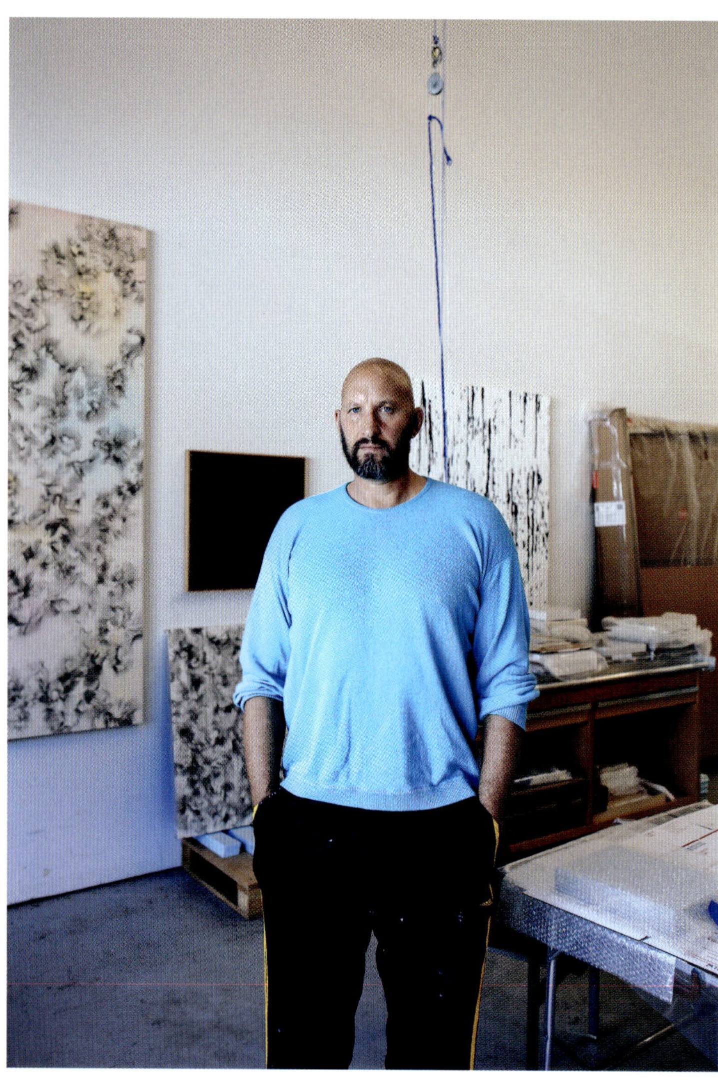

LEFT

Satz's studio is located in an industrial space in East Hampton. He chose to live here to be near the ocean and for the solitude, which enables him to work without distractions.

BELOW

The artist works in series—each a creative exploration of a method—from his sensual *Smoke* paintings to abstract pieces with flypaper, tar-and-feather, or rolled linen strands hanging from or dripping below the canvas.

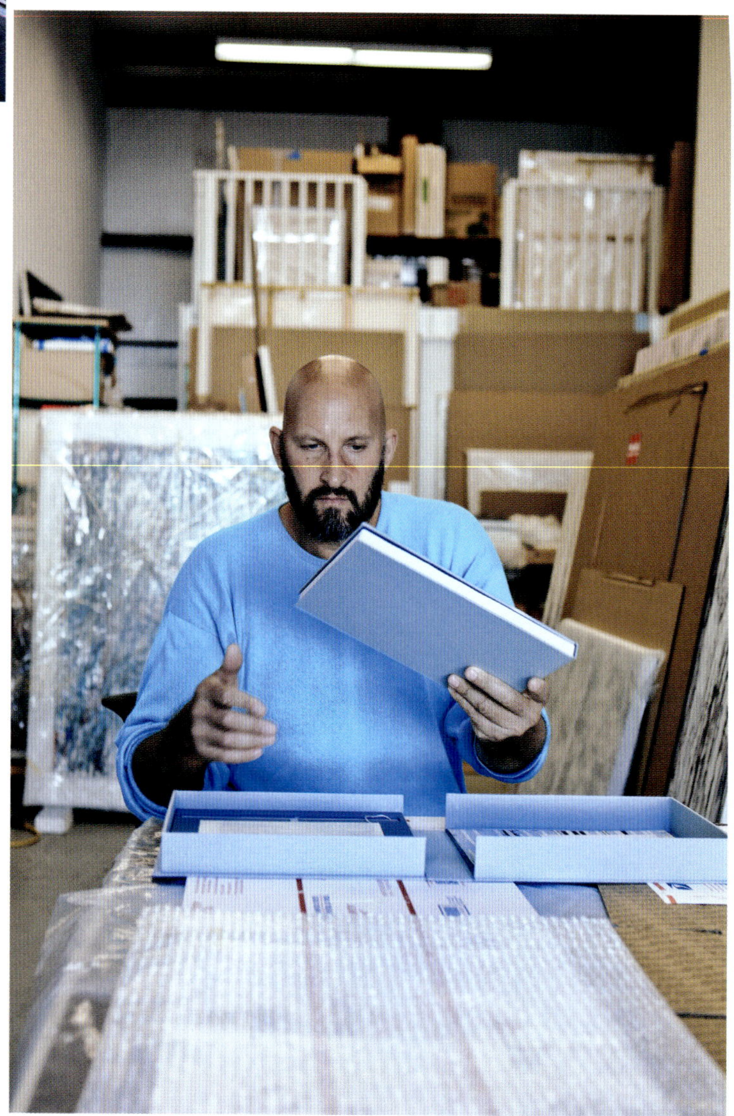

In 1994, a year after earning his degree in fine arts at Brandeis University, Satz came to the East End to take the Jimmy Ernst Artists Alliance studio tour. "I met Terry Elkins, a painter from Texas. He shared his work and the history of his home and studio, an amazing potato barn on the railroad tracks in Sagaponack. With his Southern charm and honesty, he gave me the confidence and mental support to move out east, as I knew no one here at the time." Not long thereafter, Satz set up a studio in East Hampton. "If I was going to face hardship and struggle, I was determined to do it near the beach."

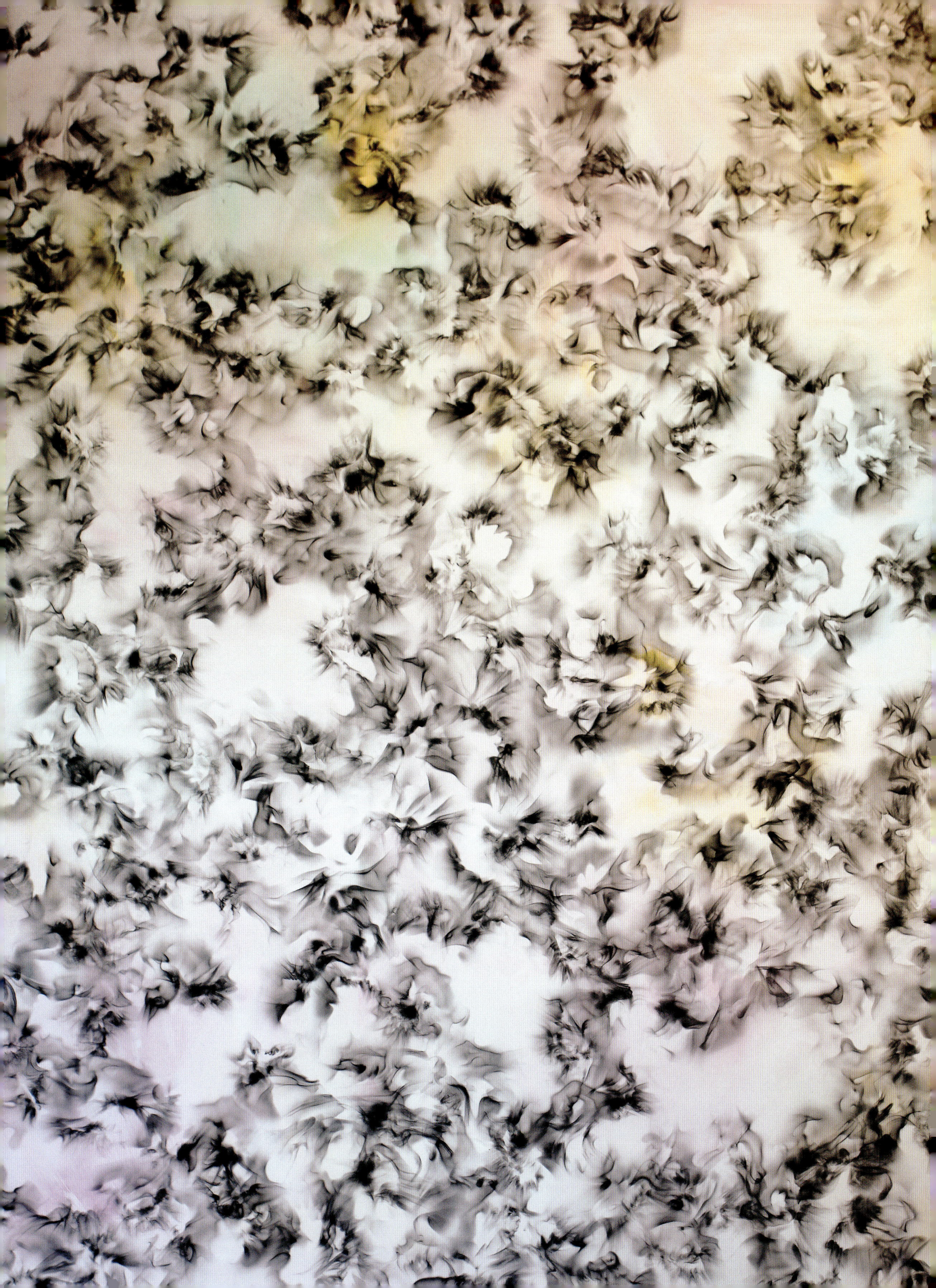

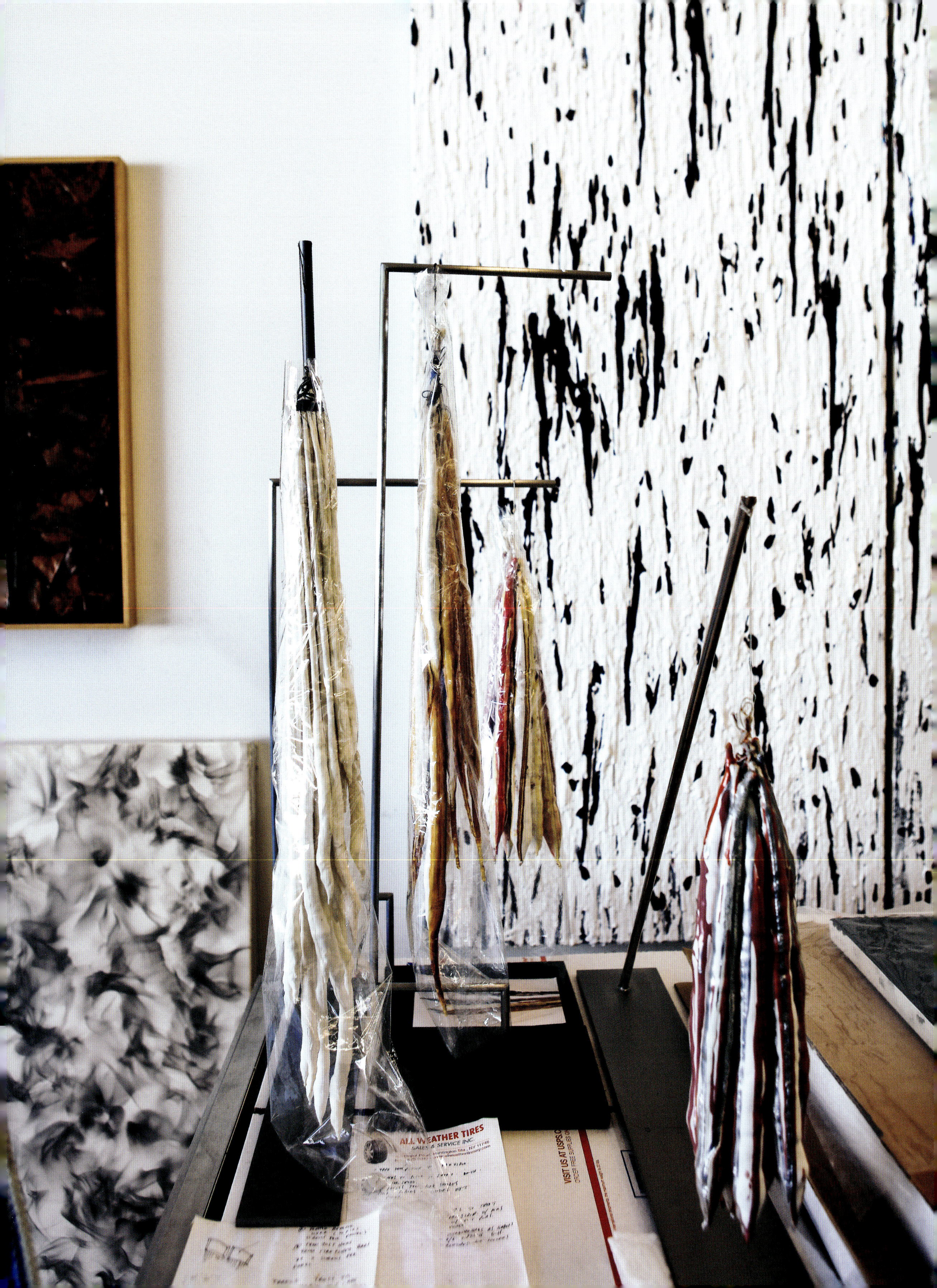
ALL WEATHER TIRES
SALES & SERVICE INC.

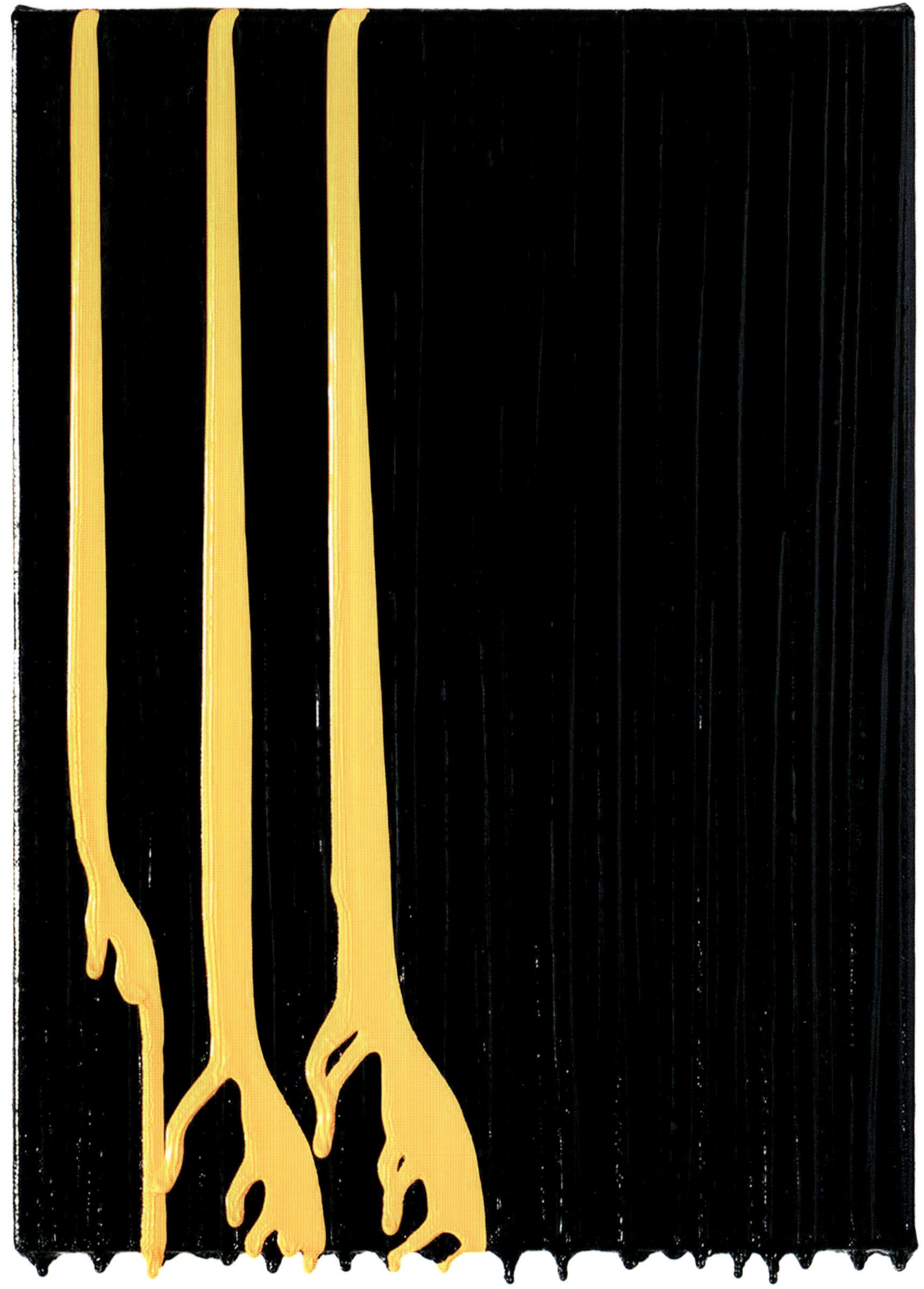

"My interests lie in engaging in an art-historical dialogue in which I'm able to present intelligent, if not elegant, solutions to problems. I'm interested in pioneering and building upon a lineage of artists who have pursued solutions to age-old issues. There are still niches and voids in this specific history, and it is within these parameters that I am determined to function effectively—to leave a mark, a signature. I aim to make work in which concept dictates process, and the end result determines the aesthetic."

When I began working from my collection of found stones, my art changed dramatically, shifting from a reverence for Culture and Nature to a connection with Paleolithic standing stones.

NED SMYTH

Brought up in New Jersey and Italy, Smyth went to Kenyon College in Ohio, where he studied art before moving to New York City in 1971. He hadn't thought much about visiting the East End, but when he finally came to the Hamptons in the early 1990s, he went to Gibson Beach in Sagaponack and ran into a lot of artists he'd already met in the city. In 1994, he moved to Sag Harbor and a few years later built a large studio on Shelter Island to accommodate his large-scale public commissions. "When I moved my storage there, I discovered a number of milk crates filled with stones. I had no memory of collecting them, but they were amazing shapes, and I started walking the beaches to collect more."

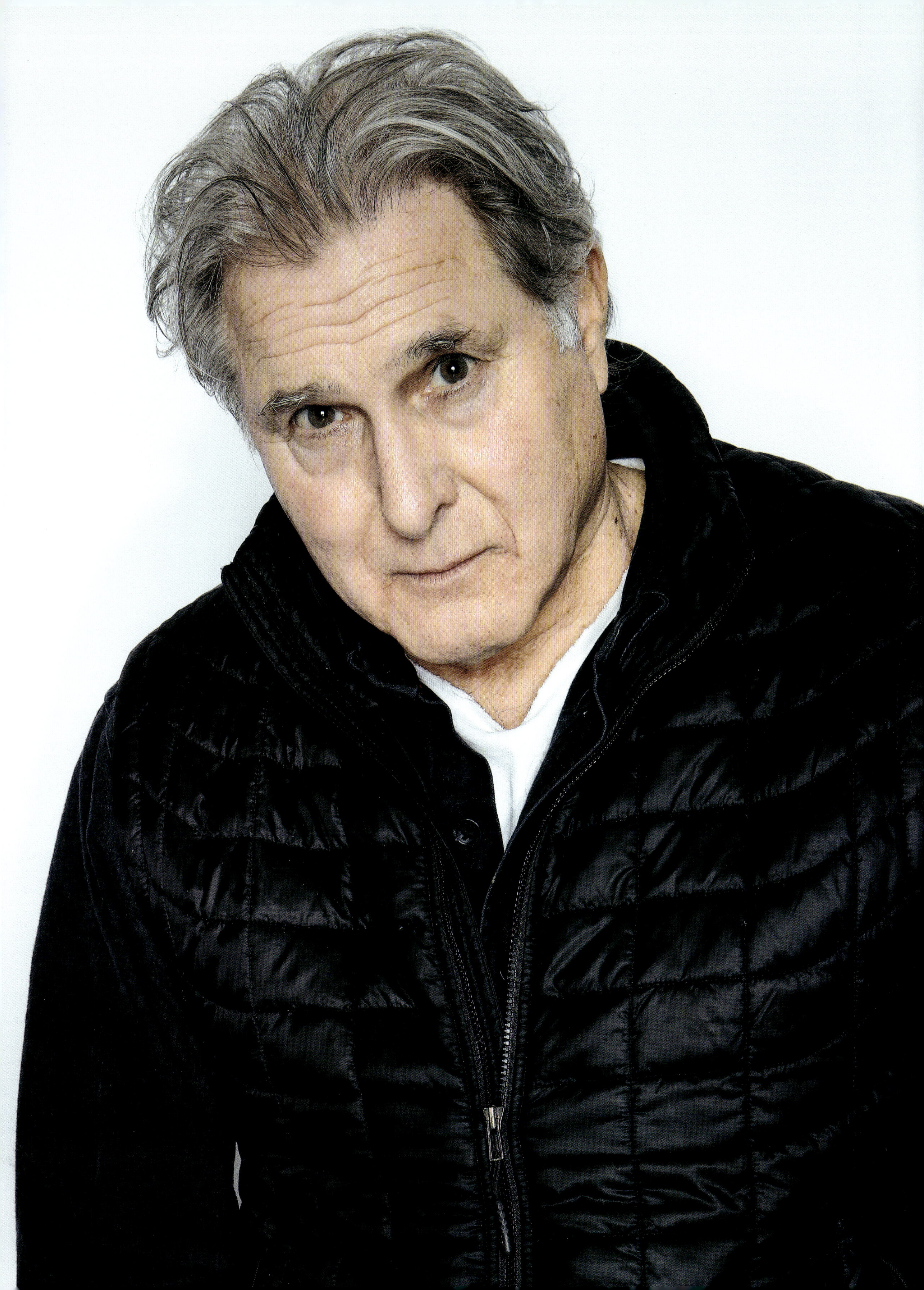

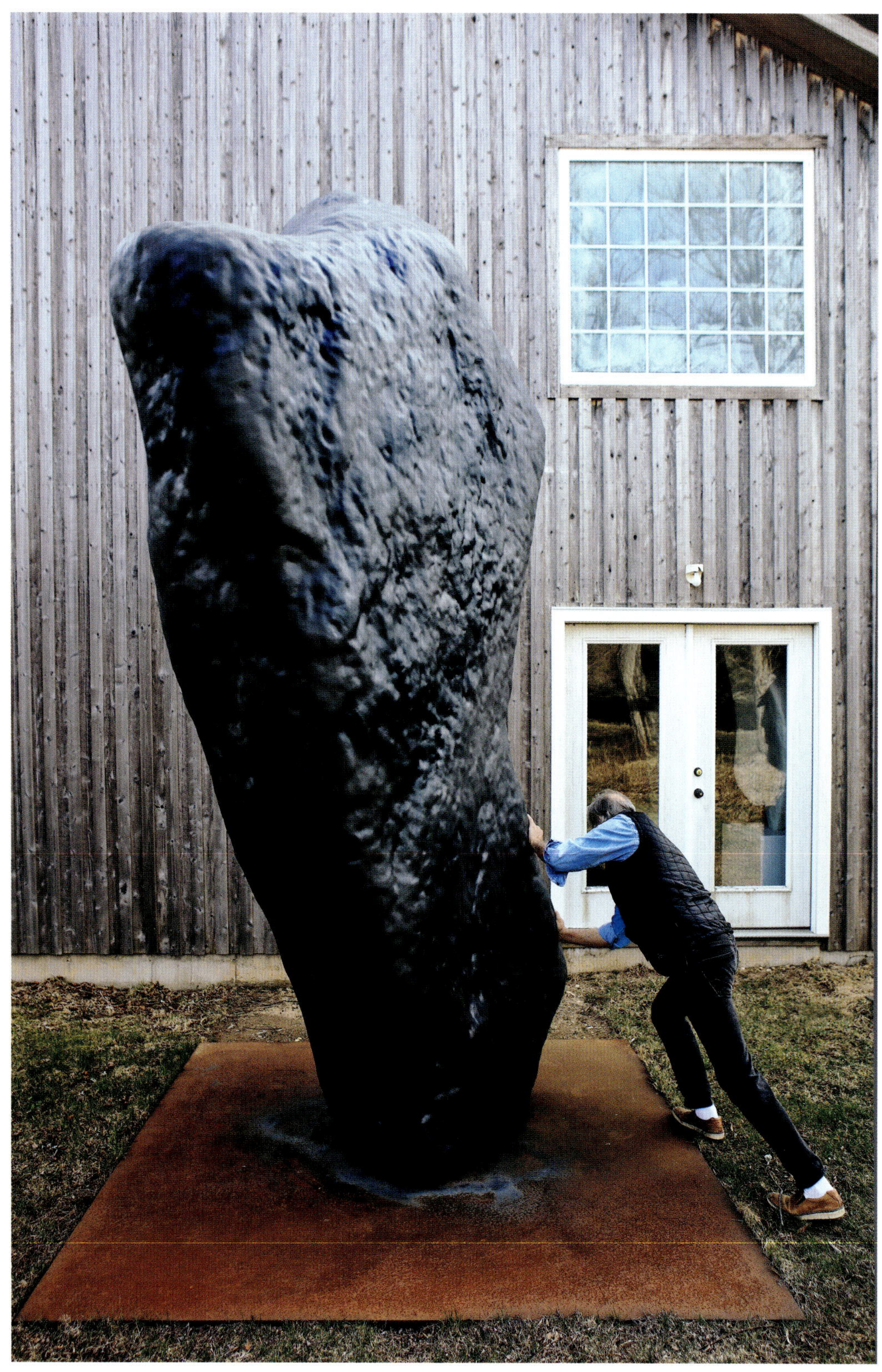

"I decided to make 3-D scans of the stones I found, stones already 'sculpted' by nature—formed by glaciers and rounded on the bay beaches here. With the 3-D scans, I could carve those models at any size. The carvings were then used to cast large bronze sculptures. At a certain point on my walks, I no longer found any stones. But I did find twigs that had washed up on the beaches, so I started making 3-D scans of the twigs, which I could then make into 3-D models. I cast those smaller pieces in bronze as well."

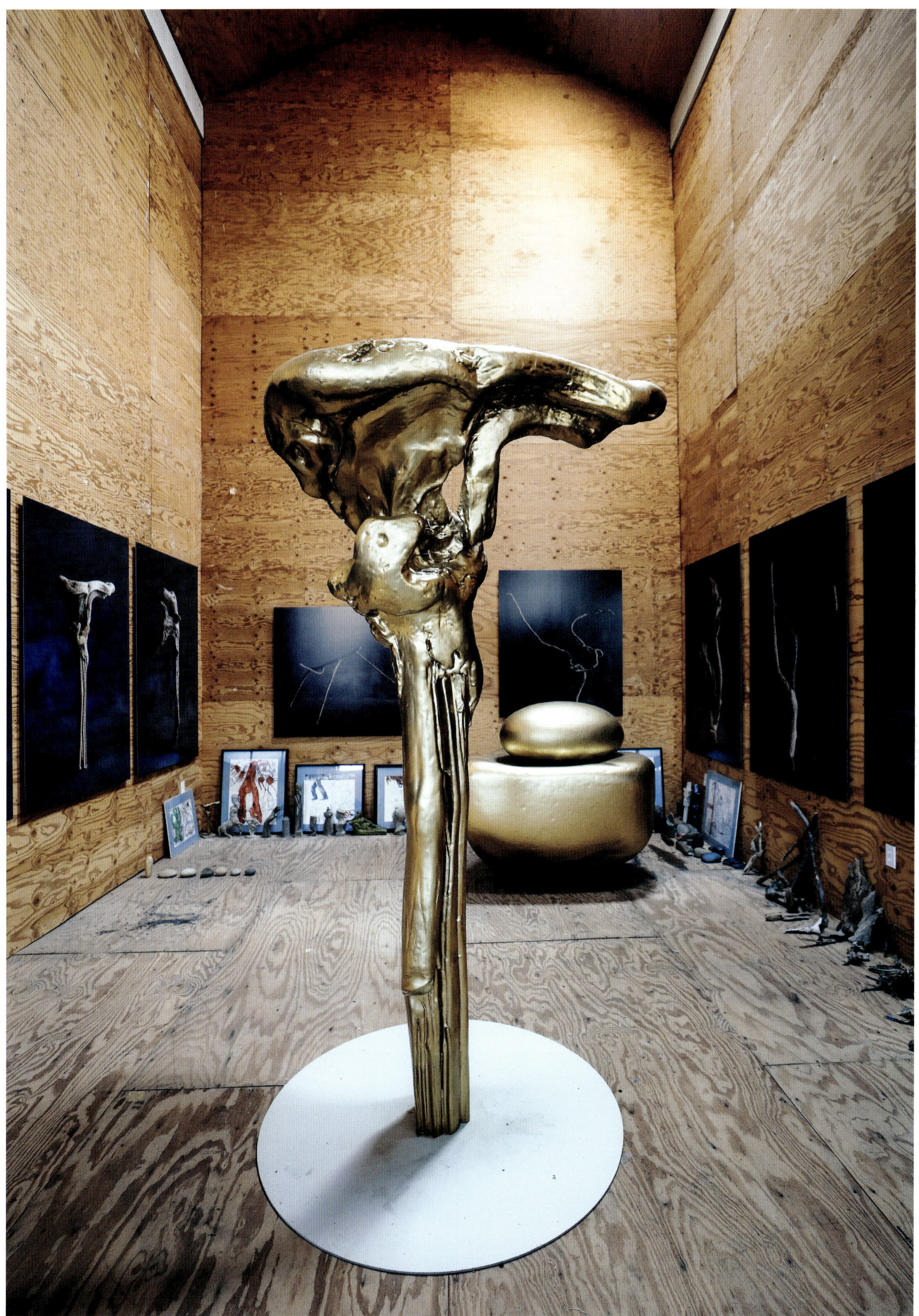

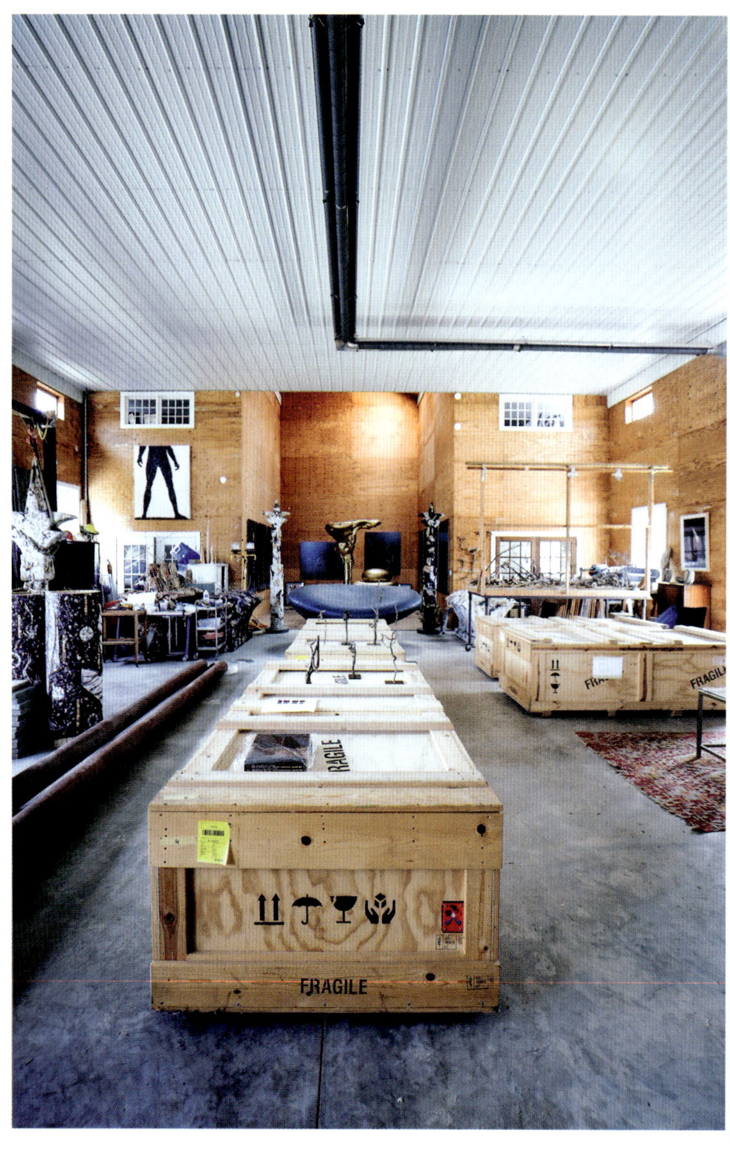

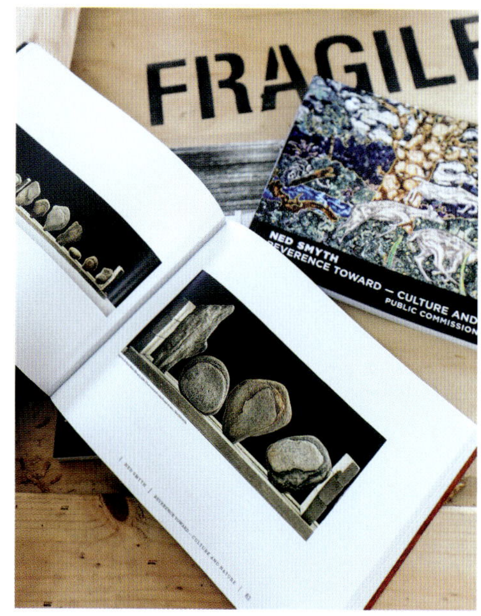

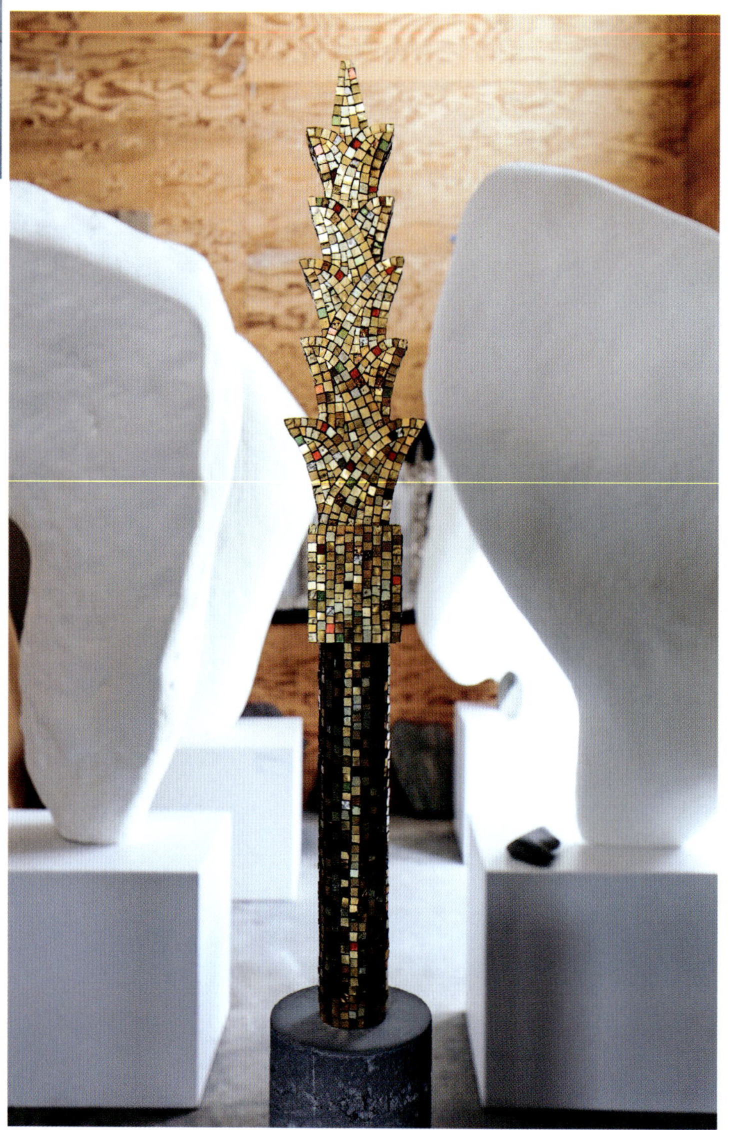

Around the same time that Smyth started doing scans of the stones, he began photographing them to see them at a larger size. "I used a very powerful camera to blow them up. This helped me decide whether or not to cast them in a bigger size." Smyth has done large-scale commissions for architects, landscape architects, and interior designers. "I recently made a twenty-four-ton stone sculpture for a new house in Florida, and a ten-foot-tall bronze stone for a house on the North Fork."

ABOVE

When Smyth moved his entire body of work to the massive studio he built on Shelter Island, where he now also lives, he discovered crates of stones he'd collected long ago—inspiring the next phase of his sculptural and photographic work.

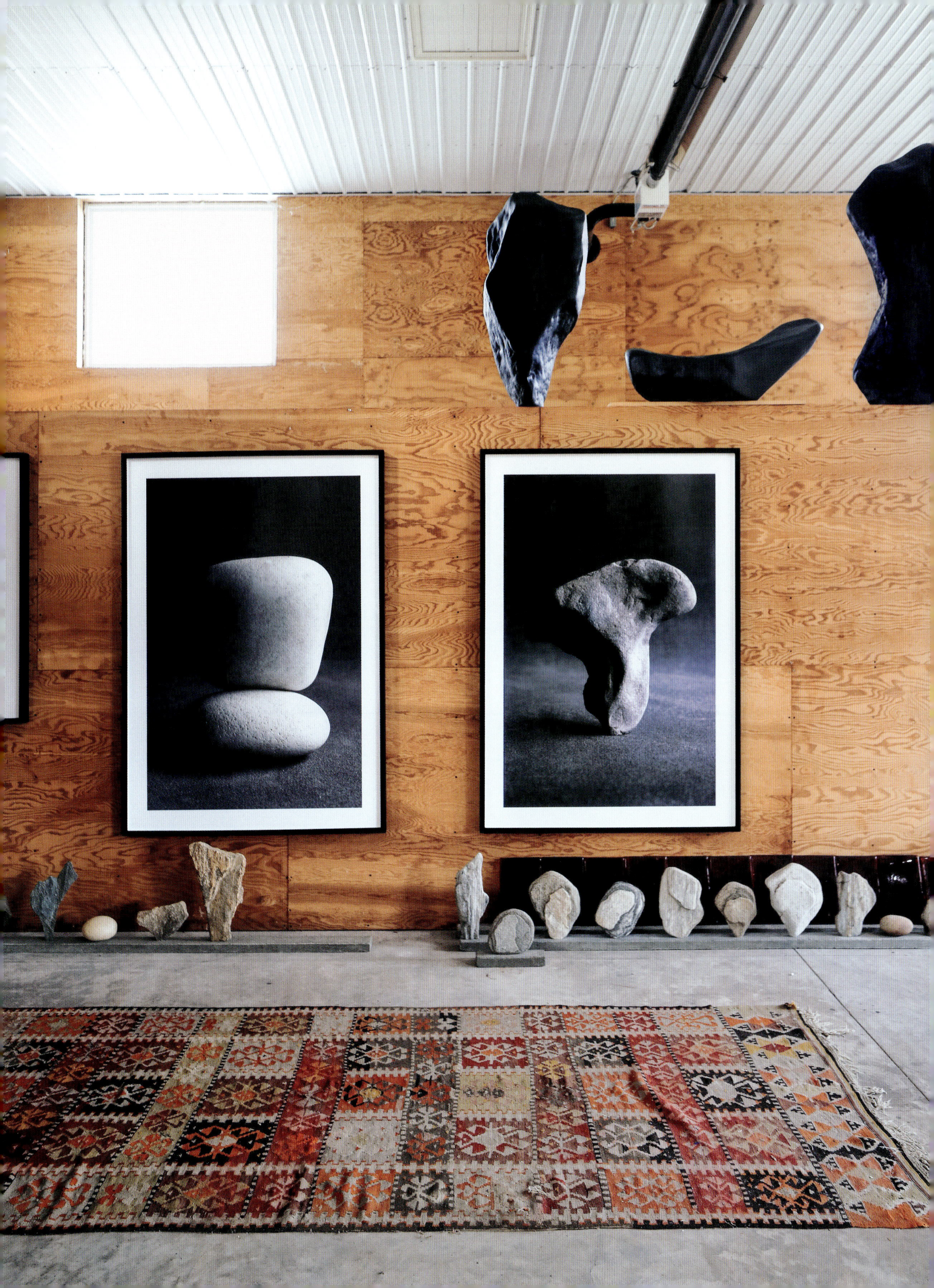

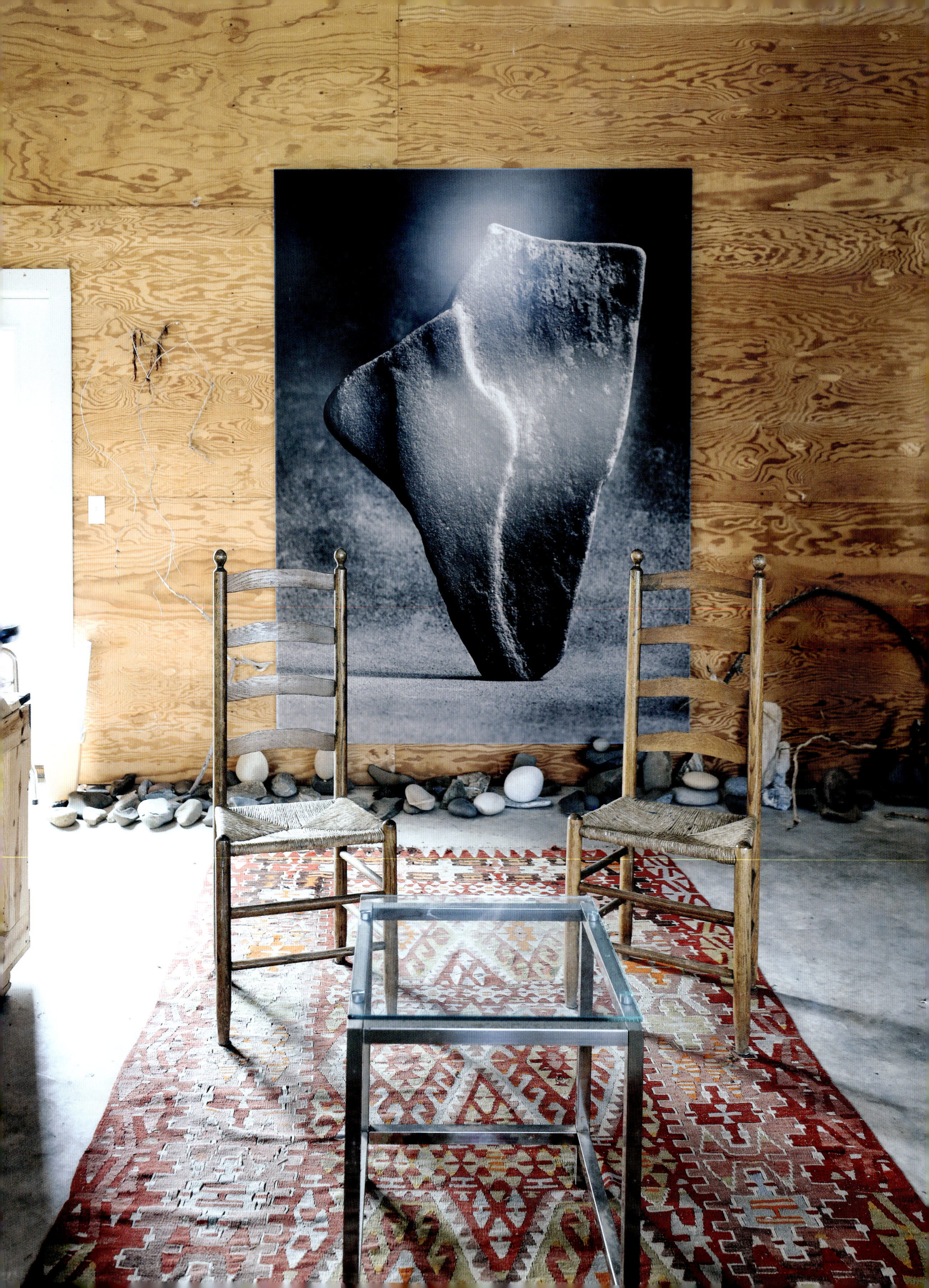

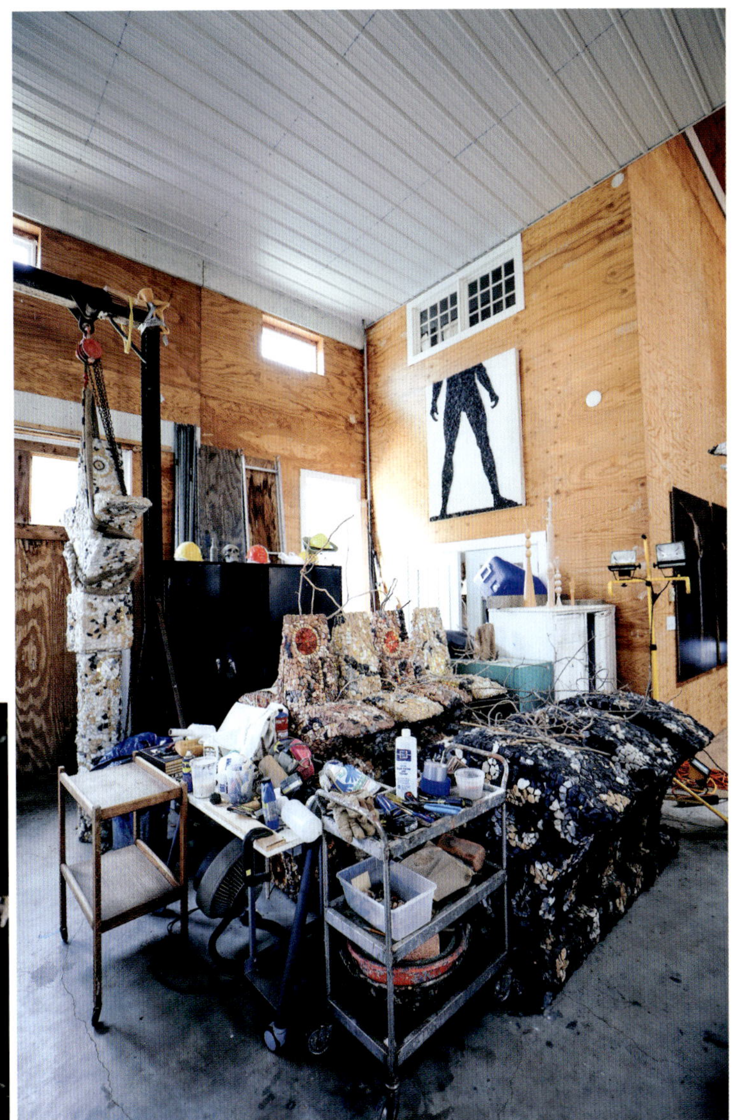

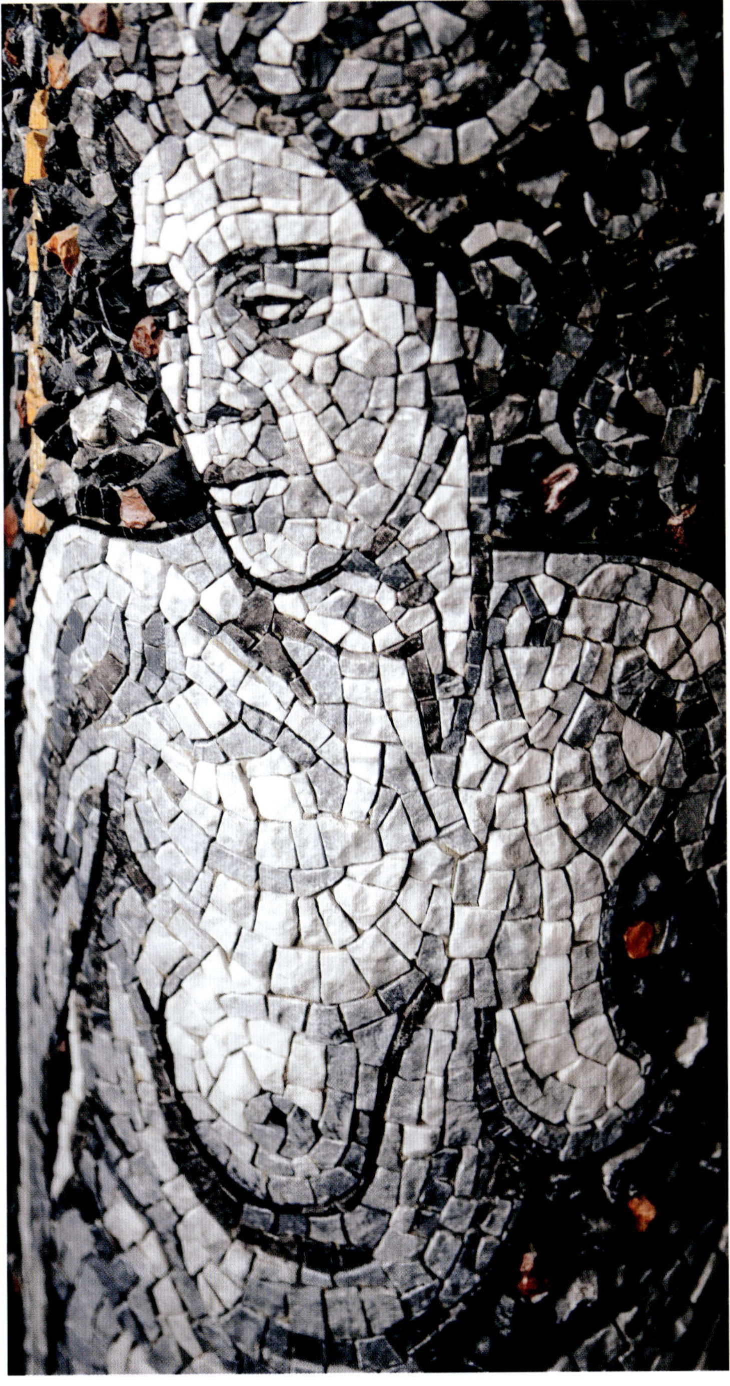

OPPOSITE AND ABOVE

Once he moved to Shelter Island, Smyth transitioned from making concrete and mosaic sculptures to working with stones already "sculpted" by nature—those formed by glaciers and rounded on the bay beaches here.

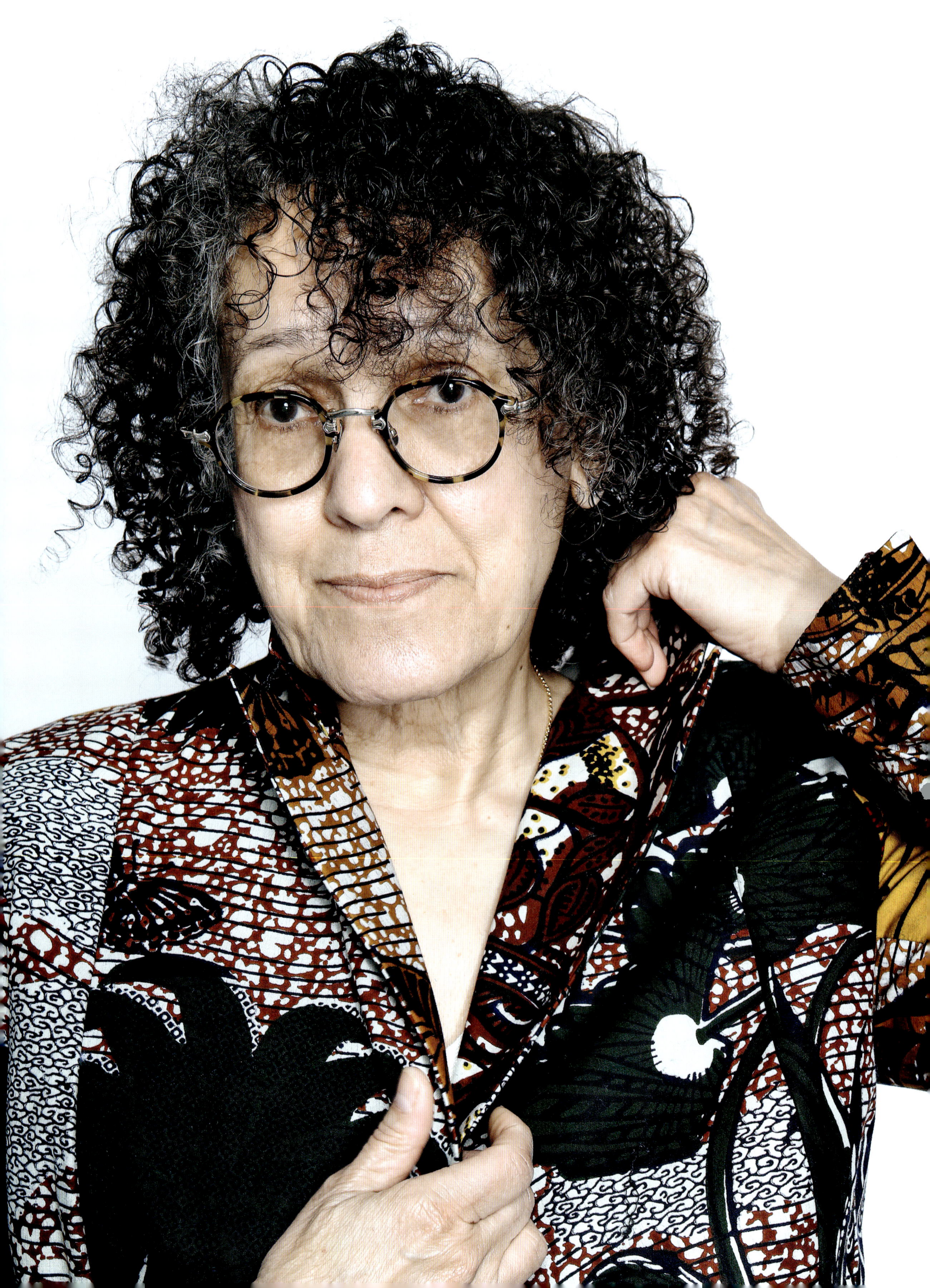

My inspiration to go to the studio is the need to express what I am experiencing in everyday life. It's my job.

LESLEE STRADFORD

Stradford studied painting at the Art Institute of Chicago. "I have always loved the arts. Several family members were artists, so it came naturally, and it was encouraged." She went on to earn a doctorate in educational administration, which allowed her to work in museums, universities, and art galleries. In 2021, Stratford and her partner, the painter Claude Lawrence, were living in France when they were both invited to be artists in residence at The Church in Sag Harbor. They decided to stay. "There have been so many famous artists living here for more than a century, it's hard not to be somewhat in awe, knowing you are now sharing the same space they embraced."

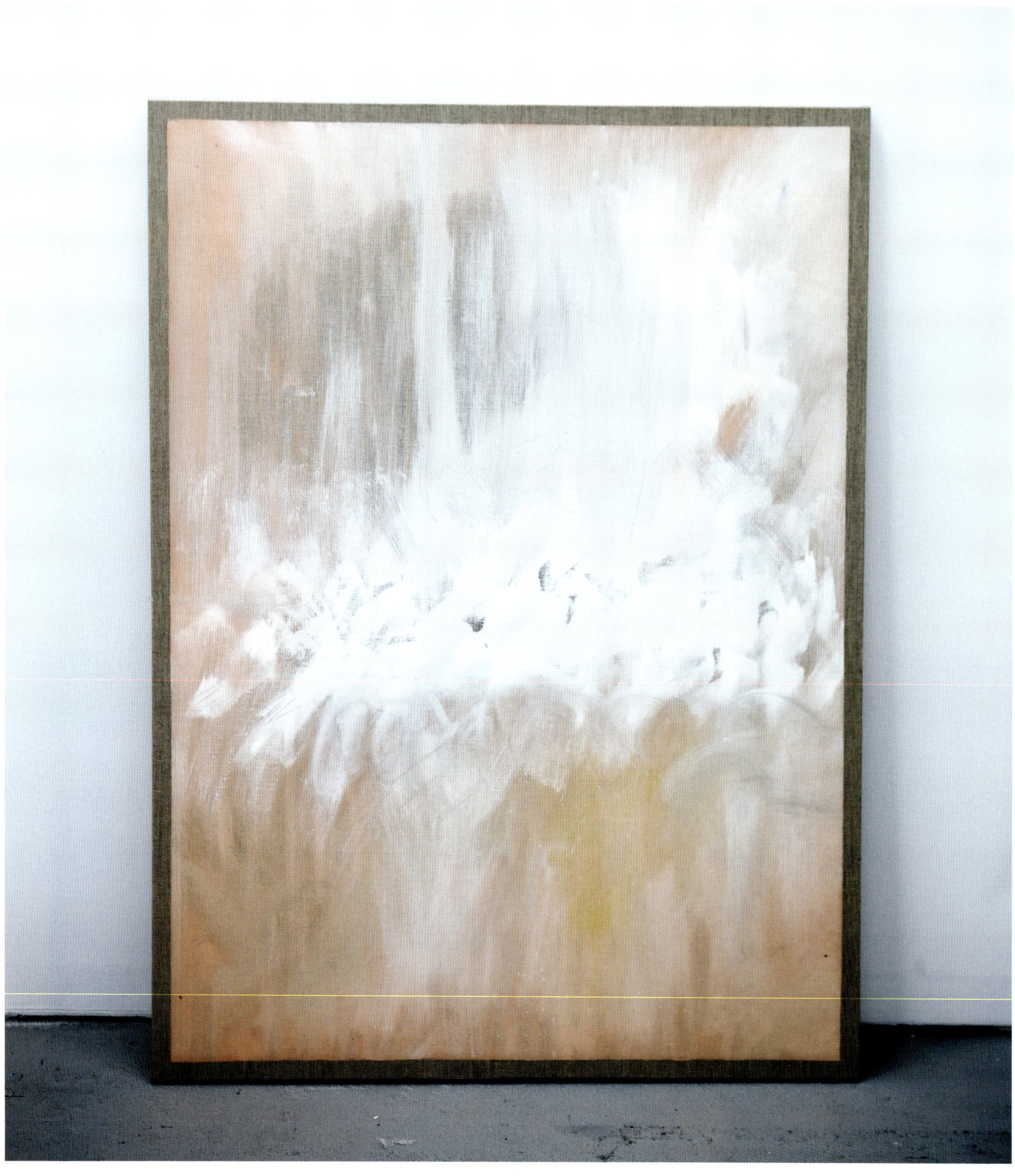

"I consider myself an Abstract Expressionist. I have taught many modes of artistic expression, but when I paint freely, that's what comes. My work has gone through phases. It has become more mature and, in some ways, simpler. Working in various styles and disciplines and using modern technology has informed content and expression. 'Less is more' has taken on a new perspective that removes the superfluous."

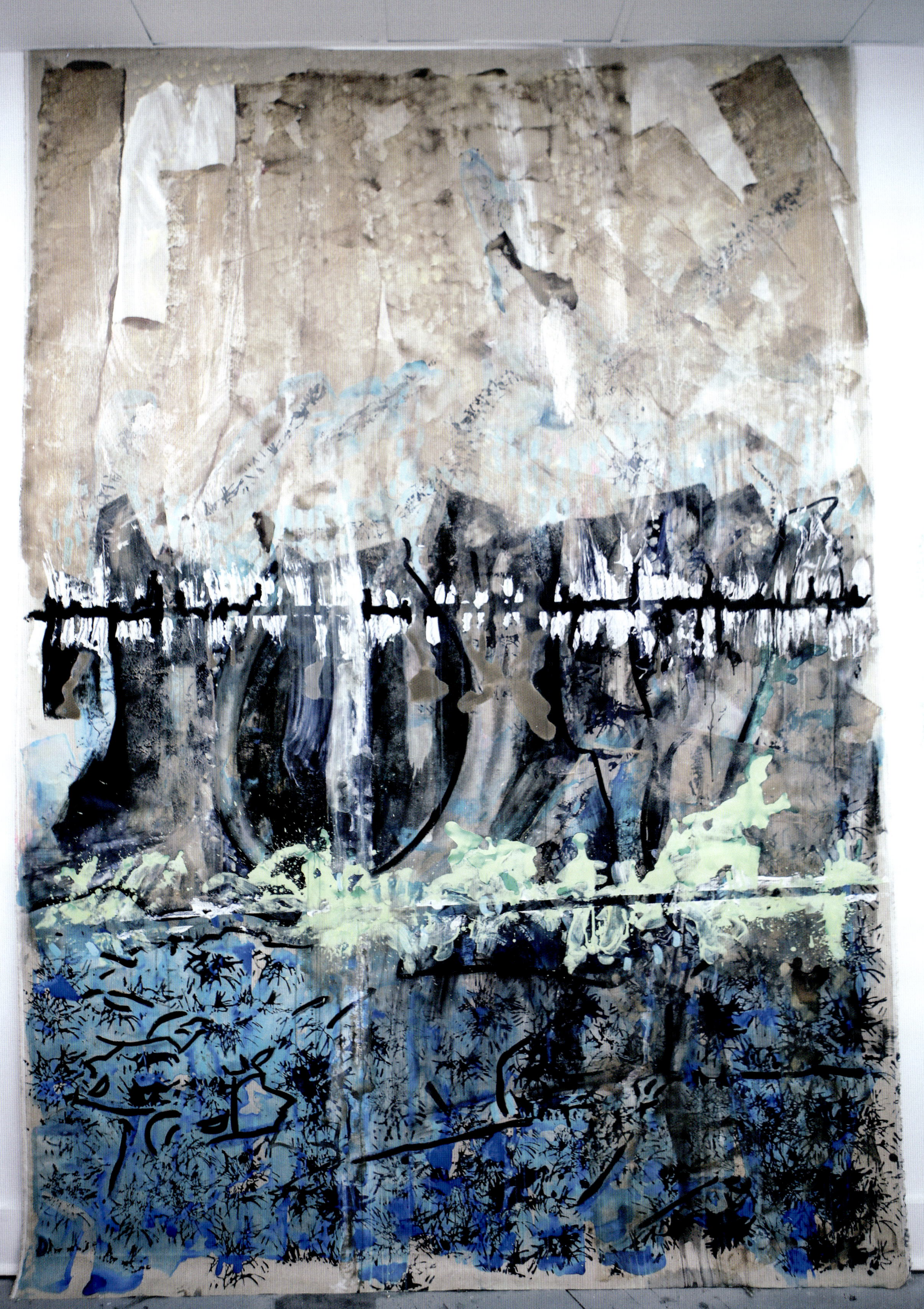

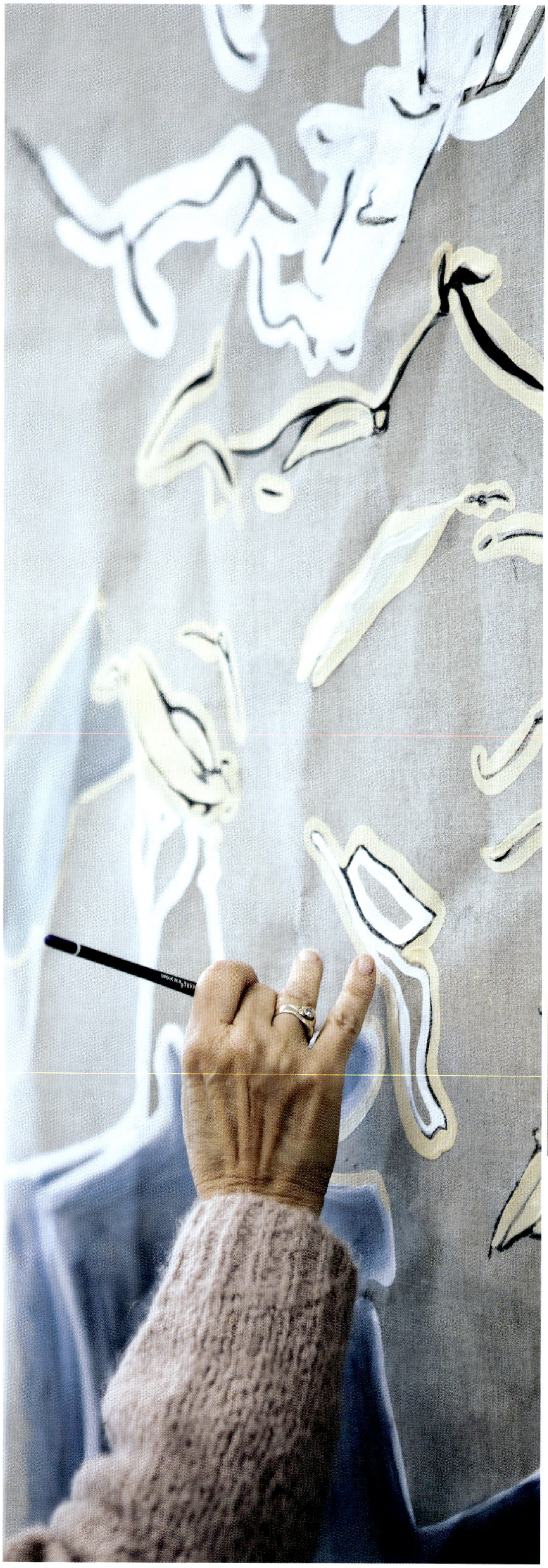

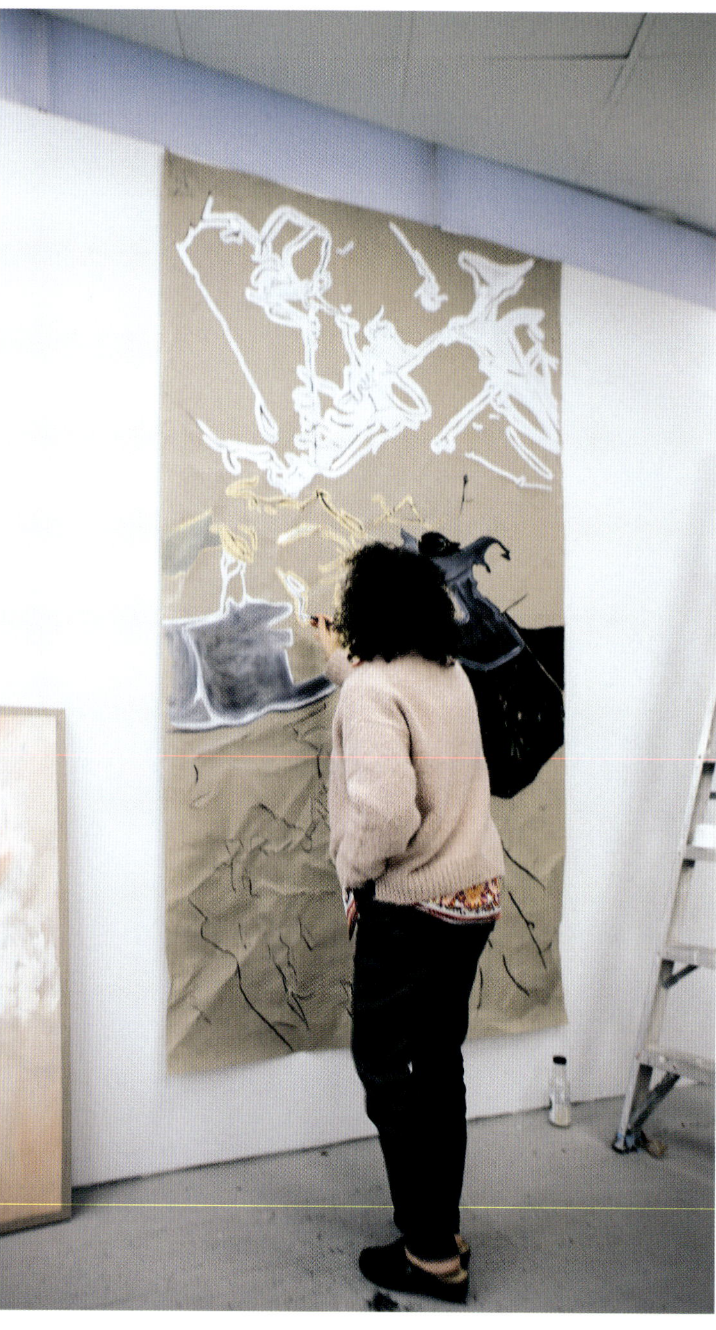

LEFT AND ABOVE

A self-described Abstract Expressionist, Stradford's works are mostly large-scale paintings in oil on linen or digital prints on silk.

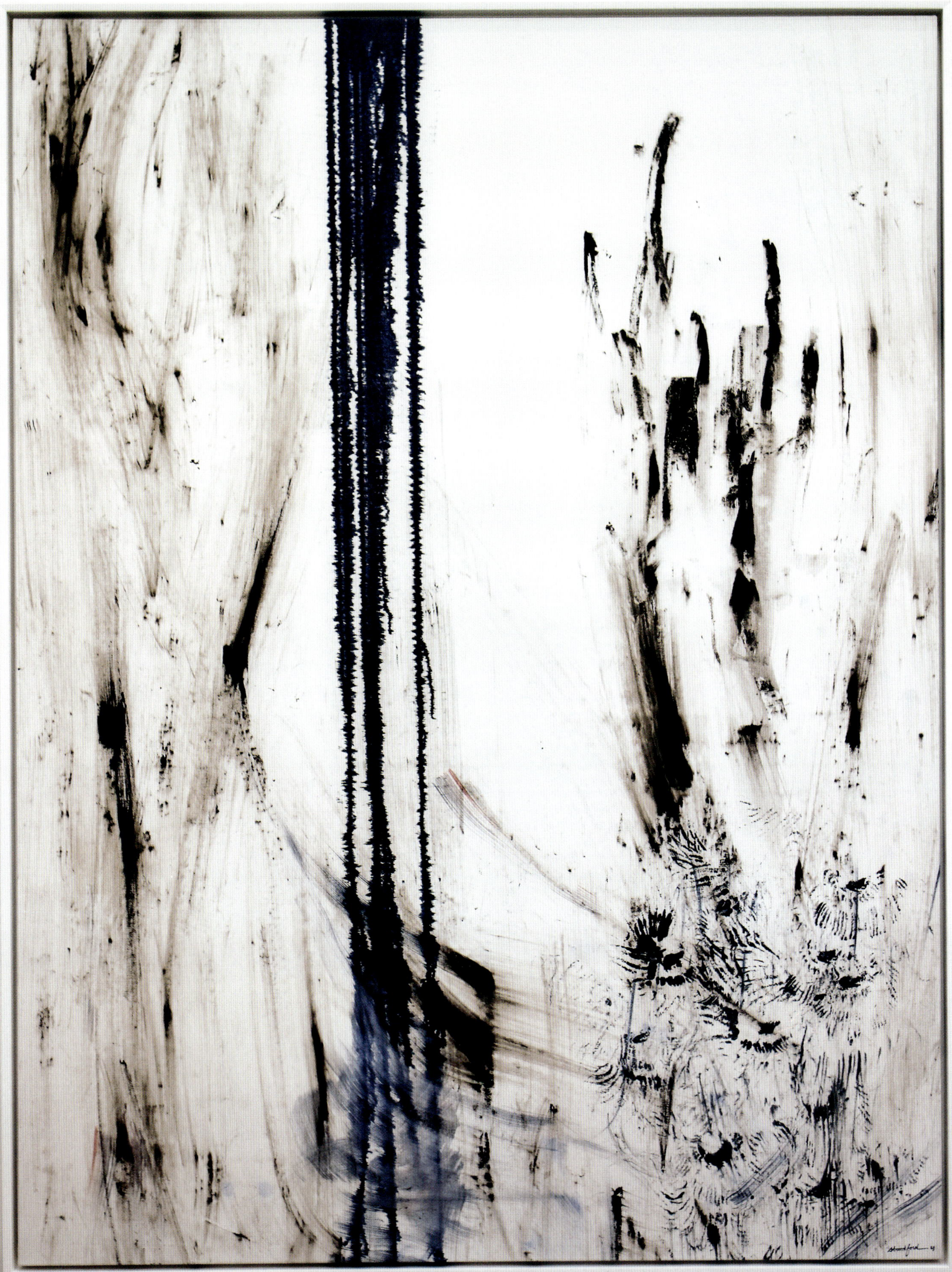

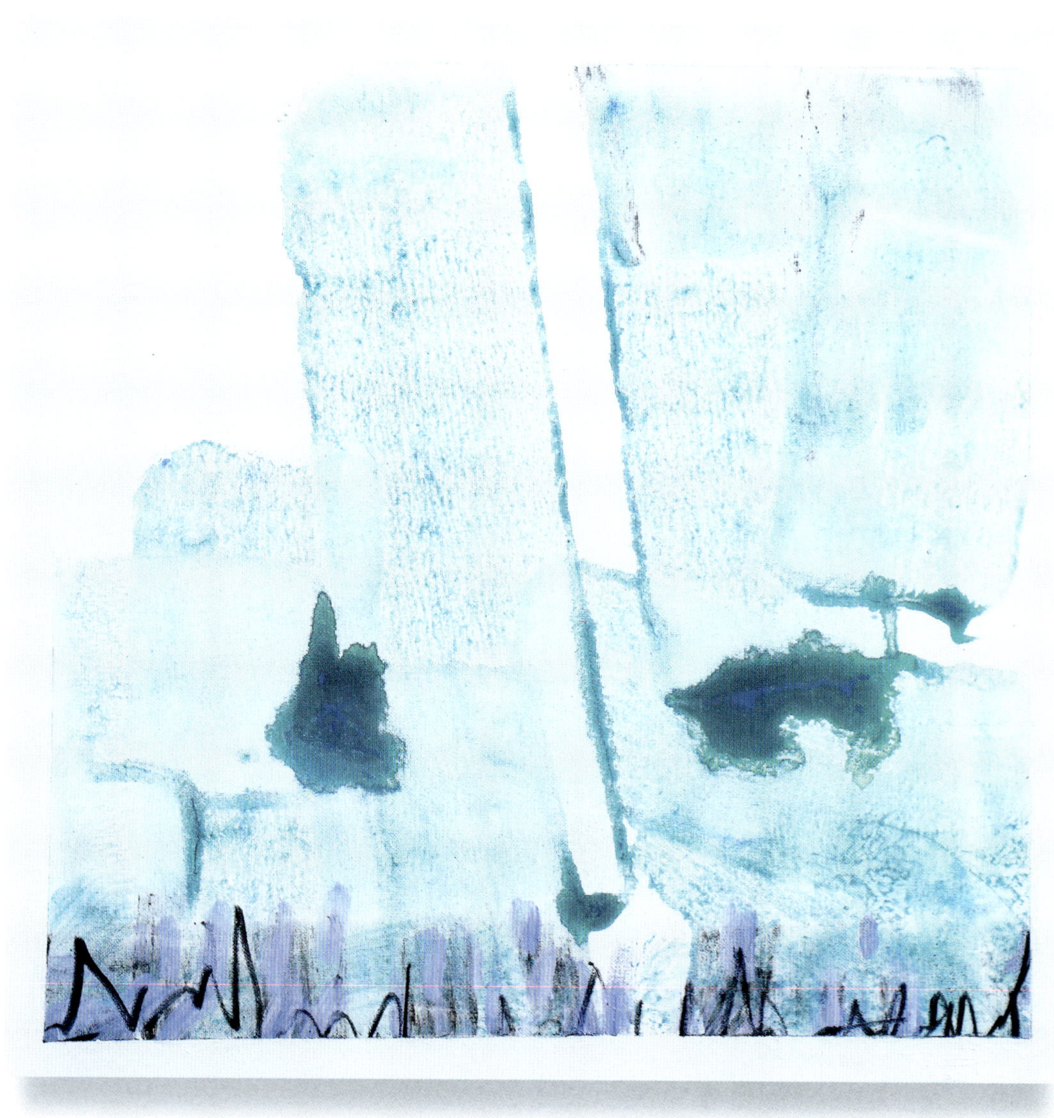

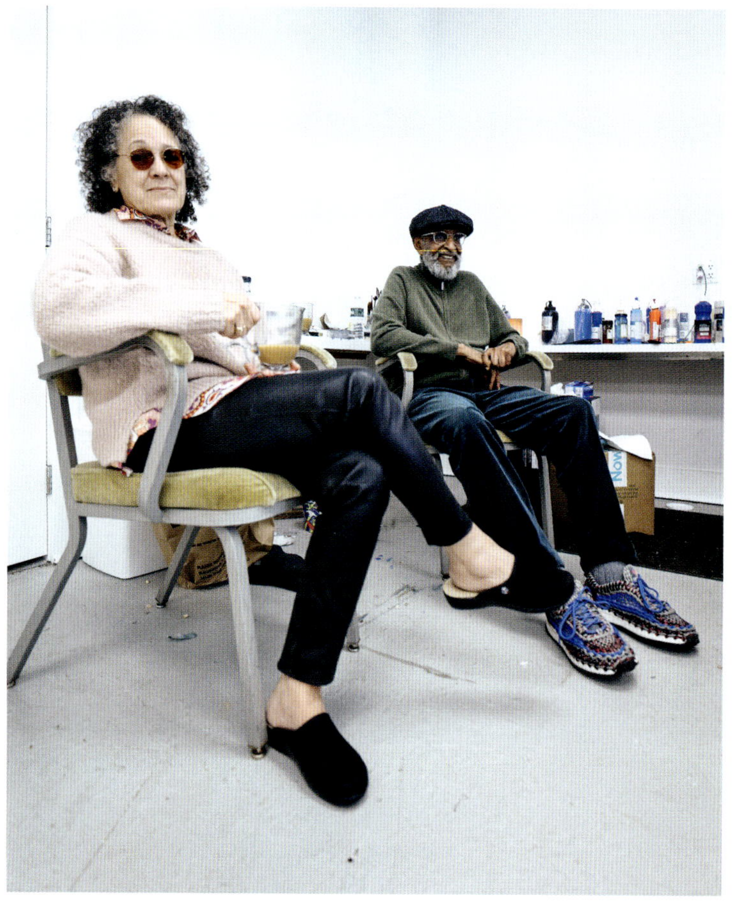

Stradford works in two modes: oil on linen and digital prints on silk. Her tools range from squeeze bottles to brushes to sponges and rollers. "I like working large. It challenges spontaneity. However, some of my smaller canvases have been dense and visually deeper." Do she and Claude influence each other's work? "Absolutely. My approach is very different from his, but we learn from and appreciate each other's expressions."

LEFT

Stradford and her husband, the painter Claude Lawrence, share an East Hampton studio space. Though their work is very different, they say each inspires the other.

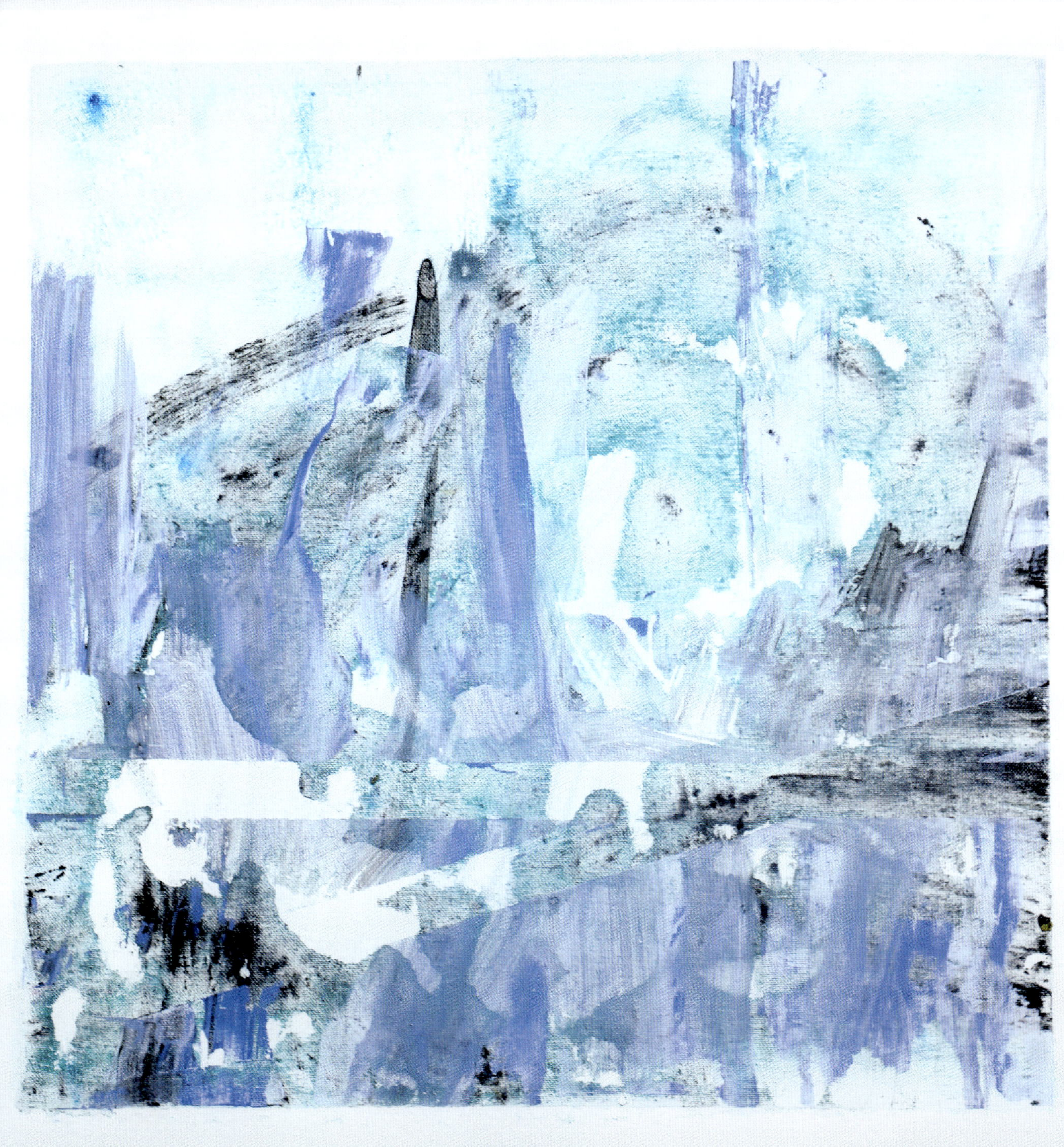

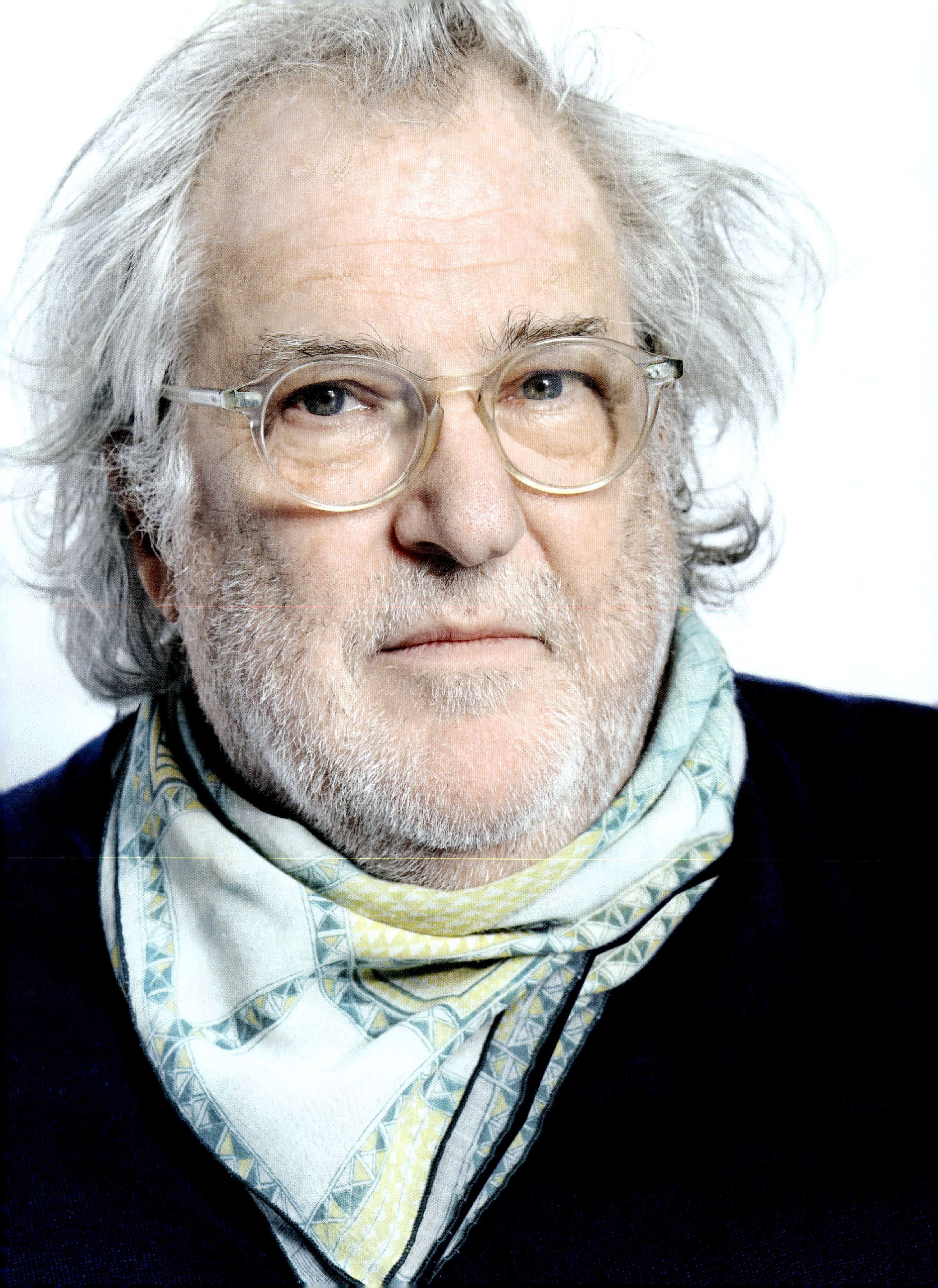

The motifs I use are engineered, like the fruits you find in the supermarket or flowers grown in a hothouse. The man-made world is my biggest inspiration.

DONALD SULTAN

Born and raised in Asheville, North Carolina, Sultan went to boarding school in Wilbraham, Massachusetts. "From the time I was thirteen, I worked in theater—both in school and in summer stock on Cape Cod. I went to the University of North Carolina, ostensibly for the theater program, but switched out after the first day and moved over to the Radio, Television, and Motion Picture Department with the idea of being involved with film. Then I switched again—to the Fine Arts Department, which required fewer people to realize my art." Sultan's theater background reveals itself in his work. "My painting structure is a vertical platform, a kind of stage. The painting itself is the performance."

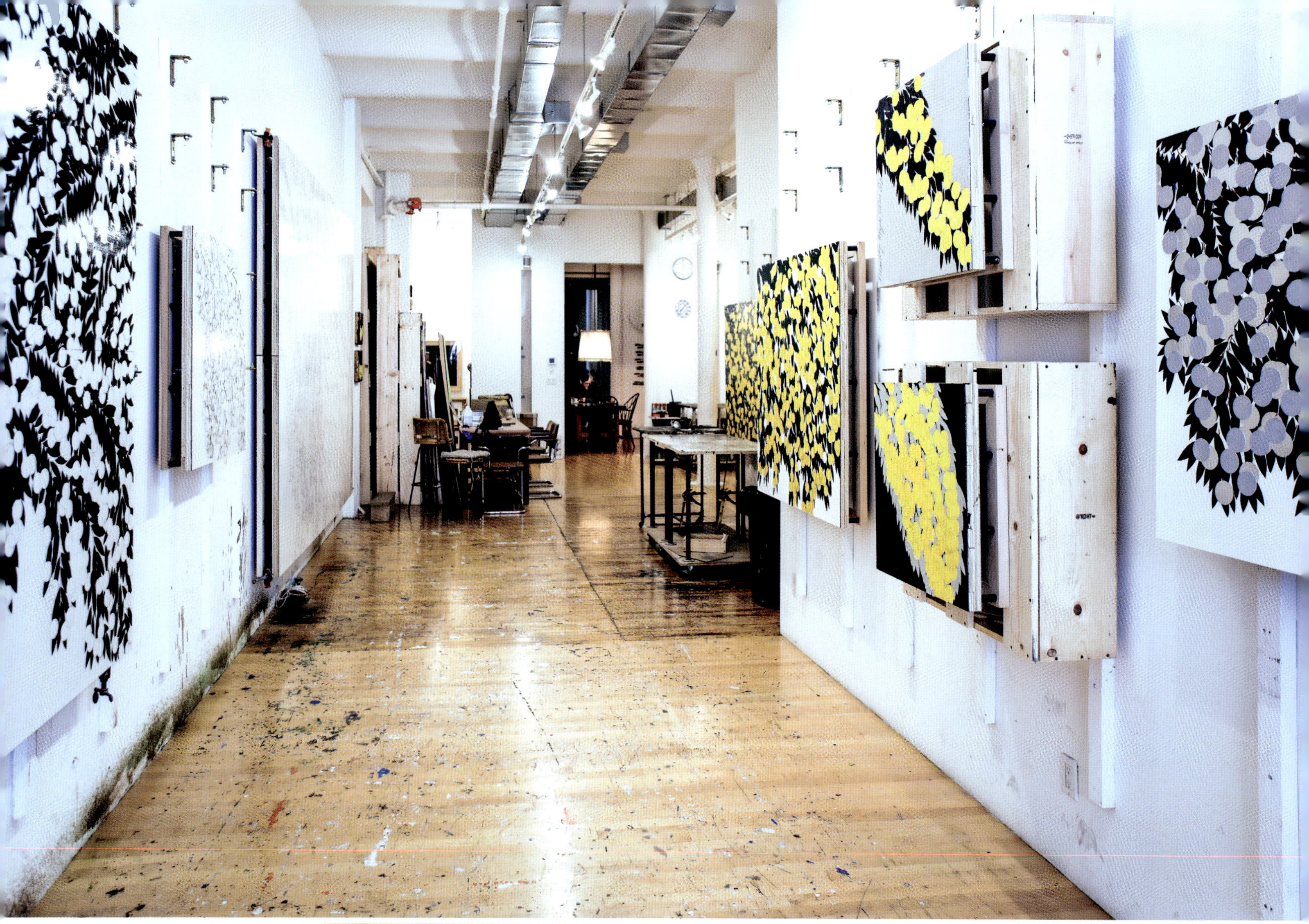

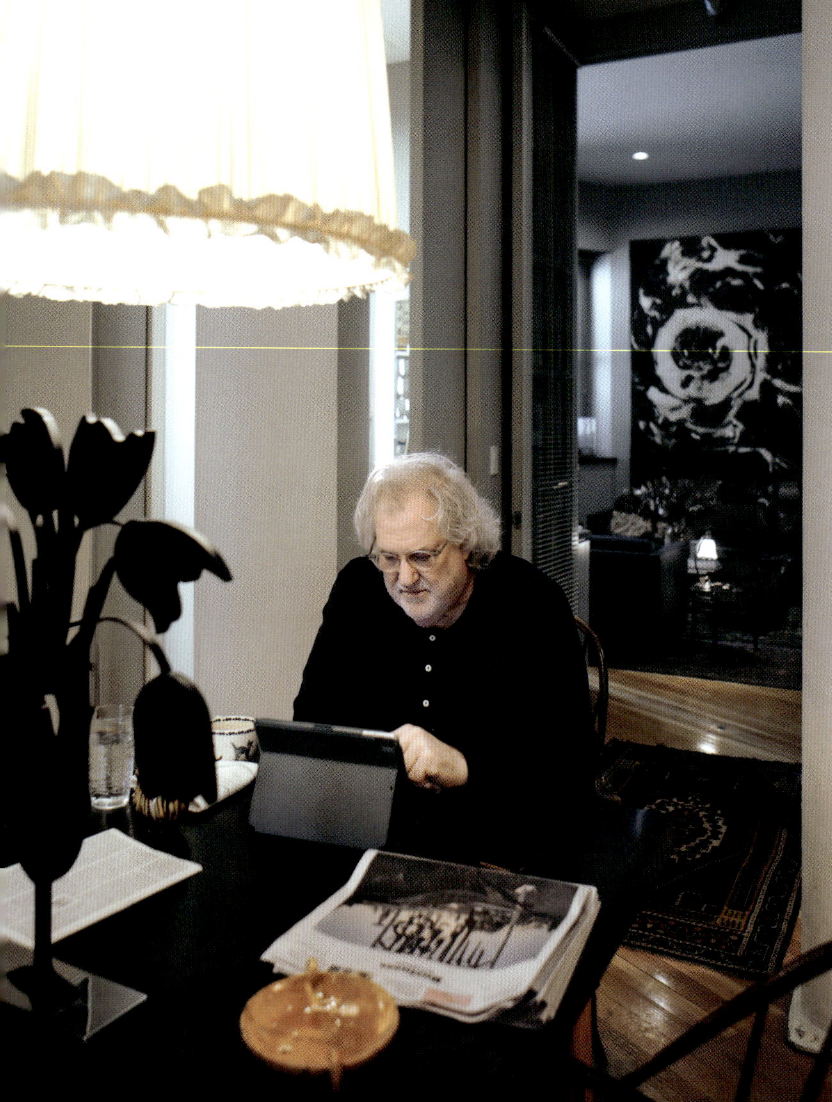

After getting his MFA at the Art Institute of Chicago, Sultan moved to New York City. "By this time, I was committed to being a painter and a part of the New York art world." He started coming to the Hamptons in 1981 after his daughter was born. "We rented a house in Amagansett for the summer. It rained every day, so I wasn't completely sold yet on the Hamptons, but I did spend a lot of time meeting really interesting people and playing poker with some of the year-rounders. The next couple of summers we spent in Saint-Tropez, but my then wife wanted a place in the Hamptons, so we rented a house in Sag Harbor for the winter. We liked Sag Harbor so much that I decided to buy a house when one came on the market across the street. Later on, I bought the house next door because we needed more space, and it is in these two houses that we remain to this day."

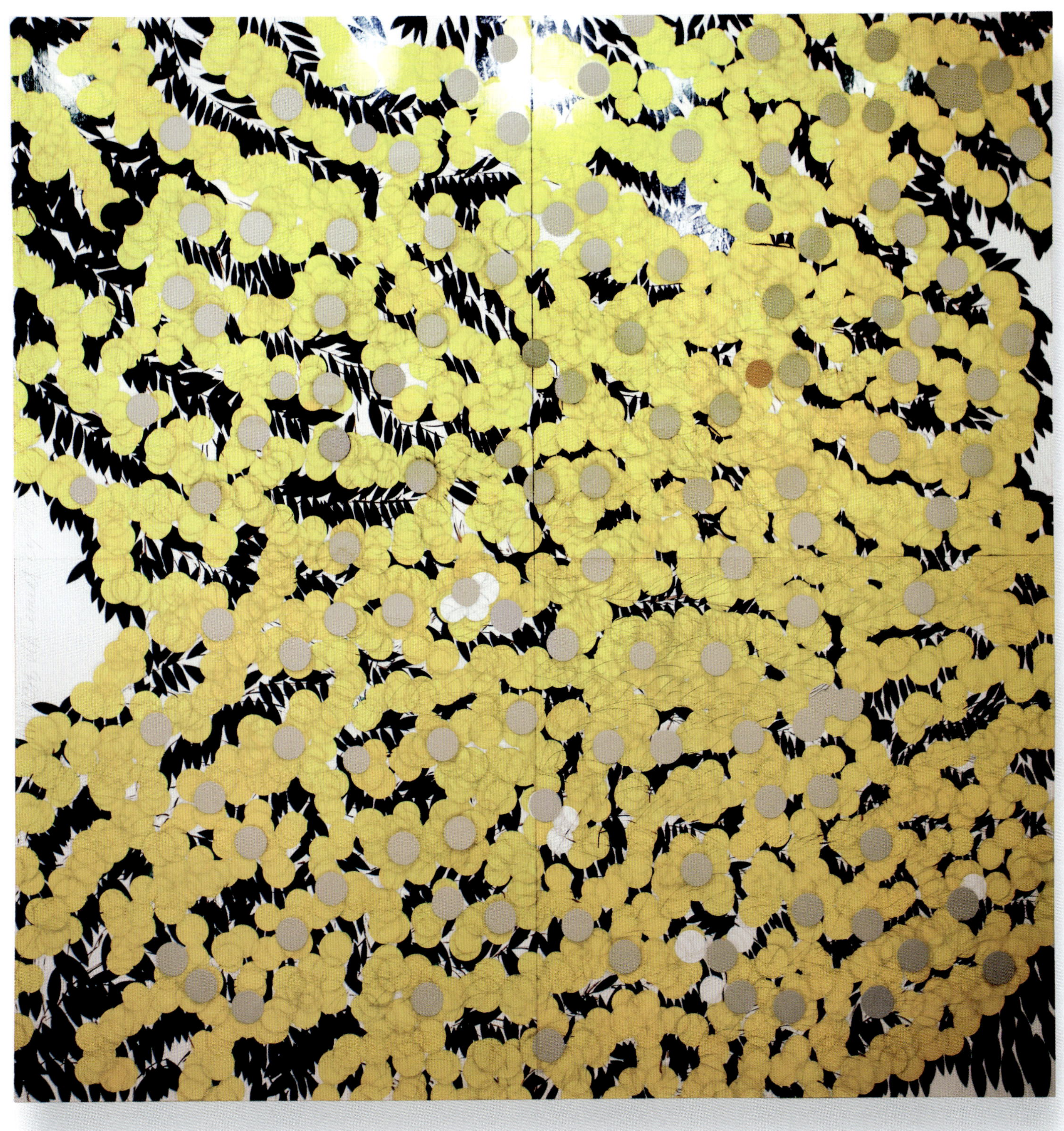

OPPOSITE TOP Though natural light is not an important factor in Sultan's studio life—whether in New York City or in Sag Harbor—wall space is, since much of his work is large-scale. **OPPOSITE BOTTOM** Sultan's ideas for his paintings often come from imagery he finds in books or newspapers.

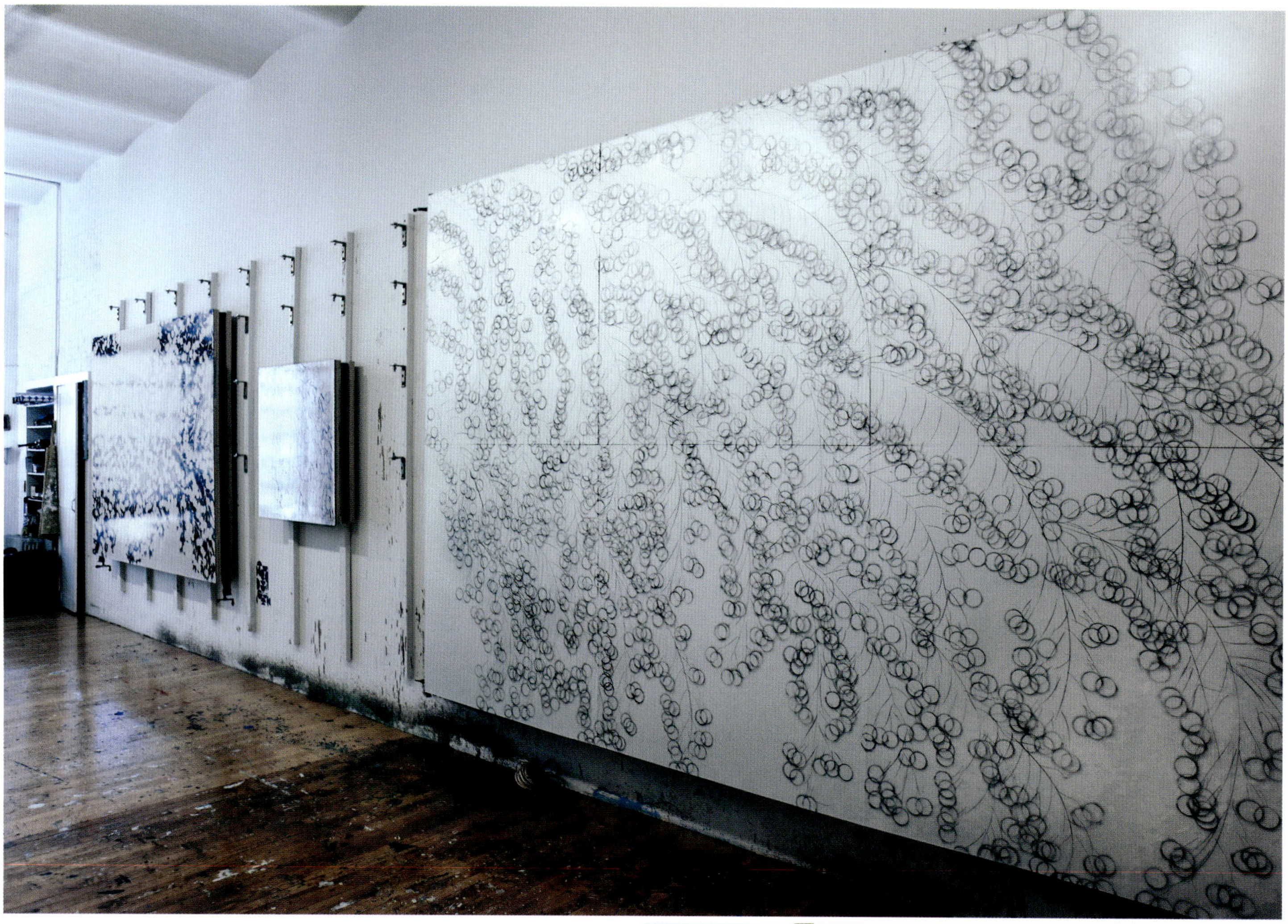

"I'm not influenced by using what you might call natural light. I usually work in a studio. My themes are the classic themes in the Western canon: still lifes, flowers, and landscapes. I more or less elaborate on imagery I find in newspapers or in quick Polaroids that I take of the still lifes I make up in the studio. Some might have, for example, a black lemon inserted in them. I'll find a lemon and paint it black or a brown egg and paint it white. I alter the natural order of the objects. And I make some of the images on a gargantuan scale that keeps them from being natural. Even though they are two-dimensional, I give both the image and the surface itself architectural and sculptural weight."

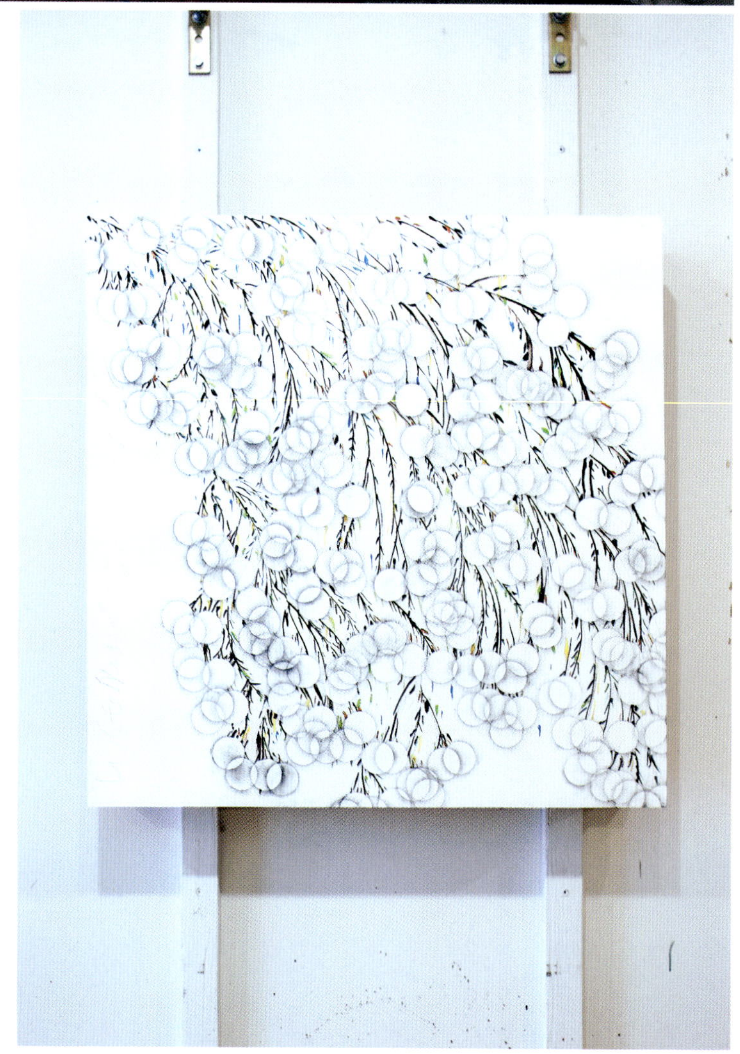

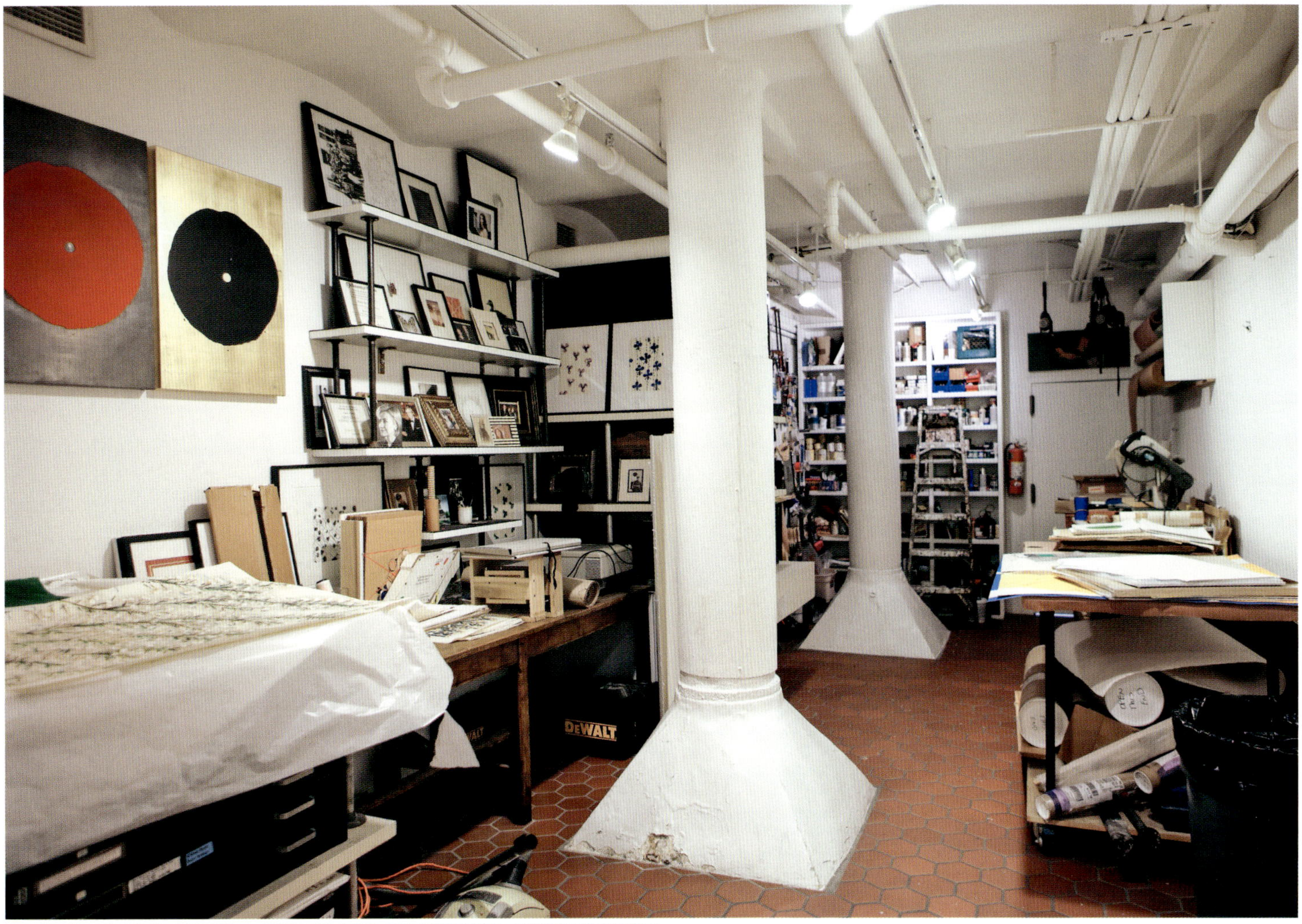

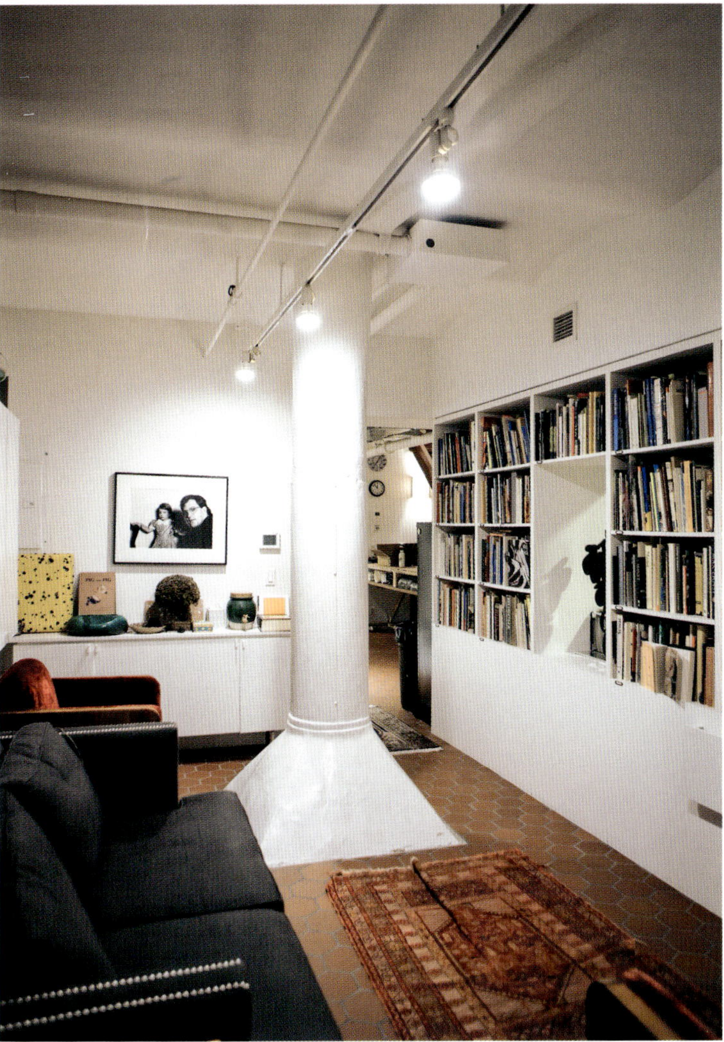

OPPOSITE TOP AND THIS PAGE

Rooms in Sultan's large New York City studio. Spending part of his time in Sag Harbor balances his city life and feeds his nature-based imagery, even if he alters that imagery in scale or color to make it read as something other than natural.

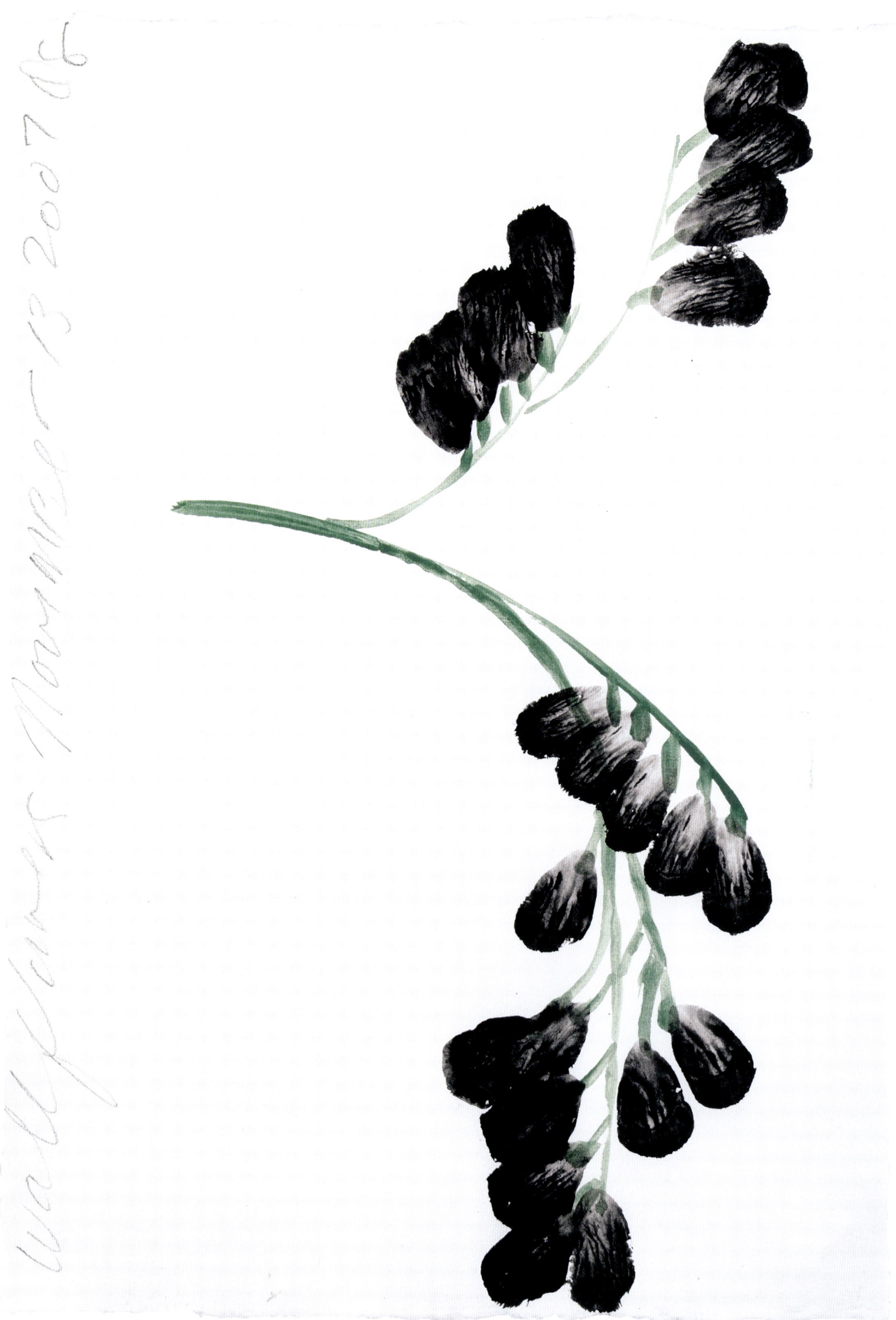

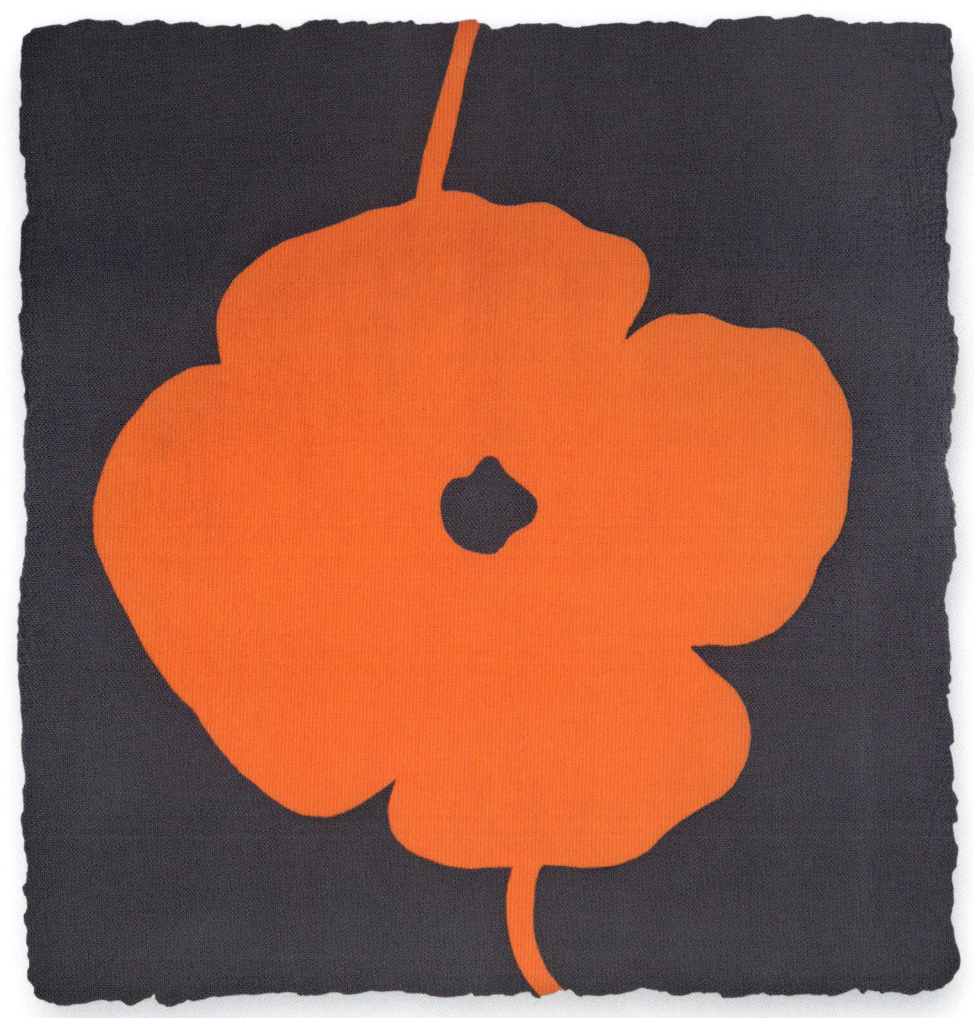

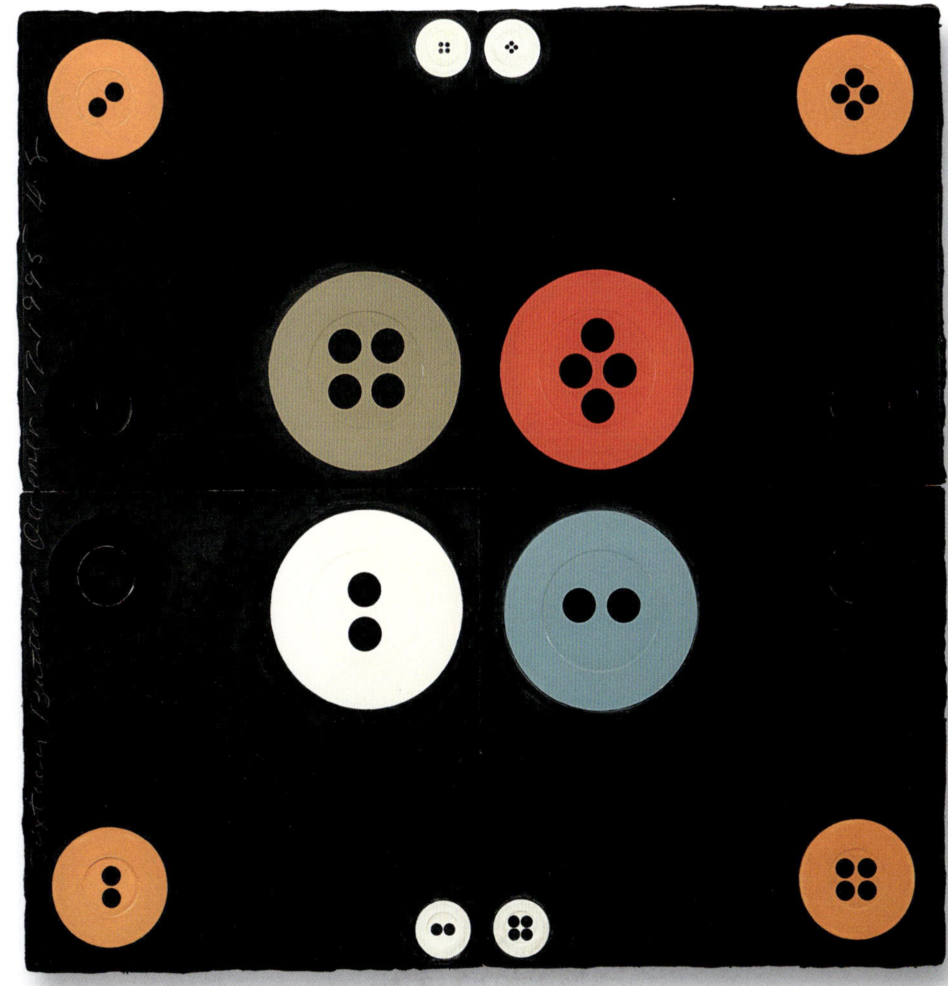

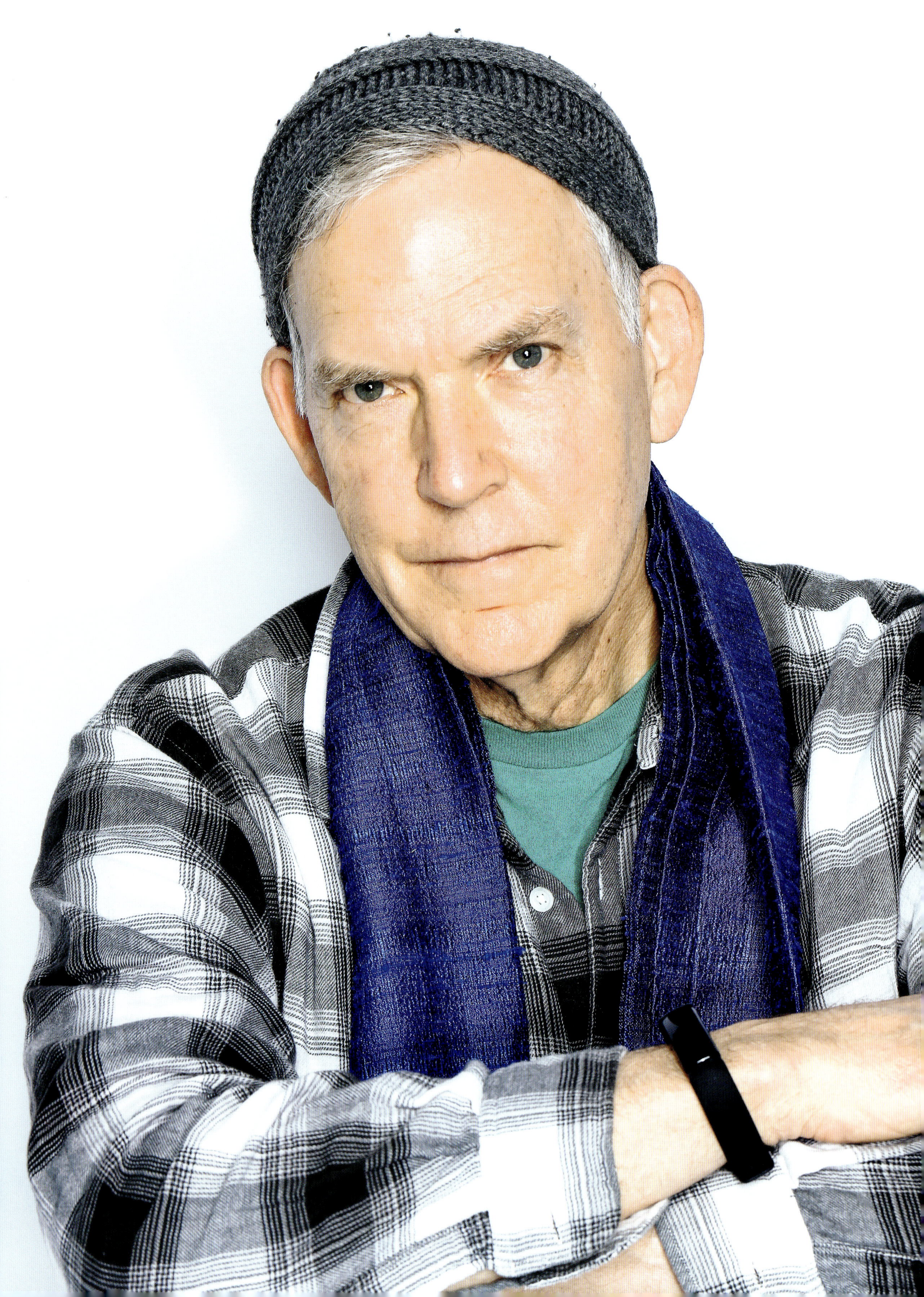

My main tools are language, design, and a decent bristle brush. . . . All the other tools are invisible.

KEVIN TEARE

Teare began painting in Indiana, his birthplace. "One of the first places I exhibited, in the seventies, was the Indianapolis Museum of Art. I didn't see anywhere to go from there, so in 1976 I moved to New York." In 1992, he and his and wife, Mary Boochever, also an artist, bought a house in Noyac. "I never realized we were moving here until we'd been here a number of years." His high-ceilinged studio—separate from the house and from Mary's studio—where he generally works from 3:00 to 8:00 PM, affords him solitude. "Sometimes I'll put on music when I start to work. When it's over, I rarely notice."

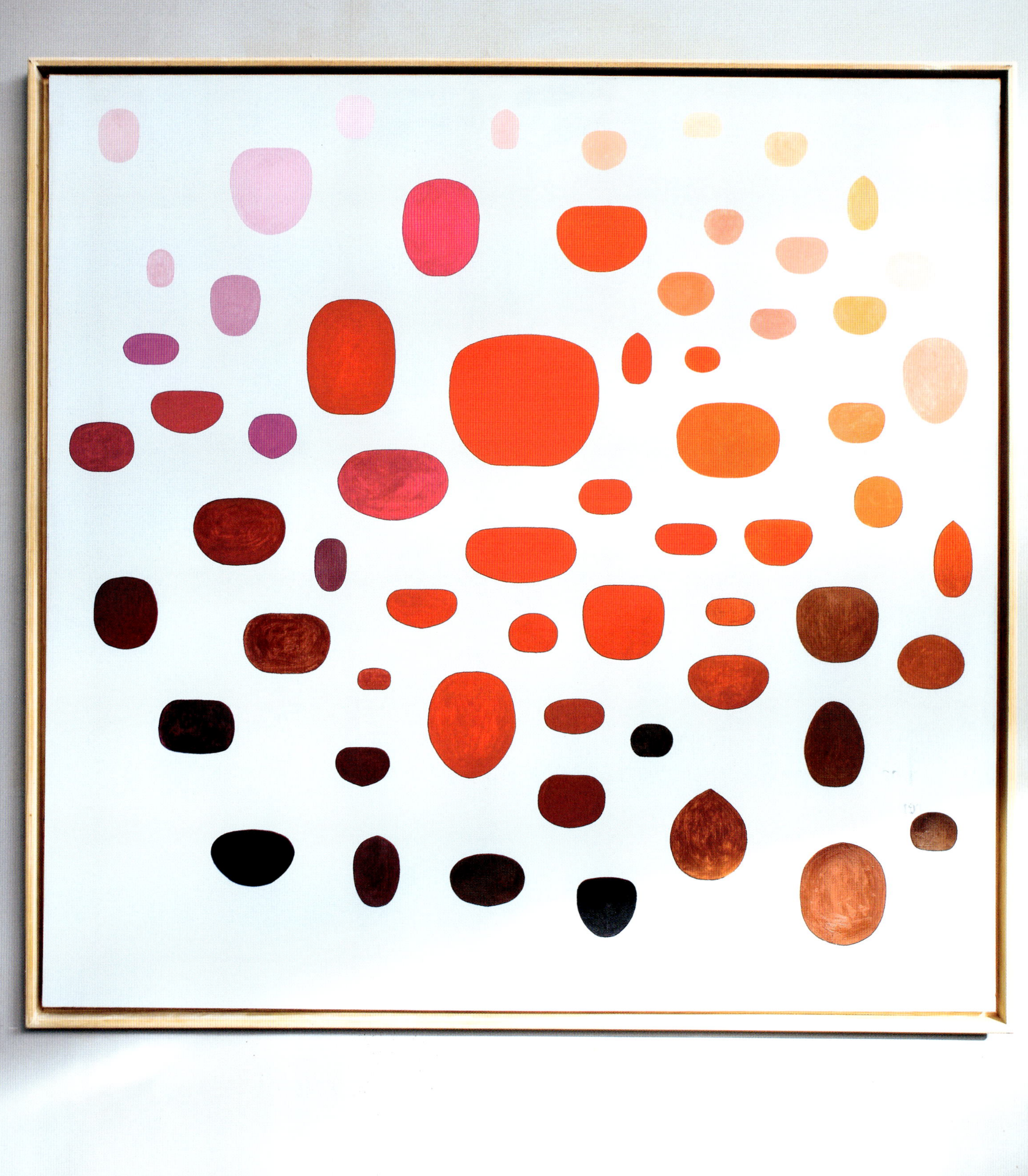

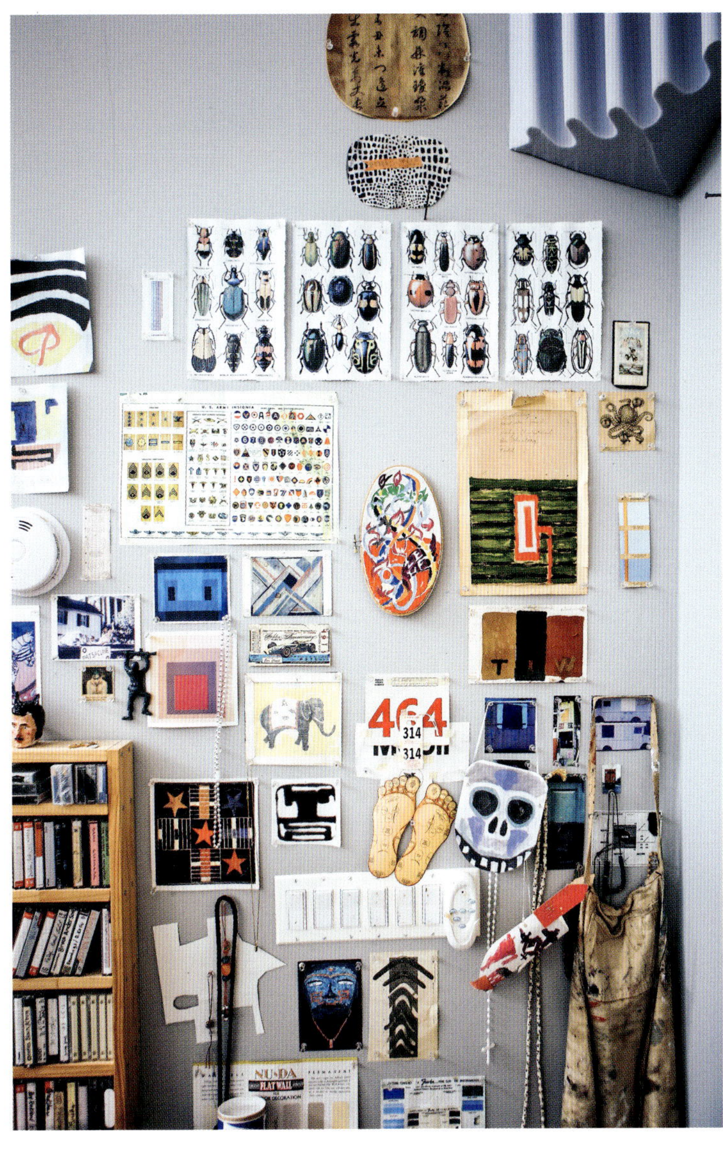

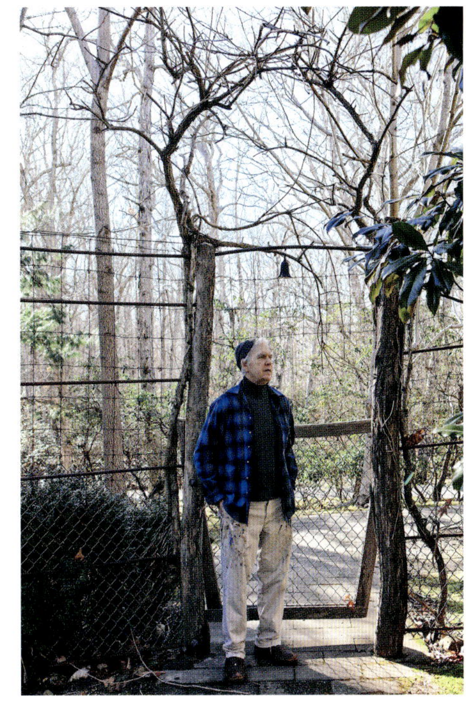

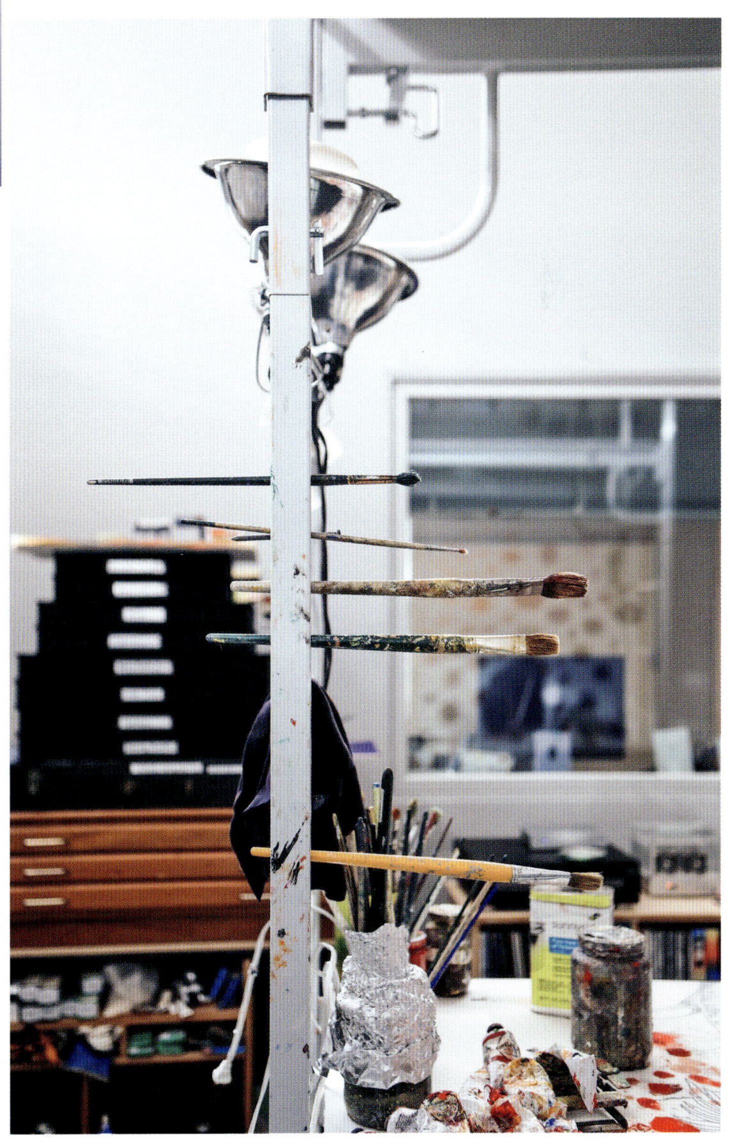

Though primarily an abstract painter, Teare's work often references his early landscape paintings. "I've worked a lot with the horizontal rectangle. That and a naturalist's sense of color are what remain from my time painting landscapes. My relationship to color is intuitive—feeling over thinking. I choose colors that are harmonic next to each other but aren't necessarily close on the color wheel." Teare works mostly in watercolor or oil on linen, canvas, or Mylar. "I like oil over acrylic because of the way light seems to reflect through it."

ABOVE AND RIGHT

The aesthetic of Teare's Noyac studio is eclectic, reflecting various influences on his art, which evolved from early landscape painting to his current abstract work.

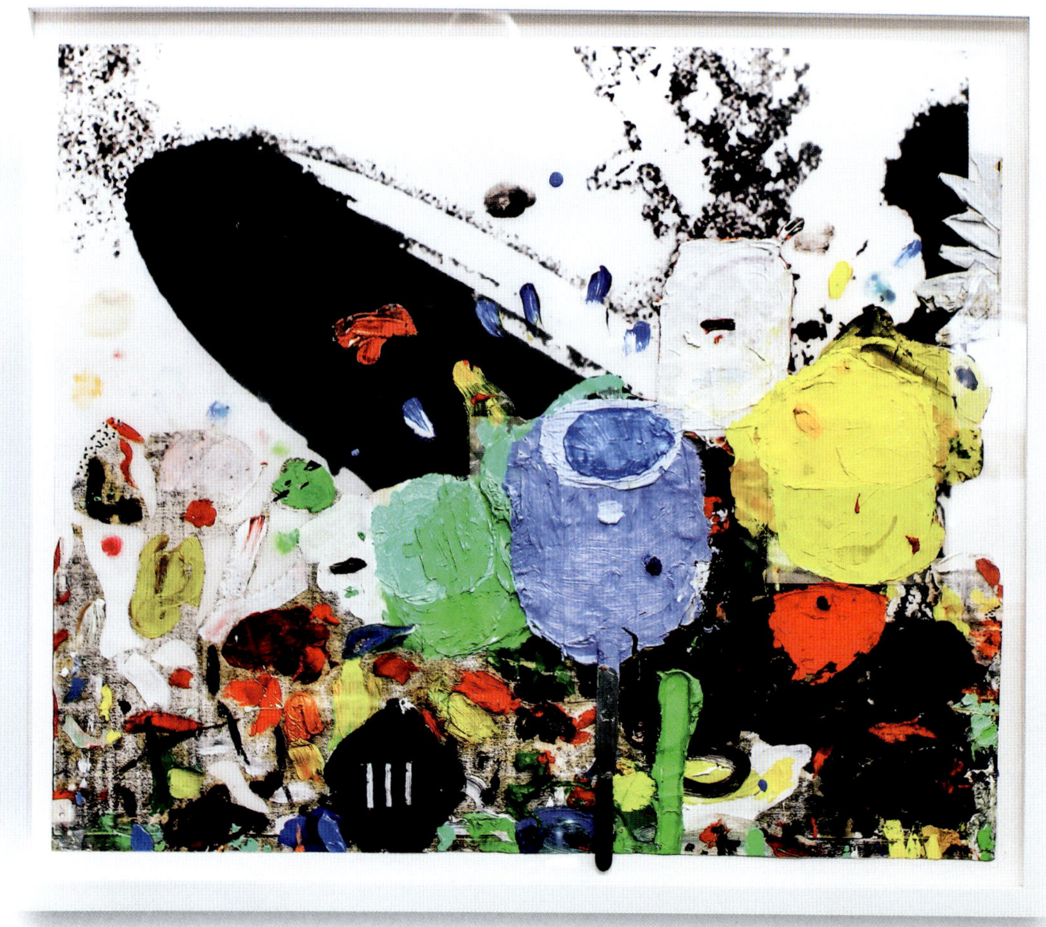

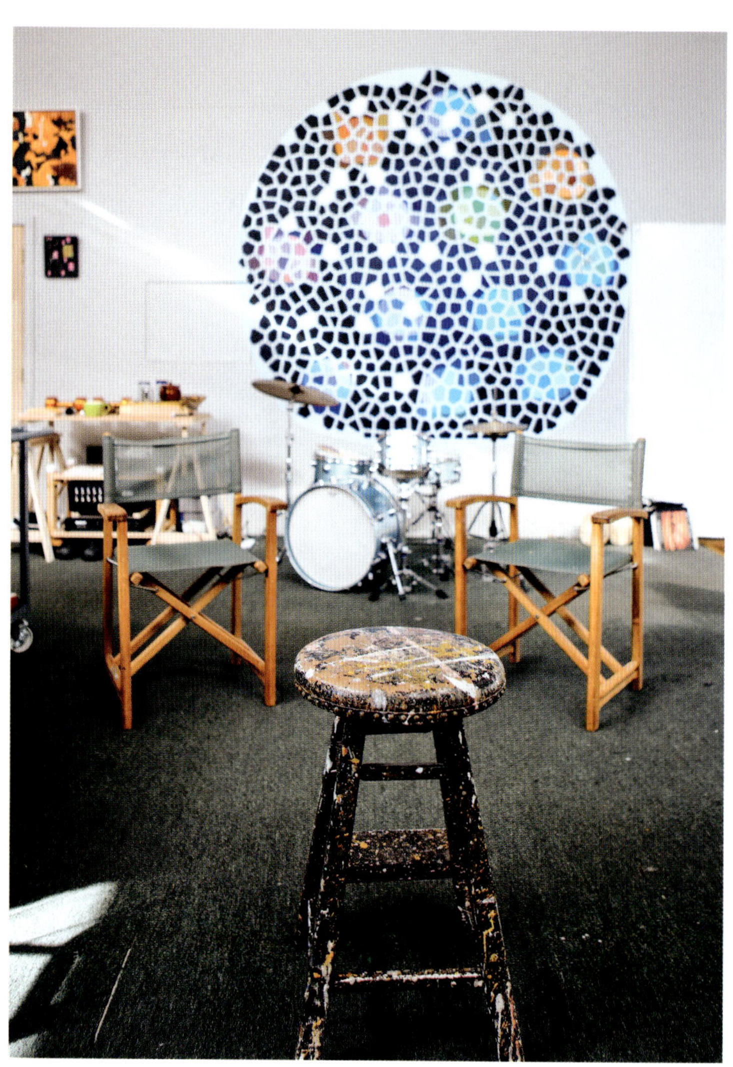

"In the seventies, I joined a rock band and began writing lyrics. When I moved to New York, I did some music reviewing for various arts publications. I've done a book of poetry and am working on a nonfiction book about dogs and love and grief. I don't see interests in music and writing as being separate from my visual work. I think the writer in me actually pushed me toward abstraction because it allowed me to explore a narrative in ways that aren't always obvious. I use flat images from time to time as symbols, but they, too, are abstracted." What inspires him? "World history, sports and military fashion, words, cartography, diagrams, and flow charts."

RIGHT AND OPPOSITE

In addition to painting, Teare plays music and writes lyrics and poetry—creative disciplines he views as intertwined with his visual work.

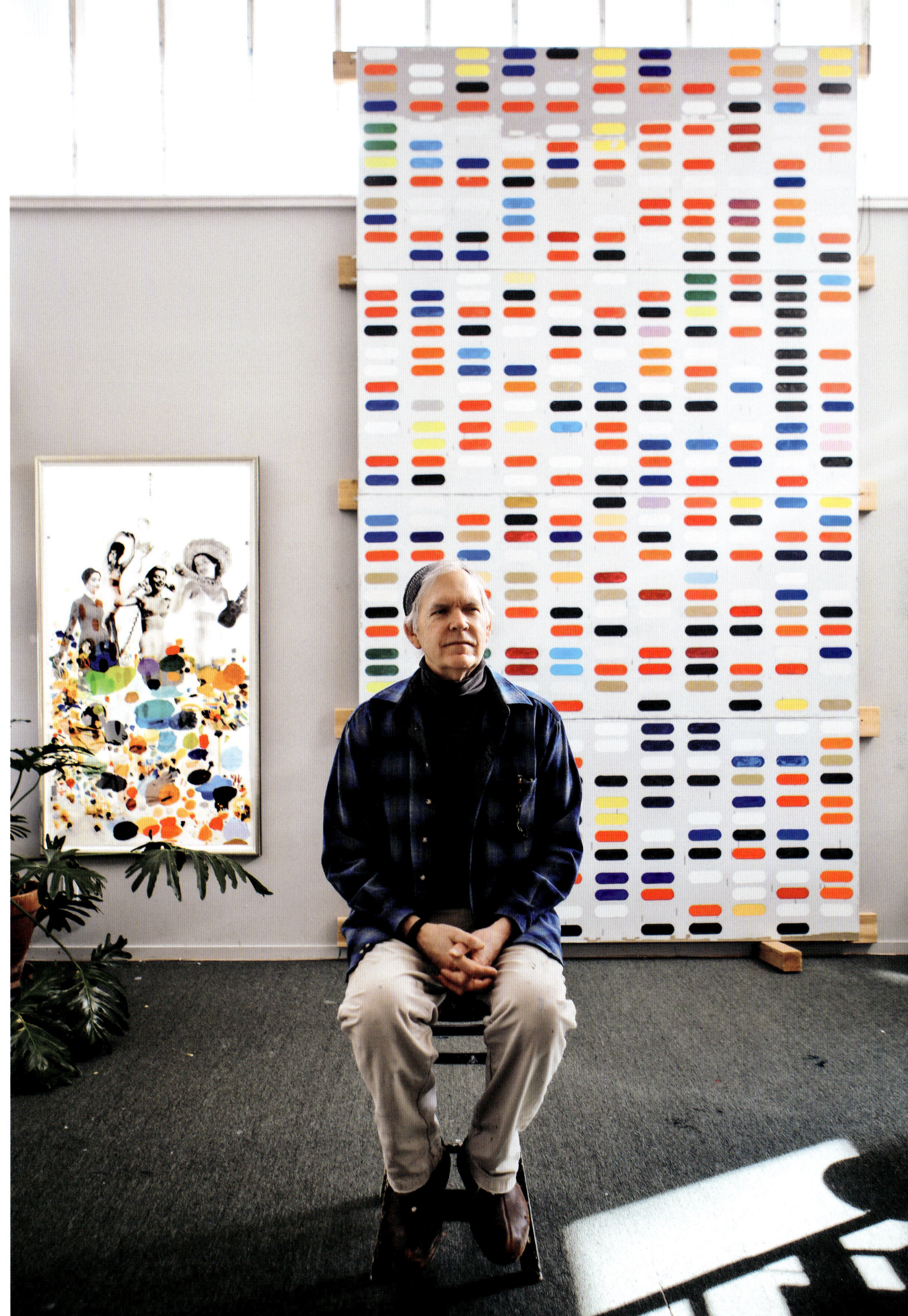

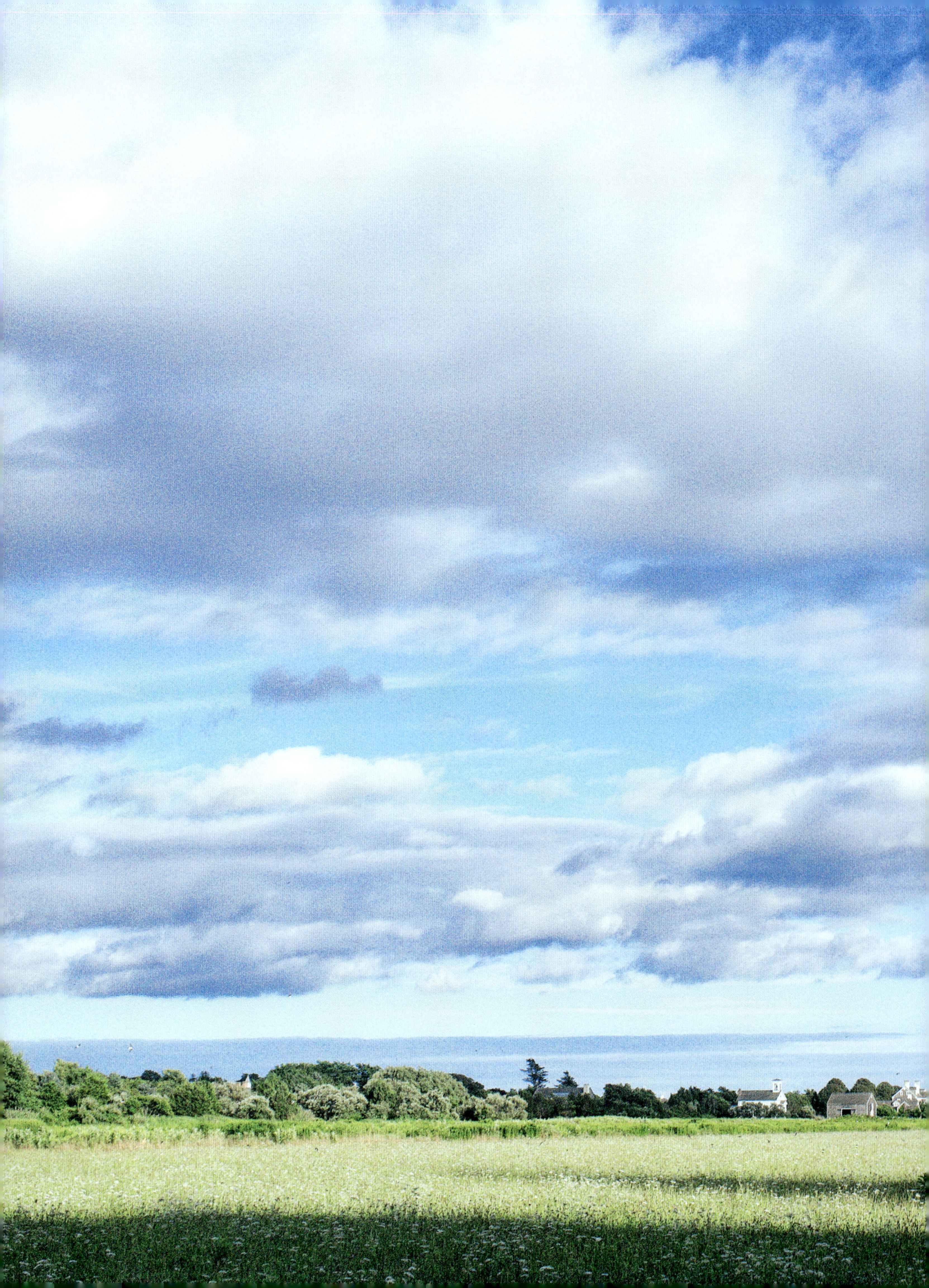

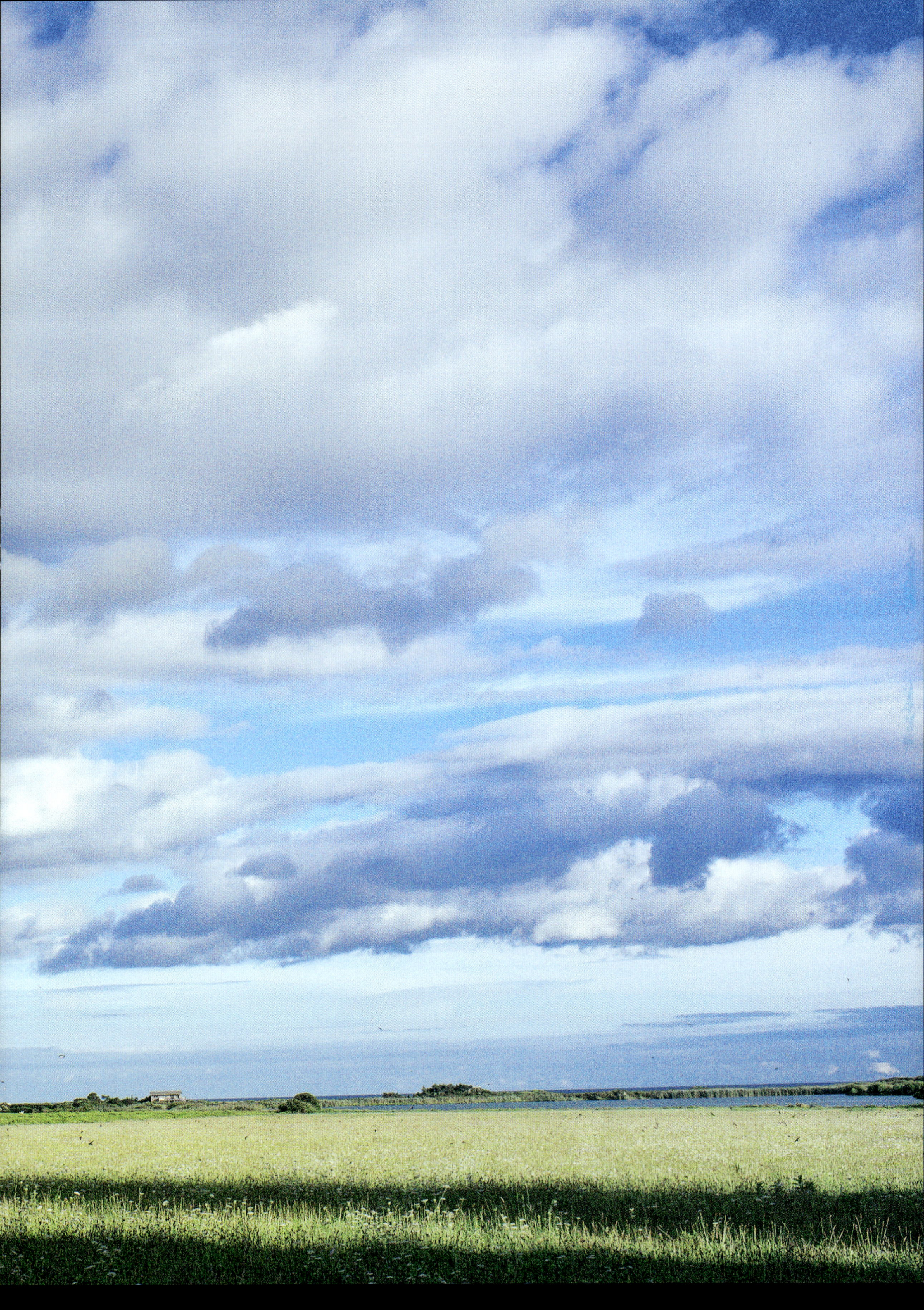

The circle, the dot, the sphere, expanding space, the Big Bang, the grid, time, and space.... All have emerged and reemerged in my life as parts of a symphony of images and ideas.

JOHN TORREANO

Torreano, born in Michigan, had his first experience with the East End as a resident at the Edward F. Albee Foundation in Montauk. "I stayed for the summer of 1969 and returned for the next one as well. The residency gave me a wonderful connection with the natural beauty of the East End and the Atlantic coast. In the early nineties, I saved enough to buy a house across from Havens Beach in Sag Harbor. In 2007, I sold that house to buy the place we have now, also in Sag Harbor, which has turned out to be one of my most productive studio/living spaces." The workspace is a combination studio and carpentry shop. "I have the usual palette of paints and brushes. But I also use a drill press, hand drills, routers, circular saws, jigsaws, and a table saw. I find I can 'draw' with cutting tools."

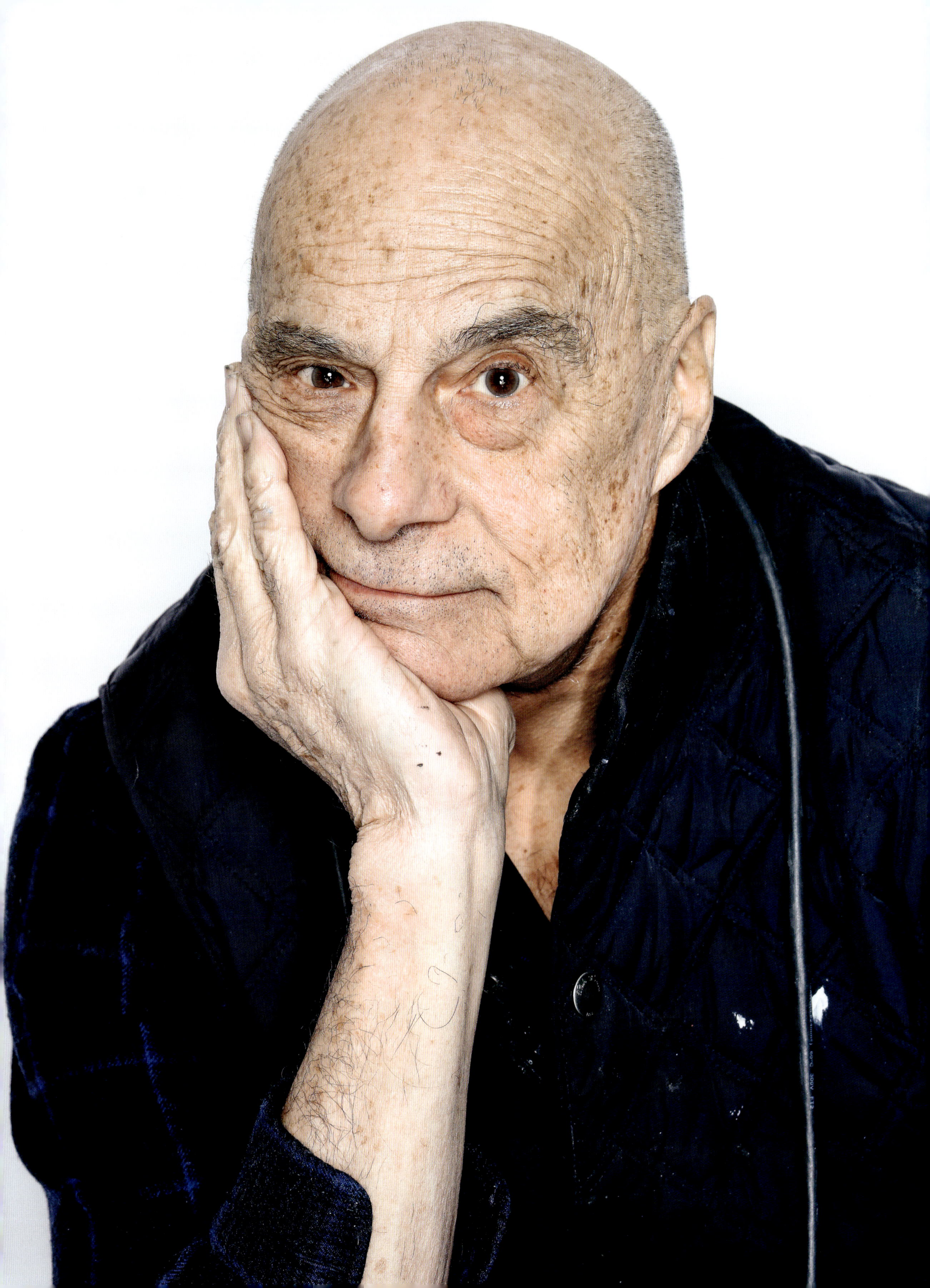

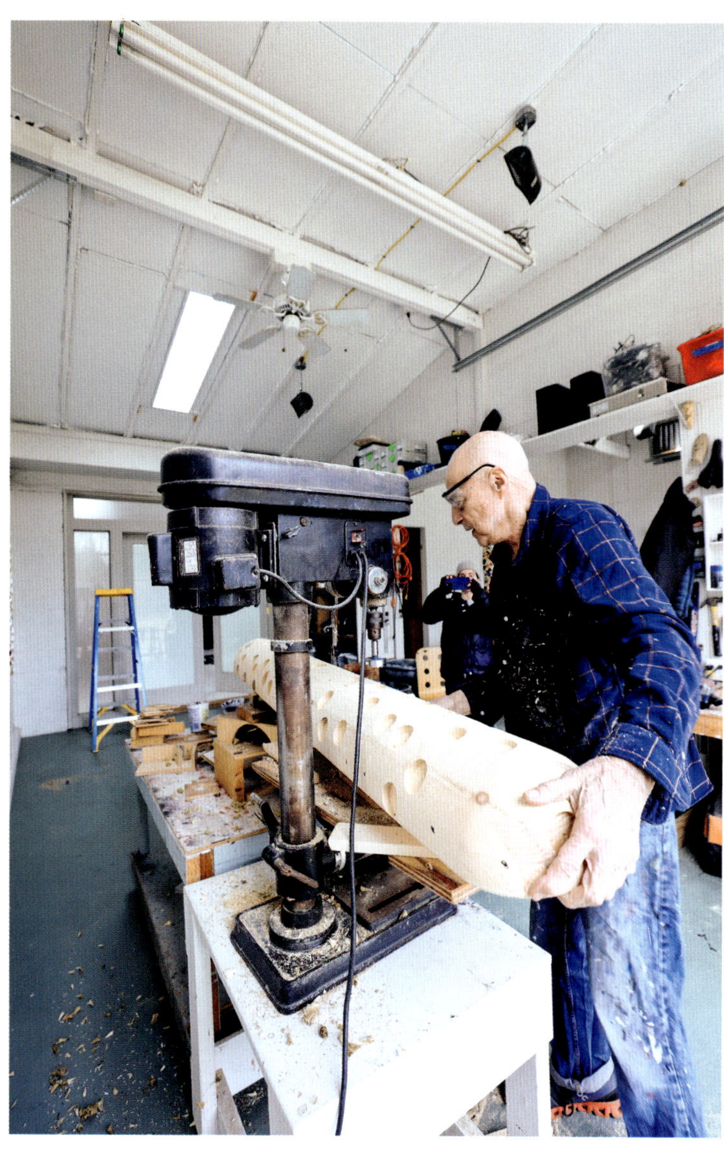

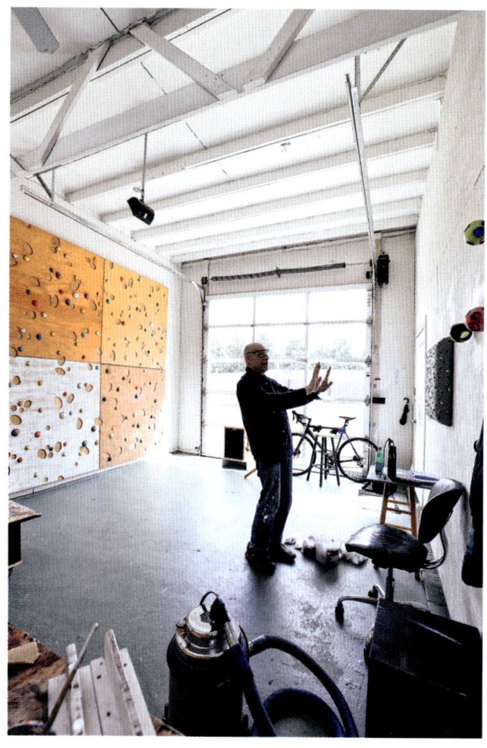

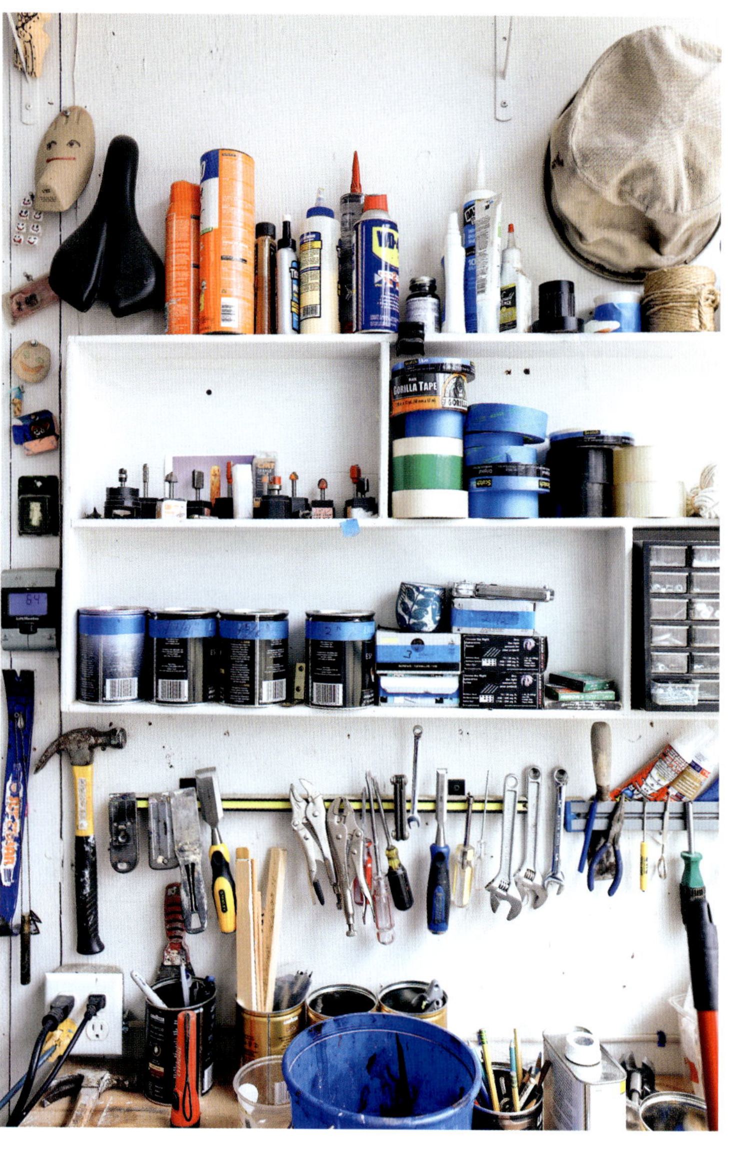

ABOVE LEFT

Torreano in his Sag Harbor studio, at work on one of his dot sculptures.

ABOVE RIGHT

The studio was previously used by a landscaper to store large machines and consisted of five bays with roof extensions to accommodate boats. The artist says that, once renovated, the building became one of the best studios he's ever had.

RIGHT

Paints, brushes, and an array of drills and cutting tools provide the artist with the means to create both paintings and sculptures.

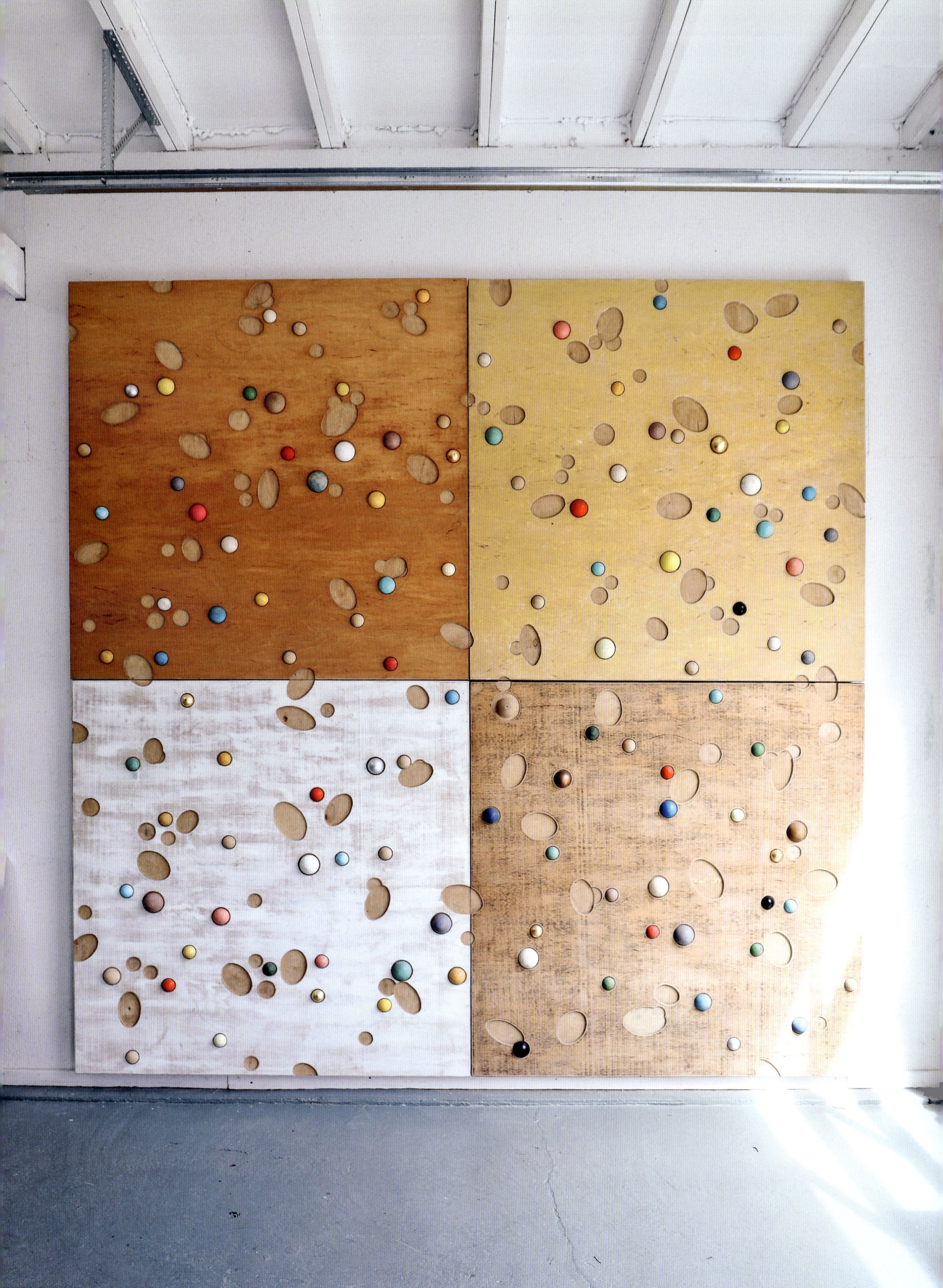

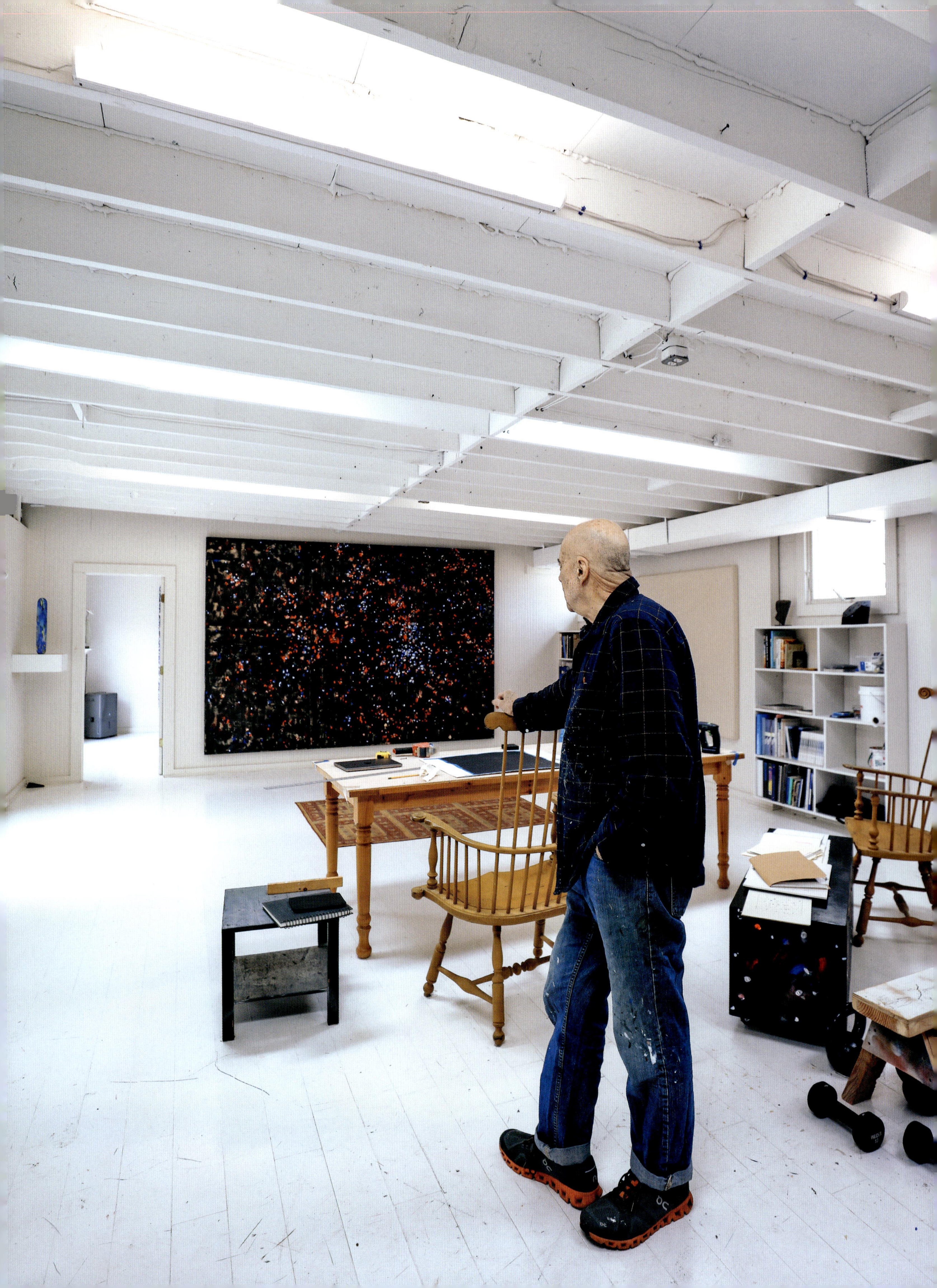

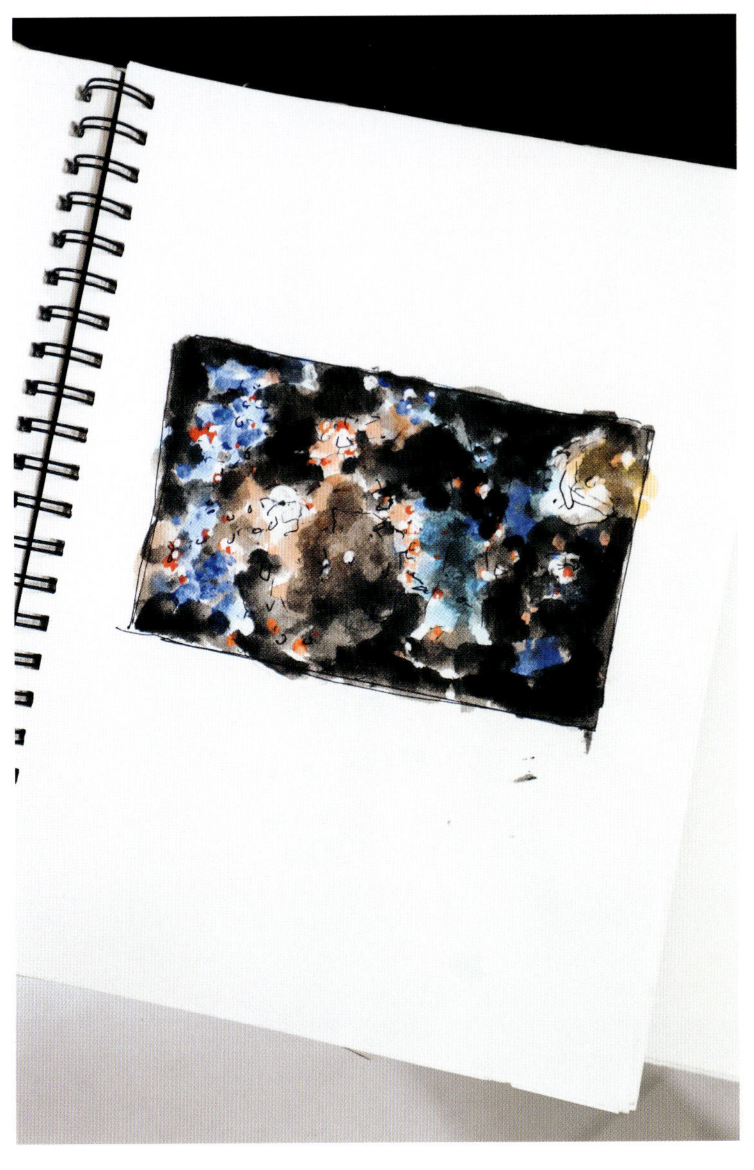

OPPOSITE
Torreano's work reveals a fascination with stars and galaxies. He calls outer space his "muse."

LEFT
A sketch in watercolor, pen, and acrylic that was inspired by a Hubble Space Telescope image of "twisters" in the Lagoon Nebula.

How did Torreano's fascination with gems begin? "In the sixties and seventies, Canal Street in Manhattan was like a Moroccan souk, with vendors selling all kinds of odds and ends. On one of my strolls, I saw a display of faceted-glass gems. They were reactive to my movements. I began doing a little dance in response to their reflections. If I stayed still, I would see one set of reflections. If I moved slightly, I would see another. Back and forth, right and left I danced. At that time, I was exploring a now-you-see-it-now-you-don't phenomenon with the use of dots in my paintings. The dots would reveal themselves according to the light and location of the viewer. These faceted gems were reacting to me in the same way, but much more explicitly. The Canal Street experience was an epiphany. It made something I had perceived unconsciously become conscious: the viewer triggers the aesthetic value of an art experience—not the artist. In other words, 'Beauty is in the eye of the beholder.'"

"The gems led me to stars. I'd done a series of eighteen-by-eighteen-inch plywood plaques covered with stretched felt. I glued the gems in a random pattern on the felt. But I soon realized that my distributions were cliché. I needed something to look at that would help make the distributions less predictable, more unique. What in nature is like a dot? Stars! I began to read about them, and my journey from a dot to outer space commenced. I discovered that astronomical concepts like curvature, time, and space aligned with my understanding of painterly space. I had found my muse."

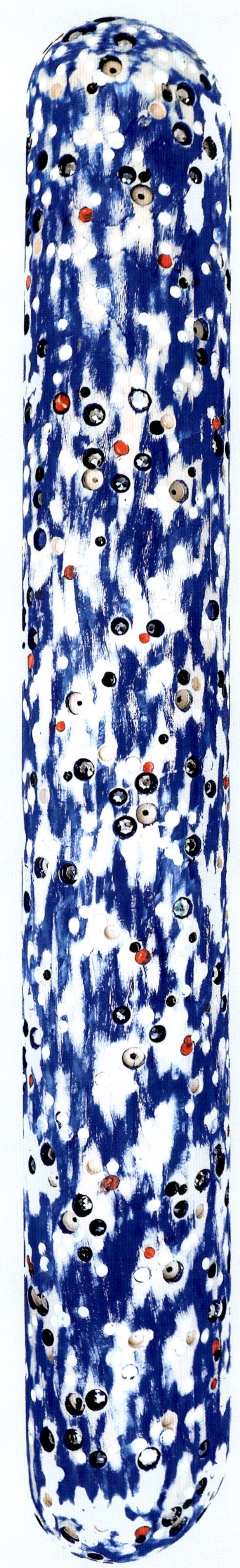

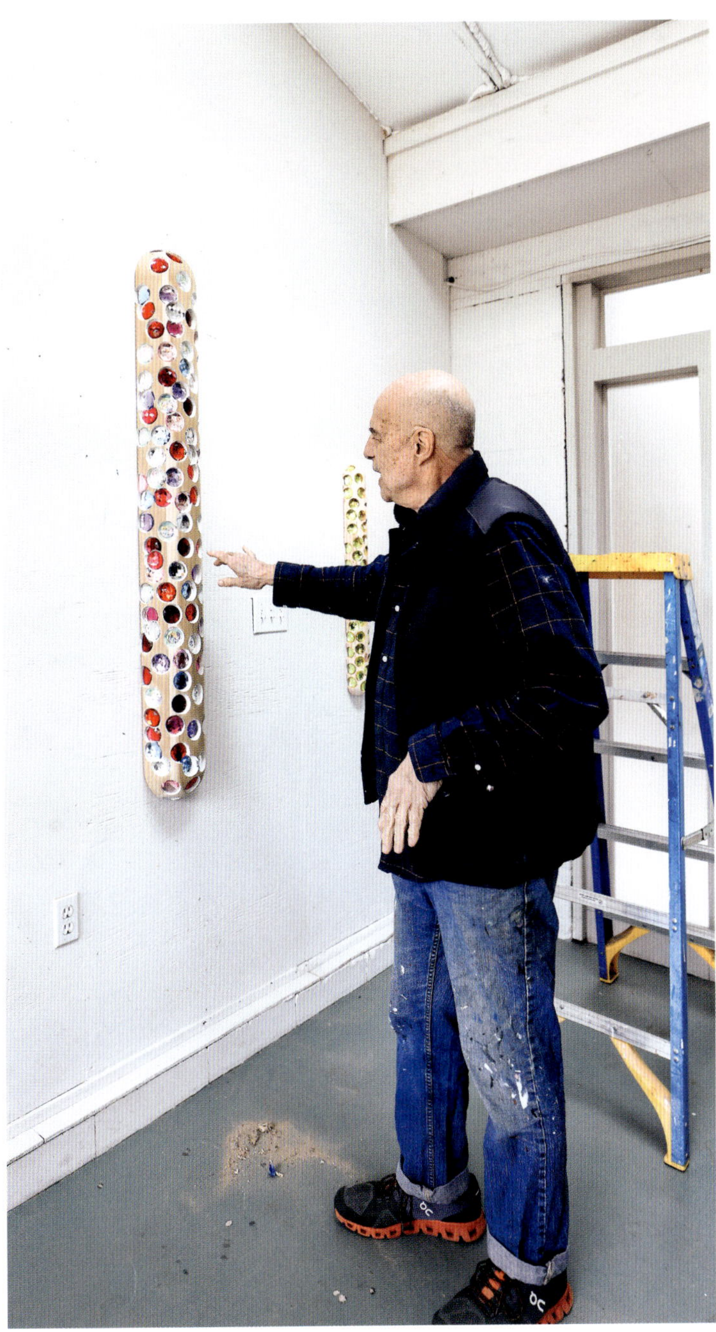

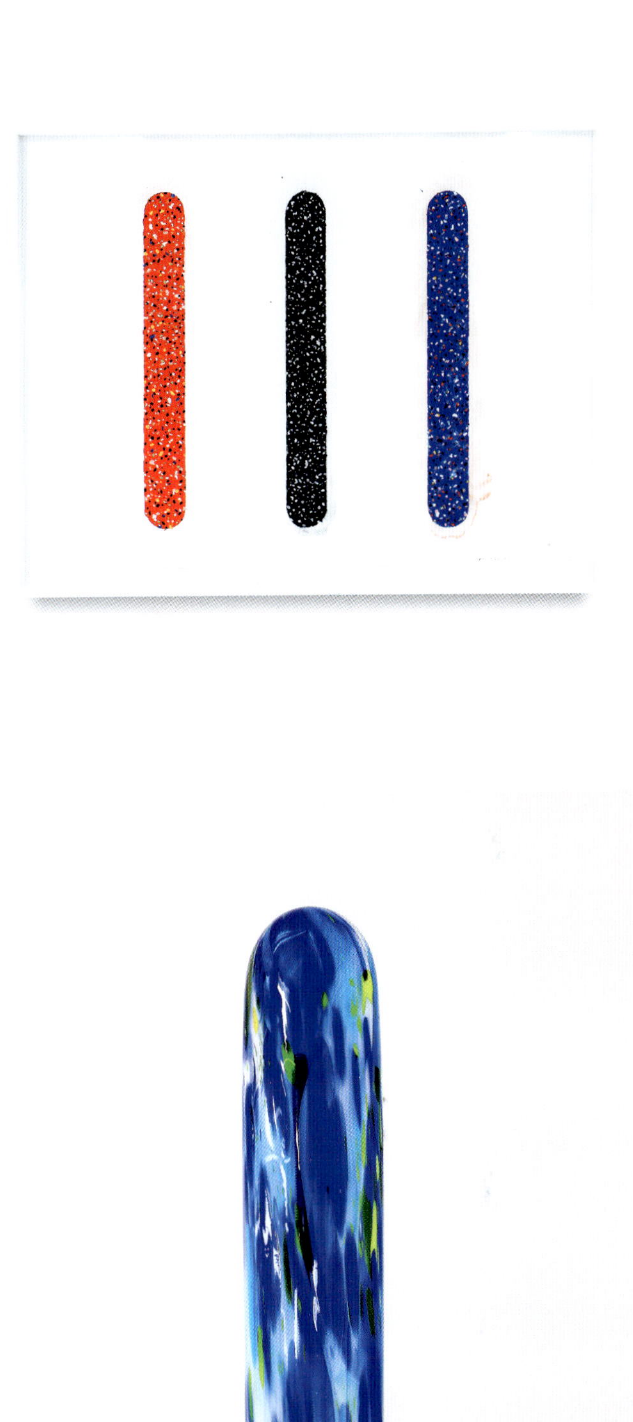

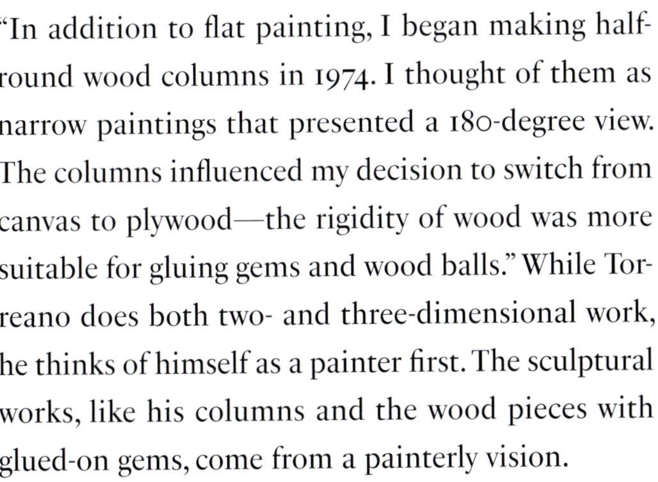

"In addition to flat painting, I began making half-round wood columns in 1974. I thought of them as narrow paintings that presented a 180-degree view. The columns influenced my decision to switch from canvas to plywood—the rigidity of wood was more suitable for gluing gems and wood balls." While Torreano does both two- and three-dimensional work, he thinks of himself as a painter first. The sculptural works, like his columns and the wood pieces with glued-on gems, come from a painterly vision.

I look at work by a lot of different artists and I study mythology and religion, the works of tribal people and their beautiful shapes. I start doodling, and that's when I'll come up with an idea.

HANS VAN DE BOVENKAMP

Van de Bovenkamp's abstract sculptures, in bronze, steel, and aluminum, are elegant, dynamic, and often anthropomorphic. The monolithic pieces are feats of scale and substance. "I trained as an architect and engineer and spent years designing fountains before concentrating on steel and aluminum sculptures." His monumental sculptures have been installed all over the world.

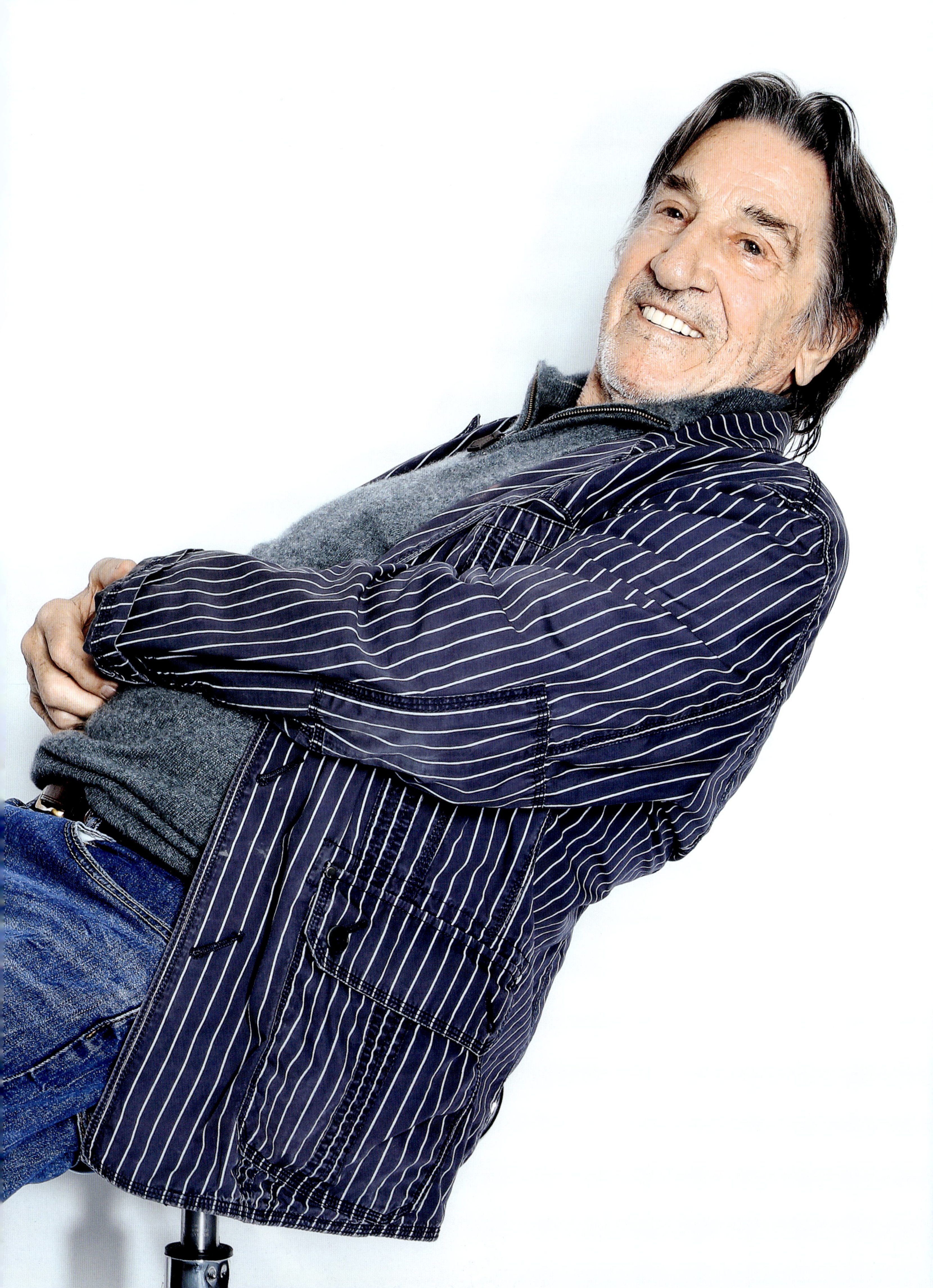

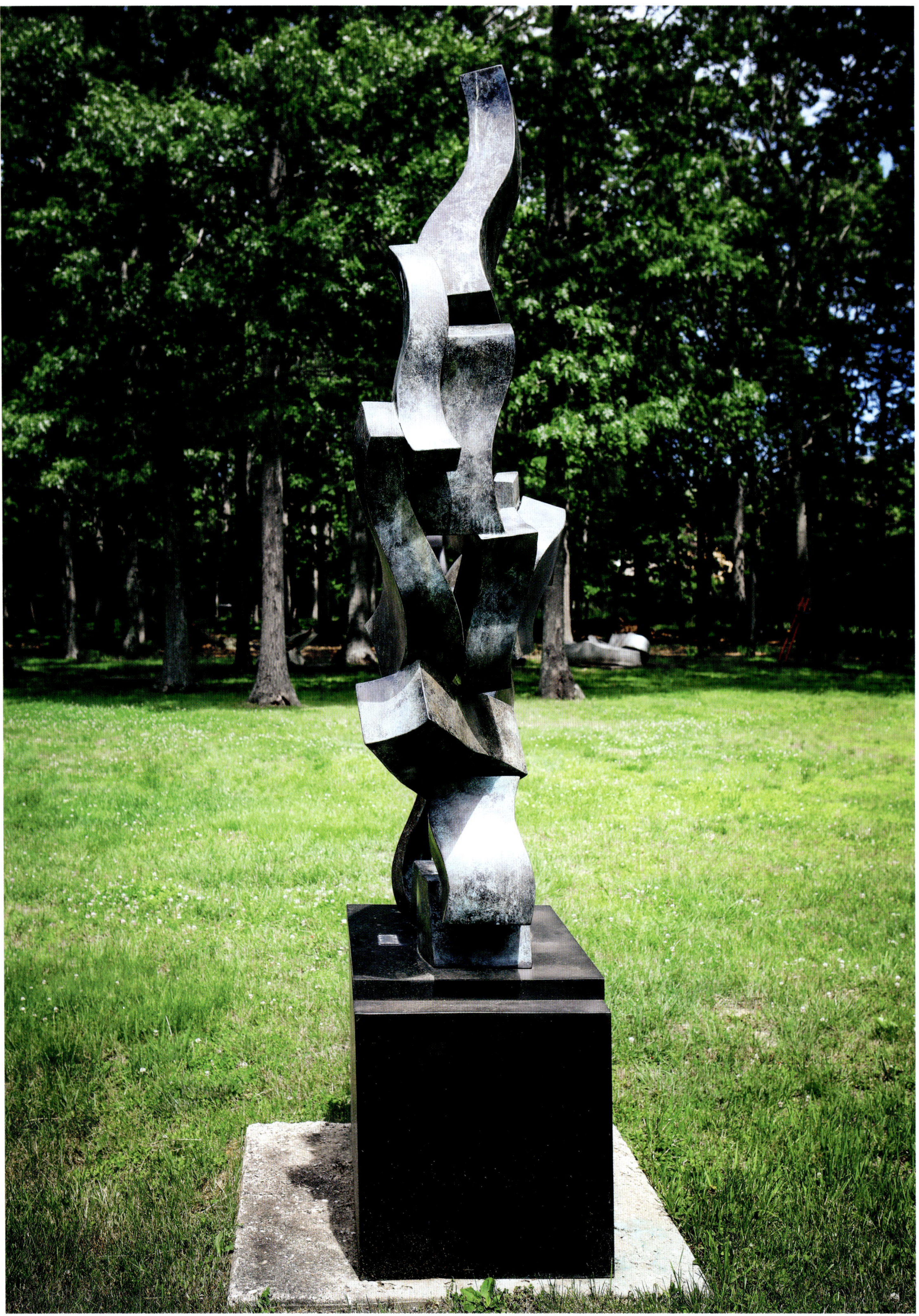

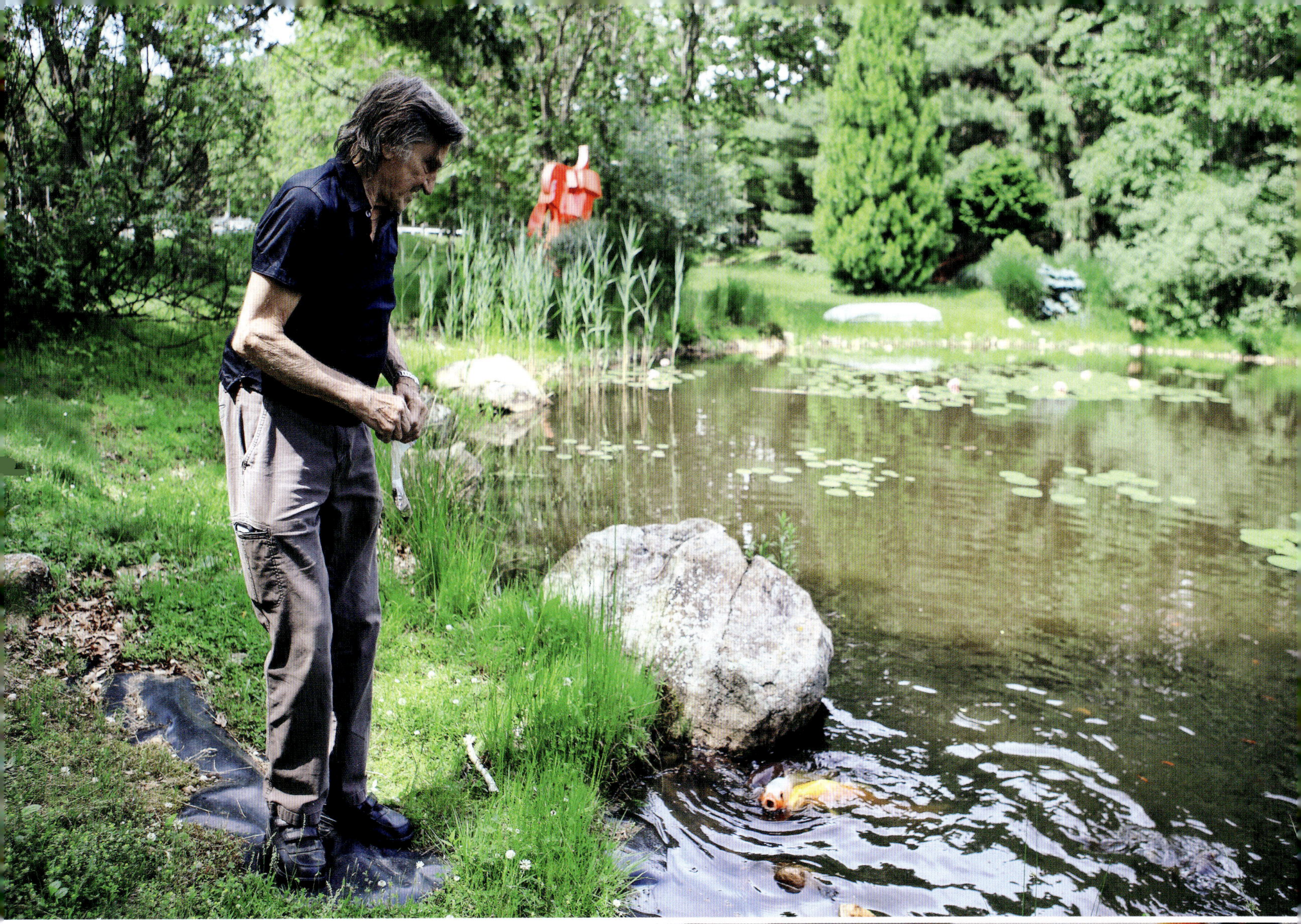

Born in Holland, Van de Bovenkamp moved to Canada in 1957, then to New York City in the 1960s. He first visited the East End in 1963, when he delivered a sculpture that he'd sold to Edward Albee, who was living in Montauk. The nature and architecture of the Hamptons attracted him immediately, as did the community of artists he met. "I rented a beach house in Amagansett and in 2002 moved full-time to Sagaponack, where I created an art compound comprised of my house, several studios, and a large sculpture garden on the rural, farm-like property. The low horizons of Sagaponack make the sculptures soar."

ABOVE The artist on his bucolic, farm-like property in Sagaponack.

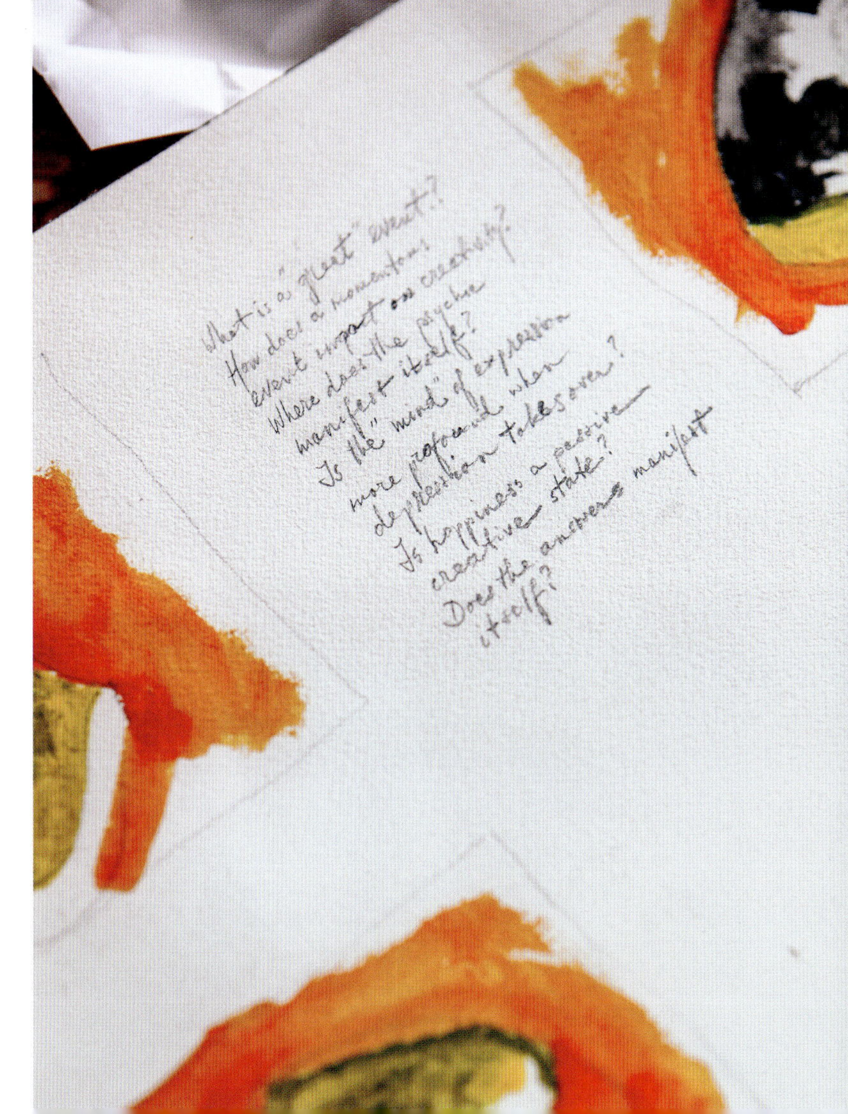

RIGHT

Van de Bovenkamp's spacious studio barn, which he opens up to visitors and friends and where he sometimes hosts exhibitions of other artists' work.

BELOW

The artist's office is home to archives of thousands of photos, slides, and digital files, as well as an array of books by his late wife, Siv Cedering, and an eclectic mix of artifacts from his extensive travels.

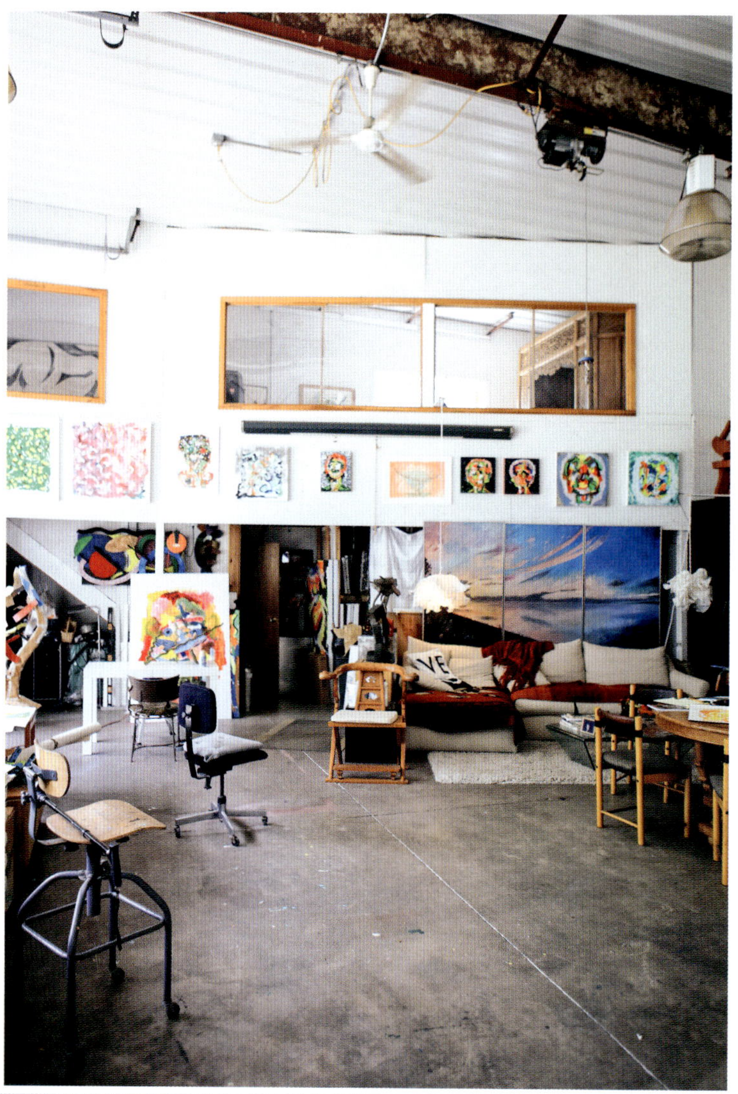

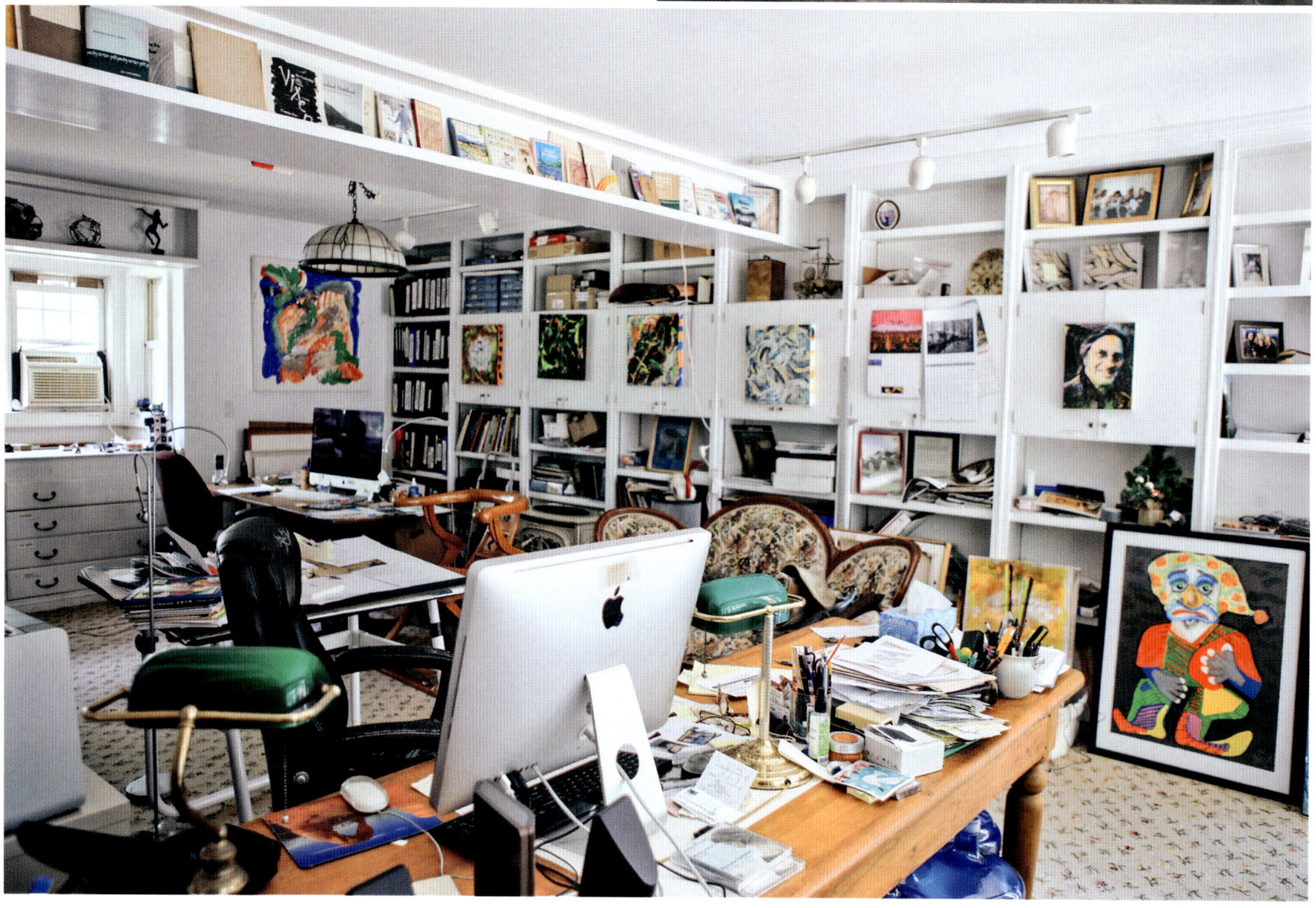

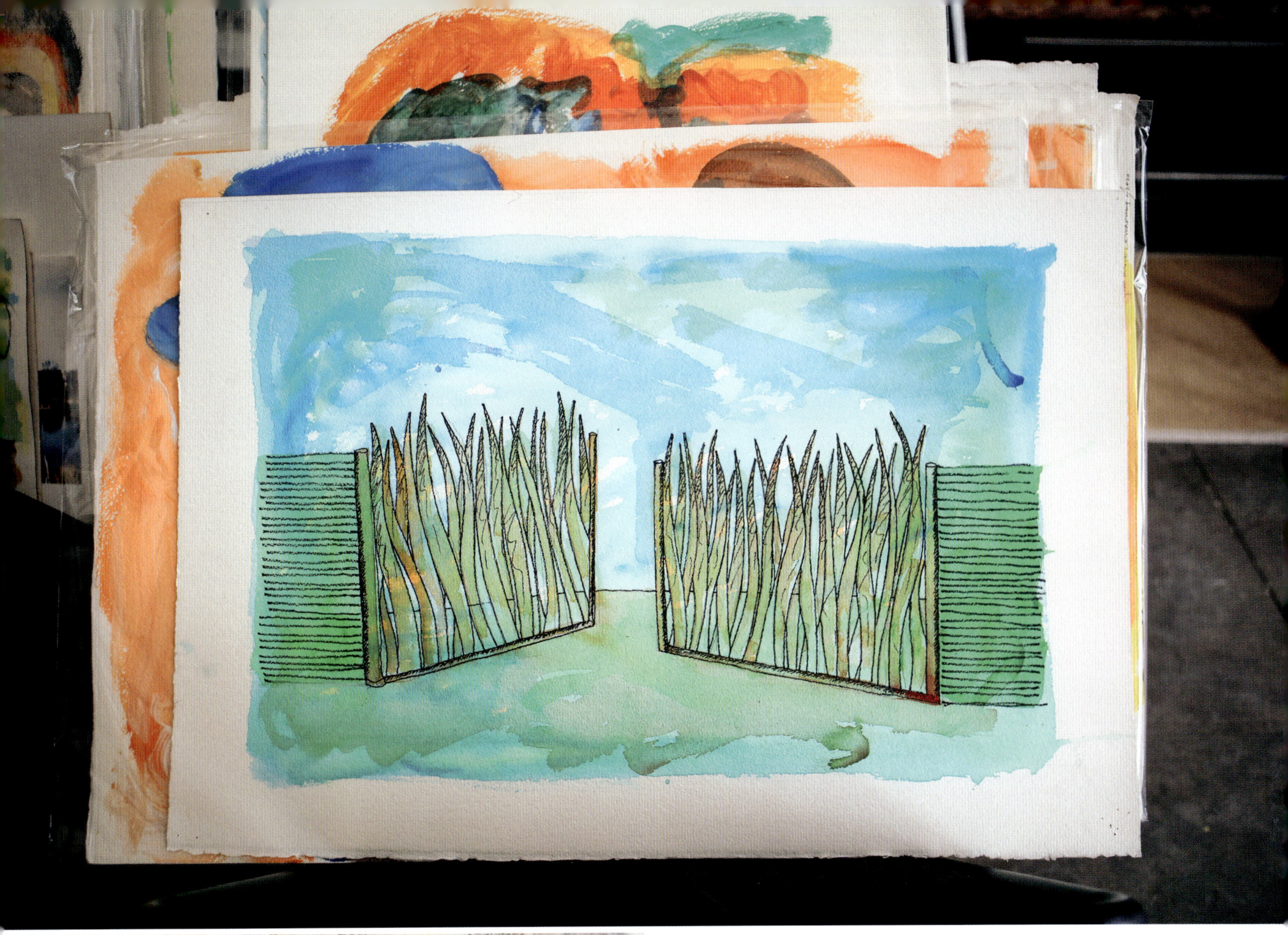

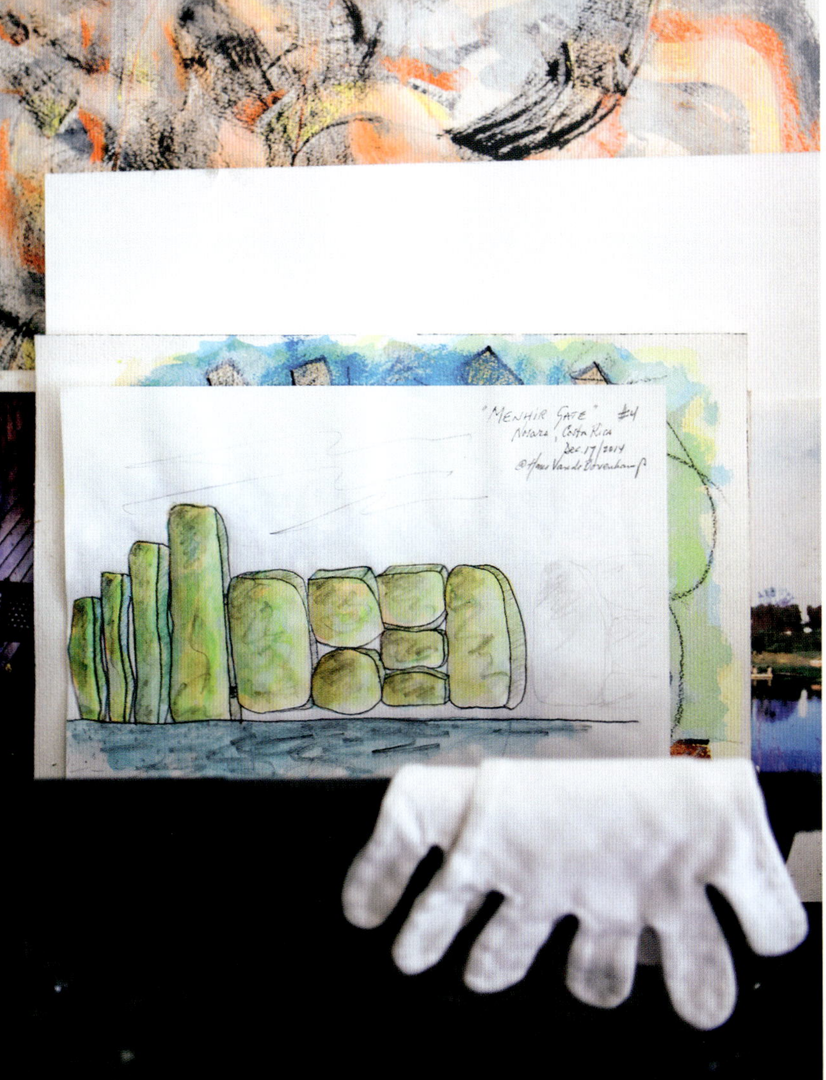

"Nature is the most important thing in my work. I've spent a lot of time contemplating and learning from it. Looking at the three-dimensional leaves teaches you about depth. Wind is beautiful when it activates the trees. On the surface of a pond, you see a lot of action. And nature gives you qualities of light and dark that translate into sculpture. Bronze absorbs light. Steel reflects it, and by making small scratches in the surface you can pick up on the sun's rays."

ABOVE AND LEFT

The artist now spends more time drawing and painting than welding sculptures.

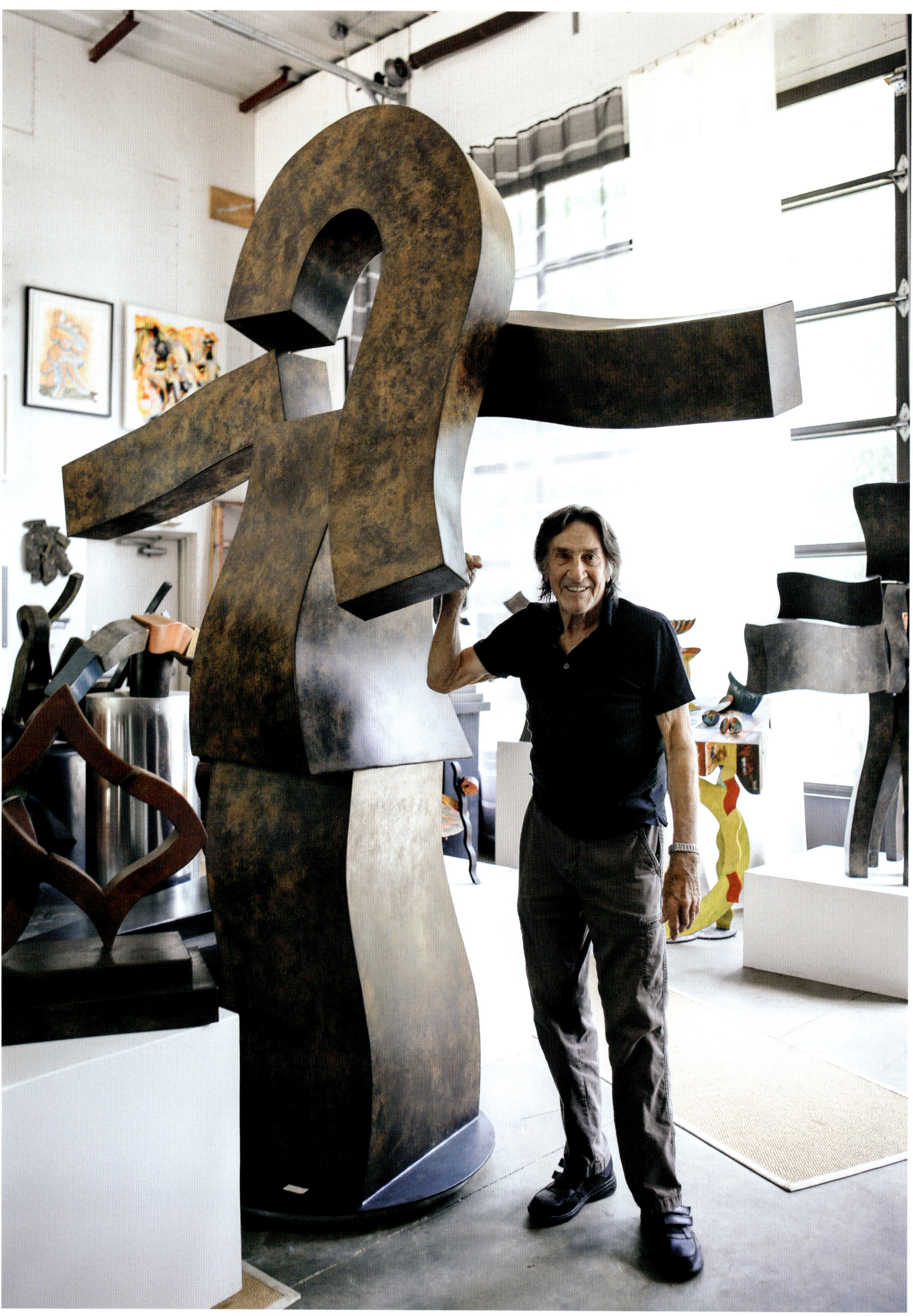

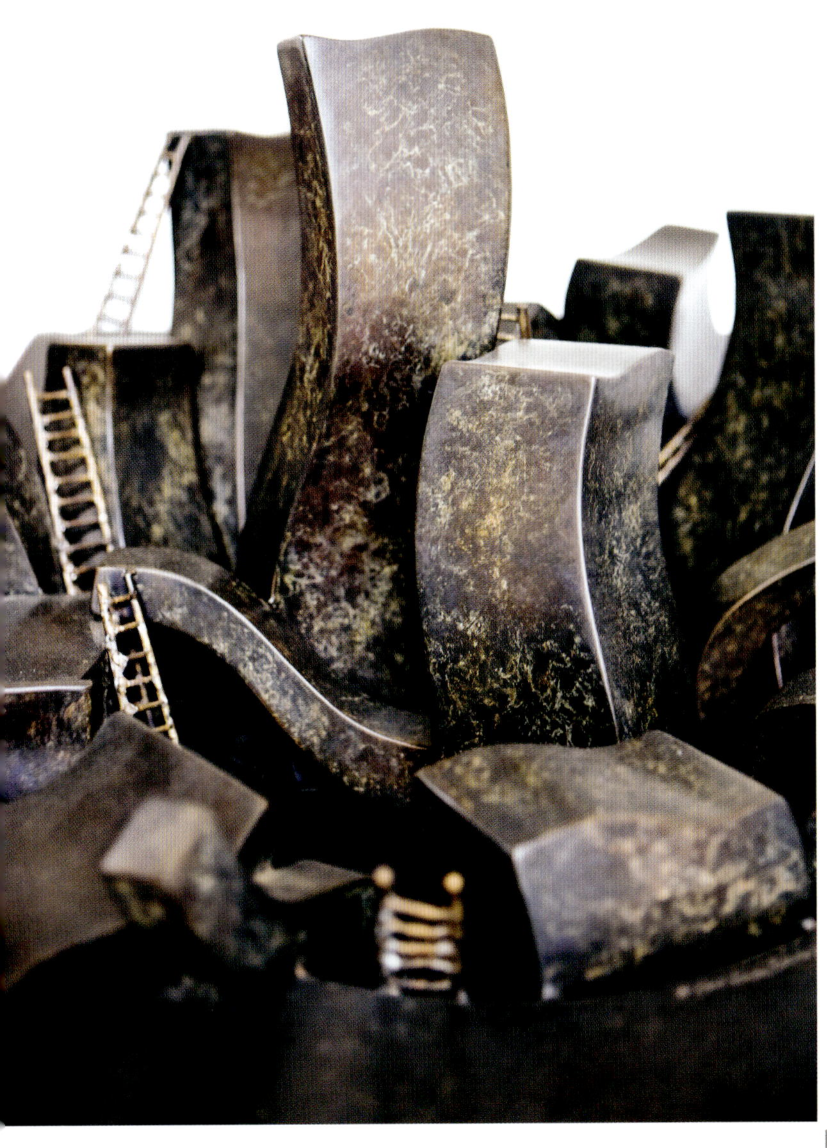

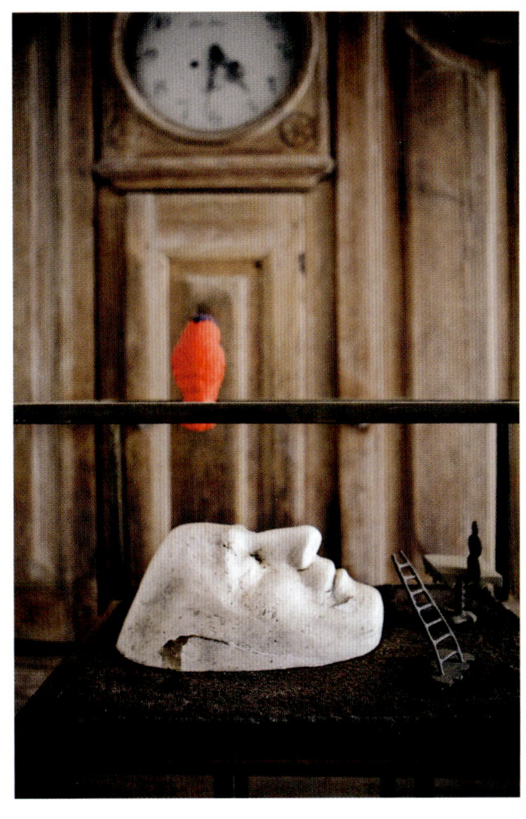

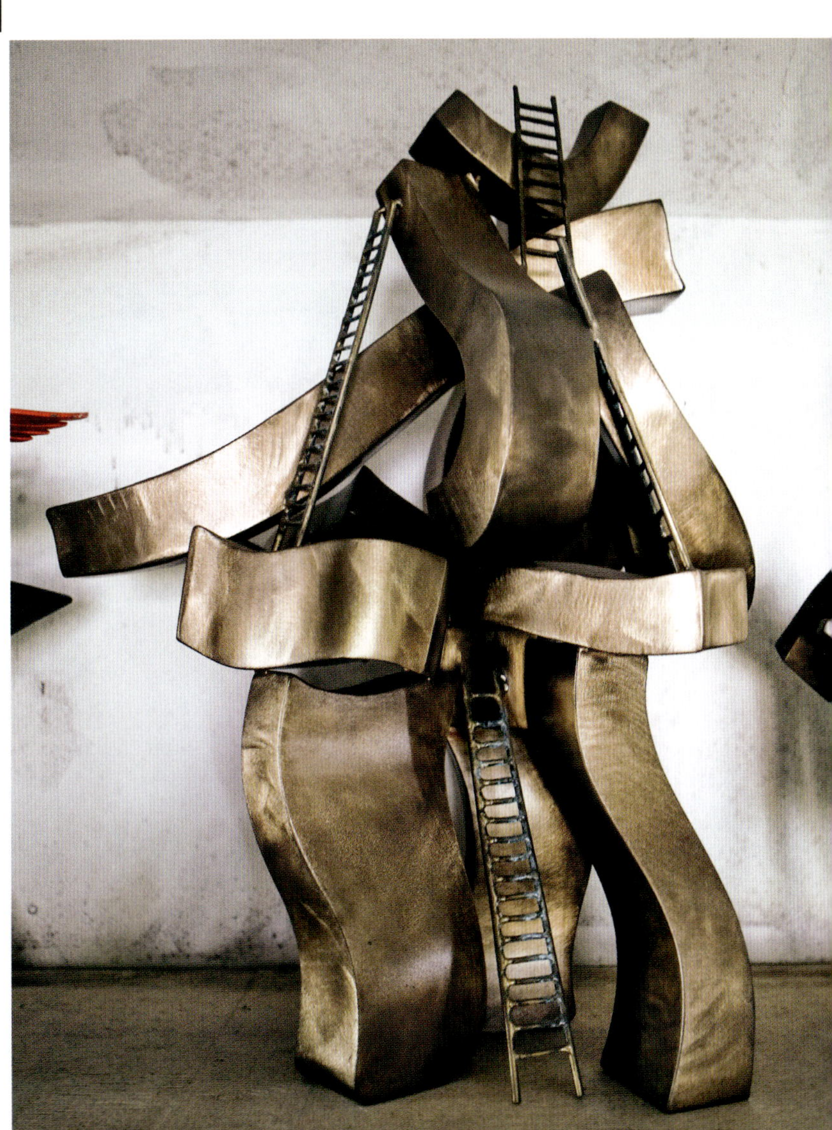

OPPOSITE AND THIS PAGE

Van de Bovenkamp is known for his large—often monumental—bronze and steel abstract sculptures, which have been commissioned and installed all over the world.

When I moved here, I understood why artists had been painting out east since the 1800s. You look at the sky of a Thomas Moran painting and the sky looks like that today.

SUSAN VECSEY

Vecsey grew up in New Jersey and went to college and graduate school in New York City. "At that time, I didn't really know you could be an artist. I didn't really know about any living or working artists until much later." She eventually created a body of work and put on her own show, which led to getting a dealer. Vecsey first came to the Hamptons in her twenties. "I remember going to beach parties and visiting galleries and museums. In 2000, I bought a weekend place in East Hampton and over the years have spent more and more time here. Now it's home."

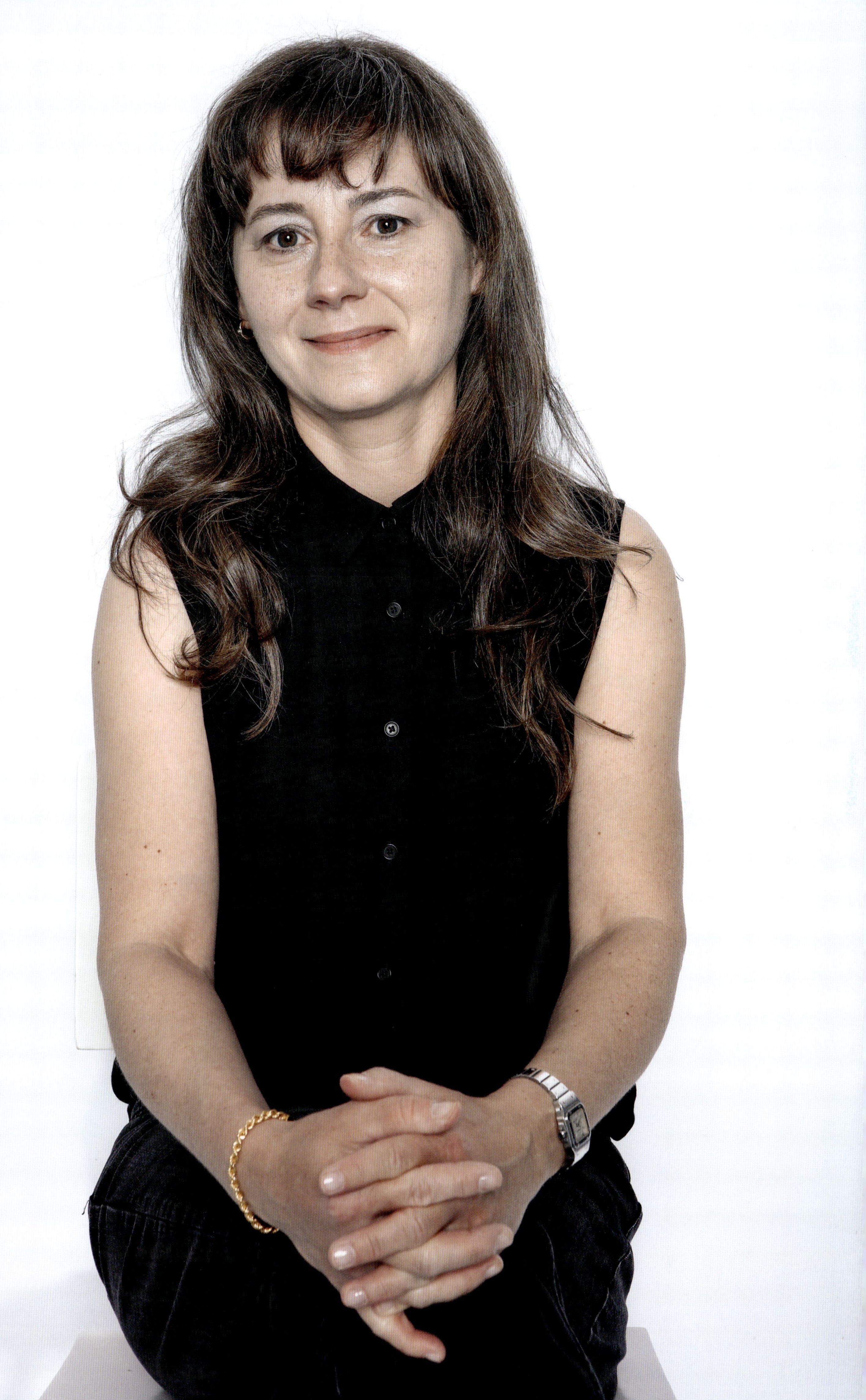

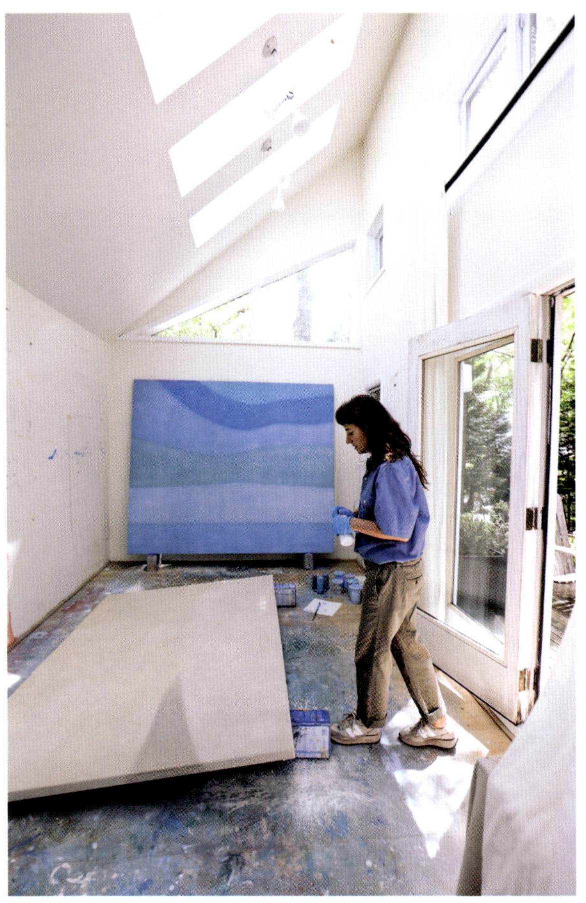

“I always wanted to create paintings with beautiful surfaces without brush marks. To me that meant working with diluted oil paint and no brushes. Working flat on the floor helps to control the flow of the paint. I primarily work with oil on linen. I pour thin layers of paint, staining the linen somewhat like the Color Field painters of the 1960s. It’s one-shot action painting, day after day in an iterative process, until the layers build up to saturated color.”

ABOVE

Vecsey lays her canvases on the floor so she can control the flow of paint and achieve a surface devoid of brush marks.

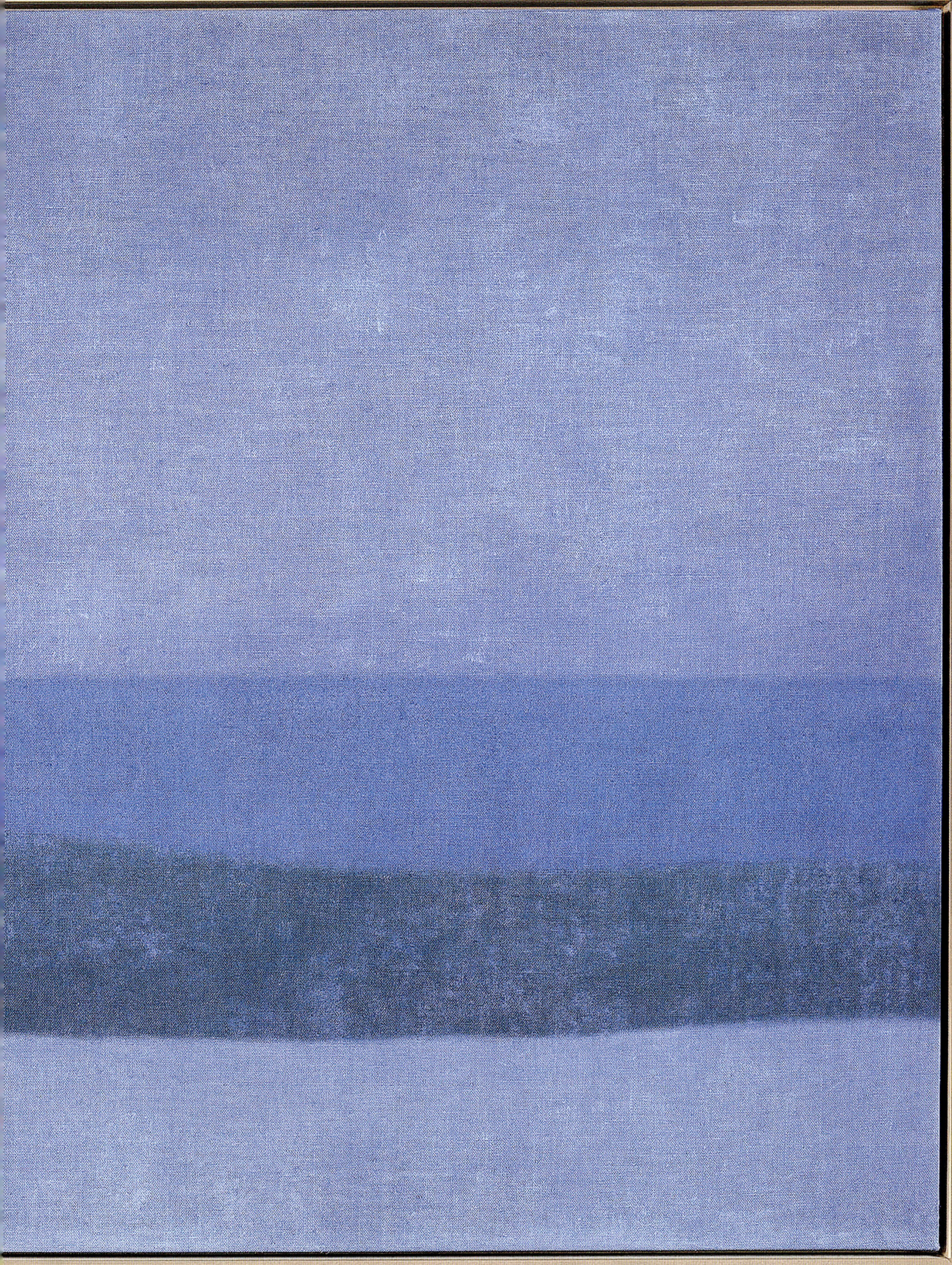

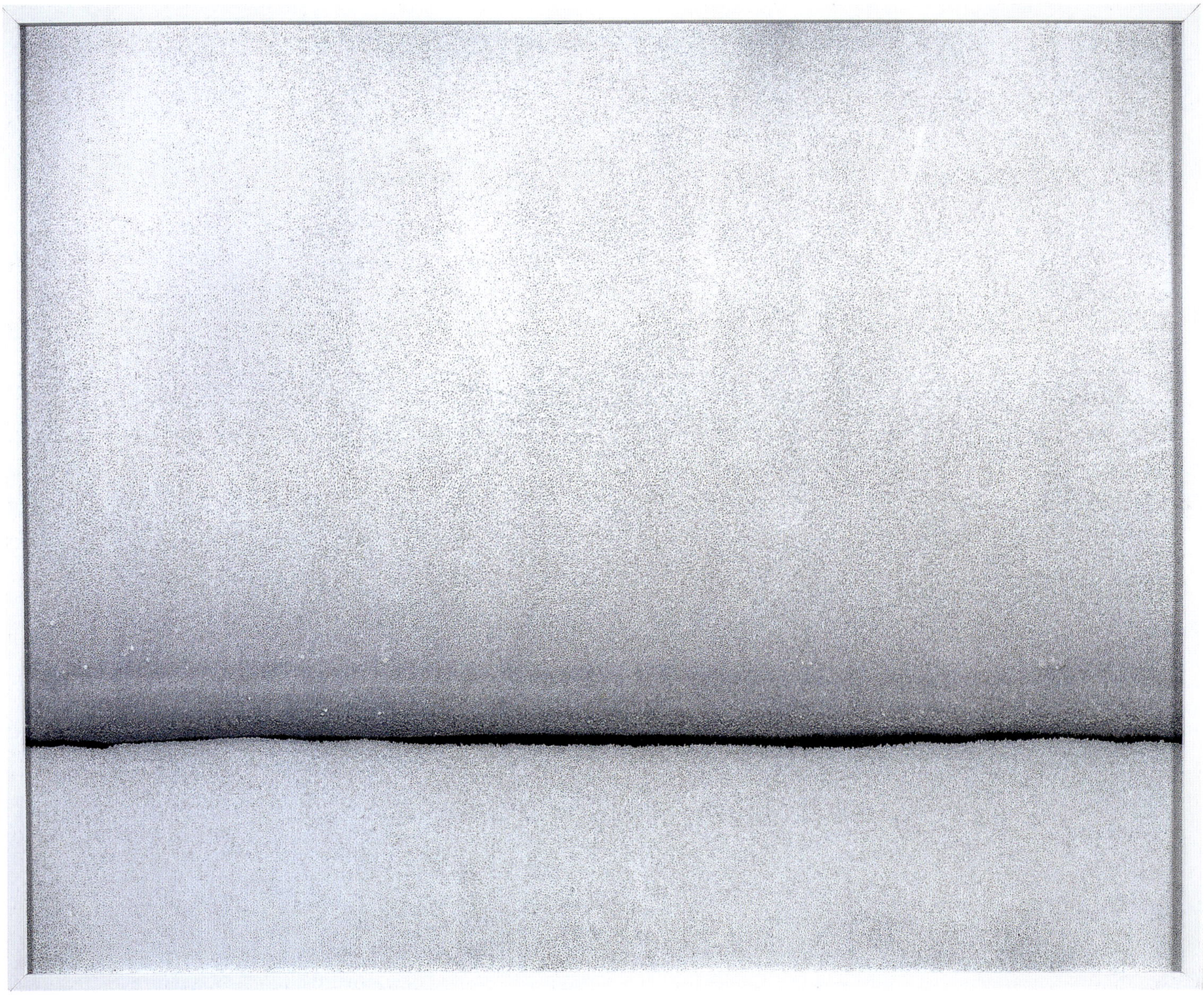

"For me, the landscape is a vehicle into painting. Over the years, my compositions have become more minimal and abstract, yet I still use the horizon line and the symbolism of the horizon line." Vecsey works from observation. "I draw outdoors and take those drawings back to the studio. Then I think about the right size for a composition and build the stretcher and stretch the linen. Finally, I think about the colors for that composition, which usually requires many color studies to find four or five colors that will lock together visually. I don't always use color in a literal way, but the quality of it is definitely informed by the light here. You can't really get away from it; it's in everything you see."

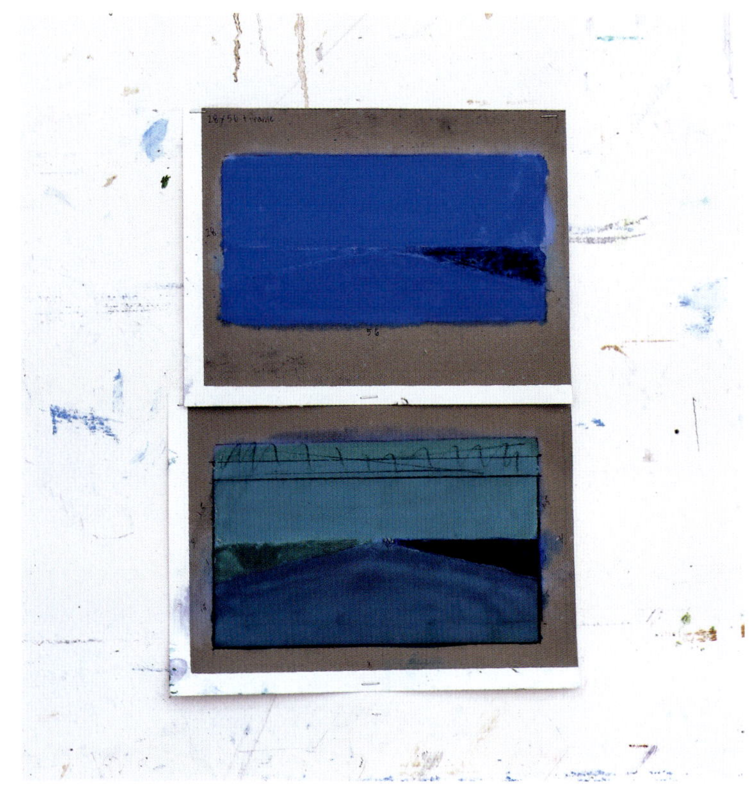

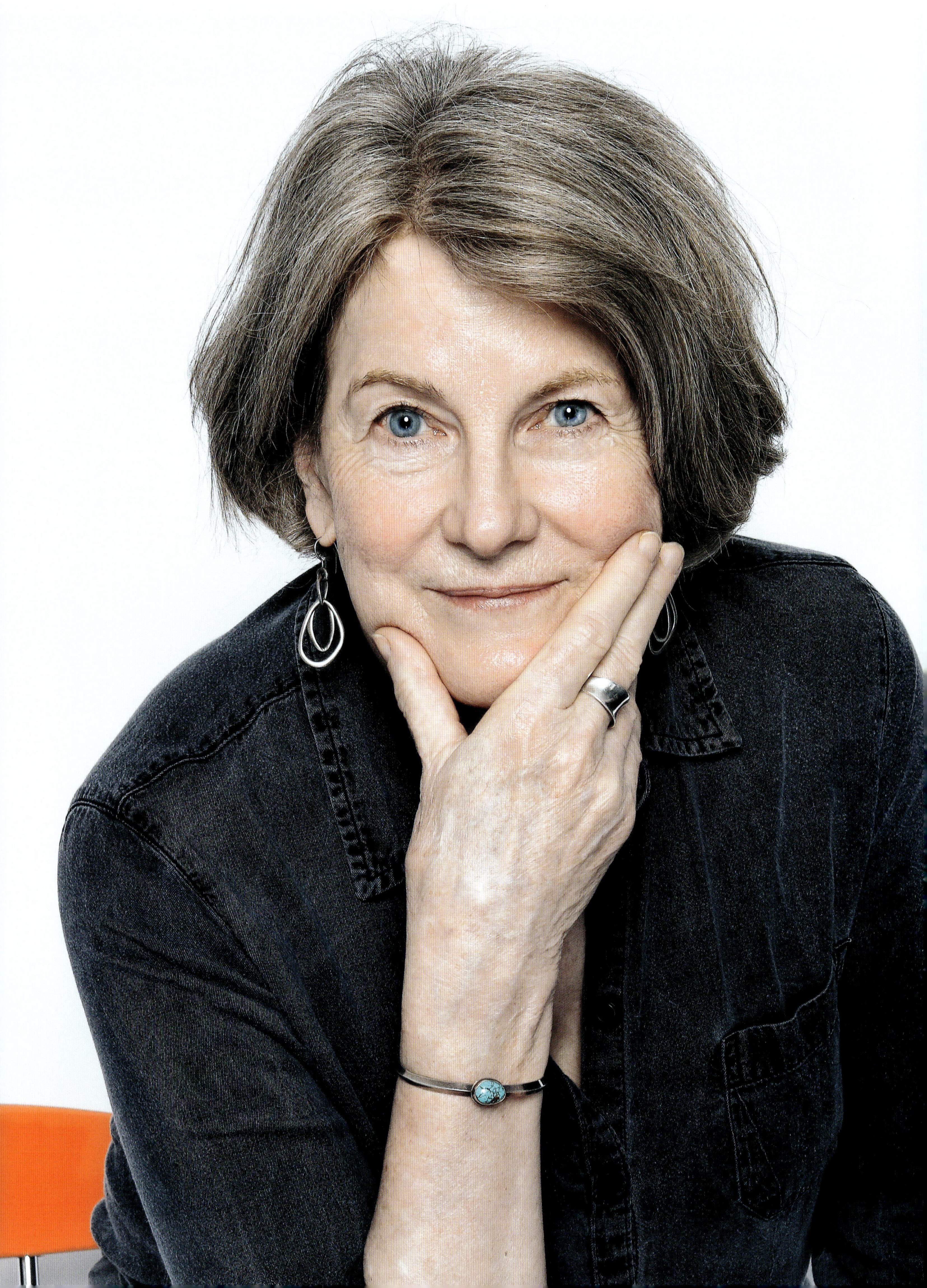

I grapple with the physical and
tactile qualities of the leather,
and the poetry of its multiple histories.

CLAIRE WATSON

Watson moved from Austin, Texas, to Manhattan in 1984 after graduate school. She and her husband married in 1990 and started building their house in Water Mill while living in the city. "We did most of the work ourselves over a period of about ten years. Our two sons grew up with scaffolding in the living room. And even though it was not quite finished, the house became our full-time home in 1996. We raised our sons here; our studios are here—we feel deeply connected to this place."

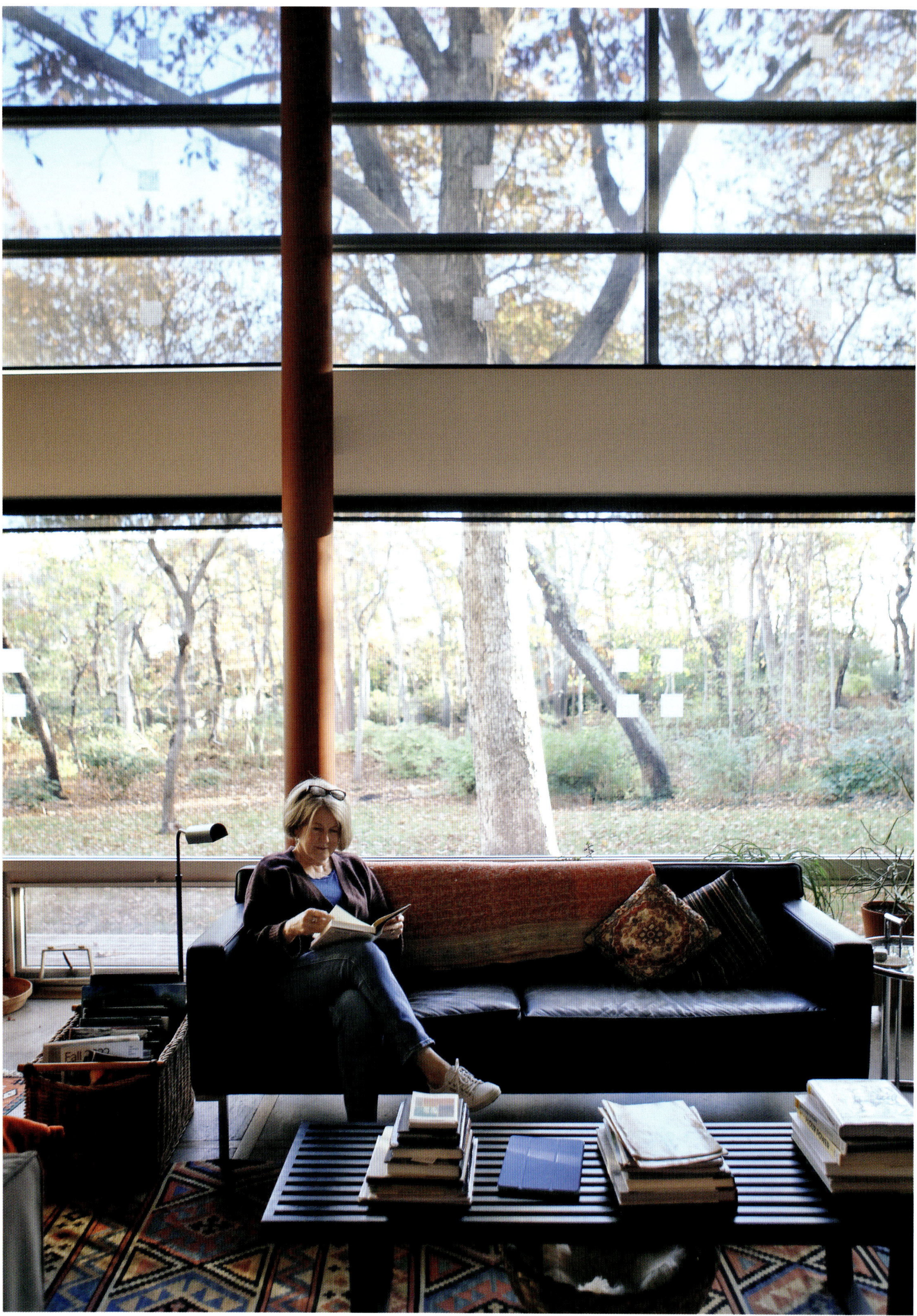

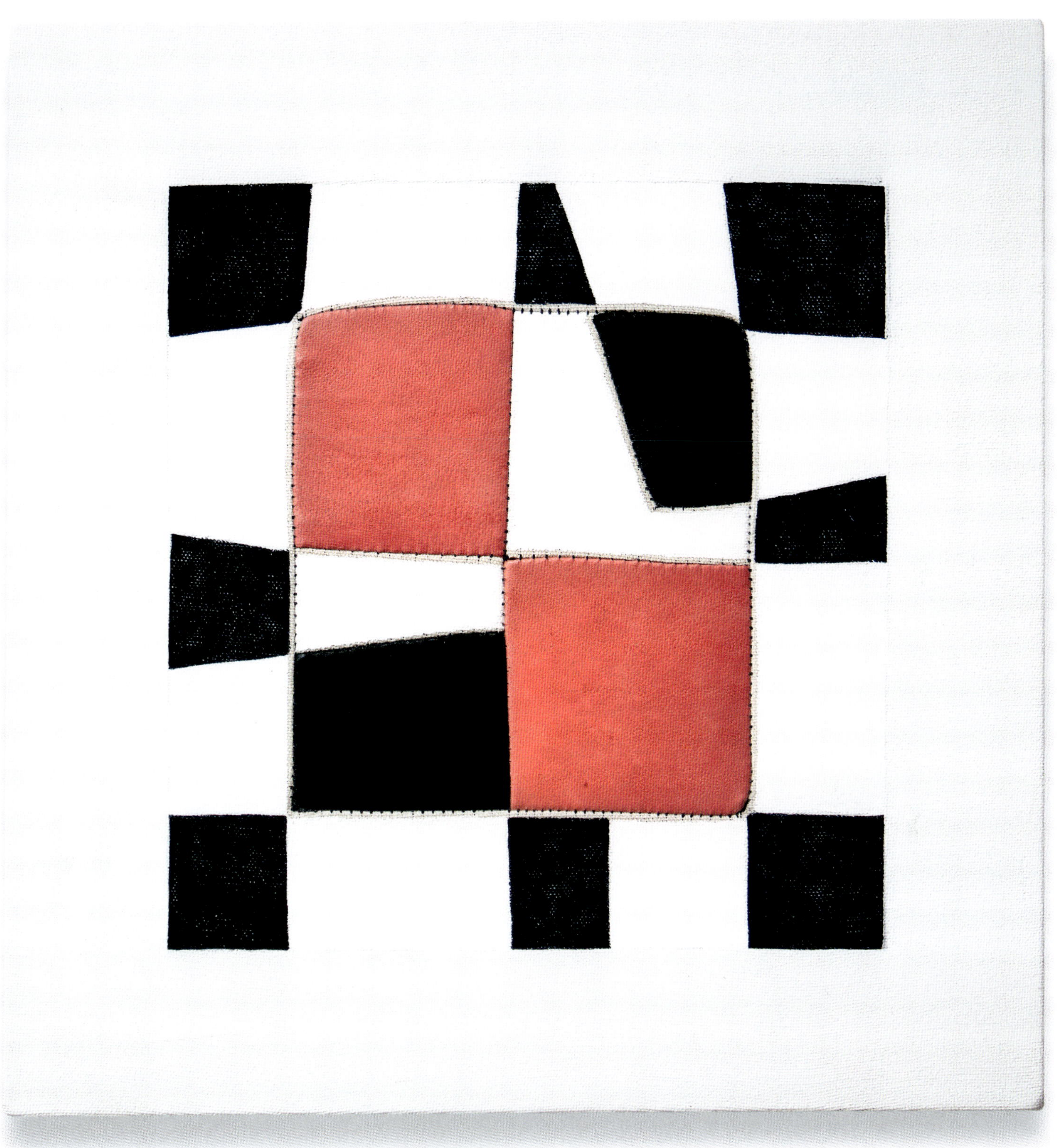

OPPOSITE

Watson's studio is in the basement of her Water Mill house. She takes breaks upstairs, where she can relax and read in the lofty, light-filled living space.

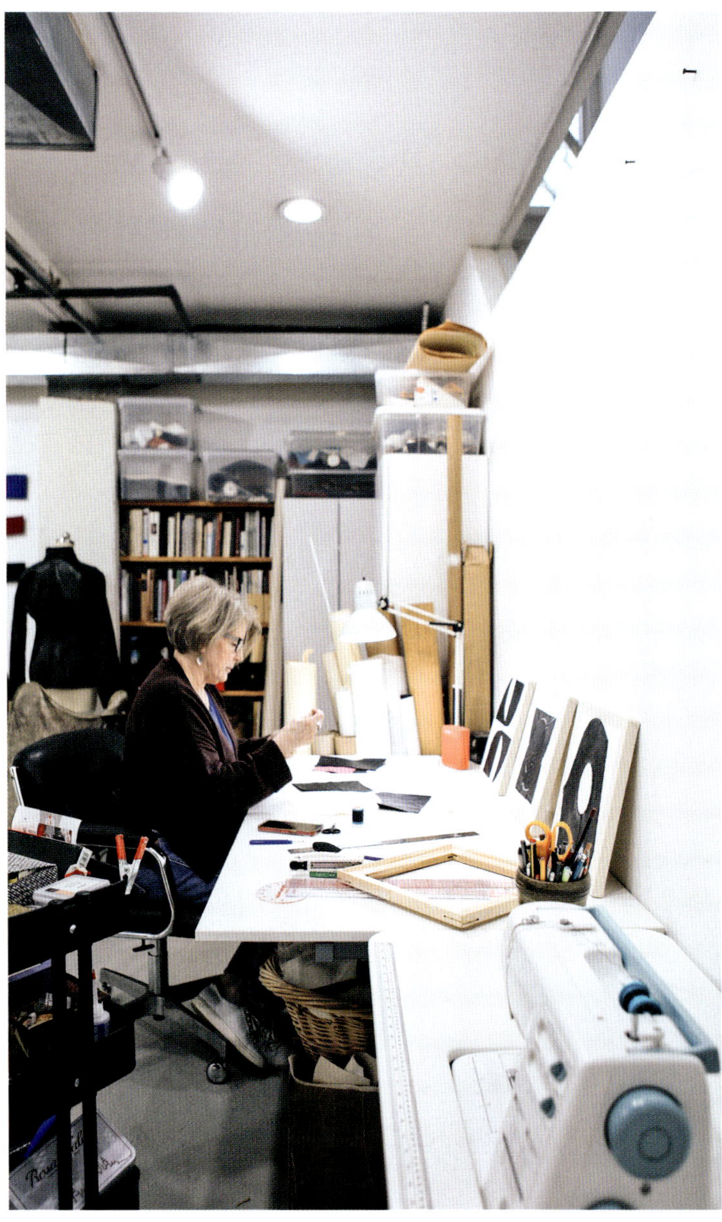

THIS PAGE AND OPPOSITE
One of Watson's main mediums is leather, which she cuts from real garments, lays on the floor to envision the composition, and then sews onto canvas.

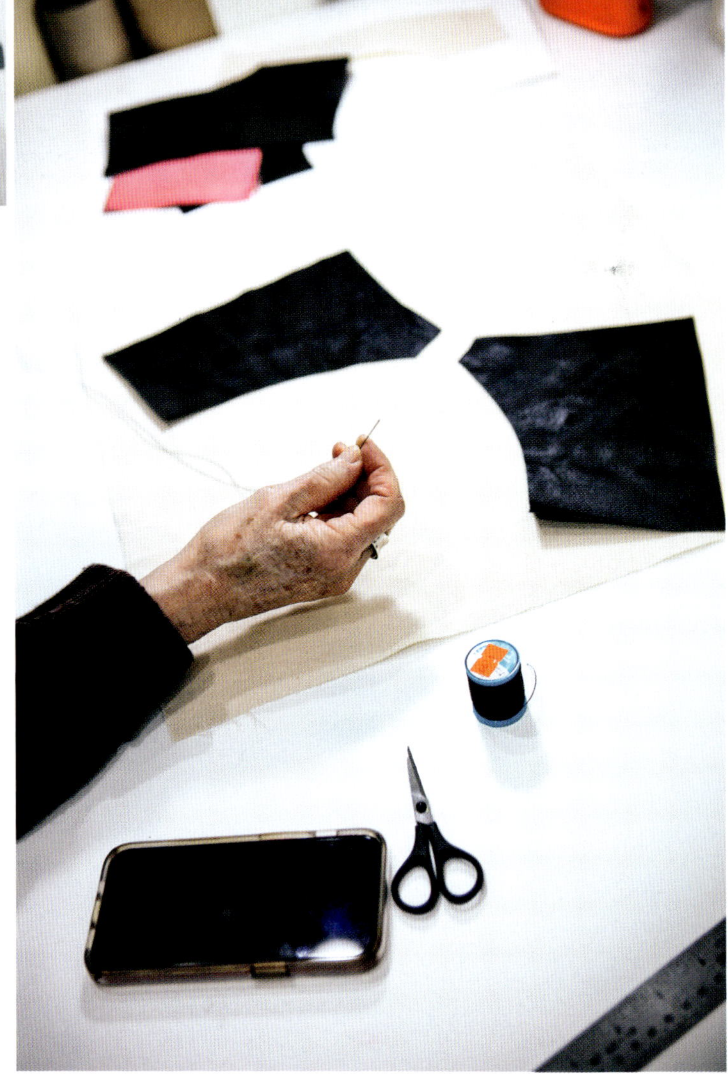

"I dismantle the garments, and the shapes of the pieces generate the compositions. Reconfigured into new juxtapositions, they can become abstract reflections of the human form. My process is improvisatory and intuitive. I lay the pieces across the floor and spend a long time moving them around and looking. When I begin to reassemble them, I use more technical methods of pattern cutting, tailoring, and sewing. But the process is also forgiving; I frequently disassemble the works with a seam ripper and start again."

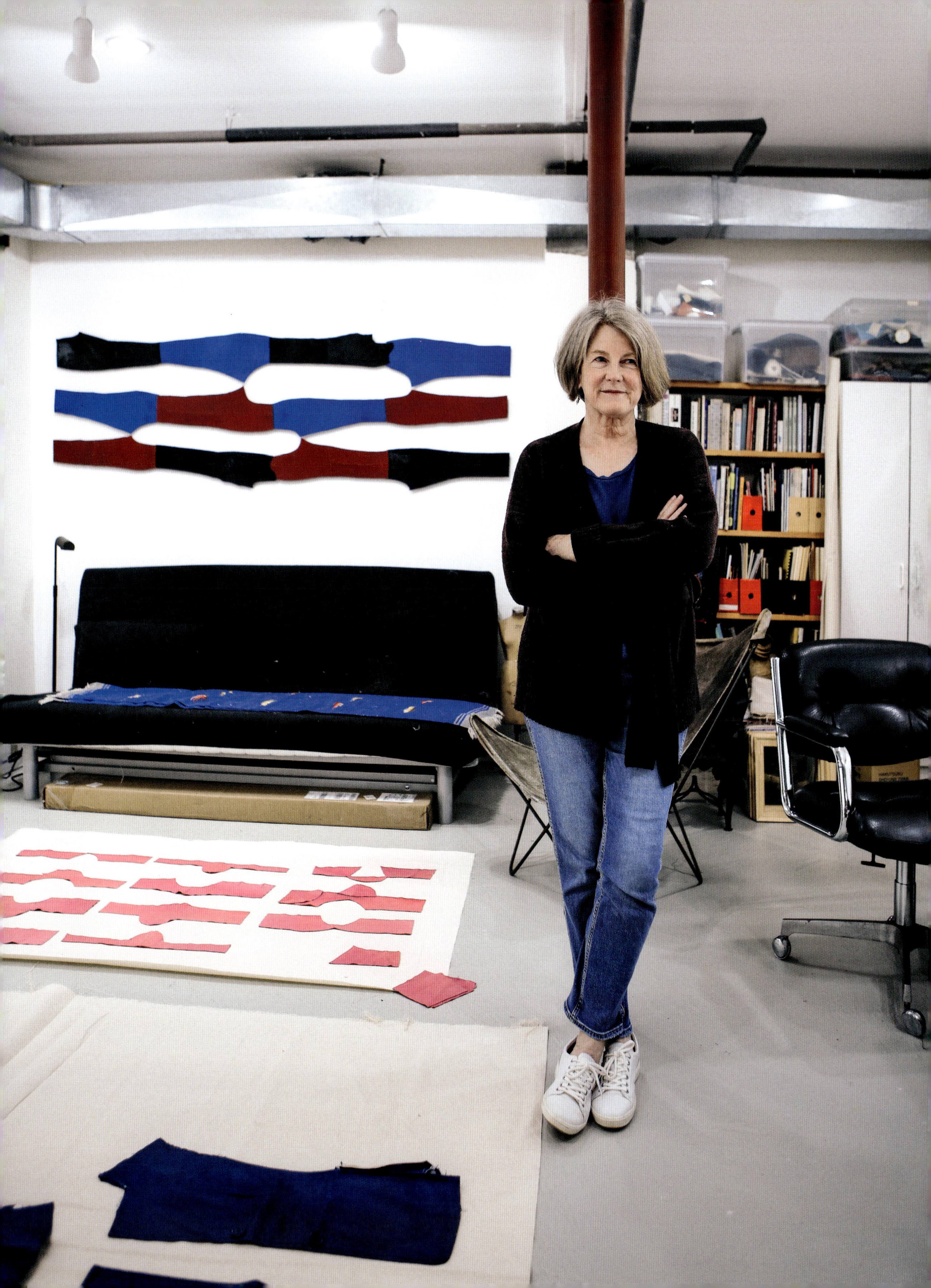

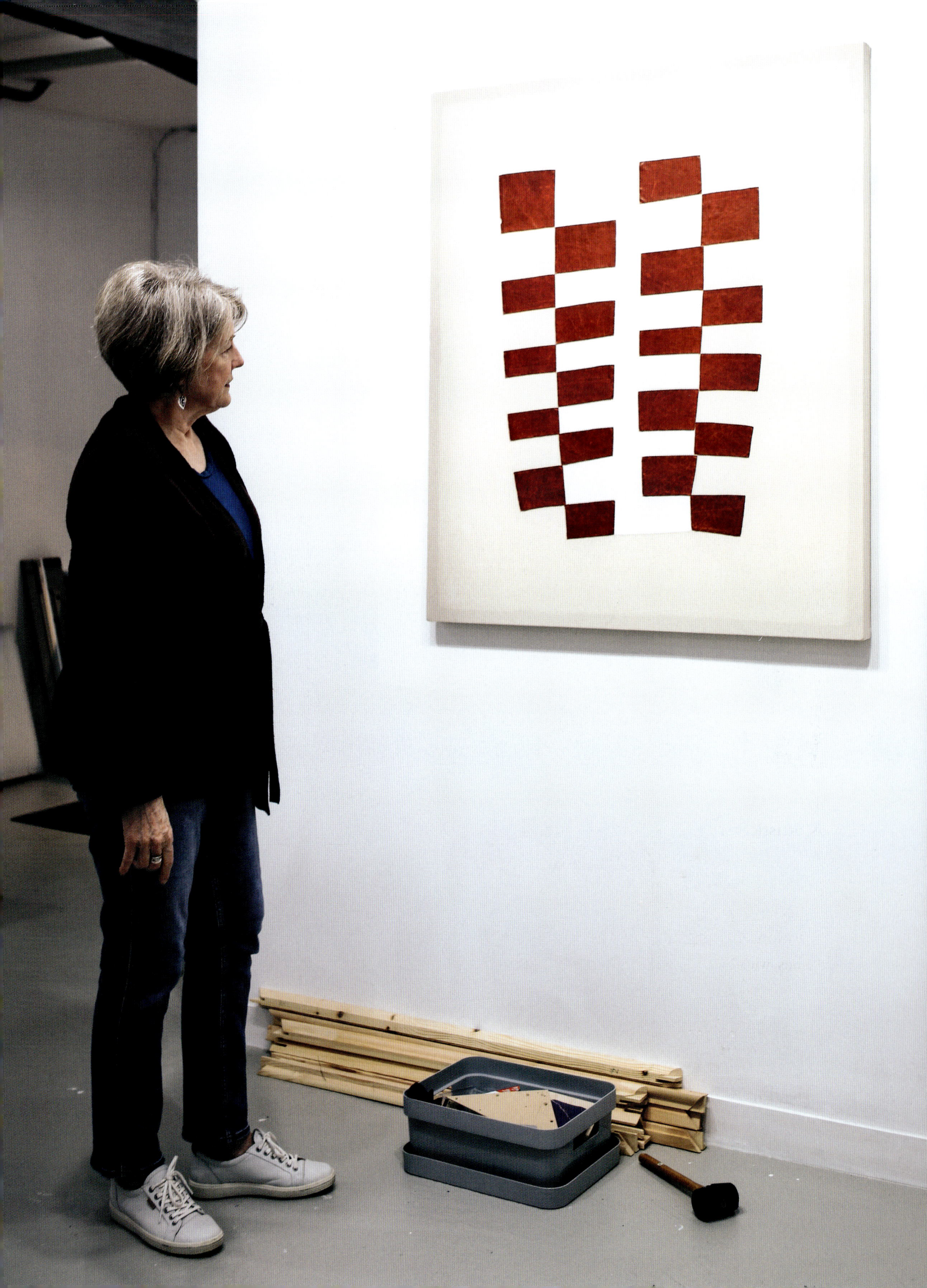

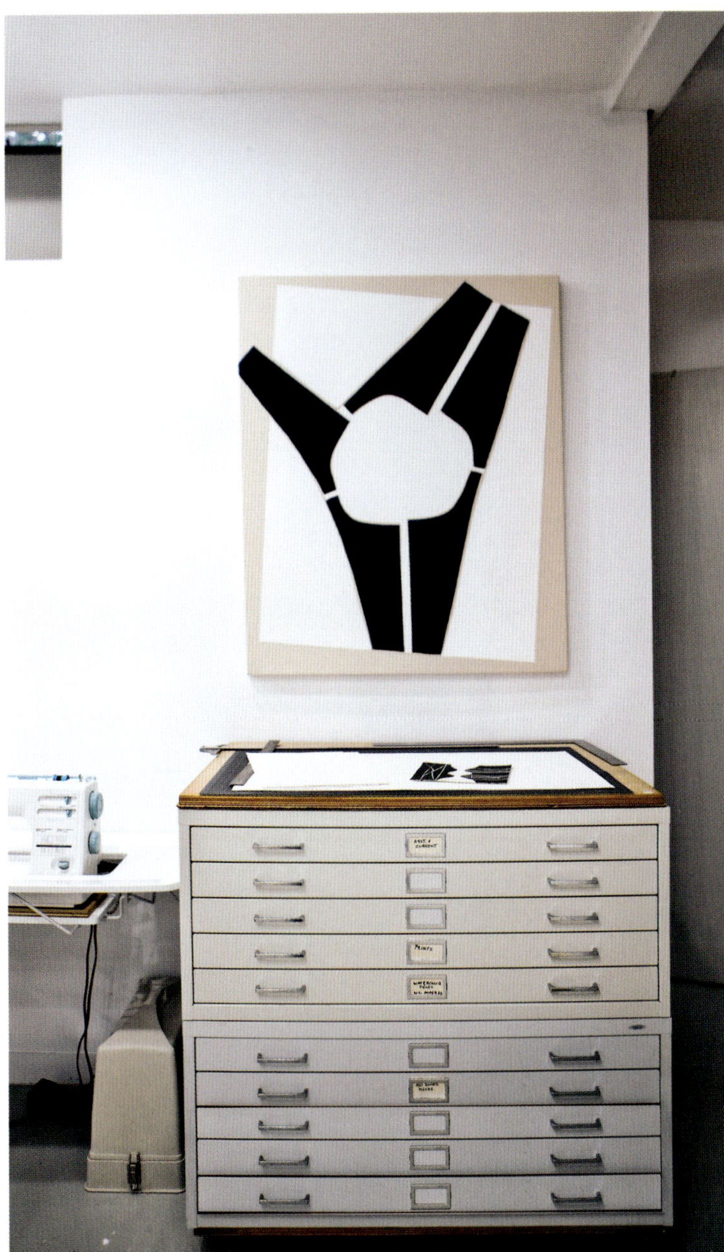

OPPOSITE AND THIS PAGE

For Watson, the salvaged leather pieces are not only about the clothes they once were but also about the animals that provided them—recycling and repurposing being a major theme of her work.

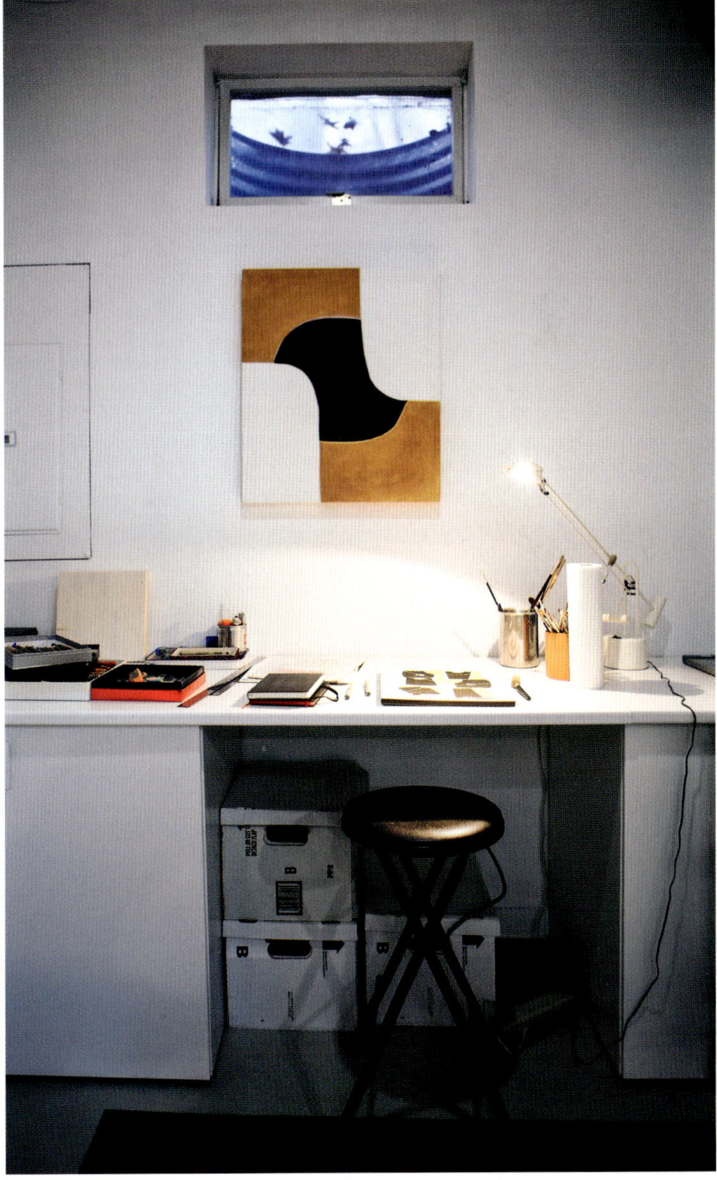

Watson's artistic process is focused on the transformation of found and repurposed materials. "I work in series, using objects that carry social or cultural references, especially those associated with traditional notions of gender, such as tobacco pipes, paintbrushes, wigs, and kid gloves. The worn leather clothing at the heart of much of my work is salvaged from thrift stores or given to me by friends. I'm fascinated with the leather garments because they project human personality and identity as elements of fashion, but also carry the visible scars of their prior animal life—and they are vestiges of the very earliest forms of clothing."

Joseph Beuys would be my art guru if there were such a thing. His famous statement "Everyone is an artist" speaks to me. It's not what you do but how you do it that brings the artist in us all to life.

MARK WILSON

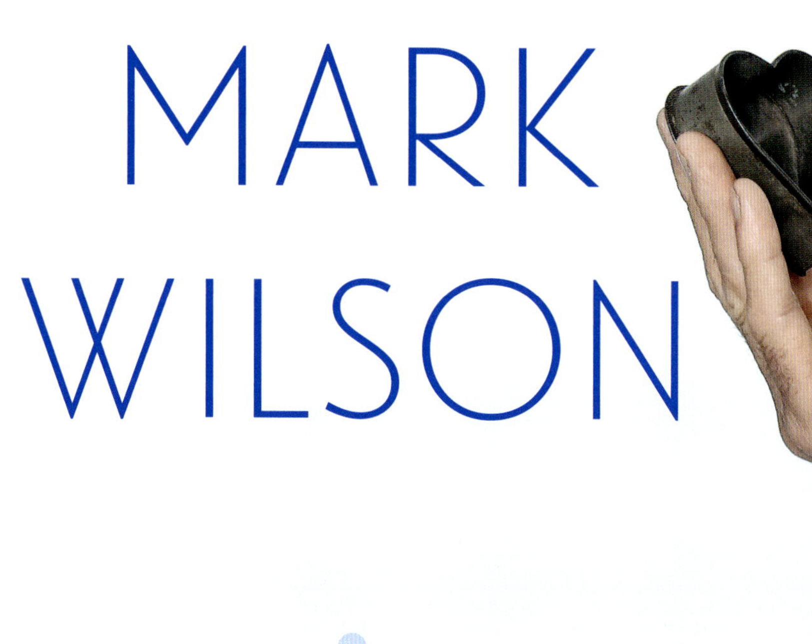

Australian-born, Wilson first came to the Hamptons in 1984. "I'd never heard of the Hamptons before when I found myself on board a helicopter with Sidney Lumet, whose movies I'd never seen. That weekend I met Julian Schnabel, and we went surfing. I had no clue what kind of work he did, but I was taken by the beauty and serendipity of this place. I was going with the flow. It all had a natural magic to it. In 1990, I moved to Mastic, Long Island. I was a struggling artist, about to have my second child. I applied for a Pollock-Krasner grant and won. I now live a mile away from their house in Springs."

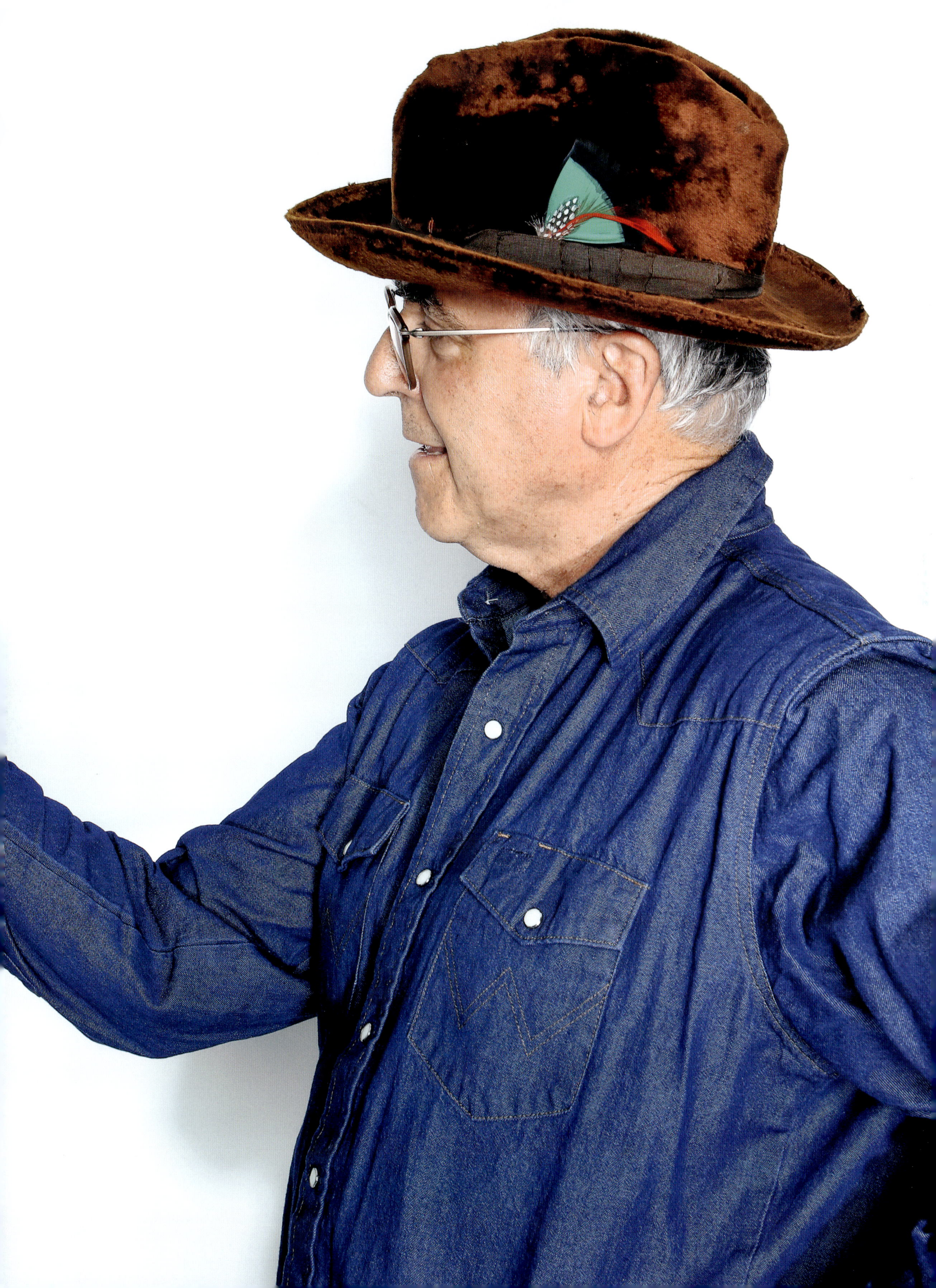

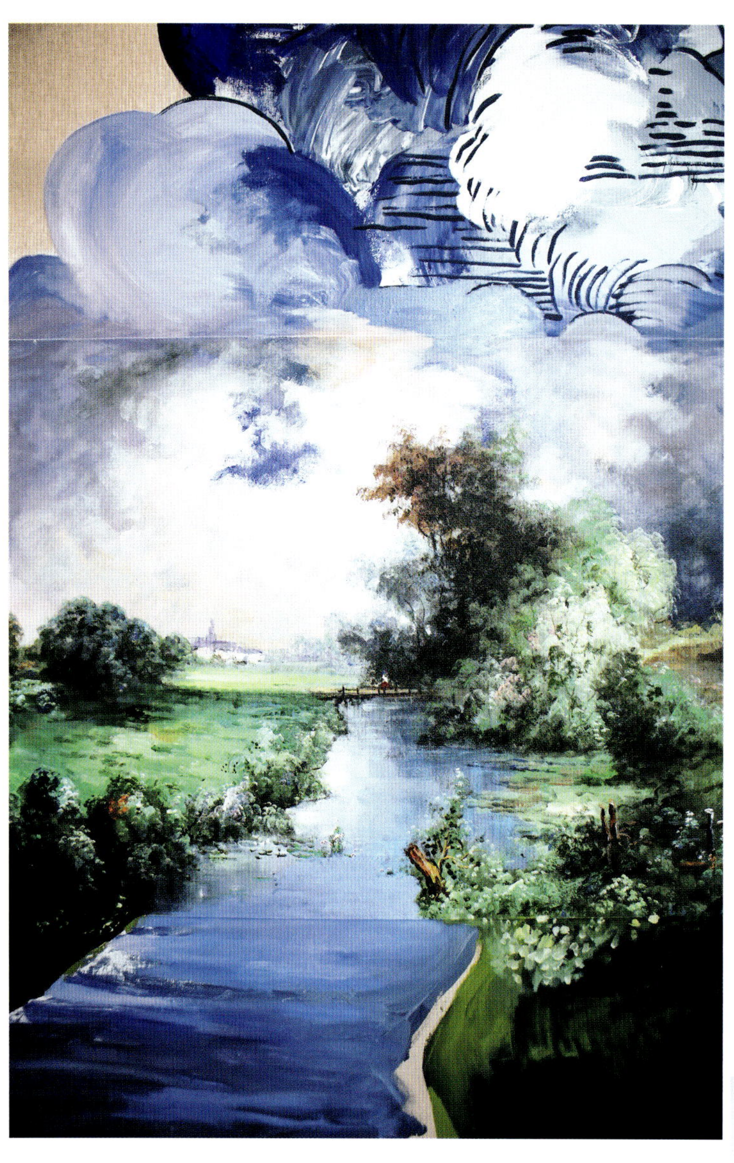

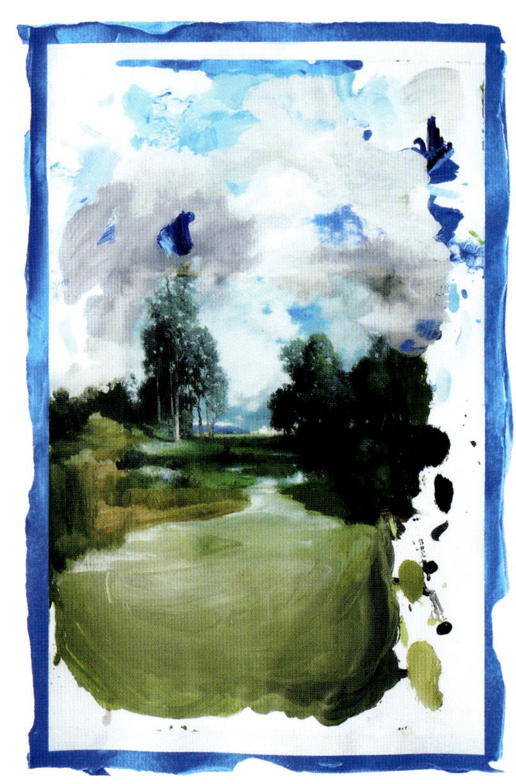

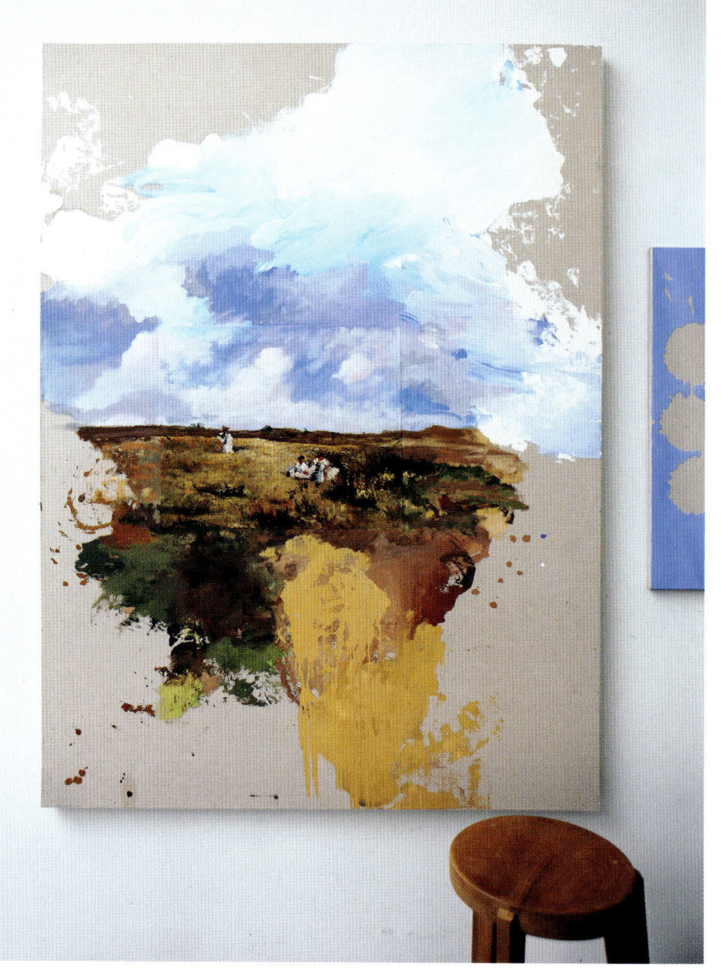

"Since the start of the twenty-first century, I have been making paintings within paintings—working with the concept of time expansion. I place a painting or reproduction of a painting at the center of a canvas and, using the same color palette, expand out from it with my own painting. Often I use nineteenth-century works, such as landscapes by William Merritt Chase and Thomas Moran. Because of the consistent color and light in the overall piece, one's perception is that it is a single piece done in a consistent time and place. In this way, I create a work in which the past and present coexist."

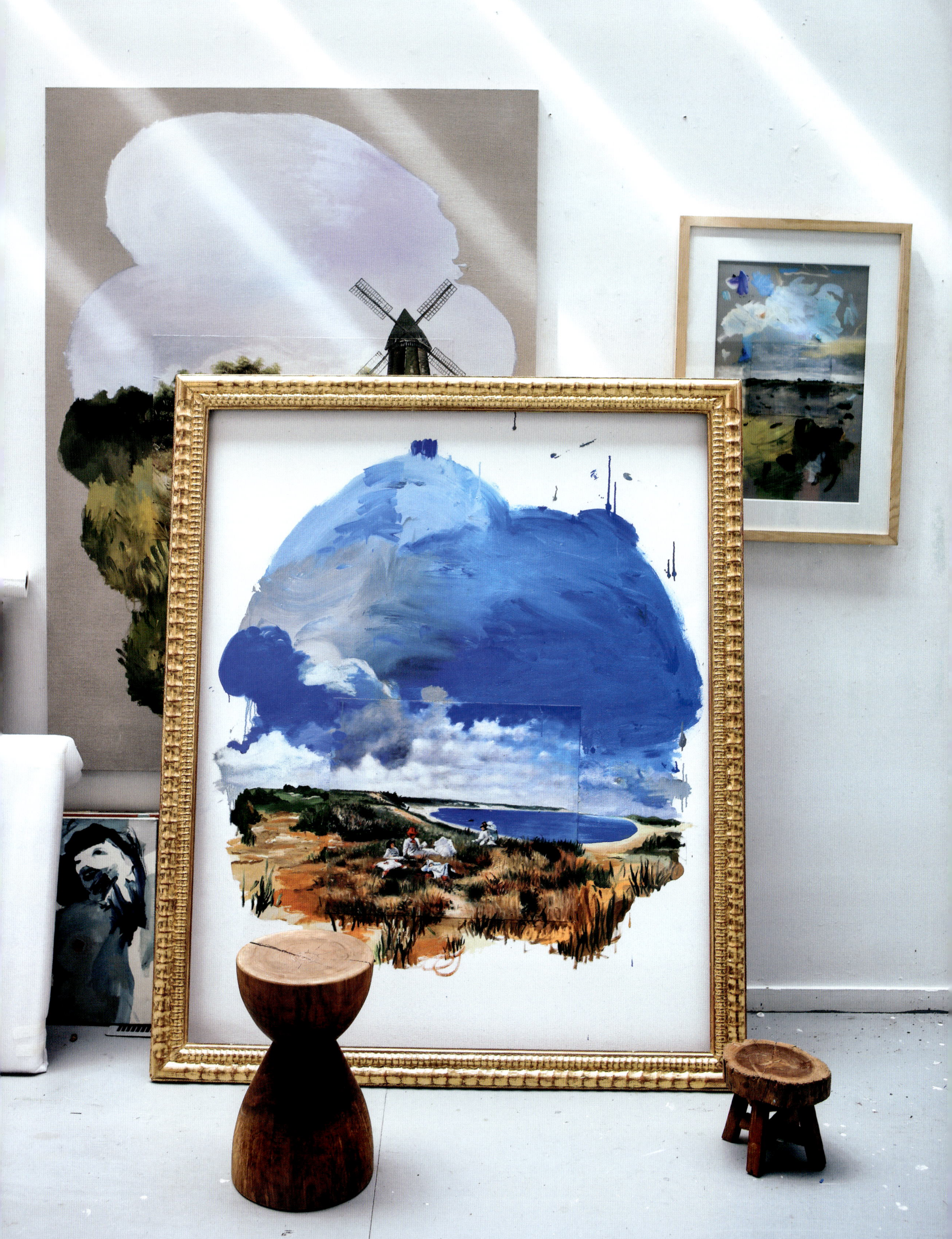

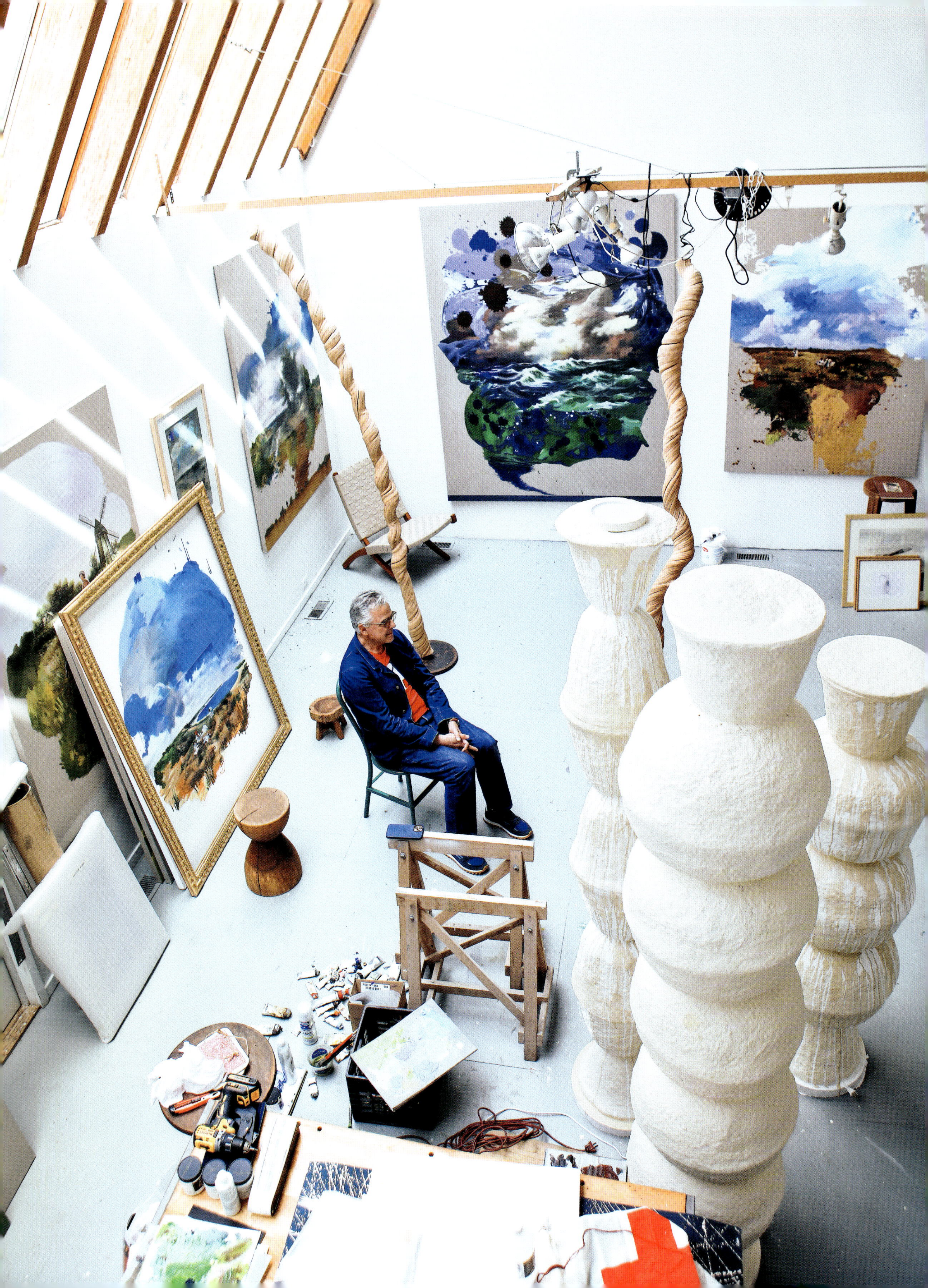

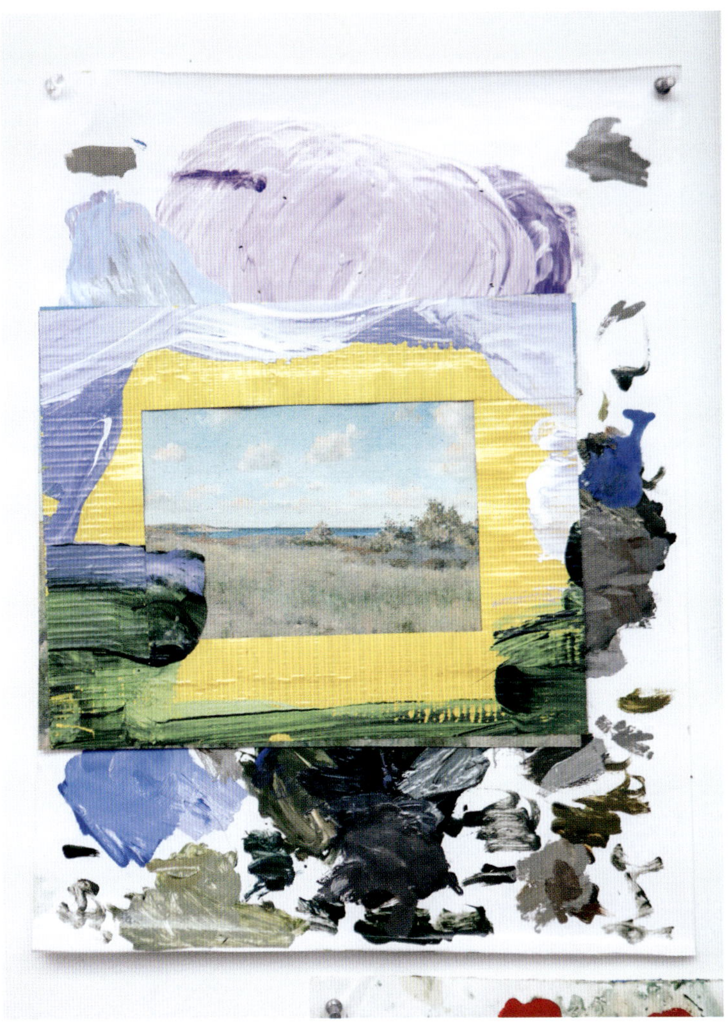

Wilson found his Springs house in 2000. "The moment I saw the house and crossed the threshold of the studio, I knew this was the place for me. The studio has an enormous, north-facing skylight. It's all about the light!" The spacious workplace is filled with his collection of books, found objects, and outsider art. "Collecting feeds my curiosity," he says. Self-taught, Wilson doesn't paint with a plan. "I make it up as I go along. For me, it's all happening in the moment. I start by mixing a color—usually the sky. The application is secondary—the paint often simply describes itself."

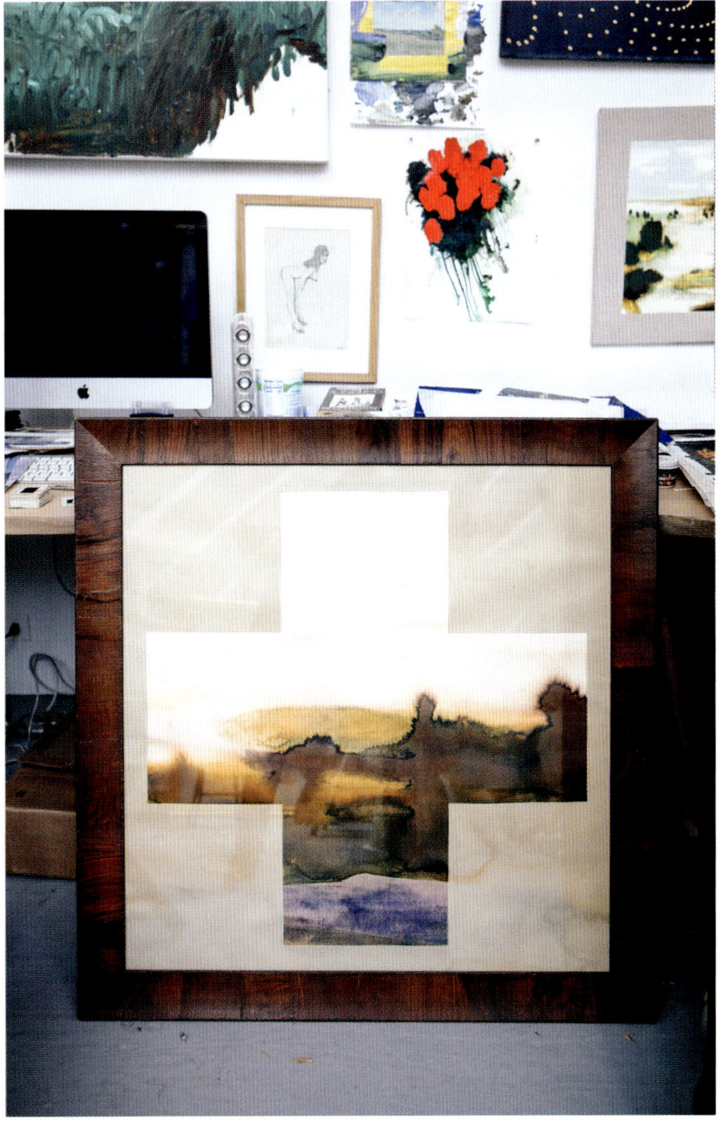

OPPOSITE

Wilson's high-ceilinged studio in East Hampton accommodates not only his paintings but also his collection of found objects, such as the spiraling trees, and his papier-mâché column creations—a play on Brancusi's *Endless Column* but turned into standing lamps.

I start with a single stroke on the canvas and see what feeling that evokes, where it naturally takes me. I think of painting as creating controlled accidents.

FRANK WIMBERLEY

As a child growing up in the New Jersey suburbs, Wimberley was drawn to music and art. In 1945, after serving in the army, he studied painting at Howard University and became involved with jazz, listening to it and playing it. "My improvisational painting method is much like jazz, which is a constant theme in my art." With texture and motion key to the work, Wimberley expresses music with his brushstrokes.

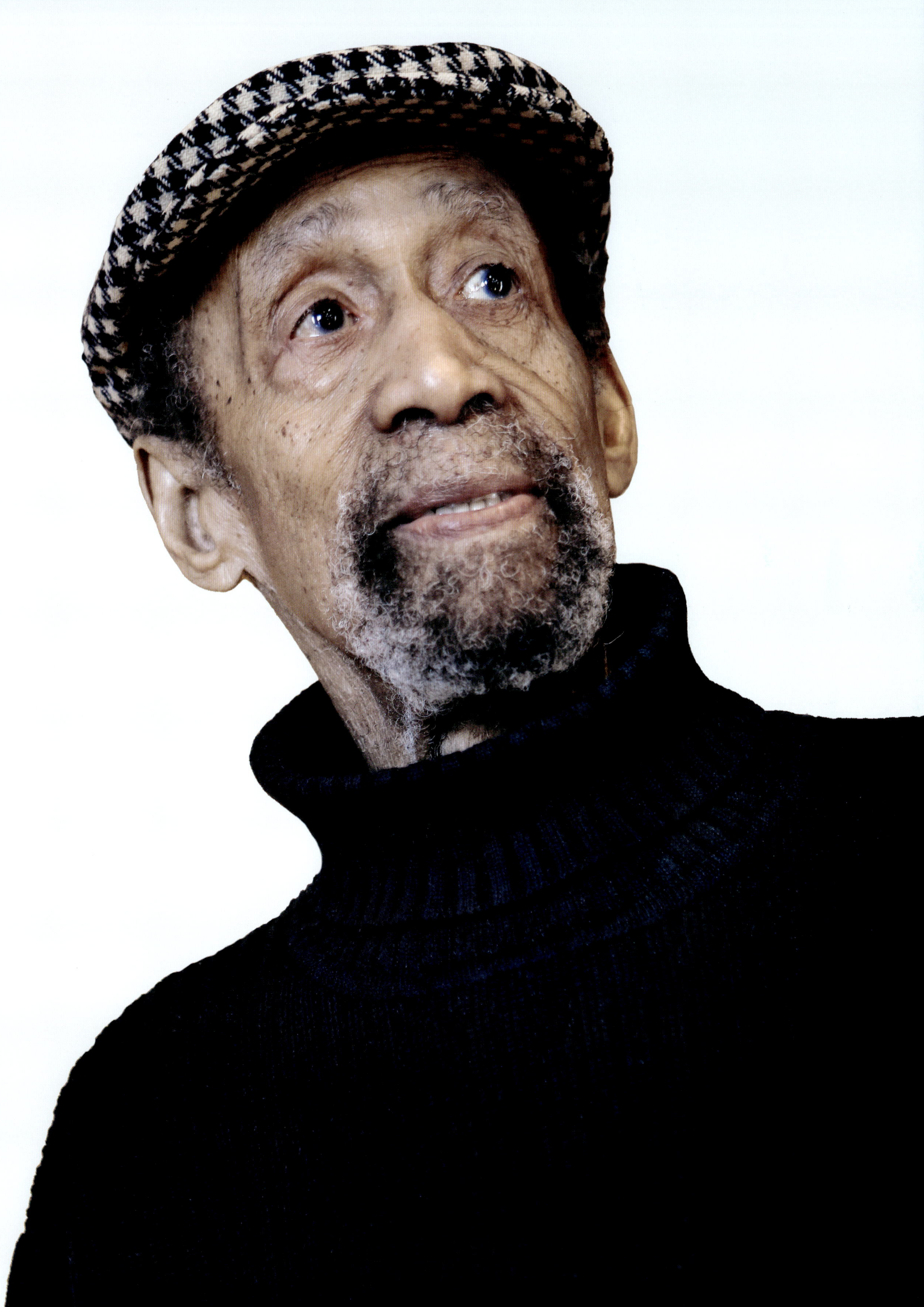

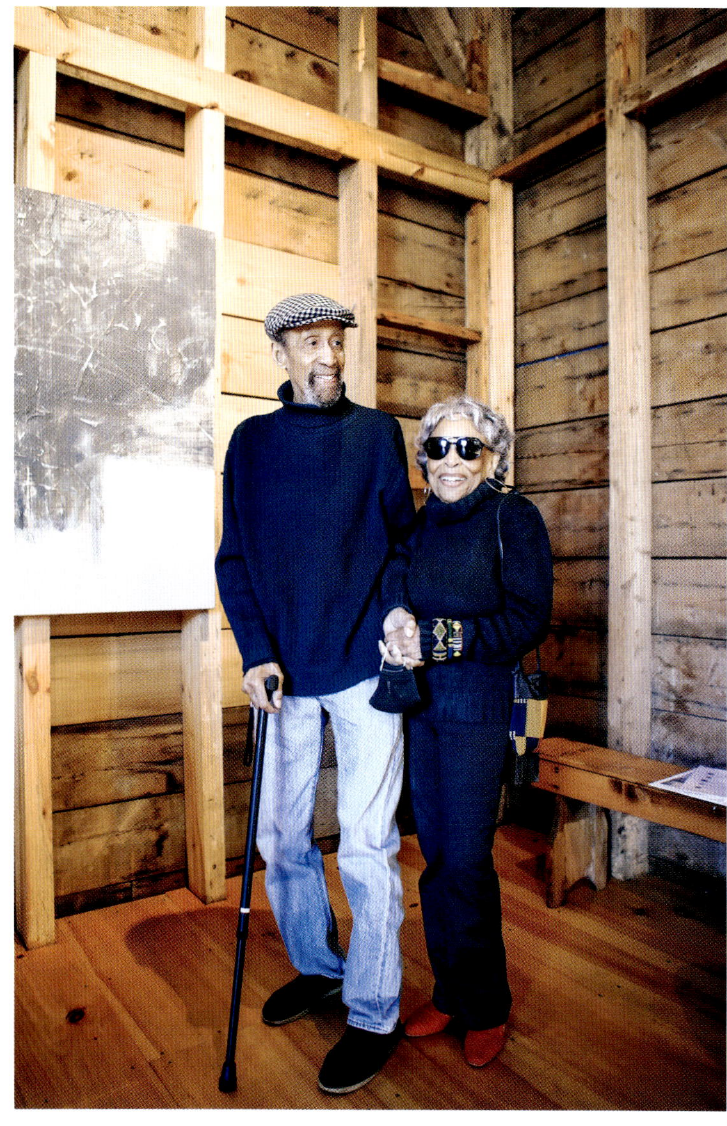

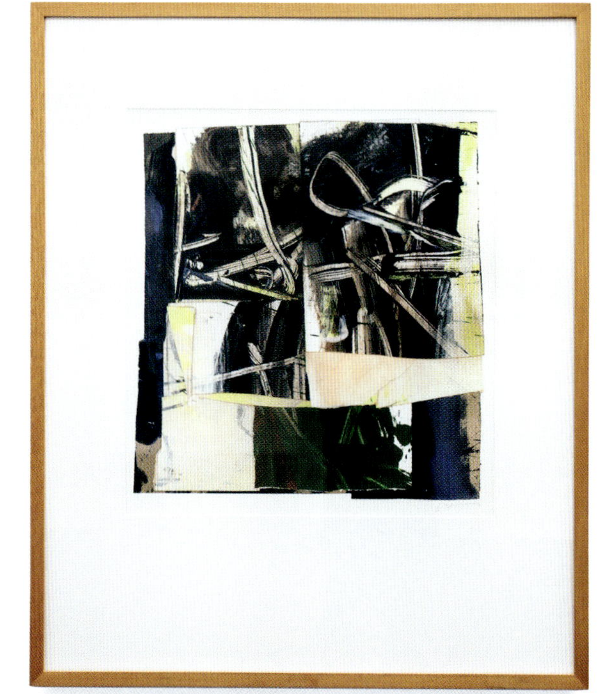

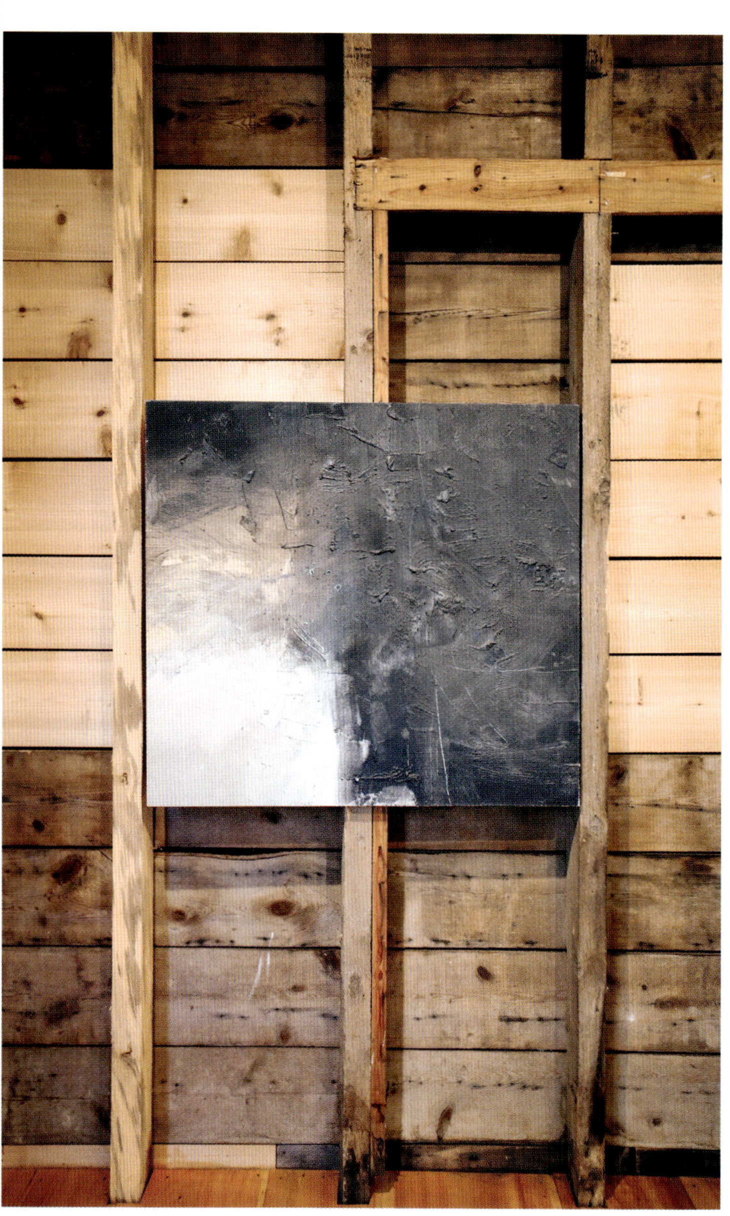

"I've always been intrigued by the legacy of artists on the East End and especially the history of Sag Harbor's African Americans, who settled in the area in the 1600s." After working and painting in Queens for many years, Wimberley and his wife began vacationing in Sag Harbor, and in 1965 they bought land and designed a modern, sky-lit house with a Japanese-inspired simplicity. Wimberley connected with other local artists, who were supportive of his work, and it wasn't long before he became a strong presence on the East End and a central figure in the African American art world.

ABOVE

Wimberly, with his wife, Juanita, in the gallery-barn at Duck Creek in Springs, where he had a solo show in the summer of 2022.

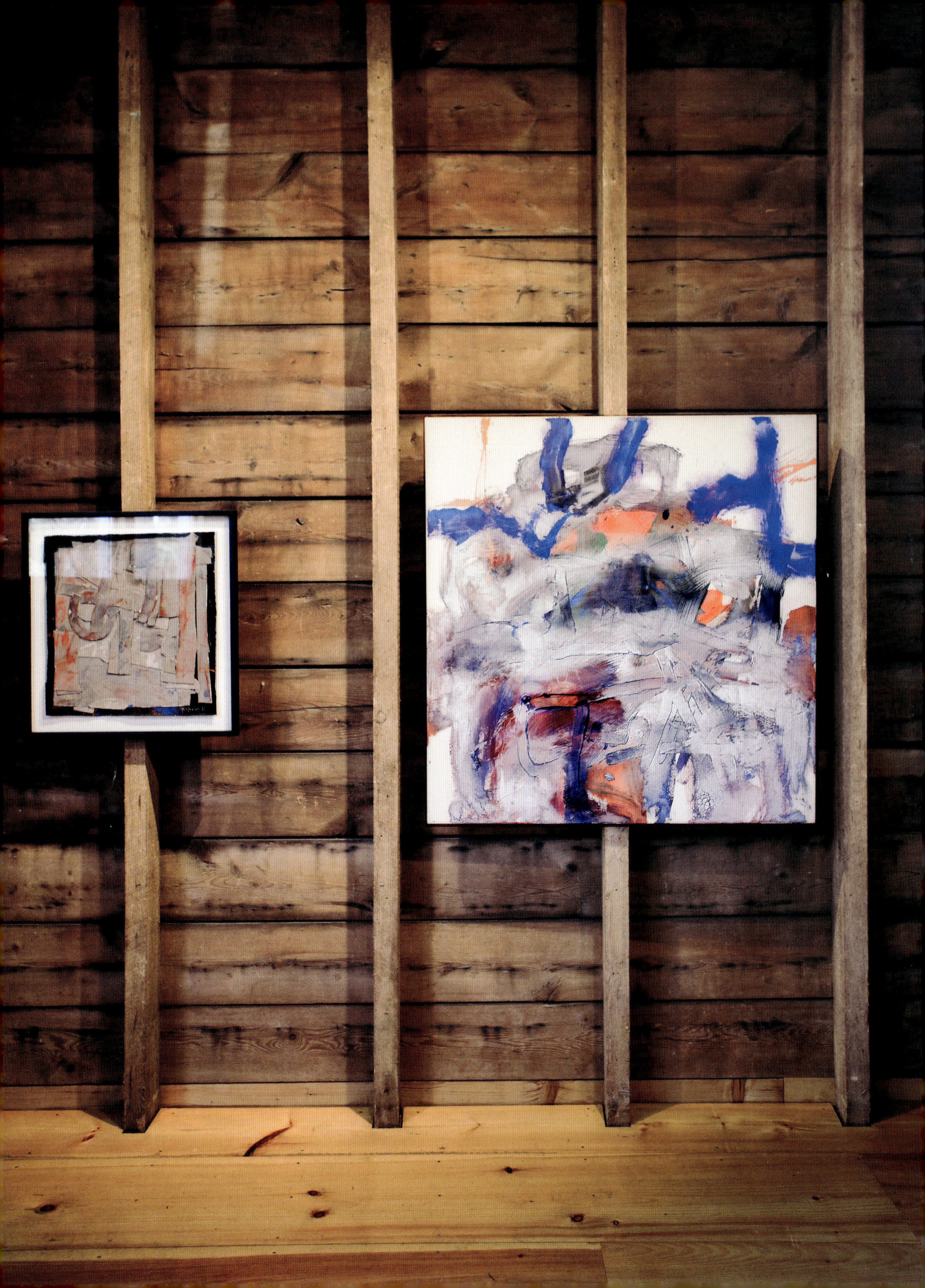

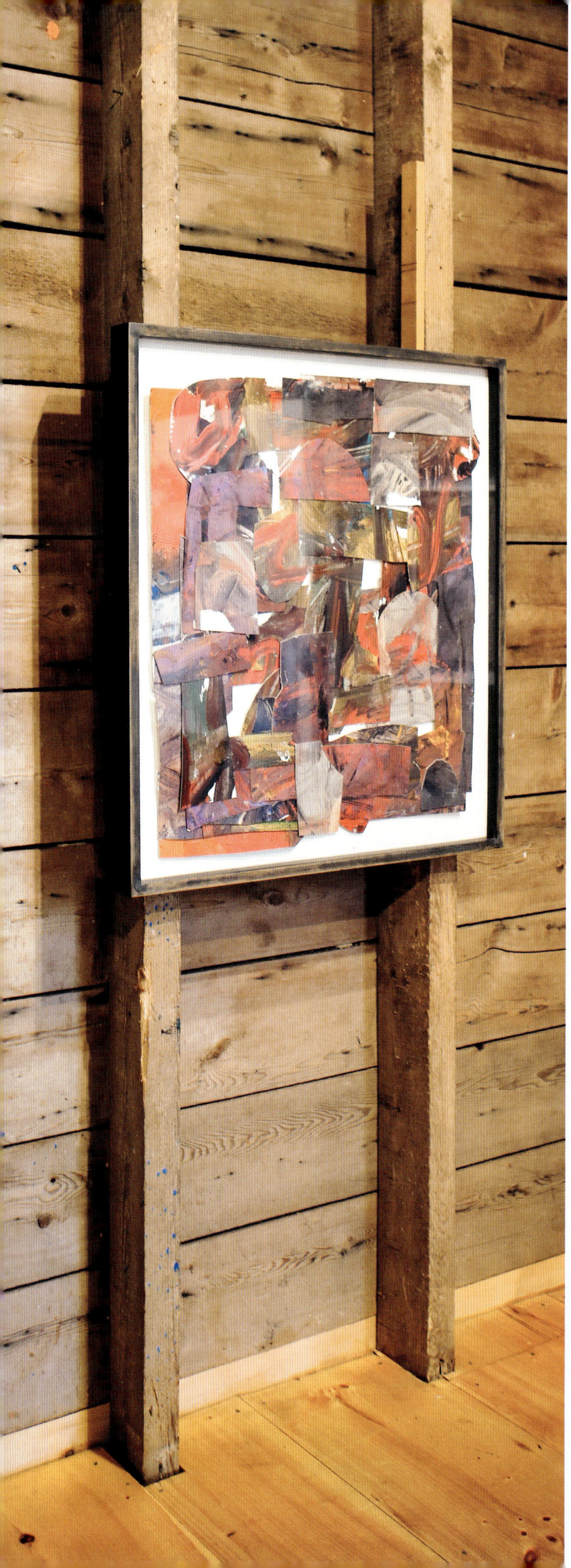

Throughout his long career, Wimberley has maintained a strong connection to the art of the Abstract Expressionists. His multilayered paintings are exuberant and lush, with a sculptural quality created by thick applications of pigment that are often raked or scratched. His tools include scrapers, spatulas, pumice, and brushes. "I like using a big, floppy brush to get the movement in the paint."

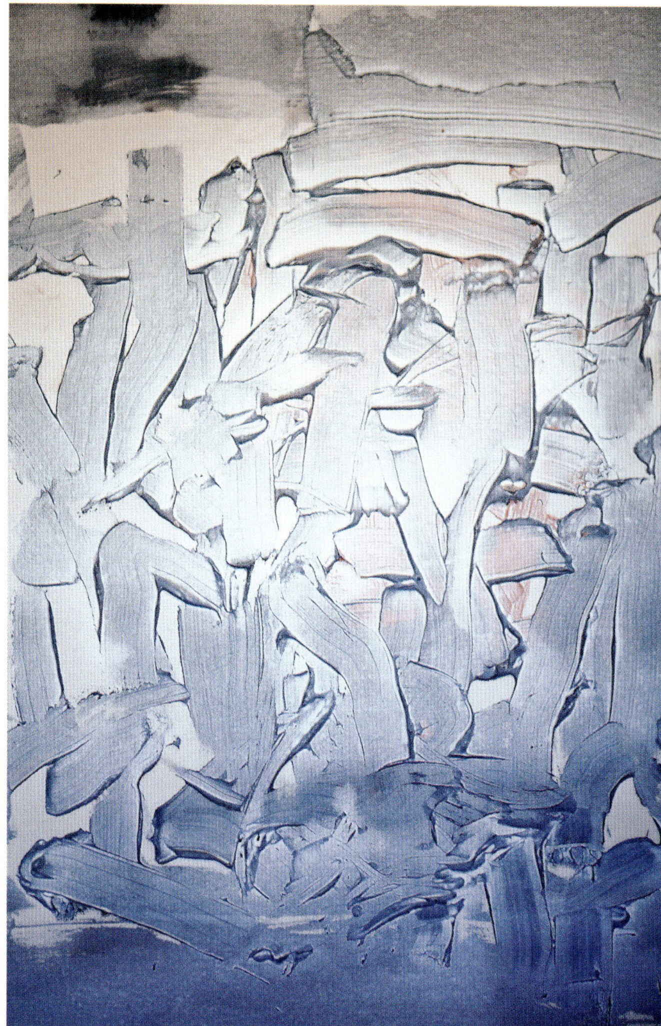

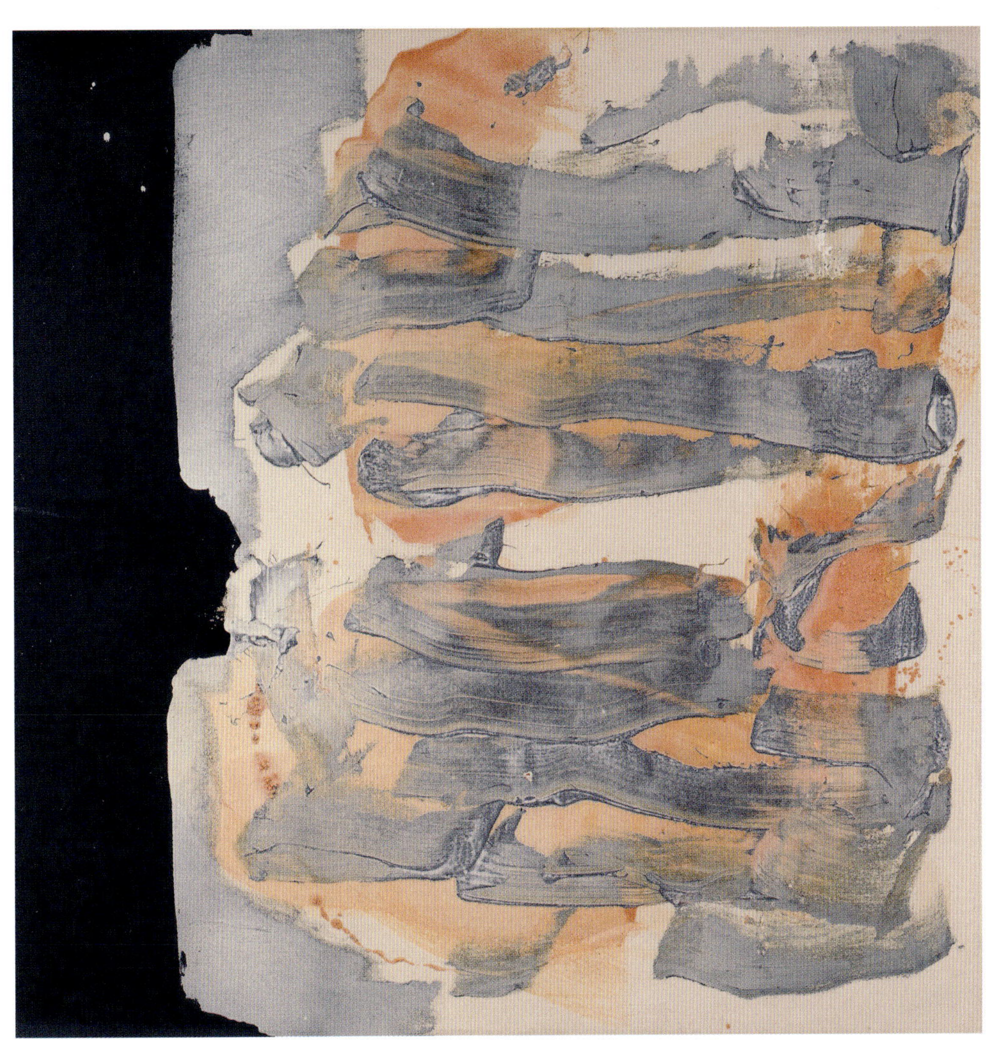

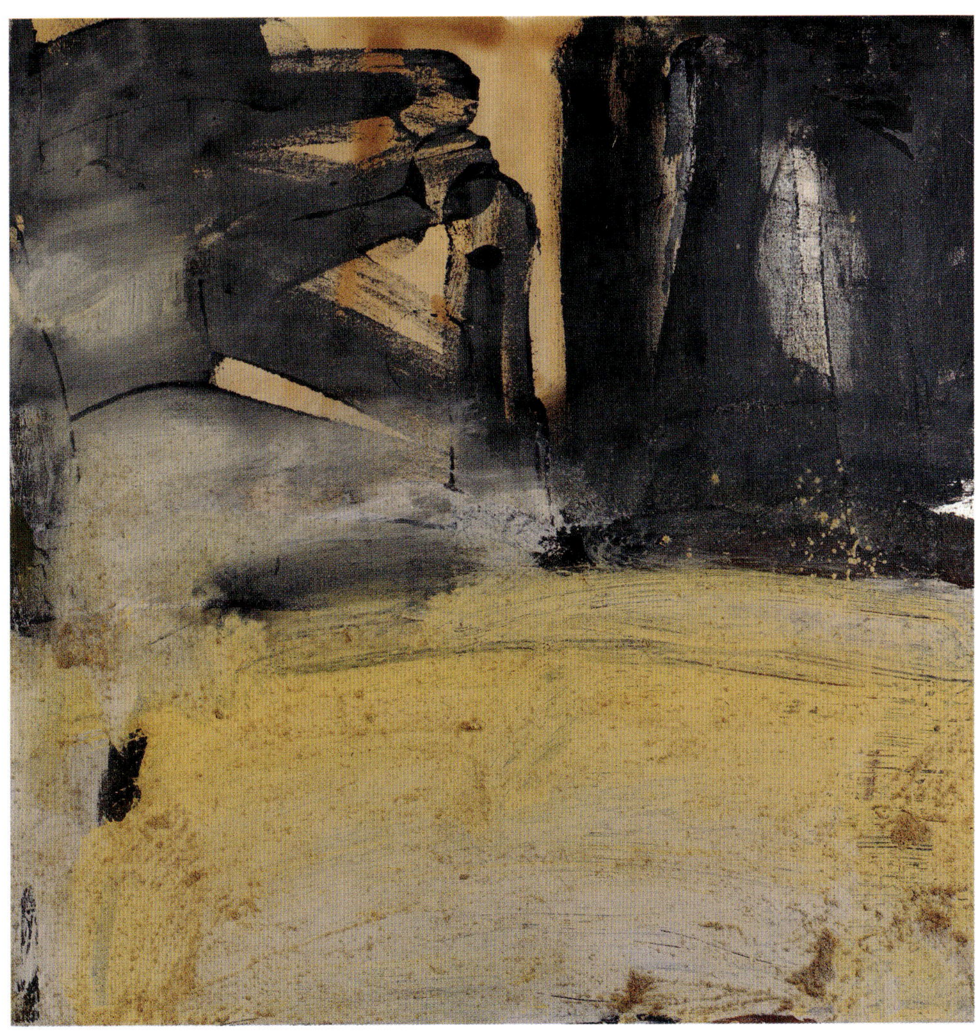

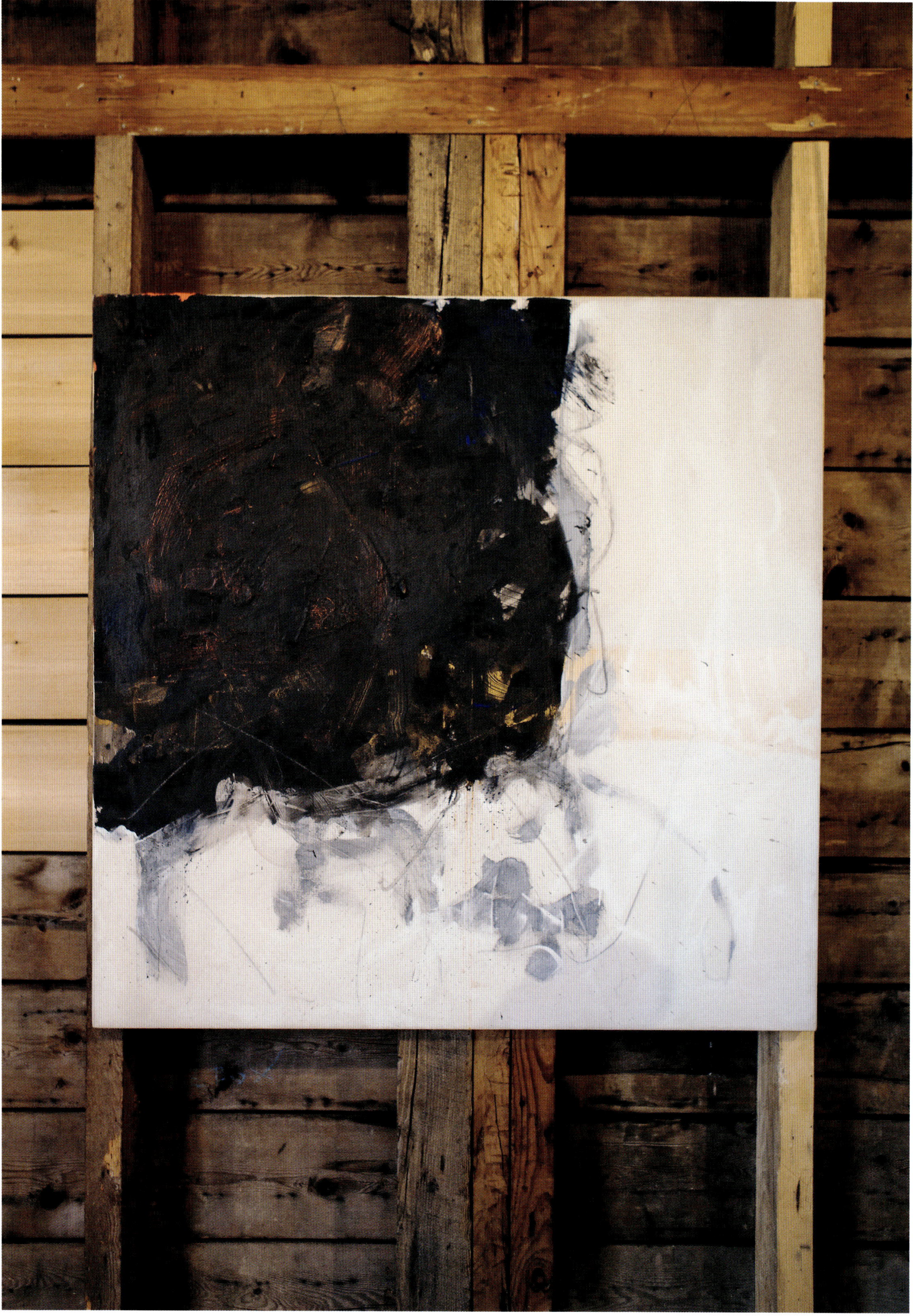

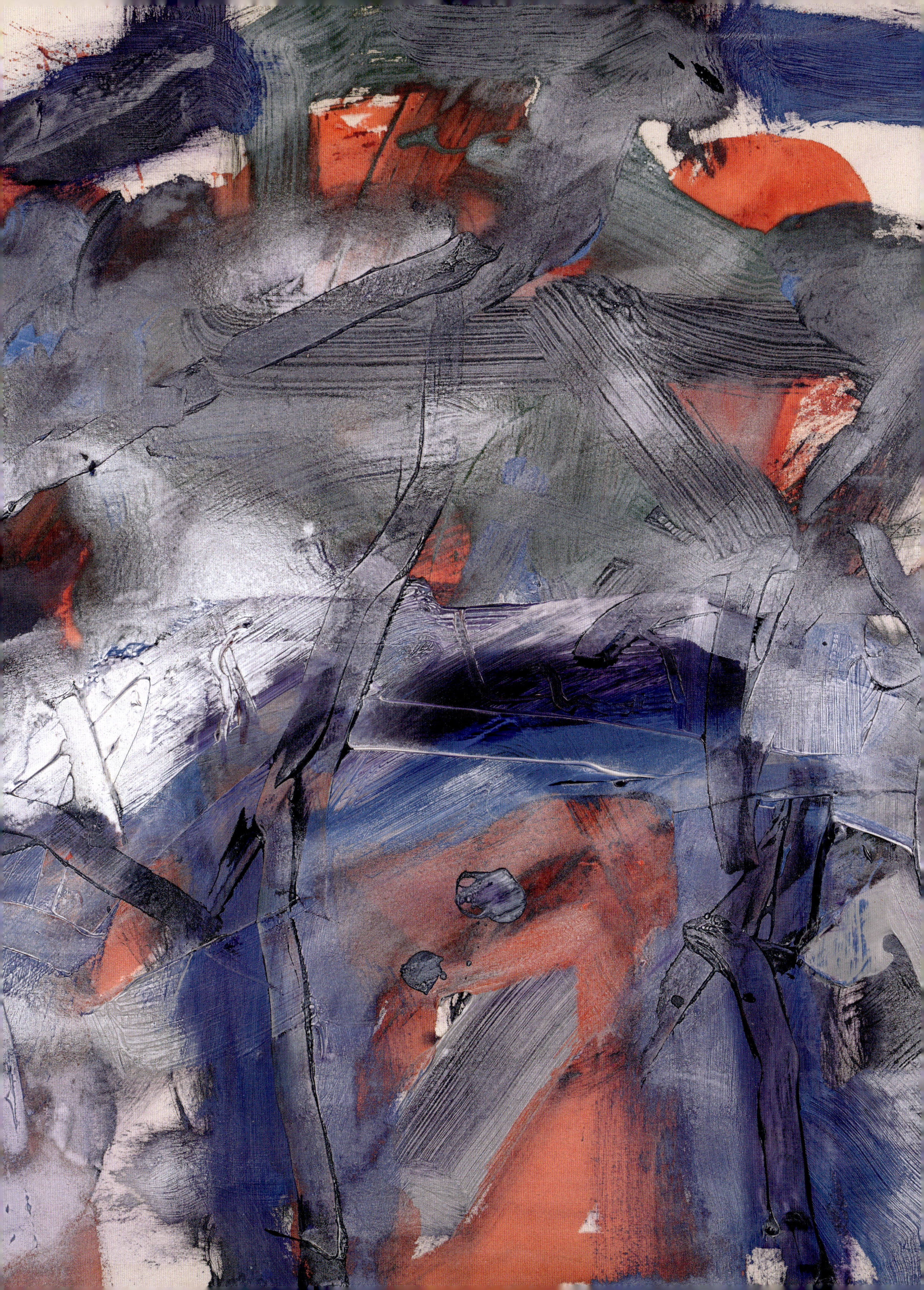

My restless hand wants to paint something new, and I'm not sure if that means slowing down the process or speeding it up.

DARIUS YEKTAI

"My medium is paint on canvas, but I extend and invert the traditional processes. Varnish, which was used by the old masters to 'finish' a painting's surface, becomes an intermediary thick layer of resin that sits between what was painted under it and over it—a varnish exploded in motion, a thousand times thicker and highly reflective. The resulting surface catches and throws light, and anything painted on it interrupts the reflection and stands out as matte in a sea of gloss."

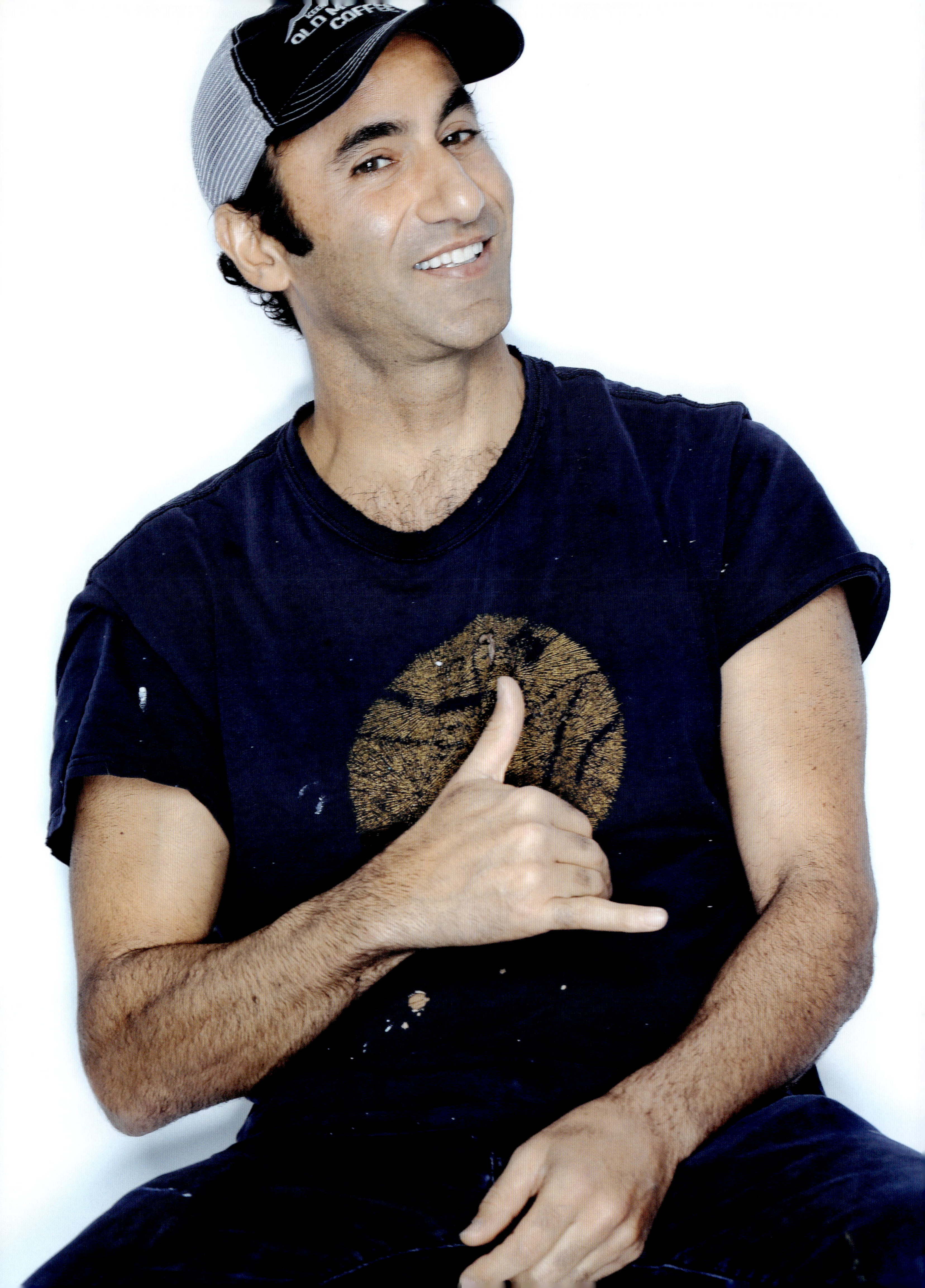

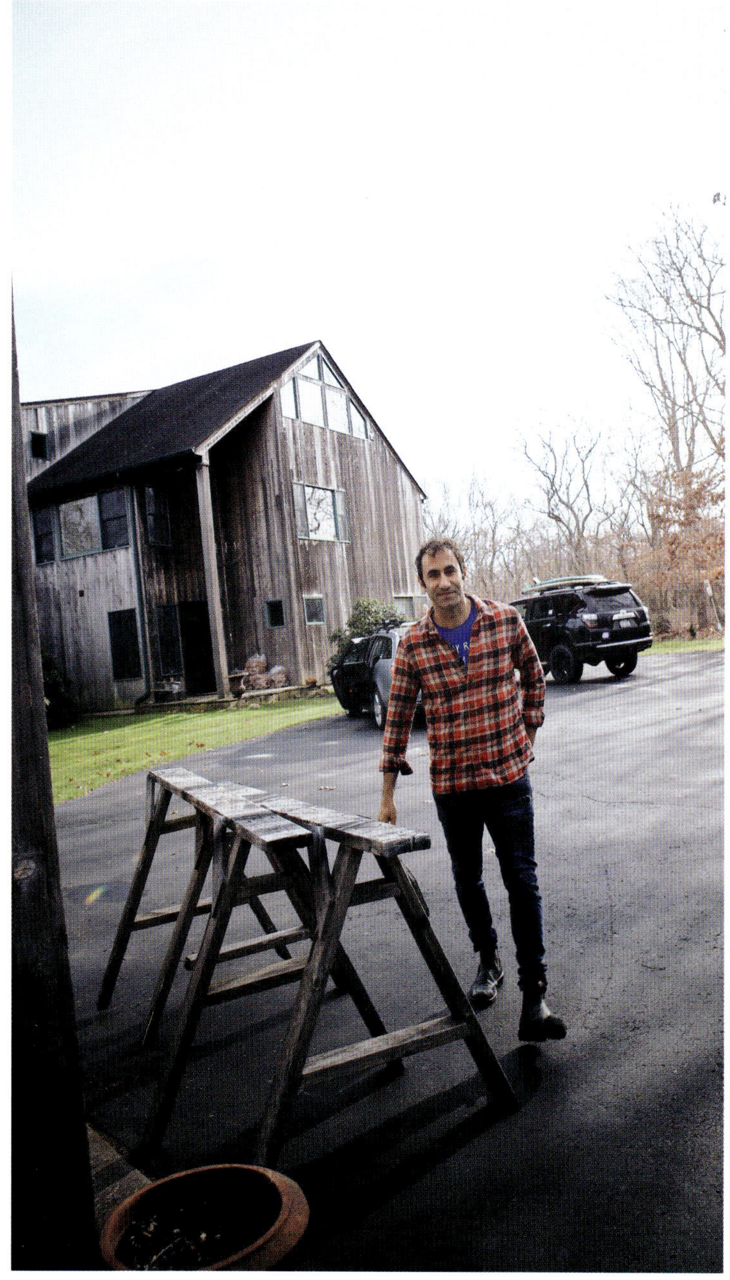

LEFT

Yektai grew up coming to Bridgehampton every summer and always knew he would return to the area after living in New York City and studying in Paris. He settled in Sagaponack more than two decades ago.

BELOW

Nature is a big part of the artist's work and life. He wakes up early, feeds his dog and two cats, refills his bird feeder, and then heads to the ocean to surf.

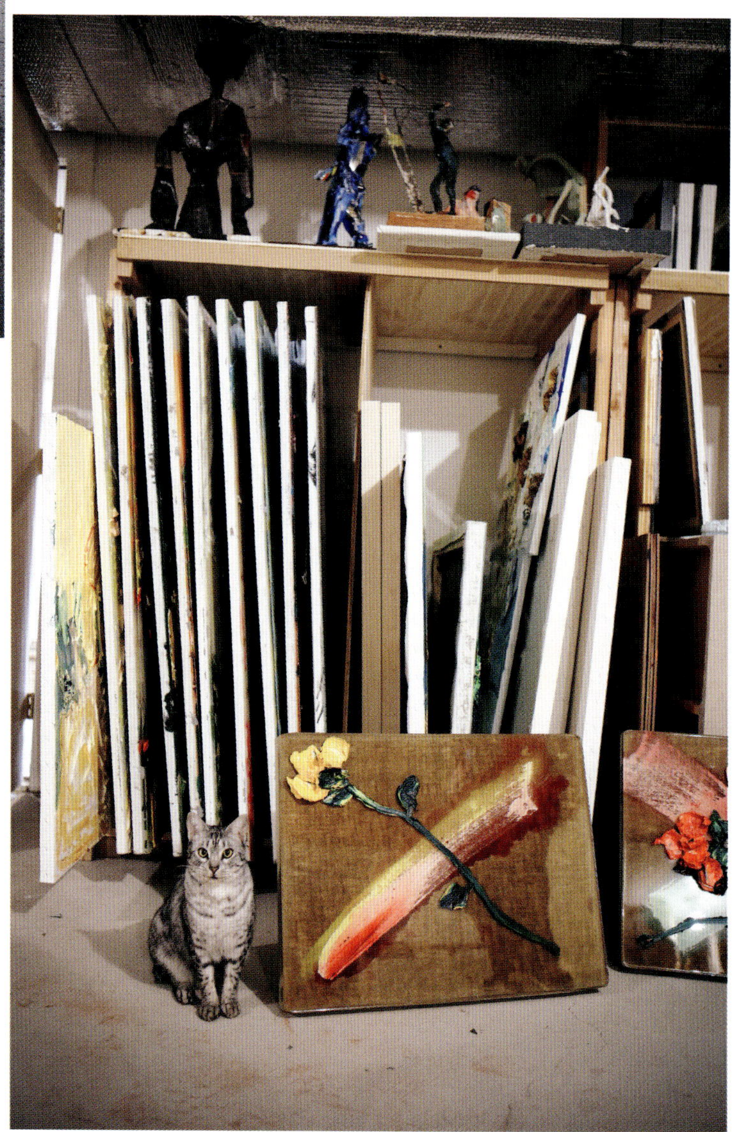

Born in Southampton, Yektai grew up in New York City and spent the summers in Bridgehampton. "I looked forward to being in nature and exploring the local swamps and ponds and beaches." He studied art history at the American University in Paris and eventually came back to the East End. "Like a salmon swimming upstream, I knew I wasn't going to be happy until I moved my young family here, which I did, more than twenty years ago. I found that many of the artists I'd been studying and admiring while I was in Paris lived out here. I started going to openings and meeting them and began to feel part of something."

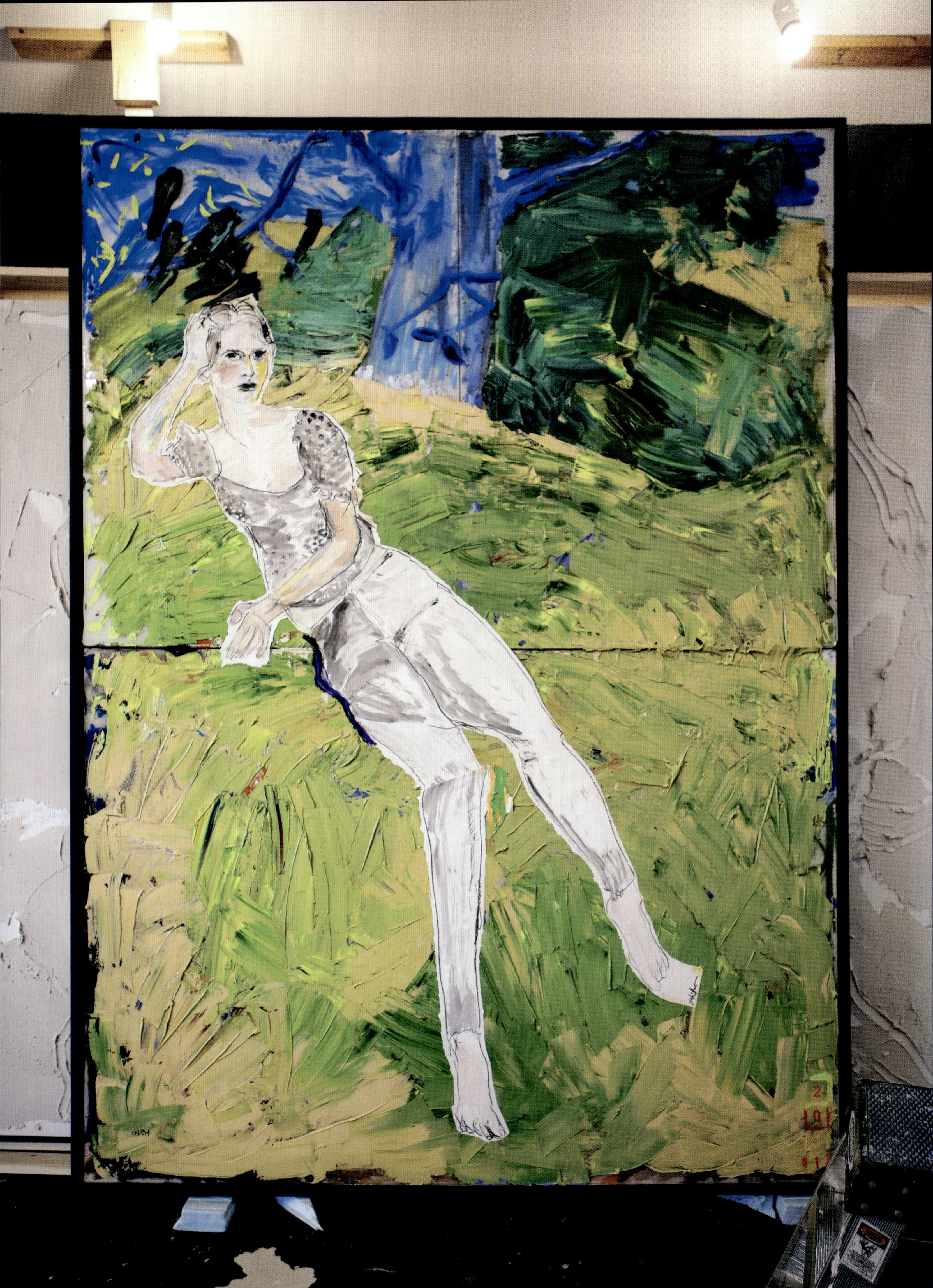

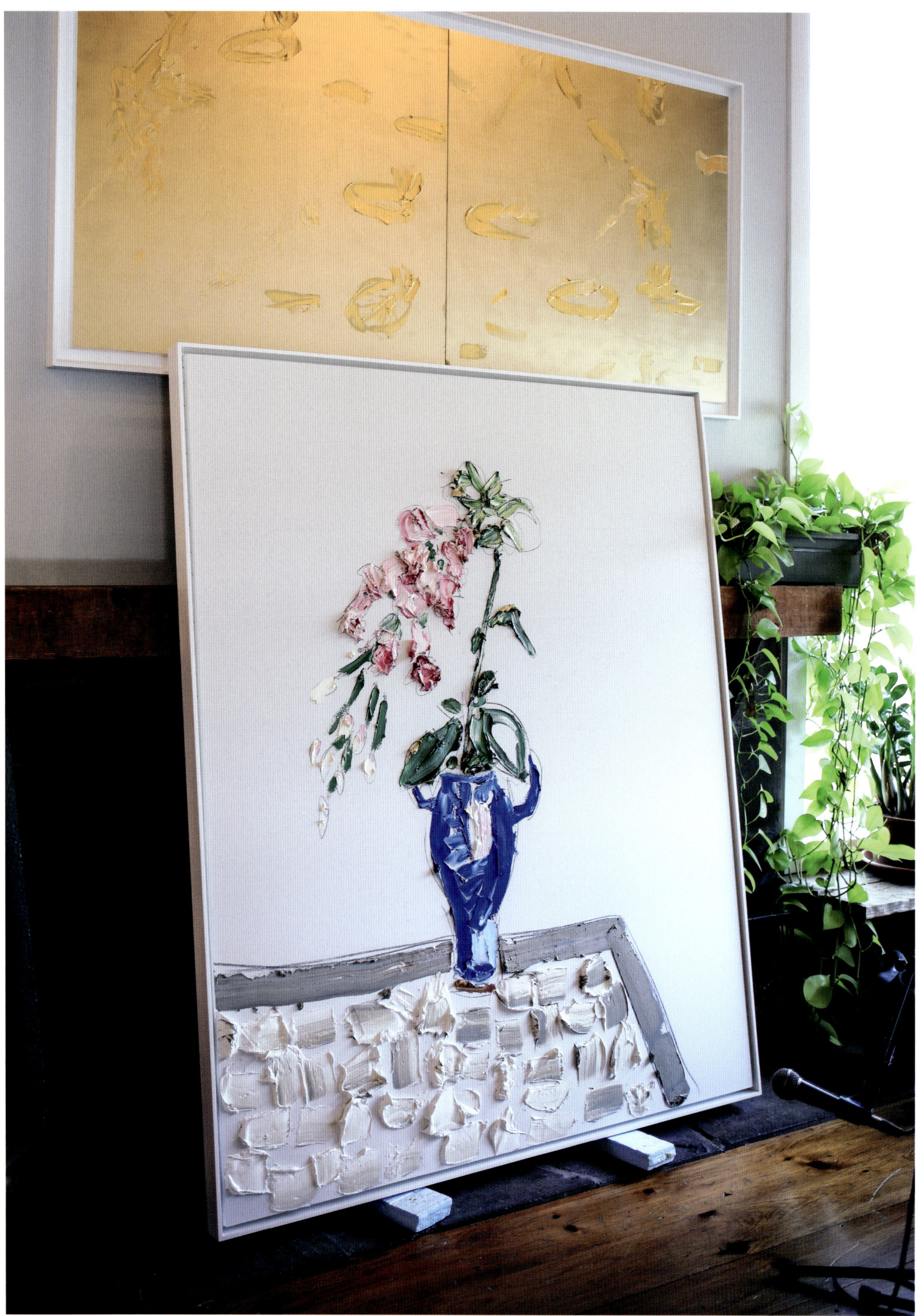

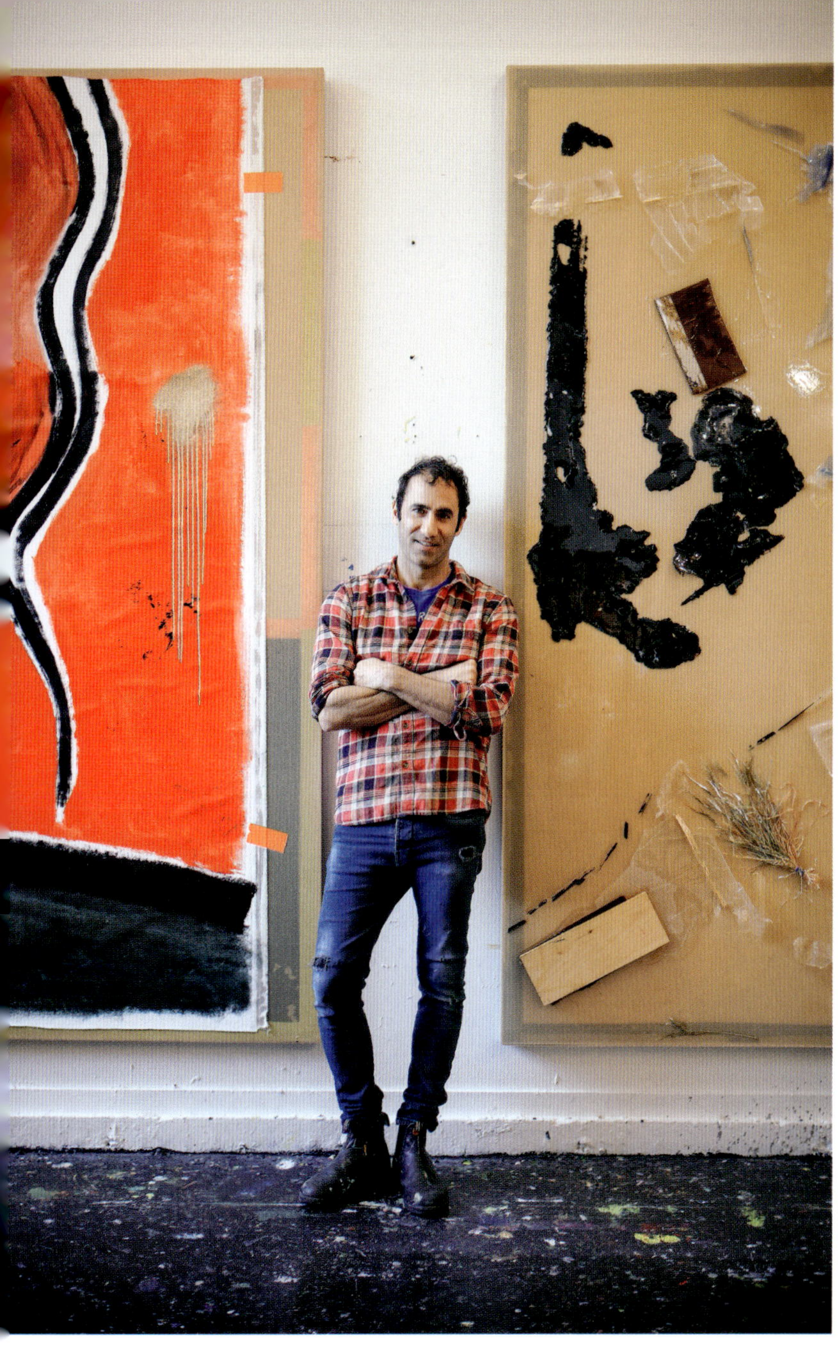

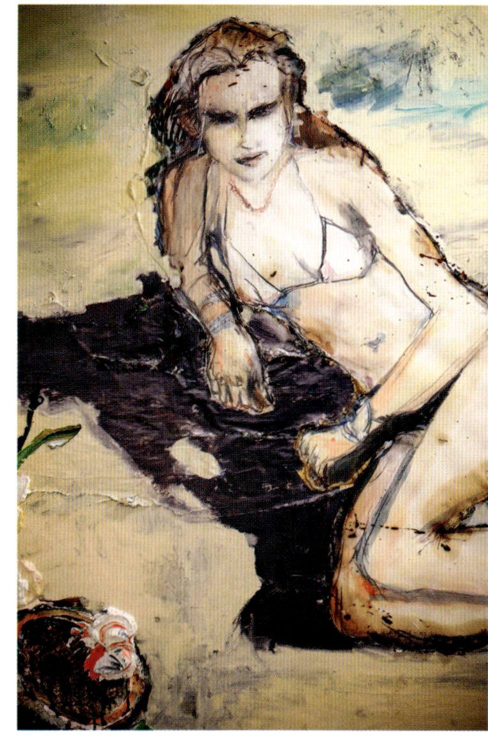

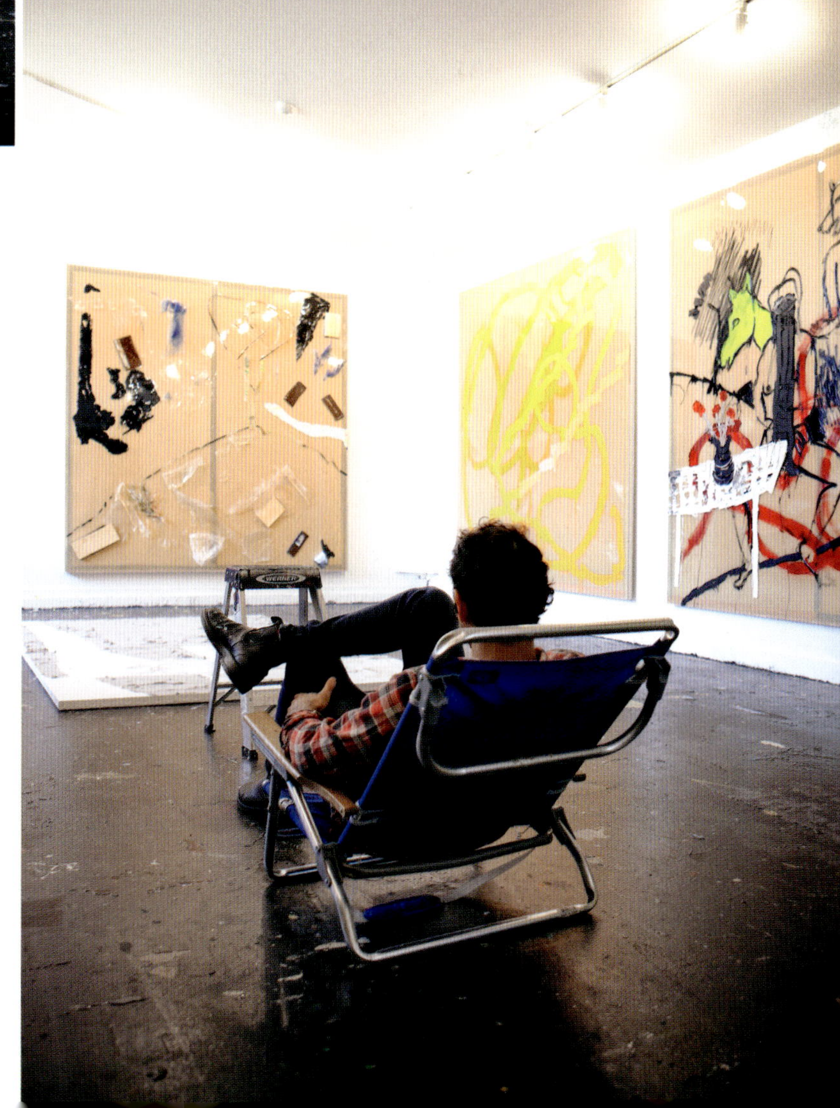

ABOVE

Yektai's main medium is oil, but he expresses himself in a variety of subjects and styles—landscapes, still lifes, florals, figuration, and abstraction.

RIGHT

The artist begins the day sitting in his studio with coffee.

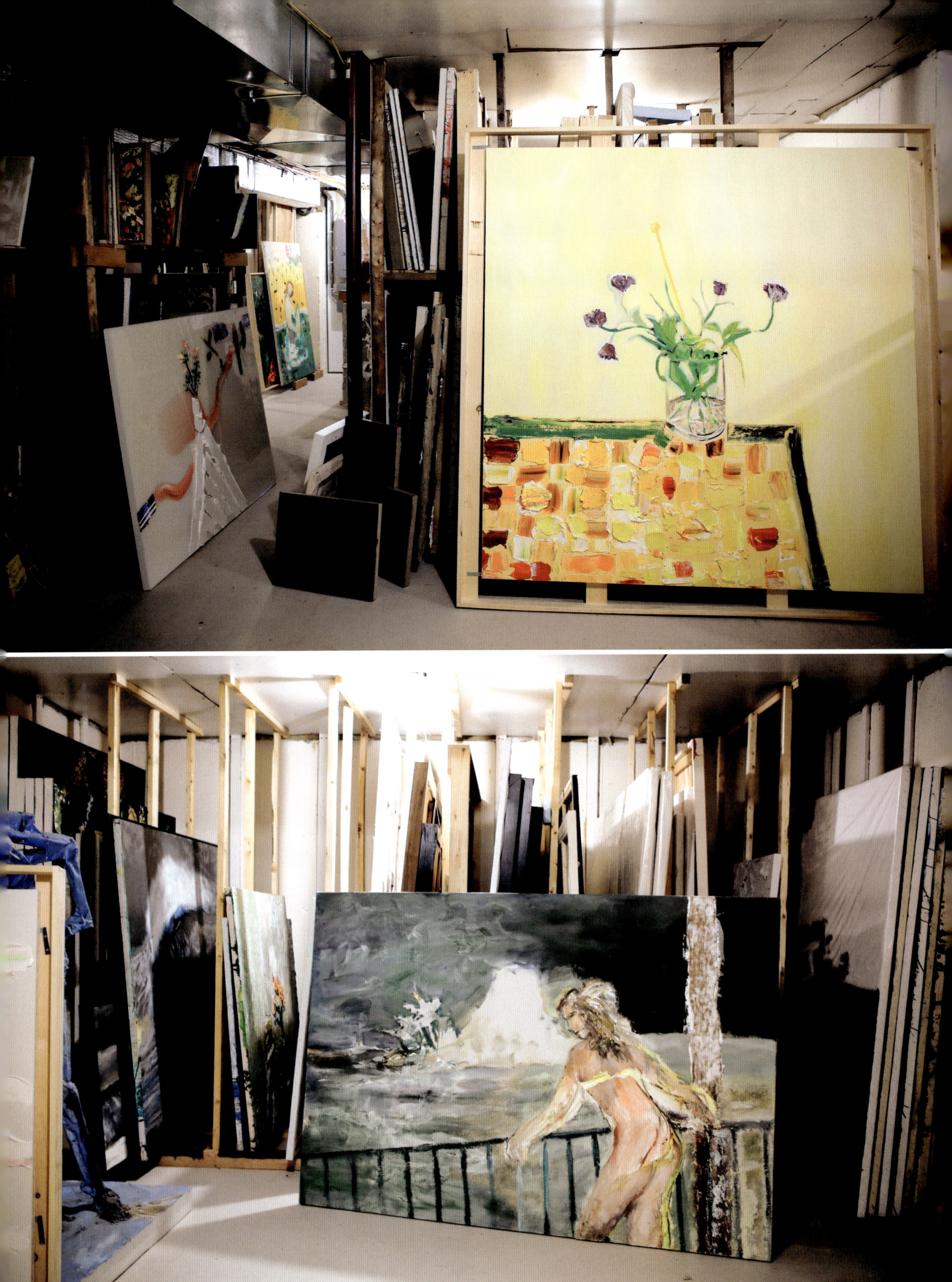

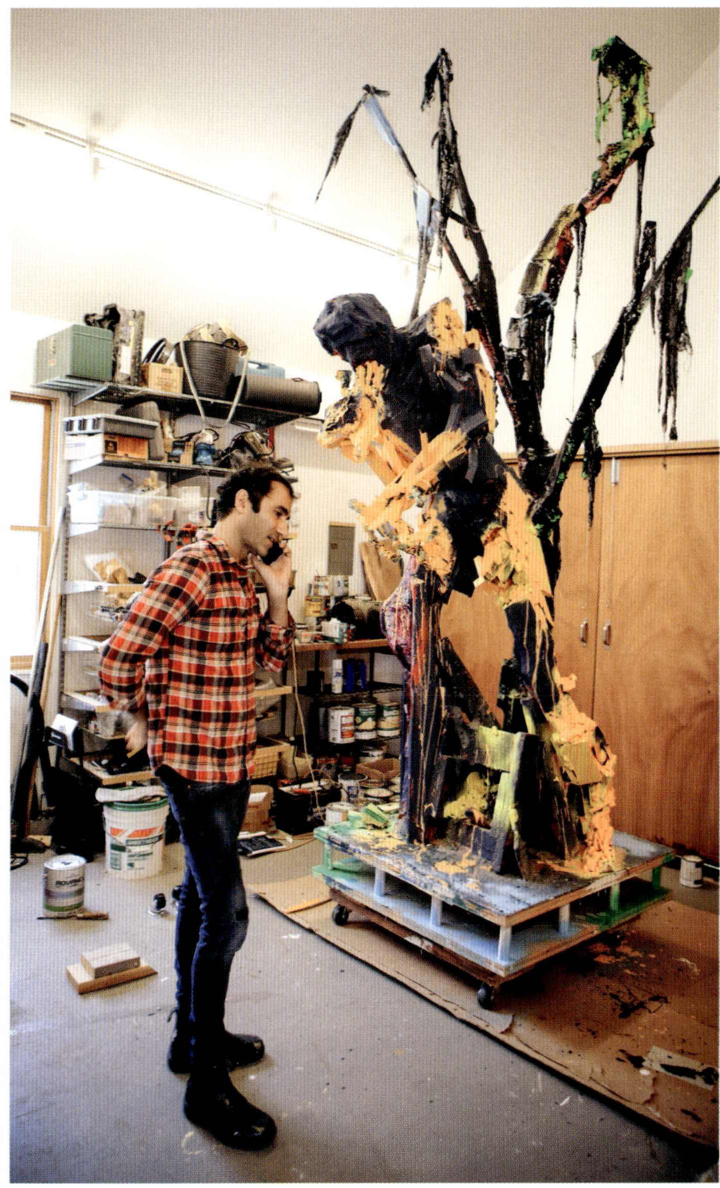

LEFT

Yektai's father, also an artist, had a big influence on Yektai. Their nature walks and conversations grounded Yektai, enabling him to become the artist he is.

Yektai's work—a mix of landscapes, still lifes, florals, figuration, and abstractions—are created in his large, airy Sagaponack studio. "I wake up early, feed my animals—two cats and a German Shepherd—and refill the bird feeder. Then I sit in the studio with coffee. When the waves are up, my dog and I drive onto the beach and surf. Then it's back to the studio. It all feels like a walking meditation. In my thoughts are the paintings I'm working on. When I notice that a thought doesn't go away, I'm pushed to move on it. This is how a series of fifteen-foot, dark self-portraits developed, and how the desire to develop an abstract language of my own was born."

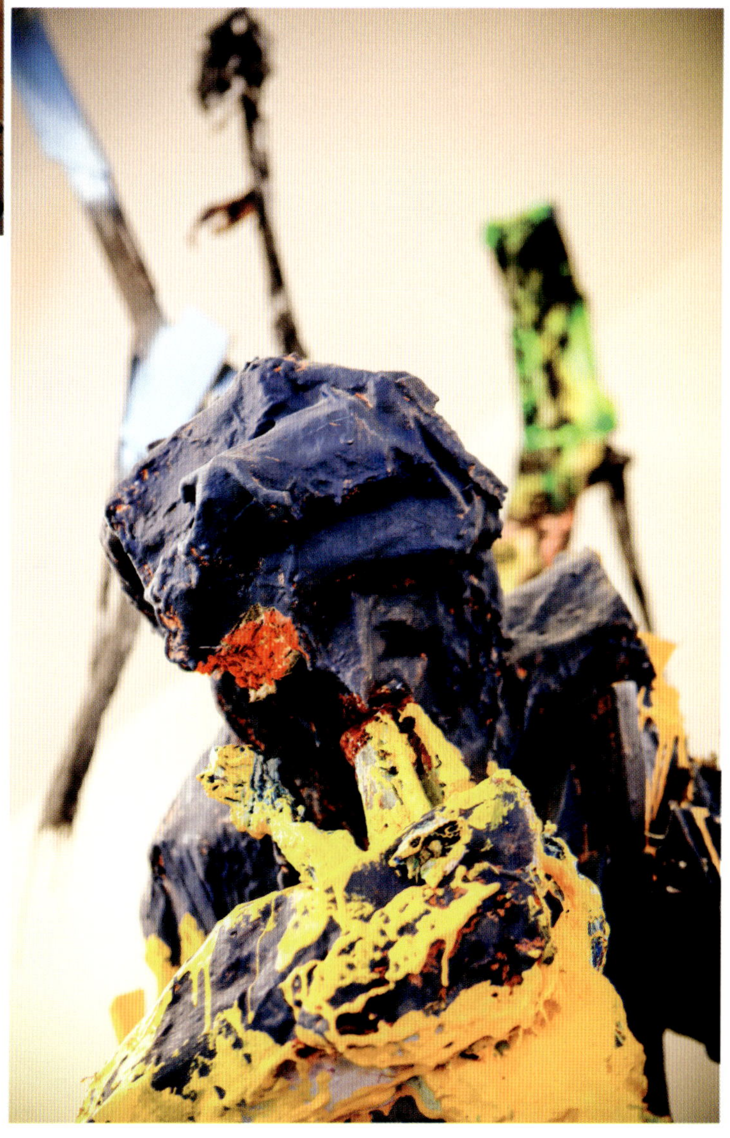

If something doesn't work, I move on.
The failure remains.
There's no way of painting it out.

JOE ZUCKER

Born in Chicago, Zucker went to graduate school at the Art Institute of Chicago and taught art in the Midwest before moving to New York City. "By 1982, I had grown tired of the New York art scene and frustrated by the lack of space. There was tremendous social pressure. Most people who spent fifteen years in the city wanted to get out. My wife and I chose a plot of land in the middle of a wooded area in East Hampton, accessible only by a rocky, rutted dirt road. It was secluded, and we wanted seclusion. My mother's family is from Wisconsin, and I had a romantic attraction to the woods. We built a house and studio connected by a glass structure, and it has been my base of operations ever since."

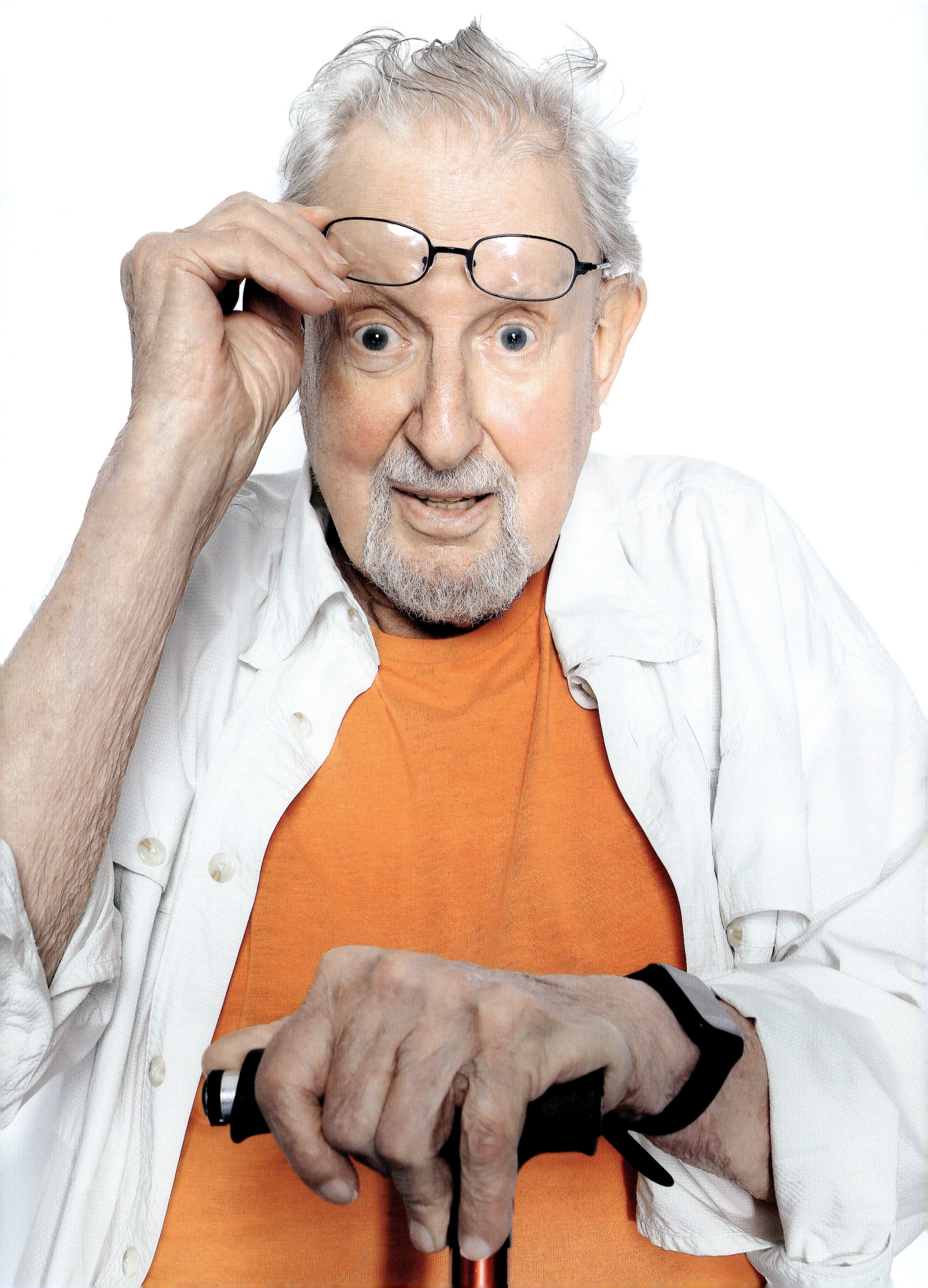

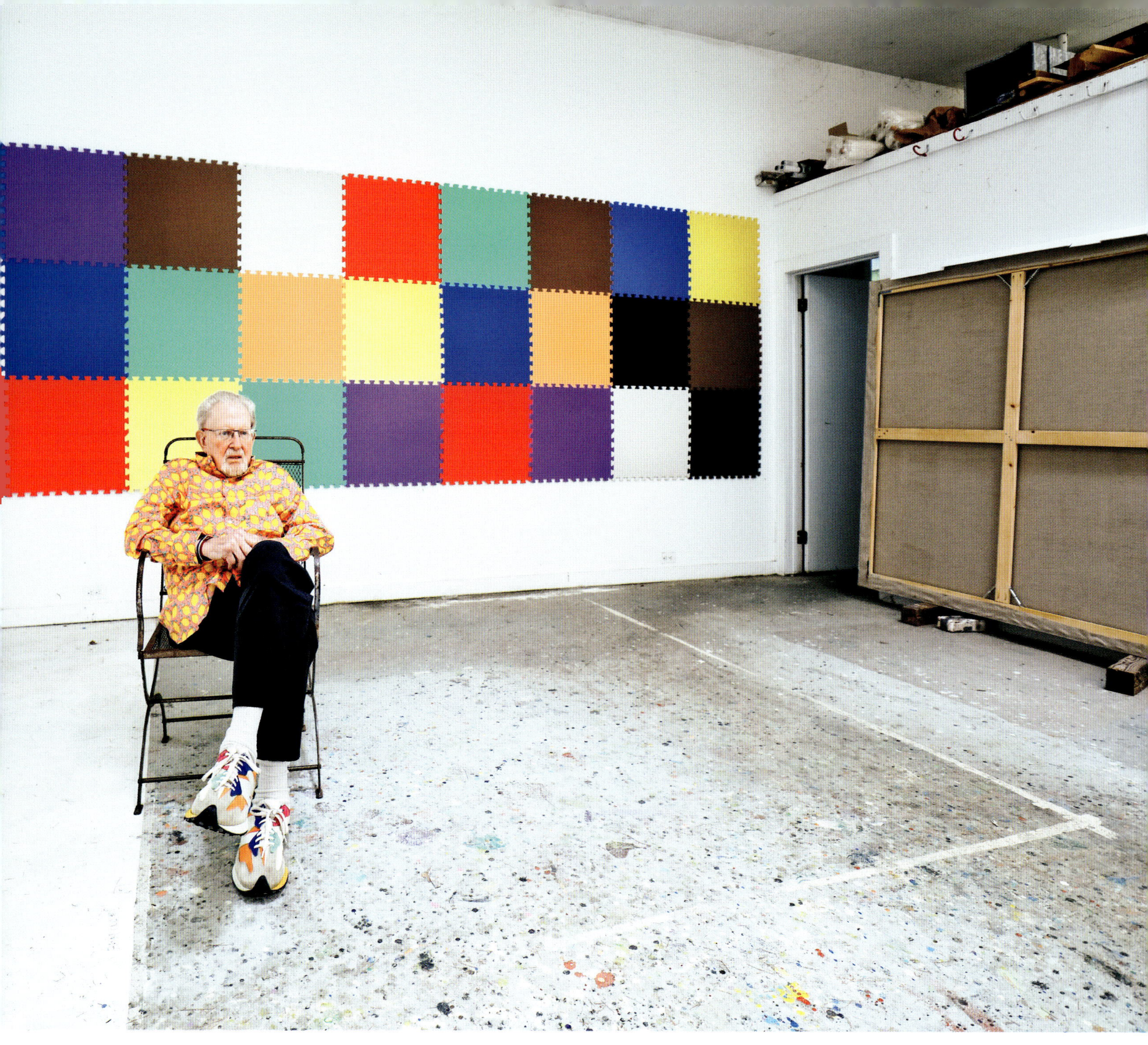

"Out here I can indulge in my love of sports and fishing off Montauk Point." Zucker became assistant coach for the Killer Bees basketball team at Bridgehampton High School. "I love the language of sports and the language of fishing. They are competitive things. I'm very competitive. I like excellence. I was a good basketball player, and I'm a very good fisherman. Painting is not an indulgence to me; it's a competitive activity—competing against yourself and with history."

ABOVE

The spacious East Hampton studio where Zucker created both abstract and figurative works, always aware of a tension between the two stylistic approaches.

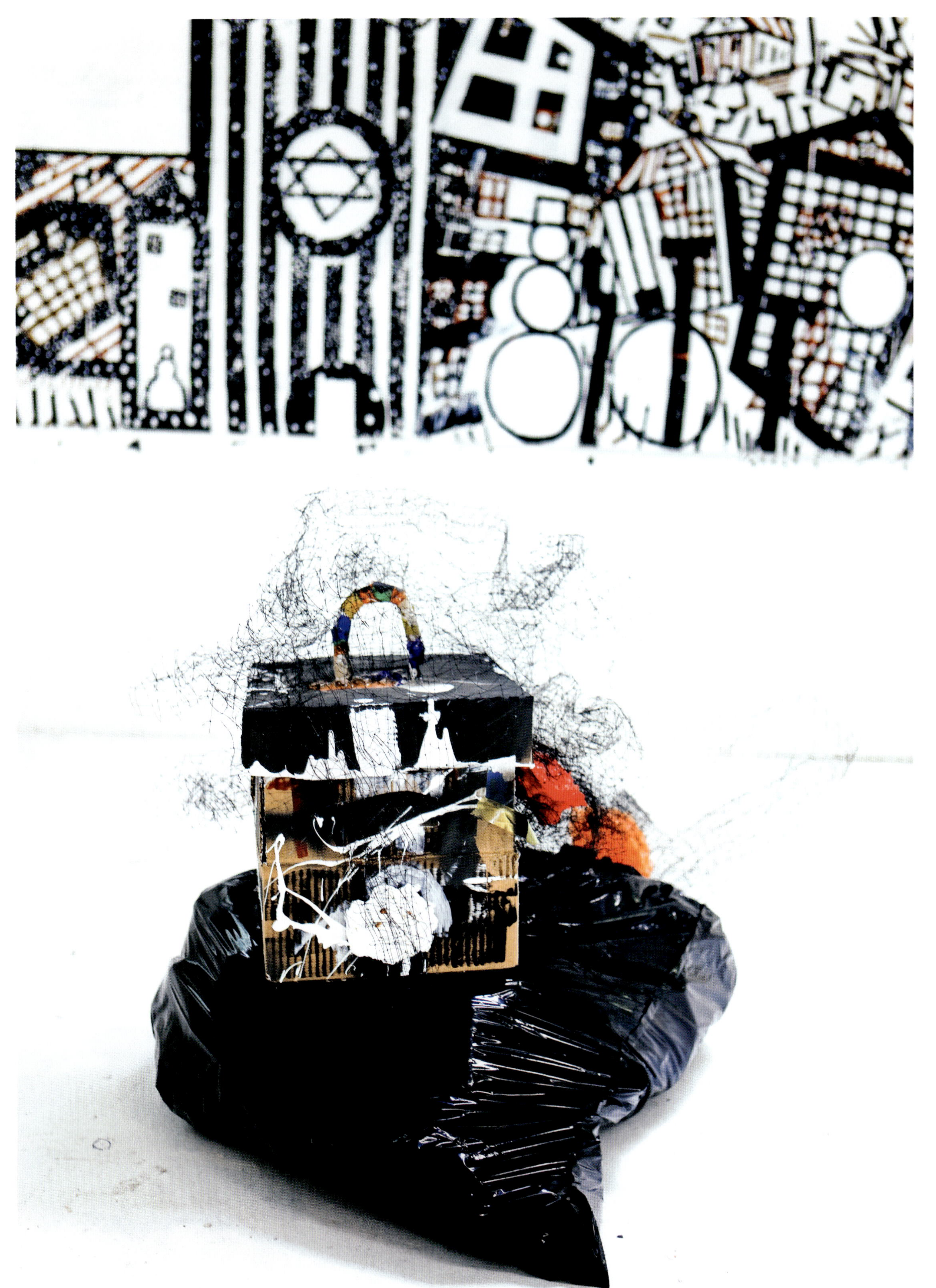

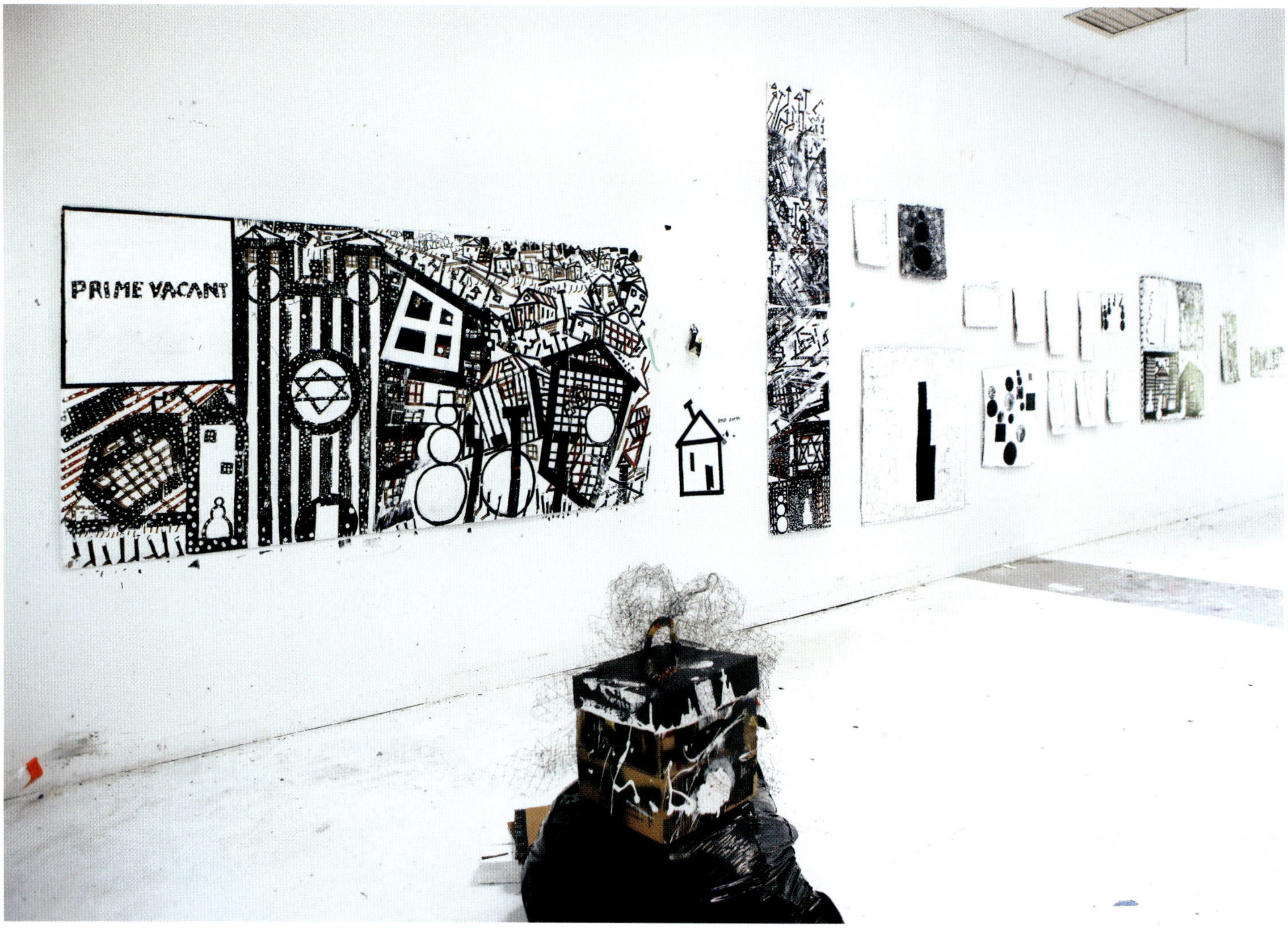

Zucker's expansive studio allowed him to work on a large scale and in a variety of mediums—cotton balls, foil, twine, wood, watercolor, acrylic, and enamel were all fodder for his creativity. "What matters is how I can use different means to continue on." To understand Joe's work, you have to look at it in its entirety: two-dimensional and three-dimensional, from representational to abstract. "I jump party lines. Ultimately, I'm interested in the struggle between figurative work and pure abstraction. Some say nobody cares about that anymore, but for me, the struggle is always there."

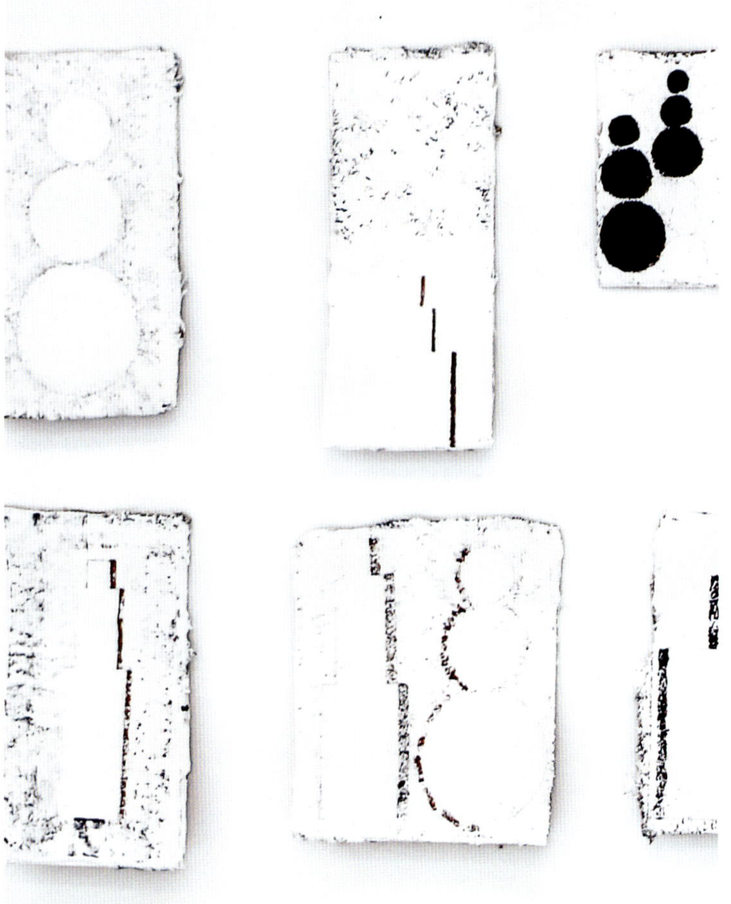

NOTE

Joe Zucker passed away in East Hampton just about a year to the day after the photo shoot in his studio.

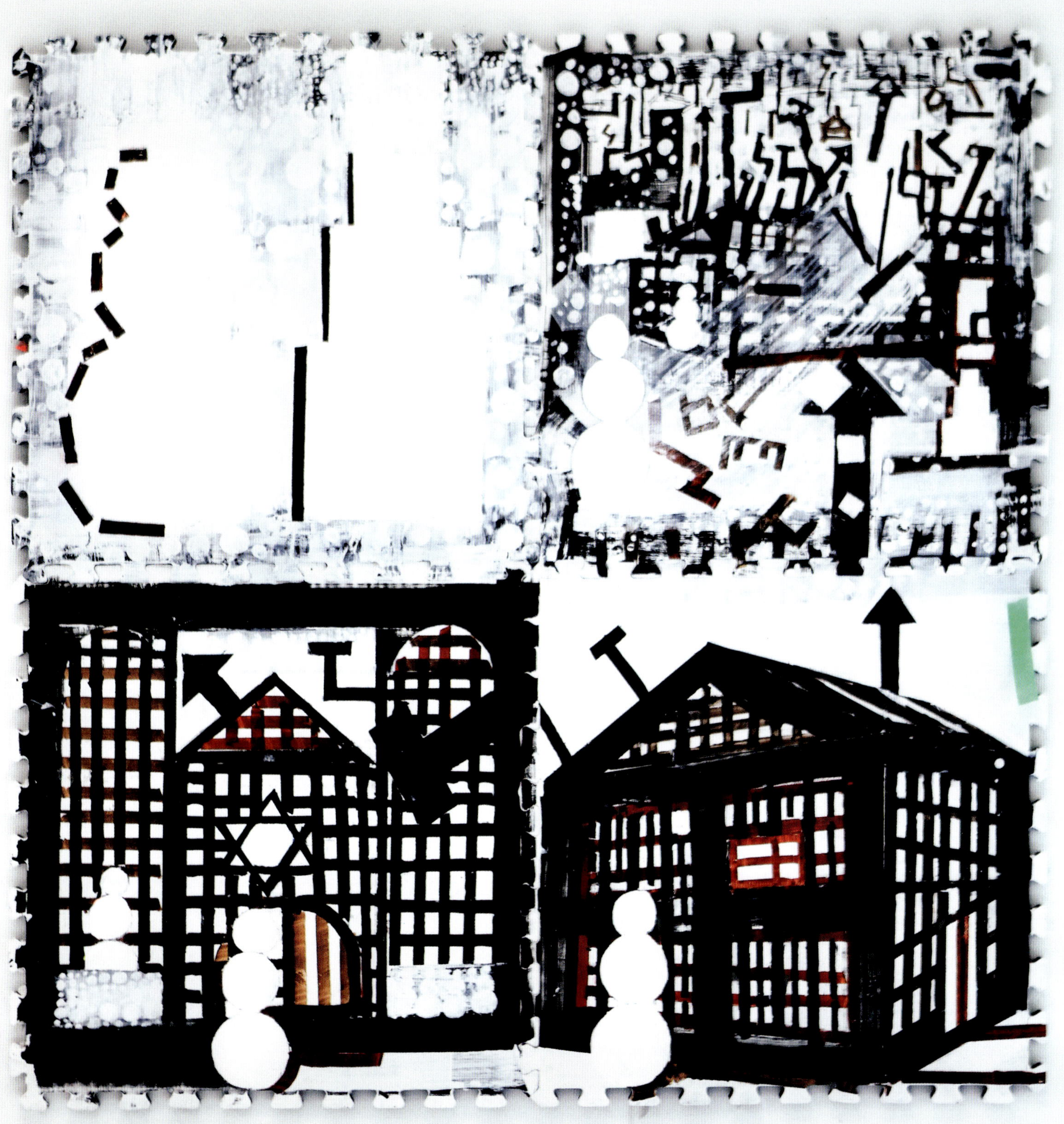

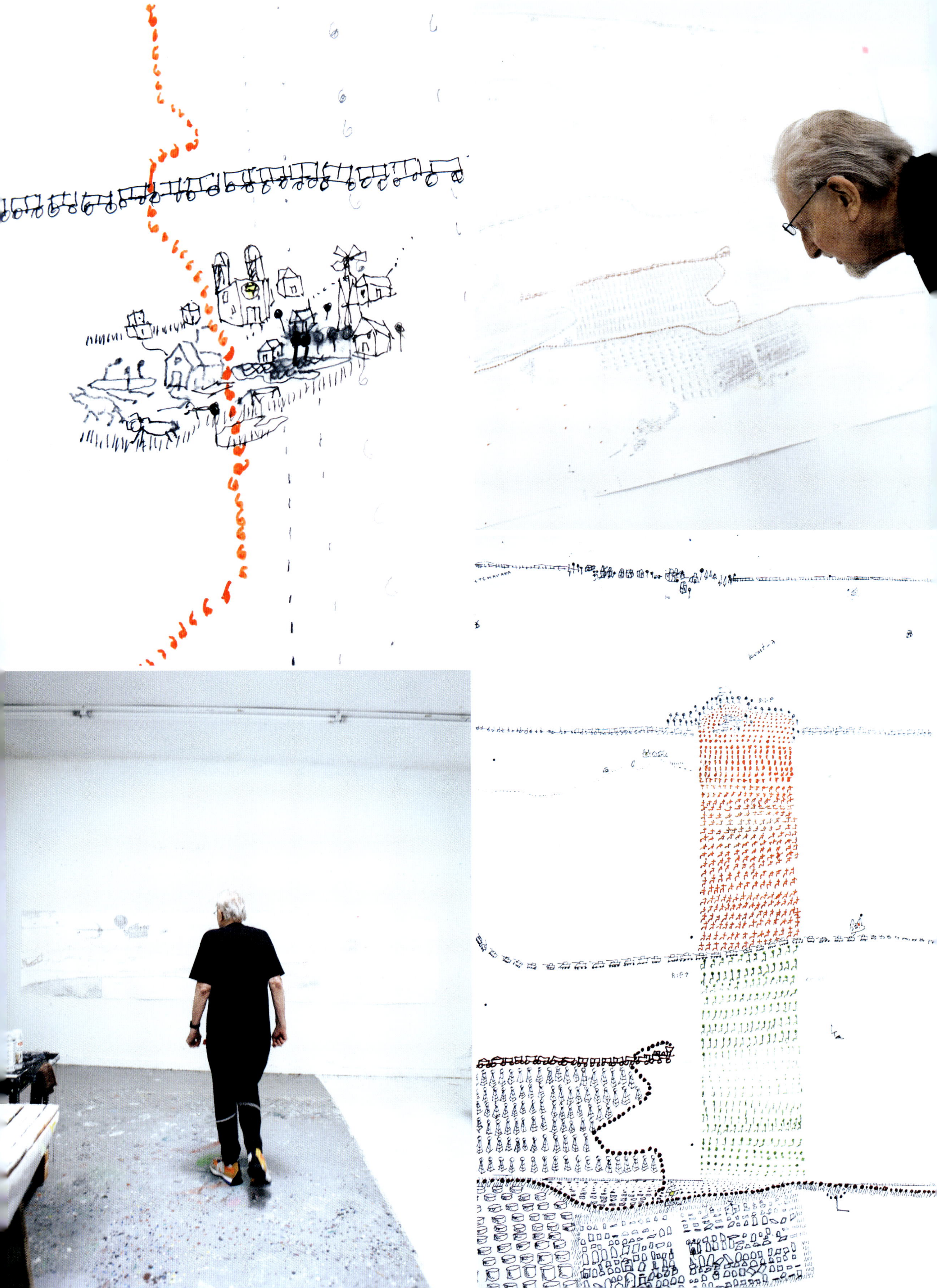

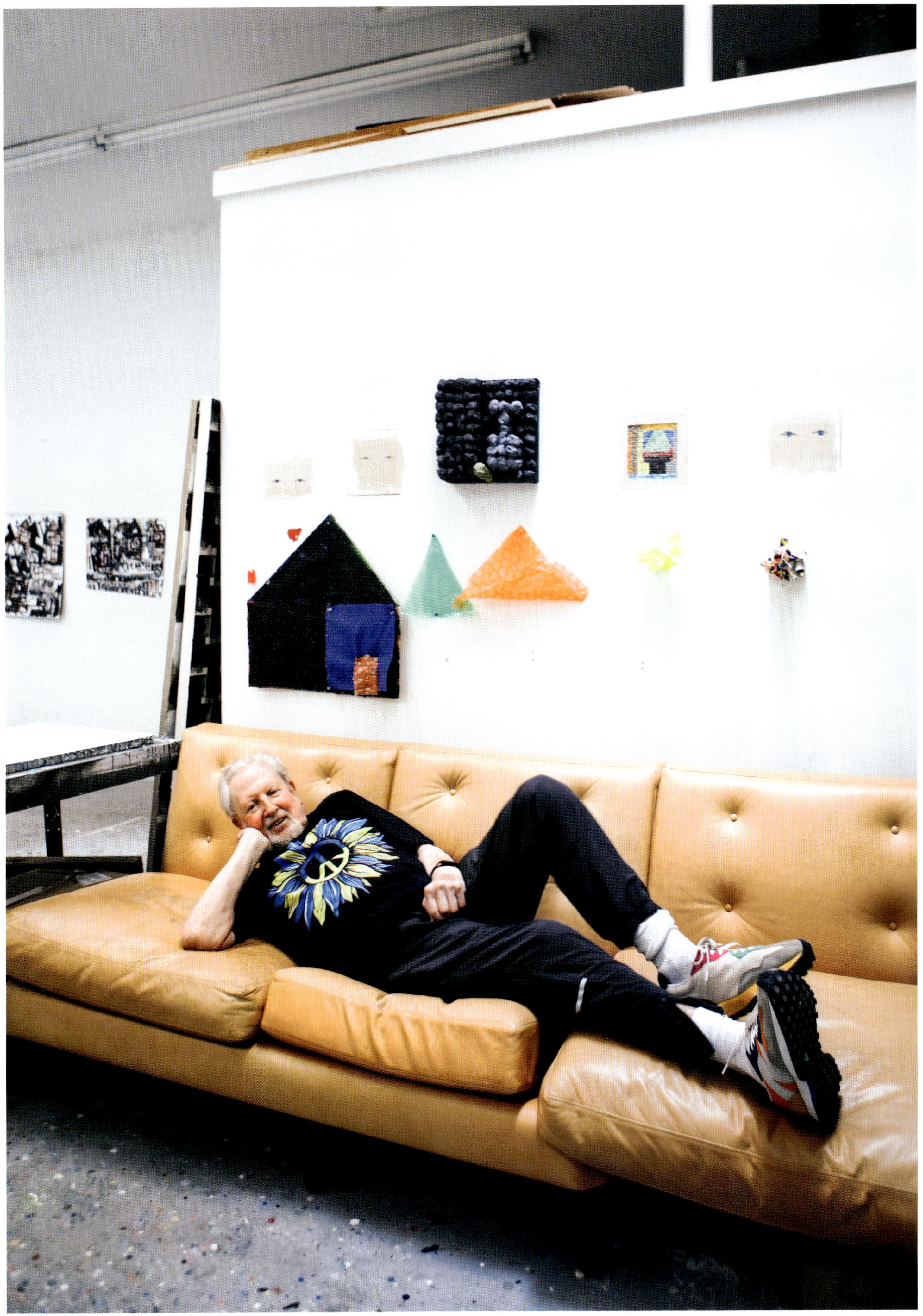

Acknowledgments

Jaime Lopez

We could not start anything without our parents' involvement. I owe them and the rest of my family much gratitude for helping me get to the path I'm on.

Among all the brilliant artists, photographers, and thinkers who have influenced me on the art of seeing—too many to mention—one is always on my mind, and I am deeply grateful for his influence: fashion photographer Alex Chatelain not only paved the way for my professional life as a photographer but also questioned my path and encouraged me to pursue and achieve it with passion.

I also have to thank him for changing my life in a different way. When I was his assistant, Alex had the brilliant idea of booking the beautifully talented model Marilyn Clark, who soon became my wife, life companion, most supportive friend, and the mother of our two daughters. They are my reasons for trying harder.

Then there's Coco. Her collaboration on the creation of these images, her brilliant interviews, and her help in getting us to the finish line were invaluable. Coco's partner, Arthur Bijur, helped us every step of the way with his enthusiastic, often humorous, but right-on-point and generous support, especially in those moments of doubt when one needs it most.

Thank you to the team at the Parrish Art Museum in Water Mill, New York, for the encouragement to do this project, with special thanks to Mónica Ramírez-Montagut for writing the book's foreword and to Corinne Erni and Jan Schluger for their encouragement to continue pointing the camera at artists.

Stephen Ducker was an immense force who generously and enthusiastically introduced us to Mark Magowan at Vendome Press. During my initial conversation with Mark about books, the creative life, and the business of publishing and spreading these beautiful messages, I knew we had a special connection and that this project would be in the best hands.

Then came the pleasure of meeting all the people at Vendome—what an incredibly positive and talented group of professionals: editor Jackie Decter, designer Mark Melnick, production director Jim Spivey, publicity manager Meghan Phillips, and sales liaison Marti Malovany.

Finally, to the artists, I just say this: thank you for being who you are, for seeing the world as you see it, and for using art to express your dreams for a better world. Many more thanks for the commitment to making art your lives. Friends (you know who you are!), I hope that I successfully translated your energy into these pages. My gratitude goes beyond words. I hope that together we will be bringing a positive message to our world.

Love art.

Coco Myers

Let me start by thanking my partner in this project, Jaime Lopez, whose vision, energy, and conviction helped propel this book into being. He photographed the artists of our community—their personalities, studios, and artworks—with great skill and a contagiously positive spirit. I loved watching him get the artists to relax in front of the camera just by being himself. Jaime is a true pro, and it shows in the character of the photographs.

Huge appreciation goes to my partner in life, Arthur Bijur, for his unending support throughout the project. His critical eye and ear helped us enormously as the book began to take shape. He was also a particularly good sounding board for me while I was writing the text and captions, as was my friend and frequent collaborator, Susan Carlton. Big thanks also go to Marilyn Clark, Jaime's wife and our good friend, for her enthusiasm and insights over many months and many meetings—often over a cocktail.

A very special thanks to Stephen Drucker, who introduced our project to Vendome. While Stephen is part of the community out here, I first knew him in another context—in my early days as a staff writer in New York at *Self* magazine. Stephen was my first boss and became my mentor and friend. It was Stephen, an enormously talented writer and editor, who taught me how to write and I owe him much gratitude.

I'd like to thank the entire team at Vendome: editor Jacqueline Decter for her smart word skills, positive attitude, and professionalism. And thanks to publisher Mark Magowan for his vision and guidance on this project, as well as to designer Mark Melnick, production director Jim Spivey, publicity manager Meghan Phillips, and sales liaison Marti Malovany.

I'm grateful to everyone at the Parrish Art Museum in Water Mill, New York, for their enthusiasm and in particular to executive director Mónica Ramírez-Montagut for writing the book's illuminating foreword.

And of course, the book could not exist without the artists themselves. They invited us into their homes and studios and happily sat for their portraits without attitude or prima donna behavior. I came away knowing them better as both artists and people. My world is enriched by the relationships that have grown out of this project.

I'd also like to acknowledge the East End community itself. I grew up in East Hampton and returned here years later to raise my three sons. It's where I began a second career representing and exhibiting local artists. The Hamptons have always been supportive of the arts, and art has always been part of my life. For that I thank my parents, Astrid and David Myers, who moved our family here in the early 1960s and befriended the large group of Abstract Expressionists living on this spit of land. Many of my earliest memories are of gallery openings and artists' beach gatherings—still lively happenings within the current community of artists, who are as integral as ever to the fabric of this unique hamlet by the sea.

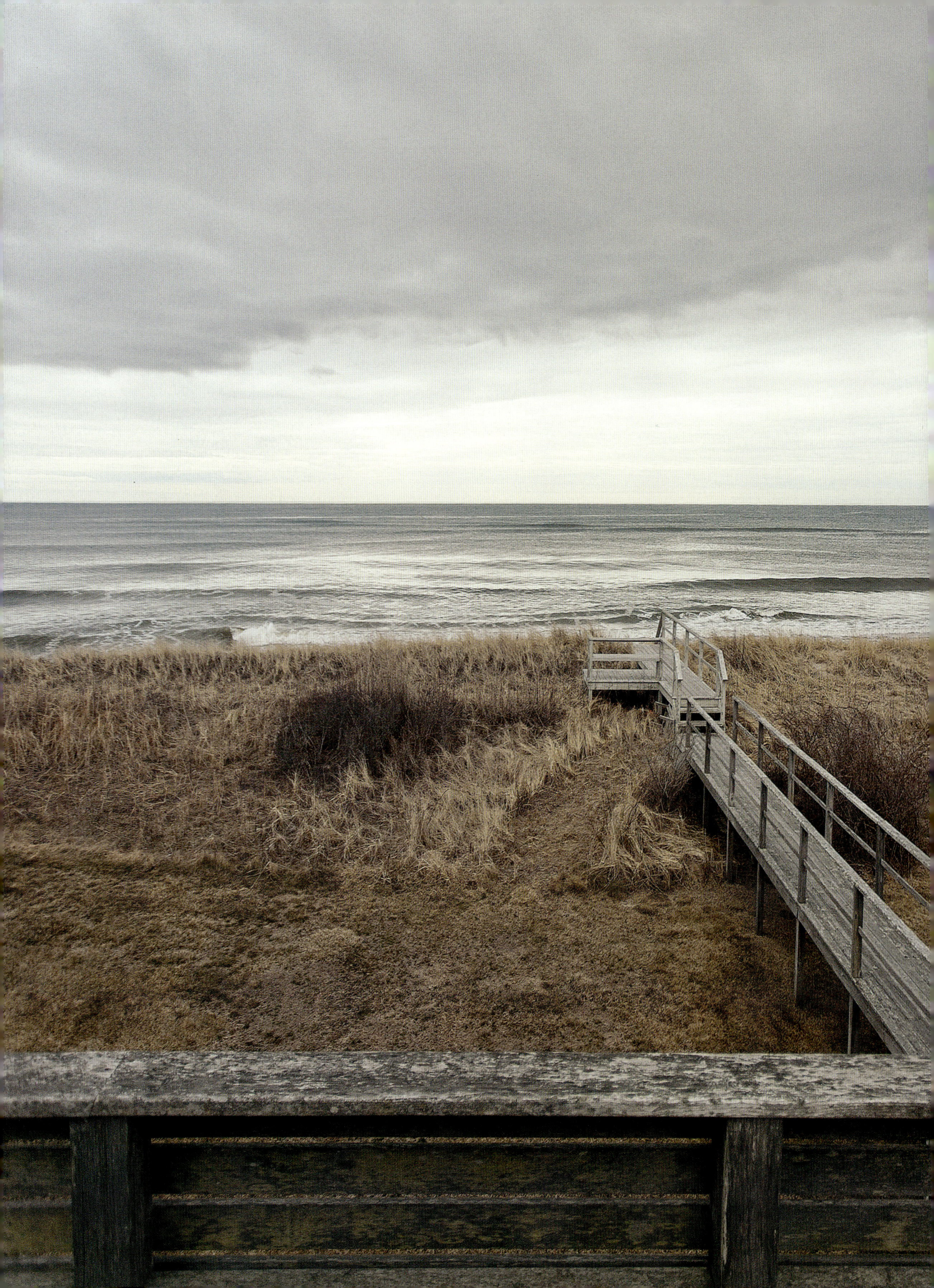

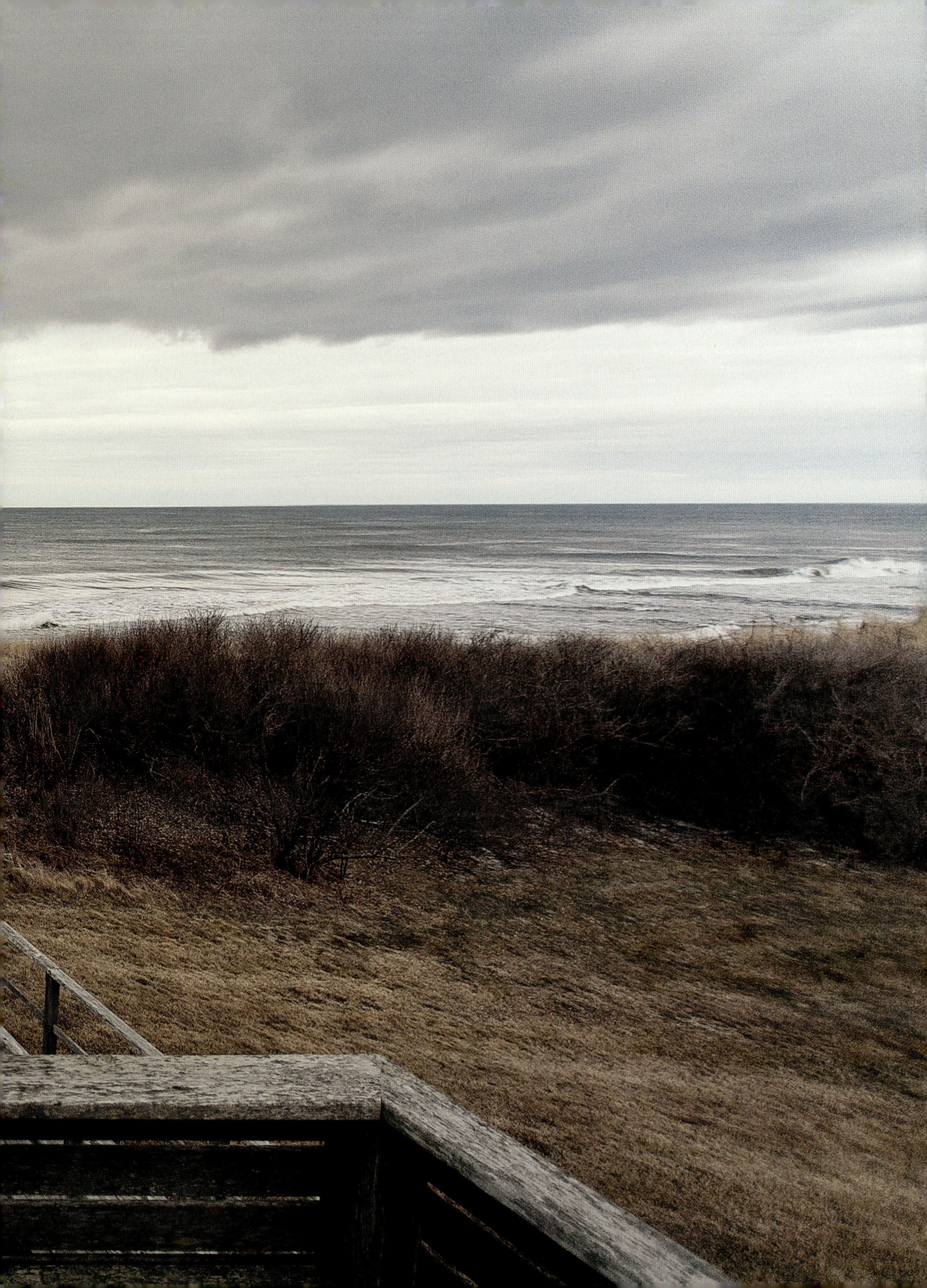

Light, Sand, and Sea: Hamptons Artists and Their Studios
First published in 2025 by The Vendome Press
Vendome is a registered trademark of The Vendome Press LLC

VENDOME PRESS US
P.O. Box 566
Palm Beach, FL 33480

VENDOME PRESS UK
Worlds End Studio
132-134 Lots Road
London, SW10 0RJ

www.vendomepress.com

ISBN 978-0-86565-472-3

Publishers: Beatrice Vincenzini, Mark Magowan, and Francesco Venturi
Editor: Jacqueline Decter · **Production Director:** Jim Spivey · **Designer:** Mark Melnick

Library of Congress Cataloging-in-Publication Data
available upon request

Printed and bound in China

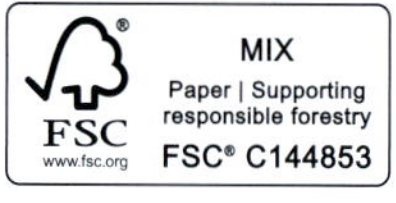

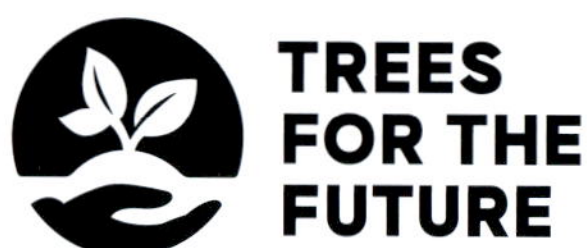

FIRST PRINTING

Endpapers: Jaime Lopez, *Sagg Main Dream 2*, Sagaponack, NY. · **Pages 2–3:** In Mark Wilson's East Hampton studio, his own paintings and sculptures mix with found pieces from nature (see pages 366–71). · **Pages 4–5:** The bucolic view from Idoline Duke's Springs studio (see pages 104–11). · **Pages 6–7:** Creativity abounds in Quentin Curry's spacious Sagaponack studio (see pages 82–89). · **Pages 8–9:** Jaime Lopez, *Sagg Main Lifeguard 1*, Sagaponack, NY. · **Pages 10–11:** Jaime Lopez, *Long Beach #2*, Sag Harbor, NY. · **Page 12:** Matthew Satz driving home after a portrait shoot in Jaime Lopez's Sagaponack studio. · **Page 15:** Jaime Lopez, *Sagg Main Grasses*, Sagaponack, NY. · **Pages 22–23:** Jaime Lopez, *Warhol's Beach 1*, Montauk, NY. · **Pages 80–81:** Jaime Lopez, *Sagg Main Beach 1*, Sagaponack, NY. · **Pages 152–53:** Jaime Lopez, *Wainscott Beach*, Wainscott, NY. · **Pages 214–15:** Jaime Lopez, *Ocean Wave 1*, Sagaponack, NY. · **Pages 274–75:** Jaime Lopez, *Mecox Bay Dream*, Bridgehampton, NY. · **Pages 334–35:** Jaime Lopez, *Wainscott Field*, Wainscott, NY. · **Pages 398–99:** Jaime Lopez, *Jim Tree's Deck*, Sagaponack, NY.